Blender for Beginners
Part 1
Third Edition

A reference guide to 3D modeling, shading, and animating workflows with Blender 4.5 LTS

3D Tudor (Neil Ian Bettison)
Vanessa Haralambous

‹packt›

Blender for Beginners
Part 1
Third Edition

Portfolio Director: Rohit Rajkumar
Relationship Lead: Kaustubh Manglurkar
Project Manager: Sandip Tadge
Content Engineer: Anuradha Joglekar
Technical Editor: Tejas Vijay Mhasvekar
Copy Editor: Safis Editing
Indexer: Manju Arasan
Proofreader: Anuradha Joglekar
Production Designer: Shantanu Zagade
Growth Lead: Lee Booth
Marketing Owner: Nivedita Pandey

First edition: June 2012
Second edition: August 2014
Third edition: November 2025

Production reference: 1261125

Published by Packt Publishing Ltd.
Grosvenor House
11 St Paul's Square
Birmingham
B3 1RB, UK.

ISBN 978-1-83763-109-4
www.packtpub.com

We would like to dedicate this book to our two daughters who we hold most dear, to Luke, and all the people, seen and unseen, who helped put this book together.

— Vanessa & Neil

Contributors

About the authors

3D Tudor is an online course creator team publishing courses on 3D modeling, game design, and animation. Founded and led by **Neil I. Bettison** in 2019, 3D Tudor brings with it over 10 years of specialist experience. The focus of 3D Tudor is on teaching 3D modeling and animation through free and accessible software, including Blender and Unreal Engine 5, to over 250,000 students from all backgrounds. The team publishes courses, 3D models, and game props, and also runs a YouTube channel where free Blender-to–Unreal Engine 5 environment tutorials are posted. The 3D Tudor headquarters are in Paphos, Cyprus, and Neil holds a Computer Games Art BA (Hons) degree from the University for the Creative Arts.

Vanessa A. B Haralambous is an academic writing specialist with over 10 years of experience. Since 2010, she has taught academic writing and proofreading techniques to university students from different levels and disciplines, including the humanities and arts. Between 2019 and 2020, Vanessa published two courses on academic writing for university students. Vanessa offers ad hoc copywriting support to 3D Tudor and holds a Psychology with Criminology BSc (Hons) degree and a Forensic Psychology MSc degree.

I would like to extend my thanks to Vanessa and Vanessa would like to extend her thanks to me (pun intended!) for working together to write the book around us both looking after the girls and keeping them off the keyboard. Because let's face it; they are far too young to be keyboard warriors. We would like to wholeheartedly thank our partner in 3D Tudor and real friend for many reasons he no longer needs to prove, Lukas Partaukas—the technical genius behind image creation and fact-checking for this book. Special thanks to the different editors who worked with us while we wrote this book, including Hayden Edwards, Rashi Dubey, and Anuradha Joglekar—for their valuable input and time reviewing this book. Also, extending our dearest thanks to the entire Packt team for their support during the course of writing this book.

About the reviewers

Skylar Jetton is a multidisciplinary artist whose career has spanned professional ballet, manga illustration, and VR technology. Today, he is the Creative Director of Spookhaus, where he guides narrative and art direction while creating photorealistic 3D characters for film and games. He specializes in Look Development using Maya, Blender, Unreal Engine, Mari, and the Substance Suite. The author of a book on ballet technique, he now spends his free time composing orchestral scores and playing narrative-heavy video games. He is based out of Los Angeles, California.

I would like to sincerely thank Namita for inviting me onto this project and welcoming me into the Packt Publishing family. My gratitude also goes to Sonam and Rashi for their kindness, incredible support, and expert guidance throughout the editing process.

Jane Suteerawanit is a Senior Character Artist at Gameloft Brisbane. Originally from Perth, she holds a Bachelor's in Animation and Game Design from Curtin University, where she earned the Best Portfolio Award and Academic Award for high achievement. Her career began with an internship at Landshark Games in Singapore, creating low-poly characters and assets. In 2021, she joined Flying Bark Productions, contributing to *100% Wolf: The Book of Hath* on ABC ME. Her recent game credits include *My Little Pony: Mane Merge (2022)* and *Carmen Sandiego (2025)*, where she modeled the iconic title character.

Jane also previously contributed as a reviewer on *Low Poly 3D Modeling in Blender* by Samuel Sullins.

Table of Contents

Chapter 3: Exploring Blender's Properties Panel for Optimal 3D Creativity   51

Chapter 4: Unleashing the Potential of Blender's Outliner and Add-On Ecosystem   95

Chapter 9: Discovering Must-Know Advanced Blender Modeling Techniques

Chapter 12: Introducing Digital Sculpting and Brushing Up on Your Retopology Skills 461

Preface

When I first opened Blender many years ago, I did exactly what you have probably done. I clicked around, lost the camera somewhere and I thought it was gone forever, accidentally deleted the default cube, and wondered how on earth people were making beautiful game environments and film shots with this thing.

Fast forward a good few years, a lot of late nights, and a fair amount of tea, and I have now taught well over a quarter of a million students Blender and 3D art through 3D Tudor courses and YouTube. Over the time, I kept seeing the same patterns: artists burning out on huge "dream projects," beginners bouncing between random YouTube videos like a headless chicken, and a lot of people who were clearly talented creatively, but were slowed down by the basics of navigation, topology, and shading. This book, *Blender for Beginners*, *Parts 1* and *2*, grew out of that experience.

Blender is free, powerful, and very forgiving once you know how to drive it. The problem is that the first weeks (and often the first year) can feel like you are trying to learn to fly a plane by pressing every button in the cockpit in random order.

I wanted to create a guide that does the opposite of that.

Instead of dropping you straight into one giant "hero project" and hoping you survive, this book takes a tools-first, habits-first approach. You will still build real things – props, small sets, simple animations, finished shots – but every project is there to show you why a particular tool, setting, or workflow matters, not just what buttons to press.

It is written by artists for artists. That means a lot of clear images, concrete examples, and practical advice about how things actually look under lighting, not long theoretical detours. You will see where the tools live, what they do to your mesh, and how they behave when you send that mesh into a game engine or a render.

Packt has split the material into two volumes, but it is one learning journey. *Part 1* is all about foundations and everyday workflows. You will:

- Set up Blender so it stops fighting you: status bar, sensible workspaces, overlays, Outliner filters, and a viewport that tells you what is actually going on.

- Learn to move around in 3D confidently, read the different shading modes, and understand why objects sometimes "move weirdly" when origins and pivots are off.

- Build up from simple modelling into mid-level techniques: extrude, inset, bevel, loop cuts, knife, spin, slide, shear, and rip, along with curves, basic generators, and deformers.

- Keep meshes clean and shading-friendly with good topology, sharps, Auto Smooth, and sensible use of n-gons.

- Unwrap your models properly with seams and projections, understand texel density, and get used to trim sheets, atlases, and the basics of UDIMs.

- Build principled PBR materials with Node Wrangler and a few quality-of-life tricks, so your models stop looking like grey clay and start behaving under light.

By the end of *Part 1*, your files will be organized, your models will hold up when you add light, and you will have the sort of clean assets that are actually ready to animate or send to a client, not just "nice screenshots." *Part 2* picks up from there and moves you into motion, systems, and final look-dev.

Take your time, do the exercises, and do not be afraid to make ugly work on the way to better work. Everyone does. If a chapter feels dense, put the kettle on, come back to it, and try again. The only real mistake is to give up too early.

Thanks very much for picking up Blender for Beginners. I hope it becomes a book that you not only read once but keep coming back to when you want to push your skills a little further.

Until next time, happy modeling, everyone!

– 3D Tudor (Neil Bettison) & Vanessa Haralambous

Who this book is for

If you are a video games enthusiast looking to gain experience in 3D modelling, game design, and animation for game props, assets, and environments, this is the book for you. Character artists, game designers, motion graphics designers, animators, environment artists, or other technical artists would also benefit from this book.3D modelling artists already familiar with video game assets, prop, and environment design will be able to learn new workflows that maximize their productivity using Blender.

This book teaches 3D modelling techniques using Blender—a type of free, open-source software. From familiarizing you with the user interface to all kinds of digital creations, taken together, *Parts 1* and *2* of *Blender for Beginners* will take you on a journey up and including rendering your 3D art for your portfolio.

What this book covers

Chapter 1, Understanding Camera Control and Viewport Navigation in Blender, lets you get comfortable moving around the 3D world. You will learn how to orbit, pan, and zoom with confidence, snap to orthographic views, and frame your objects properly so you are not constantly losing things off-screen.

Chapter 2, Optimizing Workflow with the Status Bar, Workspaces, and File Options, helps you tidy up how Blender behaves day to day. You will explore the status bar, create and customize workspaces for different tasks, and learn sensible file options so that saving, loading, and recovering work becomes reliable and predictable.

Chapter 3, Exploring Blender's Properties Panel for Optimal 3D Creativity, dives into the Properties editor and understand what all those tabs actually control. You will learn where to adjust render settings, world and lighting options, object data, modifiers, constraints, and how these panels shape the behavior of your scenes.

Chapter 4, Unleashing the Potential of Blender's Outliner and Add-On Ecosystem, teaches you to manage complex scenes without getting lost. You will use the Outliner to organize objects, collections, and visibility, and you will explore how enabling the right add-ons can extend Blender.

Chapter 5, Going Over Proportional Editing, Transform Orientation, and Viewport Shaders, guides you in refining how you move and shape objects. You will use Proportional Editing to make soft, organic changes, switch transform orientations to work in local or global space and understand viewport shading modes so you can judge form and lighting while you model.

Chapter 6, Discovering Essential Tools for 3D Modeling in Blender, builds up a toolkit of core modelling operations. You will work with extrude, inset, bevel, loop cuts, the knife tool, and other bread-and-butter tools that underpin almost every hard-surface and environment project you will create.

Chapter 7, Elevating Your Craft with Mid-Level Blender Modeling Techniques, levels you up so you can move beyond simple block-outs. You will start to care about good topology, build cleaner transitions, use more advanced edit tools, and begin shaping meshes that hold up when smoothed, lit, and seen from multiple angles.

Chapter 8, Refining Your Mid-Level Blender Modeling Techniques, polishes the skills from the previous chapter. You will focus on tightening edge flow, simplifying messy areas, resolving pinching and stretching, and using Blender's tools to refine models so they are efficient as well as good-looking.

Chapter 9, Discovering Must-Know Advanced Blender Modeling Techniques, explores higher-end modelling workflows. You will use tools and tricks that make repeating details, complex shapes, and tricky intersections much more manageable, and you will see where advanced techniques fit into a real production pipeline.

Chapter 10, Leveling Up with More Advanced Blender Modeling Techniques, transports you a step further into advanced modelling. You will combine multiple tools and modifiers, tackle more demanding shapes, and learn to think about modelling as a layered process rather than a single pass from start to finish.

Chapter 11, Exploring Blender's Particle System, welcomes you into procedural detail. You will create and control particle systems for things like hair, grass, debris, and other repeated elements, and you will learn how to keep them performant and art-directable rather than random and chaotic.

Chapter 12, Introducing Digital Sculpting and Brushing Up on Your Retopology Skills, lets you explore Blender's sculpting side. You will use brushes to push and pull forms, experiment with dynamesh-style remeshing, and then retopologize sculpted shapes into cleaner, animation-friendly meshes ready for UVs and shading.

Chapter 13, Introducing Shaders in Blender, turns grey clay into believable materials. You will work in the Shader Editor, use the Principled BSDF, plug in basic texture maps, and start building a mental model of how light, color, roughness, and normal detail come together.

Chapter 14, Mastering Seams and Sharps in Blender, prepares meshes for clean shading and texturing. You will mark seams in sensible places, manage sharp edges and Auto Smooth, and understand how these decisions affect both your UV unwrap and the way your model catches highlights.

Chapter 15, Mastering the Art of UV Unwrapping in Blender, teaches you to tackle UVs properly. You will unwrap a range of shapes, troubleshoot stretching, pack islands efficiently, and gain the confidence to produce UV layouts that work well with tiled textures, trim sheets, and custom texture painting.

Chapter 16, Animating Your First Scene in Blender, pulls everything together in motion. You will keyframe transforms and camera moves, adjust timing and interpolation, and create a simple, finished animation that shows off your modelling and shading work in a way that feels like a real shot, not just a static render.

To get the most out of this book

Before you dive into *Part 1*, it helps to be clear about what I am assuming you already know – and what you absolutely do not need to know yet.

For *Part 1*, I am assuming:

- You are comfortable with basic computer use: opening and saving files, using folders, installing software, copy–paste, that sort of thing.
- You can use a mouse and keyboard together without thinking about it too much.
- You have a basic feel for how 2D images work (JPGs, PNGs) and that 3D is "a different thing," even if you have never touched it.

You do not need:

- Any previous experience with Blender or any other 3D software.
- Any math background beyond everyday common sense.
- Any drawing or traditional art training (it helps later, but it is not required to start).

If you have never opened Blender before, *Part 1* is exactly where you should begin. If you have opened Blender and bounced off it because the interface felt like an aircraft cockpit, you are also in the right place, and when you are ready, you can move on to *Part 2* of *Blender for Beginners*.

Before we begin, do not forget to check out the full technical specifications for Blender in *Chapter 1*—nothing fancy in terms of computer specs, but make sure you got the basics.

Download the color images

We also provide a PDF file that has color images of the screenshots/diagrams used in this book. You can download it here: `https://packt.link/gbp/9781837631094`.

This book contains long screenshots captured to provide you with an overview of the entire Blender interface. As a result, the text on these images may appear small at 100% zoom. We recommend referring to the graphics bundle for the ease of understanding.

Conventions used

There are a number of text conventions used throughout this book.

`CodeInText`: Indicates code words in text, database table names, folder names, filenames, file extensions, pathnames, dummy URLs, user input, and Twitter handles. For example: "Open your custom `.blend` file in Blender."

Bold: Indicates a new term, an important word, or words that you see on the screen. For instance, words in menus or dialog boxes appear in the text like this. For example: "**Object** mode in Blender is one of the primary modes available for working with 3D objects."

Warnings or important notes appear like this.

Tips and tricks appear like this.

Get in touch

Feedback from our readers is always welcome.

General feedback: If you have questions about any aspect of this book or have any general feedback, please email us at customercare@packt.com and mention the book's title in the subject of your message. If you have feedback on content, you can email the authors at bettison.gamedesign@gmail.com or vanessa.haralambous@gmail.com.

Errata: Although we have taken every care to ensure the accuracy of our content, mistakes do happen. If you have found a mistake in this book, we would be grateful if you reported this to us. Please visit http://www.packt.com/submit-errata, click **Submit Errata**, and fill in the form.

Piracy: If you come across any illegal copies of our works in any form on the internet, we would be grateful if you would provide us with the location address or website name. Please contact us at copyright@packt.com with a link to the material.

If you are interested in becoming an author: If there is a topic that you have expertise in and you are interested in either writing or contributing to a book, please visit http://authors.packt.com/.

Share your thoughts

Once you've read *Blender for Beginners, Part 1*, we'd love to hear your thoughts! Scan the QR code below to go straight to the Amazon review page for this book and share your feedback.

https://packt.link/r/1837631093

Your review is important to us and the tech community and will help us make sure we're delivering excellent quality content.

Free Benefits with Your Book

This book comes with free benefits to support your learning. Activate them now for instant access (see the "*How to Unlock*" section for instructions).

Here's a quick overview of what you can instantly unlock with your purchase:

PDF and ePub Copies   **Next-Gen Web-Based Reader**

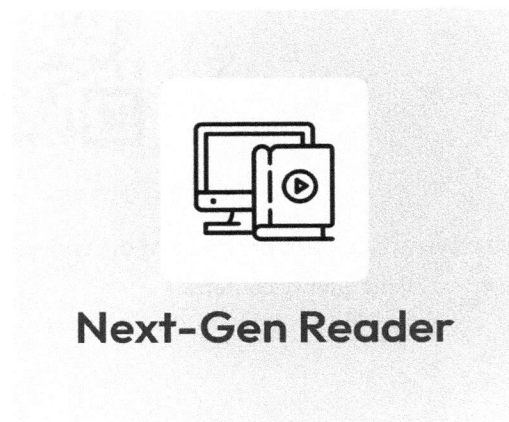

Free PDF and ePub versions   **Next-Gen Reader**

Access a DRM-free PDF copy of this book to read anywhere, on any device.

Use a DRM-free ePub version with your favorite e-reader.

Multi-device progress sync: Pick up where you left off, on any device.

Highlighting and notetaking: Capture ideas and turn reading into lasting knowledge.

Bookmarking: Save and revisit key sections whenever you need them.

Dark mode: Reduce eye strain by switching to dark or sepia themes.

How to Unlock

UNLOCK NOW

Scan the QR code (or go to packtpub.com/unlock). Search for this book by name, confirm the edition, and then follow the steps on the page.

Note: Keep your invoice handy. Purchases made directly from Packt don't require one.

1

Understanding Camera Control and Viewport Navigation in Blender

Welcome to Blender, a beast of a tool, but once tamed, it becomes your best mate in the world of 3D.

Now, if you're anything like me when I first opened Blender, you probably stared at the interface like it was the cockpit of a spaceship. So many buttons. So many panels. So many opportunities to completely crash your scene without knowing how you did it.

But here's the thing: Blender is *free*. Not "free trial," not "give us your card, and we'll charge you in 7 days," just *free*, open source goodness. It was developed and continues to be updated and maintained by the Blender Foundation. The Blender Foundation is a non-profit organization that was founded by Ton Roosendaal in 2002. Its goal is to be a free and accessible toolset for artists, designers, and researchers in various industries. Blender is popular with professionals because it is cost-effective and versatile. Compared to heavyweights such as Autodesk Maya, which costs a small fortune and updates at the pace of a sloth on a coffee break, Blender moves fast.

Now, before we start slapping materials onto dragons and building medieval taverns with infinite barrels, we have to get through the basics. Yes, I know. But trust me, you *need* to know how to move around in Blender first. This chapter will walk you through the Blender interface, what all those buttons do and how to get comfortable with cameras, including how to move around Blender's 3D Viewport and how to use cameras in Blender.

Mastering the UI early on will save you hours down the line, and possibly a few gray hairs.

So, without further ado, this chapter will cover the following topics:

- Opening Blender
- Differentiating Blender's **Object Mode** and **Edit Mode**
- Explaining the XYZ axes
- Operationalizing Blender's 3D Cursor
- Conceptualizing the **Perspective** and **Orthographic** views
- Learning Blender's 3D Viewport controls
- Grasping Blender camera essentials

Free Benefits with Your Book

Your purchase includes a free PDF copy *Your Book* section in the Preface to un-
of this book along with other exclusive lock them instantly and maximize your
benefits. Check the *Free Benefits with* learning experience.

Technical requirements

As for **Blender 4.5 LTS (Long-Term Support)**, the general requirements include the following:

- **macOS:** minimum now ~11.2+ (Apple Silicon supported natively).
- **Linux:** glibc baseline rises from ~2.17 to ~2.28+
- **CPU:** instruction set reference updated from **SSE2** to **SSE4.2** (newer CPUs)
- **RAM:** practical minimum **8 GB** (32 GB recommended for heavy scenes)
- **GPU/OpenGL:** OpenGL 4.3; VRAM **2 GB+** (more recommended)
- **GPU backends:** include **Metal (macOS), AMD HIP, Intel oneAPI**, alongside **CUDA/OptiX**
- **Practical notes:** Full HD display recommended; app footprint ≈1 GB; SSD recommended

Because Blender is constantly evolving and these technical requirements might change, the stuff you need to run it might change over time. This list should give you a good idea of what you will need to get started, but I would still recommend checking Blender's official documentation (https://www.blender.org/download/requirements/) to make sure you have the latest info before installing it.

Opening Blender

Alright, so you've launched Blender. First thing that pops up? The splash screen you can see in *Figure 1.1.*

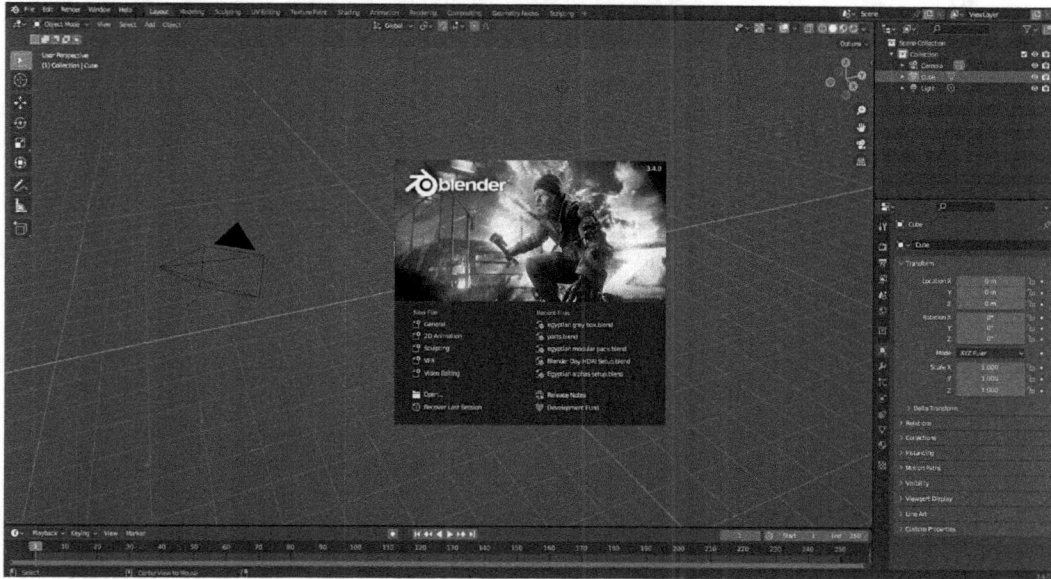

Figure 1.1: Blender splash screen

Think of it as Blender's way of saying, "Hey, welcome back!" before throwing you into the deep end. The Blender splash screen can help you recover your last session and access the Blender release notes; and, most importantly, it has a direct link to the Blender manual online. Even if you did not manage to check which version of Blender you are using before the flash screen disappeared, Blender will still display that key information on its status bar, at the bottom right of the screen.

Once the splash screen vanishes, you are dropped into the mysterious world of the **default startup scene**. It contains the holy trinity: a camera, a cube, and a light. This is called the default startup Blender window, and is shown in *Figure 1.2*.

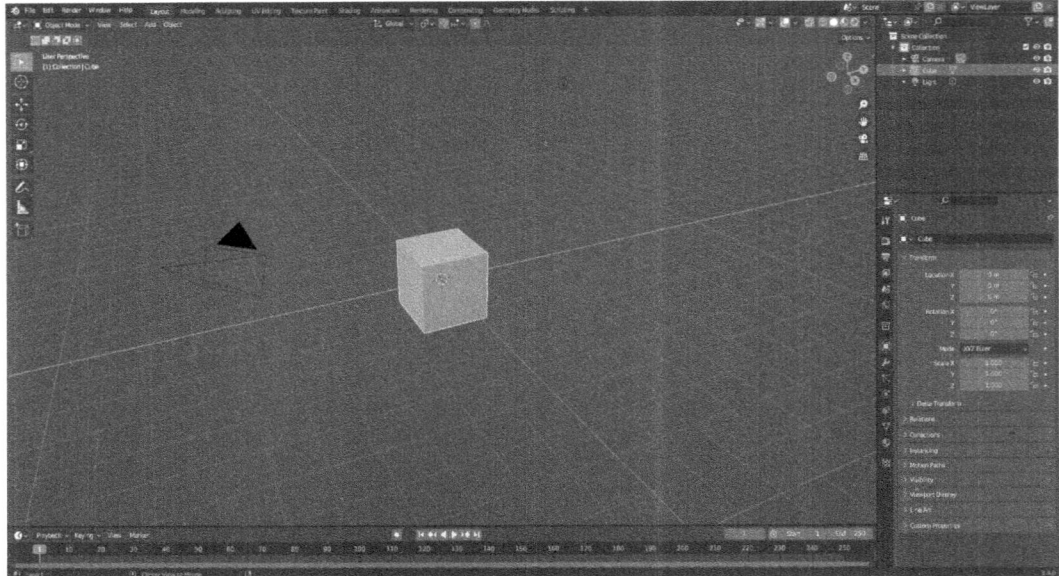

Figure 1.2: Default startup window

The default startup Blender window makes up the core of Blender's UI. It is made up of the topbar at the very top, and it includes tabs that let you perform essential functions within Blender, such as saving, importing, or exporting files, rendering, and settings configuration. Under the Topbar, you will find the Areas Bar, containing options that will help you make the most of Blender.

The next thing you will come across is the **3D Viewport**. The best way to define it would be as the entire space the Blender application occupies on your screen. It is where all the modeling, texturing, animating, and world-building magic happens. You can tumble around the scene, zoom in to inspect tiny details, or spin the camera like a dramatic director looking for the perfect shot.

You can also use the 3D Viewport space to add more lights, cameras, and objects to optimize your workspace and scene. The 3D Viewport is an essential part of the Blender UI, and it is where you will be spending most of your time as a 3D modeling artist immersed in the creation process. Just to reassure you, we will be talking about additional parts of the Blender UI, such as the **Properties** tab and the **Animation** tab, later on in this book as well.

Do not worry if it still feels like a maze right now. We are going to walk you through it all. Let us begin by defining key terms and functions in Blender. Even though these have many uses, you will gradually come to see how Blender functions help you navigate the 3D Viewport and set up cameras later on.

Differentiating Blender's Object Mode and Edit Mode

Before we dive into camera controls (which I promise we'll get to in a second), we need to talk about something absolutely fundamental in Blender: the difference between **Object Mode** and **Edit Mode**.

Now, if you have ever wondered why clicking on your mesh sometimes lets you move it around and other times lets you poke at its little dots and lines, this is why.

Object Mode in Blender is one of the primary modes available for working with 3D objects. In **Object Mode**, you can move the objects around your 3D Viewport, as well as rotate, scale, or duplicate them. This mode is mainly used to position and arrange objects in a 3D environment or to apply **modifiers** (i.e., automatic operations or effects that can be applied to 3D objects without altering the underlying mesh) and **properties** (i.e., various settings related to objects, materials, textures, and lighting) to them.

Figure 1.3 shows you what an object looks like in **Object Mode**:

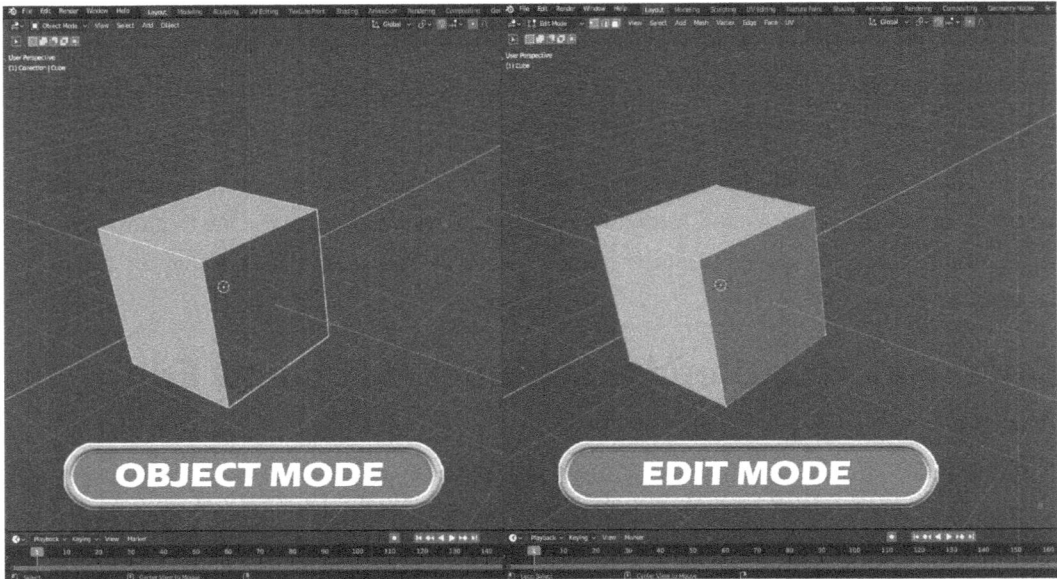

Figure 1.3: Object Mode versus Edit Mode in Blender

Now, let us flip the switch.

Edit Mode is where you *really* get into the details.

Figure 1.3 also shows **Edit Mode**. **Edit Mode** in Blender is used for modifying the underlying structure and topology of 3D objects, including vertices, edges, and faces.

You can jump into **Edit Mode** in a couple of ways. You can switch to **Edit Mode** manually by either clicking on **Edit Mode** in the **Mode Select** menu in the top-left corner of the 3D Viewport or manually by pressing *Tab* to switch between the two modes. This is important to know before you start exploring Blender's UI, because selecting options such as a 3D model's vertices, edges, and faces by *left-click*ing on those icons in the **Areas** tab is only available in **Edit Mode**.

Basically, do not stress about which workspace you are in. You do not have to be in the dedicated **Modeling** tab to do this stuff, any layout that includes a 3D Viewport will work fine, as long as you are in the right mode.

In *Figure 1.4*, you will see what parts of a cube the terms vertex, edge, and face refer to (we will discuss them in more detail in *Chapter 6* in *Part 1* of this book:

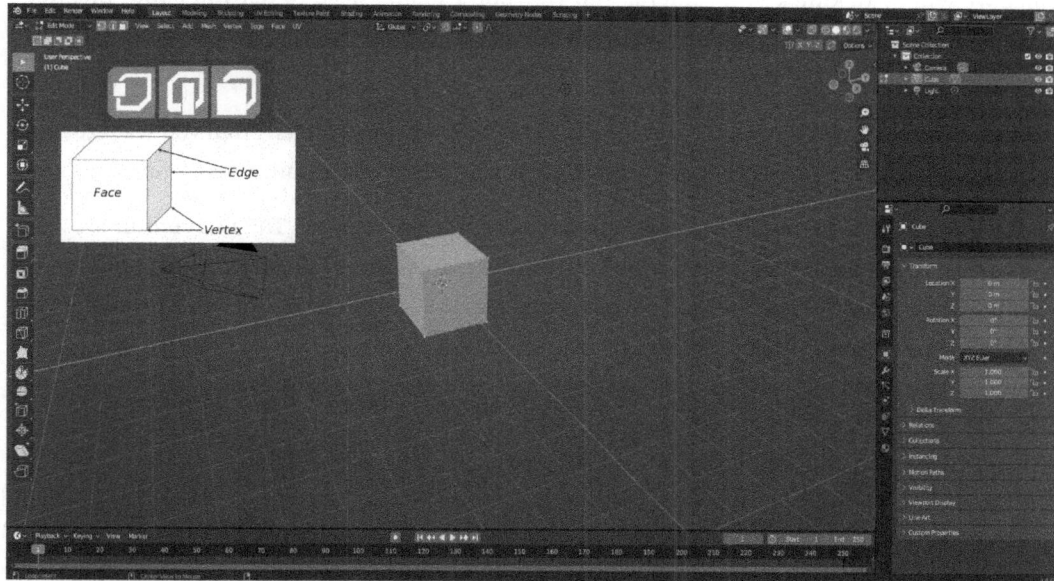

Figure 1.4: Conceptualizing vertices, edges, and faces in Blender

Blender's **Edit Mode** and **Object Mode** work together to provide a comprehensive workflow for creating and modifying 3D objects in a scene. To recap, **Object Mode** focuses on the basic manipulation of entire objects, whereas **Edit Mode** allows you to dive deeper into the structure of individual objects using tools that modify the mesh.

This can be summarized as follows:

- **Object Mode** = move, scale, rotate, and organize your objects like chess pieces
- **Edit Mode** = zoom in, slice up objects, reshape them, and get creative with geometry

To use these modes effectively, it is important to learn how to use coordinates for accurate positioning in 3D space. Next up, we will start talking about cameras, coordinates, and how not to lose your scene in the Blender void. Let's keep going.

Explaining the XYZ axes

Since we will be talking about cameras and viewports soon, I need to tell you about Blender's axes. Blender is based on a **coordinate system** represented by the *X*, *Y*, and *Z* axes, which you can see in *Figure 1.5*.

Now, do not worry, this is not going to turn into a math lesson (I promise). But if you want to move stuff around in Blender without it going haywire, you've got to understand what direction is what.

Blender's coordinate system is an essential part of its 3D environment. The XYZ coordinates help define the position and orientation of objects, vertices, and other elements within your scene. It is important to understand and be able to visualize their location in 3D space, especially if your project is based on real-life proportions.

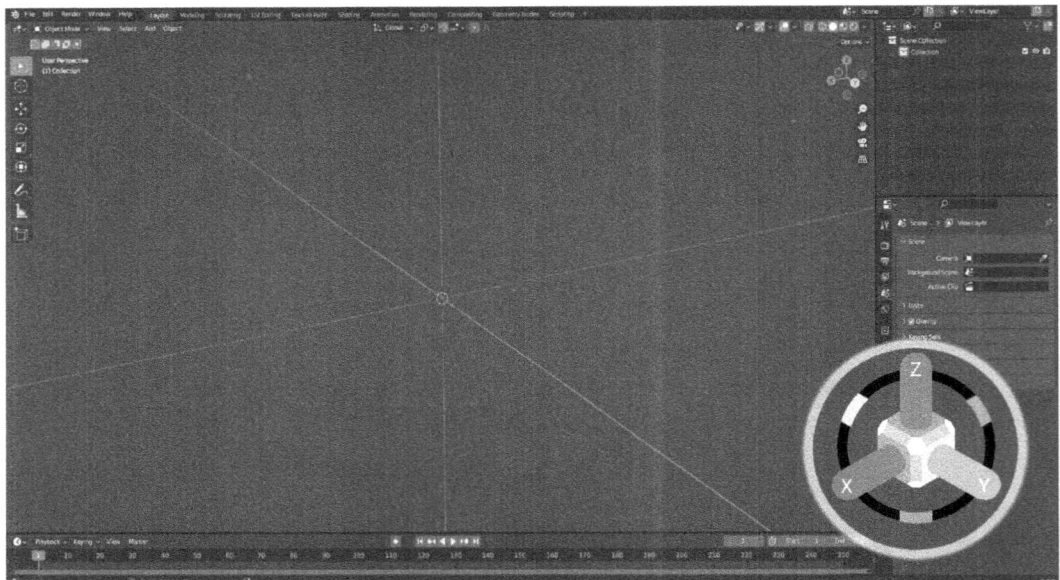

Figure 1.5: Blender XYZ coordinate system

The *X* axis is horizontal and runs from left to right; positive values are positioned to the right and negative values to the left. The *Y* axis is vertical and runs from front to back; positive values are positioned to the back, and negative values to the front. The *Z* axis is based on depth and runs from top to bottom; its positive values run upward and its negative values downward. Blender's coordinate system is mathematical, and it uses each object's values on the *X*, *Y*, and *Z* axes to define its exact position in 3D space.

Put simply, here is how it works:

- **X** is your left-to-right axis. Move right? That's **positive X**. Move left? That's **negative X**.
- **Y** is your front-to-back axis. Push something away from you? That's **positive Y**. Pull it toward you? **Negative Y**.
- **Z** is up and down. Yep, you guessed it: **positive Z** is up (floating in the sky), and **negative Z** is down (buried underground, or just clipping through your floor).

This coordinate system helps Blender users manipulate objects in a number of ways:

- Positioning, scaling, and rotating objects in 3D space
- Positioning sets of objects in a 3D scene and aligning them
- Controlling cameras and lights to create renders or videos of scenes with correct lighting and perspective, including direction, intensity, and falloff of light sources
- Managing the movement of objects through space
- Rigging characters and objects

You will be learning more about advanced uses of the XYZ coordinate system later, in *Chapter 5* in *Part 1* of this book, where snapping tools such as vertex snapping and grid snapping would not function the way they do if it were not for the accurate placement that Blender's coordinate system facilitates.

The coordinate system is an integral part of using the software, and it interacts with other tools in Blender. So yeah, it might not be flashy, but understanding Blender's coordinates is like learning how to drive before getting behind the wheel of a Formula 1 car.

One of the other tools we need to talk about in Blender is its **3D Cursor**: a reference point for different operations. Because it is placed on specific locations on the coordinate system, Blender's 3D Cursor effectively links your actions with the tools you have at your disposal.

Operationalizing Blender's 3D Cursor

Blender's 3D Cursor is an essential tool in its interface. It is a small circle with a crosshair in the center and acts as a visual marker for a specific point in 3D space.

It might look like a tiny bullseye someone forgot to clean up, but do not underestimate it; it is actually one of the most useful tools in Blender. If the 3D Viewport is your sandbox, the 3D Cursor is the flag you plant in it.

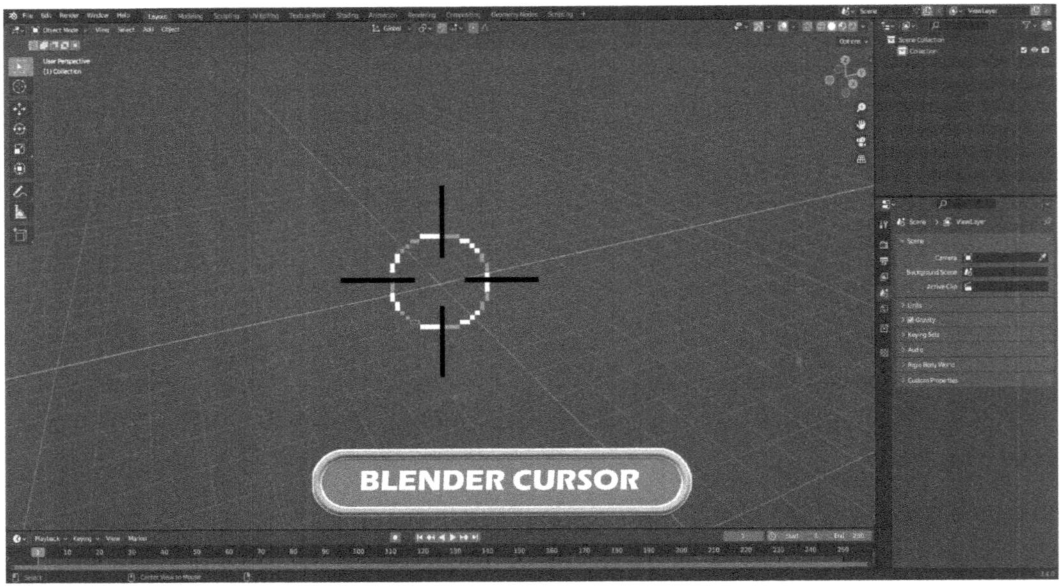

Figure 1.6: Blender 3D Cursor

For example, when you are parenting objects (shown in *Figure 1.7*), it is important to have worked out exact object locations using the 3D Cursor. This is because parenting (i.e., establishing a hierarchical relationship between two or more objects) makes them interdependent in regard to rotation, movement, and scale. In other words, by using the 3D Cursor and Blender's coordinate system and understanding their synergy, you are making sure that the one object (i.e., the parent) is influencing the other object (i.e., the child) the way you want them to.

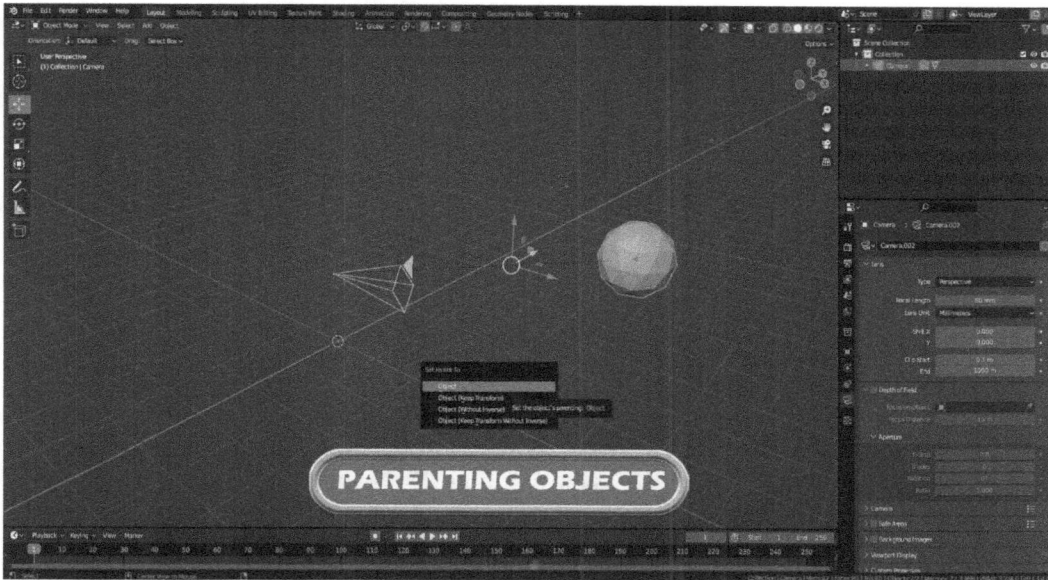

Figure 1.7: Parenting objects in Blender

Blender's 3D Cursor can be used for different Blender functions, including, but not limited to, the following:

- Modeling, animation, and scene composition
- Acting as the anchor point for viewport navigation
- Creating new objects since all new objects will be placed at Blender's 3D Cursor location
- A reference point for snapping to align objects to their location or as a pivot point for object transformations (e.g., scaling and rotation) so that the objects are transformed around that center point

To move the 3D Cursor, *Shift + right-click* anywhere in the 3D Viewport or press *Shift + S* to open the snap menu and position the 3D Cursor based on different snapping options (e.g., **Cursor to selected**, which moves your 3D Cursor to the center of a selected object). Also, should you want to manually define your 3D Cursor coordinates on the *X*, *Y*, and *Z* axes, you can do the following:

Press the *N* button. Use the sidebar to access the **Property** panel under the **View** tab, as in *Figure 1.8*:

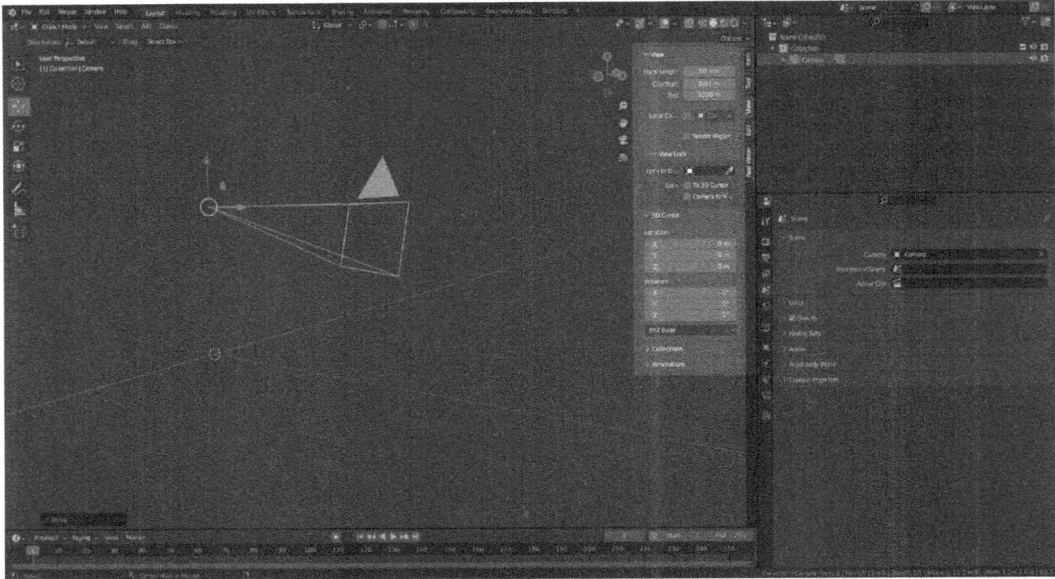

Figure 1.8: Sidebar (Property panel)

The better you get at using the 3D Cursor, the more you will come to realize that it is like having a cheat code for efficiency. Whether you are snapping pieces together, laying out a scene, or rigging characters, it helps you stay clean, accurate, and in control. The good news is that we will be discussing how to use the 3D Cursor more as we move through the book.

As you get a deeper understanding of Blender's UI, it is important to learn about different visualization techniques. Although Blender's 3D Cursor is not directly related to the **Perspective** and **Orthographic** views, which we will discuss next, it does serve as a super useful reference point when navigating or placing your camera.

Conceptualizing the Perspective and Orthographic views

Alright, let us take a quick detour to talk about two really important ways Blender shows you your 3D scene: the difference between the **Perspective** and **Orthographic** views.

The **Perspective** view depicts how the human eye would see a 3D scene. Objects further away in the distance appear smaller, and this allows users to judge depth and spatial relationships between objects more easily.

In the **Orthographic** view, the distortion of making objects look smaller when they are further away from the camera is removed. Hence, all objects appear the same size independent of camera distance. The same object in both views is shown in *Figure 1.9*.

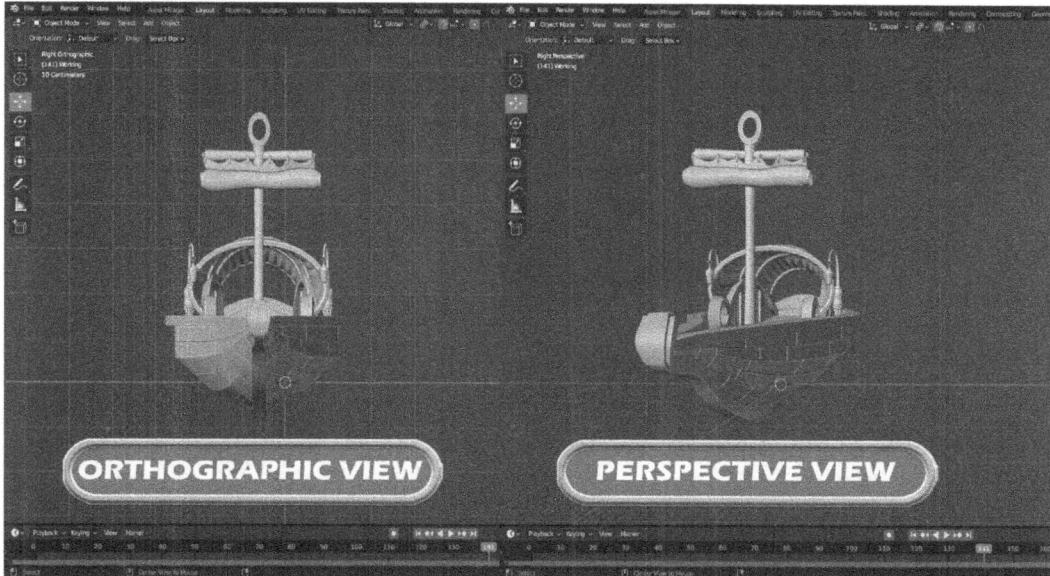

Figure 1.9: Perspective versus Orthographic view

In Blender, the main difference between the **Orthographic** and **Perspective** views is that **Orthographic** is how to visualize depth, whereas the **Perspective** view gives a sense of space. Things that are closer to the camera look bigger, and you can move inside a model, such as into the mouth of a character, to see the inside clearly. The **Orthographic** view does not have this kind of sense of depth. Everything stays the same size no matter how far it is from the camera. For example, in the **Perspective** view, the front of a ship will look larger if it is closer to the camera. In the **Orthographic** view, the ship stays the same size all over, no matter the distance.

By pressing *5* on your number pad, or going to **View | Perspective/Orthographic**, you will reactivate the **Perspective** view (i.e., the default view in Blender), and here, you cannot zoom into the inside of your model. Press it once, you are in **Perspective**. Press it again, bam, you are in **Orthographic**.

Also, do not stress about this affecting your final renders. Being in the **Orthographic** view will not affect rendering because rendering uses the **Perspective** view by default.

Discussing the **Perspective** and **Orthographic** views laid the foundation for introducing different ways for Blender users to navigate its UI. Now, as we delve deeper into understanding Blender's UI, you will come to understand how to use Blender's 3D Viewport controls. This will help you effectively navigate, manipulate objects, and increase your productivity.

Learning Blender's 3D Viewport controls

Before we jump into the fun stuff, such as using cameras and getting cinematic, it is super important to get comfortable moving around Blender's 3D Viewport. Think of this as learning to drive before taking your car down a mountain road. We will begin with some viewport navigation methods and shortcuts.

Viewport navigation methods and shortcuts

The 3D Viewport is Blender's primary window and displays your 3D scene: the place where you'll do 90% of your work. The main ways of 3D Viewport navigation include orbiting, panning, and zooming, and you can use a keyboard shortcut or navigate to those options via the Blender menu, depending on your personal preference.

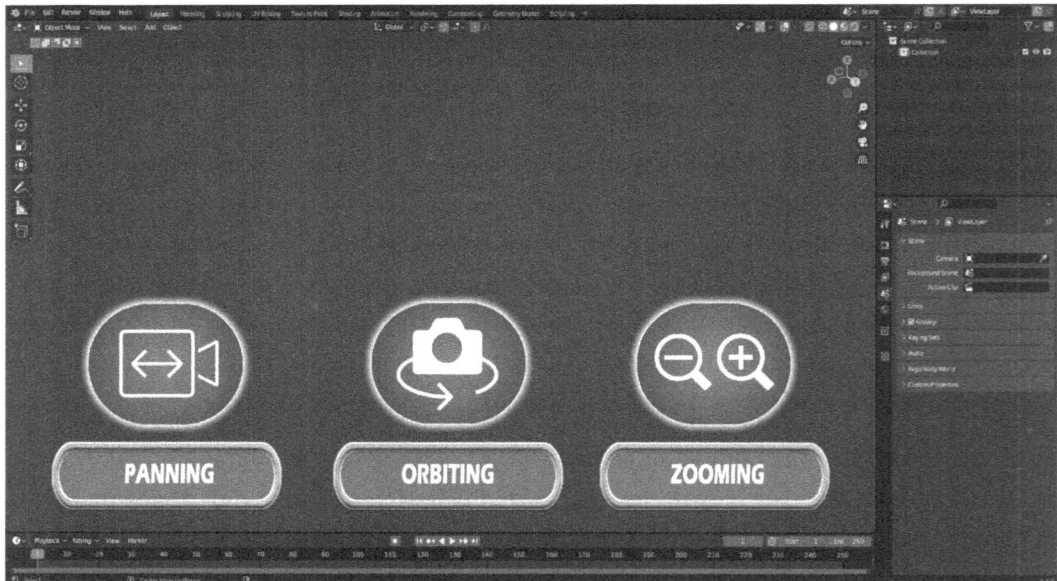

Figure 1.10: Panning, orbiting, and zooming in Blender

Let's look at some viewport controls and the shortcuts to use them:

- **Orbit**: To orbit around the 3D scene, hold the *MMB* and drag the mouse. This rotates the view around the scene's focal point.

- **Pan**: To pan the view, hold *Shift + MMB* and drag the mouse. This moves the view parallel to the 3D Viewport plane.

- **Zoom**: To zoom in and out, use the scroll wheel on your *MMB*. This adjusts the distance between the viewport camera and the scene's focal point.

- **Slow Zoom**: To zoom in and out slowly, use the scroll wheel, or press *Ctrl + MMB*.

- **Frame Selected**: Press the period key (.) on the number pad to frame the selected object(s) in the 3D Viewport. This focuses the view on the selected object(s) and adjusts the orbiting center. The orbiting center will always be the object's orientation point, which you will see as a small yellow dot (you can see this in *Figure 1.11*).

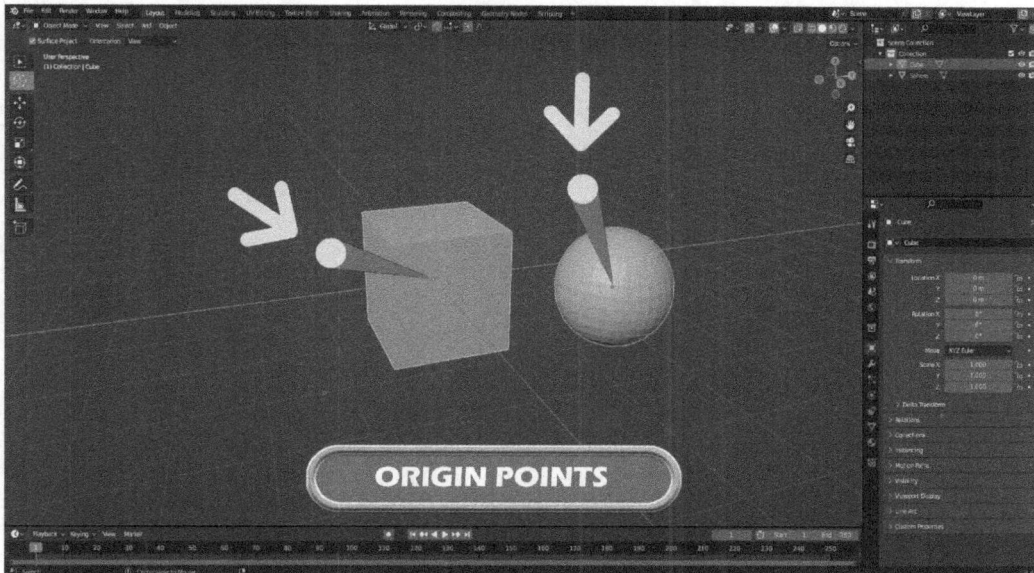

Figure 1.11: Blender origin points

- **Frame All**: Press the *Home* key to frame all objects in the 3D Viewport.

- **Viewport Views**: Press the number pad keys to switch between different views:

    - **Front view**: *1*

    - **Right view**: *3*

    - **Top view**: *7*

- **Back view**: *Ctrl + 1*
- **Left view**: *Ctrl + 3*
- **Bottom view**: *Ctrl + 7*
- **Perspective/Orthographic toggle**: *5*

You can also navigate Blender's 3D Viewport using the navigation gizmo (shown in *Figure 1.12*), which you can find in the top-right corner of the 3D Viewport. It gives you the tools to orbit, pan, and zoom in an alternative way as well:

- To orbit, click and drag the circle around the gizmo
- To pan, click and drag the hand icon
- To zoom, click and drag the magnifying glass icon

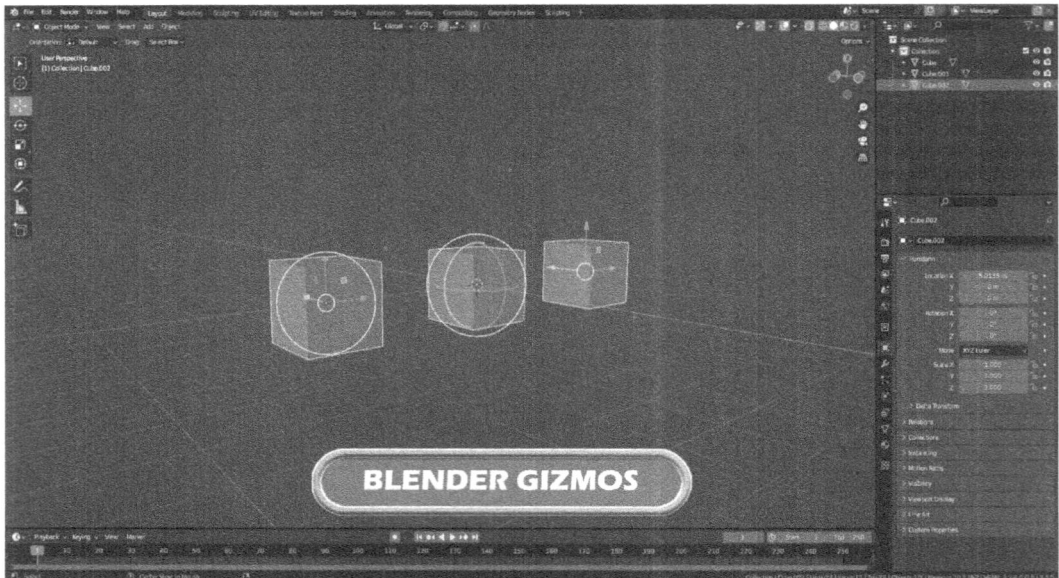

Figure 1.12: Blender gizmos

There's also another set of gizmos that pop up when you activate **Scale**, **Rotate**, or **Move**. These tools let you change the size, angle, or position of your object. *Figure 1.12* shows what each of those gizmos looks like when they are active. Just to note, this is different from the navigation gizmo in the top left, which helps you move the camera view and shows the colored axes.

Additional Blender 3D Viewport controls

You can use the sidebar (**Property** panel) by pressing *N*, giving you access to additional options, such as camera lens settings, 3D Cursor location, and background images, as in *Figure 1.13*.

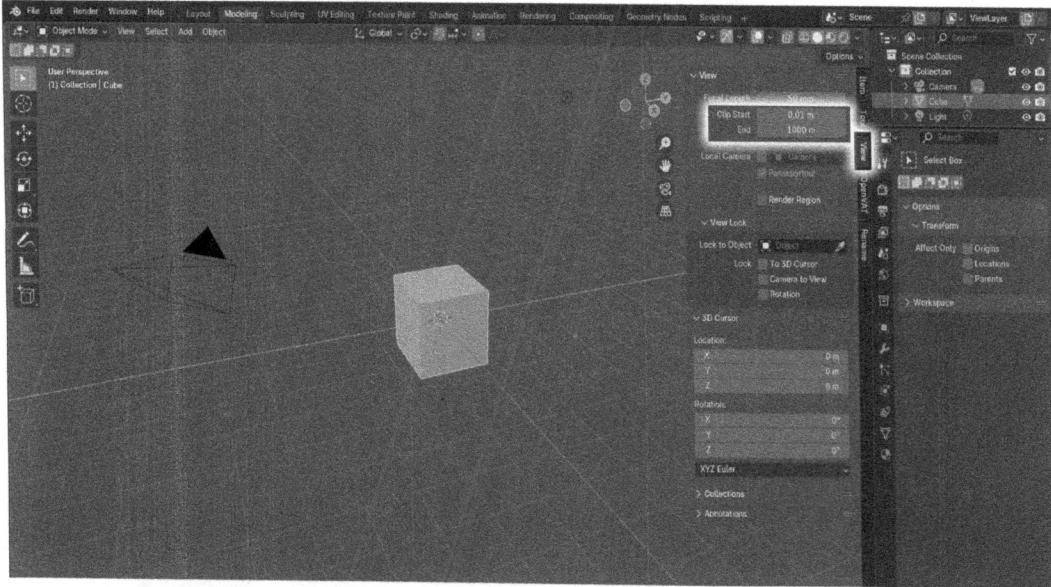

Figure 1.13: Pressing N to access the Property panel in Blender

Using the properties editor, you can clip distances and adjust focal length.

Clipping distances, accessed through the **View** tab, help you define the distance at which objects are visible in Blender's 3D Viewport. By defining the visibility range of objects, you are ensuring that objects that are closer or farther from the specified distance are not displayed. There are two types of distances:

- **Clip Start:** This value sets the minimum distance from the viewport camera at which objects become visible. Objects closer to the camera than the clip start distance will not be displayed.

- **Clip End:** This value sets the maximum distance from the viewport camera at which objects are visible. Objects farther from the camera than the clip end distance will not be displayed.

Important note

Clipping distances help you optimize your Blender 3D Viewport's performance, especially with complex scenes that include many objects. Adjusting your clipping distances can also prevent issues such as Z-fighting (i.e., overlapping surfaces flickering due to depth buffer imprecision).

Focal Length changes the "lens" you're viewing through. This changes the field of view, and objects appear in the **Perspective** view. A lower **Focal Length** value results in a wider field of view, while a higher **Focal Length** value results in a narrower field of view. Modifying the **Focal Length** can help you achieve specific visual effects or mimic real-world camera lenses in the 3D Viewport.

Other 3D Viewport options that could improve your 3D modeling workflow include **Lock to Object** and **Lock to 3D Cursor**.

Lock to Object allows you to lock the 3D Viewport camera to a specific object, as shown in *Figure 1.14*.

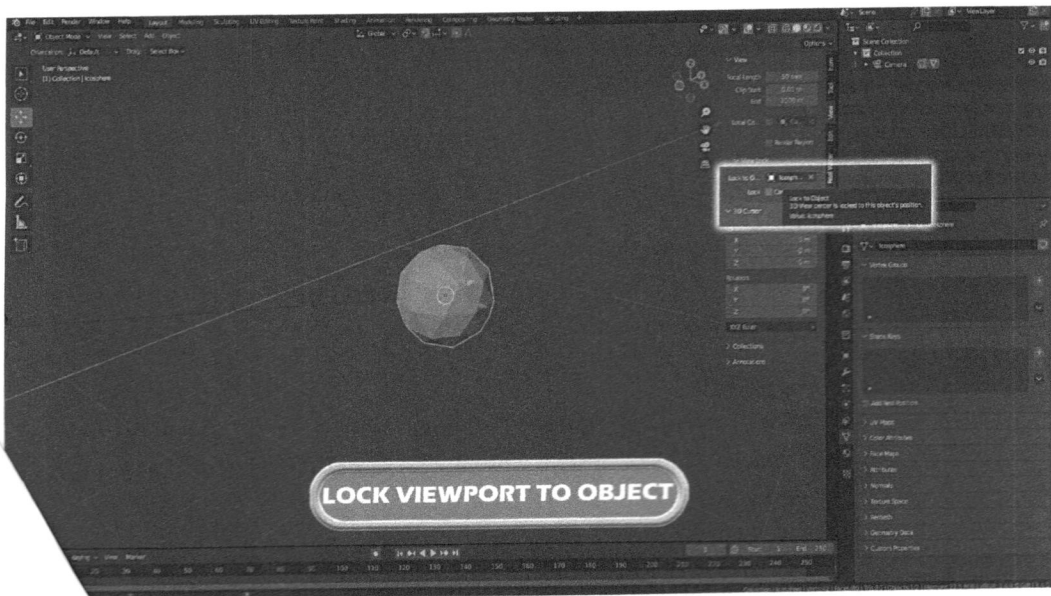

Figure 1.14: Lock viewport to object

To use **Lock to Object**, follow these steps:

1. Select the object you want to lock the viewport to.

2. Click on the object in the viewport or select it in the Outliner (i.e., a Blender menu shown in *Figure 1.15* that will be discussed in more detail in *Chapter 2* in *Part 1* of this book):

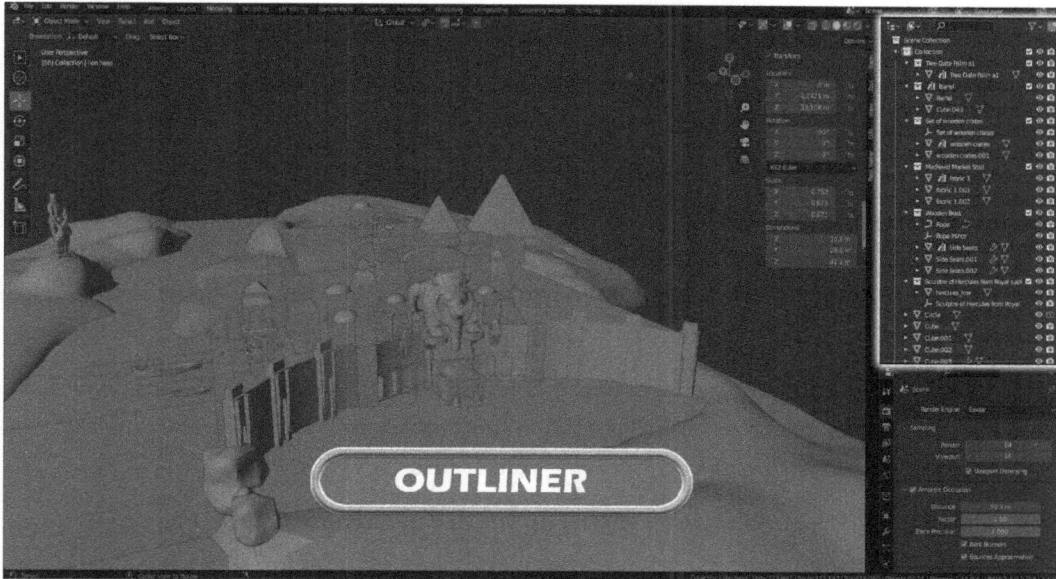

Figure 1.15: Outliner menu in Blender

3. Press *N* to open the sidebar panel on the right side of the 3D Viewport.

4. Click on the **View** tab to access the viewport settings.

5. Locate the **Lock to Object** drop-down menu.

6. Find the object in the Outliner or select the object you want to lock the 3D Viewport to. You can do this by choosing it from the drop-down list, or even easier, click the little eye-dropper icon next to the menu, then click on the object directly in the 3D Viewport. That is a handy way to quickly pick what you want.

7. You can click the **X** icon next to the object name to clear the lock and reset the view.

> Note
>
> Do not worry if the scene in *Figure 1.14* looks a bit busy. It is just a glimpse of what a full 3D scene can look like. It is totally normal for things to get a little complex sometimes, and you will get used to it as you go.

If you follow these steps, your 3D Viewport will always be centered on the selected object even if you move around the scene or you move the object elsewhere. To unlock the 3D Viewport from the object, go back to the **Lock to Object** drop-down menu and click on the **X** icon or choose another object to use the **Lock to Object** option on.

Tip

Lock to Object only affects navigation in Blender's 3D Viewport. It does not affect object transformations or other actions.

When **Lock to Object** is enabled, the 3D Viewport camera will follow the object as it moves or rotates. The 3D Viewport camera will maintain the same relative position and orientation as the object. **Lock to 3D Cursor** will lock the 3D Viewport camera to the Blender's cursor instead. This will make the 3D Viewport camera orbit around the 3D Cursor and not the scene's focal point.

Understanding Blender's 3D Viewport controls is essential to developing your camera know-how. Both topics are interconnected since Blender's 3D Viewport controls and understanding cameras are both essential to visualizing and rendering your scenes:

- Navigating the 3D Viewport lets you position and manipulate objects effectively.
- A good understanding of cameras helps you create renders the way you imagined them, based on framing, perspective, and depth.

So, take your time with this. Practice orbiting, panning, and locking your view. Soon, it will feel second nature, and your scenes will thank you for it.

Let us keep going. Cameras are up next, and things are about to get cinematic.

Grasping Blender camera essentials

Camera control is important to all 3D modeling artists. Whether you are creating a game asset, a cinematic short, or a snazzy turntable for *ArtStation* (https://www.artstation.com/), camera control is what makes your work shine.

Think of the camera as your audience's eyes. It tells them *what* to look at, *how* to feel about it, and *where* to focus. And in Blender, the camera is not just a passive viewer, it is something you can fully control, tweak, and animate. Blender is well equipped for camera control, allowing you to fine-tune settings to a high degree using keyboard shortcuts and specialized menus.

All Blender users should know how to use Blender cameras to create stunning visuals, animations, and renders of final scenes. Here is the truth: no matter how good your model is, if the camera angle is off, your work won't hit as hard.

This section offers a thorough overview of using cameras in Blender, including spawning, locking the camera to view, shortcut keys, and alternative menus.

Using cameras for games and film

Learning how to spawn, move, and control cameras in Blender is a must for everyone, whether you are aiming for stylized renders or full-blown animations.

For example, you can use panning to track character movement. You could also pan from one character to another to create tension in a 3D model or environment showreel video. Then again, you can use the dolly shot (i.e., moving the camera forward or backward to create a sense of depth) to take interesting camera shots using Blender's rendering options to showcase the depth and scale of an environment such as a castle keep (*Figure 1.16*).

Figure 1.16: Using Blender cameras to showcase depth in a scene

As another example, if you are working on an animation of a character, you can use a dolly shot to focus on a character in a way that encourages the audience to think about what they are thinking.

On the other hand, an orbit camera follows a circular path, moving around a target in a similar way to a potter's wheel. It allows you to view the 3D object while the orbit camera turns around in a turntable style (*Figure 1.17*).

Figure 1.17: Use for orbiting in Blender

It can be very effective for showing object or scene details using a smooth 360° shot for moving and still objects. Hence, an orbit camera could be useful for one of the most traditional videos that 3D modeling artists use to display their artwork on popular online portfolio platforms, such as Behance (https://www.behance.net/) and ArtStation (https://www.artstation.com/).

Spawning a camera in Blender

When you are creating a new scene in Blender, a default camera is already present. You can select and manipulate this camera like any other object in the scene.

To add a new camera to your scene, follow these steps:

1. Press *Shift + A* or click on the **Add** menu at the top of your 3D Viewport.

2. Choose a camera from the list of objects, as in *Figure 1.18*.

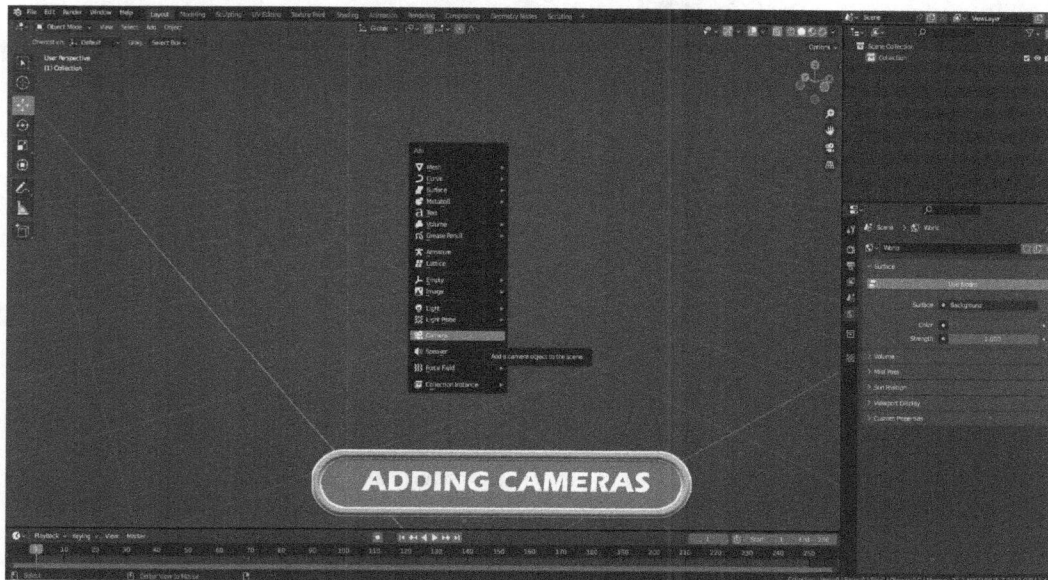

Figure 1.18: Adding cameras in Blender

You can see the added camera in the next subsection, along with how to navigate and manipulate cameras.

Camera navigation and manipulation

To learn about camera navigation, it is important to learn to differentiate certain Blender features, such as the ones provided here:

- **Activate Camera View**: Press the *0* key on the number pad to switch to the active camera's view.

- **Select Active Camera**: Press *Ctrl + 0* (number pad) with a camera selected to set it as the active camera, as in *Figure 1.19*.

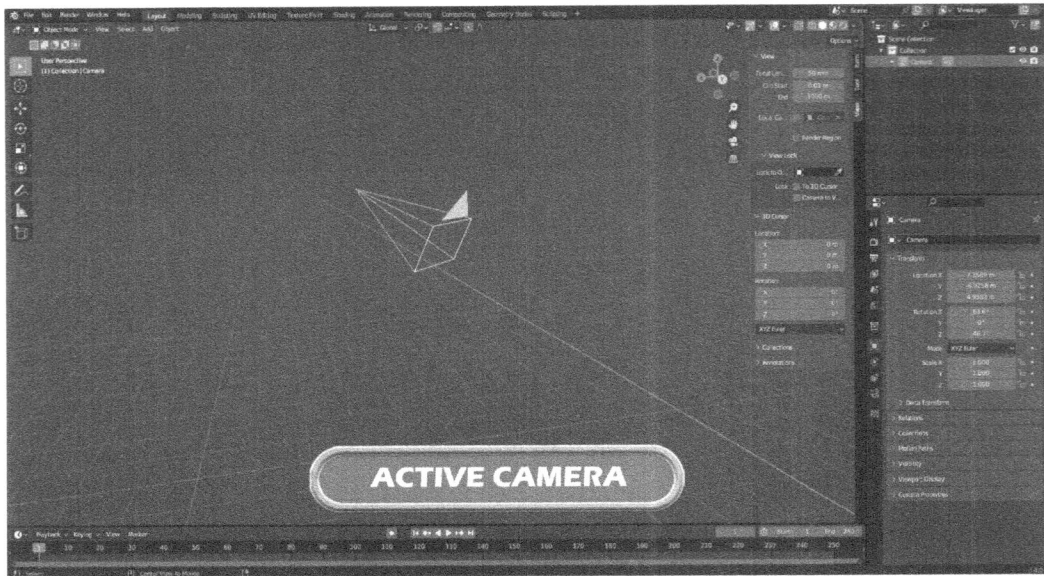

Figure 1.19: Active Camera in Blender

- **Lock Camera to View**: Press *N* to open the sidebar, navigate to the **View** tab, and enable the **Lock Camera to View** option. This allows you to navigate the 3D Viewport while looking through the camera, adjusting the camera's position and orientation in real time, as we did in *Figure 1.20*.

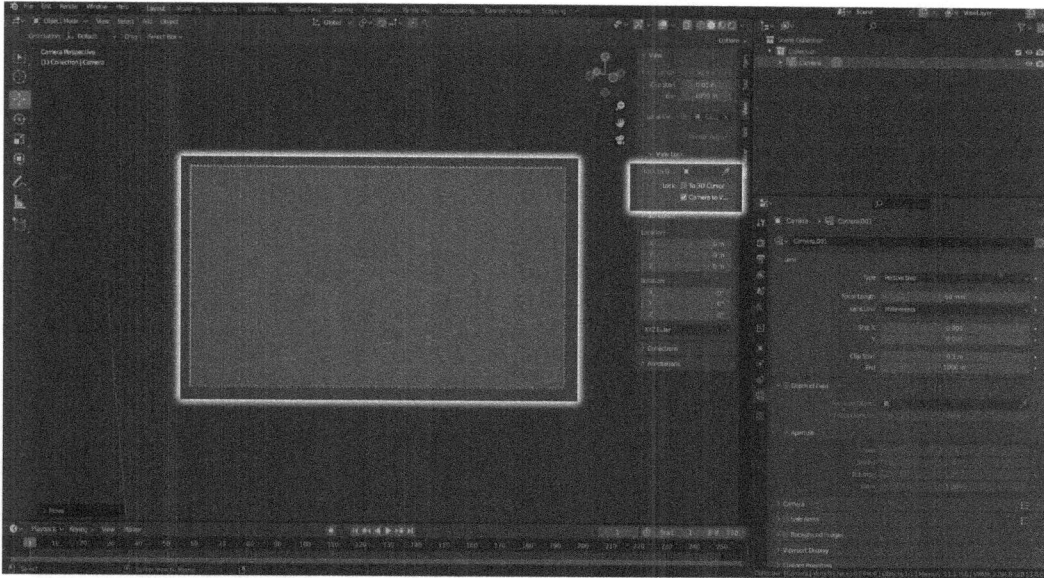

Figure 1.20: Lock Camera to View

Also, to transform your camera, you will find the following keyboard shortcuts and explanations useful:

- **Move**: Press the *G* key to move the camera or use the transform gizmo in the 3D Viewport.
- **Rotate**: Press the *R* key to rotate the camera or use the transform gizmo in the 3D Viewport.
- **Scale**: Although scaling does not apply to cameras, you can adjust the camera's focal length and depth of field settings to achieve different visual effects.

Tip

All options relating to transforming the camera work alongside the XYZ coordinates. You can move, scale, or rotate along the *X*, *Y*, and *Z* axes depending on your needs.

The following menus can also help with camera navigation and manipulation, and they each have specialized functions you should know about:

- **Properties editor**((*1* in *Figure 1.21*): In the **Camera** tab of the properties editor, as shown in *Figure 1.21*, you can access various camera settings, such as focal length, depth of field, and sensor size.

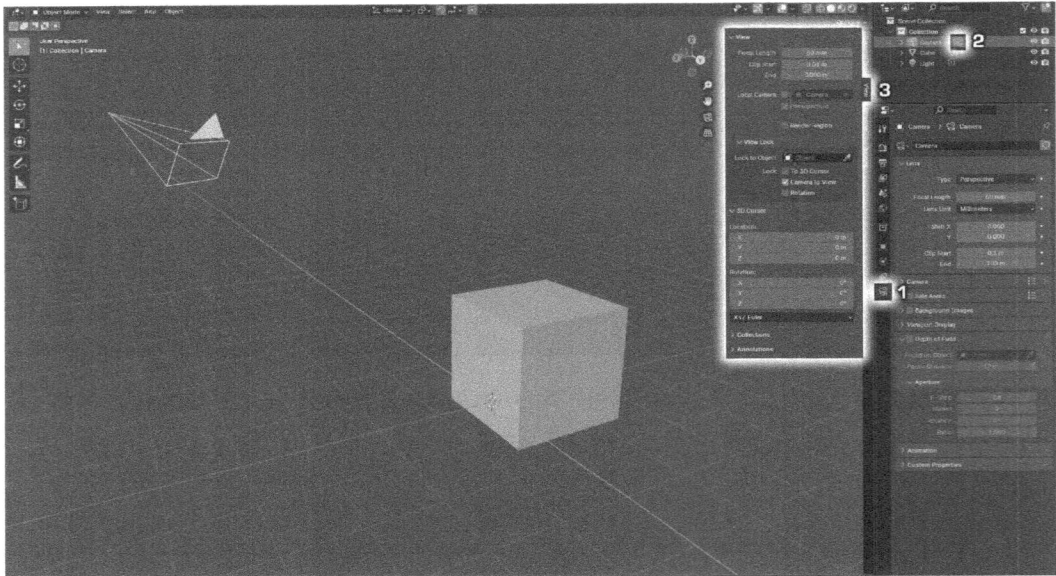

Figure 1.21: A Visual Overview of Blender's Camera Tab

- **Outliner** (*2* in *Figure 1.21*): Use the Outliner to select and manage cameras in your scene. You can also use the Outliner to enable or disable visibility and rendering for specific cameras.
- **View** menu (*3* in *Figure 1.21*): In the 3D Viewport **View** menu, select **Align View** and choose **Align Active Camera to View** to position the active camera to match the current 3D Viewport view.

Blender also allows you to change camera properties based on rendering settings. These will be discussed later in *Chapter 5* in *Part 2* of this book. You will see that you can adjust the camera's focal length, sensor size, and sensor fit to control the field of view and perspective. These options will also allow you to set **Focus Distance**, **F-stop**, and **Blade Count** to create realistic depth-of-field effects. Also, you will learn how to define the near and far clipping planes to control the visible range of the camera for rendering.

Congratulations! You now have a solid grip on Blender's camera system. You have learned how to do the following:

- Spawn and switch between cameras
- Lock the view for easy navigation
- Create dynamic shots such as dolly, pan, and orbit
- Use menus and shortcuts to control every angle

And that's just the beginning.

As you learn more about using them, you will be able to develop your skills and get accurate previews of your 3D models, use multiple camera angles in projects such as showreels, and use optimal rendering settings, ultimately resulting in high-quality images and animations.

Summary

Alright, you've just made it through your first chapter in Blender, and that's no small feat. So, if your brain feels a bit fried, don't worry... that's completely normal. You've just covered a lot of ground, and it's the kind of stuff that every 3D artist needs under their belt.

We kicked things off by launching Blender and introducing you to two of its fundamental modes, **Object Mode** and **Edit Mode**. Next, you discovered the importance of the XYZ coordinate system in Blender and started using the 3D Cursor, familiarizing yourself with its various functions, including object creation, pivot point, snapping, object parenting, and 3D Viewport navigation. The chapter then moved on to explaining how to navigate the 3D Viewport, switching between the **Perspective** and **Orthographic** views, and finally, the basics of using cameras in Blender.

So, what is the key takeaway?

You now know your way around Blender's core interface. You have got a grip on how to move in 3D space, how the camera works, and how to keep things organized and efficient with tools such as the 3D Cursor.

Through this, you also started on your journey to understanding basic Blender shortcuts, UI menu options, and key bindings; this will help you optimize your workflow as a 3D modeling artist and will lay the foundation for your skill acquisition going forward.

In the next chapter, we will dig deeper into Blender's UI and keep building your confidence, helping you optimize your workflow.

Subscribe to Game Dev Assembly!

We are excited to introduce **Game Dev Assembly**, our brand-new newsletter dedicated to everything game development. Whether you're coding, designing, animating, or managing a studio, we've got insights, trends, and expert advice to help you create, innovate, and thrive. Sign up now and get exciting benefits.

https://packt.link/gamedev-newsletter

Get This Book's PDF Version and Exclusive Extras

UNLOCK NOW

Scan the QR code (or go to packtpub.com/unlock). Search for this book by name, confirm the edition, and then follow the steps on the page.

Note: Keep your invoice handy. Purchases made directly from Packt don't require an invoice.

2

Optimizing Workflow with the Status Bar, Workspaces, and File Options

Blender is built to shape the way you work as a 3D artist, and the beauty of it is, it is completely customizable. That means one of the first things you should do (before diving head-first into modeling your dream castle or sci-fi hallway) is set up the interface so it actually works for you. Blender is like a giant toolbox, and there is no point fumbling around for a hammer when you can pin it right to your belt.

We will start with Blender's **Workspaces** and the **Status Bar**. Workspaces address different specialized aspects of the creation process of 3D modeling. The Status Bar is where you go to get information for optimizing the process itself. You will also learn how to overcome common challenges in 3D modeling such as losing your work. For that, you will see how to save files, create backups, and how to recover them. Our crowning jewel will be to delve into the process of exporting models or scenes from Blender to other software.

This chapter is all about getting your workspace in order and building habits that will save you a ton of time down the road. By learning how to navigate and tweak Blender's features to fit your workflow, you will not only speed things up but also make the whole process feel a lot smoother.

So, in this chapter, we will cover the following topics:

- Reading the Status Bar
- Differentiating overhead tabs

- Adding, arranging, and customizing Workspaces

- Saving and recovering Blender files

- Setting up a default Blender file

- Differentiating between common file formats for exporting

- Using Blender to export scenes and models

Technical requirements

As for **Blender 4.5 LTS (Long-Term Support)**, the general requirements include a macOS 11.2 or newer (Apple Silicon supported natively) operating system, or a Linux (64-bit, glibc 2.28 or newer) operating system. Blender now requires a CPU with the SSE4.2 instruction set, at least 8 GB of RAM (32 GB recommended for heavy scenes), and a GPU supporting OpenGL 4.3 with a minimum of 2 GB of VRAM.

For a full list of technical requirements, please refer back to *Chapter 1* of this part.

Reading the Status Bar

You will find the Status Bar at the bottom of the application window:

Collection | Cube | Verts:216 | Faces:218 | Tris:428 | Objects:1/3 | Memory: 31.3 MiB | VRAM: 6.4/12.0 GiB | 3.4.1

Figure 2.1: Status Bar overview

The Status Bar is useful because it displays different types of data, as shown in *Figure 2.1*. This data includes the following:

- **Scene statistics:** On the left side of the Status Bar, you can see the number of vertices, edges, faces, and objects in the scene. This information is helpful if your scene is complex and you are looking to hide certain objects, for example.

- **Tooltips:** The middle of the Status Bar displays context-sensitive tooltips. You can see those if you hover your mouse over interface elements in Blender. These tooltips will let you know what each interface element does, making it easier to understand and use Blender's features.

- **Notifications:** You will see important notifications, warnings, or error messages. For example, if an action cannot be performed, the Status Bar might display a notification to point you towards the issue.

- **Mode-specific information**: Whether you are in **Edit** mode or **Object** mode, the Status Bar displays additional information related to that mode. For example, in **Edit** mode, you will see the current selection mode (i.e., vertex, edge, or face).

- **Progress indicator**: When Blender is executing actions that take some time to complete (e.g., rendering), the Status Bar will feature a progress bar.

- **Blender version and memory usage**: On the right side of the Status Bar, you will see the current Blender version and the memory usage of the application.

Tip

Remember that the contents of the **Status Bar** could be different depending on your current context and mode, so make sure to check it frequently, especially if you need to troubleshoot a problem.

You can see all the Status Bar options in its preferences panel, as shown in *Figure 2.2*. To access it so that you can modify it, you need to click on **File**, **Edit**, **Preferences**, and **Choose Interface**.

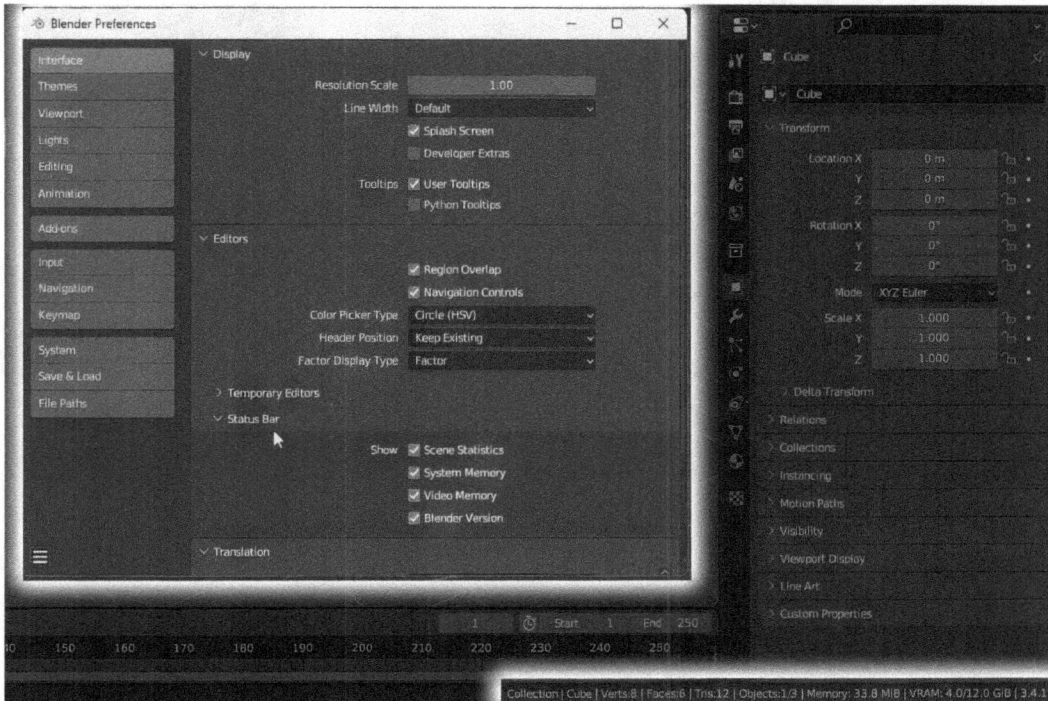

Figure 2.2: Status Bar options

The Status Bar might seem like just a little strip at the bottom of your screen, but it is actually packed with useful info. It shows things such as scene stats, tooltips, memory usage, the current Blender version, and even little indicators to let you know what is going on behind the scenes. Once you get used to checking it, it can really help you spot problems early and keep things running smoothly, like a mini dashboard for your whole project.

But that is just the beginning. If you really want to get comfortable in Blender and build a solid workflow, you will need to get to grips with the overhead tabs. Each one controls a different part of your workspace, and knowing how to customize and use them properly is a massive step toward making Blender work your way, not the other way around.

Differentiating overhead tabs

Blender's **Overhead Tabs** are called Workspaces, and they can be found at the top of the application window, as shown in *Figure 2.3*.

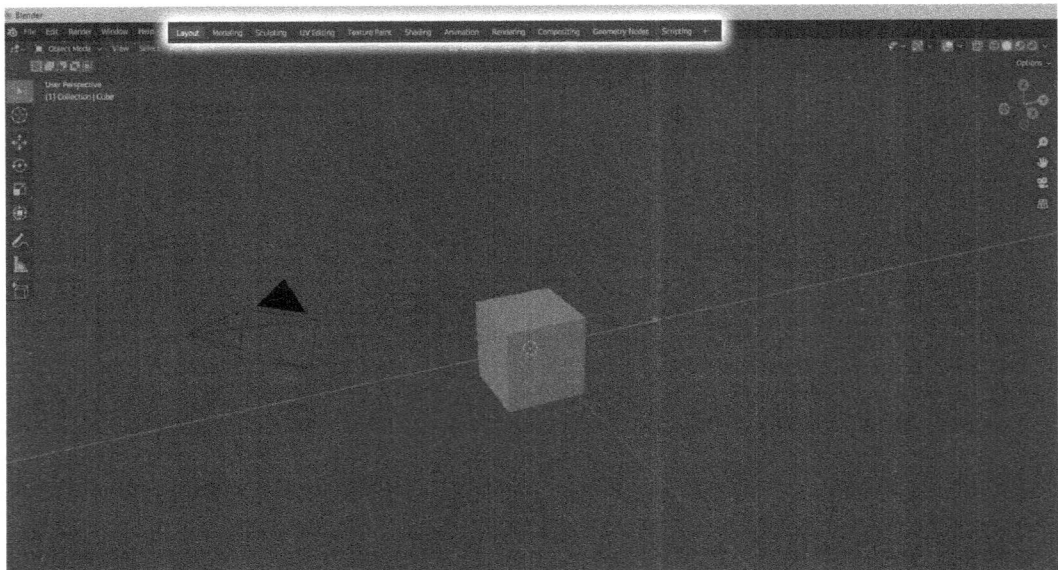

Figure 2.3: Blender's overhead tabs

Blender's default Workspaces are among the most important interface tools for using Blender, each one preconfigured to serve different purposes. You will understand more about them as we discuss the following Workspaces and their synergy, and you can see a quick preview of each one in *Figure 2.4*:

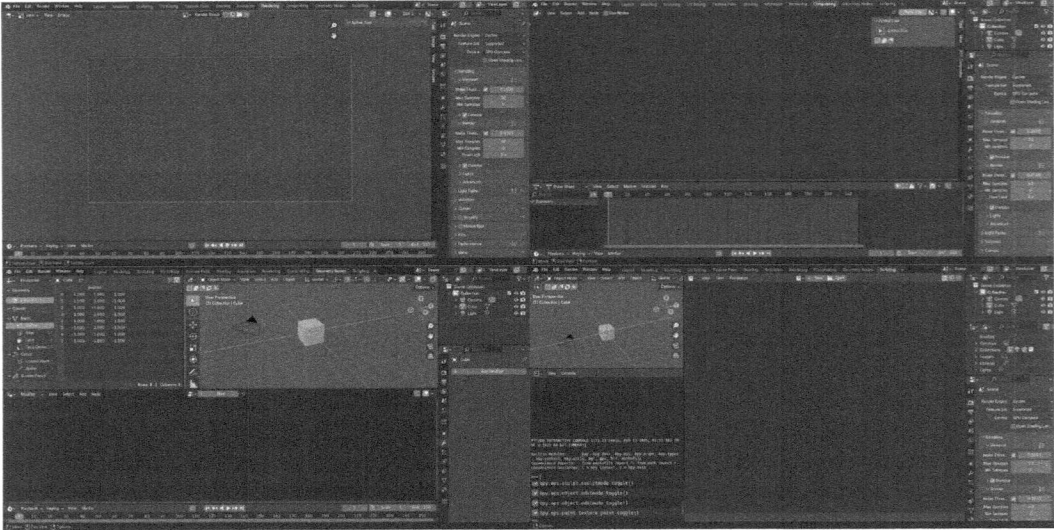

Figure 2.4: Differentiating between Blender's overhead tabs

Let's take a look at each of Blender's default workspaces:

- **Layout**: This workspace controls Blender's general scene layout and object manipulation. It includes Blender's **3D Viewport**, **Outliner**, and **Properties** panel, all of which were discussed in *Chapter 1* in this part of book. These functions help you position, scale, and rotate objects, and manage cameras, lights, and other scene elements.

- **Modeling**: As the name suggests, this workspace is tailored for 3D modeling. It provides a more prominent **3D Viewport** and quick access to tools and settings for mesh editing and object creation. You can find more details about the **Modeling** workspace in *Chapter 6* in *Part 1* of this book.

- **Sculpting**: This workspace is optimized for digital sculpting. You will find a large **3D Viewport** and **Tool Shelf**, containing a variety of brushes and sculpting options (as shown in *Figure 2.5*).

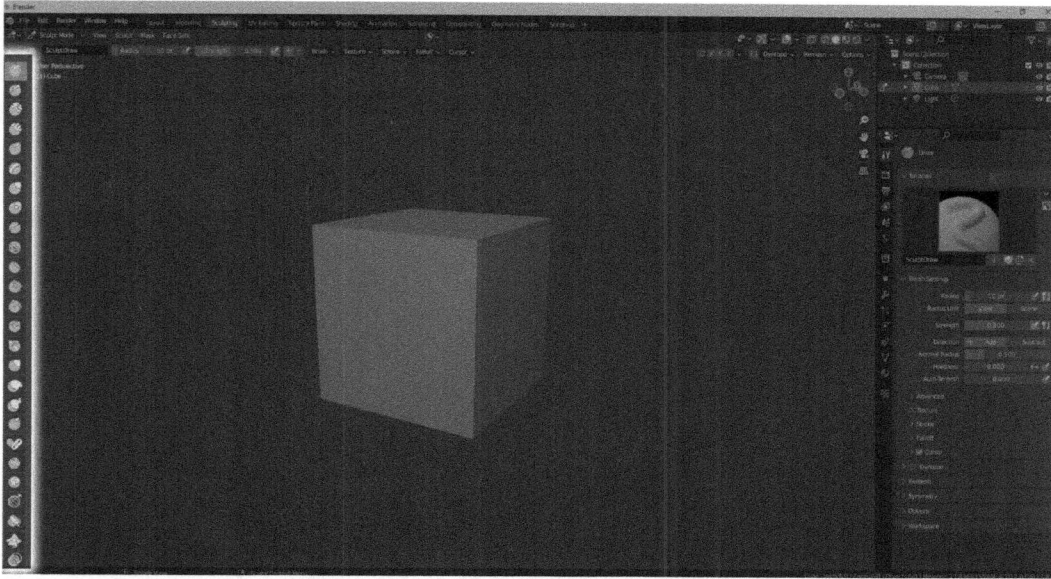

Figure 2.5: Sculpting Tool Shelf

You can find more details about the **Sculpting** Workspace in *Chapter 12* in *Part 1* of this book.

- **UV Editing**: This Workspace is designed for unwrapping and editing 3D models' UV coordinates. It features a split-screen layout with a **3D Viewport** on one side and a **UV/Image Editor** on the other, making it easy to visualize and adjust how textures are mapped onto your model. You can find more details about this workspace in *Chapter 15* in *Part 1* of this book.

- **Texture Paint**: This Workspace is dedicated to painting textures directly onto 3D models. This Workspace's **3D Viewport** contains painting tools and settings that are readily available. You can use the **Texture Paint** workspace to paint color, bump, or other types of texture maps directly onto your models.

- **Shading**: The **Shading** Workspace is focused on creating and editing materials and shaders for your 3D models. Here, you will find a large **Shader Editor** (i.e., **Node Editor**, a node-based editor allowing you to create and edit shaders) and a **3D Viewport** in rendered mode, providing real-time feedback on how the materials look on your 3D models. Shaders determine how light interacts with a surface, including its color, texture, reflectivity, and transparency, and we will cover this in more detail in *Chapter 13* in *Part 1* of this book.

- **Animation:** This Workspace specializes in animating objects, characters, and cameras. It includes a large **3D Viewport, Timeline, Dope Sheet,** and **Graph Editor,** giving you control over keyframes, timing, and interpolation of your animations (*Figure 2.6*). You can find more details about the **Animation** Workspace and find detailed definitions and explanations of its components in *Chapter 16* in *Part 1* of this book.

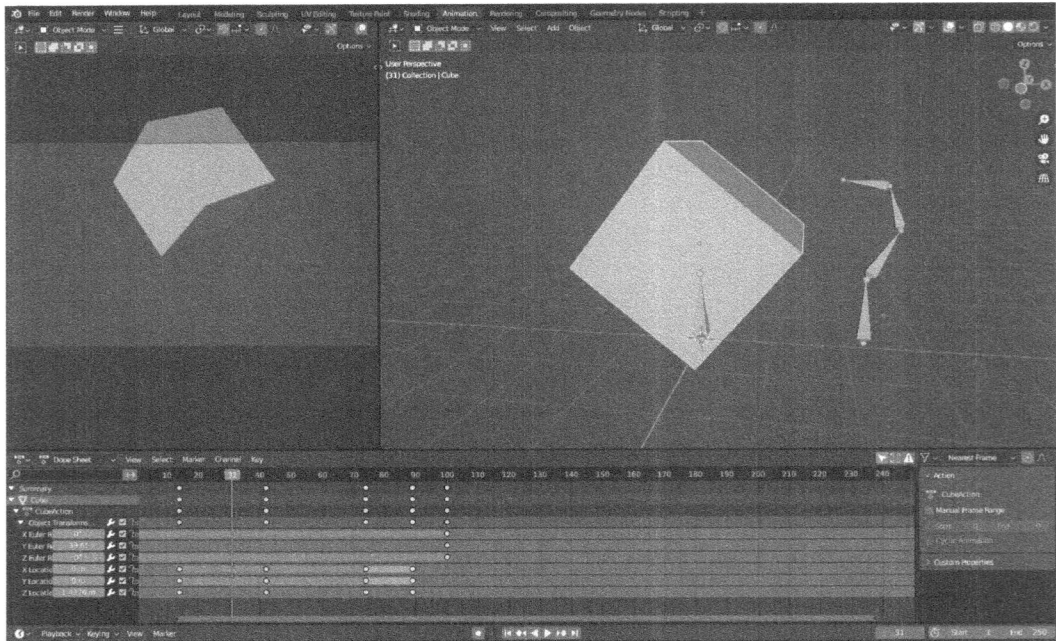

Figure 2.6: Animation Workspace

- **Rendering:** The **Rendering** Workspace is designed for setting up and fine-tuning your final render of your 3D model or scene (*Figure 2.7*). It includes a **3D Viewport** in rendered mode, panels for adjusting render settings, output formats, and post-processing options. You can find more details about the **Rendering** Workspace in *Chapter 5* in *Part 2* of this book.

Figure 2.7: Rendering Workspace

- **Compositing**: This Workspace is dedicated to post-processing and compositing rendered images or image sequences. It includes a **Node Editor** configured for compositing nodes, an **Image Editor** for previewing the result, and a **Properties** panel for adjusting settings. You can find more details about the **Compositing** Workspace and find detailed definitions and explanations of its components in *Chapter 7* in *Part 2* of this book.

- **Geometry Nodes**: This Workspace will help you create, manipulate, and distribute geometry using a node-based system. Using the **Geometry Node editor**, you can build procedural networks by connecting nodes to create or modify 3D objects. You can find more details about the **Geometry Nodes** workspace in *Chapter 2* in *Part 2* of this book.

- **Scripting**: The **Scripting** Workspace is useful if you want to write custom scripts or create add-ons for Blender using Python (*Figure 2.8*). This Workspace includes a **Text editor** for writing code, a **Python Console** for testing, and an **Info editor** to view Blender's internal operations.

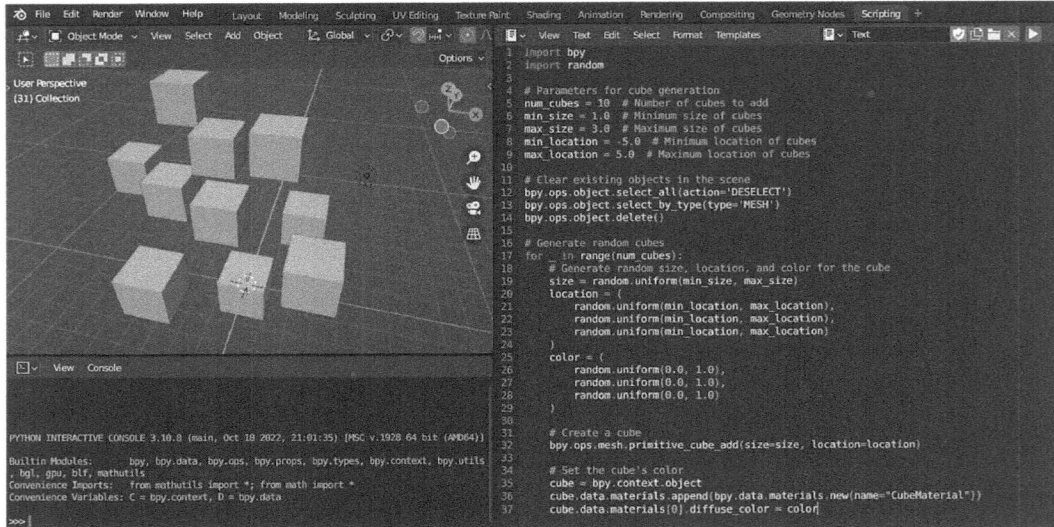

Figure 2.8: Scripting Workspace

Blender's default Workspaces are actually pretty well thought out. They cover everything from modeling and sculpting to animation, rendering, and a few things you might not even have heard of yet. Getting familiar with what each one does is like getting the lay of the land before heading off on your next big 3D project. Once you know where things live, you will feel a lot less lost.

From there, learning how to add or customize your own Workspaces is the next big step. This is where you start making Blender feel like your Blender. Bit by bit, you will shape the software around how you like to work, and that is when things will really start to click.

Adding, arranging, and customizing Workspaces

If you want to add new Workspaces or customize them, follow these steps:

1. To add a new Workspace, click the + icon located on the right side of the existing Workspaces, as shown in *Figure 2.9*. You can then create a new Workspace from an existing one by selecting **Duplicate Current**.

Figure 2.9: Adding a new Workspace in Blender

Another way to add a new Workspace is to *right-click* on an existing Workspace tab and select **Duplicate**.

2. To rename a Workspace, *right-click* on its tab and select **Rename**. Enter a new name for the Workspace in the text field and press *Enter* to save it.

3. To rearrange the order of Workspaces, click and drag the desired Workspace tab to a new location.

4. If you want to remove a Workspace, *right-click* on its tab and select **Delete**. Be careful, though, because deleting a Workspace cannot be undone!

5. In your new Workspace, you can now customize the layout by resizing, splitting, or joining different areas (i.e., windows) within the Workspace:

    •   **Resize**: Click and drag the panel edges to adjust the size of an area.

    •   **Split**: To create a new area, *right-click* on the edge between two areas and select **Split Area**. Then, drag the line to define the size of the new area (*Figure 2.10*).

    •   **Join**: To merge two areas, *right-click* on the edge between them and select **Join Area**. Then, drag the highlighted arrow over the area you want to merge with.

> Tip
>
> Hover your mouse over the corner of any editor tab. You will notice a small diagonal stripe icon appear. Click and drag from this corner to split the current area into two. If you want this new window to exist outside of Blender's main interface, click and drag that corner out of the main Blender window. This will kind of tear off the panel, creating a floating window that you can move to another screen or position. This tip will become your bread and butter if you are using two screens or more!

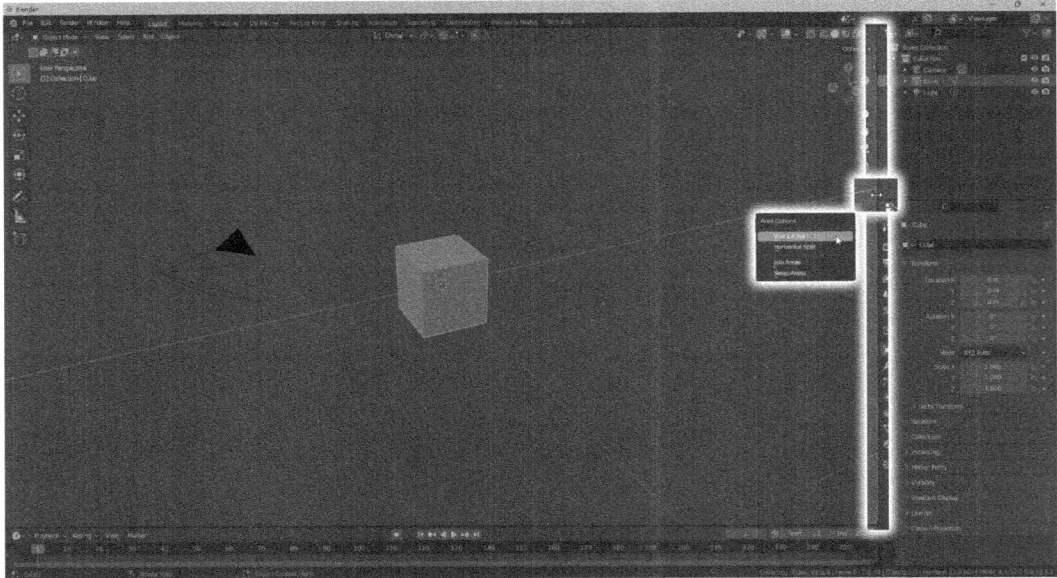

Figure 2.10: Split area demonstration

- You can also change the editor type by clicking the drop-down icon in the top-left corner of each panel. To do this, click the drop-down icon in the top-left corner of each panel and select the desired editor type from the list (e.g., **3D Viewport**, **UV/ Image Editor**, **Shader Editor**, **Timeline**, and **Outliner**), as shown in *Figure 2.11*:

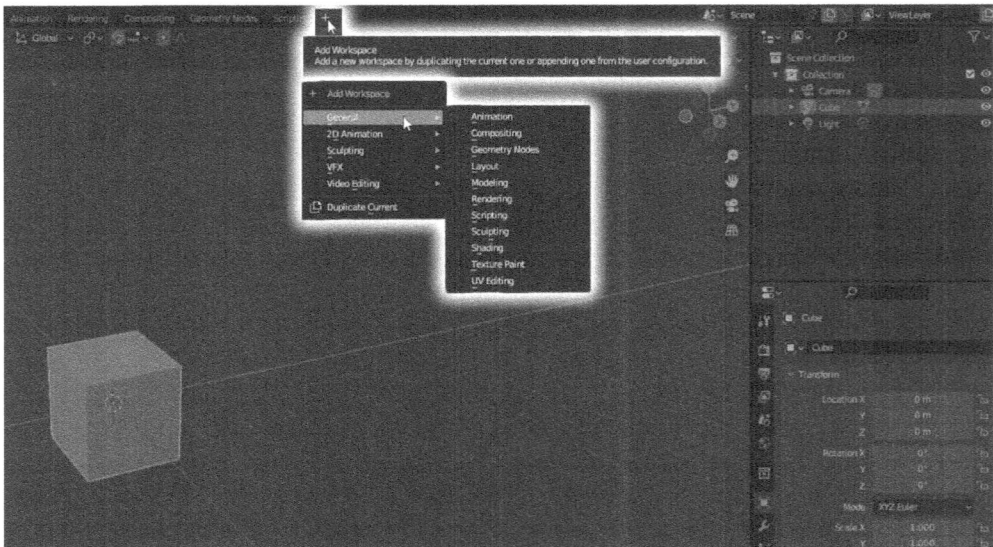

Figure 2.11: Customizing a Workspace in Blender

Tip

Workspaces are unique to each .blend file. If you want to create custom Workspaces for all your projects, you'll need to save them in your startup file. To do this, after customizing your Workspaces, go to **File** | **Defaults** | **Save Startup File** in the main menu. This will save your current layout and Workspaces as the default setup for all new Blender projects.

Blender's overhead tabs, also known as Workspaces, are absolutely key when it comes to organizing how you work, no matter what your focus is. Whether you are into sculpting fantasy creatures or piecing together modular environments, these tabs let you build a layout that actually suits you. The whole system is designed to be bent, shaped, and customized to fit the way you like to work, and honestly, that is one of Blender's biggest strengths.

That said, even with everything perfectly set up, things can (and will) go wrong. Blender, in my opinion, is one of the most stable 3D programs out there, but let's be honest, no software is perfect. Crashes, glitches, the occasional "why is this not working?" moment... they are all part of the journey. The important thing is to be ready for them when they do happen, so you are not sat there panicking at 2 a.m. with a half-finished dragon and no idea what went wrong.

In the next section, we will move on to explaining how to manage, save, and recover files to ensure that you can troubleshoot errors or take a few steps back in the creation process if you need to.

Saving and recovering Blender files

The **Topbar** in Blender is a horizontal panel located at the top of the user interface that provides access to tools and settings related to your active Workspace. One of the first things you need to know about Blender's Topbar is how to manage and save your files.

To save your work, follow these steps:

1. Go to the **File** menu in the top-left corner of Blender, and select **Save** or **Save As**.
2. Choose a location on your computer, give your file a name, and click **Save Blender File** (i.e., .blend).

You can also use the shortcuts *Ctrl + S* (for **Save**) and *Shift + Ctrl + S* for **Save As.**

Tip

At this point, you should note that .blend files are already in a format that can be used by other graphics programs and game engines. This kind of flexibility makes it much easier to collaborate with others or slot Blender into a larger workflow. Whether you are moving assets into *Unreal Engine* or *Unity 3D*, working alongside someone using *Maya*, or just bouncing between different tools, Blender plays surprisingly well with others, once you know how to handle the formats.

To recover lost work, you can try the following recovery options:

- Blender's got your back when it comes to saving. It automatically backs up your work in the background every couple of minutes (every 2 minutes by default). So, even if the worst happens and Blender crashes mid-project, there is a good chance you will still have a recent version tucked away, ready to recover.

    a. To recover a recent auto-save, go to **File | Recover | Auto Save**. A window will open, showing a list of automatically saved files. Find the most recent file, select it, and click **Recover**. Check the recovered file and save it as a new .blend file if it contains the work you want to recover.

- If Blender crashed or closed unexpectedly, you could try to recover your last session. Go to **File | Recover | Last Session**. Blender will try to open the state of your project just before the crash. If your work is recovered, save it as a new .blend file.

- It is very important to manually create backups of your work occasionally. You can create a backup by going to **File | Save a Copy** or **Save As**. Save your file with a different name or in a separate folder. In case you lose your work, you can revert to the most recent backup file and recover your project that way.

- If you cannot find your work using these options, check the temporary files folder on your computer where Blender saves some files. Look for files with a .blend extension and open them in Blender to see if they contain your lost work. Use the following folder paths to help:

    - *Windows*: C:\Users<username>\AppData\Local\Temp\
    - *macOS*: /private/var/tmp/

- *Linux*: /tmp/
- In all cases, if you find your work, save it as a new .blend file.

At the end of the day, knowing how to save, recover, and manage your files in Blender is one of the most important habits you can build. Not just for peace of mind, but to keep your workflow running smoothly. Losing hours of work because you forgot to save (or didn't know where to find a backup) is one of those mistakes that only needs to happen once before you start getting serious about file management. By learning about Blender's recovery options and backup features early on, you are not just protecting your work; you are saving yourself a lot of frustration down the road.

> Important note
>
> Another handy part of Blender's file management system is the ability to link and append files between projects. These might sound a bit technical at first, but they are powerful tools once you get the hang of them. Whether you want to reuse an asset across multiple scenes or keep everything consistent in a big project, knowing when to link or append can save you a lot of time and help keep things organized. **Link** allows you to link data from a Blender file in your library to your current one, while **Append** lets you copy new data from an existing Blender file without linking it to it. File management using **Link** or **Append** can be helpful if you are integrating items from two projects into one (e.g., assets from project one into an environment from project two).

To make you even faster after the initial set up and customization options you read in the previous sections, you will now get a brief overview of how to set up a default Blender file.

Setting up a default Blender file

To set your custom .blend file as the default startup file in Blender, follow these steps:

1. Open your custom .blend file in Blender.
2. Set up the Workspace, user preferences, and any other settings you want to have as your default (e.g., custom Workspace layouts, render settings, materials, or any other configurations).
3. In the main menu, go to **File | Defaults | Save Startup File**.
4. A confirmation dialog will appear, asking if you want to overwrite the existing startup file. Click **Save Startup File** to confirm.

Henceforth, every time you open Blender, it will resemble your custom .blend file, settings, and new Workspace layouts.

Tip

Saving your custom Blender startup file will override your previous startup file. If you need to revert to the default Blender startup file, you'll need to reset Blender to factory settings by going to **File | Defaults | Load Factory Settings**. After resetting, you can save the factory settings as the startup file if needed.

By now, you should have Blender set up to suit the way you work, nice one! That's a huge first step out of the way. So what's next? Well, it is time to talk about exporting your work. As a 3D artist, you rarely just use one piece of software forever.

Blender is brilliant for a lot of the creative process, but there will come a time when you need to move your models or scenes into something else, whether it is a game engine such as Unreal, a renderer, or even another artist's pipeline. That is where understanding export formats becomes essential. Knowing which format to use (and when) will save you a lot of trial and error and help you work like a pro right from the start.

Differentiating between common file formats for exporting

Blender's file menu lets you import and export files in .obj and .fbx formats created through other graphics programs such as *Autodesk Maya*, *Autodesk 3ds Max*, *ZBrush*, *Unity*, and *Unreal Engine*.

FBX and OBJ are two popular 3D file formats that can be used to export models and scenes from Blender. Each format has its own strengths and limitations, which makes them most suitable for different uses: this means it is context-dependent on when you may use each format.

Tip

If you are working with **Blender 4.2 or higher**, you can now import files by simply dragging and dropping files directly into Blender.

Let's take a look at the .fbx file format first. *Table 2.1* shows its advantages and disadvantages:

Pros	Cons
FBX is a widely supported format across various 3D applications, and game engines with (e.g., Godot) or without the use of external tools (e.g., Unity, Unreal Engine, Cinema 4D).	FBX is a proprietary format owned by Autodesk, which might lead to compatibility issues between different software versions.
It can store complex data such as meshes, armatures, animations, materials, textures, and even cameras and lights.	The format can be more complex and may result in larger file sizes.
FBX can handle multiple objects and their hierarchy, which is useful when exporting entire scenes or complex models.	
It supports both skeletal and vertex animations, making it suitable for character animations and moving inanimate content.	

Table 2.1: Pros and cons of choosing .FBX files

Now let's take a look at the second file format, .obj. *Table 2.2* shows a comparison of the advantages and disadvantages of this format:

Pros	Cons
OBJ is a simple, widely supported format that can be used across various 3D applications with few software compatibility concerns.	OBJ does not support animations, making it unsuitable for dynamic content.
It is well-suited for static 3D models and their associated materials, making it ideal for basic objects and scenes.	It does not store complex data such as cameras, lights, or object hierarchy.
The format is easy to read and edit since it is text-based.	The format does not handle advanced shading features and could require you to make manual adjustments when importing materials into other software.
OBJ files are small.	

Table 2.2: Pros and cons of choosing .obj files

To sum things up, FBX files are generally the go-to when you are working with complex scenes, animations, or anything heading into a game engine; they handle skeletal rigs and keyframes like a champ. OBJ files, on the other hand, are more like the reliable old toolbox you reach for when all you need is a static model with basic materials. They are simpler, more widely compatible, and just work across most platforms. So, if you are exporting a character with bones and a walk cycle into *Unreal Engine*, go with FBX. But if it is a barrel, a rock, or a crate (and let's face it, we all need crates), then OBJ will probably do the trick. As you go deeper into your 3D journey, you will find yourself using both of them.

Just ask yourself, "What am I trying to do here?" and pick the format that makes the most sense. No need to overthink it, keep it simple and crack on.

In the next section, you will find out about the technical steps for exporting files.

Using Blender to export scenes and models

As you will have gathered from the previous section, most of the time, you will be exporting in .fbx and .obj formats, as these are used in most graphics software popular among 3D modeling artists. Here, I will walk you through what steps to take to export files.

To export scenes and models in Blender, follow these steps:

1. In the **3D Viewport** or the **Outliner**, select the object(s) you want to export. If you want to export the entire scene, you can skip to the next step without a specific selection.

2. In the main menu, go to **File | Export**. A list of available export formats will appear, as shown in *Figure 2.12*. Some common formats include the following:

    *   **FBX (.fbx)**: A widely used format, compatible with many 3D applications and game engines
    *   **OBJ (.obj)**: A popular format for static 3D models and their associated materials
    *   **Alembic (.abc)**: A format for exchanging animated 3D data between various software applications
    *   **glTF (.gltf/.glb)**: A modern format designed for the exchange of 3D models, frequently used for web-based applications
    *   **COLLADA (.dae)**: An XML-based format for exchanging 3D data between different software applications

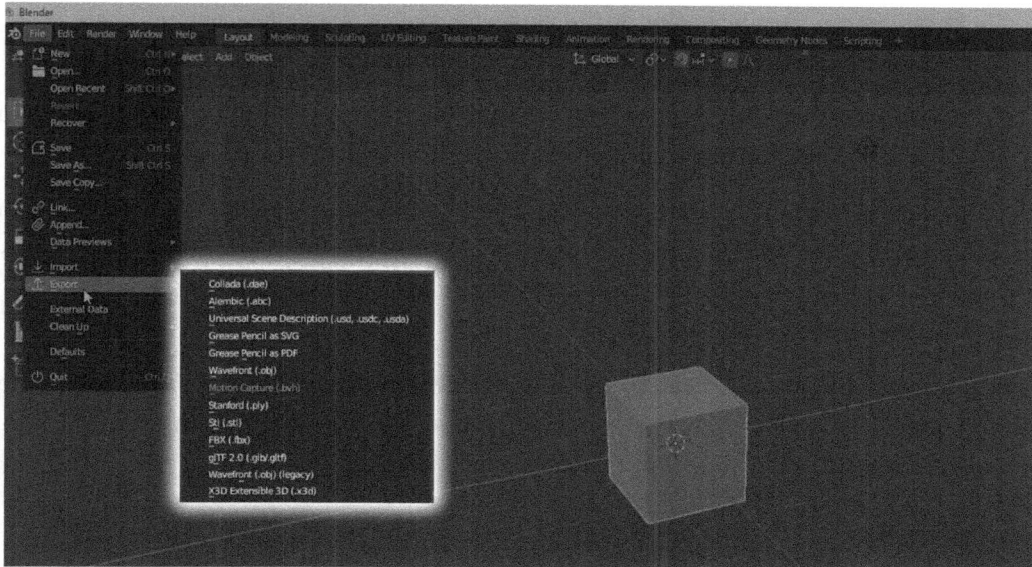

Figure 2.12: Blender's available export file formats

3. Click on the desired export format. A file dialog window will open, allowing you to choose the location and file name for the exported file. You can also customize the export settings in the lower-left corner of the file dialog window, as shown in *Figure 2.13*: these settings include applying modifiers and selecting object types.

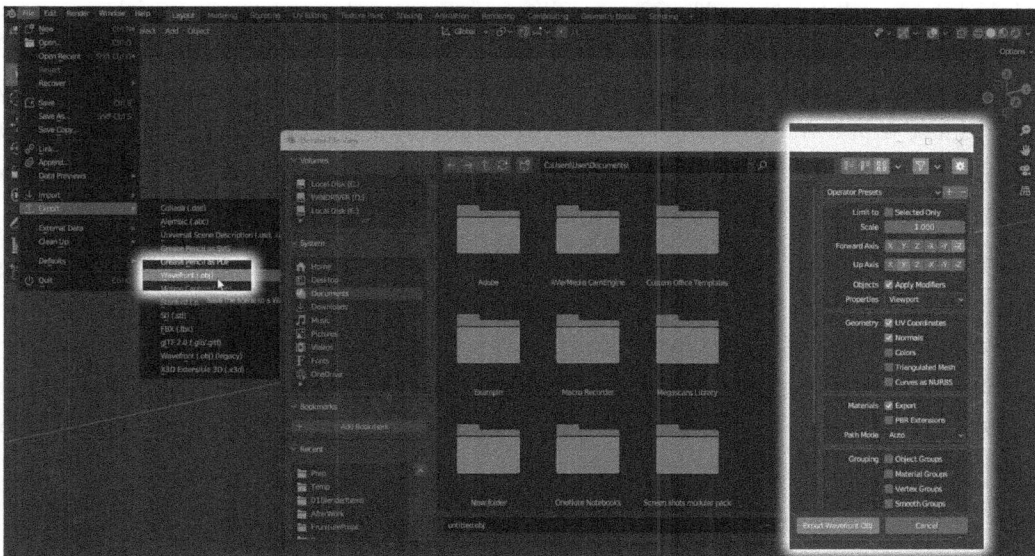

Figure 2.13: Export menu options in Blender

These settings vary depending on the chosen format but may include options for exporting specific object types, applying modifiers, exporting animations, or adjusting the scale.

4.   Once the file name and location have been completed, along with any export settings you wish to set, click the **Export** button to save the file in the chosen format.

In this section, we walked through how to export your 3D models and scenes from Blender, from selecting your objects, choosing the right format, tweaking a few export settings, and finally hitting **Save**. It might seem like a small step, but it is a crucial one, especially if you are planning to use your work in other software or game engines.

As we wrap up this chapter, the main takeaway is this: Blender's export tools are flexible enough to handle pretty much whatever you throw at them. Once you get the hang of it, exporting becomes second nature, just another part of your creative pipeline.

Summary

Blender's packed with features designed to make your life easier, but one of the best ways to speed things up and work smarter is through *customization*. From the moment you open Blender, it gives you tools to tailor the experience to suit how *you* like to work. Take the Status Bar at the bottom, it might not look like much, but it quietly keeps you updated with scene stats, memory usage, and helpful prompts while you work. Then there are the Workspaces up top, in the Toolbar, which are pre-built layouts designed for specific jobs such as modeling, animating, or scripting. Think of them as different workbenches for different tasks, ready to go right out of the box. You can customize, add, or rearrange these Workspaces, including but not limited to **Layout**, **Modeling**, **Sculpting**, **UV Editing**, and **Animation**. If you have followed along, you will now know how to customize your own Workspaces and even save them into your default startup file; so every time you open Blender, it is already set up just the way you like it. Trust me, this will save you a ton of time down the line.

Now, because Blender is such a powerful tool (and 3D modeling is no walk in the park), knowing how to save and recover your work properly is absolutely essential. Whether it is using auto-save, recovering your last session, or digging into those sneaky temp folders, being able to rescue your project when something goes wrong can be a real lifesaver. We also looked at how to lock in your custom .blend file so your setup is ready to roll every time you launch Blender, a small step with a big impact on your workflow.

We then wrapped things up by diving into Blender's export options. You now know that FBX is your friend for complex scenes, game assets, and animations, while OBJ is great for simpler, static models. By putting these tips into practice, you are well on your way to working smarter, not harder, and that is going to make a big difference in your productivity as a 3D artist.

In the next chapter, we will head into the Blender **Properties** panel, basically the control center for your entire project. This is where the real power starts to be unlocked, so let's dive in and get to grips with everything it can do.

Subscribe to Game Dev Assembly!

We are excited to introduce **Game Dev Assembly**, our brand-new newsletter dedicated to everything game development. Whether you're coding, designing, animating, or managing a studio, we've got insights, trends, and expert advice to help you create, innovate, and thrive. Sign up now and get exciting benefits.

https://packt.link/gamedev-newsletter

Join the 3D Tudor Channel Discord Server!

Join the 3D Tudor Channel Discord Server, a creative hub for learning Blender, Unreal Engine, Substance Painter, and 3D modeling, for discussions with the authors and other readers:

https://discord.gg/5EkjT36vUj

3

Exploring Blender's Properties Panel for Optimal 3D Creativity

In this chapter, we will explore the essential features and functions of the Blender **Properties** panel, which acts as the control center for various aspects of working on a 3D model or scene. This includes gaining an overview of the different tabs in the **Properties** panel, including the **Active Tool and Workspace Settings**, **Output Properties**, and **View Layer Properties** tabs, seeing how these features will enhance your workflow. By getting to know these sections early on, you will save time hunting through menus and instead focus on building your scenes with confidence. Once these become second nature, navigating Blender will start to feel a lot more intuitive.

Later, we will highlight the importance of managing collections, object properties, non-destructive modifiers, particle systems, and physics simulations through the **Collection**, **Object**, **Modifier**, **Particle**, and **Physics Properties** tabs. We will also discuss the options within the **Object Constraints Properties** tab, which is involved in animations, as well as tabs that can help you customize object appearance, behavior, and function (i.e., the **Object Data**, **Materials**, and **Texture Properties** tabs). These tabs are the behind-the-scenes tools that give your objects personality, function, and structure.

By the end of this chapter, you will have a solid grasp of how the **Properties** panel ties into almost every part of the 3D workflow. Whether you are adjusting materials, applying modifiers, or fine-tuning a simulation, this panel is where the magic happens, and once you are comfortable using it, you will start to feel properly at home inside Blender.

So, in this chapter, we will cover the following topics:

- Defining the **Properties** panel
- Using the **Active Tool and Workspace Settings** tab
- Configuring specialized settings using the **Output Properties** tab
- Splitting up and organizing your scene using the **View Layer Properties** tab
- Exploring the **Scene Properties** tab
- Navigating the **World Properties** tab
- Deciphering scene complexity using the **Collection Properties** tab
- Getting down to the nitty-gritty details with the **Object Properties** tab
- Making object alterations using the **Modifier Properties** tab
- Bringing your 3D models to life using the **Particle Properties** tab
- Maximizing realism using the **Physics Properties** tab
- Establishing rules using the **Object Constraints Properties** tab
- Finding out about the **Object Data Properties** tab
- Customizing appearance through the **Materials Properties** tab
- Upscaling your 3D models via the **Texture Properties** tab

Technical requirements

As for **Blender 4.5 LTS (Long-Term Support)**, the general requirements include a macOS 11.2 or newer (Apple Silicon supported natively) operating system, or a Linux (64-bit, glibc 2.28 or newer) operating system. Blender now requires a CPU with the SSE4.2 instruction set, at least 8 GB of RAM (32 GB recommended for heavy scenes), and a GPU supporting OpenGL 4.3 with a minimum of 2 GB of VRAM.

For a full list of technical requirements, please refer back to *Chapter 1* of this part.

Defining the Properties panel

The **Properties** panel in Blender is an essential part of the UI, and its role is to help you access and modify various settings related to the objects, materials, textures, and more in the scene you are creating. It is located on the right side of the Blender's default UI and consists of several tabs, each with a specialized purpose.

In this section, you will read a brief overview of each tab before we explore these tabs in detail in other parts of this chapter. *Figure 3.1* includes screenshots of the tab options for some of the **Properties** panel tabs we will be discussing:

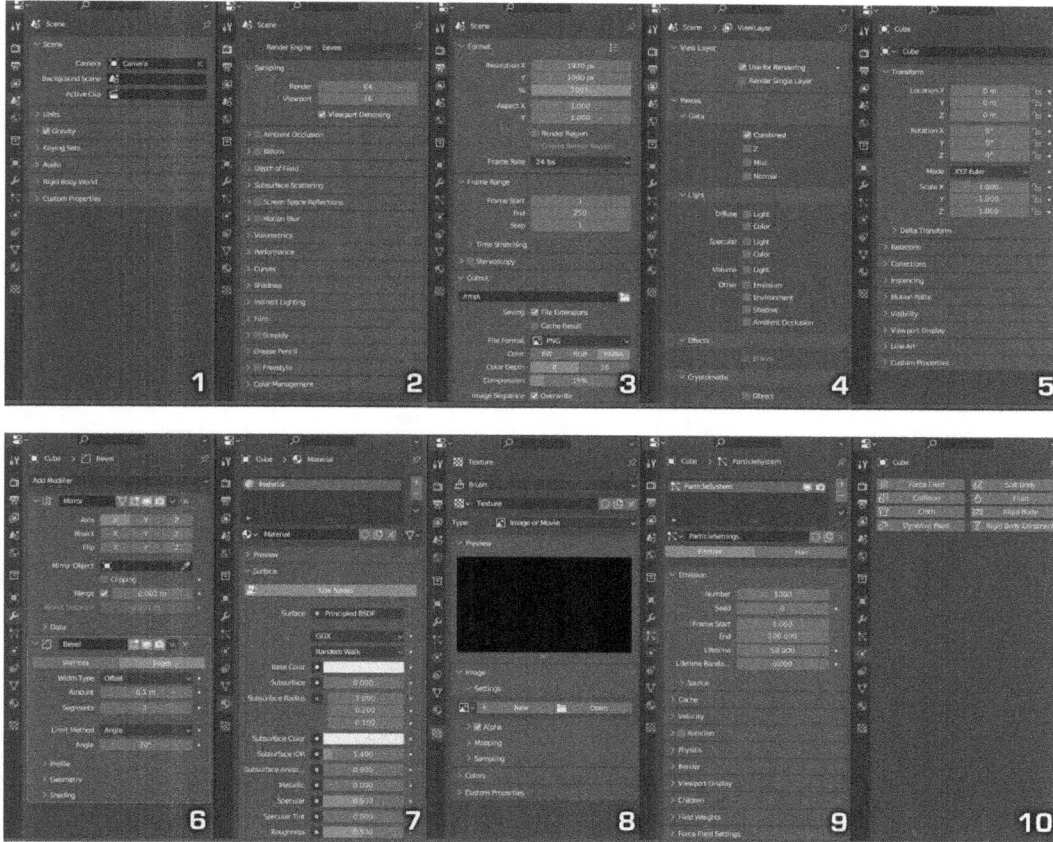

Figure 3.1: Properties panel tabs

So, key tabs within the **Properties** panel include the following:

1. **Scene Properties**: Manage scene settings such as units, gravity, and other global parameters.

2. **Render Properties**: Adjust settings for rendering (e.g., type of render engine, output resolution, file format, and render layers). The **Render Properties** tab will be the foundation of *Chapter 5* in *Part 2* of this book.

3. **Output Properties**: Configure settings for output, including file format, compression, color depth, and output path.

4. **View Layer Properties**: Control settings for view layers to organize your scene for more effective compositing and rendering.

5. **Object Properties**: Modify properties for selected objects (e.g., location, rotation, scale, and visibility).

6. **Modifier Properties**: Add and manage modifiers to objects. You can use modifiers to change the geometry, animation, or other properties of a 3D object in a non-destructive way.

7. **Material Properties**: Create, assign, and edit materials and shaders for 3D objects.

8. **Texture Properties**: Manage textures and their settings, including mapping, image source, and various attributes.

9. **Particle Properties**: Control particle systems, such as hair, fur, or particle simulations.

10. **Physics Properties**: Add and configure physics simulations for objects (i.e., rigid body, soft body, cloth, fluid, and smoke simulations).

Once you get the hang of Blender's **Properties** panel, you will be able to manage and tweak nearly every part of your scene, from the way objects behave to how they look and interact. It is a key part of turning basic models into detailed, believable creations, and it gives you full control over the finer details that make your projects stand out.

As mentioned, we are now going to dive into each of the tabs in more detail. First up is the **Active Tool and Workspace Settings** tab: this one lets you adjust settings based on the tool you are currently using and helps you fine-tune your workspace to better suit the task at hand. It is a great way to stay focused and keep things running smoothly as you switch between different parts of your project.

Using the Active Tool and Workspace Settings tab

The **Active Tool and Workspace Settings** tab in Blender lets you adjust settings related to your currently selected tool and active workspace (*Figure 3.2*). It is part of the **Properties** panel and gives you access to context-sensitive options, depending on the selected tool or mode. This can be useful because it allows you to speed up the workflow process of your 3D modeling.

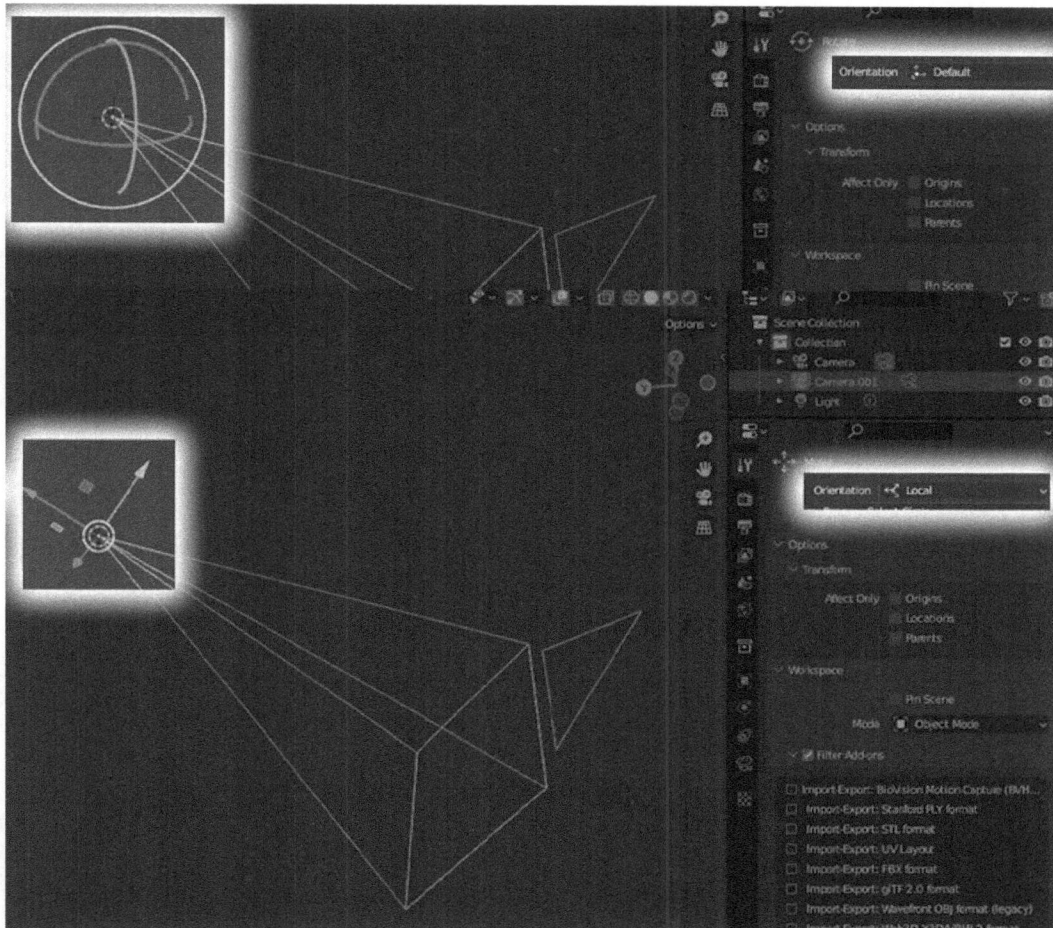

Figure 3.2: Active Tool and Workspace Settings tab

Think of the **Active Tool and Workspace Settings** tab like a control room where you can tweak how your tools and workspace behave, based on what you are doing at the moment. This can be handy because it makes working with your 3D model a bit faster and smoother.

Now, let's consider an example. You know how a map has a compass showing north, south, east, and west? Well, in Blender, you can change the direction of your compass (i.e., axis) to align with your object rather than the whole 3D world. To do this, you change the axis for your **Move** tool to **Local**. Everything else stays the same, normally aligned to the global axis of the whole 3D world. But now, when you use the **Move** tool, you can shift the object based on its alignment, not the world's. This is useful when you're working with something such as a camera control. It lets you move the camera frame without affecting its other axis when the camera is tilted. In this way, you can still use other tools, such as the **Rotate** tool, in the normal way. So, if you rotate the camera on the z axis, it does not affect the frame's alignment.

Equipped with this example, let us explore other key uses of the **Active Tool and Workspace Settings** tab that will come in handy as we progress through this book:

- **Active Tool Settings**: Here, you can find settings specific to the currently selected tool in the **3D Viewport**. For example, if you are using the **Move** tool, **Active Tool Settings** will help you adjust its axis constraints and snapping settings. Regardless of the tool you are using, these settings allow you to tailor its behavior to your needs.

- **Workspace Settings**: These settings let you adjust your active workspace. You can alter shading mode settings, overlays, and gizmos, making Blender more comfortable and efficient for you.

Every 3D modeling artist can streamline their workflow by capitalizing on options and settings provided by the **Active Tool and Workspace Settings** tab in Blender. By quickly accessing and modifying settings relevant to your current task, you will manage your tools and workspace better.

Next, we will move away from workspace settings and focus more on specific types of tasks, such as rendering file output and animation. This is where the **Output Properties** tab will come in handy.

Configuring specialized settings using the Output Properties tab

Blender's **Output Properties** tab manages settings related to rendering, file output, and animation. Unlike other tabs within the **Properties** panel, this tab specializes in configuring parameters that affect the final result of 3D models or scenes.

Key features of the **Output Properties** tab include the following:

- **Resolution**: This section helps you adjust the dimensions (e.g., width and height) of your rendered image or animation in pixels (i.e., px). This is important if you are creating test renders or if you are previewing animation sequences. The **Resolution** features allow you to adjust the percentage scale to render at a fraction of the full resolution, meaning that it is done quicker.

- **Frame Range**: Use this option to determine the start and end frames for your animation, and the frame step (i.e., the process of moving through an animation one frame at a time).

- **Frame Rate:** This option lets you define the **frames per second (FPS)** for your animation. This is useful if you are trying to change the speed of your animation to make it more dramatic, for example.

- **Output:** This section is related to saving your rendered images or animations. You can use it to define the file format (e.g., `.png`, `.jpeg`, `.exr`, or video formats such as `.avi`, `.mpeg`, or `.qtff`) and file path.

- **Metadata:** In this section, you can choose to embed metadata (e.g., author, copyright, and creation date). By adding these to your rendered images or animations, you can define ownership and track the date you created rendered items if necessary.

- **Post Processing:** This **Output Properties** tab area lets you control how your rendered images or animations are processed and combined with other elements. You can do that by compositing and by using the sequencer. We will discuss **Post Processing** in more detail in *Chapter 7* in *Part 2* of this book.

Using all the tools in the **Output Properties** tab will help you manage and fine-tune key parts of your render settings, from resolution and frame range to file output and format. Getting this right means your final render, animation, or showreel will hit the brief and work seamlessly with whatever software or platform you are delivering to.

Next, let's take a look at how to split up and organize your scene using the **View Layer Properties** tab, as we shift back into some of the more general-purpose tools found in the **Properties** panel. This is where things start to come together, especially when working on complex scenes or layered compositions.

Splitting up and organizing your scene using the View Layer Properties tab

Blender's **View Layer Properties** tab lets you control various render settings specific to each view layer in your project. Using the **View Layer Properties** tab, you will be able to configure how individual view layers are processed and combined during rendering. This will help you create advanced compositing workflows and improve your video editing process through non-destructive editing (i.e., editing whereby the original content is not changed or lost permanently).

Key features of the **View Layer Properties** tab include the following:

- **View Layer Passes:** Using this, you can choose if specific render passes (e.g., **Diffuse, Glossy, Ambient Occlusion**, or **Z-depth**) are available for compositing. By selecting specific passes, you can improve your postprocessing workflow because you can make your composites more complex and flexible. This can be useful for breaking down images to change the lighting or shading in an image by breaking it down into layers.

- **Filter:** This section lets you control which object types are included or excluded from rendering in the current view layer so that you can choose which elements of your scene will be rendered at any one time. By using **Filter**, you can toggle options such as **Mesh**, **Light**, or **Camera** to see how the look of your scene changes and to optimize it to match the mood or aesthetic you are looking for.

- **Collections:** This area is similar to **Filter** but provides you with options for managing the visibility, selectability, and renderability of collections rather than individual items within the current view layer. The **Collections** area lets you override the default settings for each collection, meaning that you can create unique configurations for various render passes or compositing setups.

- **Overrides:** As the name suggests, here you can apply material or data overrides to the current view layer. This is useful if you are looking to create variations of your scene without duplicating objects or materials. You can use **Overrides** to proactively cut down the polygon count of your scene by replacing materials, object data, or other properties with alternative versions. This option tab is only available in **Cycles**.

- **Freestyle:** This section lets you create stylized line art using pre-existing content from your 3D scene. You can use it to create non-photorealistic renders, such as cartoons, technical drawings, or other artistic styles.

The **View Layer Properties** tab in Blender helps you become flexible in how you create 3D art. Among other options, it lets you manage and customize the rendering process for each view layer in your project. In the next section, we will take your ability to configure properties of your projects further, using the **Scene Properties** tab to configure your entire scene.

Exploring the Scene Properties tab

The **Scene Properties** tab in Blender moves away from settings that apply to smaller aspects of the scene and gives you access to global settings and properties. This tab offers options to manage and configure your entire scene by adjusting details such as units, gravity, and color management.

Key features of the **Scene Properties** tab include the following:

- **Units**: This section allows you to set the measurement system (i.e., metric or imperial) and unit scale for your 3D scene in Blender. This is essential in creating realistic models for accurate modeling and consistent measurements across different objects and components.

- **Gravity**: Using these settings, you can adjust the force of gravity in your scene. This will impact physics simulations (e.g., rigid body dynamics, cloth, or particles) and make movements more realistic or stylized (e.g., if you want to give a character model a funny or cartoon look).

- **Audio**: You can use this section to optimize global audio settings in your scene, including volume, pitch, and the audio device used for playback, as shown in *Figure 3.3*. These settings are essential for animations and simulations since they will allow you to synchronize and mix audio effectively.

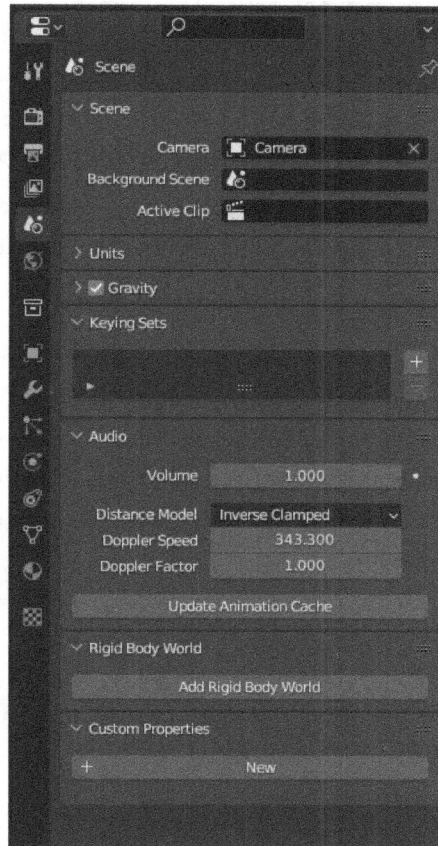

Figure 3.3: Scene Properties – Audio options

- **Rigid Body World**: Using these settings, you can adjust options such as **Simulation Steps**, **Solver Iterations**, and **Cache Options** to optimize how realistic the details in your physics simulations look. These settings will be discussed in detail in *Chapter 16* in *Part 1* of this book.

- **Custom Properties**: Here, you can add, edit, or remove user-defined properties to the current scene. This feature can be useful for a wide range of projects, particularly those requiring a high degree of customization and control over various elements within the scene. If you are using Blender to create interactive content or game assets, **Custom Properties** can be used to store and manipulate game-related data such as health points, scores, and character states.

The **Scene Properties** tab helps you manage and customize various global settings and properties for your entire project. Using the tab's options will enhance your workflow since you will be ensuring consistency, accuracy, and optimal performance across different aspects of your 3D scene. The **World Properties** tab, which will be discussed next, complements this well, and you will learn how to control and modify the global environment settings for your 3D scene.

Navigating the World Properties tab

The **World Properties** tab in Blender allows you to manipulate the global environment settings of your 3D scene, including the background color, environment lighting, volumetric effects, and more.

Key features of the **World Properties** tab include the following:

- **Surface**: This is the section where you can set the background color or add an environment texture (e.g., a **high dynamic range** (**HDR**) image) to your scene. HDR images are useful for adding environmental features, such as a sky with clouds, to your scene and can quickly and easily make your scene look more realistic. In *Figure 3.4*, you can see that by changing our skybox shader to emissive, we are able to make the sky glow, bringing more light into our scene.

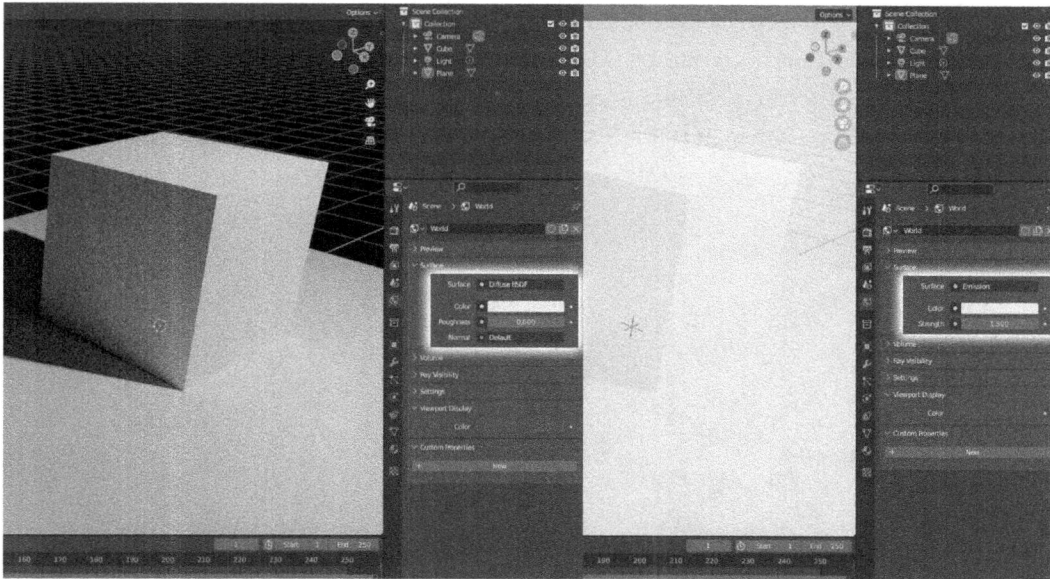

Figure 3.4: A visual comparison of surface and color World Properties tab options

- **Color:** Here, you can choose a solid color for the background of your scene (*Figure 3.4*). You can use a color background to influence your scene's aesthetics since color interacts with the overall ambient lighting and reflections, depending on the settings used.

- **Strength:** These settings relate to the intensity of the environment lighting in your scene. This helps you balance the lighting of multiple lighting sources.

- **Volumetrics:** You can use **Volumetrics** for adding and controlling volumetric effects such as fog, atmospheric scattering, or smoke in your scene. These effects contribute to the overall visual aesthetics of your scene and could be used to create a godrays lighting effect, for example, as shown in *Figure 3.5*:

Figure 3.5: Godrays effect example from "Blender 3 Beginners Step-by-Step Guide to Isometric Rooms" by 3D Tudor

- **Custom Properties:** This area gives you control over user-defined or other custom settings and options you have enabled in Blender. **Custom Properties** is a one-stop shop for adding, editing, or removing user-defined properties for the world settings.

Blender's **World Properties** tab is a management and customization tool for various global environment settings. You can use it to enhance the overall visual appearance, lighting, and atmosphere of your scene.

As we delve into more tabs found in the **Properties** panel, the degree to which they can be used to control your scene increases. The **Collection Properties** tab, which will be discussed next, is essential for every 3D modeler working on complex scenes.

Deciphering scene complexity using the Collection Properties tab

The **Collection Properties** tab is important for managing collections in your Blender scene. You can use collections to group and organize objects in a hierarchical order, which is useful for complex scenes such as a furnished room example (such as the one shown in *Figure 3.6*). The **Collection Properties** tab is part of the **Properties** panel.

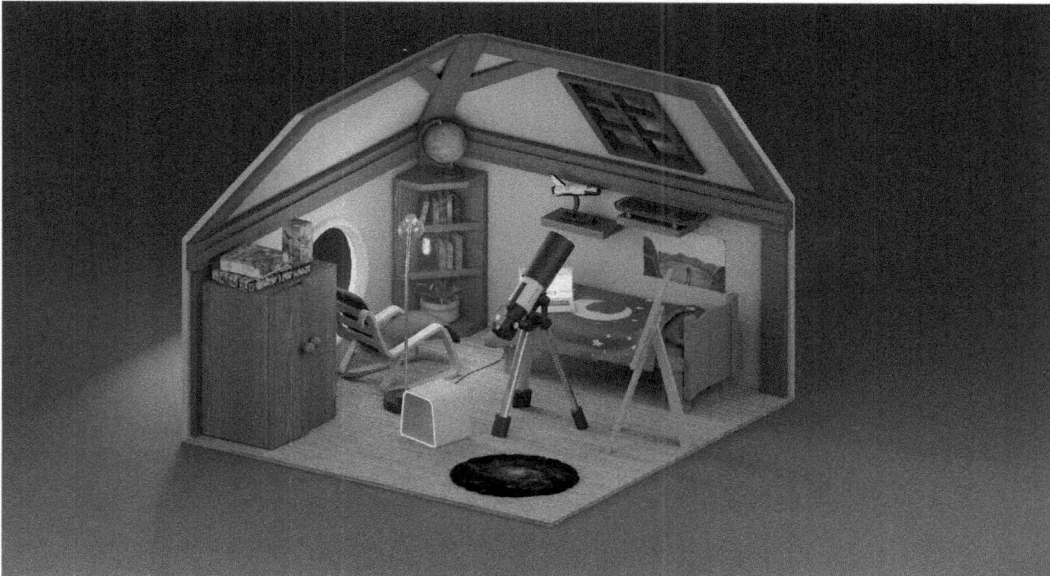

Figure 3.6: Furnished room example from "Mastering the Art of Isometric Room Design in Blender 3" by 3D Tudor

Key features of the **Collection Properties** tab include the following:

- **Collection Name**: As the name suggests, you can use this area to rename the selected collection. You can rename it by either double-clicking on the collection name in the **Outliner** or by pressing *F2*. The updated name will automatically reflect in the **Collection Properties** tab. Renaming collections is helpful if the name of each collection is meaningful, such as if you have multiple rooms where each object collection relates to a specific room (as in *Figure 3.7*).

Figure 3.7: Blender collections for Building Medieval Worlds - Unreal Engine 5 Modular Kitbash by 3D Tudor

- **View Layer Visibility**: Here, you can control the visibility of the collection in the active view layer. To do so, you can use textboxes, and you can either change the visibility of the entire collection or the visibility of individual items.

> Tip
>
> **View Layer Visibility** is controlled from the **Outliner** by *right-clicking* the collection, going to **View Layer**, and selecting **Enable** or **Disable** in **View Layer**. You can also use the checkbox in the **Outliner** to disable the collection in **View Layer**. This can't be done for individual items in the collection, though. **Holdout** and **Indirect View Layer** options are available in the **Properties** tab, however.

- **Restriction Toggles**: This area helps you control the selectability, renderability, and other restrictions for the collection, giving you the tools to change how your collection responds in different contexts. For example, you can use selection restrictions on collections so that when you are creating a scene with multiple objects, only some of them are selected.

- **Instance Offset**: Put simply, these settings let you determine an offset for instances of the collection. To make this clearer, after creating a collection instance and placing it in your scene, you can use **Instance Offset** to quickly adjust the placement of the instance. This is useful if you want to offset an object from the ground using a Z-value to make sure that the assets are not clipping through the ground; by creating item collections, you are able to create a pack of assets. If you were to simply copy it, you would create a new version of the selected collection, but by creating an instance, you are able to create a duplicate of the original. By changing the original, you are able to simultaneously change all of its instances as well. In *Figure 3.8*, you can see how to offset collection instances. This is particularly useful when you already have instance objects placed in your scene and you would like to offset their position, such as raising them from the ground.

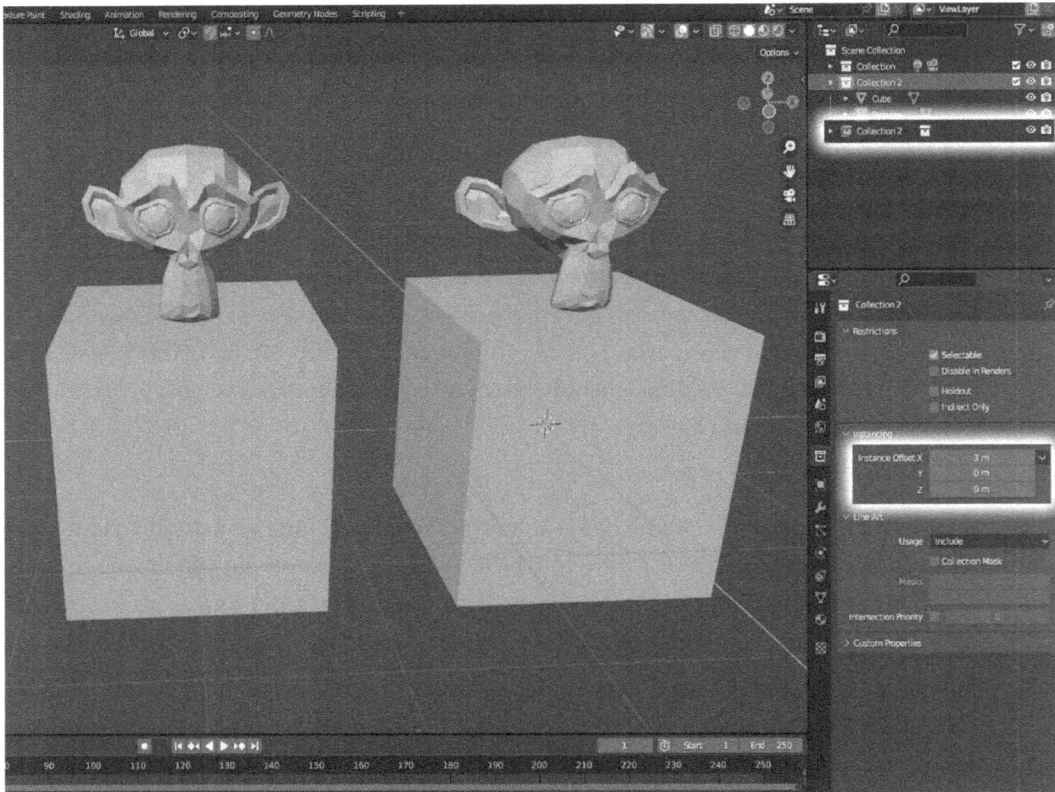

Figure 3.8: Instance Offset options

- **Custom Properties:** This area is helpful if you are thinking of using drivers, scripts, or add-ons to store and manage additional information or attributes for your collection. In a few words, you can use **Custom Properties** to add, edit, or remove user-defined properties.

The **Collection Properties** tab will be your organizational lifesaver when it comes to complex scenes. With a bit of planning and some creative thinking, you can use collections to control how your scene is structured, displayed, and managed, making everything far easier to work with. Now that we have covered how to manage the scene as a whole, let's move on to the next **Properties** panel tab, which shifts the focus to editing and managing individual objects.

Getting down to the nitty-gritty details with the Object Properties tab

The **Object Properties** tab in Blender allows you to manage and edit the properties of the currently selected object(s) in your scene.

Key features of the **Object Properties** tab include the following:

- **Transform**: This section relates to Blender's coordinate system, discussed in *Chapter 1* in this part of the book. You can use these settings to adjust the location, rotation, and scale of the selected object numerically. Alternatively, you can input exact values for each axis (x, y, z) to make the process more accurate.

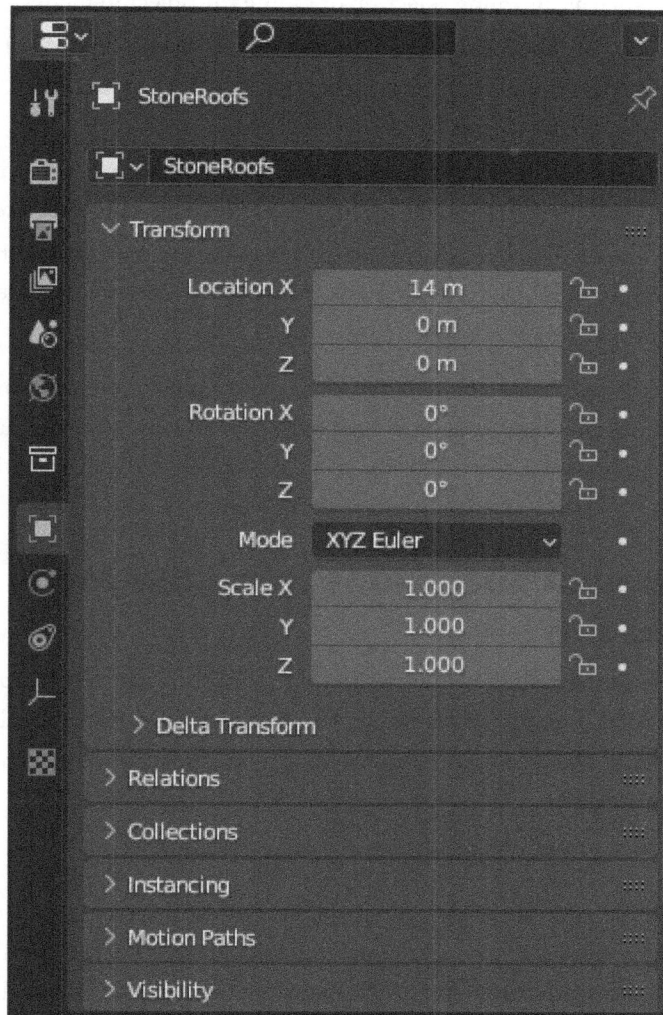

Figure 3.9: Object Properties tab – Transform options

- **Relations:** You can use this section to manage relationships between objects, such as parenting, linking, or instancing, as discussed in *Chapter 8* in *Part 2* of this book. You can also use **Relations** options to organize your scene by assigning objects to specific collections.

- **Visibility:** This section is like the process of layering, allowing you to change the visibility of the object in the viewport, render, and specific view layers. You can adjust visibility settings, such as disabling selection or hiding the object in renders.

- **Display As:** This option allows you to choose how the object is displayed in the viewport. This is based on different display modes, such as **Wireframe**, **Solid**, or **Bounding Box**, as discussed in *Chapter 1* in this part of the book.

- **Motion Paths:** This area is linked to animation settings. You can use it to calculate motion paths, update them, and adjust settings such as frame range and step size.

- **Custom Properties:** You can use this area to store and manage additional information or attributes for an object. Afterward, you can access and manipulate them using drivers, scripts, or add-ons.

Blender's **Object Properties** tab is essential for streamlining your workflow and making it easier to work with complex projects. Now that you know how to edit and manage the properties of objects in your 3D scene, we will move on to modifying and manipulating your objects in a non-destructive way using the **Modifier Properties** tab.

Making object alterations using the Modifier Properties tab

The **Modifier Properties** tab in Blender allows you to non-destructively modify and manipulate objects by applying a sequence of modifiers. The **Modifier Properties** tab is located in the **Properties** panel and offers a wide range of options for altering the geometry, animation, or simulation of objects in your scene.

Key features of the **Modifier Properties** tab include the following:

- **Modifier list:** This area displays a list of modifiers applied to the selected object. You can add new modifiers, rearrange the order of modifiers in the stack, and toggle their visibility in the **3D Viewport** and render. The order of the modifiers affects the final result as they are applied sequentially, top to bottom.

- **Modifier types:** Blender offers a variety of modifier types, categorized into four main groups, as shown in *Figure 3.10*:

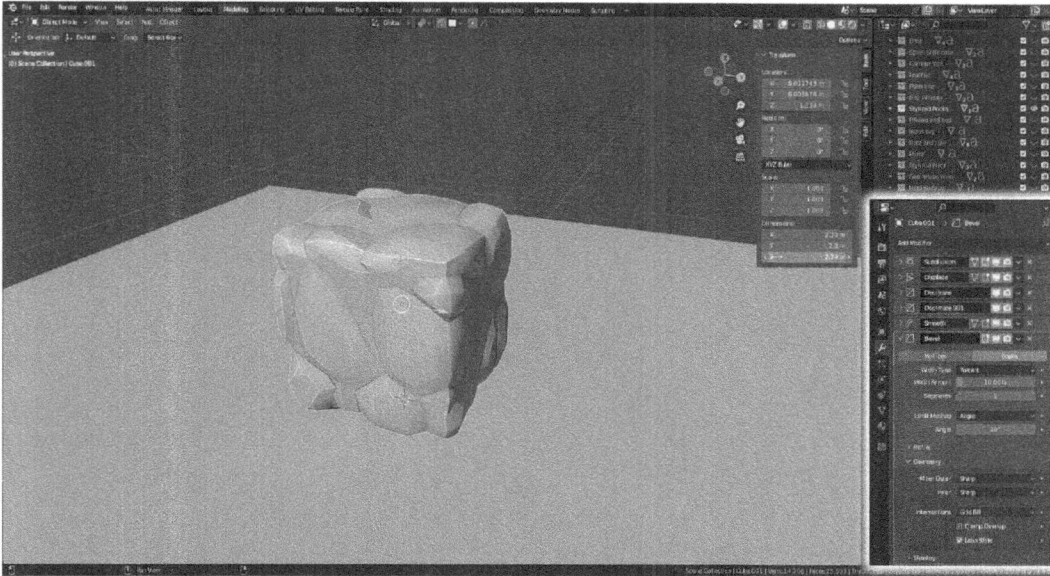

Figure 3.10: Modifier types

- **Generate:** These modifiers create or manipulate mesh geometry, such as the **Array**, **Bevel**, **Boolean**, **Mirror**, **Solidify**, and **Subdivision Surface** modifiers.

- **Deform:** Modifiers in this category are used to deform an object's geometry, such as the **Armature**, **Cast**, **Curve**, **Displace**, **Lattice**, and **Simple Deform** modifiers.

- **Simulate:** These modifiers are associated with physics simulations and include the **Cloth**, **Collision**, **Dynamic Paint**, **Fluid**, **Ocean**, **Particle System**, and **Soft Body** modifiers.

- **Modify:** Modifiers in this group perform operations on the object data, such as the **Data Transfer**, **Decimate**, **Edge Split**, **Mask**, **Multiresolution**, and **UV Project** modifiers.

- **Modifier settings:** Each modifier type comes with a unique set of settings and options, which can be adjusted in this tab. You can use these settings to control various aspects of a modifier's parameters, influence, or fall-off, as shown in *Figure 3.11*.

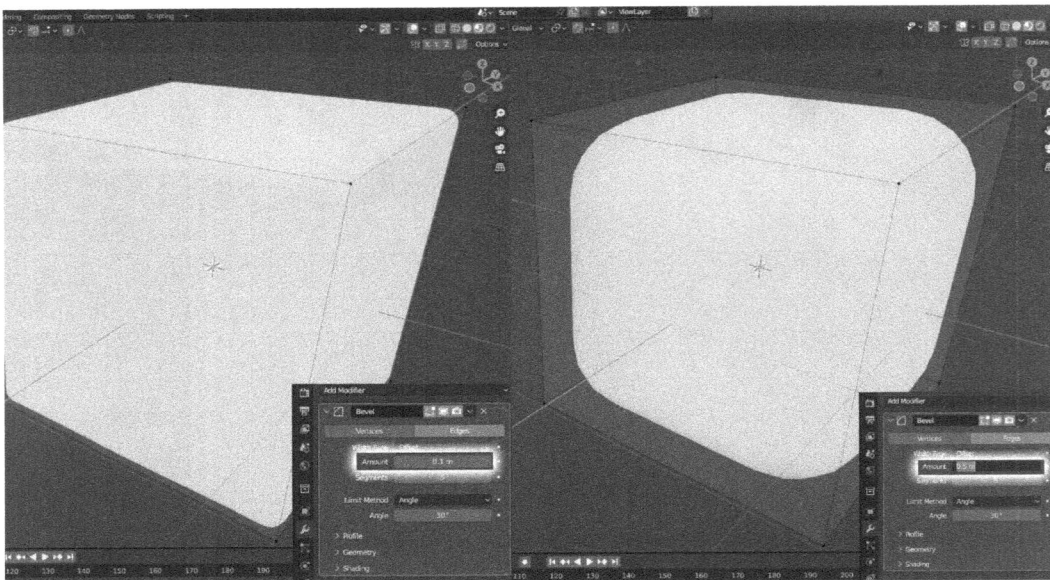

Figure 3.11: Modifier settings example

- **Modifier visibility:** Provides controls for the visibility of the modifier's effect in the **3D Viewport**, **Render Mode**, and **Edit Mode**. You can enable or disable the modifier's visibility in each mode separately, as shown in *Figure 3.12*.

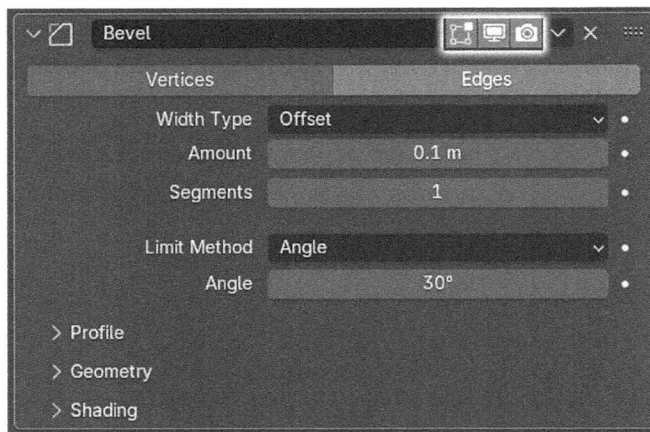

Figure 3.12: A close-up of Blender's modifier visibility options

- **Apply modifiers**: You can apply a modifier permanently to the object's data by clicking the **Apply** button in the **Modifier Properties** tab (*Figure 3.13*). You can find the **Apply** button to the right of the **Visibility** options: it looks like an arrow and expands **Modifier** options.

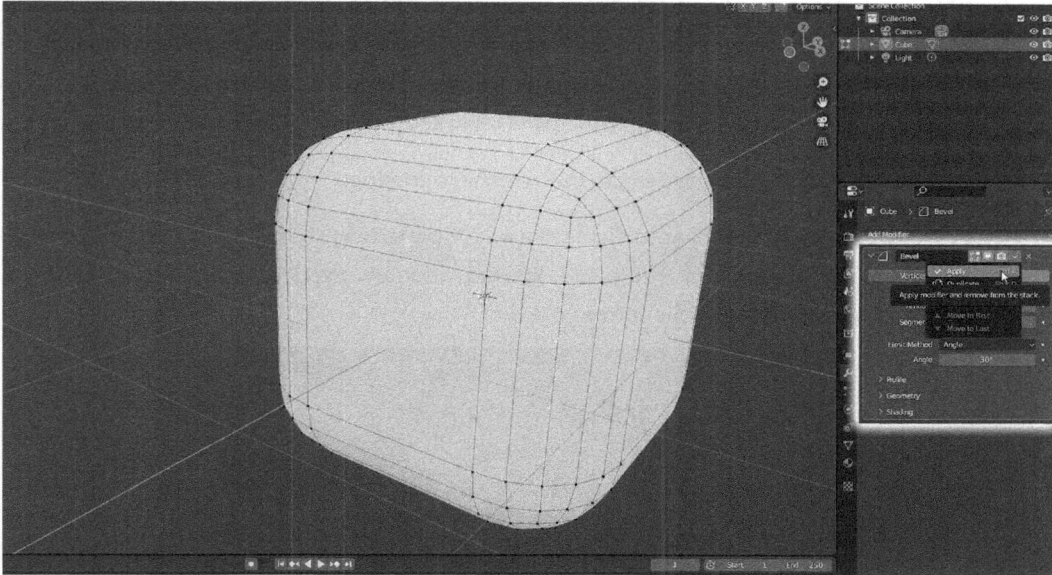

Figure 3.13: Apply modifiers location

This action cannot be undone, and it will remove the modifier from the stack, merging the modifier's effect into the object's geometry or data. This highlights the importance of creating backup versions of your .blend file, as discussed in *Chapter 2* in this part of the book.

The **Modifier Properties** tab in Blender is one of your most powerful allies; it lets you make non-destructive edits to your objects, meaning you can experiment and tweak without permanently changing the base model. Modifiers give you a ton of flexibility and control for adjusting shapes, generating geometry, or creating complex animations and simulations. Now that you know how to do this with objects, let's look at how to apply the same kind of control to particle systems using the **Particle Properties** tab.

Bringing your 3D models to life using the Particle Properties tab

The **Particle Properties** tab is a dedicated section of Blender's UI that allows you to create, control, and manipulate particle systems for your 3D objects. **Particle systems** control effects, such as simulating hair, fur, grass, smoke, fire, or other natural phenomena. The **Particle Properties** tab is in the **Properties** panel and offers a comprehensive set of settings to manage your particle systems.

Key features of the **Particle Properties** tab include the following:

- **Particle system list**: This area displays a list of particle systems associated with the selected object, as shown in *Figure 3.14*. You can add new particle systems, rename them, duplicate them, or delete them from the list.

Figure 3.14: Particle system list

- **Particle system type:** Blender offers two main types of particle systems, as shown in *Figure 3.15*. These are as follows:

  - **Emitter:** This type of particle system emits particles from the surface of an object, such as to simulate smoke, fire, or rain.

  - **Hair:** The **Hair** particle system creates hair strands, fur, or grass on an object's surface. Blender's **grooming tools** allow you to comb, cut, or style these.

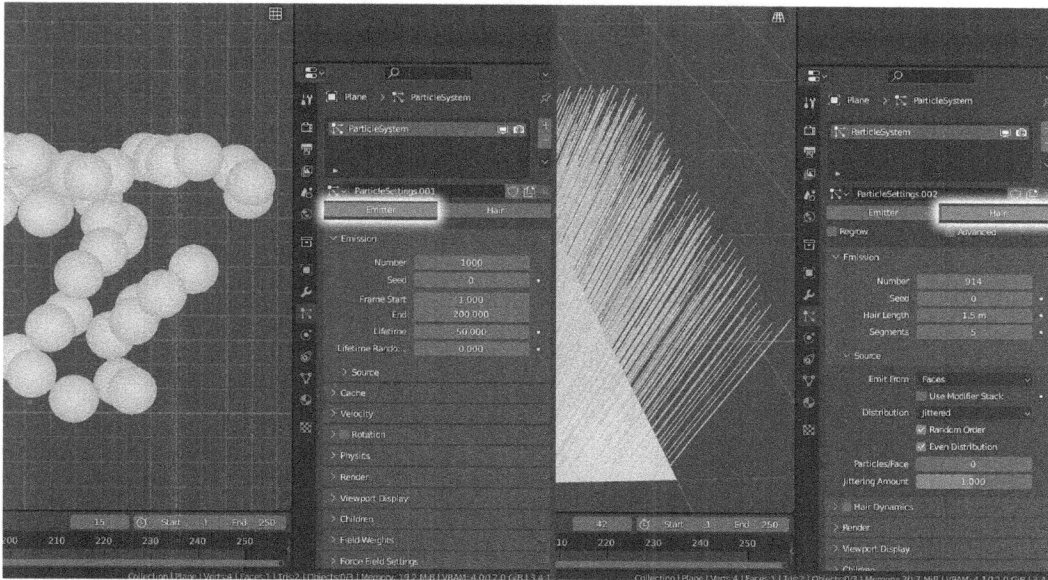

Figure 3.15: Emitter and Hair particle systems comparison

- **Emission settings:** These settings control the emission of particles, such as the particle number, the start and end frames of the emission, the lifetime of the particles, and the method for distributing them across the object's surface.

- **Physics settings:** These settings determine how particles behave and interact with their environment. You can choose from various physics types, such as **Newtonian**, **Keyed**, or **Fluid**, and adjust parameters such as **Mass**, **Drag**, or **Damp**, as shown in *Figure 3.16*:

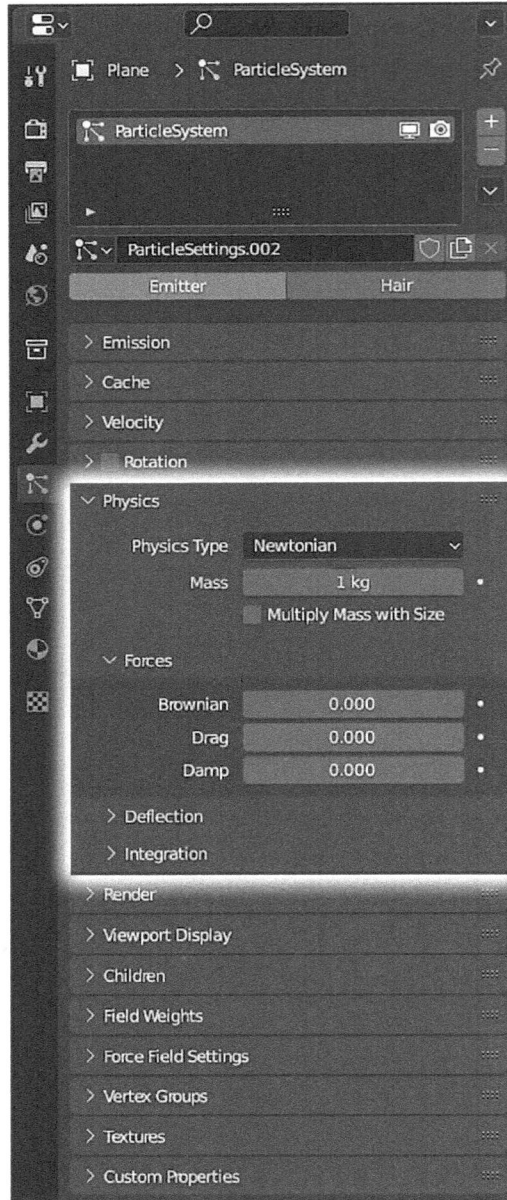

Figure 3.16: Physics settings

- These settings can be useful in projects where you are trying to simulate the function of a real-world object, such as a windmill. Here, you would use the **Physics** settings to change **Physics Type** to **Fluid** to make the dynamic particles behave like liquid during the simulation, like the one shown in *Figure 3.17*:

Figure 3.17: Dynamic particles example

- **Render settings:** These options let you control the appearance of particles in the final render, as shown in *Figure 3.18*. You can choose how particles are displayed, such as **Halo**, **Line**, **Path**, or **Object**, and modify their size, color, or material.

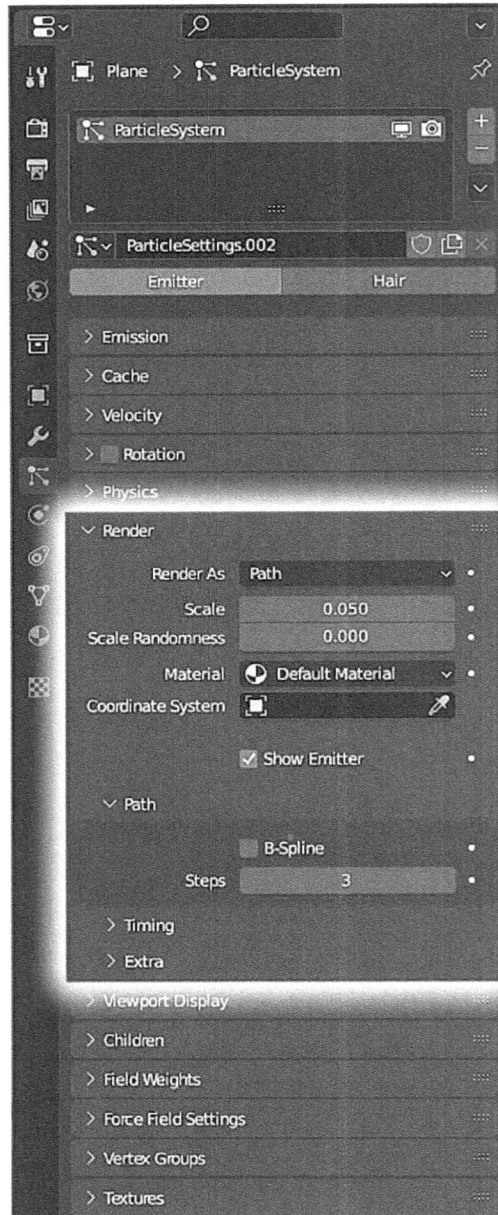

Figure 3.18: Particle Properties tab – Render settings

- **Field Weights:** Use these settings to change the influence of various force fields on the particle system, such as gravity, wind, turbulence, or vortex. Adjusting the **Field Weights** settings allows you to create complex and dynamic particle animations. This could help you simulate the function of a weathercock, for example, as you can see in *Figure 3.19*:

Figure 3.19: Illustrating Field Weights settings with a weathercock

- **Vertex Groups:** You can use **Vertex Groups** to define specific areas on your mesh that will emit particles or be affected by them:

Figure 3.20: Particle Properties tab – Vertex Groups

Assigning vertex groups gives you greater control over the distribution and behavior of particles on your object's surface. Using weight paint information of individual vertices, you can gain finer control over the vertices in a mesh. For example, you could control the length of hair particles based on the part of the mesh it is applied to. This is useful if you want to make a character's hair curly near the tips but keep the rest straight.

The **Particle Properties** tab in Blender is a powerful and versatile tool that enables you to create and manage particle systems for a wide range of visual effects. This will be part of your bread-and-butter skills as a 3D modeling artist looking to upscale the realism and detail of your 3D scenes, animations, or simulations.

Next, we will turn our gaze to a related area that also focuses on realism, based on real-life physics: the **Physics Properties** tab.

Maximizing realism using the Physics Properties tab

The **Physics Properties** tab in Blender gives you the tools to add and control various physics simulations for your 3D objects. These simulations can bring realistic motion and interaction to objects in your scene, creating more dynamic and engaging animations. The **Physics Properties** tab offers a range of options to manage different types of physics simulations.

Key features of the **Physics Properties** tab include the following:

- **Physics types**: Blender offers several types of physics simulations that you can apply to your objects, which you can see in _Figure 3.21_:

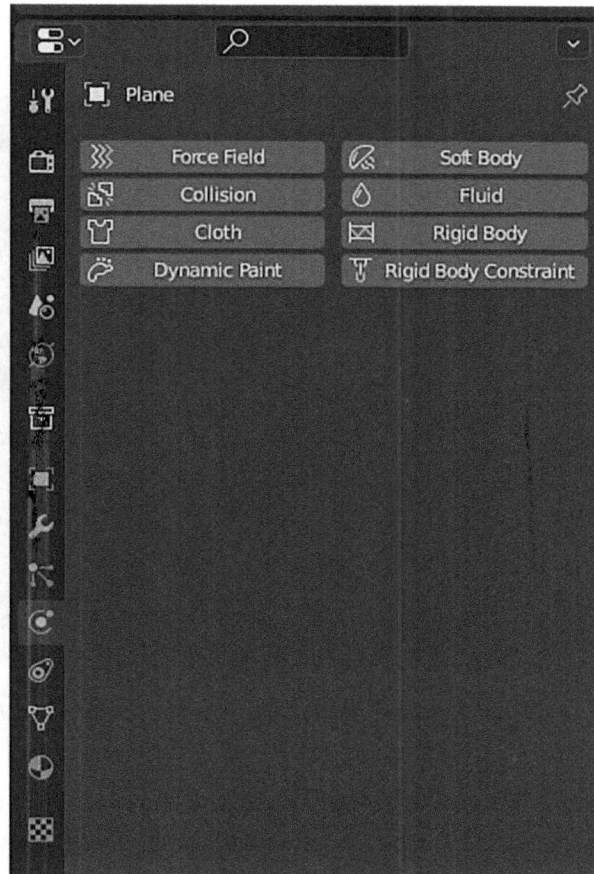

Figure 3.21: Physics properties available

Some of the most common types are as follows:

- **Rigid Body**: Simulates the motion and collision of solid objects with mass and real-world physics properties (e.g., friction and bounciness).

- **Soft Body**: Simulates the behavior of flexible, deformable objects such as cloth, rubber, or other elastic materials.

- **Fluid**: Simulates the behavior of fluids, such as water or smoke, letting you simulate gas or liquids; we can see this in *Figure 3.22*:

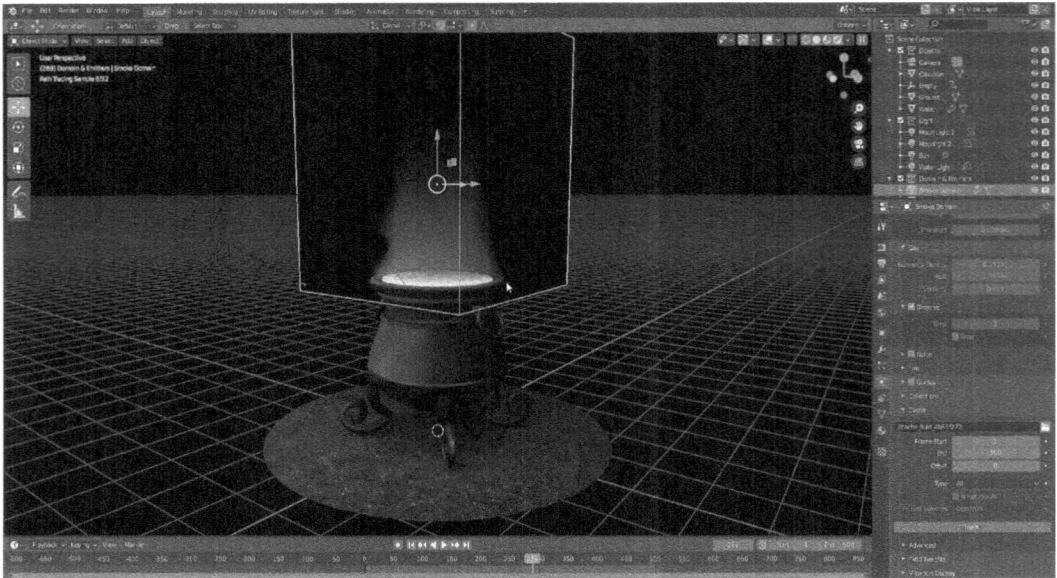

Figure 3.22: Fluid physics simulation from Blender VFX Liquid Smoke & Fire by 3D Tudor

- **Cloth**: Simulates the behavior of fabric materials, such as clothing, curtains, or flags, allowing them to interact with other objects and react to forces such as wind or gravity.

- **Dynamic Paint**: Allows objects to paint or displace other objects' surfaces dynamically, creating effects such as footprints in the sand, paint splatters, or ripples on water.

- **Physics settings**: Each physics type has its unique set of settings that control the behavior of the simulation. These settings are integral in customizing every part of the simulation, including mass, stiffness, damping, collision properties, and forces.

- **Cache**: You can use these settings to manage the storage and playback of your physics simulations. Set the start and end frames, cache the simulation data for faster playback, and save the cache to disk so that you can share it or use it later.

- **Field Weights**: Use these settings to control the influence of forces such as gravity, wind, turbulence, or vortex on your physics simulation, as shown in *Figure 3.23*.

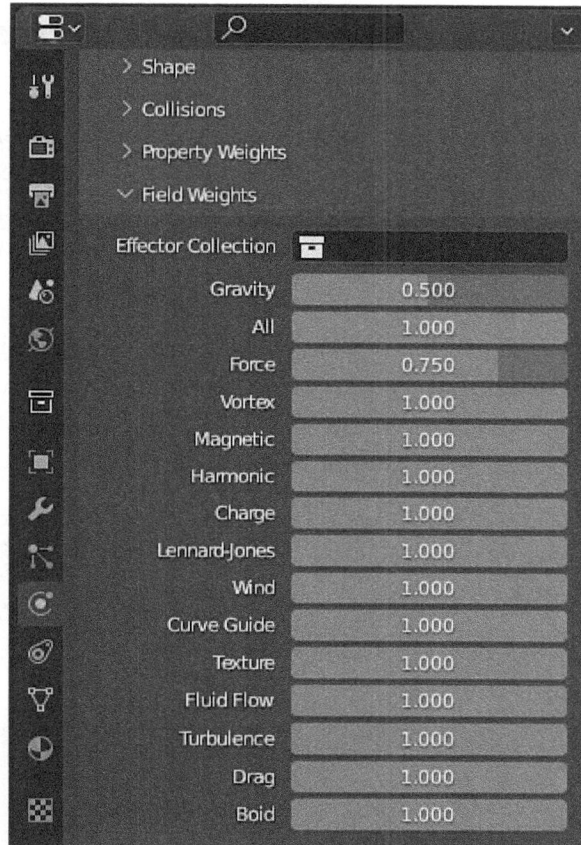

Figure 3.23: Physics Properties tab – Field Weights options

The **Physics Properties** tab is where things start to feel properly alive. Whether it is bouncing objects, flowing cloth, or a full-on destruction sim, this tab lets you bring real-world motion into your scene. And yeah, getting things to behave just right takes a bit of precision, but you have already started building those skills by making it this far through the chapter. Now, let's take it up a notch.

The next stop is the **Object Constraints Properties** tab, where you get to lay down the rules, what an object can do, what it cannot do, and how it reacts to other stuff in your scene. It is all about control without the chaos.

Establishing rules using the Object Constraints Properties tab

The **Object Constraints Properties** tab is dedicated to adding and managing constraints for your 3D objects. **Constraints** are limitations that rules place to control an object's position, rotation, or scale in relation to other objects, specific values, or mathematical expressions. They are a powerful way to create complex and precise object interactions, rigging systems, and animations without needing to manually keyframe everything.

Keyframes are specific points in time where you record the value of a property, such as location, rotation, or scale, so that Blender can interpolate the changes between them. For example, you might set a keyframe at frame 1 with a cube at the origin, and another at frame 100 with the cube moved to the right. Blender will then animate the motion in between.

Using constraints can save you from having to set all those keyframes yourself. This is especially useful for things such as tank tracks rolling through a 3D environment, where you want precise, repeatable motion driven by logic rather than endless manual input.

The **Object Constraints Properties** tab will give you the tools for the tracks to be affected by the height of an environment (see *Figure 3.24*).

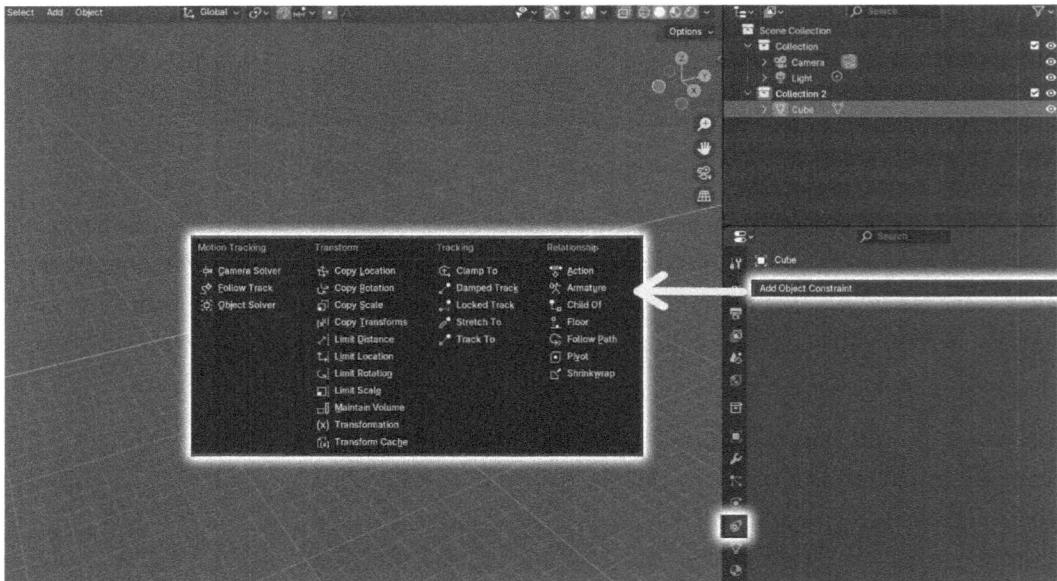

Figure 3.24: Where to find the Object Constraints Properties tab

This will ensure that whenever the vehicle moves, it will automatically touch the ground with precision, without any mesh overlapping issues.

Key features of the **Object Constraints Properties** tab include the following:

- **Constraint types:** Blender offers a variety of specialized constraint types. Their functions can include controlling object relationships, limiting object transformations, or creating complex rigging setups. Some common constraint types are as follows:

    - **Copy Location, Rotation,** or **Scale:** Copies the transformation (location, rotation, or scale) of one object to another.

    - **Limit Location, Rotation,** or **Scale:** Restricts an object's transformation within a specified range.

    - **Track To, Damped Track,** or **Locked Track:** Makes an object point to or follow another object or target.

    - **Inverse Kinematics:** Calculates the position and rotation of a chain of objects based on the position of a target object, often used in character rigging.

    - **Child Of:** Makes an object behave like a child of another object, inheriting its transformations.

- **Constraint settings:** You can use these settings to control how a constraint behaves in Blender. These settings include parameters such as target objects, sub-targets (e.g., bones), influence, space (i.e., local or world), or axis limitations.

- **Influence and blending:** The **Influence** slider is one of the most intuitive ways to control the strength of a constraint's effect on your target object. Blending is the process of combining multiple constraints with different influences.

- **Stacking and order:** Constraints can be stacked and applied in a specific order to create complex rigging and animation systems. The way you order the constraints in the **Object Constraints Properties** tab determines the order in which they are evaluated, thereby changing the final result.

The **Object Constraints Properties** tab in Blender is an essential and versatile tool for creating precise object interactions, complex rigging, and advanced animation systems. Now that you have implemented constraints on your objects and have established what they should not do, it is a good time to change their properties so that they fit your vision. To do that, we will explore the **Object Data Properties** tab.

Finding out about the Object Data Properties tab

The **Object Data Properties** tab is integral to the Blender UI because it contains settings and options specific to the selected object type, such as meshes, curves, text, cameras, or lights. It is your main point of call for modifying and managing the object's internal data (i.e., geometry or properties) and customizing its appearance, behavior, and functionality.

Key features of the **Object Data Properties** tab include the following:

- **Geometry Data**: This section is equipped with tools for rigging, morphing, and vertex painting mesh objects, as shown in *Figure 3.25*.

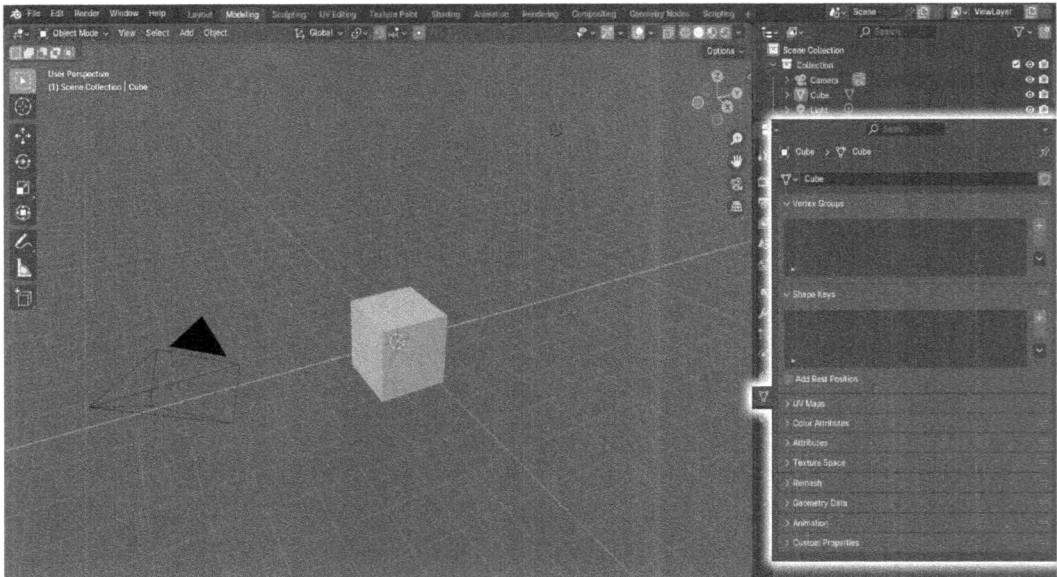

Figure 3.25: Locating the Geometry Data section in the Object Properties tab

- Settings included in this section focus on vertex groups, shape keys, UV maps, and vertex colors. Please note that this book features an in-depth discussion of the related topic of **Geometry Nodes** in *Chapter 2* in *Part 2* of this book.

- **Curve Data**: For curve objects, this section lets you manage curve properties such as shape, resolution, fill mode, and bevel depth. If your object also includes text, you can change its properties such as font, size, alignment, and spacing. This will be discussed in more detail in *Chapter 8* in *Part 1* of this book.

- **Camera Data:** Here, you can adjust the camera's properties, such as its focal length or depth of field. Using these settings, you will have full control over the camera's field of view, perspective, and rendering output. You will find more information about **Camera Data** in *Chapter 5* in *Part 2* of this book.

- **Light Data:** Using this section, you can modify the light's type, color, intensity, falloff, and shadow properties. Lighting can be a very powerful setting that impacts the mood of your scene. For example, warm lighting with settings that make it look like it is lighting a torch can make a scene, such as a dungeon, appear more ominous (see *Figure 3.26*).

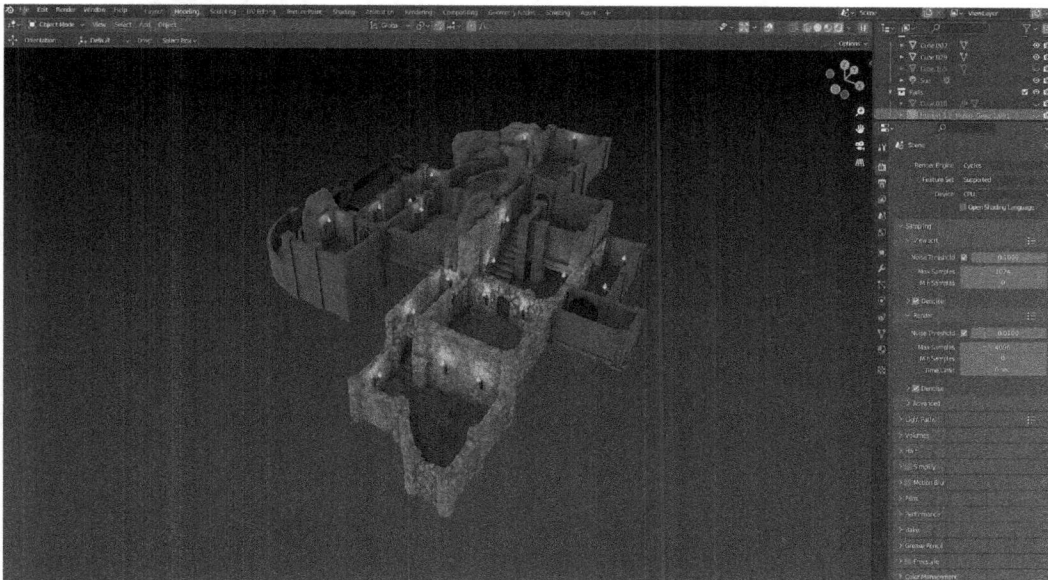

Figure 3.26: Light Data settings example from "Blender 3 to Unreal Engine 5 Dungeon Modular Kitbash" by 3D Tudor

You will find more information about **Light Data** in *Chapter 6* in *Part 2* of this book.

- **Custom Properties:** This section lets you create and manage custom properties for your objects. These are user-defined attributes that you could use for animations, controlling modifiers, or scripting, for example.

- **Normals and Geometry Data:** The **Object Data Properties** tab also provides options for managing an object's normals, which are important for shading and rendering and will be discussed in more detail in *Chapters 13* and *14* in *Part 1* of this book. Here, you can control normals' display or enable auto-smoothing, for instance.

- The **Object Data Properties** tab contains settings for other object types as well, such as **Lattice**, **Metaball**, **Armature**, or **Grease Pencil** objects. These settings allow you to manage unique properties and data related to each object type.

Blender's **Object Data Properties** tab is essential for managing and customizing the properties and data of objects in your scene. Now that you have found out how to do this for objects, we will move on to an overview of the same type of settings, but for materials. These settings can also be accessed in the **Properties** panel using the **Materials Properties** tab.

Customizing appearance through the Materials Properties tab

The **Material Properties** tab is dedicated to creating, managing, and modifying materials applied to objects in your scene. Materials are what determine the appearance of objects, including color, texture, reflection, transparency, and other surface properties. This tab allows you to create realistic or stylized materials for various 3D objects, enhancing the overall visual quality of your project.

Key features of the **Material Properties** tab include the following:

- **Material Slots**: This section lists all materials assigned to your objects, shown separately for each one, as shown in *Figure 3.27*.

Figure 3.27: Materials Properties tab – Material Slots options

You can add, remove, or reorder material slots. This is useful if you want to assign multiple materials to a single object.

- **Material creation:** You can create new materials by clicking the **New** button in the **Material Properties** tab. This action will bring up a default material that you can customize further, as shown in *Figure 3.28*.

Figure 3.28: Materials Properties tab – material creation options

- **Surface/shader presets:** Blender includes built-in presets for material use, such as the **Principled BSDF** and **Hair BSDF** presets. You can use them to create your materials via the drop-down menu in the **Material Properties** tab.

- **Shader settings:** Applying shaders can change the appearance and behavior of your materials. These settings include, but are not limited to, surface properties (e.g., **Base Color**, **Roughness**, **Metallic**), transparency (e.g., **Alpha**), subsurface scattering, or clearcoat. You will learn about each of these in more detail in *Chapter 13* in *Part 1* of this book.

- **Textures:** You can use the input slots in the **Material Properties** tab to apply textures to materials by adding images or procedural textures, as shown in *Figure 3.29*. This process can help you add details such as color variations, bumpiness, or reflections.

Figure 3.29: Applying textures

- **Displacement: Displacement** can add depth and detail to your object's surface, making it appear more three-dimensional. Use a **Displacement** map or procedural texture to control your object's surface displacement. This is useful for projects involving pebble walkways.
- **Custom Properties:** As with all other tabs in the **Properties** panel, you can create and manage custom properties for your materials.

Material Preview: When working with larger environments that have fixed lighting, it is sometimes hard to tell if the material has the right setup, especially in shadowed areas. The **Material Preview** window displays a real-time preview of the material applied to a default object, helping you see your material in different lighting conditions and with different surface properties. To imagine this better, in *Figure 3.30*, we are using **Material Preview** to determine the overall glossiness of a stained-glass window:

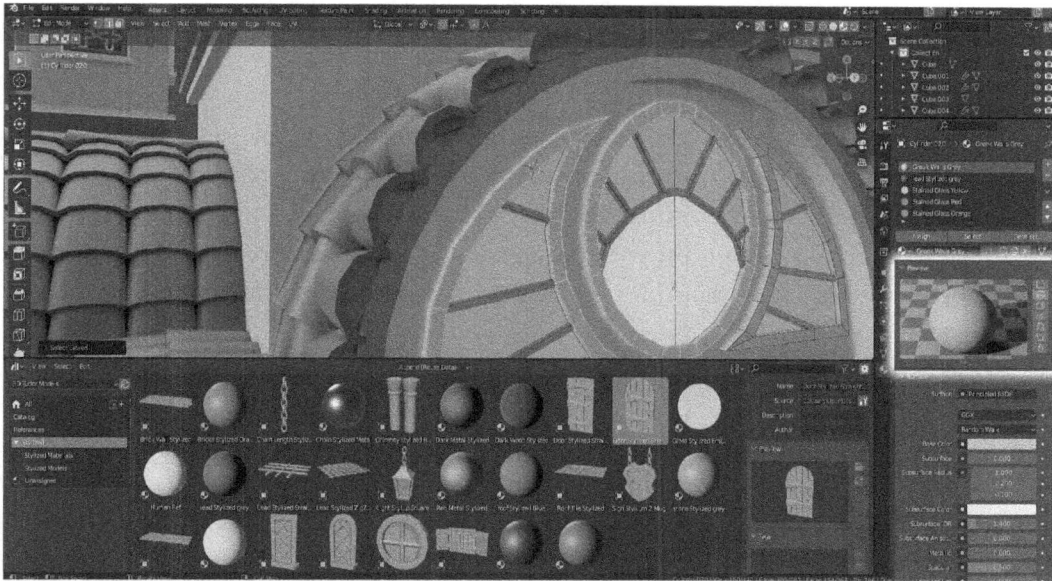

Figure 3.30: Stained-glass example from "Blender 3.0 Stylized Greek Church 3D Model Build with Commentary" by 3D Tudor

> **Note**
>
> *Figure 3.30* is a screenshot from a 3D Tudor YouTube tutorial, which can be found here: https://www.youtube.com/watch?v=HxBsVnVUBuQ. This is the complete modeling part of a stylized asset build – the build was done mainly using Blender 3.0, but a small portion was done using ZBrush (we could have used Blender, but it would have taken a little longer). This process has also been sped up around 5x; otherwise, the video would be simply too long, and it is also why we focused mainly on the modeling side of things.

The **Material Properties** tab is where your models start to come to life. This is where you create, manage, and tweak materials to give your objects the look and feel you are after, whether that is shiny metal, rough stone, or anything in between. These settings are key to making your project visually stand out. But this tab is really just the start when it comes to materials and textures in Blender. To finish off the chapter, we are going to dive into the **Texture Properties** tab and see how it fits into the bigger picture.

Upscaling your 3D models via the Texture Properties tab

Since Blender 4.4, the **Texture Properties** tab is not shown by default, and you have to go to **Texturing** mode first to see it. The **Texture Properties** tab complements the **Material Properties** tab by acting as your assistant for creating, managing, and modifying textures applied to materials, particles, or various other elements within your scene. Textures are 2D images or procedural patterns that boost the appearance of 3D objects by making them look more varied, stylized, or realistic.

Key features of the **Texture Properties** tab include the following:

- **Texture Selection**: This section lists all the available textures in your project, as seen in *Figure 3.28*. You can add, remove, or rename textures, as well as select the one you want to edit.

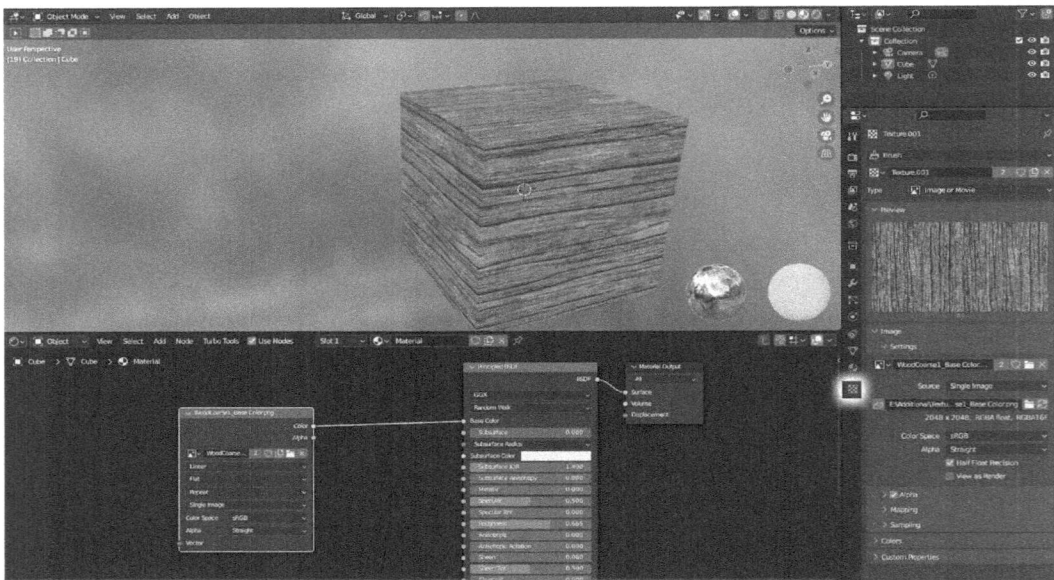

Figure 3.31: Texture Properties tab – Texture Selection options

- **Texture Type:** Here, you can choose between **Image and Movie Textures** or **Procedural Textures**. The former are based on image files or video sequences, while the latter are algorithmically generated patterns. As we move on to *Chapter 13* in *Part 1* of this book, you will see how to create procedural textures and why they are useful.

- **Image settings:** These settings are useful for image and movie textures. You can make more of them by loading an external image file or selecting an image from the available resources in your project. You can also adjust image mapping, such as tiling, interpolation, or alpha handling settings. These can be useful for adjusting the color and texture of an object to make it fit in better with the color scheme used in the scene it appears in.

- **Procedural settings:** These settings are important to the process of creating procedural textures. You can select **Procedural Textures** from the **Type** drop-down menu, and you will find properties unique to each texture. Here, you can choose from various patterns such as **Clouds**, **Marble**, **Musgrave**, **Noise**, **Stucci**, **Voronoi**, or **Wood**. Each procedural texture is fully customizable based on its unique set of parameters.

- **Mapping:** The **Texture Properties** tab gives you control over the process of mapping. This controls how the texture is mapped onto the object's surface. You can choose from mapping methods such as **UV**, **Generated**, or **Object Coordinates**. Afterward, you can also adjust the scaling, rotation, and offset of the texture: a process we will cover in detail in *Chapter 15* in *Part 1* of this book.

- **Influence:** Here, you can define which material, particle, or other properties the texture will affect.

- **Preview:** The **Texture Properties** tab includes a **Preview** window that displays a real-time preview of the texture on a default object. This preview allows you to visualize how the texture will look when applied to an object under different lighting conditions.

The **Texture Properties** tab in Blender is a critical tool for creating, managing, and customizing textures for your 3D objects and other elements in your scene. It is the sealing deal that completes your 3D modeling artist toolkit for understanding how to take advantage of Blender's UI options to maximize the quality of your next project.

Summary

The Blender **Properties** panel becomes the cornerstone of your 3D creativity, offering users a multitude of tabs for controlling various aspects of their projects. This chapter gave you an overview of the different tabs in the **Properties** panel, including the **Active Tool and Workspace Settings**, **Output Properties**, and **View Layer Properties** tabs, and more. When you put it all together, everything you have learned in this chapter gives you the tools to take full control of your scene, from tweaking individual objects and materials to managing lighting, cameras, and everything in between. It is all about building confidence in your workflow and knowing exactly where to go when you want to make things look (and behave) the way you imagined.

As every 3D modeling artist comes to know, creating and managing complex scenes comes with the territory; it can be a challenging process to understand and master. With the help of settings such as the **View Layer Properties** tab, you can control what can or cannot be seen in individual renders of your scene, hiding and highlighting objects as you wish. Like with other tabs discussed in this chapter, you must know about these options available to you before you put pen to paper.

Using this chapter's analytical overviews of different **Properties** panel tabs, you have prepared yourself for several different areas in a 3D modeling artist's workflow. This knowledge will be the backbone of your skills for using Blender, and you will keep returning to this chapter as your reference guide as we move on.

In the next chapter, we will discuss Blender's **Outliner** and **Add-On** ecosystem, which will supercharge your workflow and help you create more advanced projects with ease.

Subscribe to Game Dev Assembly!

We are excited to introduce **Game Dev Assembly**, our brand-new newsletter dedicated to everything game development. Whether you're coding, designing, animating, or managing a studio, we've got insights, trends, and expert advice to help you create, innovate, and thrive. Sign up now and get exciting benefits.

`https://packt.link/gamedev-newsletter`

Get This Book's PDF Version and Exclusive Extras

UNLOCK NOW

Scan the QR code (or go to packtpub.com/unlock). Search for this book by name, confirm the edition, and then follow the steps on the page.

Note: Keep your invoice handy. Purchases made directly from Packt don't require an invoice.

4

Unleashing the Potential of Blender's Outliner and Add-On Ecosystem

Alright, this chapter is where we stop winging it and finally get our Blender scenes under control. If your **Outliner** is a mess, your collections are all over the place, or you have ever lost an object to the abyss of your **3D Viewport**, this one is for you. I like to think of it as Blender's version of Marie Kondo's *The Life-Changing Magic of Tidying Up*, but with fewer folded socks and more hidden empties and duplicated cubes. It is all about asking the right questions: What does this object do? Do I need it? Can I make Blender less of a headache and more of a creative playground?

We will start with the Outliner, which you briefly met back in *Chapter 1*, but this time, we are doing more than just waving at it. The Blender Outliner is the backbone of this powerful software; it provides a hierarchical representation of all objects, materials, and data blocks in a scene, making selecting, organizing, and manipulating different elements quick and easy. You will find out how to enhance your project management skills through a discussion on how to display modes and search bar filter options. Think of it like Windows Explorer: just as you can expand folders to see files and subfolders, the Outliner lets you expand collections to view objects and their associated data. This familiar folder-like structure helps keep even the most complex Blender scenes organized.

But we are not stopping there. This chapter is also your gateway into Blender's add-on ecosystem, a treasure chest of workflow boosters that will make your life a whole lot easier. From official built-ins to weird-but-wonderful third-party gems, we will look at how to enable, install, and actually use these things to their full potential.

Blender's add-on ecosystem is another treasure trove waiting to be discovered. The open source nature of Blender has created a world of never-ending possibilities where its built-in add-ons are complemented by a vibrant community of third-party developers. Blender add-ons will help you unlock new features and optimize your workflow at the same time. This chapter will be your introduction to enabling built-in add-ons and importing third-party offerings, maximizing compatibility with Blender.

You will also get a proper tour of Blender's 3D Viewport customization, stuff such as toggling X-Ray, hiding object types, and configuring overlay settings. Basically, all the switches that let you declutter your view and focus on what matters. By the end of this chapter, you will have the tools to keep your scenes clean, efficient, and way less painful to navigate. This is the foundation you need before diving into anything more complex. Get this part wrong, and everything else gets messy. Get it right, and you're off to the races.

So, in this chapter, we will cover the following topics:

- Mastering the Blender Outliner
- Organizing your Blender projects
- Creating and managing assets with Blender's Asset Manager
- Expanding Blender's functionality with built-in and third-party add-ons
- Customizing your 3D Viewport experience with Viewport overlays

Technical requirements

As for **Blender 4.5 LTS (Long-Term Support)**, the general requirements include a macOS 11.2 or newer (Apple Silicon supported natively) operating system, or a Linux (64-bit, glibc 2.28 or newer) operating system. Blender now requires a CPU with the SSE4.2 instruction set, at least 8 GB of RAM (32 GB recommended for heavy scenes), and a GPU supporting OpenGL 4.3 with a minimum of 2 GB of VRAM.

For a full list of technical requirements, please refer back to *Chapter 1* of this part.

Mastering the Blender Outliner

Blender's Outliner is designed to help you manage and navigate different aspects of your project. You will find it on the right side of Blender's UI by default, but you can customize its location as discussed in *Chapter 3* in this part of the book. Outliner options are displayed using a hierarchical model, showing all of the objects, materials, and data blocks in your scene in order, which you can see in *Figure 4.1*.

Figure 4.1: Blender's Outliner options

A visual hierarchy is helpful because it simplifies the process of object selection, organization, and manipulation. By presenting the elements in a hierarchical model, the Outliner allows you to see the relationships and structure of the components within their scene at a glance. Whether it is grouping objects by function, location, or any other criteria, the visual hierarchy of the Outliner promotes effective project organization.

Taking this further, the hierarchical model in the Outliner reflects the parent-child relationships between objects. This means that modifications made to parent objects propagate to their children, allowing for efficient global changes. For example, scaling a parent object automatically scales its children as well. By visually representing these relationships, the Outliner lets you see the effects of your actions on the entire hierarchy, saving time and effort.

It is hard to focus when all the elements are visible in the 3D Viewport at once. Even if they are broken into sections, it can still feel overwhelming until you have had more time to understand how everything connects.

Within the Outliner, you will also find the display mode, search bar, and filter:

- **Display mode**: The display mode determines what types of data are shown in the hierarchy view. You can change the display mode using the drop-down menu located at the top left of the Outliner window (*Figure 4.2*).

Figure 4.2: Changing the display mode

Some common display modes include the following:

- **View Layer**: Here, you can see the objects in your scene organized by view layers. This is the default mode. You will find it useful if you are managing objects and their visibility in a scene.

- **Blender File**: Enabling this mode will let you see all the data blocks in your .blend file, regardless of whether they are being used in the scene or not. It is useful for managing and cleaning up your project's data.

- **Orphan Data**: This mode displays all data blocks that are not being used by any objects in the scene. It helps identify and delete unused data so that you can maximize your computer's performance capabilities.

- **Data API**: This mode shows the Blender data structure hierarchically. You will be able to see all the data blocks, properties, and their relationships. Although we will not discuss this in this book, if you are an advanced user, this mode will help you access specific data properties and settings.

- **Search bar**: The search bar is located in the top-right corner of the Outliner window. You can use it to quickly find specific elements within the Outliner using keywords. As you type, the Outliner will filter the displayed items to show only those that match your current search. This feature is useful if you have a complex scene with many objects and need to locate a specific element quickly, as shown in *Figure 4.3*.

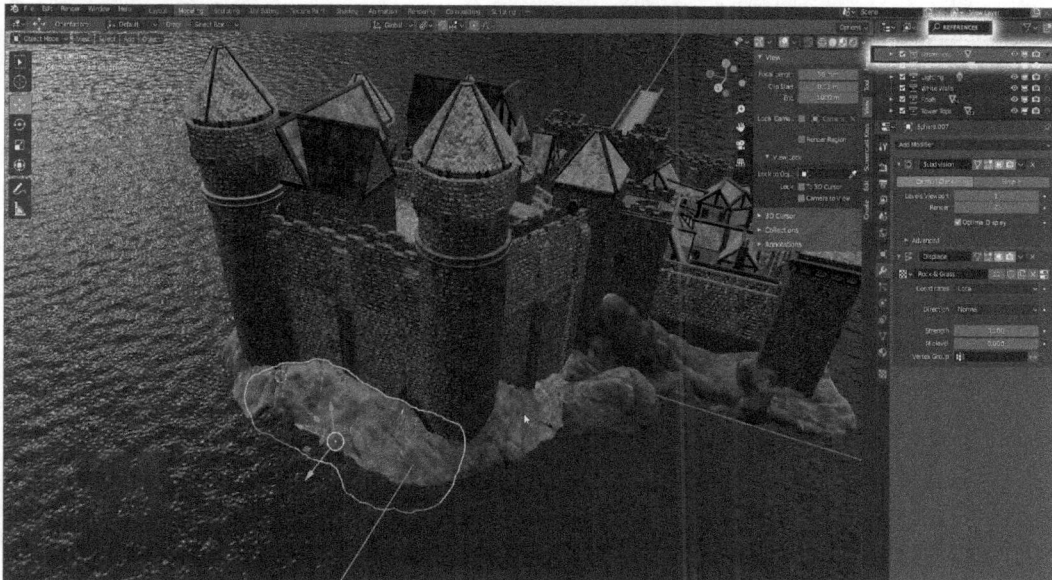

Figure 4.3: The Outliner search bar

- **Filter**: The **Filter** options are located just to the left of the search bar, represented by a funnel icon (*Figure 4.4*).

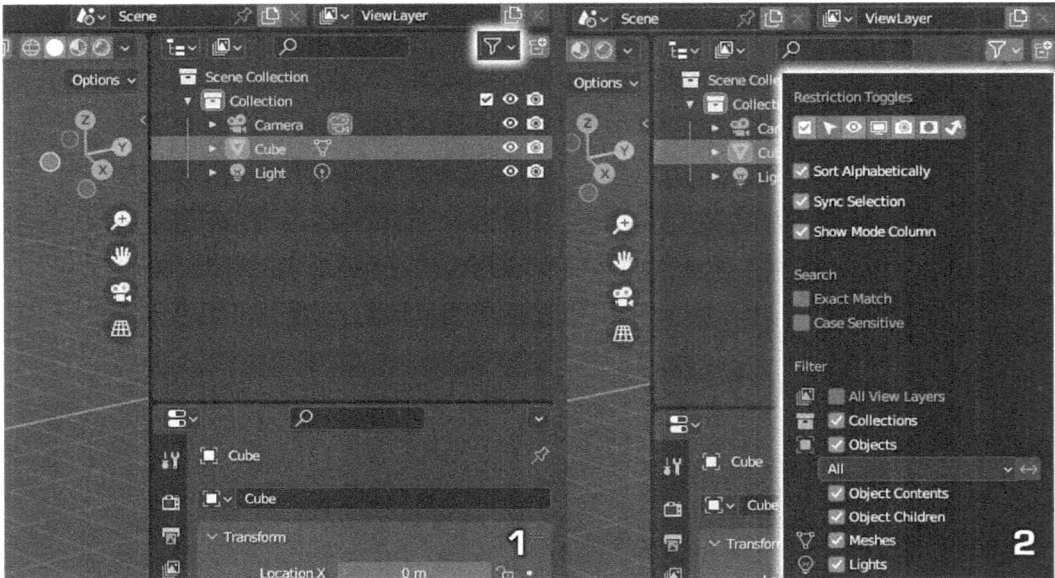

Figure 4.4: The Outliner Filter options

Clicking on the filter icon opens a drop-down menu with various filtering options that you can enable or disable (labeled *1* in *Figure 4.4*). Restriction toggles (labelled *2* in *Figure 4.4*) are options that allow you to control what is displayed in the Outliner, making it easier to focus on smaller project components. Some common filter options include the following:

- **Restriction toggles**: Enable or disable the visibility of specific toggles, such as visibility, selectability, and renderability. This allows you to focus on specific aspects of your objects. For example, you can model the interior of a building with its roof mesh hidden away, even though it is visible in the **Render** view, as shown in *Figure 4.5*.

Figure 4.5: Using restriction toggles in Blender to Unreal Engine 3D Props Medieval Market Stall by 3D Tudor

- **Object types:** Show or hide specific object types (e.g., mesh objects, lights, cameras). This is useful when you want to focus on a particular type of object in your scene.

- **Library overrides:** Display or hide library overrides, which are useful for managing linked data from external `.blend` files.

> **Note**
>
> We will not be discussing collections here because they warrant a separate, comprehensive explanation in the next section.

As you become more proficient in using the Outliner to gain control over your scene using the display mode, search bar, and filter options, you will significantly enhance your workflow. These three options will prepare you for understanding what collections are and why they are so powerful, whether you are an organization mastermind already or not. Collections will be discussed in the next section.

Organizing your Blender projects

Collections are essential to organizing and managing objects within a Blender scene. They are like a folder on your computer, since they allow you to group, categorize, and move objects in an organized way. Collections are a powerhouse of opportunities because they can let you create, manage, and utilize your project. This is helpful if you are populating a town with different assets in different areas based on a larger overall collection of 3D objects, as shown in *Figure 4.6*.

Figure 4.6: Collections in Blender to Unreal Engine Become a Dungeon Prop Artist by 3D Tudor

To create a new collection, follow these steps:

1. In the Outliner, *right-click* the parent collection (i.e., the original collection with other collections within it) or **Scene Collection**.

2. Select **New** from the context menu to create a new collection. This will create a nested collection.

> **Tip**
>
> To create a new collection (that is not nested), you would want to *right-click* **Scene Collection** or in an open space in the Outliner.

3. Rename the collection by double-clicking its name in the Outliner.

You can add objects to collections in several ways:

- Drag and drop: In the Outliner, click and drag an object onto the target collection.
- *M* key: The *M* hotkey opens the **Move to Collection** menu, so this will create a new collection and add the selected object to it. Select an object in the 3D Viewport or the Outliner, press the *M* key, and then choose the target collection from the list.
- The *right-click* menu: Select an object in the Viewport or the Outliner, *right-click* it, select **Move to Collection**, and then choose the target collection.

Collections can also be nested (**nested collections**). This means that Blender allows you to create collections within other collections for better organization.

To create a nested collection, *right-click* the parent collection and choose **New** from the context menu (*Figure 4.7*).

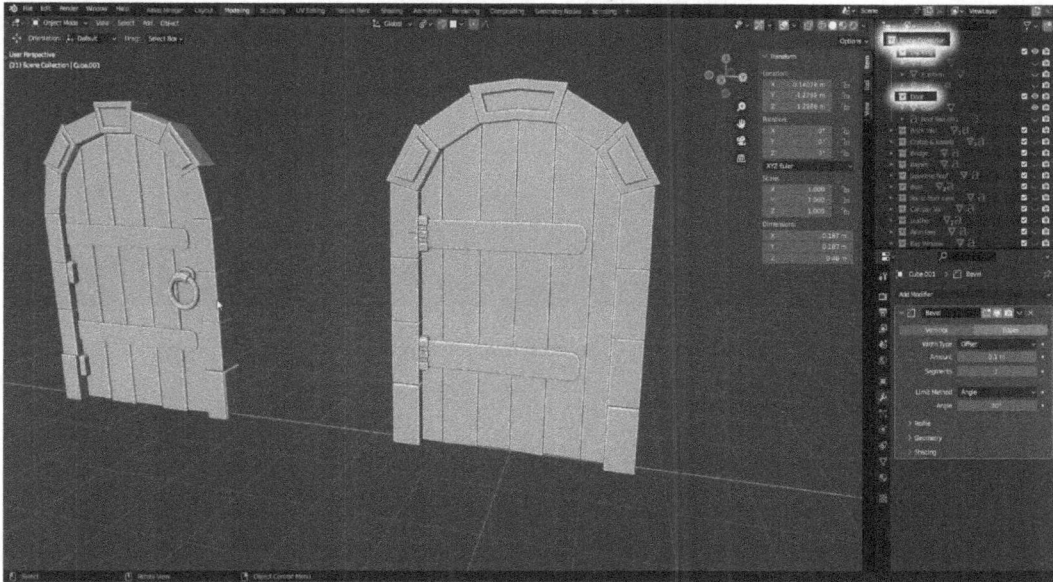

Figure 4.7: Creating nested collections in Blender

Each collection has **Collection Visibility** and **Collection Selectability** settings that can be toggled on or off. For example, these settings are useful if you have a stack of props that you would like to hide away while creating variations of your rendered images. You can find these settings in the Outliner next to the collection name:

- *Eye icon*: Controls the visibility of the collection in the Viewport

- *Arrow icon*: Controls the selectability of the collection in the Viewport
- *Camera icon*: Controls whether the collection is rendered or not

Moving on, a **collection instance** is a powerful feature that allows you to create multiple copies of a collection without duplicating its objects. This helps optimize performance when you need to replicate complex objects or groups of objects multiple times, such as in *Figure 4.8*.

Figure 4.8: Collection instances in Blender

To create a collection instance, follow these steps:

1. In the 3D Viewport, press *Shift + A* to open the **Add** menu.
2. Select **Collection Instance** and choose the desired collection from the list.
3. Position and scale the collection instance based on your needs.

> Tip
>
> You can also *right-click* the collection in the Outliner and select **Instance to Scene**.

Linking collections enables you to share collections across multiple .blend files. This can be helpful if you have two or more projects that share assets. For example, the assets from our **Egypt Themed Stylized 3D Modular Pack** can be easily brought into different environments featuring content with a similar style (see *Figure 4.9*).

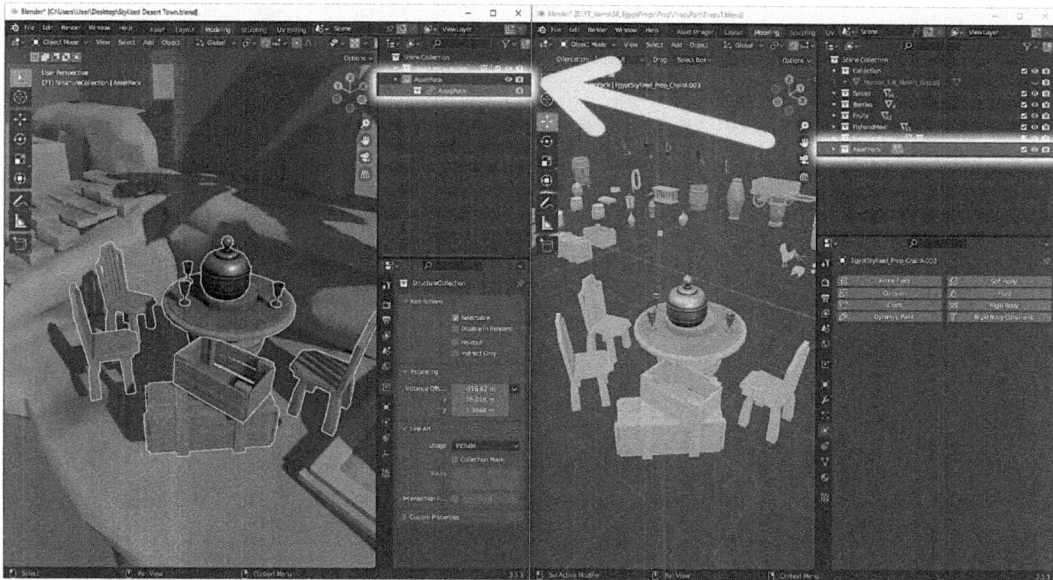

Figure 4.9: Linking collections

Linking collections will save you a lot of time when you get to populating these rooms. To link a collection from an external file, follow these steps:

1. In the top menu of your 3D Viewport, go to **File** and select **Link** to open the file browser.

2. Navigate to the .blend file containing the desired collection, then click on **Collection** in the file.

3. Select the collection you want to link and click **Link** in the top-right corner.

Grasping and applying the concept of collections in Blender will help you be organized, even if that is not part of your artistic persona. Using organized projects lets you streamline your workflow and boost performance, especially when handling numerous objects or instances. Collections and Blender's Asset Manager are like two peas in a pod, and for that reason, it is essential that you find out how to harness their power and link the two tools together.

Creating and managing assets with Blender's Asset Manager

If you thought that Blender's collections were the next big thing for your 3D modeling artist's bag of tricks, you were mistaken, Blender's **Asset Manager** is even more powerful. It has long-term usability potential since it lets you organize, manage, and access assets (e.g., objects, materials, and textures) from within your project without a lot of work required from you. The Asset Manager will save you time because you will use it to centralize all your assets in a dedicated .blend file for all future projects. In this way, you will be importing, exporting, and reusing assets across different 3D scenes and projects.

In this part of the chapter, we will comprehensively walk through how to set up an Asset Manager .blend file and how to use it, including relevant keyboard shortcuts and menus.

Now, get ready for a step-by-step walk-through:

1. Create an Asset Manager .blend file as follows:

    a. Open Blender and create a new, empty project. Save this project with a descriptive name, such as Asset_Manager.blend, to easily identify it as your central Asset Manager file on your computer.

    b. Use collections to organize your assets by category or theme, such as furniture, architectural elements, materials, or textures, as shown in *Figure 4.10*.

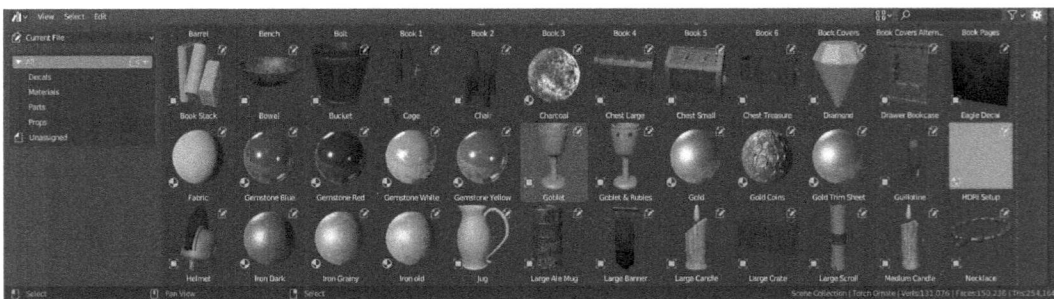

Figure 4.10: An example Asset Manager window in Blender

    c. To create a new collection, *right-click* **Scene Collection** in the Outliner and select **New**.

2. Import and organize assets as follows:

   a. Open your existing Blender projects and append or link the assets you want to include in the Asset Manager .blend file. Go to **File | Append** or **File | Link**, then navigate to the .blend file with the assets you are looking for. Select the assets and click **Append** or **Link**, depending on the option you chose before.

   b. After importing the assets into the Asset Manager .blend file, organize them into the appropriate collections.

3. Access the Asset Manager as follows:

   a. To access the Asset Manager, go to Blender's top menu and click the **Editor Type** icon, then select **Asset Browser** from the drop-down menu.

   b. You could also change any existing editor window to the Asset Browser using the **Editor Type** drop-down menu in the top-left corner of the window, as shown in *Figure 4.11.*

Figure 4.11: Accessing the Asset Manager

4. Manage asset libraries and categories as follows:

    a. Assets in the Asset Manager are organized into libraries and categories. Libraries are essentially folders containing assets, while categories help you filter assets based on their type (e.g., materials, objects, or textures).

    b. To create a new library, go to the Asset Browser, click on the folder icon in the top-left corner, and select **Create New Library**.

    c. To switch between categories, use the drop-down menu in the top-left corner of the Asset Browser, as shown in *Figure 4.12*.

Figure 4.12: The Asset Browser in Blender

5. Add, use, and remove assets as follows:

    a. To add assets to the Asset Manager, select the asset you want to add to your scene, such as an object or material. Just *right-click* the asset in the Outliner and choose **ID Data | Mark Asset**.

b. To use an asset from the Asset Manager in your scene, make sure you are in **Object Mode**. Look for the asset in the Asset Browser, then click and drag it to the 3D Viewport or the appropriate editor (e.g., **Shader Editor** for materials).

c. To remove an asset from the Asset Manager, *right-click* the asset in the Asset Browser and select **Clear Asset**.

6. **Asset Preview, Metadata**, and sharing:

a. In the Asset Browser, preview thumbnails of each asset to help you identify them quickly.

b. Add **metadata** (i.e., data about data), such as descriptions or tags that can act as background data for search engines to find your work or assets, for more efficient organization. To do this, select the asset in the Asset Browser, then press *N* or go to **View** | **Asset Details** to open the **Metadata** sidebar and make your changes.

c. To export assets for sharing across projects or with other Blender users, create a new .blend file, import the assets you want to export, and save the file.

By setting up a dedicated Asset Manager .blend file and understanding how to use the Asset Manager, you can greatly improve your workflow. Familiarizing yourself with the relevant shortcuts and menus will further enhance your productivity and efficiency, and will help you be more consistent when working with assets in Blender across all your 3D projects.

> Tip
>
> You can also create your own asset library by setting a directory on your hard drive and linking it in Blender's **Preferences** under the **File Paths** section. This allows you to save any objects or .blend files to that folder and access them easily from the Asset Browser drop-down menu.

Now that we have wrangled the chaos and got our Blender scenes nice and tidy, it is time to level up. In this next bit, we are going to look at how to supercharge Blender with built-in and third-party add-ons, which basically give Blender a few new tricks up its sleeve.

Expanding Blender's functionality with built-in and third-party add-ons

Blender has many built-in add-ons that boost its functionality through customization. Since Blender is open source software, you will come to know that many of these add-ons, as shown in *Figure 4.13*, were created by the Blender community.

Figure 4.13: Built-in add-ons

This bit is important because these add-ons were made by Blender users for Blender users, so they actually make sense. You can turn them on or off whenever you like, depending on what you need. But it does not stop there. Blender also lets you bring in third-party add-ons from outside the official ecosystem, opening the door to all sorts of extra tools and clever shortcuts. In the next section, we are going to walk through how to use Blender's built-in add-ons and how to get those third-party gems up and running.

Reviewing built-in add-ons

Blender comes with numerous built-in add-ons, covering a broad range of functionality such as mesh editing, animation, import/export, and scripting. Some popular built-in add-ons include the following:

- **Archipack**: A toolset for creating architectural elements

- **Animation Nodes:** A node-based visual scripting system to create complex animations
- **Bool Tool:** A tool that streamlines the process of using Boolean operations in Blender
- **F2:** An advanced tool for filling and creating faces in **Edit Mode**
- **Node Wrangler:** A collection of utilities to enhance the node editing workflow in the Shader Editor

Enabling built-in add-ons

To enable a built-in add-on, follow these steps:

1. Open Blender and go to **Edit | Preferences**.
2. In the **Preferences** window, click on the **Add-ons** tab.
3. Use the search bar or browse through the categories to find the add-on you are looking for.
4. Check the box next to the add-on to enable it.
5. Some add-ons might need you to configure them. You will find additional settings if you click on the arrow next to the add-on name, as shown in *Figure 4.14*.

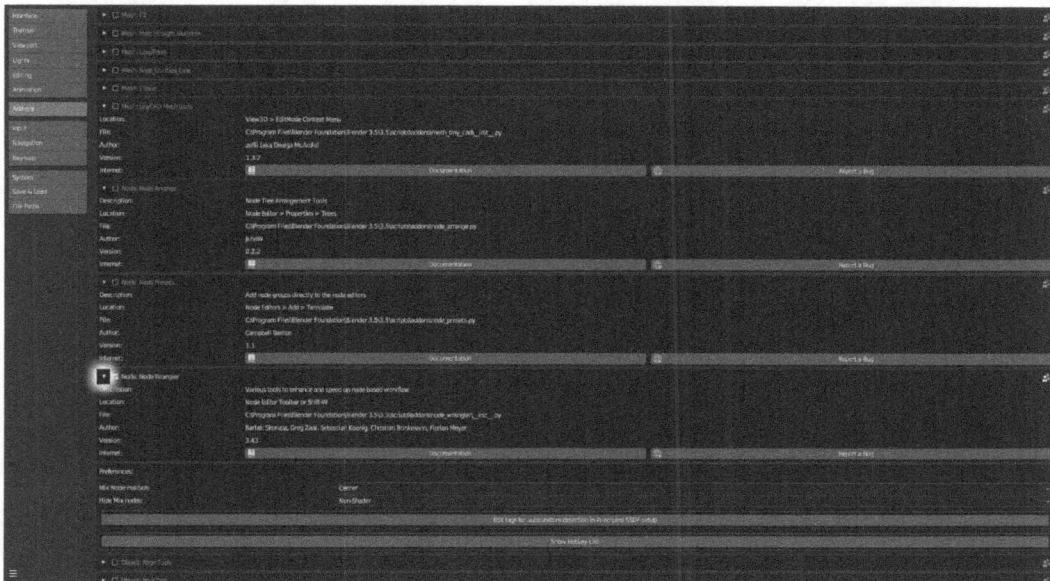

Figure 4.14: Third-party add-on settings

Importing new add-ons from outside Blender

Blender lets you import and use third-party add-ons, which can be downloaded from various sources such as Blender Market (`https://blendermarket.com/`) and Gumroad (`https://gumroad.com/`), or directly from the developers' websites. To import a new add-on, follow these steps:

1. Download the add-on file, such as a `.zip` archive.

2. Open Blender and go to **Edit** | **Preferences**.

3. In the **Preferences** window, click on the **Add-ons** tab.

4. Click on **Install** at the top right of the window.

5. Browse to the location where you downloaded the add-on file and select the `.zip` archive. You do not need to unzip it or extract the files. Then click **Install Add-on**, as shown in *Figure 4.15*.

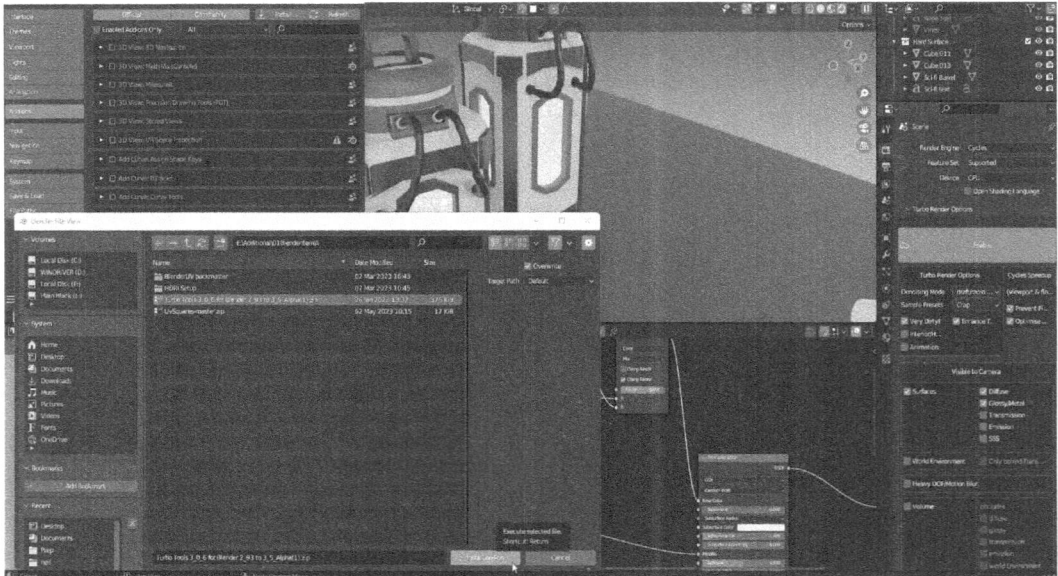

Figure 4.15: Installing an add-on

6. Once installed, the add-on will appear in the list. Check the box next to the add-on to enable it, the same as with all of Blender's built-in add-ons.

7. Some add-ons might need you to configure them. You will find additional settings if you click on the arrow next to the add-on name.

> **Note**
>
> Remember that not all add-ons are compatible with every version of Blender. So, do some research and make sure that the add-on you want to use is compatible with your Blender version before installing it.

Exploring and utilizing Blender's built-in add-ons and other third-party add-ons can enhance your workflow, unlock new capabilities, and help you create more advanced projects in Blender.

We will move on to discussing a different type of customization, this time, for Blender's 3D Viewport features. These features include **View Object Types**, **Show Gizmo**, **Show Overlays**, and **Toggle X-Ray**. Understanding these elements will help you gain better visibility of elements within your models and scenes.

Customizing your 3D Viewport experience with Viewport overlays

In this section, we will explore the exciting realm of **Viewport overlays** and discover how they can transform your 3D Viewport experience. In Blender, overlays refer to the visual elements that can be displayed on top of the 3D Viewport to provide additional information or enhance your understanding of the scene. Overlays are one of those underrated features that can quietly save your sanity. Whether you are modeling, texturing, animating, or just trying to figure out what on earth is going on in your scene, Blender's overlay options help you see exactly what you need, when you need it.

From wireframes and face orientation to origins and outlines, overlays give you better control, faster decisions, and a clearer view of the scene without cluttering your screen. From displaying wireframes and measurements to visualizing face orientation and vertex weights, the possibilities are endless. Let us learn how to tailor your Blender workspace to suit your specific needs together.

View Object Types

View Object Types allows you to control the visibility of different object types within the 3D Viewport. By enabling or disabling specific object types, you can declutter your workspace, focus on specific objects in your scene, and improve your workflow by only displaying the objects that are important for the task ahead.

To access the View Object Types options, locate the **Object Types Visibility** panel in the top-right corner of the 3D Viewport. Click the eye icon to expand the panel, and you will see a list of object types, each with a checkbox next to it (*Figure 4.16*).

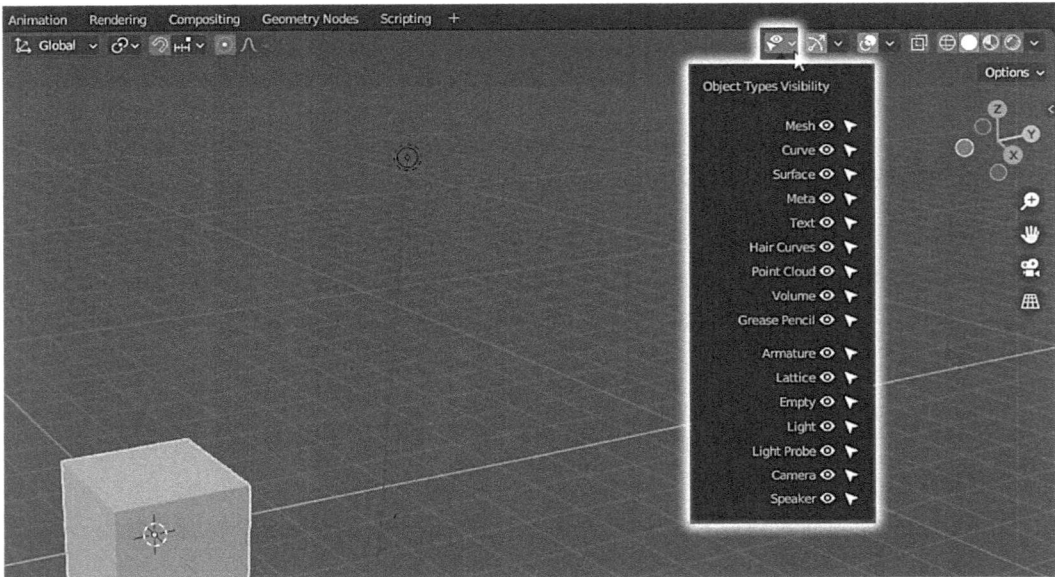

Figure 4.16: Object Types Visibility options

Here are some examples of object-type visibility in Blender:

- **Mesh**: Toggling **Mesh** visibility lets you hide or display all the 3D models in your scene. This is useful when you want to focus on other object types, including cameras or lights, such as for the project in *Figure 4.17*.

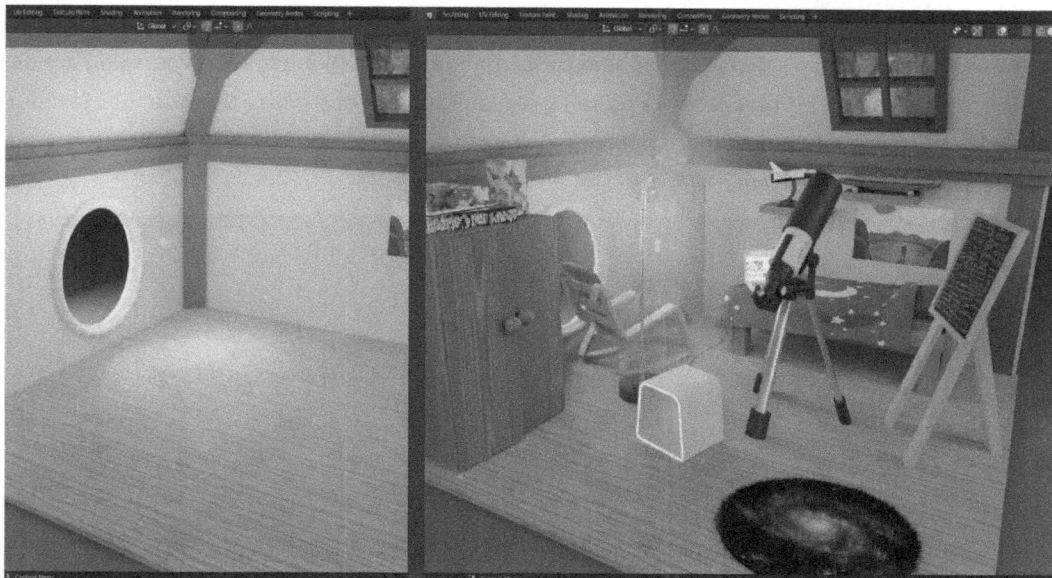

Figure 4.17: Mesh visibility options – on (right)/off (left)

- **Camera**: Toggling the **Camera** object type will hide or display all the cameras in your scene. This can be helpful when you want to focus on modeling without the cameras obstructing what you can see.

- **Light**: Adjusting the visibility of **Light** objects allows you to hide or display all the lights in your scene. This can be useful when you want to focus on modeling without the visual clutter of light sources.

- **Grease Pencil**: You can use this setting to hide or display all the 2D drawings and annotations created using the **Grease Pencil** tool.

Gizmos

In Blender, a **Gizmo** refers to a visual tool that assists users in performing specific transformations or operations on objects within the 3D Viewport. Gizmos can be interacted with directly, allowing you to translate, rotate, scale, or perform other manipulations easily. In a few words, they simplify the process of transforming objects by providing a visual representation of the transformation axes or parameters.

Show Gizmo lets you control the display of Gizmos for different object types within the 3D Viewport in Blender. Gizmos are visual feedback tools that appear in Blender's Viewport and are designed to help you manipulate objects more easily. You can also customize them so that Blender displays only those Gizmos that are relevant to your task. This is another way to declutter your workspace, as shown in *Figure 4.18*.

Figure 4.18: Show Gizmo

To access Show Gizmo options, locate the **Viewport Gizmos** panel in the top-right corner of the 3D Viewport. Click the arrow icon to expand the panel, and you will see a list of Gizmo types, each with a checkbox next to it, as you can see in *Figure 4.19*.

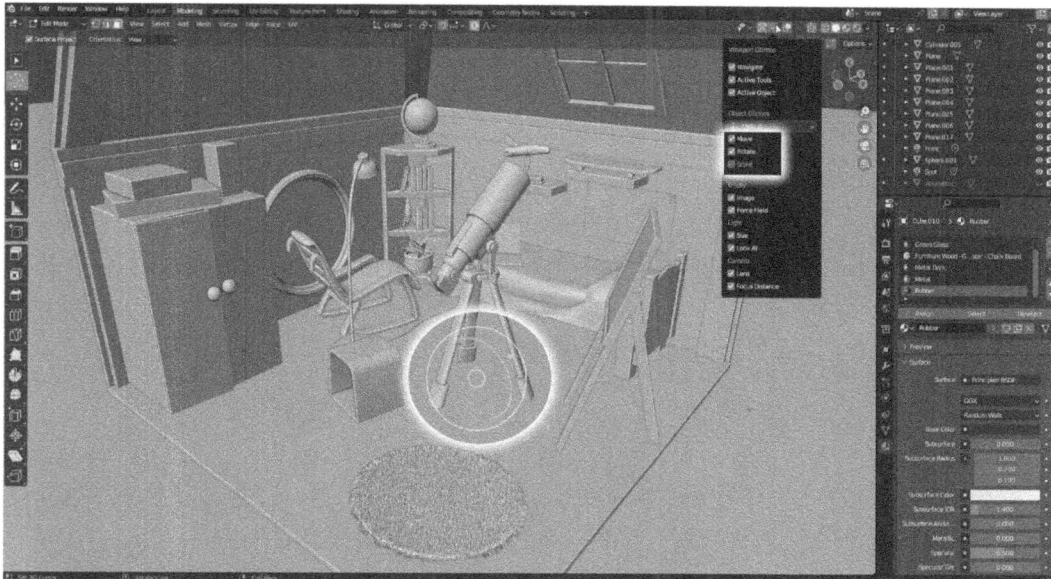

Figure 4.19: Show Gizmo options

Here are some examples of Gizmo types in Blender:

- **Transform Gizmo**: This setting will show or hide the **Move**, **Rotate**, and **Scale** Gizmos for the selected object(s). This can help you focus on other aspects of your scene, such as if you are manipulating an object for a specific task. The Transform Gizmo is helpful when you need to move and rotate an object, since it lets you tick both options.

- **Light Gizmos**: By enabling or disabling the **Light** Gizmos, you can control the visibility of the Gizmos for your lights. We will discuss this in more detail in *Chapter 6* in *Part 2* of this book.

- **Camera Gizmos**: Adjusting the visibility of the **Camera** Gizmos will show or hide the Gizmos for your cameras.

- **Empty Gizmos: Empty** Gizmos are referred to as "Empties" by Blender users, and toggling them on or off will show or hide the Gizmos associated with **empty objects** (i.e., objects without visible geometry, such as in *Figure 4.20*) in your scene.

Figure 4.20: An empty object example in Blender

Empties are often used as placeholders or as parents for other objects, and their Gizmos can help you to manipulate these objects more easily.

Show Overlays

Like Show Gizmo, Show Overlays is designed to control the display of various overlays in Blender's 3D Viewport.

As discussed at the beginning of this section, overlays are visual aids that give you extra information about your scene, such as **grid lines**, **object outlines**, and **selection highlights** (see *Figure 4.21*). Like Show Gizmo tools, overlays are meant to reduce visual clutter in your Viewport, so by displaying only those that you are interested in, you can focus your attention on them alone.

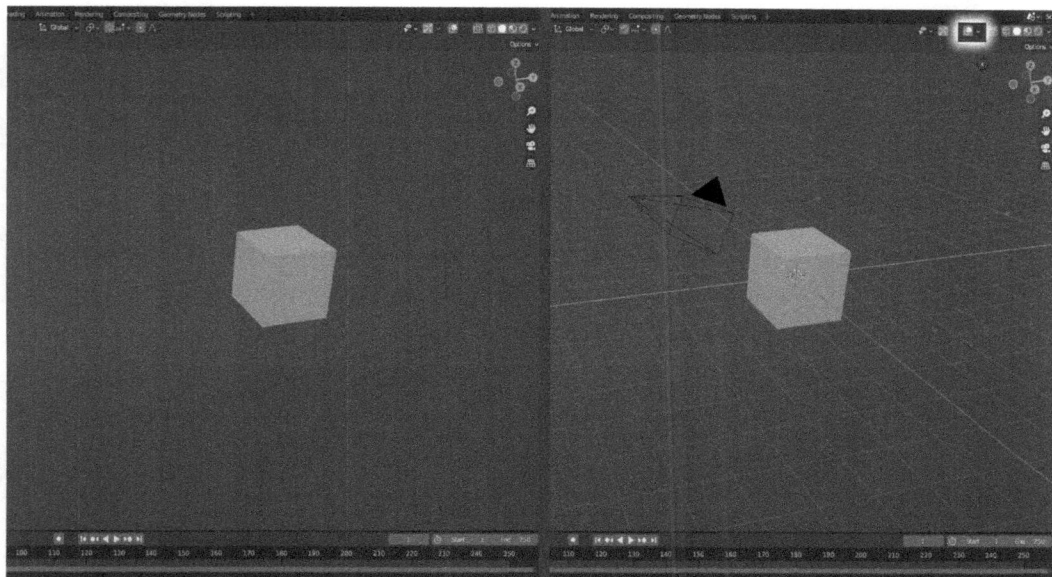

Figure 4.21: Reducing visual clutter using Blender's Show Overlays options

You can find the Show Overlays options in the **Viewport Overlays** panel in the top-right corner of the 3D Viewport. Click the **Special** menu indicated by the down arrow icon, and you will see a list of overlay types, each with a checkbox next to it, as shown in *Figure 4.22*.

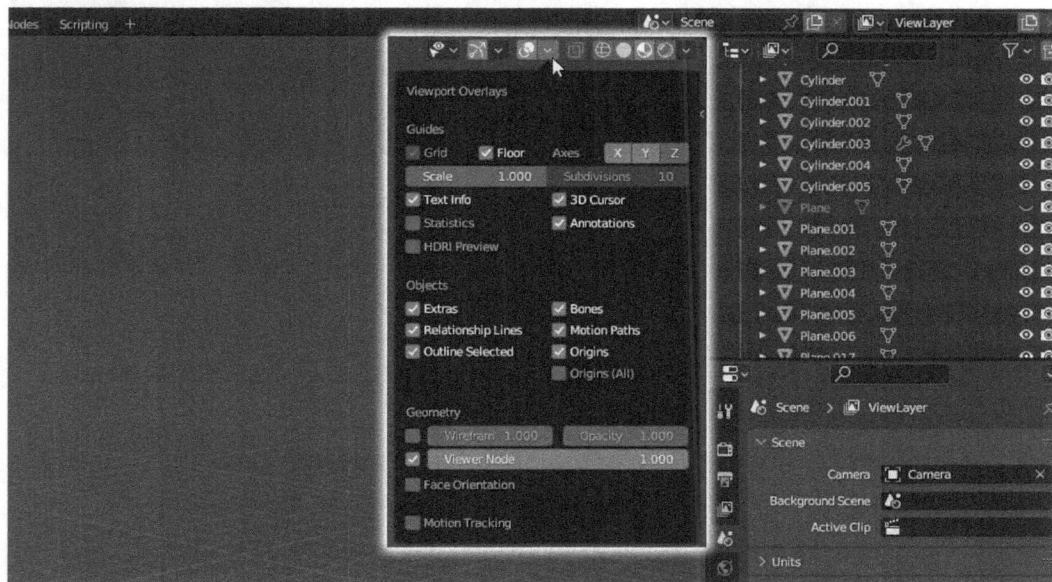

Figure 4.22: Overlay types

Note

Clicking the circle icon disables and re-enables all the overlays.

Here are some examples of overlay types in Blender:

- **Grid overlay**: This will show or hide the grid lines on the 3D Viewport floor, as shown in *Figure 4.23*. By toggling the **Grid** overlay off when the grid is not needed for positioning or aligning objects, you will have a clearer workspace.

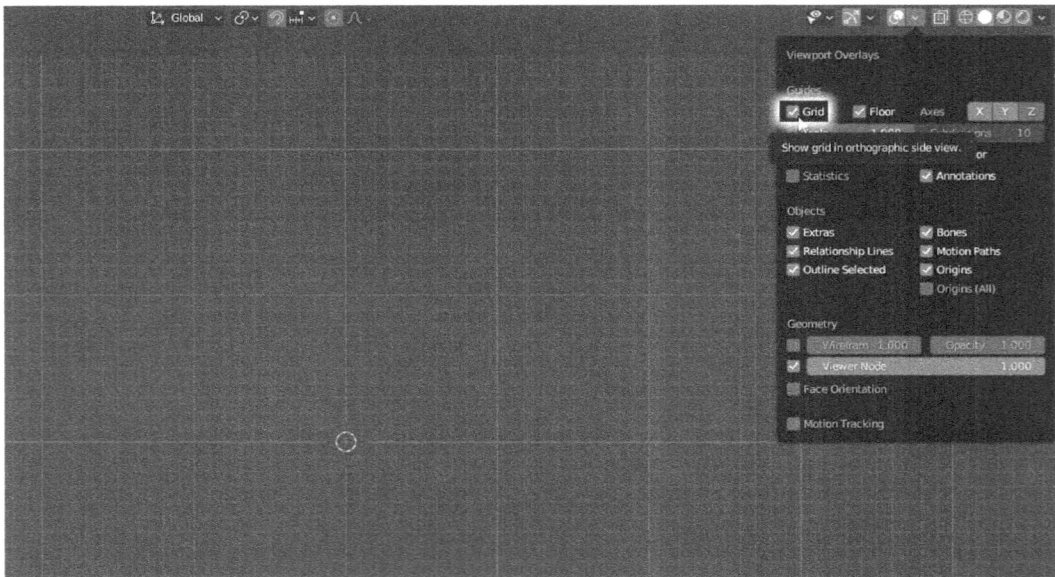

Figure 4.23: Grid lines in Blender's 3D Viewport floor

- **Wireframe overlay**: These settings control the visibility of **wireframe outlines** for objects in your scene. This can be useful when you want to see the underlying geometry of your models without the distraction of solid shading or materials. For example, you could use the **Wireframe** overlay to see the overall density of mesh within an environment and make sure you have consistent detail in your mesh shapes.

- **Face orientation overlay**: Here, you can show or hide the colored indicators that display the **normals** (i.e., the direction of faces in your mesh objects; see *Figure 4.24*).

Figure 4.24: Displaying normals in a mesh using the Face Orientation overlay

This can be helpful when you are working with real-time renderers (e.g., **EEVEE**) that use one-sided shaders instead of two-sided ones, the Blender default. If the mesh has inverted face normals, you would see straight through the mesh with a one-sided shader setup.

When using the **Face Orientation** overlay, blue faces indicate normals that are facing toward the viewer, while red faces indicate inverted normals that are pointing away: a common cause of visual errors in rendering. Note that in newer versions of Blender, the blue overlay has been removed entirely, and only red is shown to highlight problematic, reversed normals.

- **3D Cursor overlay:** You can use these settings to show or hide the **3D Cursor** overlay in the Viewport.

Toggle X-Ray

Toggle X-Ray is like a Blender superpower, letting you see through objects in the 3D Viewport by making them semi-transparent. This can be particularly useful when you are working with assets that also have topology inside them, such as a vase.

To enable or disable X-Ray mode, click on the **X-Ray** button located in the top-right corner of the 3D Viewport or use the *Alt + Z* keyboard shortcut.

Here are some examples of what X-Ray mode can be used for:

- **Selection of occluded elements**: In complex models or scenes, some vertices, edges, or faces might be hidden behind other parts of the model (i.e., occluded elements). X-Ray mode will help you see and select these occluded elements, as shown in *Figure 4.25*.

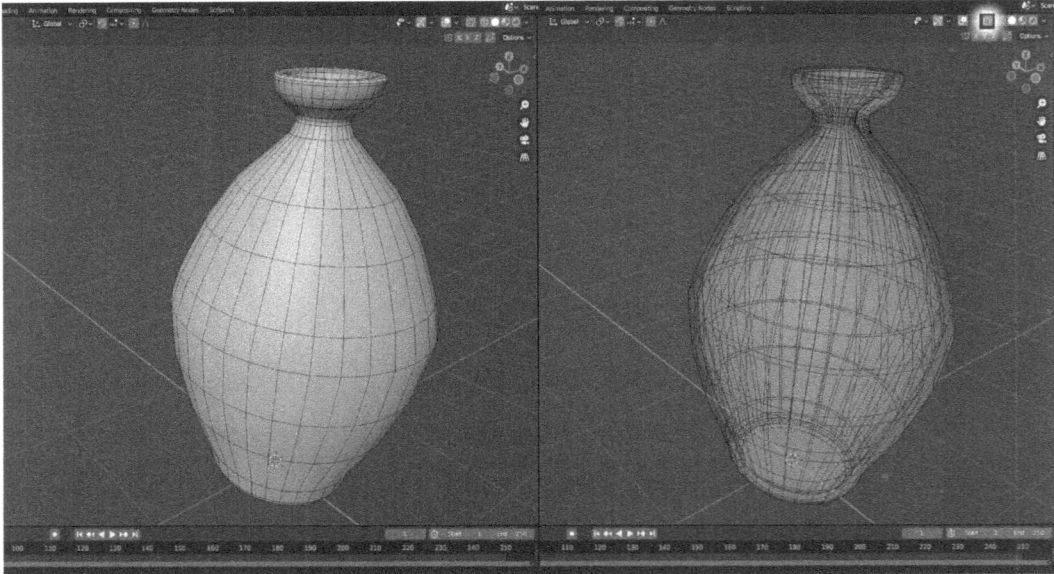

Figure 4.25: Seeing occluded elements using Blender's X-Ray mode

- **Rigging**: A clear view of the armature and bones within a mesh is essential to rigging. By enabling X-Ray mode, you can see the armature structure and manipulate it more easily.

- **Weight painting**: If you are weight painting, X-Ray mode shows you the underlying bone influences on the mesh, making it easier to paint accurate **vertex weights** (i.e., when assigning influence values to different parts of a mesh for animation purposes). We will discuss weight painting in more detail in *Chapter 1* in *Part 2* of this book.

- **Scene layout and object placement**: In a crowded scene, objects might overlap or be obscured by others, making it difficult to arrange or position them accurately. X-Ray mode helps you see through the objects in your scene, allowing for precise object placement, as shown in *Figure 4.26*.

Figure 4.26: Using X-Ray mode in "Blender 3: Stylized Scene The Ultimate Guide" by 3D Tudor

> **Tip**
>
> If you are worried that objects are accidentally placed inside one another in your scene, you can use X-Ray mode to see through objects and double-check.

Viewport overlays in Blender play a crucial role in enhancing the overall user experience and workflow efficiency. These overlays provide valuable visual information, such as wireframes, vertex colors, and face normals, allowing users to better understand the geometry and topology of their 3D models. They also enable precise measurements, grid and ruler displays, and annotation tools, facilitating accurate modeling and scene setup. You will find out more about wireframes, vertex colors, and face normals in *Chapter 10* in *Part 1* of this book.

Overall, Viewport overlays in Blender are indispensable tools for improving productivity and achieving high-quality results in 3D design and animation, which you will come to understand more and more as we move on in the book.

Summary

This chapter has given you the knowledge to create more advanced projects with ease through digital decluttering and focus. I see this chapter as the condensed version of Blender's equivalent to Marie Kondo's *The Life Changing Magic of Tidying Up*, because you know which questions to ask yourself to determine what to keep, what to remove, and how to tidy up Blender.

Through this chapter, you learned how to use the Outliner to clear your head and your 3D workspace (a.k.a., Blender's 3D Viewport). The main objective was to highlight various toggling options, allowing you to reveal or conceal segments of your scene or individual meshes.

When it comes to decluttering your Blender workspace, this chapter should be your go-to reference for the rest of your 3D modeling journey. You have picked up the essentials, from Blender's built-in features to handy third-party add-ons, and we have kept things focused and practical, especially when it came to using overlays without turning your screen into a spaghetti mess.

We also looked at Blender's Asset Manager and collections, which are key if you want to build an efficient asset library. Once you know how to organize your assets properly, it becomes much easier to drop them straight into new or ongoing projects without the usual faffing about. Even if you are not naturally the tidy type, this chapter gives you the tools to stay organized and save time, so you can spend more energy on the fun, creative stuff.

The chapter came to an end with a discussion of Blender's X-Ray mode, a tool for optimizing your 3D Viewport. I am sure this is one of the first Blender tools you will try, since it gives you a kind of superpower to look through objects and double-check whether everything is as it should be.

In the next chapter, we will be exploring the intricacies of working in Blender's 3D Viewport, giving you the foundation to start working with **Viewport shaders**, **rendering engines**, and essential tools for object manipulation.

Further reading

- If you would like more information about restriction toggles in Blender, check out *Blender to Unreal Engine 5 3D Props Medieval Market Stall* (https://www.udemy.com/course/blender-to-unreal-engine-5-3d-props/?referralCode=92DD6C744ECF6621836C)

- If you are interested in collections, you might like *Blender to Unreal Engine Become a Dungeon Prop Artist* (https://www.udemy.com/course/blender-to-unreal-engine-become-a-dungeon-prop-artist/?referralCode=979CA6D3C71A4B2BB8CD)

- If you want to try out linking collections, you can use *Egypt Themed Stylized 3D Modular Pack* (`https://3dtudor.gumroad.com/l/Egypt_Prop_Pack_Blender_Unreal_Engine_5`) as an asset set to try this out with

- Should you be looking for the perfect environment to try out Blender's X-Ray mode in, see *Blender 3: Stylized Scene The Ultimate Guide* (`https://www.udemy.com/course/blender-3-stylized-scene-the-ultimate-guide/`)

Subscribe to Game Dev Assembly!

We are excited to introduce **Game Dev Assembly**, our brand-new newsletter dedicated to everything game development. Whether you're coding, designing, animating, or managing a studio, we've got insights, trends, and expert advice to help you create, innovate, and thrive. Sign up now and get exciting benefits.

`https://packt.link/gamedev-newsletter`

Join the 3D Tudor Channel Discord Server!

Join the 3D Tudor Channel Discord Server, a creative hub for learning Blender, Unreal Engine, Substance Painter, and 3D modeling, for discussions with the authors and other readers:

`https://discord.gg/5EkjT36vUj`

5

Going Over Proportional Editing, Transform Orientation, and Viewport Shaders

In this chapter, you will explore the additional intricacies of working with Blender's **3D Viewport**. We are going to dig into some really useful stuff: getting your head around viewport shaders, understanding how rendering engines tick, and getting comfy with the core tools for moving, scaling, and rotating your objects without making a mess of things.

The first part of the chapter will discuss various shading modes available within the **3D Viewport**, such as wireframe, solid, material preview, and rendered modes. After that, we will compare and contrast the key features of Blender's rendering engines, Cycles and EEVEE, providing a solid foundation to understand their capabilities and differences. This knowledge will be developed later, in *Chapter 5* in *Part 2* of this book.

Moving beyond rendering engines, this chapter will offer you an in-depth look at Blender's **Transform Orientation** options. These options will help you gain control of the positioning and orientation of objects and components in a 3D scene. By examining options such as **Global**, **Local**, **Normal**, **Gimbal**, **View**, and **Cursor**, you will learn how to use coordinate systems to manipulate objects. Additionally, the chapter covers crucial concepts such as **Transform Pivot Points**, **Snapping**, and **Proportional Editing**.

As we wrap up this chapter, you will come away with a solid grip on these powerful tools: the kind that let you move, snap, and line things up in 3D space with the level of precision you want. Whether you are nudging a vertex into place or snapping a whole castle wall to the grid, you will be doing it with confidence and control, not just guesswork and crossed fingers.

So, in this chapter, we will cover the following topics:

- Exploring Blender viewport shaders and rendering engines
- Comparing Blender's render modes
- Understanding Transform Orientation options
- Exploring the relevance of Transform Orientation options to transform pivot points
- Guaranteeing consistency with snapping for precise 3D modeling
- Achieving smooth and organic transformations with Proportional Editing

Technical requirements

As for **Blender 4.5 LTS (Long-Term Support)**, the general requirements include a macOS 11.2 or newer (Apple Silicon supported natively) operating system, or a Linux (64-bit, glibc 2.28 or newer) operating system. Blender now requires a CPU with the SSE4.2 instruction set, at least 8 GB of RAM (32 GB recommended for heavy scenes), and a GPU supporting OpenGL 4.3 with a minimum of 2 GB of VRAM.

For a full list of technical requirements, please refer back to *Chapter 1* in this part.

Exploring Blender viewport shaders and rendering engines

Viewport shaders are responsible for displaying the materials and textures of objects within the **3D Viewport**, helping you visualize and interact with their scenes in real time, providing feedback on lighting, shading, and texturing. These are the specialized shading modes available in Blender's **3D Viewport**:

- **Wireframe mode**: This mode shows the underlying geometry of objects as a series of lines that represent their edges (*Figure 5.1*).

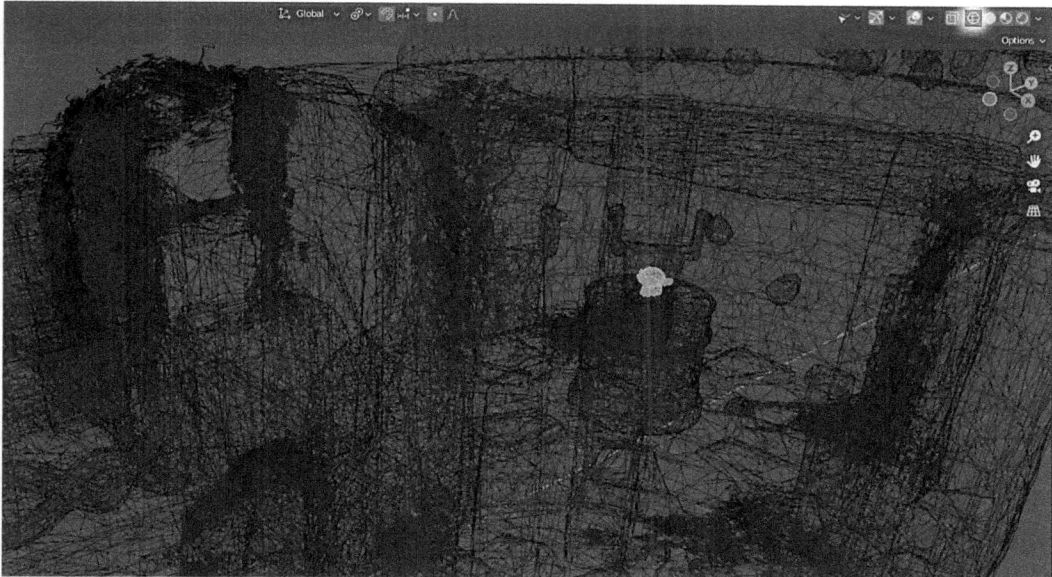

Figure 5.1: Wireframe mode of the capstone project in "The Ultimate Guide to Blender 3D Rigging and Animation" by 3D Tudor

This comes in handy when you are checking out the topology of a mesh: spotting any weird bits, problem areas, or just trying to make precise selections without going cross-eyed in a busy scene. It is like switching on X-ray vision for your geometry.

For example, when you are modeling clothing for a character, **Wireframe** mode allows you to examine the mesh's edge flow and ensure that it will deform correctly when it is animated with a cloth simulation. This is helpful because it avoids problems such as the character's body clipping through their clothing during mesh deformations when the body is moving to take on a pose.

- **Solid mode:** In this mode, all objects in your **3D Viewport** are shown using plain solid colors based on their materials or object colors (*Figure 5.2*).

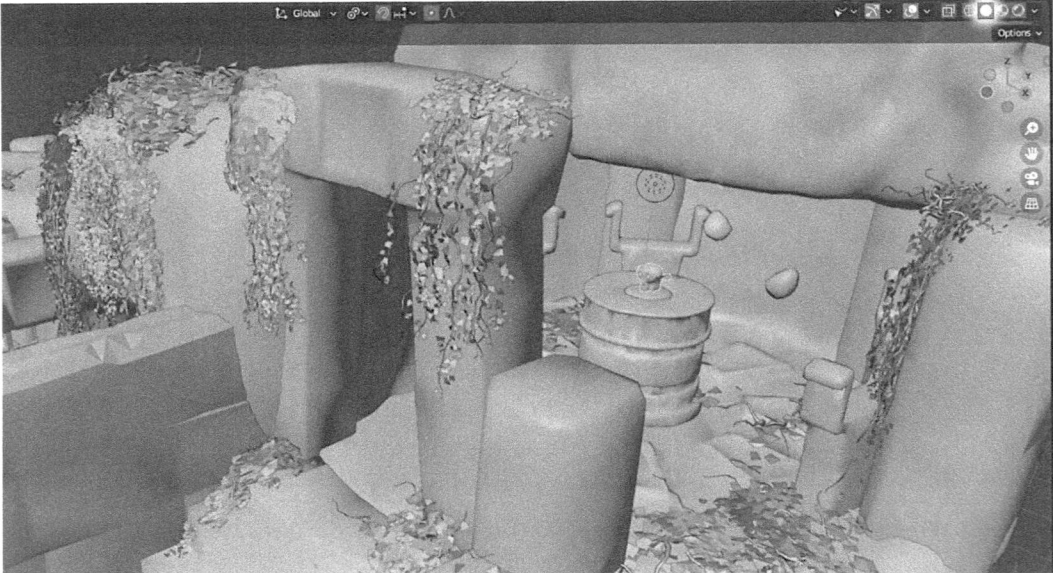

Figure 5.2: Solid mode of the capstone project in "The Ultimate Guide to Blender 3D Rigging and Animation" by 3D Tudor

As you will see in the next part of this book, this mode is your go-to mode during the early stages of modeling and positioning objects in a scene, as it is resource-efficient and provides swift performance. For example, when creating a partially transparent mesh such as foliage, **Solid** mode allows you to focus on the basic shapes and positions of objects without being distracted by textures or lighting details.

- **Material Preview mode:** Also referred to as **LookDev mode,** this mode acts as a quick, rough visualization tool, allowing you to preview materials, textures, and fundamental lighting in Blender's **3D Viewport,** as shown in *Figure 5.3*.

Figure 5.3: Material Preview mode of the capstone project in "The Ultimate Guide to Blender 3D Rigging and Animation" by 3D Tudor

Although it is not as accurate as a render, this mode can be helpful when you want to decide between one texture and another. Let's say you are designing a scene with various fabrics. The **Material Preview** mode helps you to assess how different fabric textures and colors interact with each other, making it easier to fine-tune the materials before committing to a full render.

- • **Rendered mode:** This mode displays the scene as it would appear in the final render using the chosen rendering engine (i.e., Cycles or EEVEE), as shown in *Figure 5.4*.

Figure 5.4: Rendered mode of the capstone project in "The Ultimate Guide to Blender 3D Rigging and Animation" by 3D Tudor

Like the **Material Preview** mode, the quality of a **Rendered** mode preview is not high. However, it provides a more accurate representation of materials, textures, and lighting, but it may be slower, depending on the complexity of the scene and the hardware capabilities.

The viewport shaders we discussed provide various levels of previews of the final product, but they are ultimately approximations. Now that you have a strong understanding of viewport shaders in Blender, it is time to delve deeper into the realm of Blender's rendering engines, Cycles and EEVEE. This is because Cycles and EEVEE are designed to create accurate, high-quality renders for final use, helping you get a better preview of the final product compared to what viewport shaders can do. Whether you are making a still image or an animation, Blender's rendering engines will be responsible for creating the ultimate representation of your 3D scene.

Comparing Blender's render modes

Blender provides 3D artists with multiple rendering engines, each tailored for specific needs. This includes the Cycles engine, which excels in simulating realistic light behavior to create high-quality images and animations, and EEVEE, Blender's real-time rendering engine, designed to provide fast and interactive feedback.

Now, if you have been around Blender long enough to remember when Cycles made your GPU sound like it was trying to take off into orbit, you will be glad to know we are not in Kansas anymore. Enter the new and current Cycles, the shiny, turbocharged rewrite of the old Cycles engine that landed with Blender 3.0. It is faster, smarter, and basically everything we wished rendering was back when we were chugging through frames one pixel at a time.

Each engine comes with its features and advantages, which we will explore in detail. This section will provide a brief overview of rendering in Blender, ready for *Chapter 5* in *Part 2* of this book, where we will discuss the entire process of rendering.

The Cycles render engine

Cycles is Blender's physically based rendering engine, and if you are aiming for realism, this is where the magic happens. It simulates how light actually bounces around a scene, giving you results that look much closer to reality than real-time engines such as EEVEE. Whether you are rendering still images or animations, Cycles is the go-to if you want soft shadows, global illumination, and all those subtle lighting effects that make a scene feel alive (see *Figure 5.5*).

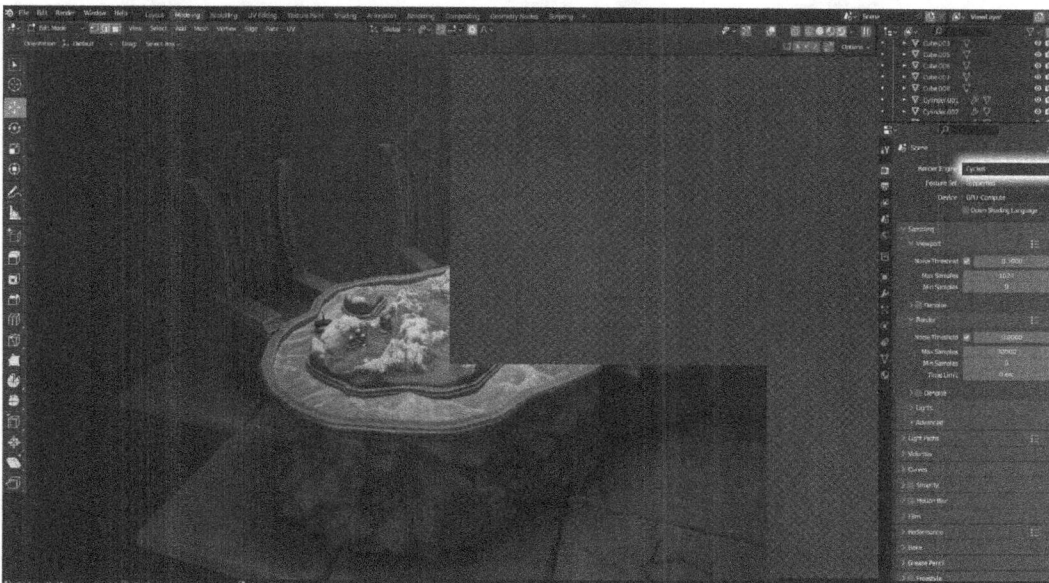

Figure 5.5: Rendering in Cycles Example from "Blender 3 Stylized Map Room 3D Environment Tutorial" by 3D Tudor

Cycles is good for rendering still images and animations. At the same time, since it uses a node-based material system, it is also good for baking textures (*Figure 5.6*).

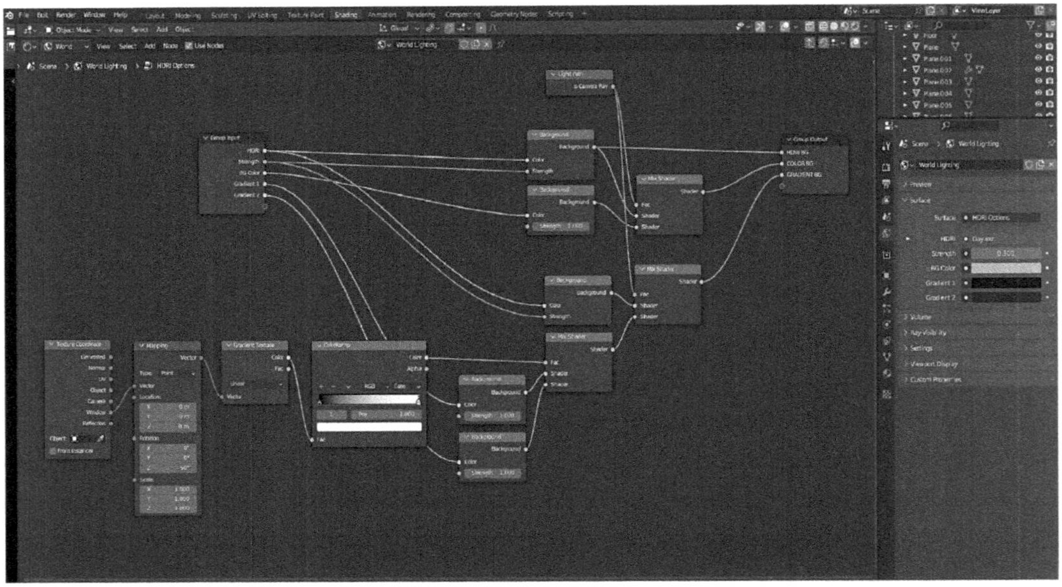

Figure 5.6: Node-based material system in Cycles

Now, I know what you are thinking: this looks like Blender's taken a course in spaghetti architecture. But do not worry! We will unravel the noodle mess in later chapters. For now, just know that this is where things start to get powerful.

Note

Back in April 2021, the Blender devs announced a major rewrite of the Cycles engine to celebrate its tenth anniversary. They called it **Cycles X** during development. By December 2021, it was fully integrated into Blender 3.0, and from that point on, it has just been called Cycles again. So, throughout this book, any reference to Cycles assumes you are using this improved, post-3.0 version. We will discuss all the uses of Blender's rendering engines in more detail in *Chapter 8* in *Part 2* of this book.

Let us say you are building a photorealistic interior or trying to show off how light bounces off a shiny sword, Cycles is built for that. Raytracing in Cycles calculates realistic light paths, handles reflections between surfaces, and even simulates how light passes through glass or fog.

So, if your project relies on accurate shadows, volumetrics, or lighting nuance, Cycles is your friend. Here is the kicker: all those lighting effects used to come with a cost, slow render times, loads of noise, and the need for beefy hardware. But since the Cycles rewrite (aka Cycles X under the hood), performance has been massively boosted.

Improvements since Blender 3.0

Here are some of the major updates and reasons why Cycles now runs better than ever:

- **Faster GPU rendering**: For complex, high-poly scenes, GPU rendering is 2–8x faster than it used to be.

- **Adaptive sampling and noise reduction**: The new sampling system adjusts automatically and speeds up previewing without needing to jump back to EEVEE.

- **Viewport responsiveness**: You can now move around your scene while rendering and still get usable feedback.

- **Denoising improvements**: Details are preserved better with the new denoising system, meaning less cleanup in post.

- **Shadow catcher rewrite**: Now supports colored indirect light and emission. This is great for things such as compositing 3D assets into real environments.

- **Scrambling distance and ray optimization**: More control over render quality versus speed, but without the confusing mess of older setups.

- **OptiX support and reduced kernel compilation**: Faster startup and better ray-traced baking (especially if you are on a supported NVIDIA GPU).

- **No more OpenCL**: Due to driver issues, OpenCL support was dropped, but AMD GPU rendering is slowly being reintroduced through updated APIs.

Let's take a look at Cycles rendering key features. *Table 5.1* shows its advantages and disadvantages:

Pros	Cons
Rendering in Cycles is 2 to 8 times faster in real-world scenes out of the box on the GPU than in the original Cycles.	As a major rewrite of Cycles, you might need time to adapt to the new system and its features.

Pros	Cons
Cycles has improved adaptive sampling. This is accompanied by a redesign of the sampling user interface and default settings. This is helpful in situations such as when you are doing quick render previews at the same time as moving your camera around. This means that there is no need to go to EEVEE. Although Cycles will be considerably noisier, you would still be able to achieve a nice composition while overseeing the raytraced lighting conditions of a scene.	Hardware vendors are working to bring back GPU rendering support with their APIs. This is in development and can be a problem because users of older graphics cards might need to update their hardware to run Cycles1 because it is very graphics card intensive.
Renders on both, with GPU acceleration via CUDA, OptiX, and new AMD API support.	You will need a decent graphics card to fully benefit: older GPUs may struggle.
Includes a powerful node system for building complex, realistic materials from scratch.	Renders take longer due to accurate light simulation, especially in complex scenes. This means Cycles is still slower than EEVEE.
Global Illumination: Cycles uses path tracing to simulate realistic light bouncing, providing accurate indirect illumination and soft shadows.	The new **Scrambling Distance** setting can cause banding artifacts if used at extreme values. However, an automatic scrambling distance feature helps mitigate this.
Denoising has been greatly improved, with detail preservation too.	Without enough samples, renders can get noisy, but this is less of a problem thanks to improved denoising.
The shadow catcher system was fully rewritten, and it can now fully handle colored indirect light and emission. For example, if you are working on an indoor scene that heavily relies on a skybox environment for lighting, using Cycles will help you improve its lighting conditions without the long wait that usually comes with raytraced indirect lighting setups.	Due to driver issues, OpenCL was dropped (but AMD support is coming back through different APIs).
Better performance when moving around your scene during rendering.	

Pros	Cons
Drastically reduced load times before rendering starts because of better **kernel compilation** (OptiX).	

Table 5.1: Pros and cons of using the Cycles rendering engine in Blender

As mentioned in *Table 5.1*, we can see a raytraced rendering result in *Figure 5.7* based on a specified sample count. Increasing the amount would fill the gaps more in between each traced pixel within the render, increasing the quality, but at the cost of increasing the render time. We can fix that artificially using the **denoiser** algorithm. The denoiser algorithm fills in the noise that is left with a low raytraced sample count by using raytraced pixels and by filling the gaps in between using machine learning.

Figure 5.7: Scrambling distance in Cycles side-by-side comparison

Imagine you are working on an indoor environment lit by a skybox. With Cycles, you will get beautifully soft shadows, subtle reflections, and accurate bounce lighting, and now you will get it without waiting for what feels like a full ice age.

So, that is Cycles, the heavyweight champ of realism in Blender. If you are after cinematic lighting, glass that actually *looks* like glass, or the kind of shadows that make people go "Ooh, nice render," Cycles is your tool. But of course, that level of realism comes at a cost: render time and hardware demand.

If you are after something faster, more responsive, and a bit more forgiving on your system, then it is time to meet Cycles' speed-obsessed little sibling...

The EEVEE render engine

EEVEE is Blender's real-time rendering engine. It is designed to provide fast and interactive feedback during the creation process, to generate visually appealing results in a short time (*Figure 5.8*).

Figure 5.8: Rendering in Eevee Example from "Blender 3 Stylized Map Room 3D Environment Tutorial" by 3D Tudor

EEVEE is particularly useful for game development, real-time animation, and rapid visualization. It is helpful for quick light intensity and direction adjustments. Doing a fast render in EEVEE gives a general understanding of your 3D scene setup, even if you plan to switch to Cycles afterwards.

The key features of EEVEE differ from Cycles, and you must consider which one to use on a case-by-case basis. *Table 5.2* shows EEVEE's advantages and disadvantages:

Pros	Cons
Real-time rendering: EEVEE provides real-time feedback in Blender's **3D Viewport**, making it easier for 3D artists to make decisions about materials, lighting, and animations.	Less physically accurate: EEVEE sacrifices some physical accuracy for speed, and therefore its renders are not as realistic as those produced by Cycles.
Physically-based materials: EEVEE supports the same node-based material system as Cycles, as shown in *Figure 5.6*.	Limitations on materials: EEVEE supports the same node-based material system as Cycles but with some limitations due to its real-time nature. For more details, see *Chapter 5* in *Part 2* of this book
Screen space reflections and refractions: EEVEE uses screen space techniques to simulate reflections and refractions, providing realistic-looking surfaces with relatively low computational costs.	Screen space effects: Some of EEVEE's effects, such as reflections and refractions, are screen-space and might not work correctly in all situations. For example, if you were working on an interior design project of a room that contains mirrors, the reflections coming from those mirrors would be considerably lower in quality in comparison to Cycles.
Volumetrics and subsurface scattering: EEVEE supports volumetric rendering and subsurface scattering for realistic lighting and shading effects. For more details, see *Chapter 5* in *Part 2* of this book	

Table 5.2: Pros and cons of using the EEVEE rendering engine in Blender

As you can see, EEVEE is all about speed and interactivity, while Cycles is built for realism. The best one to use depends entirely on your scene, your goals, and whether you are after quick feedback or photoreal final results.

Blender has got a few different rendering engines up its sleeve, each one built for a different kind of task. Whether you are after real-time speed or cinema-level realism, there is a tool for the job, you just need to pick the right one. Cycles is praised for its realistic light behavior simulation and high-quality output, but it can be slow and requires a high-performance GPU. EEVEE, Blender's real-time rendering engine, allows for quick, interactive feedback, although its real-time nature may limit some material effects. Cycles significantly improves rendering speed and responsiveness, but might require some adaptation time due to its rewrite of the original Cycles engine. Each engine has its pros and cons, suitable for different scenarios and needs, which you will come to know more about in *Chapter 5* in *Part 2* of this book.

In the next section, we will continue learning about Blender's versatility by discussing **Transform Orientation**.

Understanding Transform Orientation options in Blender

Transform Orientation is the way in which objects or components such as vertices, edges, and faces are manipulated in the 3D space using a specific coordinate system. Different **Transform Orientation** options allow you to move objects in specific directions and restrict movement in other directions, meaning that you need to decide which coordinate system best suits your needs. Learning about **Transform Orientation** before you begin 3D modeling is important because it helps in achieving precise control over the positioning and orientation of objects and components in a scene.

To access and change the **Transform Orientation** options, locate the **Transform Orientations** drop-down menu in Blender's **3D Viewport** header, next to the **Transform Pivot Point** drop-down menu (*Figure 5.9*).

Figure 5.9: Accessing the Transform Orientation options

Here is an in-depth view of the different **Transform Orientation** options available in Blender:

- **Global**: **Global** orientation is the default **Transform Orientation** mode, which uses the world coordinate system as a reference for transformations. When using **Global** orientation, the **Transformation** gizmo aligns with the world axes (i.e., X, Y, Z), as discussed in *Chapter 4* in this part of the book and illustrated in *Figure 5.10*.

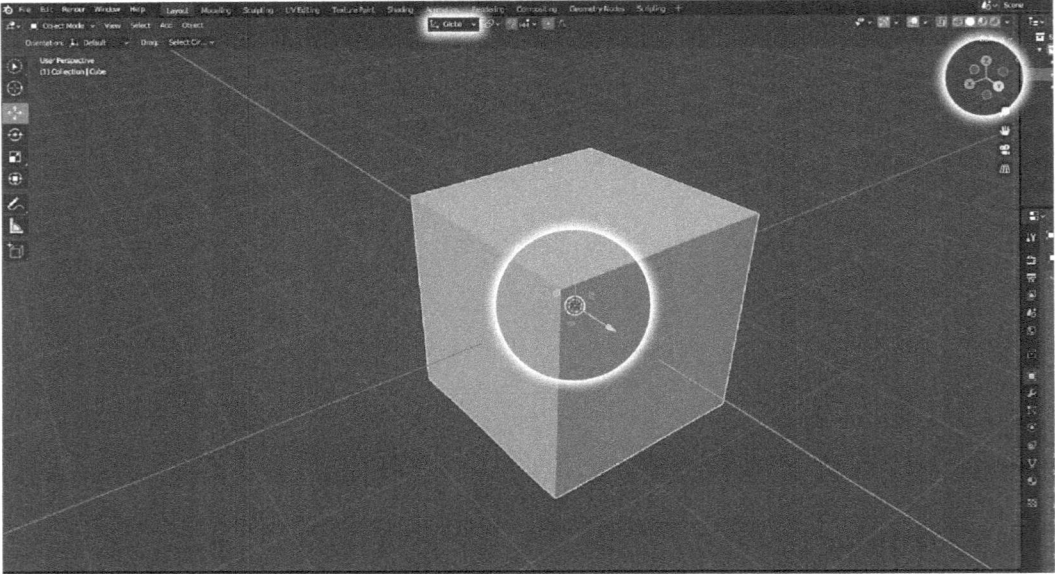

Figure 5.10: Transformation gizmo

- **Local**: **Local** orientation uses the object's coordinate system as a reference for transformations (*Figure 5.11*).

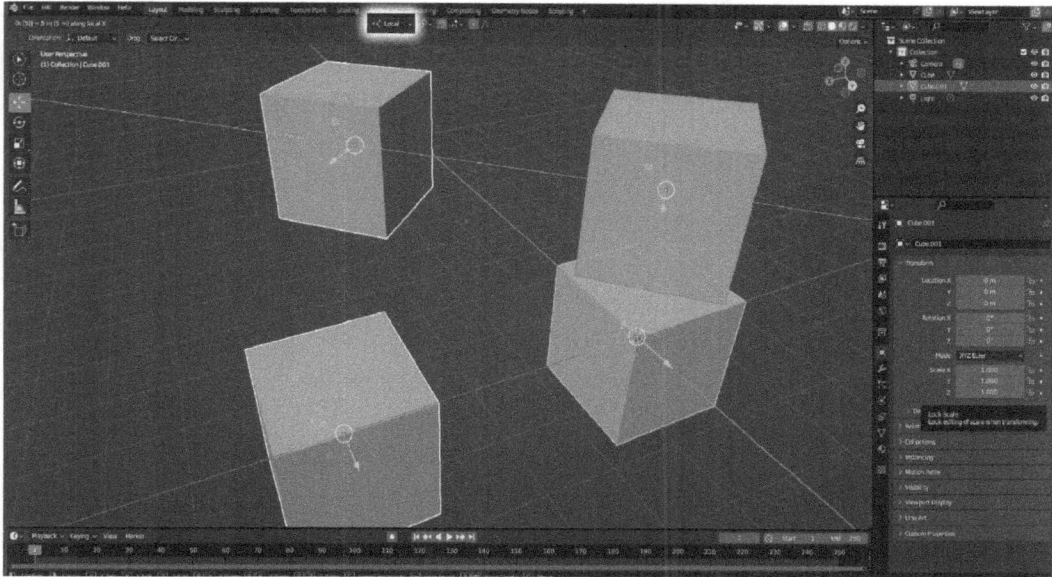

Figure 5.11: Local orientation | Transform Orientation options

You would be using **Local** orientation if you are working with multiple objects that have different rotations, and you want to manipulate them according to their specific orientations. For example, imagine a dungeon room with a diagonal wall and a bunch of light sources. With **Local** orientation, you are making sure that your wall-mounted torches can be easily offset along the mounted wall without clipping into the wall itself or making the torches float.

- **Normal**: The **Normal** orientation uses the **Normal Vector** of the selected component(s) (i.e., vertices, edges, faces) as a reference for transformations (*Figure 5.12*).

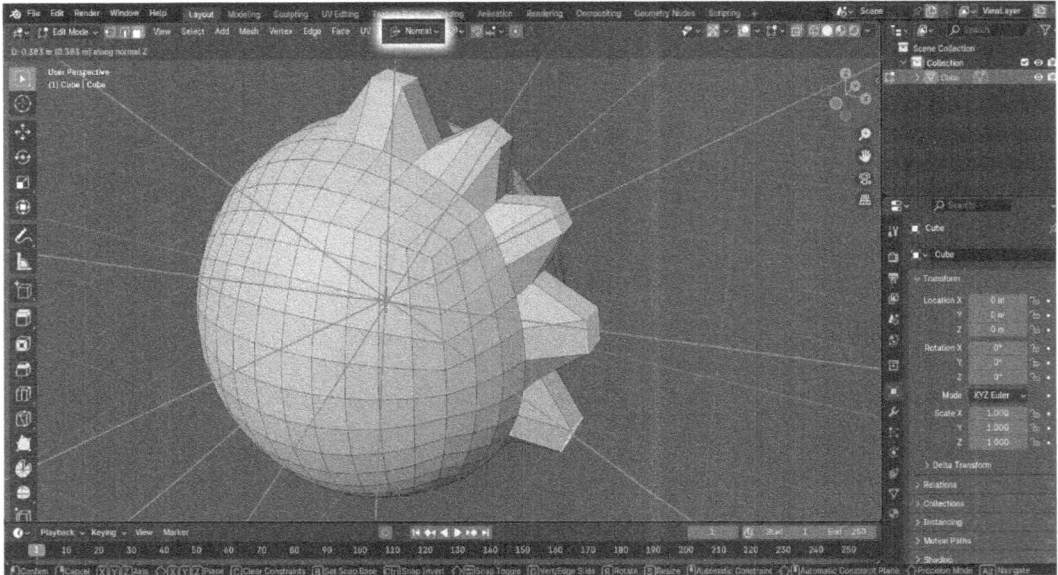

Figure 5.12: Normal Orientation

This mode is especially helpful for modeling or editing a mesh because you can control components based on their surface direction. For example, if you are working on a curved sign and you want to push out the base to make it pop out, you can move the faces along, as shown in *Figure 5.13*:

Figure 5.13: Using Normal orientation with curved signs in "Blender 3 | Unreal Engine 5 | Vintage Music Hall Building | Game Design" by 3D Tudor

When using **Normal** orientation, the **Transformation** gizmo aligns with the average normal of the selected component(s):

- **Gimbal**: The **Gimbal** orientation uses the object's current rotation order as a reference for transformations. This mode is often used in rigging and animation scenarios to avoid gimbal lock issues. When using **Gimbal** orientation, the **Transformation** gizmo aligns with the object's **Gimbal** axes, as shown in *Figure 5.14*.

Figure 5.14: Gimbal orientation | Transform Orientation options in "How I Created Indiana Jones Raider of The Lost Ark Fan Art in Blender 3(Fully Animated)" by 3D Tudor

Tip

In Blender, the **Gimbal** setting allows you to arrange the transformation axes to better understand the object's **Rotation Mode**. This is especially beneficial when using **Euler modes**, where the object undergoes rotation one axis at a time.

Switch the gizmo from **Global** or **Local** to **Gimbal** when you are animating rotations:

- It shows the real *X*, *Y*, and *Z* axes Blender uses for the object's **Euler** rotation.
- If two axes suddenly line up and you cannot rotate the way you expect, that is a gimbal lock (i.e., it just means two axes overlapped, so one direction of rotation got *lost*).

- Turn **Gimbal** on to spot this early and tweak your keyframes before it becomes a headache.

> Tip
>
> To temporarily modify the orientation during a transformation, you can utilize hot-keys along with axis locking. For example, initiating the movement of an object with *G*, followed by *X* to secure the *X* axis of the orientation, and pressing *X* once more will switch to an alternate orientation. If the original orientation was **Global** orientation, it will change to **Local** orientation (and vice versa).

- **View**: The **View** orientation uses the current viewport's camera view as a reference for transformations. This mode is useful when you want to manipulate objects or components based on the current perspective in the **3D Viewport**. When using the **View** orientation, the **Transformation** gizmo aligns with the viewport's camera axes (*Figure 5.15*).

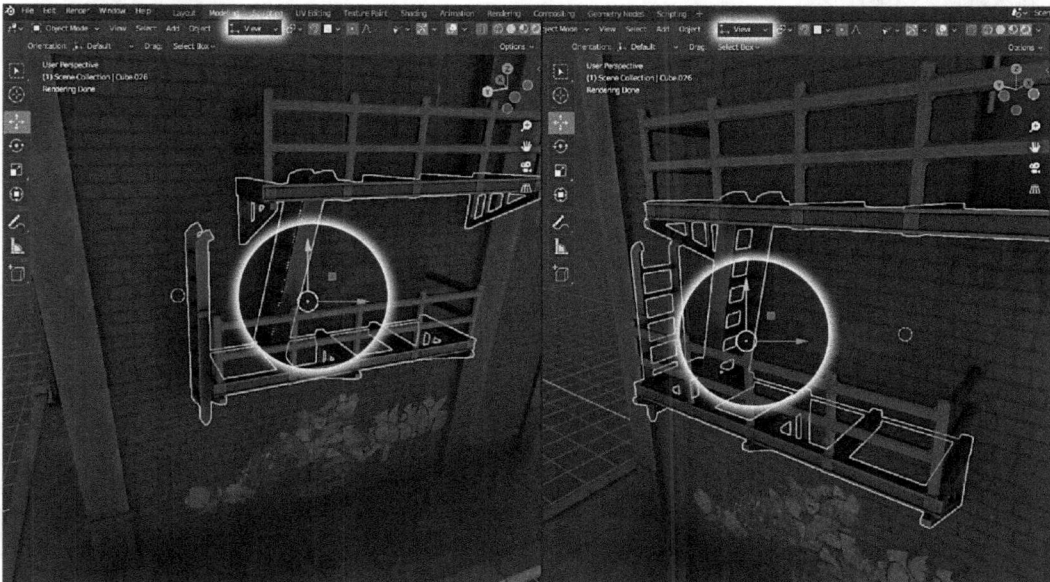

Figure 5.15: Using View orientation in "Blender 3 | Unreal Engine 5 | Vintage Music Hall Building | Game Design" by 3D Tudor

- **Cursor**: The **Cursor** orientation uses the *3D cursor's* orientation as a reference for trans-formations. When using **Cursor** orientation, the **Transformation** gizmo aligns with the 3D cursor's axes (*Figure 5.16*).

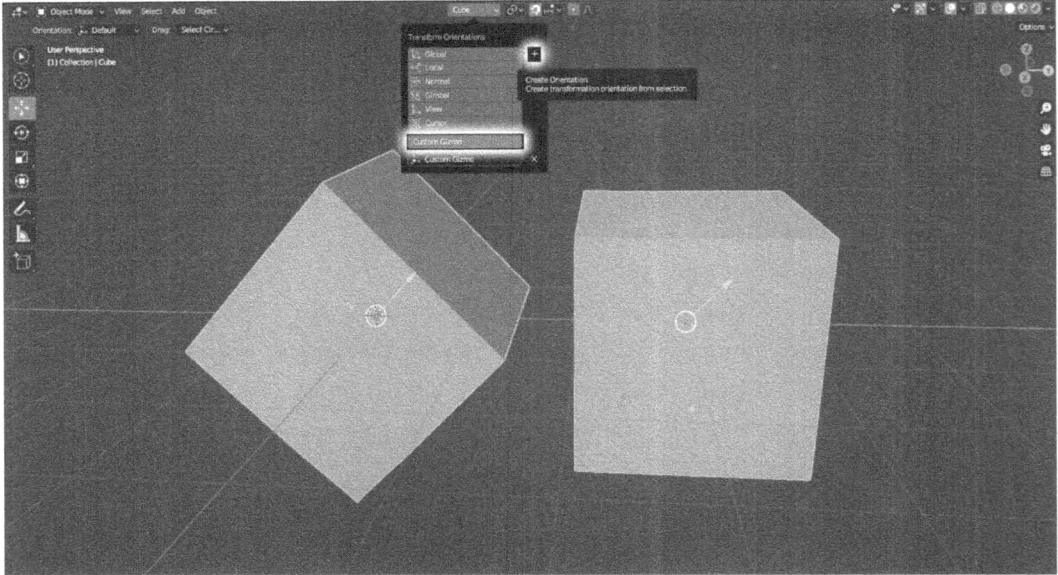

Figure 5.16: Using Cursor orientation

Tip

Blender also allows you to create custom transform orientations. You can create a new transform orientation by aligning it with the selected component(s) or by defining a custom orientation using the **3D Cursor**.

To wrap up in a few words, transform orientation refers to the manipulation of objects or components in 3D space using a specific coordinate system. The options include **Global**, **Local**, **Normal**, **Gimbal**, **View**, and **Cursor**, each offering distinct reference points for transformations.

Next, let's learn how to access these options and the importance of transform orientations to transform pivot points.

Exploring the relevance of transform orientations options to transform pivot points

Transform pivot points and transform orientations in Blender are two intertwined concepts that greatly influence how you manipulate objects in a 3D scene.

As discussed, transform orientations determine the coordinate system that is used for transforming (i.e., moving, rotating, or scaling) objects or components in 3D space. On the other hand, **transform pivot points** determine the point about which transformations are performed.

For example, when you rotate an object, the **pivot point** is the centre of that rotation. Depending on your selection, the pivot point could be the median point of the object, the individual origins of the objects, the **3D Cursor**, and so on.

Figure 5.17 shows cubes with rotation transformations set to 45 degrees for different axes. The first part of the screenshot shows the cubes with no additional rotation applied to them. The second part of the screenshot shows the rotation of all cubes simultaneously by 25 degrees in the X-axis direction (shortcut *R*) using the median points, which causes them to rotate based on their axis.

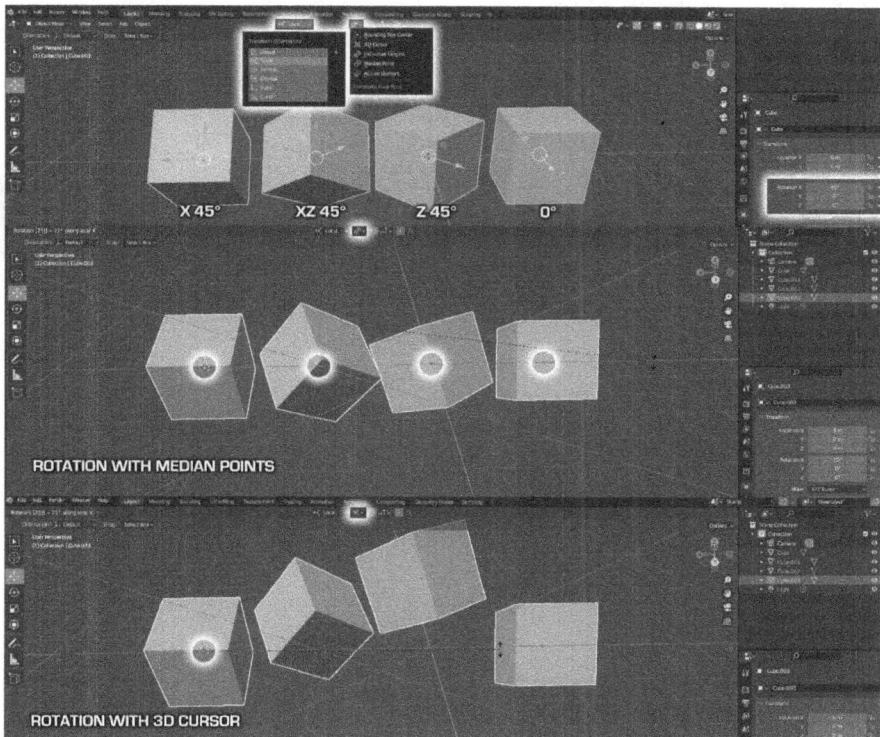

Figure 5.17: Explaining transform orientation options

The last row of *Figure 5.17* shows the same rotation of 25 degrees along the X axis with **3D Cursor** as its **Transform Orientations** point, causing objects to rotate based on their orientation while having a pivot as a **3D Cursor** placed on the first cube, causing the ones that have an angle to offset from their original locations.

The combination of **Transform Orientations** and **Pivot Point** determines the way objects in a scene are manipulated. Let's say you choose a **Local** transform orientation with an **Individual Origins** pivot point, each object in a selection would rotate around its origin following its local axes. To illustrate this further, if you had chosen a **Global** transform orientation with a **Median Point** pivot point, you would rotate all objects as a group around their shared median point following the global axes.

All in all, a transform pivot point determines the centre point around which objects or components (i.e., vertices, edges, faces) are manipulated during operations such as rotation and scaling. By changing **Pivot Point**, users can achieve more precise control over these transformations, which is especially useful in various modeling and animation tasks. For example, in animation, which we will explore in *Chapter 16* in *Part 1* of this book, you could use a custom pivot point to rotate a character's limb from the joint or scale an object from a specific location rather than from its geometric center, thus creating more natural and realistic movements.

The following list provides an in-depth view of the different transform pivot point options available in Blender:

- **Bounding Box Center**: This is the default **Pivot Point** option in Blender, and is what you will be using for most of your transformations. It calculates the center of the bounding box that encloses the selected objects and uses it as the pivot point (*Figure 5.18*).

Figure 5.18: Bounding box

- **3D Cursor**: This **Pivot Point** option uses the location of the **3D Cursor** in the scene as the pivot point.

- **Individual Origins**: This option uses the individual origins of objects as pivot points. You will find this useful when you want to rotate or scale multiple objects independently of each other, such as when you are placing furniture in a room.

- **Median Point**: This **Pivot Point** option calculates the median point of the selected objects or components and uses it as the pivot point. Based on the original mathematical concept, the **median point** is the average of the selected objects' or components' positions. **Median Point** pivot points are suitable for transformations where you want to maintain the relative spacing between individual items.

- **Active Element**: This option uses the last selected object or component as the pivot point for transformations.

To access and change the transform pivot point, locate the **Transform Pivot Point** drop-down menu in the header of the **3D Viewport**. It is usually found next to the **Transform Orientations** drop-down menu. By clicking on this drop-down menu, you can select the desired **Pivot Point** option to use during your transformations (*Figure 5.19*).

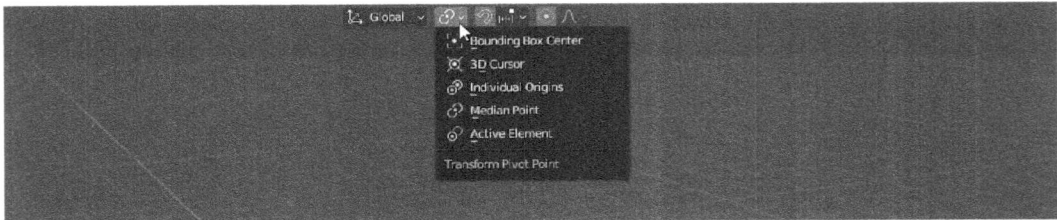

Figure 5.19: Access Transform Pivot Point

So, transform pivot points define the central point around which these transformations occur. As we move on, you will find out more about gaining precise control over transformation using the **Snapping** tool, which we will explore in the next section.

Guaranteeing consistency with Snapping for precise 3D modeling

The **Snapping** feature is a powerful tool that enables objects or components to snap to specific points within 3D space (e.g., vertices, edges, faces, or grid increments). It provides an additional level of control and precision during transformations by aligning the transformed objects to specific targets. **Snapping** helps ensure accuracy and consistency during modeling and animation (*Figure 5.20*).

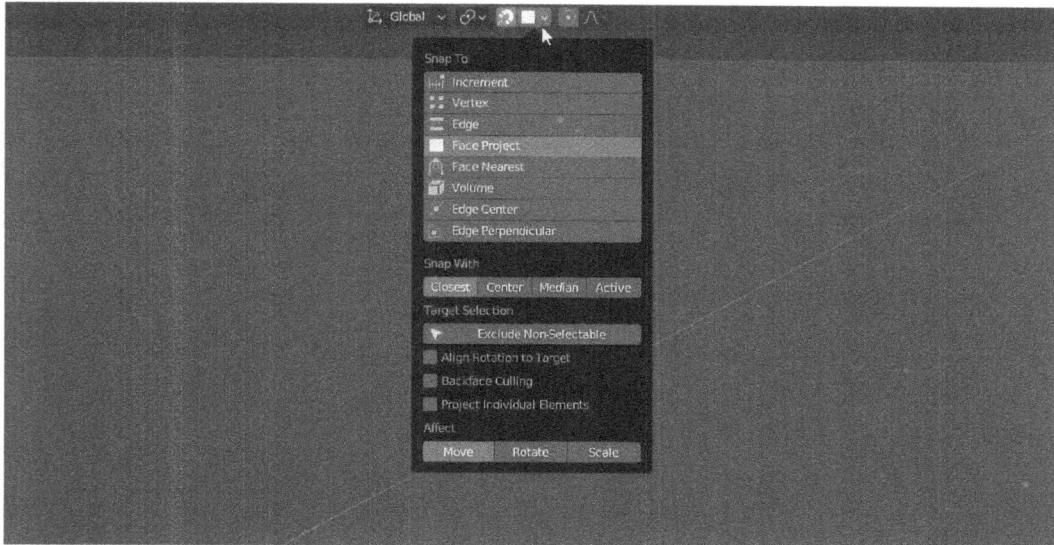

Figure 5.20: An overview of Snapping options

Blender offers different **Snapping** options for specialised uses:

- **Increment:** This option snaps objects or components to the nearest grid point, based on the configured grid scale. **Increment Snapping** is useful for 3D modeling a building with modular parts. It will ensure that individual parts always line up within the grid elements.

- **Vertex:** This snapping option aligns objects or components to the vertices of other objects in the scene. **Vertex Snapping** is particularly helpful in tasks such as retopologizing a high-poly mesh.

- **Edge: Edge Snapping** lets you snap objects or components right along the edges of other geometry in your scene, perfect for when you need things to meet up cleanly without any awkward gaps. Say you are building a floor and want it to tuck neatly into the wall without floating or clipping, this is your go-to. It is all about that nice, flush alignment that keeps your models looking solid and intentional.

- **Face**: This option snaps objects or components to the faces (i.e., surfaces) of other objects in the scene. Imagine you are gently pressing a magnetized coin onto a curved fridge door. Blender figures out the surface underneath and sticks it right there. It is perfect for making things sit naturally on complex surfaces, such as placing a decal on a wall or dropping rocks along uneven ground. **Face Project** goes one step further by projecting your object straight onto the surface based on your current view, almost like throwing a sticker at a wall and having it land perfectly flat (*Figure 5.21*).

Figure 5.21: Using Face Project in AI and 3D Art: A Course for Digital Artists by 3D Tudor

- **Volume**: This **Snapping** option aligns objects or components to the centre of the volume of other objects in the scene. **Volume Snapping** can be useful for tasks that require objects to be centred within other objects, such as when you are creating nested structures (e.g., placing a door within its frame, as in *Figure 5.22*).

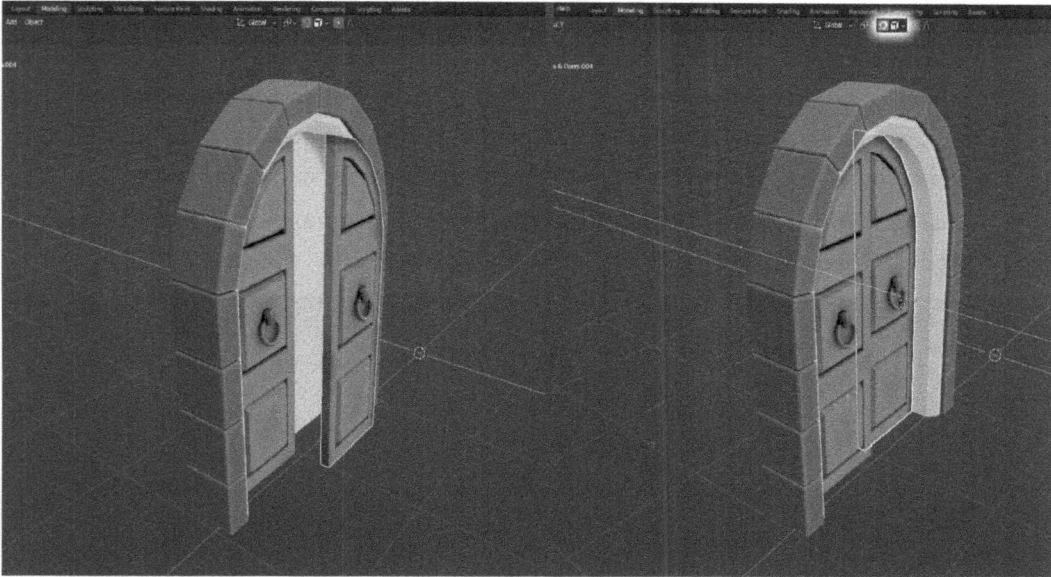

Figure 5.22: Volume Snapping with a door in "Blender 3.0 Stylized Greek Church 3D Model Build with Commentary" by 3D Tudor

- **Edge Center: Edge Center Snapping** does exactly what it says on the tin. It grabs the dead centre of an edge and snaps your object or component right to it. This is super useful when you are trying to space things out evenly, such as lining up ceiling panels, wall beams, or even bolts along a frame. There's no need to eyeball it or mess with measurements. It just locks things in, clean and tidy.

- **Edge Perpendicular:** This is one of those **Snapping** options that makes you feel like a geometry wizard. It locks your object or component so it lines up at a perfect right angle to the edge you are snapping to. This is great if you are working on clean architectural details, mechanical parts, or just trying to get things to behave properly with reference images. It also comes in handy when you are aiming for clean, accurate topology, no guesswork needed.

- **Absolute Grid Snap**: This is one of those tools that sounds a bit fancy but does exactly what it says on the tin. It snaps your object straight to the global grid, ignoring whatever random rotation or offset it had before. It is super handy when you want things perfectly lined up and behaving, especially if you are blocking out architecture or anything modular where consistency actually matters. No more wobbly walls or floating crates.

- **Absolute Grid Snap** is essential in tasks such as architectural modeling, level design, or modular asset creation, such as when you are designing a city (*Figure 5.23*).

Figure 5.23: Uses of Absolute Grid Snap in "Build Stunning Medieval Worlds with UE5's Modular Kitbash" by 3D Tudor

To enable **Absolute Grid Snap**, follow these steps:

1. Locate the **Snapping** button in the header of the **3D Viewport**. It is usually represented by a magnet icon. Click on the drop-down arrow next to the magnet icon to open the **Snapping** options menu.

2. Select the **Increment Snapping** option from the list of available modes. This will configure Blender to snap objects or components based on the grid increments.

3. Click on the **Snapping** options menu located to the right of the **Snapping** icon to access the advanced settings.

4. In the advanced settings, enable **Absolute Increment Snap** using the checkbox.

Blender's **Snapping** feature is an essential tool for achieving precise alignment of objects or components (e.g., vertices, edges, faces) in 3D modeling. It offers a variety of options, such as **Increment Snapping**, **Vertex Snapping**, **Edge Snapping**, and **Face Snapping**, each serving specific tasks, such as aligning to the nearest grid point, the vertices of other objects, or surfaces, respectively.

However, it is important to note that while **Snapping** is aimed at precise placement, **Proportional Editing**, which we will explore next, allows for a smoother, gradient effect on transformations.

Achieving smooth and organic transformations with Proportional Editing

Proportional Editing is a powerful modeling feature that gives you the power to manipulate a selected object or component at the same time as affecting the surrounding geometry, based on a predefined falloff radius. This way, you can create smooth and organic transformations that enhance the realism of your 3D art. **Proportional Editing** is particularly useful in character modeling, terrain editing, and creating complex shapes, such as in *Figure 5.24*.

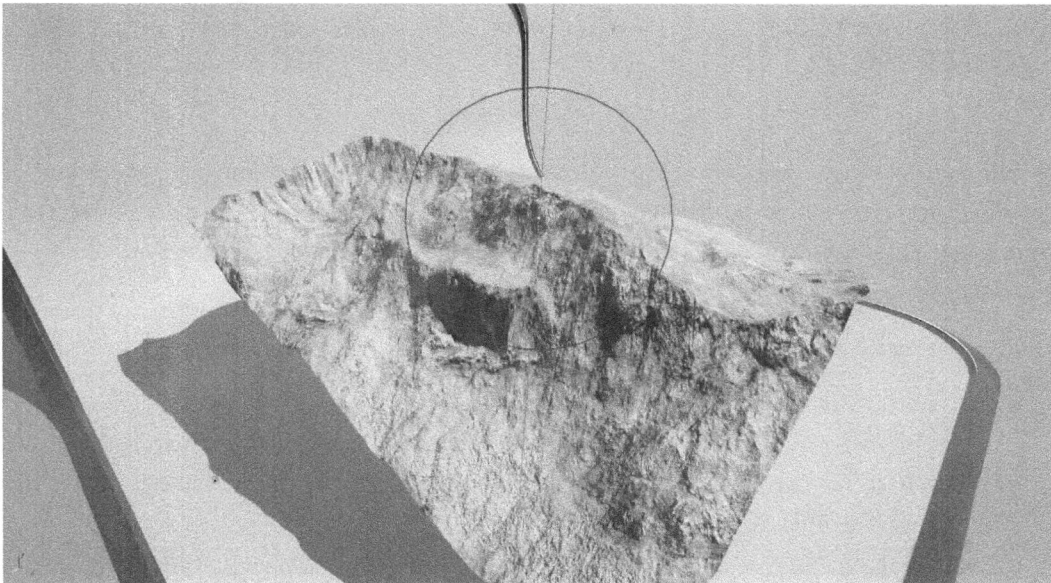

Figure 5.24: Using proportional editing to design terrain in "Creating Stunning Environments in UE5 A Game Artist Bootcamp" by 3D Tudor

To access and enable **Proportional Editing** in Blender, locate the **Proportional Editing** button in the header of the **3D Viewport**. It is represented by a circle with a dot inside, as seen in *Figure 5.25*.

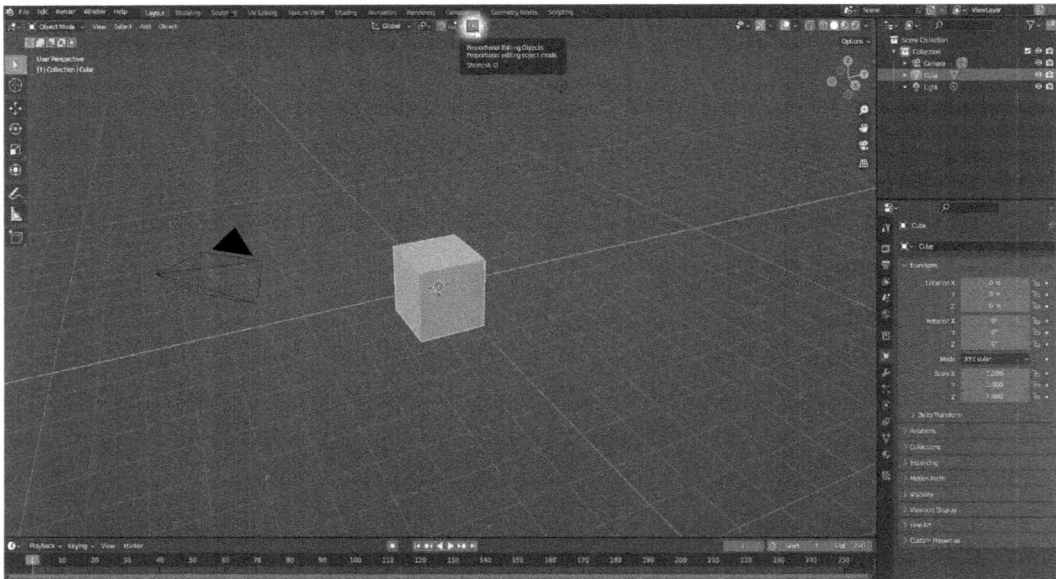

Figure 5.25: Accessing Proportional Editing options

Falloff refers to the range of effect for the transformation (i.e., moving, rotating, or scaling) of surrounding parts near your selection. **Falloff** allows you to ease off the intensity of the transform action. If in **Edit Mode**, this applies to vertices, and if in **Object Mode**, **Falloff** applies to surrounding objects.

There are several **Falloff** types available for **Proportional Editing** in Blender:

- **Smooth Falloff**: This achieves a smooth, gradual transition in the affected geometry. It is suitable for most general-purpose editing tasks. For example, by adjusting the shape of a character's arm with **Smooth Falloff**, you are preserving the smoothness of the surrounding geometry.

- **Sphere Falloff**: This generates a spherical falloff, affecting geometry within the specified radius, like on the surface of a sphere. I suggest you use this option for creating rounded, bulbous shapes. **Sphere Falloff** is useful if you are expanding a portion of terrain to create a smooth hill or mound.

- **Root Falloff:** Create a more concentrated, pointed effect in the affected geometry. This is very helpful if you are making adjustments that emphasize a specific point, as shown in *Figure 5.26*. Another use for **Root Falloff** would be if you are sculpting a mountain peak or creating a sharp ridge on a character's armor.

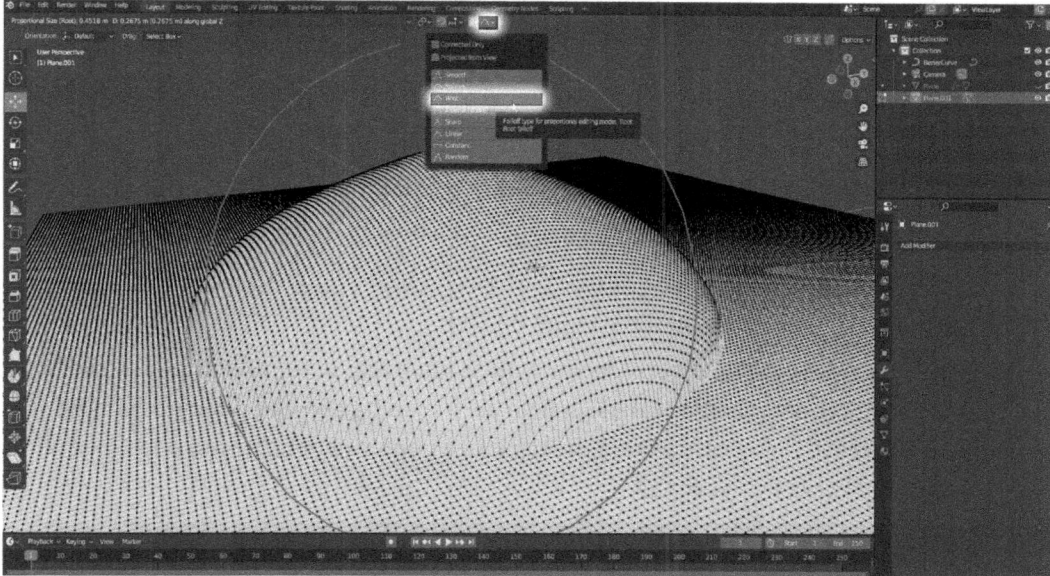

Figure 5.26: Root Falloff

- **Inverse Square Falloff:** This makes a falloff that decreases quadratically with distance. It is useful for creating a localized effect with some influence on the surrounding geometry. You can use **Inverse Square Falloff** to adjust facial features on a character model or modify a specific area of a landscape.

- **Sharp Falloff:** This generates a sharper, more pronounced transition in the affected geometry. For example, **Sharp Falloff** is the tool for you if you are shaping a character's jawline or creating a sharp crease in a piece of clothing.

- **Linear Falloff:** This applies a gradual and consistent decrease in influence as you move away from the selection. Each surrounding vertex is affected in equal, evenly spaced steps. This is useful when you want a smooth, predictable slope, such as bending a pipe or shaping a tree branch with consistent tapering.

- **Constant Falloff**: This applies the same amount of influence to every vertex within the falloff radius, regardless of distance from the selection. Every vertex within the radius gets the exact same treatment, no gentle fades or soft transitions. It is perfect when you want to move or scale a flat area evenly, such as lifting up a section of terrain without accidentally turning it into a hill. It's all or nothing, no in-betweens.

- **Random Falloff**: This manipulates a mesh with randomised intensity. **Random Falloff** is ideal if you are creating a rough terrain or giving a natural, randomized effect to the surface of an object (e.g., stubble on the face of a male character).

To control the **Proportional Editing** falloff, follow these steps:

1. Ensure **Proportional Editing** is enabled.

2. Select a **Falloff** type by clicking on the drop-down arrow next to the **Proportional Editing** button and choosing a **Falloff** type from the list.

3. After selecting a vertex, edge, or face in **Edit Mode**, begin to transform it using the *Move (G)*, *Rotate (R)*, or *Scale (S)* tools using their corresponding keyboard shortcuts. While doing so, you will see a circle around the selected component, which represents the **Falloff** radius, as shown in *Figure 5.27*.

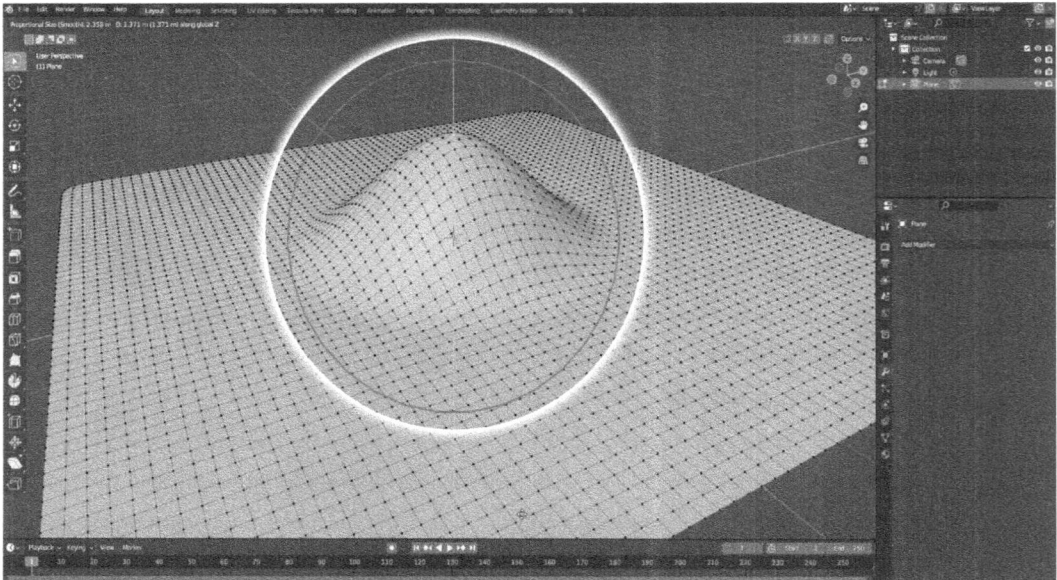

Figure 5.27: Falloff radius

4. Adjust the **Falloff** radius by scrolling the mouse wheel up or down, or by pressing the *Page Up/Page Down* keys. The **Falloff** radius determines the area of influence around the selected component, and it affects how the surrounding geometry is modified during the transformation. For example, you can create a hook by simply rotating a mesh line with **Proportional Editing** turned on, as shown in *Figure 5.28*.

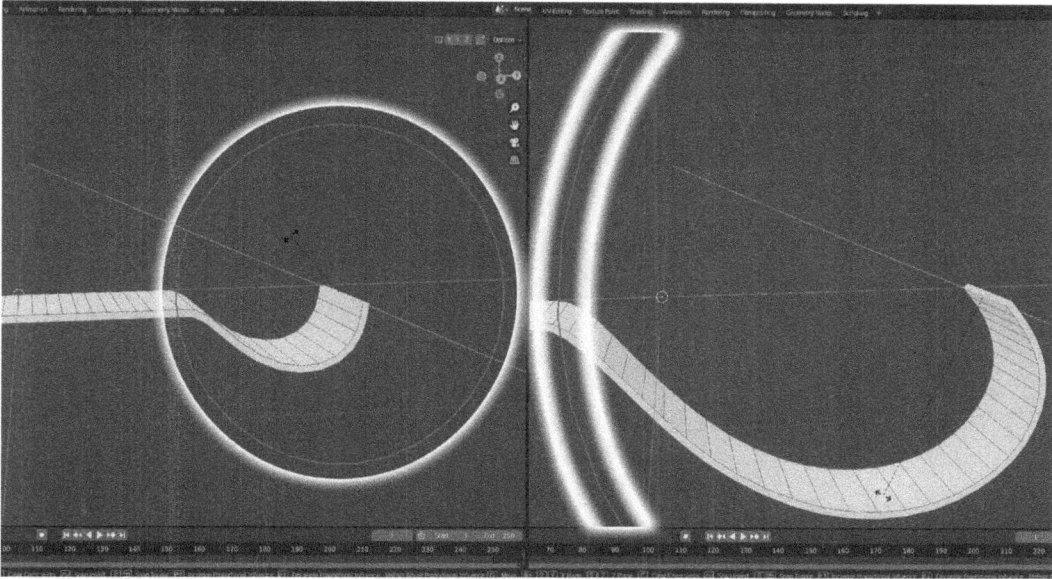

Figure 5.28: Creating a hook with Proportional Editing

5. If you need to change the **Falloff** type, you can press *Shift + O* while **Proportional Editing** is enabled. This will open the **Proportional Editing Falloff** panel in your mouse location.

Here, you can manually set the **Falloff** radius and tweak additional **Falloff** settings based on your project's needs. If you click that little drop-down arrow next to the **Proportional Editing** icon, you will find all the extra options hiding there. This is where you can dial in the **Falloff** radius manually and fine-tune how the influence fades out. It is especially useful when you are working on high-density meshes, such as something with a ton of geometry, because having precise control means you can nudge whole sections of verts around smoothly, keeping the overall shape flowing nicely instead of turning into a lumpy mess (*Figure 5.29*).

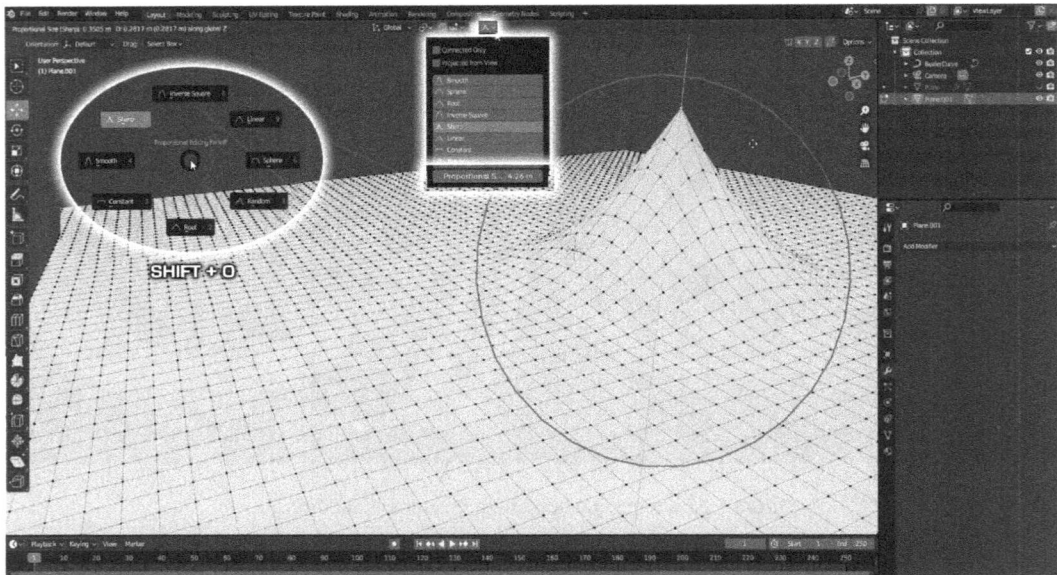

Figure 5.29: Additional Falloff settings

Tip

If you cannot see the **Proportional Editing** circle when you are trying to transform the mesh, while in **Transformation Mode**, try scrolling up your mouse wheel for either location (keyboard shortcut: *G*), rotation (keyboard shortcut: *R*), or scaling (keyboard shortcut: *S*) to make the falloff smaller. This issue can happen because Blender sometimes sets the default value too high, making the radius so large that it cannot be seen within the **3D Viewport**.

Once you get the hang of all the different **Falloff** types in Blender's **Proportional Editing** tool, you will start transforming your models with way more control. Whether you are going for smooth, organic curves or stylized, chunky shapes, picking the right falloff makes all the difference. It is like having a sculpting brush for your mesh, only smarter.

Summary

This chapter has equipped you with more knowledge about different aspects of working with Blender's **3D Viewport**, including viewport shaders and rendering engines. It began with an overview of the different shading modes available in Blender's **3D Viewport**, such as **Wireframe Mode, Solid Mode, Material Preview Mode,** and **Rendered Mode**. After understanding how viewport shaders can act as quick preview tools for your work in progress, we delved deeper into the realm of Blender's rendering engines, **Cycles** and **EEVEE**.

Before we dive into the juicy bits of 3D modeling, we need to get comfy with moving stuff around. Learning how to grab, rotate, and scale objects in your scene is like learning to walk before you run. It might not be glamorous, but it is absolutely essential if you want to build anything that is not a complete mess. To get that control, we discussed **Transform Orientations** options in Blender. These options allow you to manipulate objects or components in the 3D space using specific coordinate systems such as using **Global, Local, Normal, Gimbal, View,** and **Cursor** orientation. It might sound like overkill now, but once you start modeling seriously, picking the right one can save you a ton of time, and headaches.

We built on that foundation by jumping into some of Blender's more precise tools for moving stuff around properly, namely, transform pivot points and **Snapping**. The chapter naturally led to **Proportional Editing**. Using actionable examples, you came to understand why **Proportional Editing** is a precursor to 3D modeling. At this point, you have got the tools to not just move an object, but to shift it while shaping the geometry around it like a pro. You are no longer just dragging things around blindly; you are sculpting, nudging, and tweaking with purpose. As you wrap up this chapter, you are walking away with the know-how to create smooth, organic transformations in your mesh and loads of ways to preview those changes like a proper 3D artist in control of the scene.

In the next chapter, we will dive into the toolbox: the actual modeling tools inside Blender's **Edit** mode and how to use them properly. This will be the last chapter of this section and will be a precursor to 3D modeling in Blender.

Further reading

- If you are looking to find out more about topics not covered in this chapter such as the fundamentals of rigging and animation in video format, see *The Ultimate Guide to Blender 3D Rigging and Animation* (https://www.udemy.com/course/blender-3d-rigging-animation/?referralCode=39A1E0B8F07B474DFE0F).

- Should you be looking for a good environment to use to see the difference between rendering in Cycles or in EEVEE for yourself, take a look at *Blender 3 Stylized Map Room 3D Environment Tutorial* (https://youtu.be/3JUvCK78R58).

- As you have seen, there are many different **Transform Orientations** options. The perfect environment to try this out in is *Blender 3 | Unreal Engine 5 | Vintage Music Hall Building | Game Design* (https://youtu.be/UySRjBEaiGY) where you will get to work on different sides of the same building or *How I Created Indiana Jones Raider of The Lost Ark Fan Art in Blender 3 (Fully Animated)* (https://youtu.be/az91SYsjRB4) where you will work on different trap rooms.

- The perfect project to practice using **Face Project** with is *AI & 3D Art A Course for Digital Artists* (https://www.udemy.com/course/ai-3d-art-a-course-for-digital-artists/?referralCode=FAD4D851581CB6EAA61B), where you will apply a graffiti decal on the wall.

- You can try out **Volume Snapping** on a door in *Blender 3.0 Stylized Greek Church 3D Model Build with Commentary* (https://youtu.be/HxBsVnVUBuQ), where you will model a Greek Orthodox church.

- Try out **Absolute Grid Snap** with the models included in our *Build Stunning Medieval Worlds with UE5's Modular Kitbash* (https://www.udemy.com/course/building-medieval-worlds-unreal-engine-5-modular-kitbash/?referralCode=F936D687808F3AE55AF2) course.

- Should you be tempted to design terrain, you can get started with *Creating Stunning Environments in UE5 A Game Artist Bootcamp* (https://www.udemy.com/course/creating-stunning-environments-in-ue5-a-game-artist-bootcamp/?referralCode=BC8CF6C3160E4D3933F4).

Subscribe to Game Dev Assembly!

We are excited to introduce **Game Dev Assembly**, our brand-new newsletter dedicated to everything game development. Whether you're coding, designing, animating, or managing a studio, we've got insights, trends, and expert advice to help you create, innovate, and thrive. Sign up now and get exciting benefits.

```
https://packt.link/gamedev-newsletter
```

Get This Book's PDF Version and Exclusive Extras

UNLOCK NOW

Scan the QR code (or go to packtpub.com/unlock). Search for this book by name, confirm the edition, and then follow the steps on the page.

Note: Keep your invoice handy. Purchases made directly from Packt don't require an invoice.

6

Discovering Essential Tools for 3D Modeling in Blender

Alright, so in this chapter, we are diving into **Edit Mode**: basically, the place where all the modelling magic happens in Blender. If you remember back to *Chapter 1* in this part of the book, that is where we first dipped our toes in, but now we are going a bit deeper and exploring the actual tools that make your models come to life. This time, you will be introduced to a range of powerful tools such as the **Measure, Add Object, Loop Cut, Knife, Bevel, Poly Build, Spin, Smooth, Edge Slide, Shrink/Fatten, Shear,** and **Rip Region** tools. These tools provide options for creating and adjusting geometry, refining shapes, manipulating volumes, distorting objects, and separating mesh regions.

Reading through this chapter is really going to level up your modelling game. You will get better at tackling tricky shapes, add a whole lot more realism to your work, and just feel way more confident with the tools. These are the kinds of features that boost your speed, improve your workflow, and give you that creative edge when building detailed, believable models that actually look good onscreen.

Put simply, this chapter explores a range of powerful tools within Blender's **Edit Mode** that will give you the power to build complex, detailed models with real precision, even if you are just starting out or sitting somewhere in the middle of your 3D journey.

So, in this chapter, we will cover the following topics:

- Finding and using your Blender Tool Shelf
- Refreshing your knowledge of Blender's **Object Mode** tools
- Exploring the Tool Shelf in **Edit Mode**

Technical requirements

As for **Blender 4.5 LTS (Long-Term Support)**, the general requirements include a macOS 11.2 or newer (Apple Silicon supported natively) operating system, or a Linux (64-bit, glibc 2.28 or newer) operating system. Blender now requires a CPU with the SSE4.2 instruction set, at least 8 GB of RAM (32 GB recommended for heavy scenes), and a GPU supporting OpenGL 4.3 with a minimum of 2 GB of VRAM.

For a full list of technical requirements, please refer back to *Chapter 1* of this part.

Finding and using your Blender Tool Shelf

The **Tool Shelf**, sometimes referred to as the **Tool Panel**, is a critical part of Blender's UI, equipped with a convenient set of tools and operations that adapt according to the context. You can find it on the left side of the **3D Viewport** as shown in *Figure 6.1*.

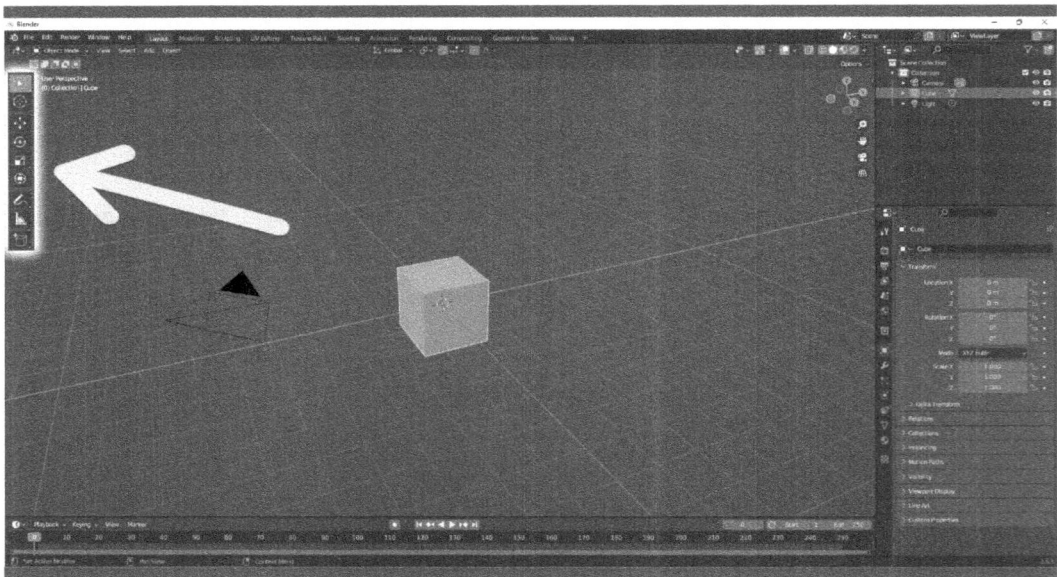

Figure 6.1: Finding the Tool Shelf

Here's how you can open and close the **Tool Shelf**:

To open the **Tool Shelf**, hover your mouse anywhere within the **3D Viewport**, and press the *T* key on your keyboard. The **Tool Shelf** will appear on the left side of the **3D Viewport**.

To close the **Tool Shelf**, press the *T* key once more while your mouse is inside the **3D Viewport**. The shelf will disappear.

> Note
>
> The **Tool Shelf** will display different tools when you are in **Object Mode** compared to when you are in **Edit Mode**, **Sculpt Mode**, or any other mode. As well as this, the **Tool Shelf** includes a wide range of sculpting brushes in **Sculpt Mode**, which we discussed in *Chapter 2* in *Part 1* of this book.

Among the tools found in the **Tool Shelf** are transformation tools such as **Move**, **Rotate**, and **Scale**. You will also find tools for mesh editing such as **Extrude**, **Bevel**, **Loop Cut**, and **Slide**, all of which we will discuss in this chapter (*Figure 6.2*).

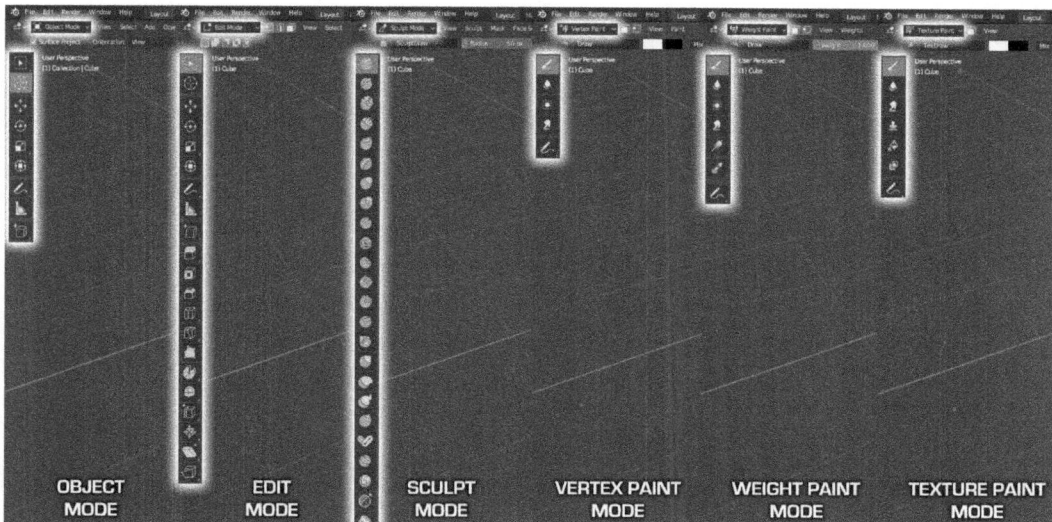

Figure 6.2: Tool Shelves in different Blender modes

The **Tool Shelf** is incredibly useful because it allows you to declutter your workspace when you do not need to see all the tools that are available to you, and then quickly bring the one you need back when you do need it. It is one of the many ways Blender allows for a highly customizable UI to suit individual workflows, as discussed in more detail in *Chapter 4* in *Part 1* of this book.

Tip

The **Tool Shelf** is scrollable, which means not all tools will be visible on your screen at the same time if there are many options available. You can scroll up and down the **Tool Shelf** to see everything. Just look in the bottom-left corner of your **3D Viewport** after using a tool. If you keep an eye on that little panel, you will find loads of hidden gems that give you more control over how each tool behaves. *Click and hold* on the button to open the menu.

Blender's **Tool Shelf** is one of those core bits of the UI that keeps everything flowing. It is dynamic, meaning what you see changes depending on what mode you are in, which is super handy once you get used to it. Now that you have got a feel for navigating and managing it properly, we are ready to jump into the next section: a proper refresher on the tools you will find in **Object Mode** and how to actually make the most of them.

Refreshing your knowledge of Blender's Object Mode tools

As we touched on back in *Chapter 1* in *Part 1* of this book, **Object Mode** is one of Blender's main workspaces; it is where you interact with whole objects in your scene. You can move them around, rotate them, scale them, change properties… basically treat each object as its own unit. We already talked about **Move**, **Rotate**, **Transform**, and the **3D Cursor**, but really getting comfortable with these tools is key to navigating and arranging stuff smoothly in Blender's 3D space.

Like with everything in Blender, the secret sauce is practice. So do not be shy! Click around, try things out, and get a feel for how these tools behave. Alright, now that we have got the basics covered, let us dive into some of the more advanced tools in **Object Mode** and see what else the **Tool Shelf** has to offer.

Familiarizing yourself with the Annotate tool in Blender

One tool that often flies under the radar but is super handy, especially if you are doing any kind of planning, storyboarding, or quick concept work, is the **Annotate** tool. It lets you scribble notes or sketch ideas right onto the **3D Viewport**, which is brilliant for visualizing things on the fly. As shown in *Figure 6.3*, it is a simple feature, but surprisingly powerful when you want to keep your thoughts in the scene without opening another app or losing your flow.

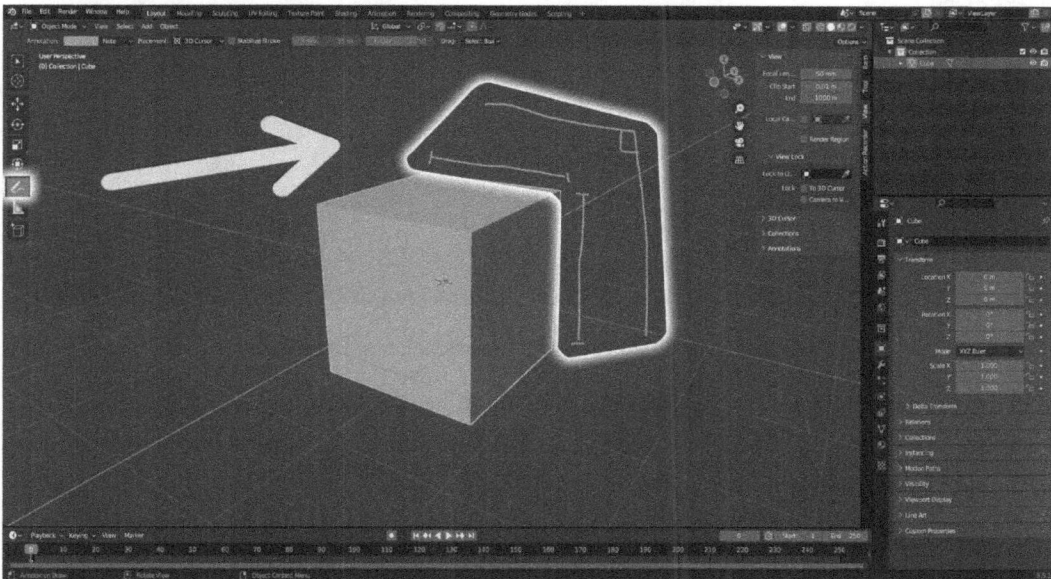

Figure 6.3: Annotate tool illustration example

Being able to jot down notes or sketch directly in Blender with the **Annotate** tool is honestly a bit of a superpower. It makes planning and visualizing your 3D scenes way easier, especially if you are someone who uses tools such as **Pureref** (https://www.pureref.com/). You can see how to use the **Annotate** tool for referencing in Blender in *Figure 6.4*.

Figure 6.4: Using the Annotate tool with a bridge reference

When you grab the **Annotate** tool from the **Tool Shelf**, your cursor turns into a little pencil icon, basically telling you, "Alright, time to draw." It lets you scribble, sketch, or make notes directly in the viewport, and honestly, it is like having a virtual notepad right inside Blender. Say you are working on a big, messy scene, such as a medieval castle with loads of moving parts (see *Figure 6.5*). Instead of trying to remember what goes where, you can just mark it out in the viewport and keep your thoughts right in front of you while you build.

Figure 6.5: Using the Annotate tool – Build Stunning Medieval Worlds with UE5's Modular Kitbash by 3D Tudor

What is even better is that you can tweak the color and thickness of your annotation lines, so it is not just scribbles; you can actually organize your notes. Whether you want bold lines for blocking out big ideas or subtle marks for fine detail, this tool's flexible enough to fit whatever you are working on.

To access these controls, follow the next steps:

1. Click and hold the **Annotate** tool. *Figure 6.6* shows different options for annotation, which can be opened by clicking and holding on the annotation button. Plus, the toolbar will be different depending on what you choose.

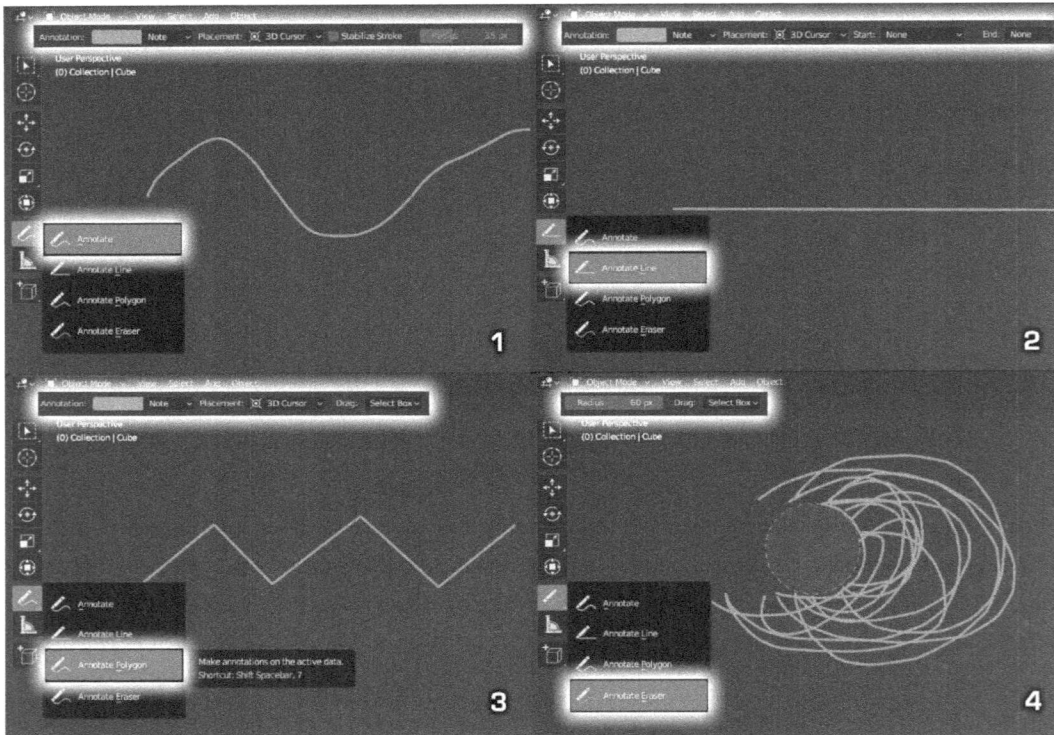

Figure 6.6: Optimizing how you use the Annotate tool's toolbar

2. As you come to make your first annotation, a drop-down menu will reveal multiple options, including color, thickness, and placement (*Figure 6.7*). In this same panel, you can also manage annotation layers: click the minus (-) icon next to a layer to remove all annotations assigned to it.

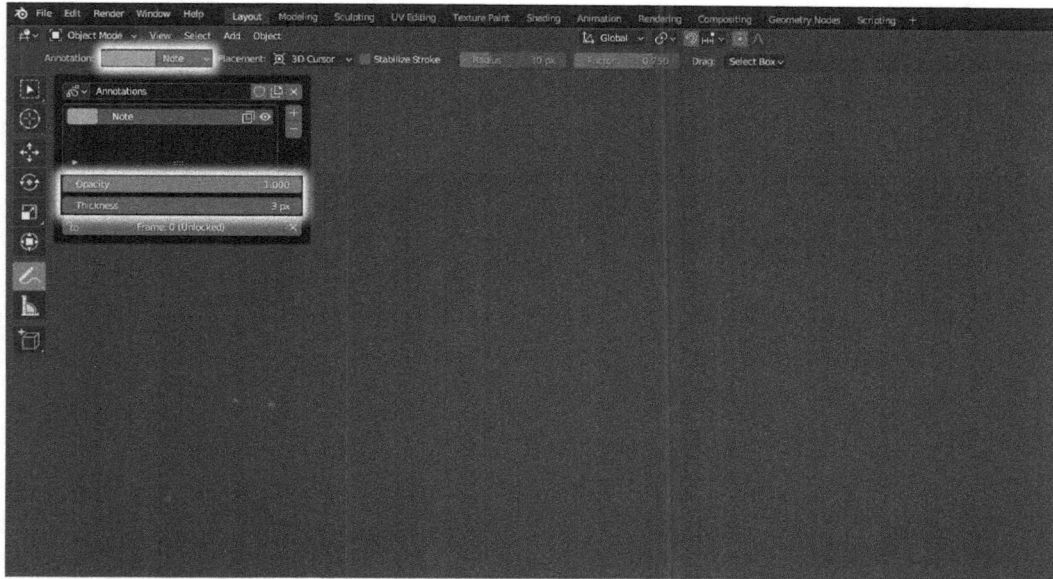

Figure 6.7: Annotate tool drop-down menu

Alright, so here is a quick one that will save you a lot of head-scratching later: **Annotations** in Blender. Now, before you go scribbling all over your scene like a caffeinated concept artist, you should know there is actually a right way to place these notes.

You have three main **Placement** options:

- **3D Cursor**: This plonks your annotation directly into 3D space, perfect if you want it to live inside your scene.
- **View**: This is more like a sticky note on your screen. It stays put no matter where your camera moves, so it's great for quick reminders or instructions to your future self.
- **Surface**: This one is clever; it actually *sticks* the annotation to the mesh itself, so it moves with your model. Ideal for those "don't forget to fix this wonky bit" notes.

If you are wondering how to manage the chaos once you have gone annotation-happy, yep, there is a panel for that. Hop over to the **Annotation** panel and boom, you can manage your layers like a pro. Want to get rid of an entire layer of notes in one go? Just hit the little minus icon. Poof, gone.

Consider a scenario where you're creating a medieval castle scene. You might want to use the **Annotate** tool to sketch out where specific elements such as towers, gates, or flags should be positioned. Using different colors for different components and adjusting the thickness for importance could be helpful here, as shown in *Figure 6.8*.

Figure 6.8: Using the Annotate tool – Build Stunning Medieval Worlds with UE5's Modular Kitbash by 3D Tudor

The **Annotate** tool's functionality is not limited to creation; you can also modify or completely remove annotations as required. This can be done via the **Annotation** panel in the sidebar, which opens up by pressing the *N* key. All in all, the **Annotate** tool in Blender proves itself to be a versatile and potent aid in the 3D creation process.

The **Annotate** tool in Blender allows users to draw and make annotations directly on the **3D Viewport**, facilitating communication and providing a visual reference for the modelling and design process. The **Annotate** tool and the **Measure** tool, which will be discussed next, both serve the same core purpose: helping you work more precisely in Blender. Whether you are laying out a scene or double-checking your dimensions, these tools are great for staying accurate and making sure your ideas are clear, especially when you are collaborating or just trying to stay organized in your own workflow.

Maximising accuracy with the Measure tool

Blender's **Measure** tool is a powerful feature for ascertaining distances, angles, and areas in the **3D Viewport**. This can be incredibly beneficial in many scenarios, such as architectural modelling, product design, or simply checking the scale and proportion in any 3D scene (e.g., see *Figure 6.9*).

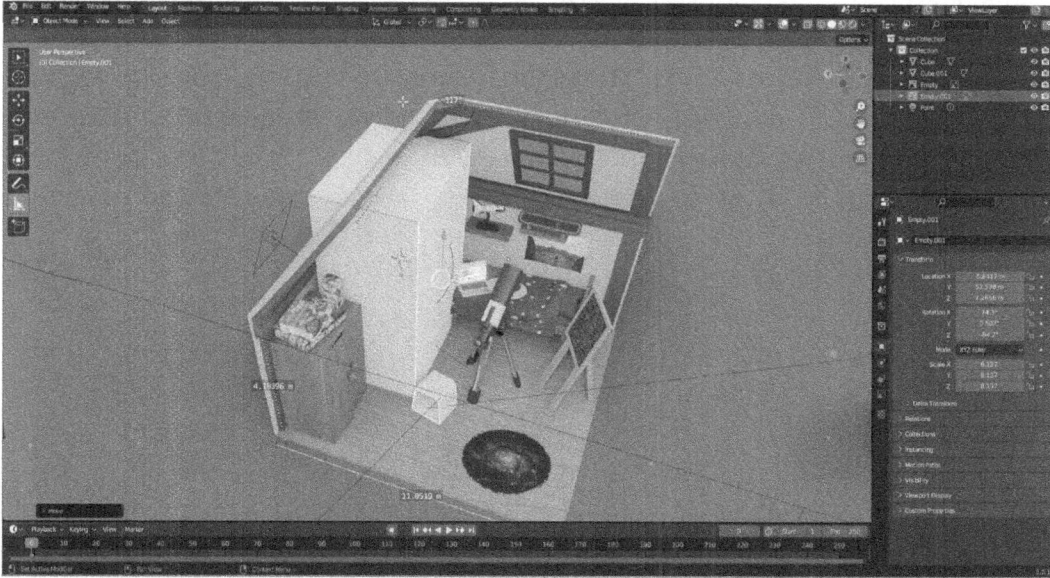

Figure 6.9: Using the Measure tool in "Mastering the Art of Isometric Room Design in Blender 3" by 3D Tudor

It is a time-saving feature because it allows you to create assets that can then be used within any correctly scaled and realistic environment in the future, especially if you add them to Blender's **Asset Manager**, as discussed in *Chapter 4* in *Part 1* of this book.

Using the **Measure** tool is straightforward. Once selected from the **Tool Shelf**, a simple click and drag in the **3D Viewport** generates a measurement line. The length of this line, represented in Blender units, is displayed instantly.

Note

Blender units are set as **metric** by default; even if they are set as **none**, it will use metric values. Another option for Blender's unit system is to use the imperial system, but that is a change you must make manually.

If you are working on creating a 3D model of a building based on architectural plans, you can use the **Measure** tool to ensure that the dimensions of your model match its specifications. Similarly, in product design, where parts need to fit together perfectly, the **Measure** tool allows you to confirm that the sizes of the individual components are correct.

The utility of the **Measure** tool is not limited to linear dimensions. You can measure angles as well. By generating a second measurement line that intersects the first, the tool immediately displays the angle between these lines. This could be useful in numerous situations, such as when you are creating slanted roofs. Angle steepness will affect how structures connect, and this will influence overall aesthetics and structural integrity, as shown in *Figure 6.10*.

Figure 6.10: Slanted roofs and Measure tool usage – Build Stunning Medieval Worlds with UE5's Modular Kitbash by 3D Tudor

The **Measure** tool can also be used in another way. While dragging the measurement, holding *Shift* lets you measure the depth of an object by drawing a straight line through its volume. If you also hold *Ctrl*, it enables snapping to edges, vertices, or faces, making it easier to measure the volume along specific geometry, such as edge-to-edge or corner-to-corner, as shown in *Figure 6.11*.

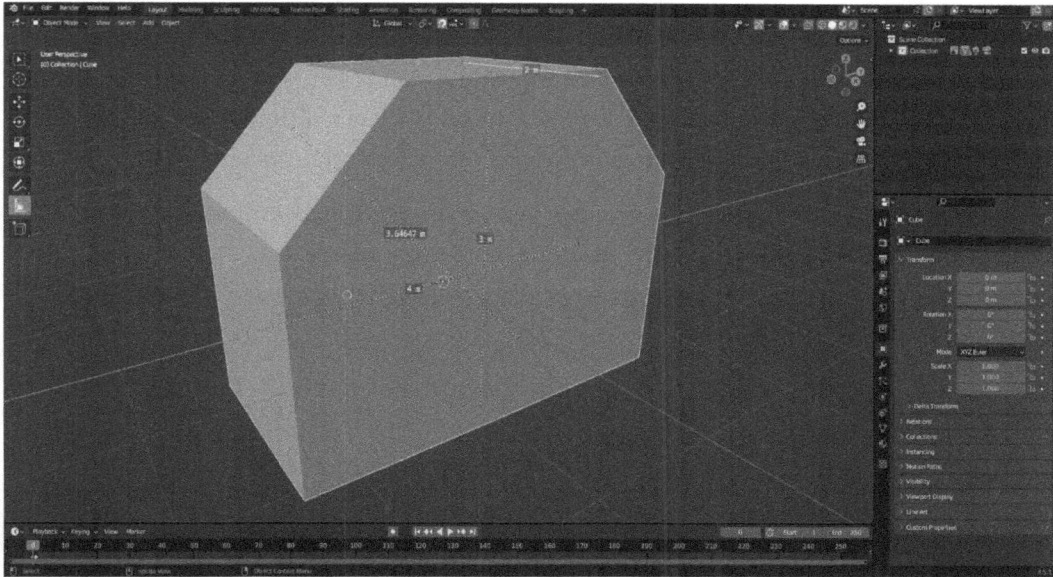

Figure 6.11: Calculating the area of an object with the Measure tool

Tip

Here is a neat little tip about Blender's **Measure** tool that might save you a bit of time (and frustration). When you are working with measurements, whether it is checking the length of a wall, aligning props, or just making sure something is not wildly out of scale, modifying those measurements is actually a breeze. If you want to adjust the length of a measurement line or change where it intersects, just grab the endpoints and drag them around. Blender makes this feel pretty intuitive, like moving regular geometry. No hidden menus, no complex steps, just click and drag. And when you are done? The measurement line behaves just like any other object in your scene. Want to clean up? Select it and hit *Delete*. That is it, no fuss.

So, the **Measure** tool in Blender enables users to accurately measure distances, angles, and dimensions between various elements in the **3D Viewport**, providing precise information for modelling and design purposes. As we move on, we will explore the **Add Object** tool. The **Add Object** tool allows you to add predefined shapes, meshes, and primitives to the scene, enhancing the creative possibilities within Blender. Even though you will be using the **Add Object** tool to import default shapes into the **3D Viewport**, your creative journey in 3D modeling would be harder without them.

Adding objects in Blender

Adding objects to your **3D Viewport** will be part and parcel of your work in Blender. Blender makes this routine task quick and convenient with its **Add Object** tool, letting you add new mesh objects into your scenes without having to navigate through multiple menus.

The **Add Object** tool, when clicked, presents a small menu populated with several options such as **Add Cube**, **Add UV Sphere**, **Add Cylinder**, and more (*Figure 6.12*).

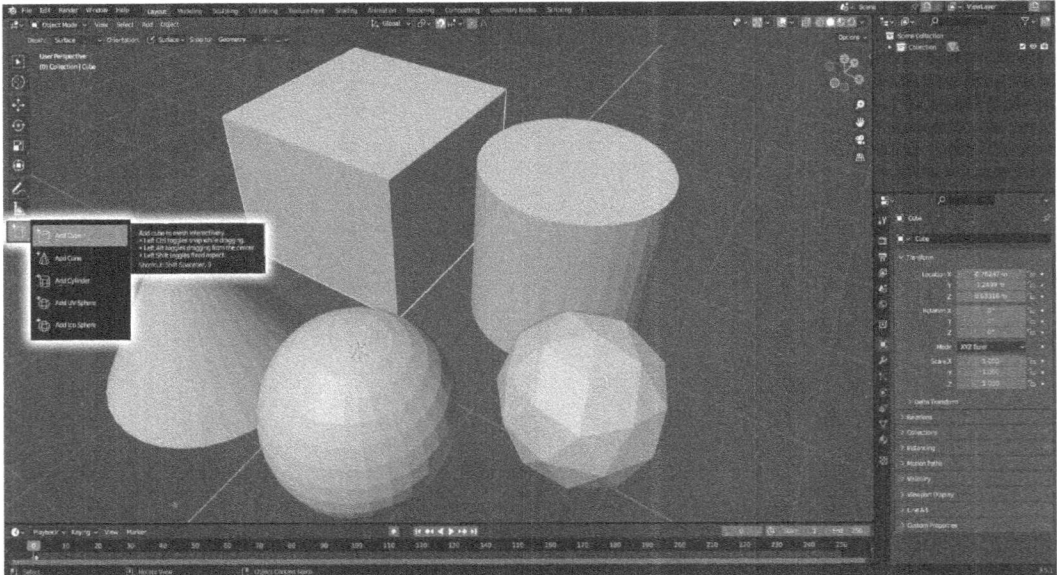

Figure 6.12: Default shapes available through the Add Object tool

Depending on your selection, the corresponding object is added to your scene at the location of the **3D Cursor**. For example, if you are building a basic room layout and need to add a cube to represent a table, you would go to the **Add Object** tool, select **Add Cube**, then click and drag in the **3D Viewport** to define the base of the cube. Release the mouse to begin adjusting the height and click again to finalize the shape. You can then modify this cube to match the dimensions and placement of the table in your scene, as shown in *Figure 6.13*.

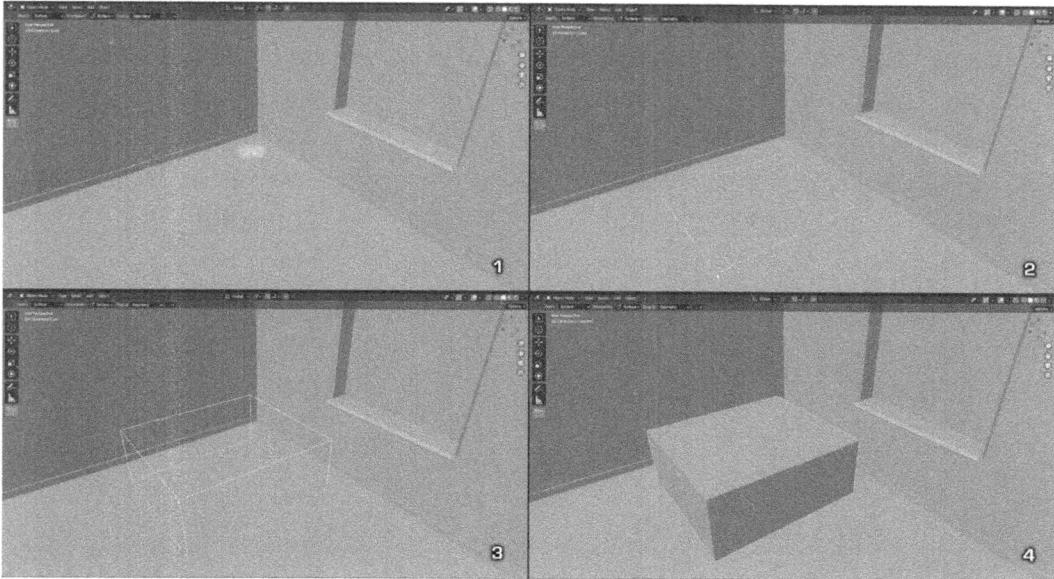

Figure 6.13: Steps involved in using the Add Object tool

Alright, so here is something that catches a lot of people out when they are starting in Blender: editing an object's properties right after you add it. The good news is Blender makes it really easy... as long as you know where to look. As soon as you drop in a new object, say a cube, a cylinder, or one of those torus shapes you swear you will use more often, you will see a little panel pop up in the bottom-left corner of the screen (*Figure 6.14*). That is the **Operator** panel, and it is your shortcut to changing things such as dimensions, location, and rotation right away. No diving into menus, no fiddling with transforms.

Now, if you are like me and have the attention span of a magpie, you might click away too fast. No worries. Just press *F9* and Blender will bring that panel back for the last object you added. This is super handy when you realise your new cylinder is five times too tall or floating halfway to the moon.

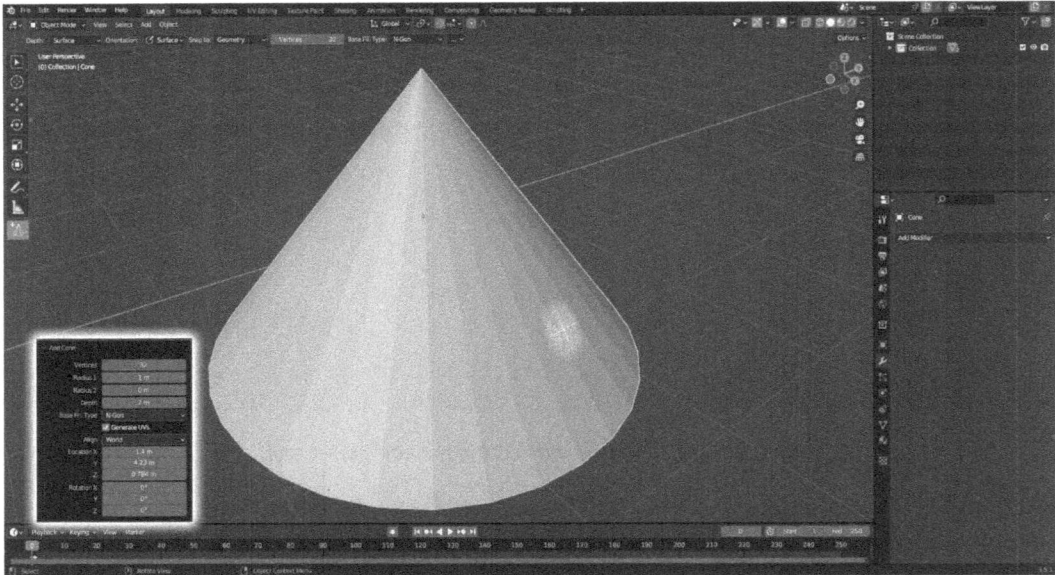

Figure 6.14: Add Object tool operator panel location

The **Add Object** tool's utility in rapid prototyping or blocking out a scene is undeniable. The time saved by avoiding navigating menus and the convenience of immediate addition and modification of objects can streamline the 3D creation process. You can build a graybox (i.e., a rough, untextured version of a 3D scene using basic shapes to block out the layout and scale) of an extensive town or city in a few hours, helping you better calculate what modular pieces you will need to build it and make a list (*Figure 6.15*).

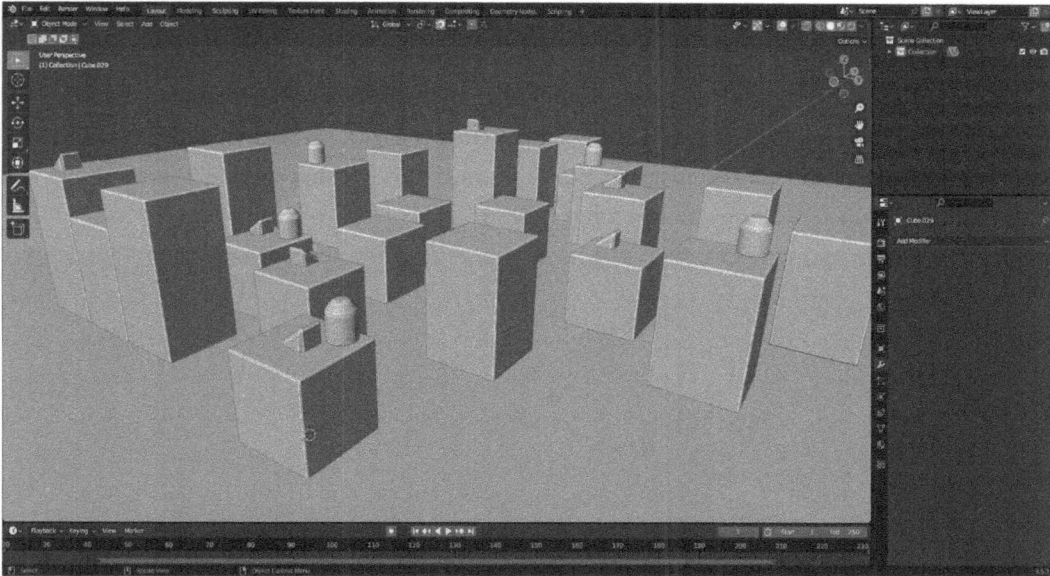

Figure 6.15: A graybox of an extensive town

In **Object Mode**, the **Tool Shelf** is a bit like your local hardware store. You pop in for one thing and end up finding loads of handy tools you did not even know you needed. From **Annotate** and **Measure** to the **Add Objects** tool, it has all the essentials to keep things ticking along nicely. Once you know your way around, it makes navigating Blender feel a lot less like herding cats. Now that you have got the hang of things in **Object** mode, we are off to **Edit** mode, where Blender throws even more buttons at you (because clearly, we were not confused enough already). But do not worry! We will break it all down and show you how these tools can take your modelling to the next level. Let us crack on, shall we?

Exploring the Tool Shelf in Edit Mode

One of the great things about working in Blender is being able to jump between **Object Mode** and **Edit Mode**: it is like switching from planning a house to actually building the walls. This switch changes up your toolset completely, which is where things start to get interesting.

Now, when you hop into **Edit Mode**, you will notice that the usual suspects, **Move**, **Scale**, and **Rotate**, are still hanging around at the top of the **Tool Shelf**. These tools are basically the bread and butter of 3D modelling, so Blender wisely keeps them close at hand, no matter what mode you are in. But here is where it gets fun: look just below the **Add Cube** tool, and you will find a whole new bunch of shiny buttons waiting to be pressed. It is like discovering a secret drawer in your toolbox. *Figure 6.16* shows exactly what I mean.

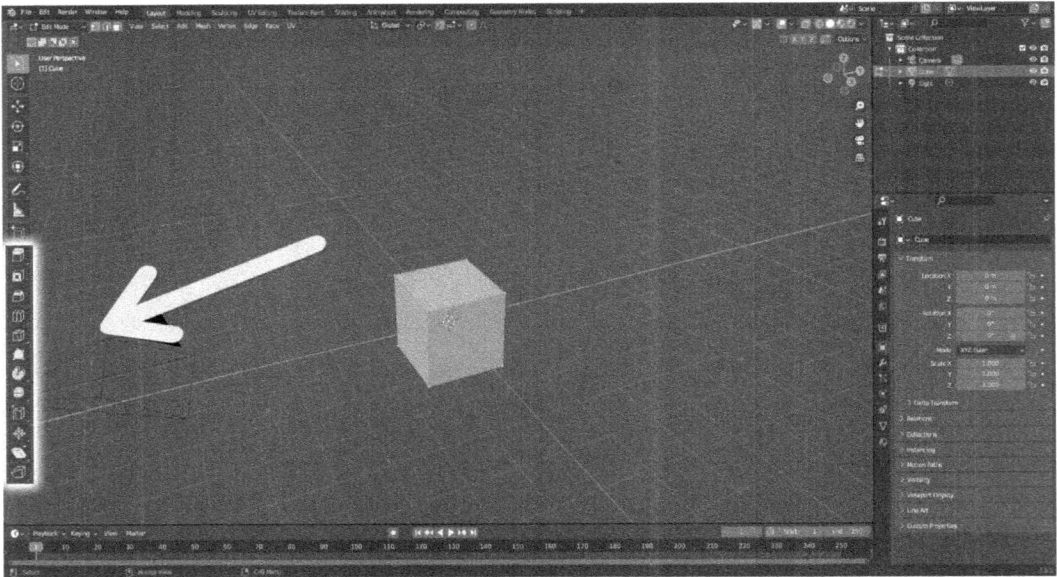

Figure 6.16: Add Cube tool options

Now, even though these next tools are not exactly fan favourites in the wider Blender community, do not write them off. They can seriously level up your modelling workflow if you give them a proper shot. What they do really well is give you finer control over your vertices, edges, and faces; so if you want to shape your models with more precision, these are the tools to check out.

But here is the thing: they only become useful once you actually start using them. Just knowing they exist will not cut it. You need to play around with them, see how they affect your mesh, and get comfortable weaving them into your day-to-day modelling. Trust me, the more you use them, the more you will realise just how powerful they are, especially for more advanced or detailed work.

So, with that said, here are the tools we will be diving into for the rest of this chapter:

- The **Extrude Region** tool
- The **Insert Faces** tool
- The **Bevel** tool
- The **Loop Cut** tool
- The **Knife** tool
- The **Poly Build** tool
- The **Spin** tool
- The **Smooth** tool
- The **Edge Slide** tool
- The **Shrink/Fatten** tool
- The **Shear** tool
- The **Rip Region** tool

Let's go through them, one by one.

Building intricate models with the Extrude Region tool

The **Extrude Region** tool is one of those **Edit Mode** essentials you will end up using all the time. It is how you take a flat shape and start turning it into something with depth. By extending selected vertices, edges, or faces along an axis, you can build out your model step by step, think of it as pulling new geometry out of thin air. *Figure 6.17* shows a classic example: extrude a 2D square's vertices along the *Z axis*, and boom, you have got yourself a cube.

This tool is a proper workhorse, whether you are knocking together industrial prototypes, sketching out a bit of furniture, or even modelling something such as a liver (because, why not?). If you want to add complexity and structure to your model, **Extrude Region** is where it all begins.

Picture yourself creating a character model. Starting with a rudimentary cylindrical shape that represents the body, your next step is to create the arms. You start by selecting the faces on the cylinder's side where you want the arm to originate. With the **Extrude Region** tool active, a *click and drag* action will extend a new section of geometry from the cylinder, forming an arm-like projection. This process can be duplicated on the cylinder's opposite side to construct another arm. As you can see, you can create more with **Extrude Region** than with any other Blender tool discussed so far.

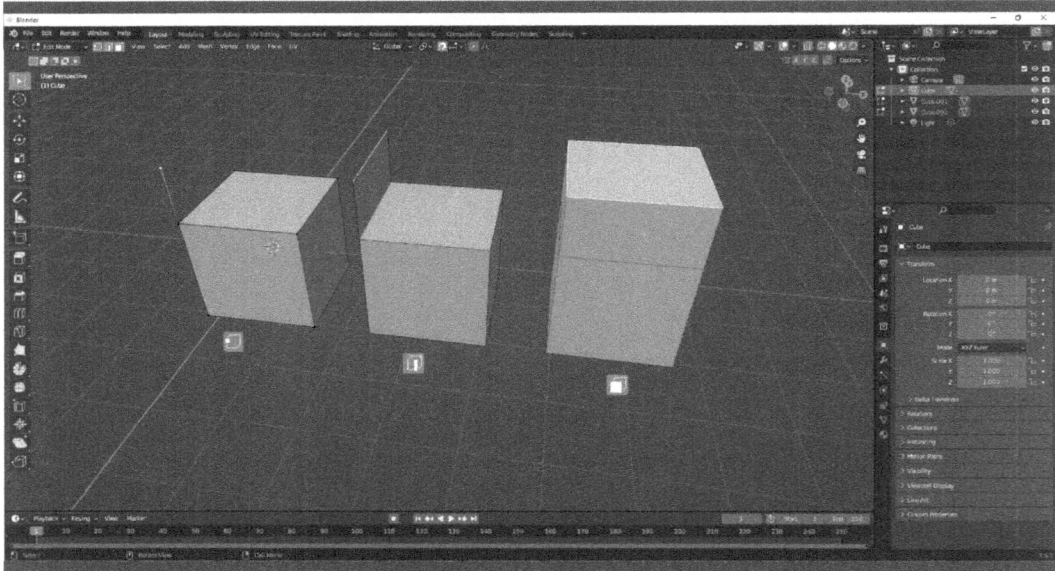

Figure 6.17: Using the Extrude Region tool in different selection modes – vertex extrusion, edge extrusion, face extrusion

Note

By default, using the **Extrude Region** tool using the keyboard shortcut *E* will put you into mouse location-based (i.e., freeform) extrusion, allowing you to extrude following the direction of your mouse. Pressing the *X*, *Y*, and *Z* shortcuts lets you switch to the *X*, *Y*, and *Z* axes in **Global Orientation**, respectively. Pressing either of these shortcuts twice will switch to **Normal Orientation** for each of those axes. If you select two vertices and there is a line in the middle, it will extrude the line. If you select four vertices surrounding a face, it will extrude a face.

One really handy thing about the **Extrude Region** tool is that you can lock your extrusion to a specific axis. Just hit *X*, *Y*, or *Z* after starting the extrusion, and Blender will keep it perfectly aligned along that direction. This is super useful when you are after clean, symmetrical shapes, such as if you are building something mechanical or architectural, say a car panel, a wall, or even a spaceship wing. It stops things from going wonky and helps keep everything neat and in proportion, which makes a huge difference when you want your model to actually look solid and intentional.

The **Extrude Region** tool is extremely versatile. Whether you are forming fingers on a hand, sculpting branches on a tree, or creating spikes on a surface, this tool is up to the task. Its applications extend beyond character modelling, proving valuable in hard surface modelling (i.e., objects with well-defined, geometrically precise surfaces such as armour plates), architectural modelling, and more. You can use the **Extrude Region** tool for some of the most exciting projects, such as unintentional skewing or misalignment of parts, if you are creating a symmetrical or mechanical object, such as a car, building, or spaceship. By constraining the extrusion to a specific axis, you ensure the extruded parts are in line with the rest of your model, thereby maintaining the proportions and symmetry needed.

By tapping the axis shortcut (*X*, *Y*, *Z*) a second time, it will extrude the mesh based on the vertice's normal orientations, allowing you to extrude multiple faces outwards from the mesh (*Figure 6.18*).

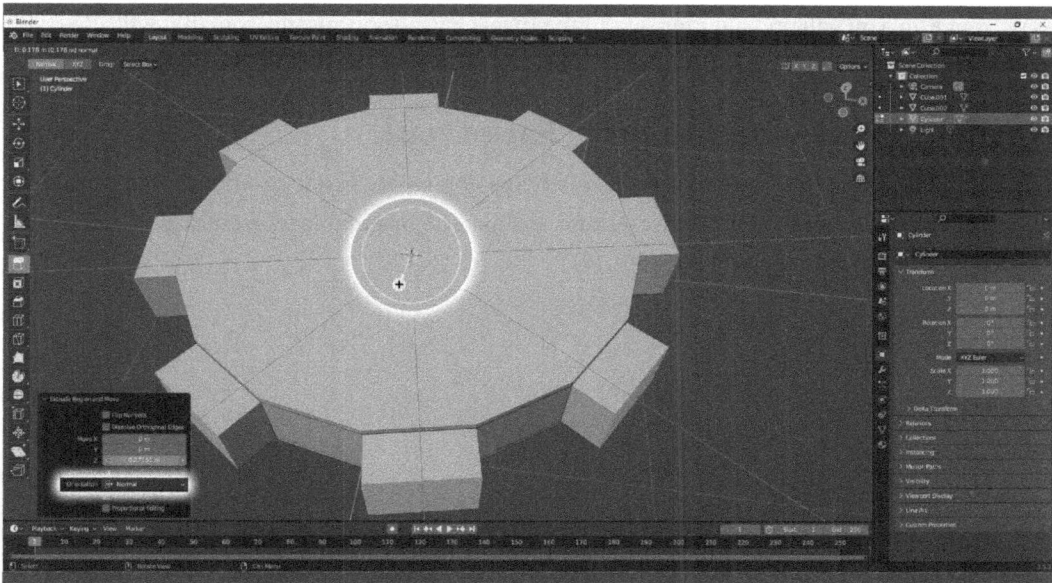

Figure 6.18: Using the Extrude Region tool to model a gear

If you click and hold on the **Extrude** tool in Blender's toolbar, you will notice it is not just a one-trick pony. You actually get access to a few different extrusion modes: **Extrude Manifold**, **Extrude Along Normals**, **Extrude Individual**, and **Extrude to Cursor**.

Each one behaves a little differently depending on what you are trying to do:

- **Extrude Manifold** is great when you want to keep the mesh watertight and avoid weird overlaps.
- **Extrude Along Normals** pushes geometry out evenly based on the surface direction.
- **Extrude Individual** lets you extrude separate faces on their own without merging them.
- **Extrude to Cursor** shoots new geometry straight toward your mouse pointer.
- **Extrude Region** helps you morph basic shapes into complex ones.

Tip

Here is a cheeky shortcut: if you are already using one of the **Extrude** tools, you can just press *Ctrl + Right-Click* to quickly extrude toward your cursor. This is super handy for placing geometry exactly where you want it without messing around with gizmos.

As we move on, you will find out more about the **Insert Faces** tool: another tool that will allow you to add depth and complexity to your 3D models, but this time, by helping you create new faces.

Nestling faces with the Inset Faces tool

The **Inset Faces** tool in Blender's **Edit Mode** helps you create insets or an inner face within a selected face of your mesh; it duplicates and shrinks the original face, resulting in a new face nestled within the existing one (*Figure 6.19*).

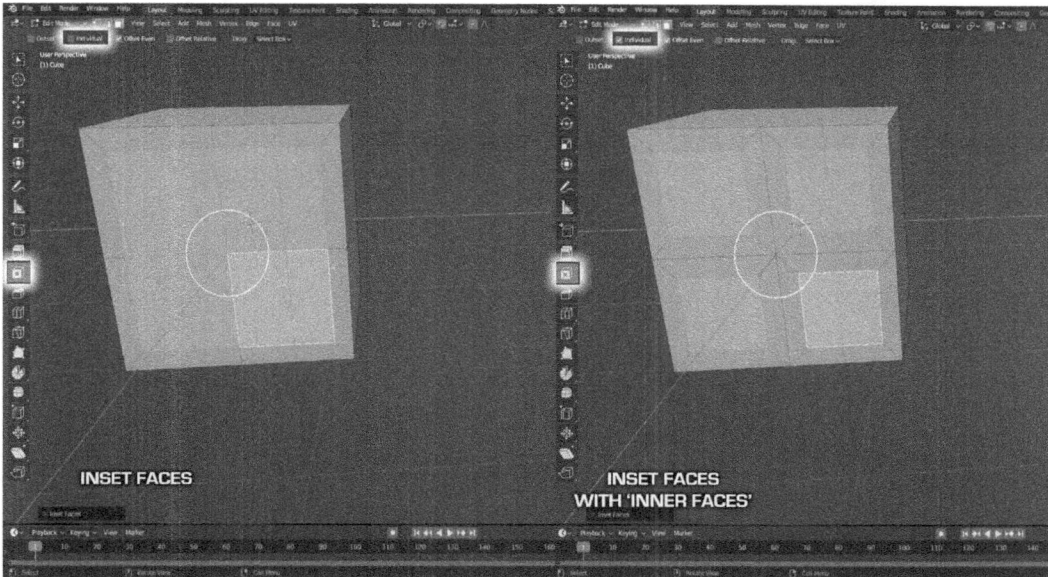

Figure 6.19: Inset Faces

Let's go through an example of using **Inset Faces**. Imagine you are building a window and you are in the process of grayboxing (i.e., blocking out the basic structure of your scene using Blender's default cubes with the default gray material to focus on layout and scale rather than detail), so your building is a simple cube:

1. Start by selecting the face where you want the window to be.
2. Activate the **Inset Faces** tool, either by clicking it on the toolbar or using the shortcut key *I*.
3. Click and drag to scale down the original face, forming a smaller, new face within the selected face.

This smaller, new face that you have just created is referred to as an inset. Essentially, an inset is a duplicate of the original face but scaled down and nested within it. You have now created an inset, and you can now manipulate it separately from the rest of the mesh.

To make an opening for the window within the wall itself, you can use the **Extrude Region** tool to push the newly created inset face into the cube and create a window-like hole in the geometry. If you are looking to create a raised detail, you can extrude the inset face outward (*Figure 6.20*).

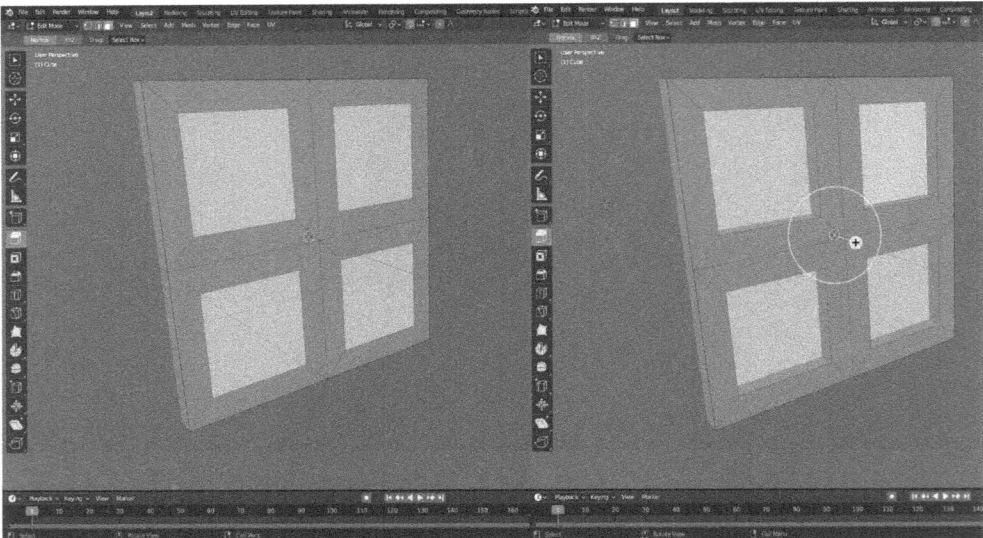

Figure 6.20: Extruding inset faces for raised detail

Another important feature of **Inset Faces** is its ability to inset multiple faces at the same time. If you press the *I* shortcut a second time, you will turn on the **Individual Faces** option, which will create an inset function for faces individually. This is especially useful if you are creating inset faces for multiple mesh faces at once, since it helps to save time because you can do it all through one action.

Note

Remember, the **Inset Faces** tool is dependent on the face selection mode. If you have selected multiple faces, all of them will be inset, forming multiple new faces at the same time. This is helpful if you want to create identical details on multiple sections of your model, such as the windows of a building or the scales of a creature.

Knowing how to create insets is part of the essential know-how every 3D modelling artist should have. Regardless of your artistic focus, whether that ranges somewhere between architectural design or organic forms, **Inset Faces** is undeniably useful. As we move on, it will become easier to imagine different 3D modelling scenarios to use your newly found knowledge.

Next, we will be discussing the **Bevel** tool.

Bevelling edges and controlling object sharpness

Most geometric shapes have sharp corners and edges. This is where the **Bevel** tool becomes handy. The **Bevel** tool helps you smooth out sharp edges and corners by creating additional geometry that forms a transition between faces. It adds a chamfer or rounded edge where two faces meet, making the model's edges appear more realistic and less sharp.

> **Note**
>
> Here is something that might surprise you: nothing in the real world has a perfectly sharp edge. Not even the sharpest kitchen knife. If you zoom in close enough, there is always a slight bevel or curve to it. Why does that matter in 3D? Adding a tiny bevel to your edges helps them catch the light more naturally when rendered. It is one of those subtle details that makes a big difference in how believable your models feel.

The best way to understand how the **Bevel** tool works is to go through a 3D modelling scenario. Let's say you are creating a simple table model. The edges of the table's surface are too sharp, and you want to soften them to give a more polished look, as shown in *Figure 6.21*.

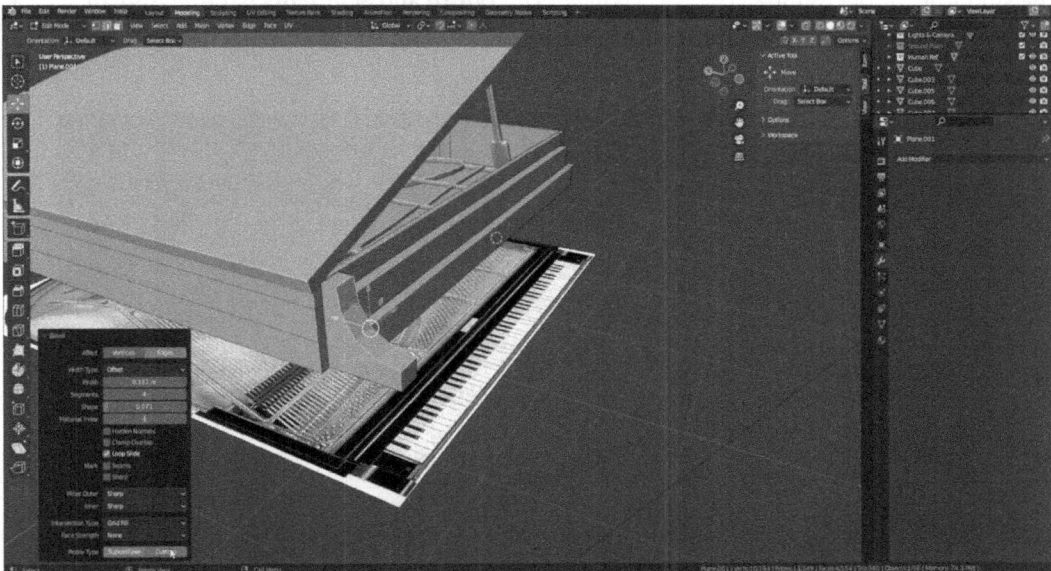

Figure 6.21: Beveled edges on a piano in "Blender 3 – Beginners Step-by-Step Guide to Isometric Rooms" by 3D Tudor

Here's how to make your piano's or any other 3D model's edges less sharp by bevelling them:

1. Select the edges you want to bevel. You can do this by entering **Edge Select** mode and clicking on the edges of the table surface.

2. Once you have selected the edges, activate the **Bevel** tool either by choosing it from the toolbar or by using the shortcut key *Ctrl + B*.

3. As you drag your cursor, you'll notice the selected edges start to split and round off, creating a bevelled, softer edge.

Note

Technically, whether you are using the **Bevel** toolbar version or the *Ctrl + B* shortcut, it is the same underlying tool, but the experience is not quite the same. When you use the **Bevel** tool from the toolbar, you need to click and drag the little handle in the **3D Viewport** to set the width and then adjust things such as segments and profile shape using the pop-up menu. It is functional, but not exactly the smoothest workflow.

You can control the amount of bevel by moving the mouse and adjusting the number of segments (i.e., levels) of the bevel by scrolling the mouse wheel up or down. The more segments you have, the smoother, more rounded the bevel will be. The **Width** and **Segments** parameters can also be adjusted from the operator panel that appears at the bottom left after using the tool, which you can see in *Figure 6.22*.

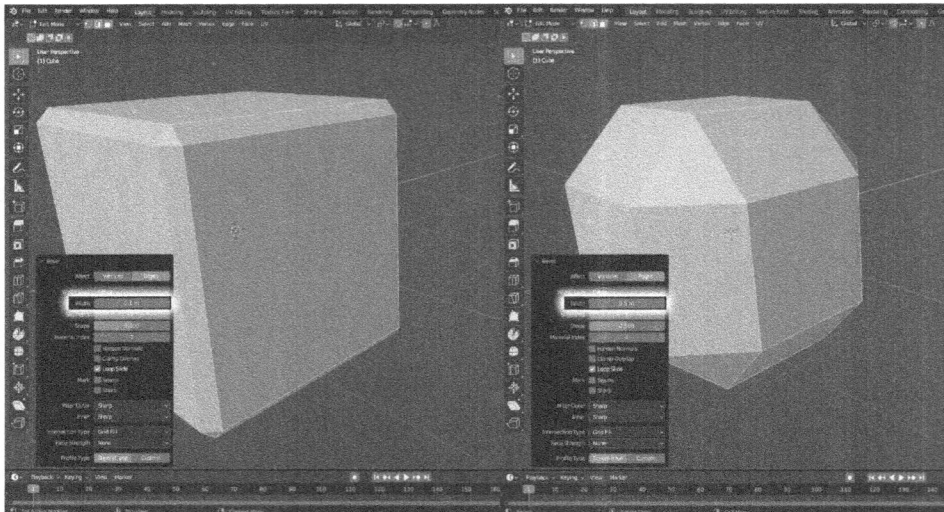

Figure 6.22: Bevel tool Width and Segments parameters

A single-segment bevel creates a chamfered edge, which might be useful for hard surface models such as machinery or furniture. A bevel with multiple segments creates a more rounded edge, often used for organic models or when a smoother transition is desired (see *Figure 6.23*).

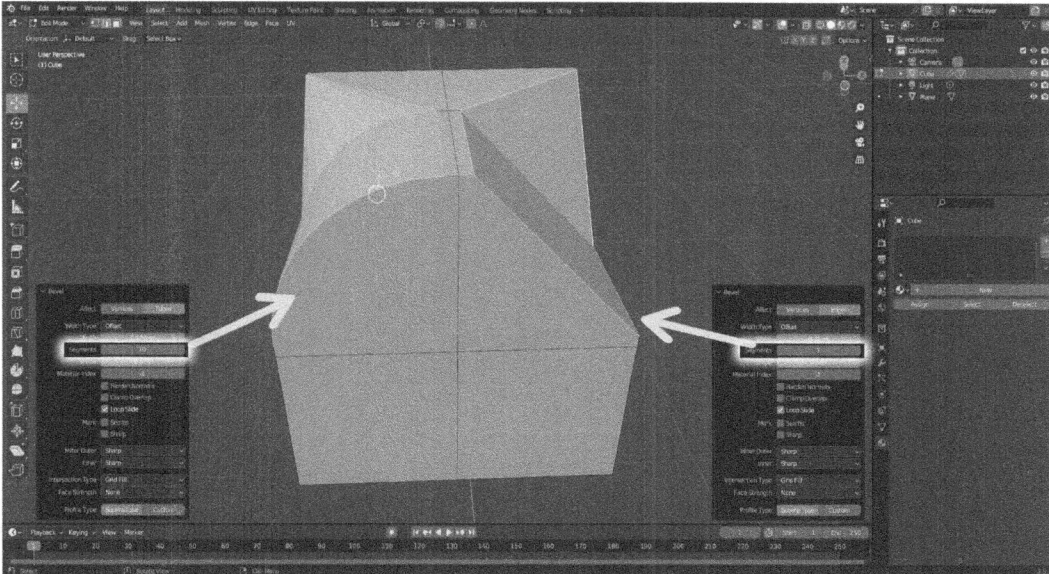

Figure 6.23: Single- versus multiple-segment bevels

This distinction happens because it adds more topology between bevelled areas, creating a smoother transition between the points.

The **Bevel** tool works with edges and vertices. Using the **Bevel** tool on a vertex creates a bevelled corner, smoothing out sharp points. This is because it tries to average out the vertices based on a corner angle and the default profile that the **Bevel** tool follows.

The **Bevel** tool is instrumental in giving your 3D models a more refined appearance. It helps you depart from the rigid and unrealistic sharpness associated with primitive shapes (i.e., the default shapes you bring in with Blender's **Add Object** tool). Bevelling helps you move toward models that feel more tangible and realistic. The **Bevel** tool is a powerful asset in your Blender toolset, and mastering it can significantly enhance the quality and realism of your 3D models.

In the next section, we will talk about how to increase the level of detail in your models with the help of the **Loop Cut** tool.

Maximising 3D model detail with Loop Cut

The **Loop Cut** tool is your answer to adding more detail to your 3D models. This is because it allows you to insert a continuous loop of edges, also referred to as an **Edge Loop**, into your mesh, subdividing the faces it passes through and increasing the level of detail in that area of the model (*Figure 6.24*).

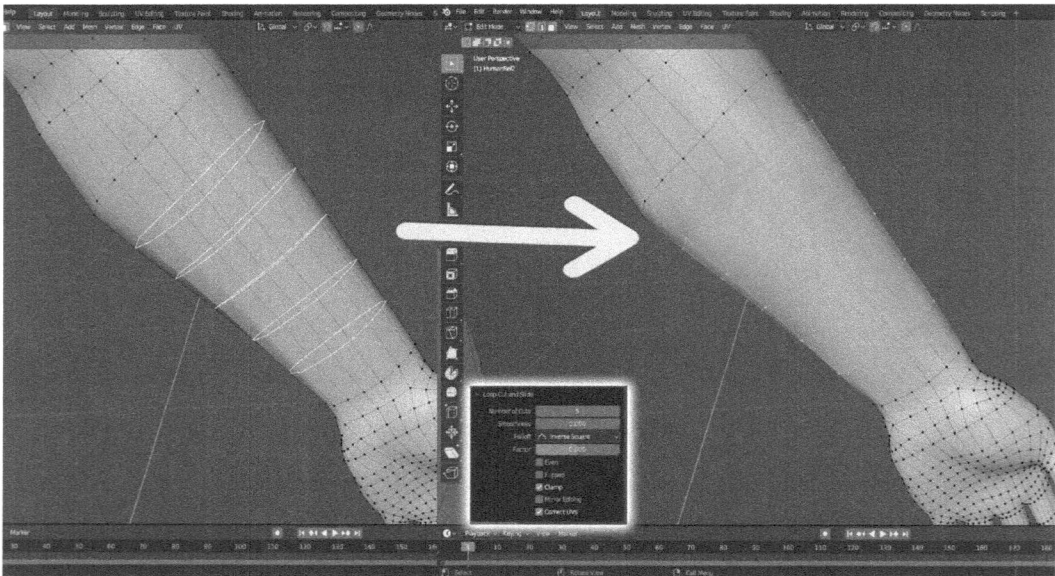

Figure 6.24: Loop cuts on a human arm model

A practical demonstration of the **Loop Cut** tool might involve the modelling of a simple character face. Imagine you have a basic head shape but need to add more detail to the eye region:

1. Start by selecting the **Loop Cut** tool from the toolbar, or by using the shortcut *Ctrl + R*.

2. When you hover your cursor over your mesh, Blender will highlight where the loop cut will be placed, usually following the flow of your geometry.

3. Move your cursor to the area around the eyes (i.e., where you wish to increase the level of detail).

4. *Left-click* to confirm the placement of the edge loop. At this point, you can still slide the new loop along the existing geometry by moving your mouse, as shown in *Figure 6.25*.

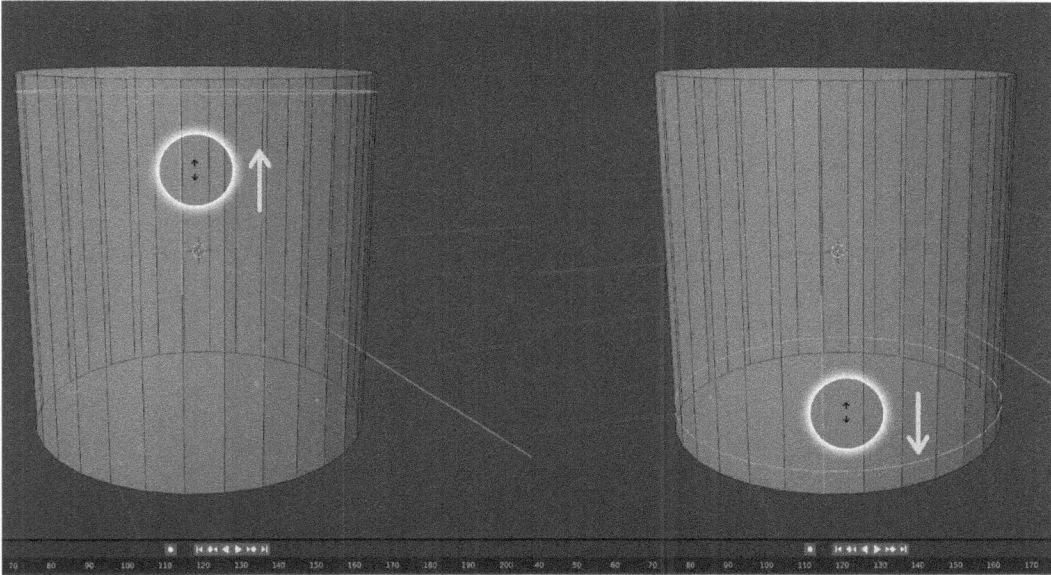

Figure 6.25: Sliding new loops along existing geometry

5. *Left-click* again to confirm the position or *right-click* to place the edge loop in the center.

The inserted edge loop has now increased the number of vertices, edges, and faces in the eye area, allowing you to further manipulate and refine the shape of the eyes. For example, you could now select individual vertices and move them to sculpt the individual eyelids.

Loop Cut also influences how a model is deformed by animations and how it looks when it is smoothed. Strategic placement of loop cuts can create sharp creases or folds, such as the corner of a mouth, or smooth bulges, such as muscles (*Figure 6.26*).

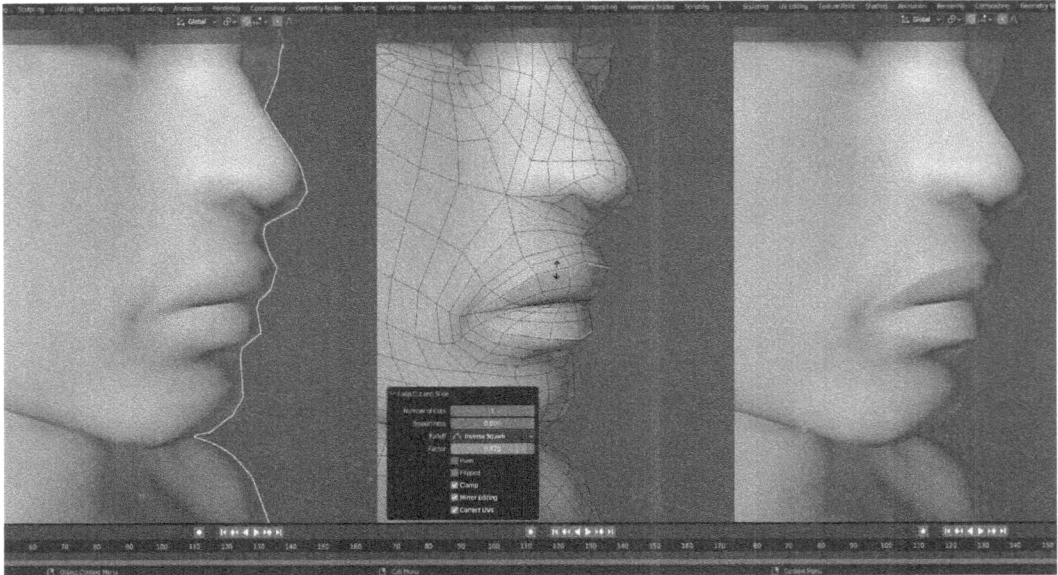

Figure 6.26: Using the Loop Cut tool for lip design

Adding more loop cuts effectively provides you with more clay to shape your model while keeping the overall form of the mesh intact.

Getting the hang of the **Loop Cut** tool is one of those core skills every Blender user should have under their belt. It gives you proper control over your topology, so your model does not just look good, but also behaves well if you ever need to animate it. Plus, it lets you add extra detail exactly where you need it, without messing up the rest of your mesh.

We will move on to discussing the **Knife** tool, which will be useful in different tasks, such as when you need to cut a mesh to fit something else within it.

Nip and tuck in Blender with the Knife tool

The **Knife** tool in Blender's **Edit Mode** is a versatile and precise feature that allows you to make custom cuts, creating new vertices, edges, and faces in your 3D model. Unlike the **Loop Cut** tool, which provides uniform cuts following the topology of your mesh, the **Knife** tool offers you full control over where and how you want to cut.

Chapter 6   197

For example, if you need to create a cutout of a logo from a plane and turn it into a 3D object, you can use the **Knife** tool to trace around a basic object to help you create a complex shape. To illustrate using the **Knife** tool in a real 3D modelling scenario, let's say you're sculpting a terrain model and want to carve a river path through it, as shown in *Figure 6.27*. Here's how to do it:

1. Activate the **Knife** tool from the toolbar or by pressing the *K* key.
2. Once the tool is active, you can start creating a custom cut by clicking on the mesh to define the start point of the cut.
3. Move your cursor across the mesh to the desired endpoint and click again.
4. A new edge is created between these two points, cutting through any faces in its path. You can add additional points to the cut by clicking on other parts of the mesh.
5. Press *Enter* to confirm the cut when you're finished.

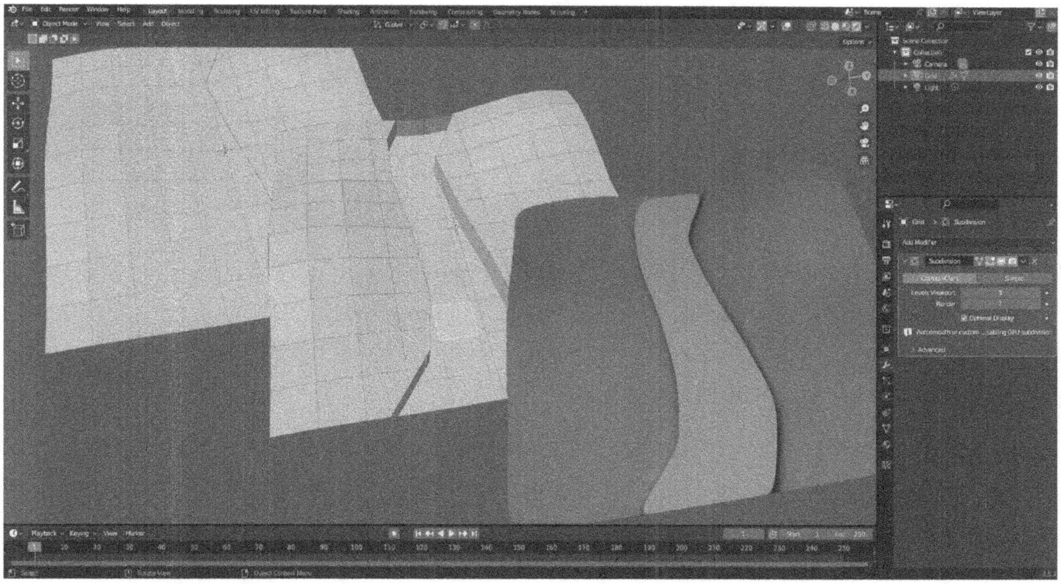

Figure 6.27: Using the Knife tool to carve out a river phase 1-3

Once the loop cut is in place and you have shaped out the river path, you can quickly select just the river section using *C* for **Circle Select**. This tool lets you paint over the faces you want to include, making it much faster than clicking each one individually. We already introduced **Circle Select** earlier, so if you have been following along, this part should feel pretty natural.

Knowing how to sculpt terrain and carve a river path through it is important because you can introduce small imperfections to your world and make it more realistic.

Tip

Here are some practical tips for using the **Knife** tool:

- Pressing *C* after activating the **Knife** tool allows the cut to slice through the entire model, not just the visible side, which can be particularly useful for creating symmetrical cuts or when working on complex models where certain areas are obscured.

- Pressing *A* after activating the **Knife** tool enables angle constraints, which can be handy if you want your cuts to be perfectly horizontal, vertical, or at a 45-degree angle, for example.

- Pressing the *right mouse button (RMB)* while using the **Knife** tool ends the continuation of your current cut, disconnecting it from the last point. This allows you to start a new, separate line from a different location, ideal for creating multiple distinct cuts in one operation. To complete the cut action, press *Enter*.

The **Knife** tool provides a powerful way to edit your meshes beyond the constraints of existing topology. It is like having a freehand tool in a drawing program but within a 3D modelling environment, making it a crucial feature in your Blender toolkit. This short introduction to using Blender's **Knife** tool is just the beginning.

In the next part of this chapter, you will find out how to use the **Poly Build** feature to create a low-poly (i.e., more optimized and more lightweight in terms of difficulty to load) version of your models.

Optimizing models for specific uses with Poly Build

Poly Build is a feature in Blender's **Edit Mode** that offers a quick and user-friendly way to create and adjust polygonal shapes. As you learn more about it, it will become essential to retopologizing your model or when you need to build geometry (e.g., in architectural design or terrain sculpting). This is because, in video games, you might end up using that same object a few thousand times, if not more, in just a single scene. Using **Poly Build**, you can make sure that you are effectively using your computer's resources to render a scene.

To showcase the utility of **Poly Build**, let's say you're retopologizing a character model. You have a high-poly sculpt and need to create a lower-poly version for efficient animation or game engine usage.

1. Start with a mesh in a scene that you want to create topology on.
2. Create a new cube object using the **Add Object** tool, and delete all of its faces except one, as seen in *Figure 6.28*.

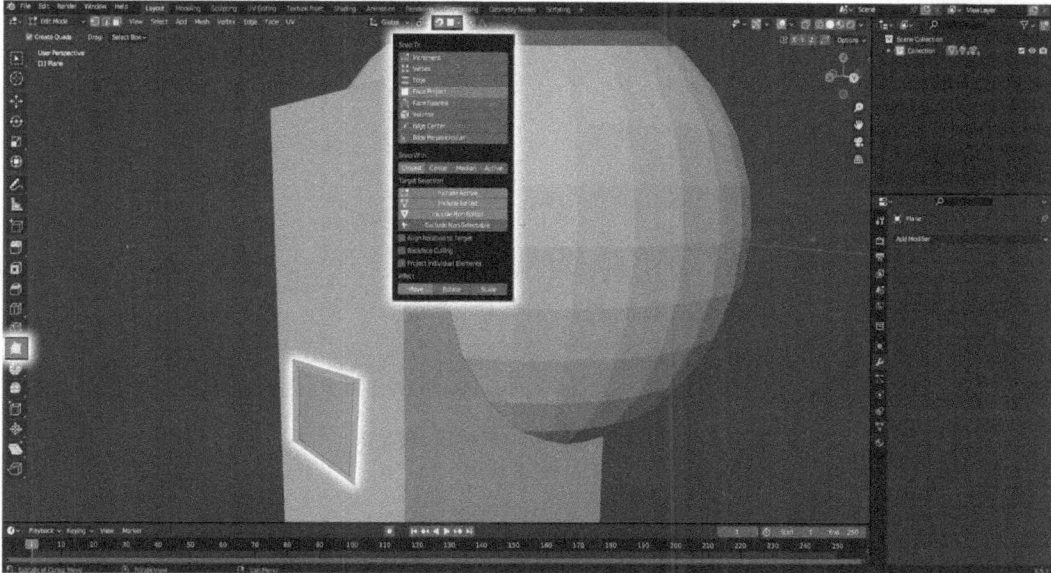

Figure 6.28: Finding the Poly Build tool

3. Switch to the **Poly Build** tool from the toolbar, or press the *Shift + Spacebar* keys and choose **Poly Build** from the pie menu. Then, enable **Snapping** and set it to **Surface** to ensure the tool interacts properly with existing geometry.

4. Hold down *Ctrl* while moving your mouse to show a new vertex being created from the already existing line, thereby creating a new triangle (*Figure 6.29*).

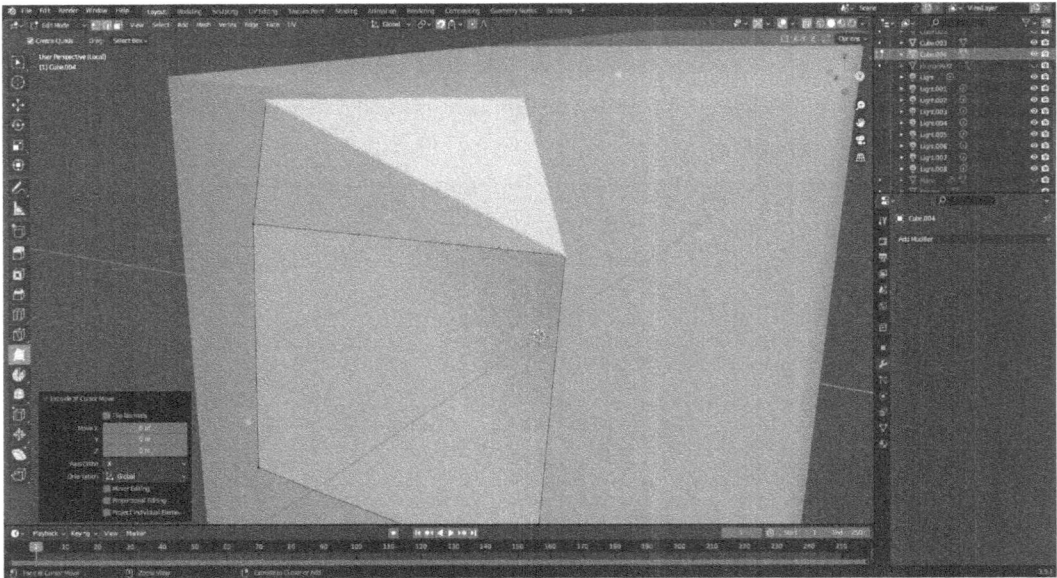

Figure 6.29: Using Poly Build in Blender

Tip

Use Blender's **X-Ray Mode** (*Alt + Z*) to see your topology from **Poly Build** better.

5. As you move the cursor around the **3D Viewport**, the new vertex of the triangle (the one not connected to any existing geometry) follows your cursor.

6. *Ctrl + clicking* again creates another triangle, connected to the one you just made. In this way, you can quickly draw the new, optimized topology over your high-poly model (*Figure 6.29*).

Note

Beyond creating new polygons, the **Poly Build** tool also provides easy ways to adjust existing topology. Simply clicking and dragging a vertex allows you to move it around. Enabling **Auto Merge** will help you use its retopology function properly. The default **Auto Merge** threshold is set low, but changing it to **0.03 m** will make it work better. This is, however, dependent on the scale of a mesh.

If you ever need to get rid of a vertex, just hold *Shift + click* on it: that will dissolve it and merge the surrounding triangles into a single face. It is a great trick when you are cleaning up a messy topology. Say you have a face that is breaking the edge flow: those kinds of areas can cause all sorts of weird artifacts when you animate. If your model is meant for animation, that is a big problem. By removing a rogue vertex, you make it way easier for Blender to follow a clean edge loop, which means smoother deformations and way less hassle down the line.

The **Poly Build** tool can seem a bit unconventional compared to other modelling tools, as it allows for a more freehand and fluid approach to creating geometry. However, with some practice, you will see that it is an invaluable resource for tasks such as retopology or any situation where you need to build up a mesh.

Our focus will now switch to another Blender tool, called the **Spin** tool. It is more specialized than the **Poly Build** tool and is primarily used for creating rotational symmetry.

Spinning your way through 3D design with Pivot Point

Blender has a unique and specialized tool for creating circular or spiral copies of your selected geometry around a **Pivot Point** (i.e., the **3D Cursor**). This is called the **Spin** tool and it is incredibly useful when you are designing models with rotational symmetry or need to create repeated elements around an axis, such as the petals of a flower or corners with complex topology, as shown in *Figure 6.30*.

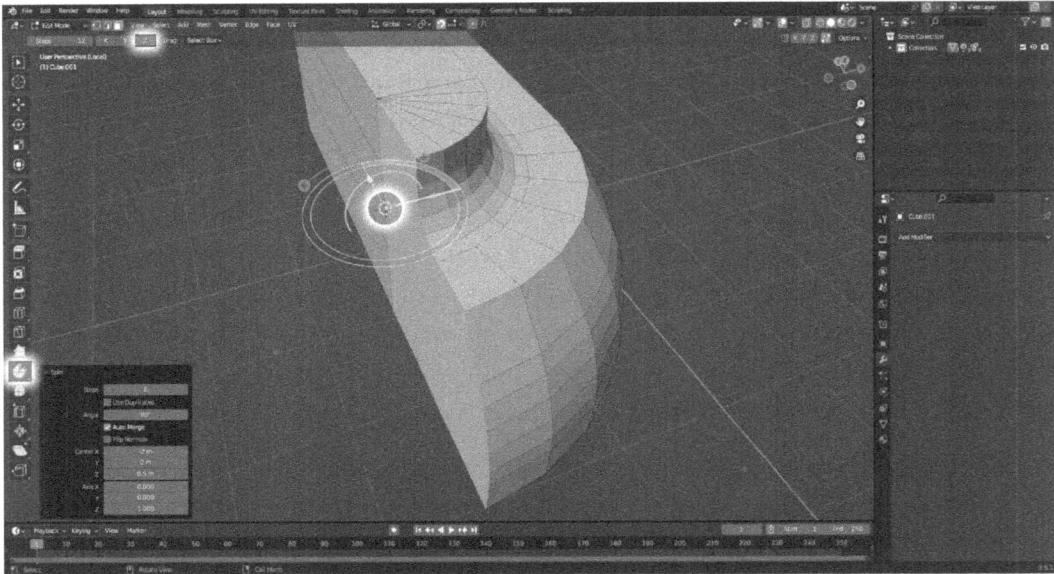

Figure 6.30: Finding the Spin tool

To illustrate using the **Spin** tool with a real 3D modelling example, imagine you're designing a classical column with fluted details, which are vertical grooves running along the length of the column.

1. First, you need to design a single flute.

2. Once that's done, select the entire geometry of the flute, then choose the **Spin** tool from the toolbar (see *Figure 6.30*), or press the *Alt + R* key.

3. When you activate the **Spin** tool, a gizmo will appear in the **3D Viewport**. The gizmo's origin is located at the **3D Cursor**, which defines the center of rotation.

4. On the gizmo, you'll see an arc that you can click and drag (*Figure 6.31*).

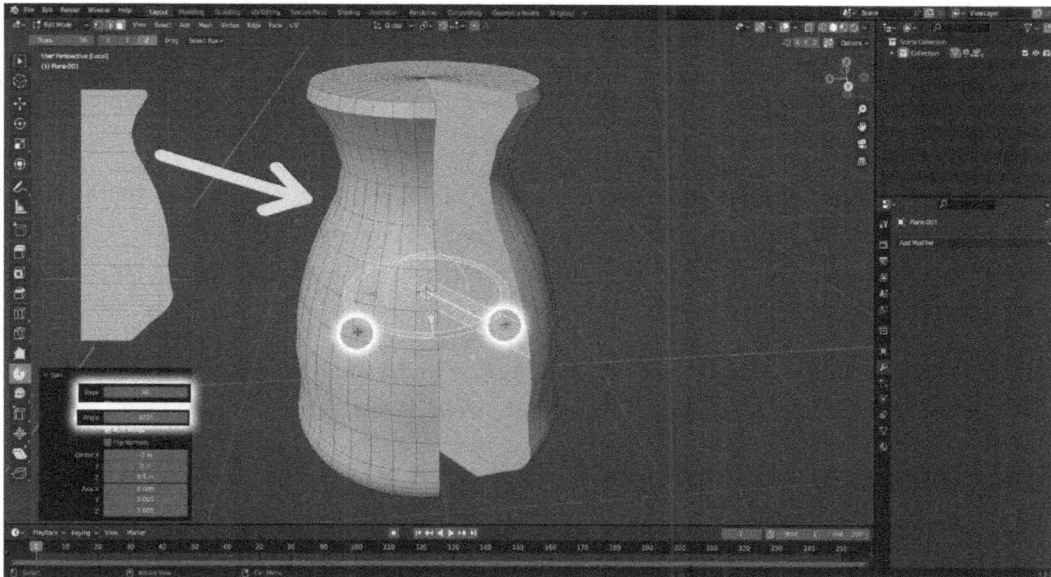

Figure 6.31: Using the Spin tool

5. As you drag, Blender will create copies of your selected geometry, rotating them around the **3D Cursor**.

6. You can also adjust the angle and number of copies directly in the operator panel or the bottom bar in the **3D Viewport**. In the end, you will come away with an easy way of creating corners or vase-like meshes.

7. If you are going for a full 360-degree spin in Blender, nice one! Just make sure you are in **Edit Mode** and using face selection. Here is the key part: as soon as the spin is done, get those original faces out of there. If you leave them in, you will get a tangled mess of overlapping geometry inside your mesh, like stuffing socks inside a teapot. No one wants that. Clean it up, and your model will thank you later!

> **Note**
>
> By default, the **Spin** tool operates on the Z axis. You can switch your view at the top left of the screen, as shown in *Figure 6.30*. You can also change the steps and the amount of topology the **Spin** tool will make use of using the options in the tab at the bottom left (see *Figure 6.31*).

The **Spin** tool is brilliant for stuff such as fluted columns. You can take one flute shape and spin it around the central axis of your column to get that nice, even detailing, without modelling each one by hand like a mad person. It saves loads of time and keeps everything perfectly symmetrical, which is a win-win in my book.

The **Spin** tool in Blender provides an efficient way to create complex, rotationally symmetrical objects or intricate details in your 3D models. This one's a bit of a workflow lifesaver. It cuts out the faff and gets you closer to what you actually want to build in Blender, faster, cleaner, and with way less frustration.

Your next chapter milestone will focus on helping you understand how and why to refine the surface appearance and smoothness of 3D models using the **Smooth** tool.

Smoothing out your presentation with Blender's Smooth tool

In **Edit Mode**, the **Smooth** tool serves as a way of giving your 3D models a smoother appearance by softening or averaging out the arrangement of selected vertices, resulting in a smoother appearance. The **Smooth** tool operates by adjusting each selected vertex's position so that it is more aligned with its immediate neighbours, which can be beneficial in numerous modelling scenarios, such as smoothing out a character's face to simplify its facial features or softening certain sharper features on an object.

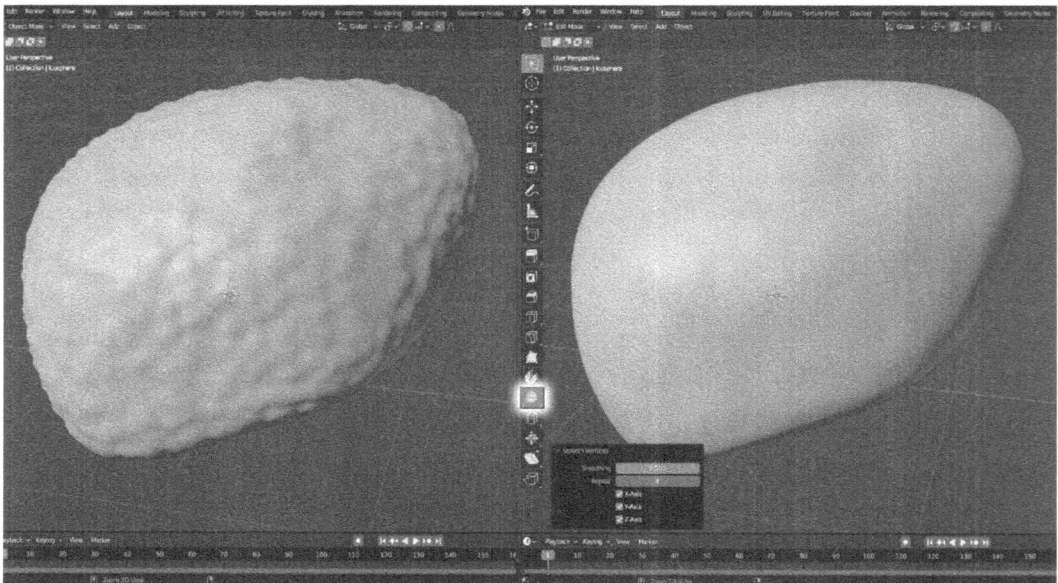

Figure 6.32: Rough versus smooth rocks using the Smooth tool

Consider a scenario where you have a rough, jagged 3D model of a rock, and you want to create a smoother version of it for a scene in the distance where details will not be prominent (*Figure 6.32*):

1. Activate the **Smooth** tool from the toolbar or use the *W* key and choose **Smooth** from the menu.

   Next, select the vertices you want to make smoother. This could be a specific region of the rock or the entire object.

2. Once you have your vertices selected, *left-click* and drag in the **3D Viewport**.

3. As you drag, the **Smooth** tool will begin averaging the positions of your selected vertices, moving them closer to their neighbours and smoothing out the geometry.

> Note
>
> You can control the intensity of the smoothing effect by how much you drag.

You can repeat the smoothing process several times until you achieve the desired level of smoothness. But be careful: overusing the **Smooth** tool can result in a loss of detail and might make your model look blob-like. It is best to use it sparingly or in combination with other tools to achieve the best results. Such tools could be the **Bevel** and **Extrude Region** tools, which will add topology and create new detail for your assets.

You can increase the **Smooth** tool value for smoothening above 1 by manually typing in the number yourself using the bottom-left corner. Please note that this will create more artifacts. To increase the smoothening result beyond a value of 1, use the **Repeat** tab slider (see *Figure 6.33*).

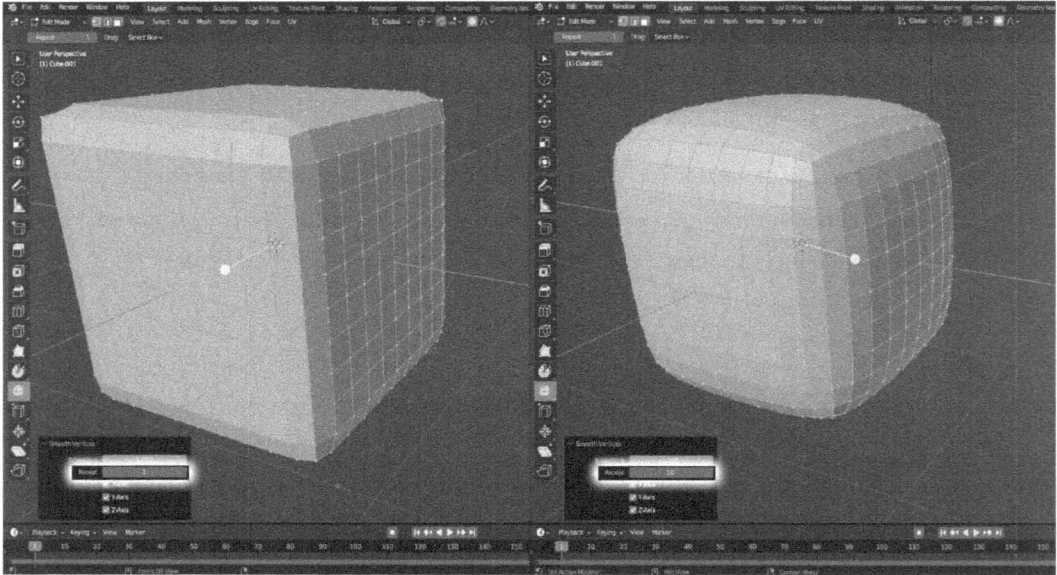

Figure 6.33: Manually altering smoothening

The **Smooth** tool is one of those underrated gems. It really shines when you are working on complex or organic models; it helps you tame any lumpiness and gives your mesh a much cleaner, more natural flow. Once you get the hang of it, it is a great way to polish things up and push your models that bit closer to realism.

Next up is the **Edge Slide** tool, and this one is all about finesse. Instead of just dragging an edge around and wrecking your topology, you can slide it neatly along the surface, keeping its shape and angle intact. It's super handy when you want to tweak edge placement without messing up the rest of your mesh.

Sliding edges to refine 3D model geometry

The **Edge Slide** tool is a highly beneficial feature in **Edit Mode** that lets you move edges along the surface of your mesh while keeping the existing topology intact. This is important because it will not affect the overall shape of a mesh and will instead conform to its volume. The **Edge Slide** tool is a fundamental part of a 3D modeller's toolkit as it aids in refining the shapes, contours, and overall geometry of the models without adding or deleting vertices, edges, or faces (*Figure 6.34*).

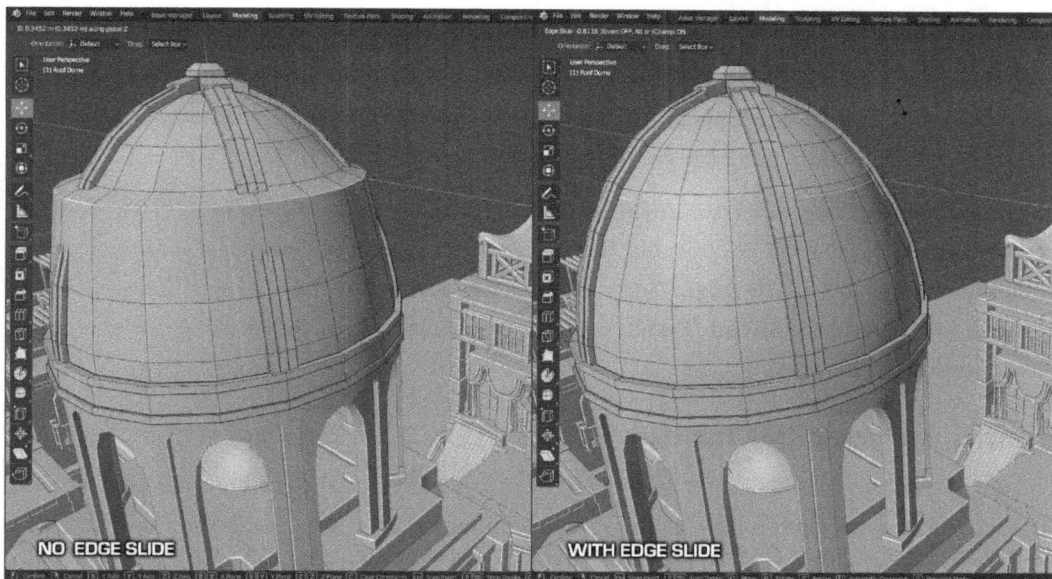

Figure 6.34: Highlighting Blender's Edge Slide tool functionality

For example, using the **Move** tool along the *Z* axis (by pressing *G*, then *Z*) on a curved roof, you will likely distort the mesh. But if you use **Edge Slide** (by pressing *G*, then *G*, and finally *Z*), the movement stays constrained to the mesh surface, preserving the shape without causing any distortion.

Now, imagine you are working on a character model and want to refine the shape of the character's nose:

1. Select the edge or edges that you want to adjust, then activate the **Edge Slide** tool from the toolbar, or by using the *G* shortcut followed by *G* again.

2. Once the tool is active, you can slide the selected edges back and forth along the adjacent faces' topology by moving your mouse.

3. The edges will remain on the surface of the model, allowing you to tweak the shape while preserving the existing structure of the mesh.

Another feature of the **Edge Slide** tool is that it allows you to create new geometry while sliding. Pressing *Ctrl* while sliding an edge snaps the motion in grid increments.

The **Edge Slide** tool is a cornerstone in 3D modelling, offering a simple yet powerful way to refine your models. Now, we will go over the **Shrink/Fatten** tool. Both tools are useful for controlling and refining edge loops. The **Edge Slide** tool helps you adjust the positioning and flow of edges within a loop, while the **Shrink/Fatten** tool can be used to adjust the thickness or size of the faces forming the loop.

Sizing up your 3D model

The **Shrink/Fatten** tool is like a volume dial for your mesh; it pushes or pulls selected vertices, edges, or faces along their normals. It's super useful when you want to bulk something up, thin it down, or add a bit of bumpy character to an otherwise flat surface. Whether you are thickening a plane or shaping out a chunky sci-fi panel, this tool does the job nicely.

Consider an example where you are shaping a character and wish to add volume to its belly.

After selecting the relevant vertices on the belly, activate the **Shrink/Fatten** tool from the toolbar, or use the shortcut *Alt* + *S* (i.e., the same shortcut we used with **Bevel**).

Once activated, moving your mouse cursor will inflate (i.e., fatten) or deflate (i.e., shrink) the selected region. This is achieved by moving the vertices along their normals: invisible lines that radiate out from the faces of the object.

What you can see in *Figure 6.35* is the result is an inflation or deflation effect, using what we said in step 1, depending on the direction you move your mouse:

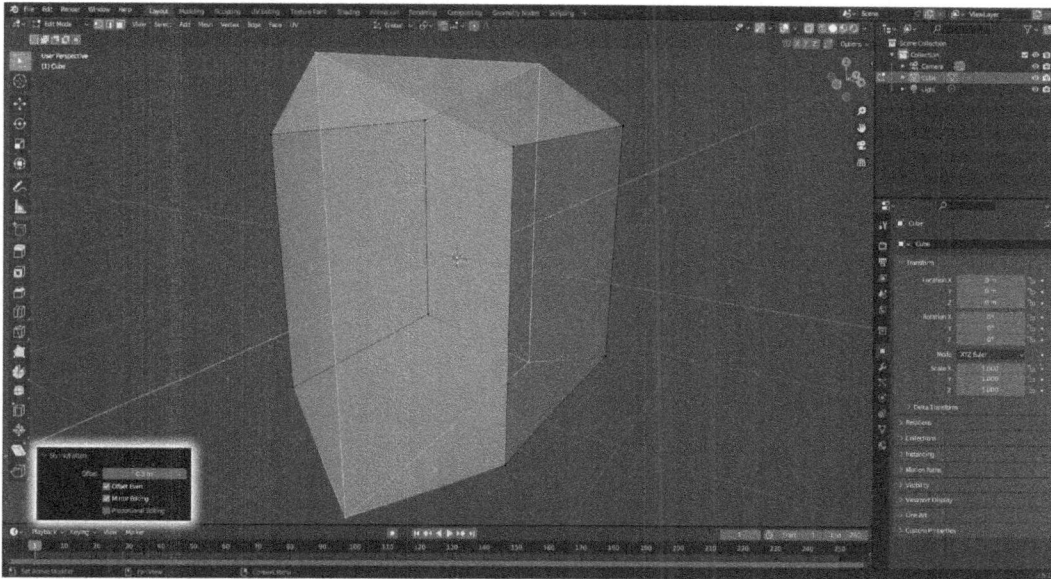

Figure 6.35: Operator panel containing Shrink/Fatten tool parameters

Tip

For more precision, look to the operator panel or bottom bar in the **3D Viewport** for the tool's parameters (*Figure 6.35*). Here, you can specify an exact distance to move the vertices, select **Offset Even** to maintain the volumes of the original shapes, or enable **Proportional Editing** to gradually influence nearby vertices.

Now, let us look at two different situations that warrant using **Offset Even** instead of **Proportional Editing** and vice versa. The **Offset Even** option can be useful in many cases, such as when you are adding thickness to a plane to create a basic wall structure. It ensures that the wall is equally thick in all parts, retaining the original face sizes and avoiding distortion, as shown in *Figure 6.36*.

*Figure 6.36: Using Offset Even in "Blender 3 to Unreal Engine 5 Dungeon Modular Kitbash"
by 3D Tudor*

On the other hand, leaving **Offset Even** off and turning **Proportional Editing** on can be handy when working on more organic forms, such as the character's belly. It results in a more gradual transition, giving the shape a natural-looking curve (*Figure 6.37*).

Figure 6.37: Using Offset Even with organic forms in Stylized Pig Farmer 3D Model by 3D Tudor

Offset adjusts how far faces are pushed along their normals. It's great for fine-tuning details such as coat thickness or surface depth.

The **Shrink/Fatten** tool is one of those underrated gems; it lets you scale things outward or inward based on their normals, which regular scaling just cannot do. It's super handy for all sorts of detailing. Now that we have got that covered, let us move on to the **Shear** tool and see what it brings to the table. While both tools allow for localized modifications, the **Shrink/Fatten** tool focuses on adjusting the thickness or size of selected faces, while the **Shear** tool focuses on deforming the geometry by skewing or tilting it along a specified axis.

Distorting objects with the Shear tool

The **Shear** tool is an often underutilized but incredibly handy feature that permits you to skew selected vertices, edges, or faces along a defined axis. It offers an alternative way of distorting an object, which can be particularly beneficial in situations such as creating slanted roofs (e.g., *Figure 6.38*), modelling italic text, or modifying the angle of an appendage on a character model.

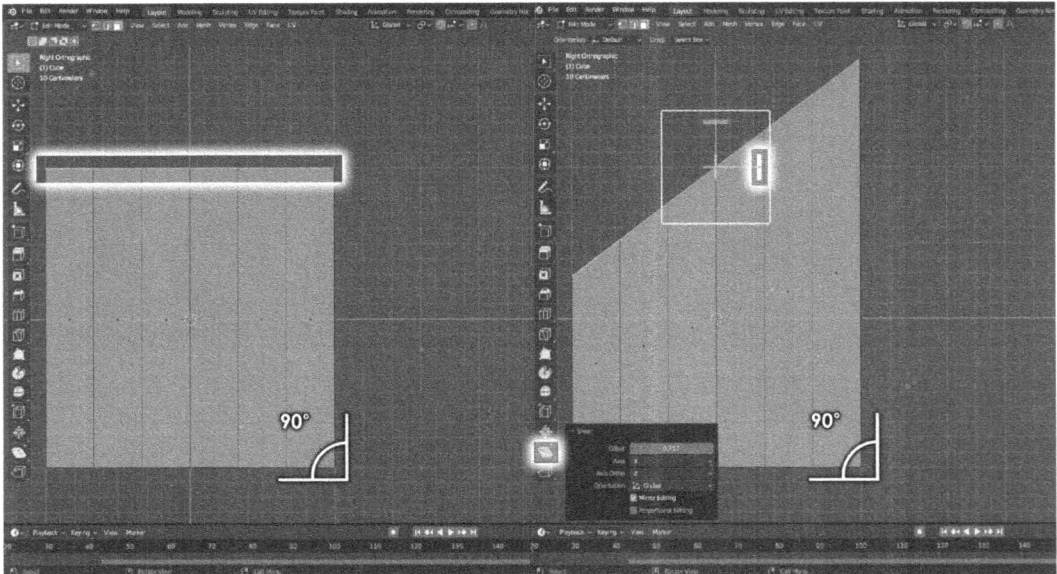

Figure 6.38: Creating slanted roofs with the Shear tool

To show you how to use the **Shear** tool, imagine modelling a house and you want to create a slanted roof. Use the following steps as a guide:

1. Begin by selecting the top edges of the walls where the roof will sit.

   Then, activate the **Shear** tool from the toolbar, or use the shortcut *Ctrl + Alt + Shift + S*.

   Note

   One thing to watch out for when using the **Shear** tool with the hotkey is that it kind of locks you into guessing the direction unless you constrain it to an axis, which can get fiddly. Honestly, I find the gizmo version from the **Tool Shelf** way more intuitive. You can actually see what is going on and control the direction properly without the guesswork.

2. Once the **Shear** tool is active, moving your mouse will start to shear or skew the selected edges. The direction and extent of the shearing depend on your mouse movement.

3. You can shear along the *X* or *Y* axis of the view by moving the mouse horizontally or vertically, respectively. Shearing the top edges of the house helps you create the slanted sides of the roof without having to manually adjust each vertex.

4. If you want the roof to have a specific angle, you can input the **Shear** value directly into the operator panel or the bottom bar in the **3D Viewport** (*Figure 6.39*).

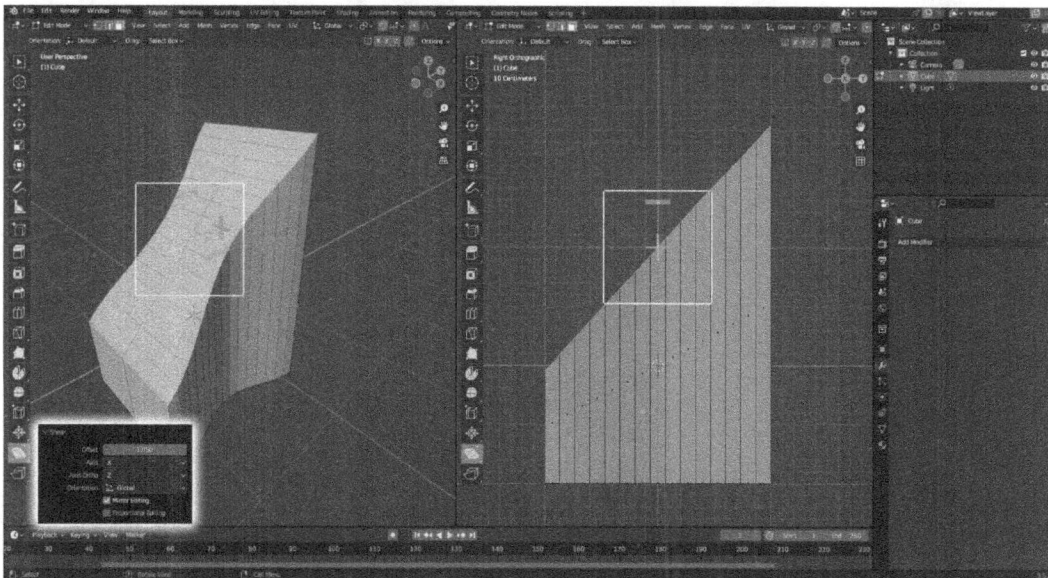

Figure 6.39: Creating roofs with specific angles using manual inputs

> 💡 **Tip**
>
> **Proportional Editing** can also be used with the **Shear** tool to affect nearby vertices and create a gradient of influence, which can yield more natural and smooth results.

The **Shear** tool, with its unique distortion capability, presents a fantastic way of manipulating your models. While it may not be used as frequently as other tools, understanding how to use it can greatly expand your modelling skills and help you navigate complex scenarios.

Before we move on, right next to the **Shear** tool in the toolbar, you will find another handy one called **To Sphere**, sometimes called *Spherify* if you are feeling fancy. You can get to it by clicking and holding on the **Shear** icon, or just hit *Ctrl + Shift + S*.

What it does is super straightforward but really useful; it reshapes your selection into a more circular or spherical form. As in *Figure 6.40*, it can take a flat chunk of geometry or part of a 3D object and smooth it out into a perfect ring or dome.

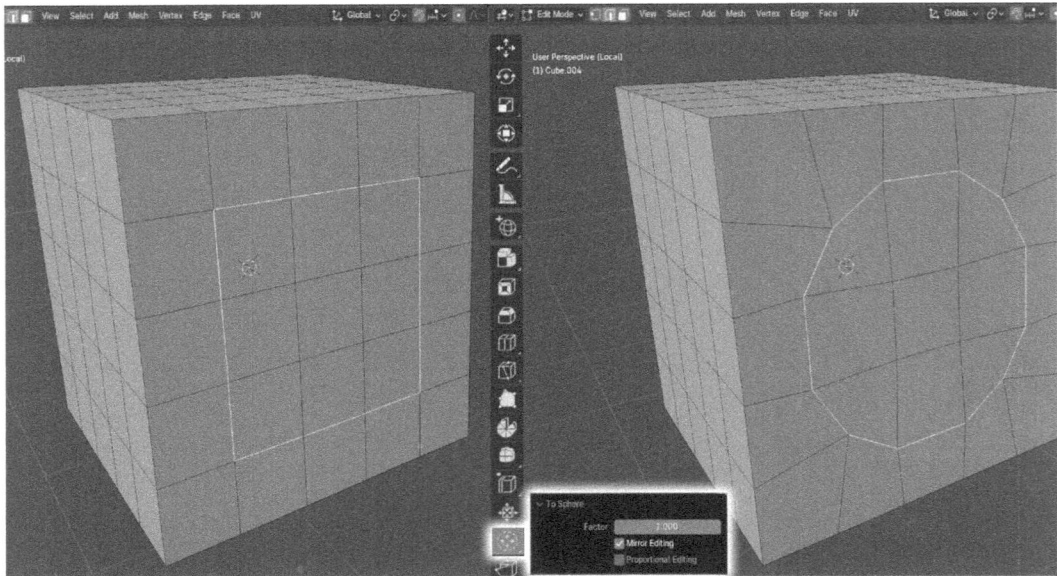

Figure 6.40: Using the To Sphere tool in Blender

On the left, a square face is selected on a subdivided cube. On the right, the **To Sphere** tool has been applied, transforming the face into a smooth, circular shape while maintaining an even edge flow, perfect for rounded features such as eyes or dials.

To Sphere is especially great when you are working on things such as eyeballs, buttons, or rounded panels, anywhere you need that clean, even edge flow to keep things looking polished.

As this chapter comes to an end, we will discuss the **Rip Region** tool.

Ripping your mesh in Blender

The **Rip Region** tool lets you separate a section of your mesh along selected edges, essentially ripping a region away from the rest of the model. This is especially useful in circumstances where you want to create a gap or split in your mesh, such as forming a mouth on a character's face, modelling torn fabric, or creating separate panels in a mechanical model (*Figure 6.41*).

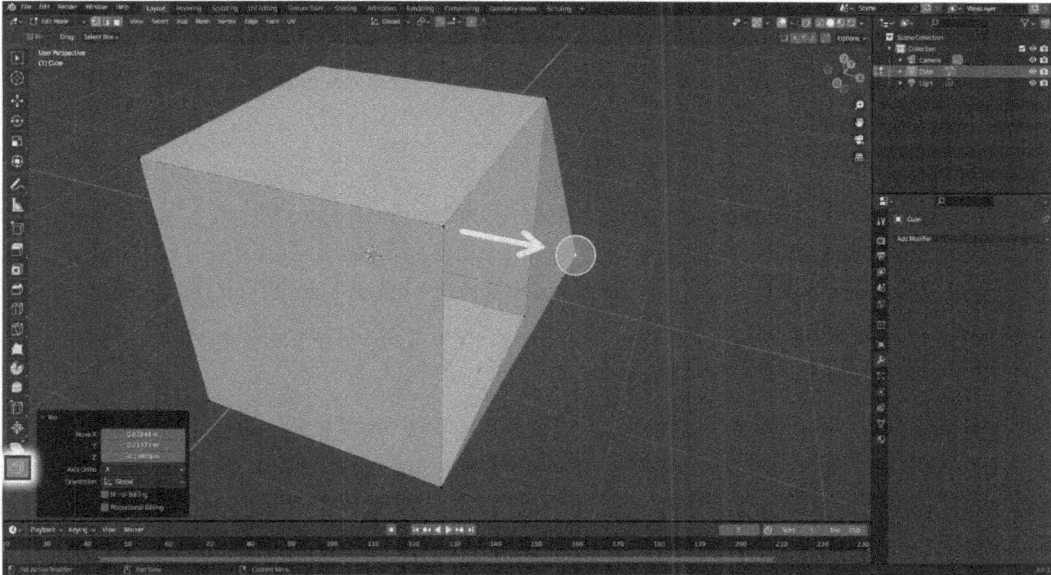

Figure 6.41: Using the Rip Region tool

Consider a situation where you are working on a character model and want to form the mouth.

1. First, select the edges that define where the mouth will be.

2. Next, activate the **Rip Region** tool from the toolbar, or use the shortcut *V*.

   After activating the tool, dragging your mouse will start to rip the selected region away from the rest of the mesh. The extent and direction of the ripping action are determined by your mouse movement.

   The result is a split or gap in your mesh where the mouth would be. This is a far more efficient and cleaner method compared to manually moving vertices to create a gap, especially for complex geometry.

3. Additionally, if you want to rip a single vertex or edge, you can use the **Rip** tool (*V*) instead of **Rip Region**. This will create a new vertex or edge and separate it from the original, allowing for further manipulation.

Tip

One thing to remember when using the **Rip Region** tool is that it creates additional geometry. Therefore, it is important to check your mesh after using the tool to ensure that it is still properly structured, especially if you plan on applying modifiers or texturing the mesh.

The **Rip Region** tool is a proper lifesaver when you need to break apart bits of your mesh cleanly. It is perfect for those times when just moving or scaling vertices is not cutting it. Think of it as your go-to when you need to peel geometry open without making a mess. It really shines when you start messing about with cloth sims too. You will see what I mean once you give it a go. It's definitely one to keep up your sleeve.

We have now concluded our detailed exploration of the **Tool Shelf** in Blender's **Edit Mode**. These tools, starting with simple vertex extrusions all the way through to shearing, spinning, and ripping, are the backbone of your modelling skillset. They are what you will rely on when it comes to creating detailed, refined, and professional-looking models. Once you get comfy navigating the **Tool Shelf**, you will start unlocking way more of what Blender has tucked away. It is like lifting the lid on a whole new level of control.

Summary

This chapter provided you with a toolkit to create, adjust, and refine your 3D models with the help of Blender's **Tool Shelf**, including a comprehensive overview of tools available in Blender's **Object Mode** and **Edit Mode**.

You will have come away with new knowledge about different ways of optimizing 3D assets and making 3D models look more realistic. The tools in **Edit Mode** are there to help you make changes to the individual vertices, edges, and faces of an object, offering high levels of control for detailed modelling. On the other hand, **Object Mode** tools will help you manipulate entire objects based on their position, rotation, scale, or relationships with other objects. Getting a solid grip on what both of Blender's modes can do really cranks up your efficiency and precision, whether you are modelling, building out full scenes, or even diving into animation. By now, you have the background knowledge you need to actually start creating. So take what you have learned, mess around with the tools, and start turning those ideas into proper 3D models. It's time to put it all into action!

The next part of your journey will be the start of *Chapter 7*, where you will explore advanced modelling tools such as the **Bridge** tool, learn about parenting hierarchies, and discover techniques for splitting and separating objects. It will also cover advanced smoothing methods, intricate vertex and edge manipulation, and geometry modification.

Further reading

- If you are looking to find out more about level design and creating a medieval dungeon in Blender and Unreal Engine 5, see *Blender 3 to Unreal Engine 5 Dungeon Modular Kitbash* (`https://www.udemy.com/course/blender-3-to-unreal-engine-5-kitbash/?referr alCode=3F43CC836F2DD9A7178D`).

- Should you want to practice using the **Annotate** tool more, *Build Stunning Medieval Worlds with UE5's Modular Kitbash* (`https://www.udemy.com/course/building-medieval-worlds-unreal-engine-5-modular-kitbash/?referralCode=F936D687808F3AE55AF2`) will be a good place for you to start because it relies on organizing space.

- If you want to start a project in interior design and give yourself the perfect project to practice using the **Measure** tool, see *Mastering the Art of Isometric Room Design in Blender 3* (`https://www.udemy.com/course/blender-3-mastering-the-art-of-isometric-room-design-in/?referralCode=663C5F3BD974A0124FB7`).

- If you want to apply what you have learned about the Bevel tool, a great place to start would be a piano such as the one found in *Blender 3 Beginners Step by Step Guide to Isometric Rooms* (`https://www.udemy.com/course/blender-3-beginners-step-by-step-guide-to-isometric-rooms/?referralCode=AB7E2519D26525F1320A`).

Subscribe to Game Dev Assembly!

We are excited to introduce **Game Dev Assembly**, our brand-new newsletter dedicated to everything game development. Whether you're coding, designing, animating, or managing a studio, we've got insights, trends, and expert advice to help you create, innovate, and thrive. Sign up now and get exciting benefits.

```
https://packt.link/gamedev-newsletter
```

Join the 3D Tudor Channel Discord Server!

Join the 3D Tudor Channel Discord Server, a creative hub for learning Blender, Unreal Engine, Substance Painter, and 3D modeling, for discussions with the authors and other readers:

```
https://discord.gg/5EkjT36vUj
```

7

Elevating Your Craft with Mid-Level Blender Modeling Techniques

Welcome to the crossroads between being a beginner and being an expert, where we begin to refine your 3D modeling skills together. Alright, so this is where things start getting interesting. We are past the stage of poking around with cubes and calling it a day. Now we are stepping into the fun middle ground between beginner and expert. If the last chapter was all about getting your feet wet, this one is where we roll up our sleeves and start digging into the proper tools that will actually make your models look good. Welcome to mid-level 3D modeling, where the real magic starts happening.

From dissecting geometry to simplifying meshes, this chapter will be a joy to read. We will cover how to use Blender's **Bridge** tool and learn more about filling faces using **Grid Fill**, **Beauty Fill**, and **Poke Faces**. You will also come to understand contextual subdivision, and you will find out about the practical reasons for you to use the **Triangulate** and **Tris to Quads** commands to convert your 3D meshes. We will also cover many other topics, such as the **Dissolve Faces** function, all the **Delete** functions available in Blender, and including but not limited to the process of rock and gear generation. Now, let us leave behind the entry-level landscape and begin refining your skills.

In this chapter, we will cover the following topics:

- Bridging gaps with Blender's Bridge tool
- Filling faces in Blender

- Subdividing mesh elements via the context menu
- Mastering mesh elements with triangulation and conversion
- Controlling surface appearance with smoothing or flattening
- Dissecting geometry using the Separate function
- Simplifying meshes with Dissolve Faces
- Refining meshes using Delete functions

Technical requirements

As for **Blender 4.5 LTS (Long-Term Support)**, the general requirements include a macOS 11.2 or newer (Apple Silicon supported natively) operating system, or a Linux (64-bit, glibc 2.28 or newer) operating system. Blender now requires a CPU with the SSE4.2 instruction set, at least 8 GB of RAM (32 GB recommended for heavy scenes), and a GPU supporting OpenGL 4.3 with a minimum of 2 GB of VRAM.

For a full list of technical requirements, please refer back to *Chapter 1* of this part.

Bridging gaps with Blender's Bridge tool

The **Bridge** tool does what it says on the tin: it connects two sets of elements (e.g., vertices, edges, or faces), so it can be used to fill gaps, join distinct parts, or form transitions in models. *Figure 7.1* shows the **Bridge** tool being used to create natural connections between two metal beams:

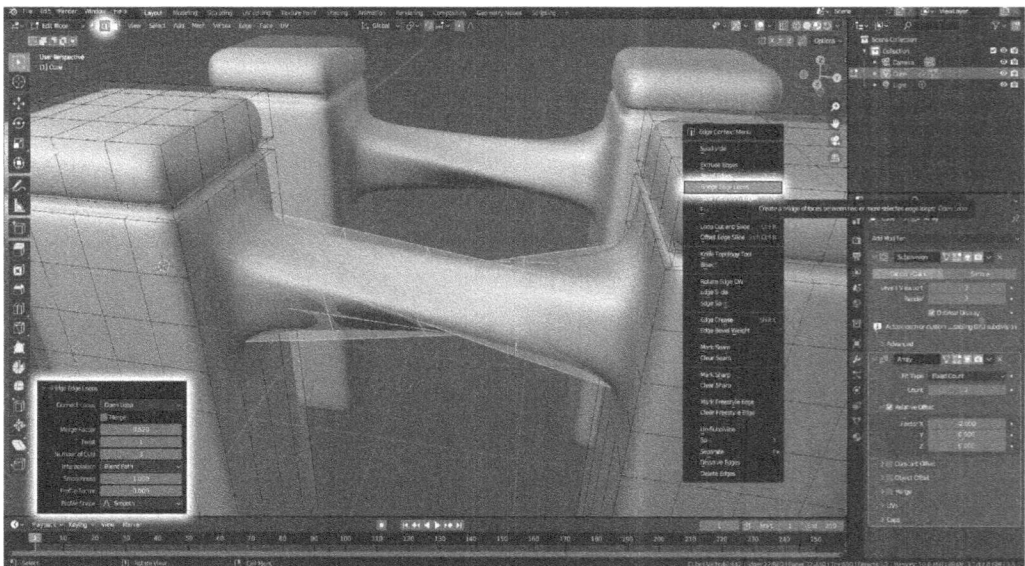

Figure 7.1: Connecting metal beams using the Bridge tool

It is useful because it allows us to make use of the **Subdivision** modifier, which averages out the vertices, thereby smoothing out the mesh.

How to access the Bridge tool

The **Bridge** tool is found in Blender's **Edit Mode**, under **Face**, which you can access by *right-clicking* while in face selection mode. Note that the **Bridge Faces** option will only appear once you have at least two separate faces selected, as shown in *Figure 7.2*:

Figure 7.2: Locating the Bridge tool

You can also access it by pressing *F3* and searching for Bridge Edge Loops, or *right-clicking* anywhere in your **3D Viewport** and selecting **Bridge Edge Loops** from the context menu.

How to use the Bridge tool and its features

To use the **Bridge** tool, follow these steps:

1. Select the two sets of elements (edges or faces) you want to bridge.

2. Access the **Bridge** tool using one of the methods mentioned in the previous section or *right-click* with faces selected.

The tool will automatically generate the needed connections between the selected elements. As you can see in the left part of *Figure 7.3*, we have selected two faces that do not touch. Then, in the middle part, we applied the bridge tool, and in the right part, we connected the edges based on our face selection. In this case, because our faces were made up of four edges each, this process created four new faces to connect the selection.

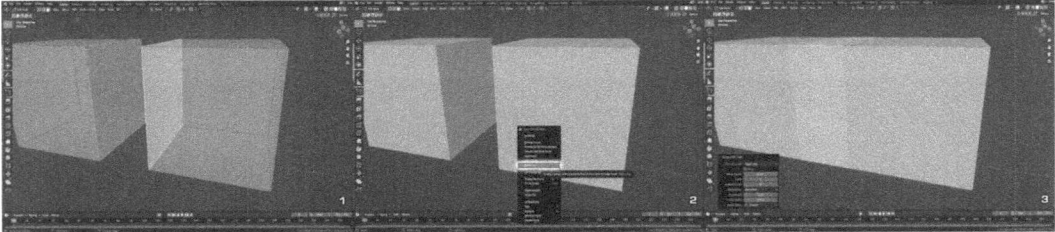

Figure 7.3: Using the Bridge tool in three steps

Note

If you want to bridge vertices, you need to select the two vertices you want to connect, *right-click*, and select **New Edge/Face from Vertices**.

3. Blender lets you specify the number of segments between the bridged elements, providing additional geometry for detailing through interpolation options, which we will go over in this chapter (*Figure 7.4*):

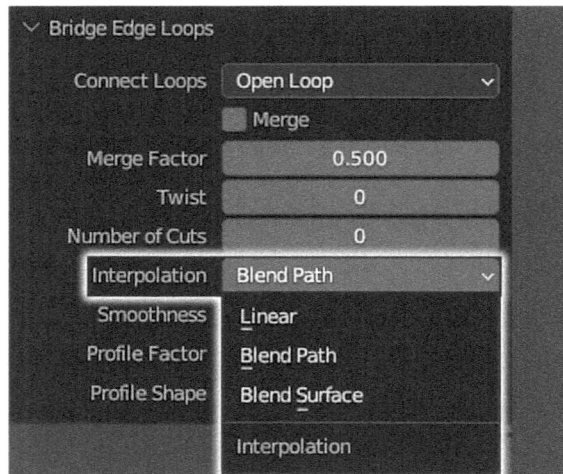

Figure 7.4: Interpolation sub-menu options

4. After you have used the **Bridge** tool, if the bridging result is not satisfactory, immediately tweak the parameters in the **Operator** panel (*Figure 7.5*). For example, increasing the **Number of Cuts** and **Smoothness** options would help to ease off a sharper angle connection. Forgetting about this step could lead to a lack of control over the connection.

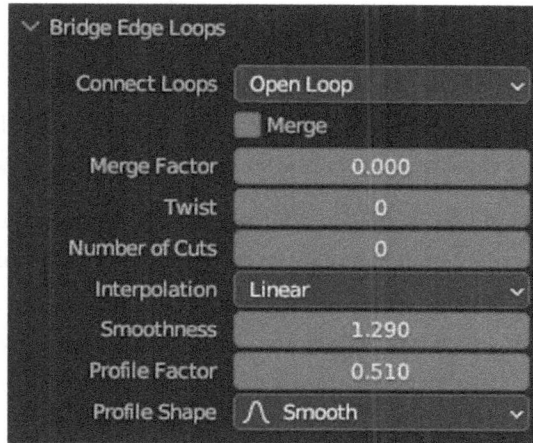

Figure 7.5: Tweaking Bridge tool parameters in the Operator panel

The **Bridge** tool is not just there to bridge gaps, it can also act as a way of enhancing the design of your model. A useful feature of the **Bridge** tool is **Bridge with Twist** (*Figure 7.6*).

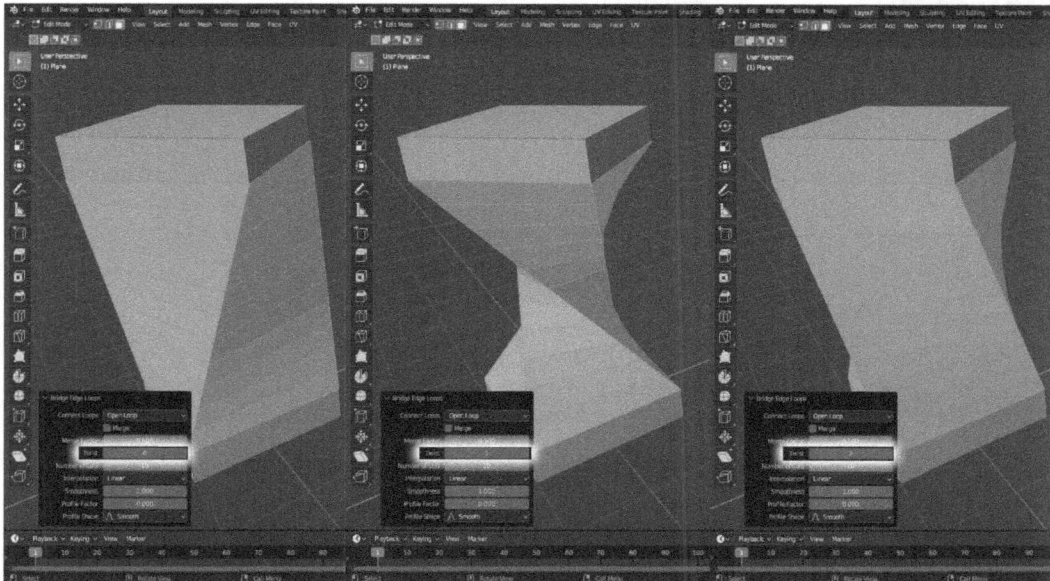

Figure 7.6: Illustrating the function of Bridge with Twist

This feature is useful for misaligned elements, adjusting connections to accommodate the misalignment. Misalignment can be a problem because vertices can connect in an unexpected way based on Blender's **Bridge** tool algorithm, creating mesh parts that overlap one another. Using **Bridge with Twist** can act as a solution because you can offset the connections to get the desired result.

Scenarios for when to use the Bridge tool

To understand the **Bridge** tool better, you need to consider practical examples of using it. The following list goes over the four most common uses for this tool:

- *Closing gaps*: Useful for sealing any unintended openings in a mesh, as discussed throughout this chapter section and as shown in *Figure 7.1*, for example.

- *Joining separate mesh parts*: An example would be bridging a character's torso to its lower body. In this situation, the **Bridge** tool is useful as it allows you to connect parts at the same time as controlling the interpolation between the shapes, giving you freedom over the form (*Figure 7.7*).

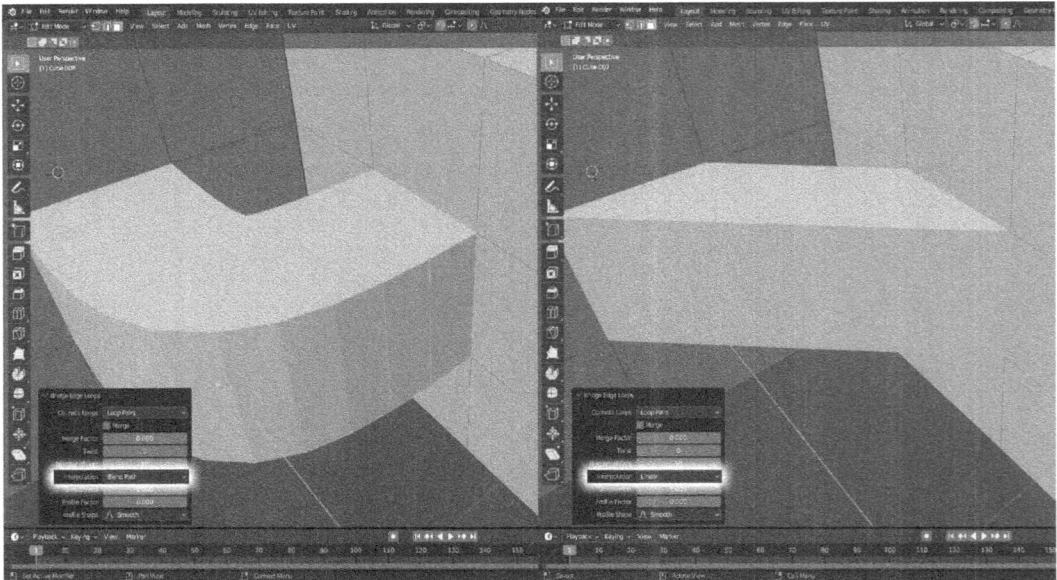

Figure 7.7: Using the Bridge tool to connect separate mesh parts

- *Adding details*: Bridging can help create features such as rings around cylindrical objects or details in architectural models, as shown in *Figure 7.8*.

Figure 7.8: Bridging in Creating a Modular Kitbash in Blender by 3D Tudor

- *Multi-element transitions*: Combining the bridging of vertices, edges, and faces in a model can lead to more complex and refined transitions. For example, you can create different architectural details for a building using the **Bridge** tool and object interactions, as shown in *Figure 7.9*.

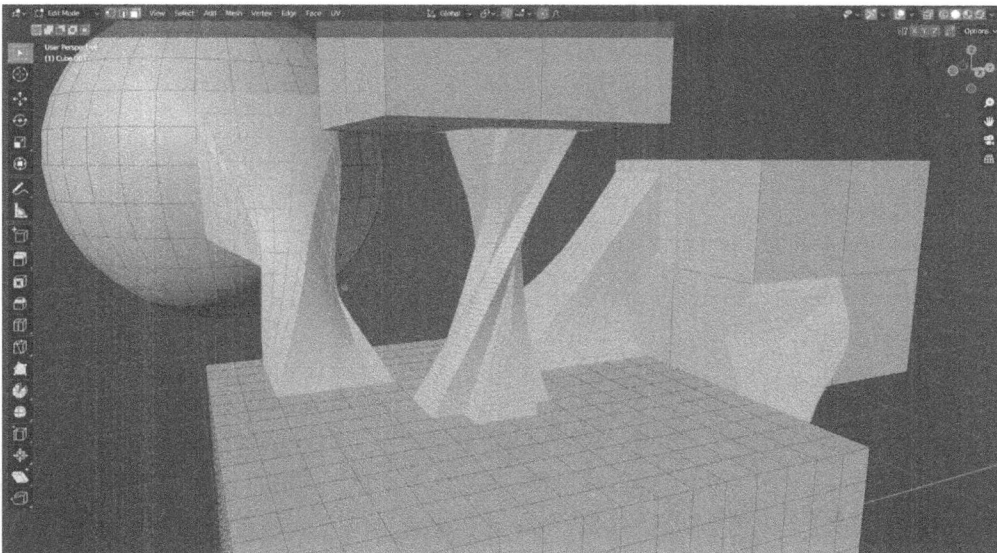

Figure 7.9: Creating Multi-element transitions with the Bridge tool

> Tip
>
> You need to match the count of vertices between two openings when you are using the **Bridge** tool. This is because your mesh is more likely to have **N-gons** (i.e., faces with more than four edges) or other artifacts if you do not. For a clean bridge, the selected elements should ideally have an equal count or can be interpolated cleanly.

Blender's **Bridge** function is more than just a tool to connect edge loops. Its flexibility in handling vertices, edges, and faces turns this tool into a Swiss Army knife for 3D modelers.

Like the **Bridge** tool, the **Filling Faces** tool is also made to help you 3D model with a focus on flexibility, allowing you to quickly close gaps in your mesh by creating faces between vertices and edges.

Filling Faces in Blender

Finding out about different techniques and tips for filling faces is part of the foundation you need as a 3D modeling artist. Whether you are building a basic shape, refining a 3D model, or adding final touches, you will need to know how to fill faces in a mesh. The different face-filling tools include **Basic Face Fill**, **Grid Fill**, **Beauty Fill**, and **Poke Faces**. Each of these tools has unique advantages and specific use cases, so the goal of this section will be to introduce you to them through practical examples and specialized scenarios.

Basic Face Fill

Basic Face Fill allows you to create a single face from a selection of vertices or edges. Its specific function makes it a quick and efficient method for closing gaps and creating a solid object, leading to it being the most commonly used 3D modeling tool for filling faces in Blender.

To use **Basic Face Fill**, follow the next steps:

1. Select the vertices or edges that define the boundary of the face you want to create while in **Edit Mode**.
2. Press *F*. This action will fill the space with a face.

Using **Basic Face Fill** saves time since, without it, you would need to manually create individual edges and vertices, or use more complex methods to accomplish the same task, which could be cumbersome and time-consuming.

The **Basic Face Fill** tool is useful for closing simple gaps. For example, if there's a hole in a mesh after deleting a face, you can use this tool to remedy the issue hassle-free.

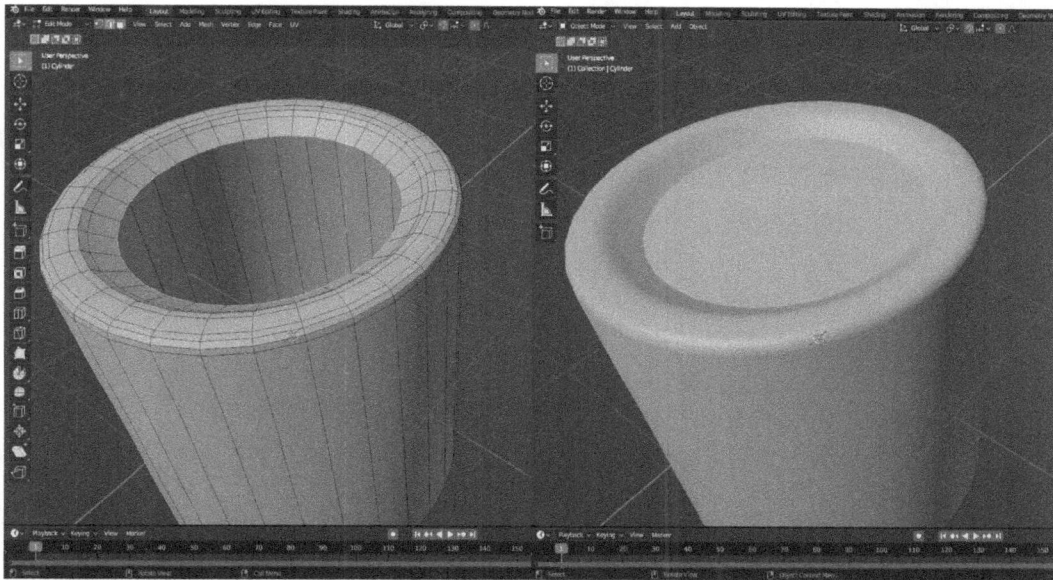

Figure 7.10: Using Basic Face Fill before (left) and after (right)

Basic Face Fill is also good for starting a flat base for you to 3D model on, such as the base of a cup, by selecting the boundary vertices and filling them, as shown in *Figure 7.10*.

Grid Fill

Here is a little gem I wish someone had explained to me sooner: **Grid Fill**. If you have got a circular hole in your mesh or two edge loops staring at each other awkwardly like they are at a school disco, this tool steps in like a geometry dance coordinator. It fills the gap with all-quad faces and lays them out in a tidy grid pattern, assuming you have got a nice even number of verts to work with. It's super handy when you are after a clean topology without wrestling the **Knife** tool for hours. Trust me, once you start using it, you will wonder why you ever did it the hard way.

To access the tool, press *F3* to access the menu and search for **Grid Fill**. Alternatively, press *Ctrl + F* and select **Grid Fill** from the menu.

To use the **Grid Fill** tool, follow the next steps:

1. Select two opposing edge loops.

2. Then press *Ctrl + F* to bring up the **Faces** menu and select **Grid Fill** (*Figure 7.11*).

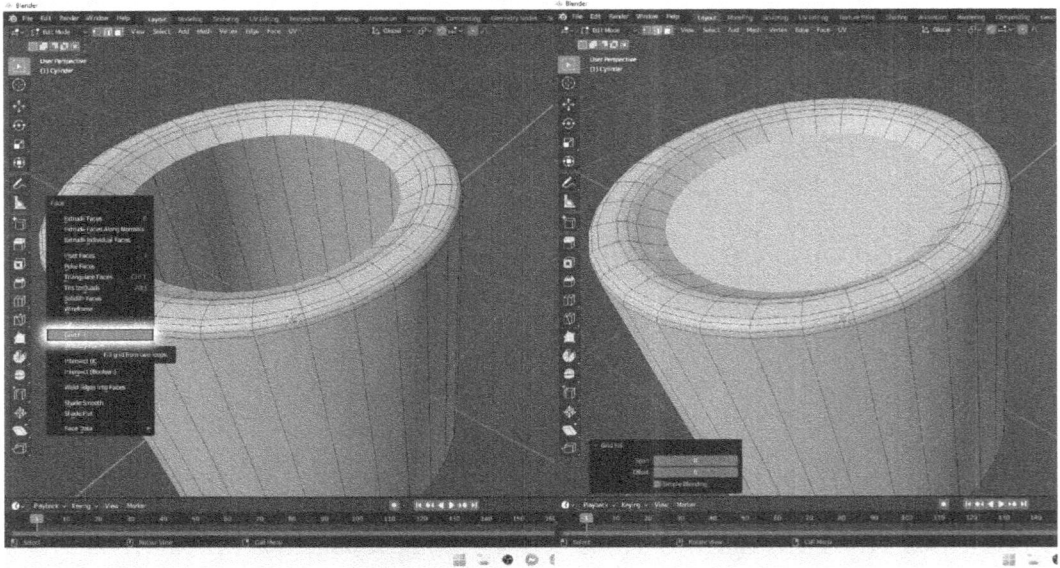

Figure 7.11: Using Grid Fill

Using **Grid Fill**, you can turn a loop into a grid of faces. For example, if you are modelling a spaceship with a cylindrical fuselage, **Grid Fill** can efficiently fill the space between the top and bottom edges of the cylinder with a grid of faces.

The **Grid Tool** will be useful if you are 3D modeling a cylinder or tube and intend to keep one of its ends open, such as with a telescope lens (*Figure 7.12*).

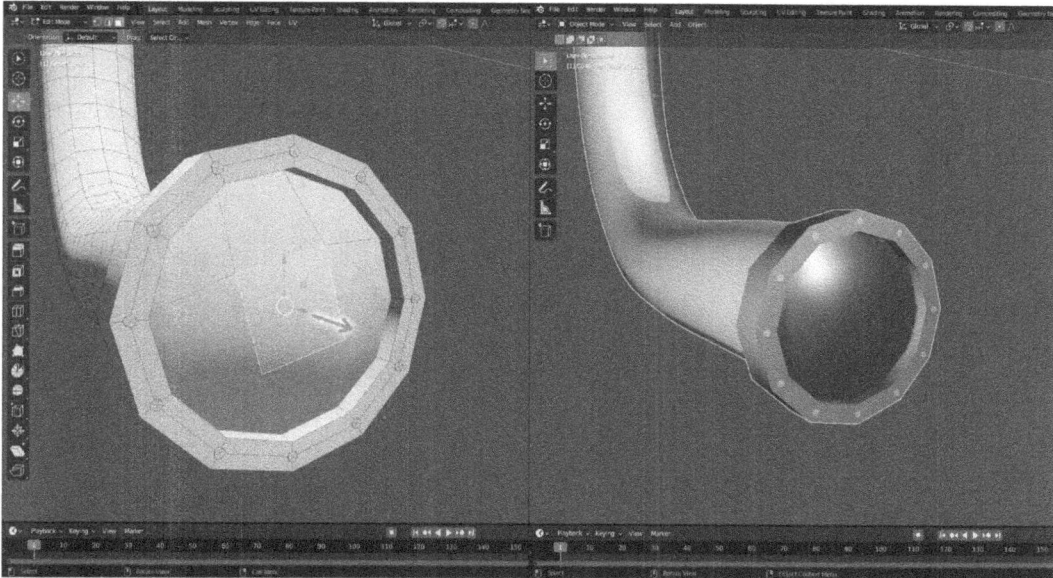

Figure 7.12: Using Grid Fill for a telescopic lens

In this scenario, **Grid Fill** will allow you to make a neat grid pattern close to it.

Note

For **Grid Fill** to work correctly, the selected edges usually need to form two loops with a similar number of vertices. If the edge counts are too uneven or if the selection does not clearly define a fillable region, the tool may fail or produce distorted geometry. It works best when the geometry forms a clean ring or gap that Blender can logically bridge with quad topology.

Likewise, **Grid Fill** is also ideal for irregularly shaped gaps, such as models of vents (*Figure 7.13*).

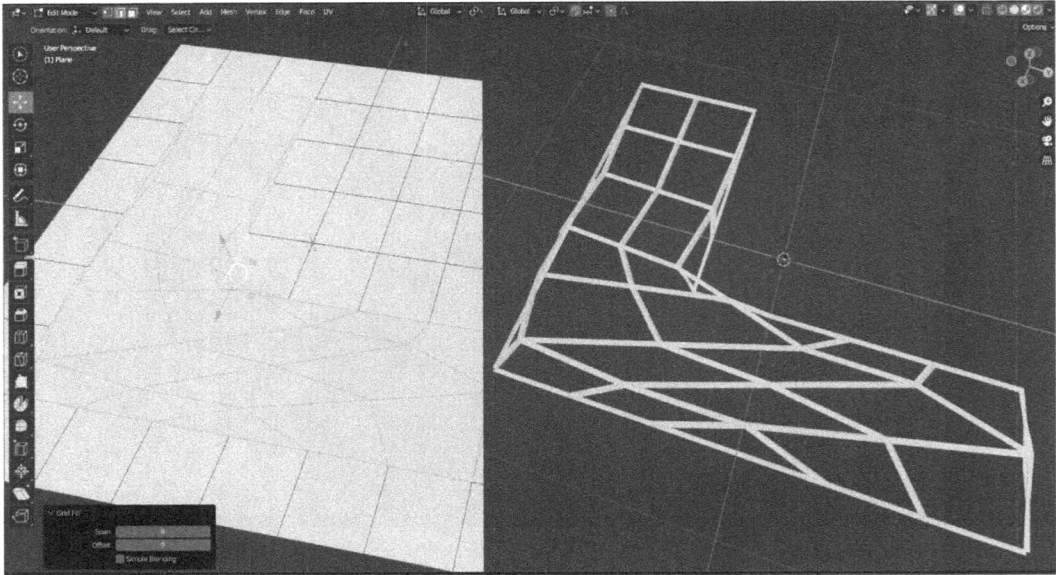

Figure 7.13: Using Grid Fill for models with irregularly shaped gaps

Beauty Fill

Blender also comes with tools that help you fill faces in a way that makes your model more manageable to work with. One such tool is **Beauty Fill**, which you can use to rearrange the resulting triangles from a fill operation into a cleaner, more aesthetically pleasing layout. Unlike **Grid Fill**, which creates quads when possible, **Beauty Fill** only produces triangles, but arranges them in a more visually organized and topology-friendly way.

By clicking *Alt + F*, you will access the fill functionalities. By default, it should have the option checked. To check whether the **Beauty Fill** functionality is being used, after using *Alt + F*, you should be able to find the **Beauty** option in the bottom left-hand corner of your **3D Viewport**.

To use **Beauty Fill**, you must be in **Edit Mode**:

1. First of all, select the faces you wish to convert.
2. Press *Alt + F* and your existing triangles will be rearranged into quads.

Rearranging existing triangles using **Beauty Fill** is helpful because it distributes them into a more evenly spaced, quad-like configuration.

Now, technically, it is still triangulated under the hood, but using **Grid Fill** gives you a much cleaner layout. What that means in practice is you are not left with those awkward, stretched-out triangles that make your mesh look like it has been through a blender, and not the good kind. It keeps things neat and avoids a load of mess when it finally comes time to triangulate properly. Just have a look at *Figure 7.14* and you will see exactly what I mean:

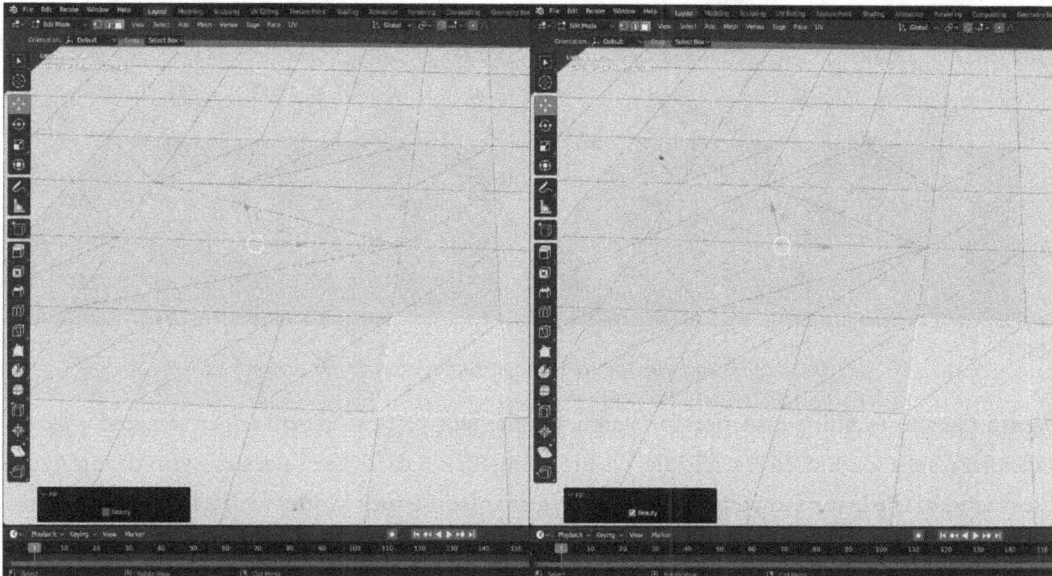

Figure 7.14: Using Beauty Fill for mesh rearrangement before (left) and after (right)

Note

Having triangles that are too long after mesh triangulation can cause problems down the line when we are moving individual vertices because mesh edges will struggle to follow the flow of the mesh itself.

To understand the purpose of **Beauty Fill** better, follow along with our next procedural illustration.

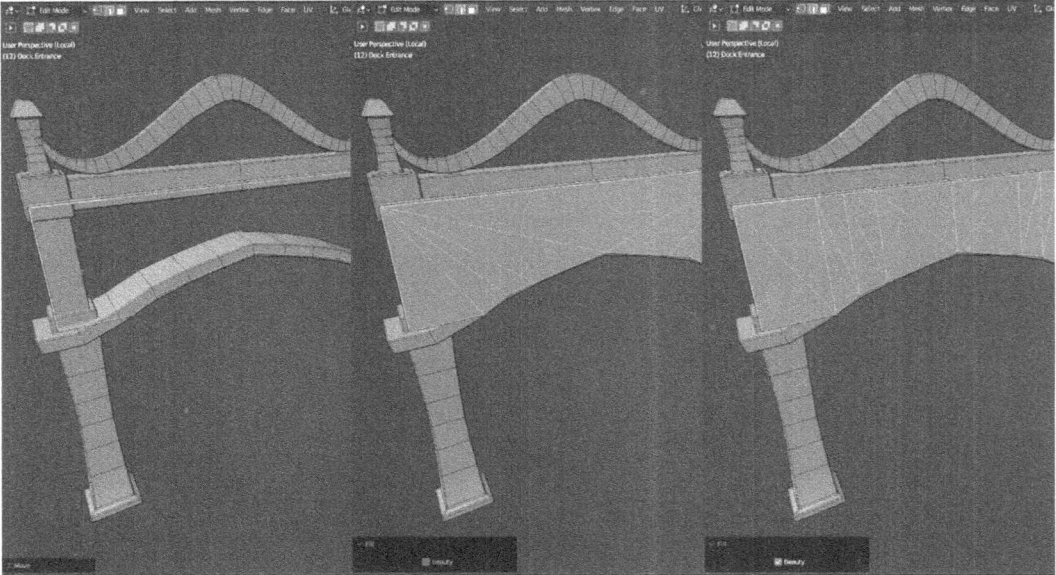

Figure 7.15: Using the Beauty Fill tool step by step on ornate arches

Figure 7.15 shows filling a section for a sign. On the left, you can see all edges selected with no faces for a sign section. In the middle, we are using *Alt* + *F* to fill the selection with triangulated faces, and in the last part, you can see we have enabled **Beauty Mode**, which better distributes those triangles.

One of the best areas to use **Beauty Fill** with is character and organic shape modeling. By rearranging triangles into quads in this context, you are setting up triangles into more manageable chunks. This is good because you can manipulate them better, especially if their shape is organic.

Poke Faces

So far, we have discussed filling faces for basic models, specific parts, characters, and organic shapes. The final way to fill faces that we will discuss is most useful for larger faces and for adding decorative elements. **Poke Faces** converts a quad or N-gon into triangles by adding a vertex in the center and connecting it to every corner.

To access **Poke Faces**, you can search for it by pressing *F3* and searching the menu for **Poke Faces**. Alternatively, you can click *Ctrl + F* and select **Poke Faces** on a newly opened tab.

To use the **Poke Faces** tool, follow the next steps:

1. Select the faces you wish to poke.

2. Press *Ctrl + F* and choose **Poke Faces**, or simply *right-click* in face selection mode to access the same menu.

Practical uses for the **Poke Faces** tool include scenarios where a model can be improved by adding additional geometry in the center of a large face. This is because when you use **Poke Faces**, you are creating a vertex at the center of each polygon, which can then be modified further (*Figure 7.16*).

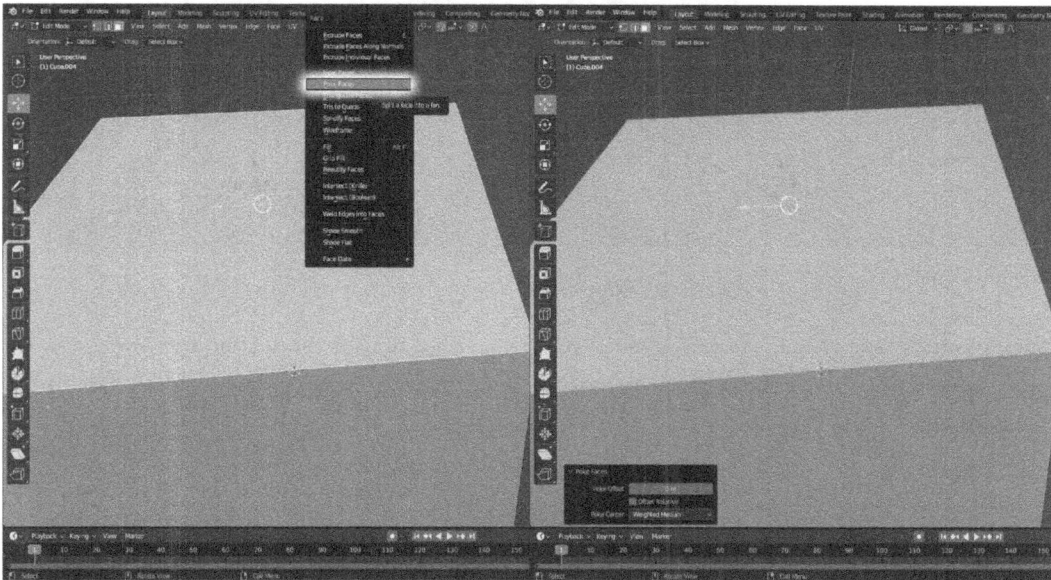

Figure 7.16: Using Poke Faces

As you can see in *Figure 7.17*, we used those points with **Vertex Beveling** (*Ctrl + Shift + B*) and **Extraction** (*E*) to create cylindrical extrusions from an object.

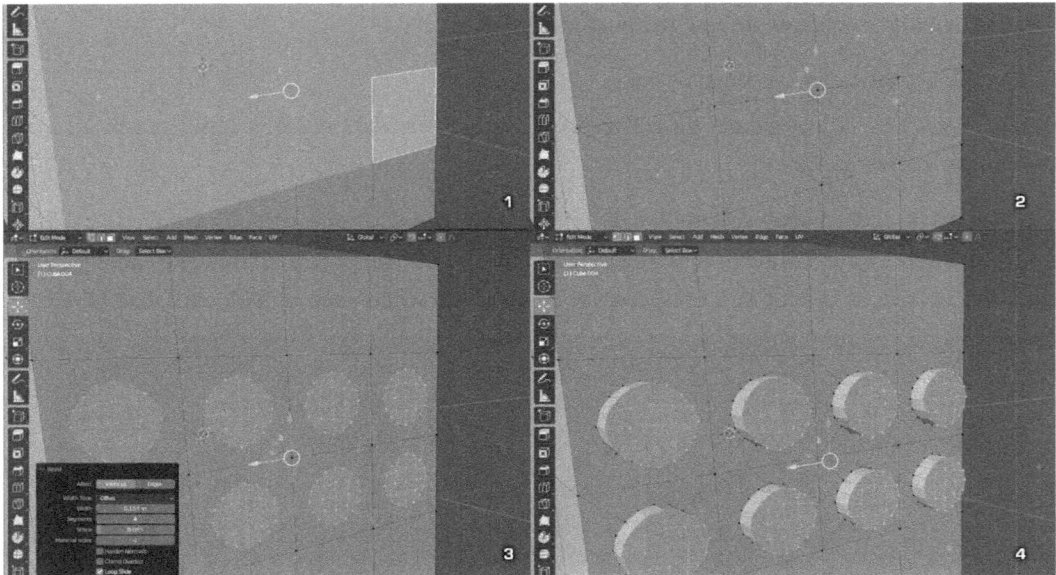

Figure 7.17: Using Vertex Beveling and Extraction to create bolt tops in Blender

The first quadrant of the image shows us selecting faces, and in the second quadrant, we are using **Poke Faces**. In the third quadrant, we are beveling the vertices of the poked faces, and in quadrant 4, we use **Extrude**.

> Tip
>
> You can use **Poke Faces** to create star patterns, which can be useful in architectural design.

Knowing when and how to use Blender's face-filling tools can be a game-changer. Over time and with practice, you will be able to go over a checklist in your head to decide which face-filling tool to use and when. Face-filling tools can help you achieve cleaner topology, mend gaps, and cater to different design aesthetics. As we move on, you will learn about subdivision and the reasons why you might need to refine your mesh.

Subdividing mesh elements via the context menu

Refining your mesh is key to creating 3D models, allowing you to perfect your designs so that they're both aesthetically pleasing and align with what you intended them to be, from the flow of the shape down to all the little details.

Local mesh refinement

Contextual Subdivision is a type of local mesh refinement, and it is a technical term that 3D artists use every time we use **Subdivide** (i.e., by *right-clicking* on the selected faces) to subdivide part of our mesh. **Contextual Subdivision** subdivides only a section of the mesh, making the changes you make contextual to your selection.

To compare, **Subdivision Surface Modifier** subdivides an entire mesh and smoothens it globally. Because it is a modifier and not a function, **Subdivision Surface Modifier** subdivides the mesh in a non-destructive way, meaning that we can still adjust our original topology at the same time as being able to see how it would look after it has been subdivided.

On the other hand, **Contextual Subdivision** gives you more control over the subdivision process. It breaks selected mesh elements (vertices, edges, faces) into smaller parts without affecting the entire mesh.

> Note
>
> In Blender, when we talk about **Contextual Subdivision**, we are really just referring to the standard **Subdivide** option (yep, the one you get from *right-clicking* in **Edit** mode). The term contextual just describes how it behaves: it subdivides based on what you have selected, whether it is faces, edges, or vertices. So, if you are wondering why we are switching between **Subdivide** and **Contextual Subdivision**, do not worry, they are the same tool, just described a bit differently depending on context.

To use **Contextual Subdivision**, in **Edit Mode**, select the mesh elements you want to subdivide (*Figure 7.18*). Then *right-click* to bring up the context menu and choose **Subdivide** from the list; in a few words, **Subdivide** will multiply the faces, splitting each face into four.

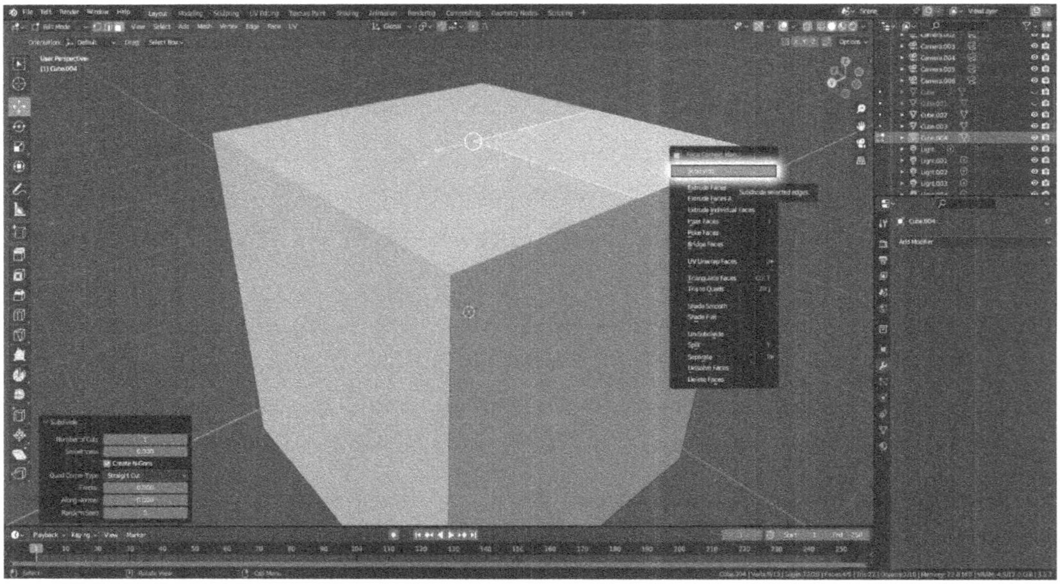

Figure 7.18: Finding Contextual Subdivision in Blender's menus

If you want additional control over the subdivision process, as soon as you have selected **Subdivide** following the preceding steps, you will be able to do so using the **Properties** panel (i.e., **N Panel**) located on the right side of the **3D Viewport**. To illustrate this tip, see *Figure 7.19*.

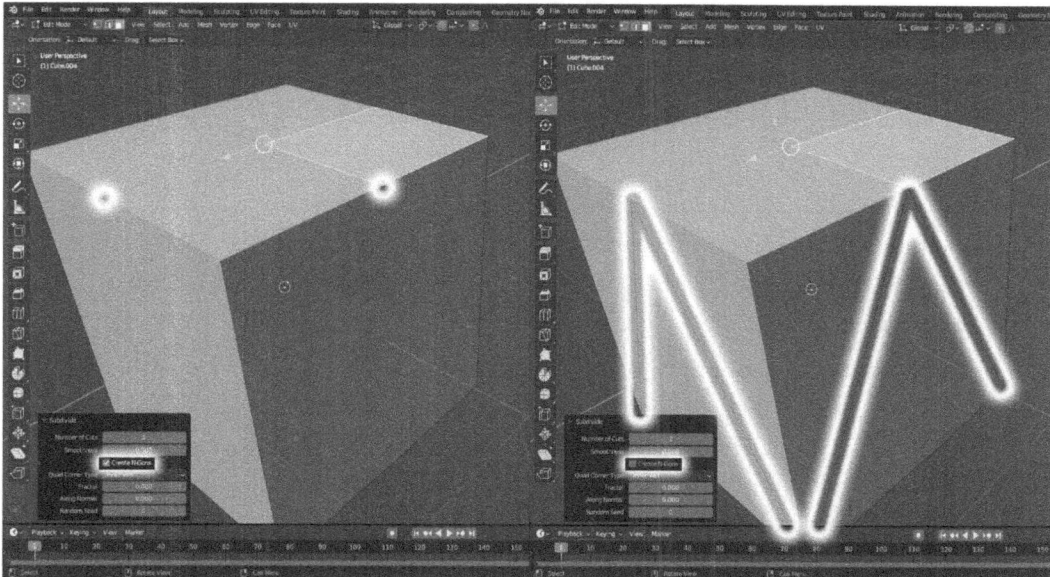

Figure 7.19: Creating N-gons through Subdivision

Here, you can see us subdividing the top face of a cube and creating four additional vertices in the middle. By leaving the **Create N-Gons** option on, we see that it leaves the vertices as is, giving us the N-gons for connected faces. On the right, we see the option off, giving us edge connections, essentially triangulating nearby surfaces, which fixes the N-gons.

If you have chosen to customize your subdivision, you can use the following list to see which key parameters the **N panel** will give you control over (*Figure 7.20*).

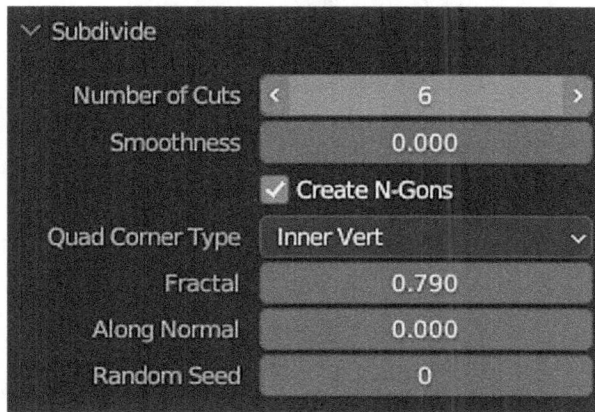

Figure 7.20: Customizable Subdivide parameters

The key parameters are as follows:

- **Number of Cuts**: Determines how many subdivisions or splits you want.

- **Smoothness**: Controls the amount of rounding or smoothing applied to the subdivided elements.

- **Fractal**: Introduces a degree of randomness to the subdivision. It works by determining the randomness offset of the vertices after subdivision. This can be helpful for models such as terrain or fabric, where random imperfection noise is needed to make their appearance more realistic.

- **Along Normal**: Determines how much randomness is added to the **Fractal** value based on the vertex normal (i.e., averaged out from the normal of adjacent faces) of the individual points. If the value is set to the maximum of **1**, it will inflate/deflate vertices randomly. This could be useful on a curved surface, such as a balloon, when you want to add height distortion without affecting the overall shape.

- **Random Seed**: Randomizes the noise applied during randomization.

- **Corner Types**: Adjusts how corners are treated during subdivision (e.g., **Straight Cut**, **Inner Vert**, **Outer Vert**). For example, you should subdivide if you have a path with a quad corner design and you would like to have smoother transitions on each corner, as shown in *Figure 7.21*. This is because when you are subdividing a mesh with the **Smooth** modifier, the edge flow will help the flow of your mesh form.

Figure 7.21: Using Subdivide for a path with a quad corner design

Mesh optimization

When creating a 3D asset, we try to keep to as low a topology as possible to increase performance and speed up the modeling process. However, in some cases, it might not be enough, and this is where subdividing your mesh might come in. The left side of *Figure 7.22* shows a circular object with low topology, where, especially around its edges, you can see each individual vertex. By subdividing its topology, like in the middle of the figure, we smooth out the edges, which gives us more of a round shape, which we can then see on the right.

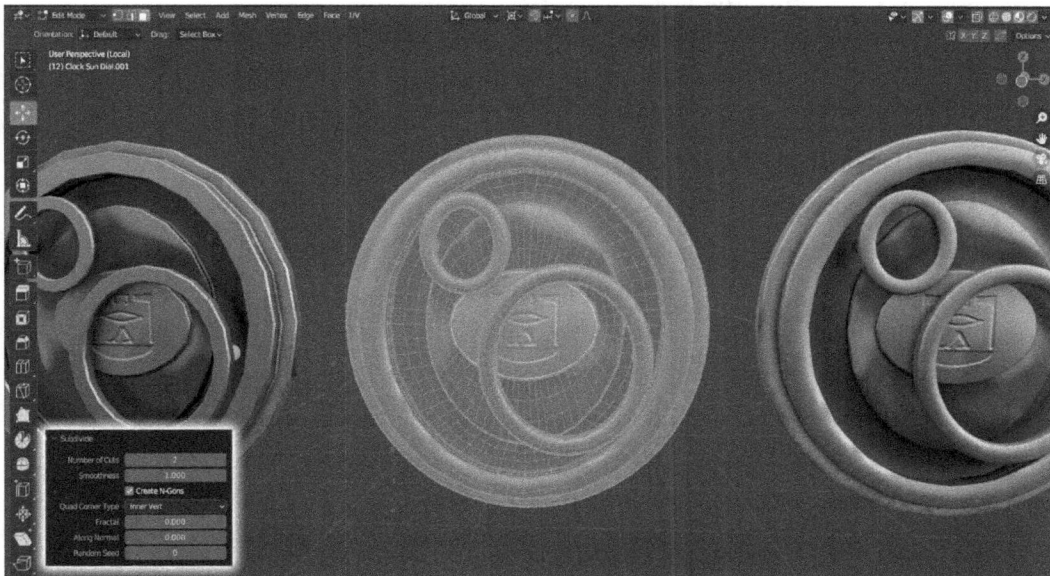

Figure 7.22: Customizing Subdivision smoothness before (left), resulting topology (middle), and after (right)

Tip

Overdoing subdivisions can lead to heavy meshes that are hard to manage and may slow down the Blender application. This is because your computer's GPU needs to determine the location of each of the vertices and the way they are connected to create the mesh shape. More vertices equal more computation power, which in turn can slow down your computer substantially.

Scenarios for when to use the tool

Let us clear this up right from the start because the naming can throw people off. In Blender, the *right-click* **Subdivide** tool in **Edit Mode** lets you split up just a specific selection, edges, faces, or verts, and that is what we are calling **Contextual Subdivision** here. It does not affect the whole mesh, only what you have selected. On the other hand, **Subdivision Surface Modifier** works globally and is used to smooth the entire model in a non-destructive way, perfect for previewing your model at higher resolution or smoothing things out for animation. So, think of **Subdivide** as the manual chisel and **Modifier** as the polish.

With that cleared up, let us talk about the real-world ways you might use the **Subdivide** tool in your modeling workflow:

- Sculpting or detailed modeling on a specific mesh area.
- Character sculpting.
- Reducing the number of unnecessary vertices your 3D models might be laden with. This is because you will have increased mesh density locally.
- If you have only started working with a simple mesh, subdividing it can help you create more complex geometries that you can detail separately on a local basis.
- Terrain management, designing rocks, and other objects with organic shapes. You can use the tool's **Fractal** and **Randomness** sliders to make surfaces irregular, as shown in *Figure 7.23*, where we are using the sliders.

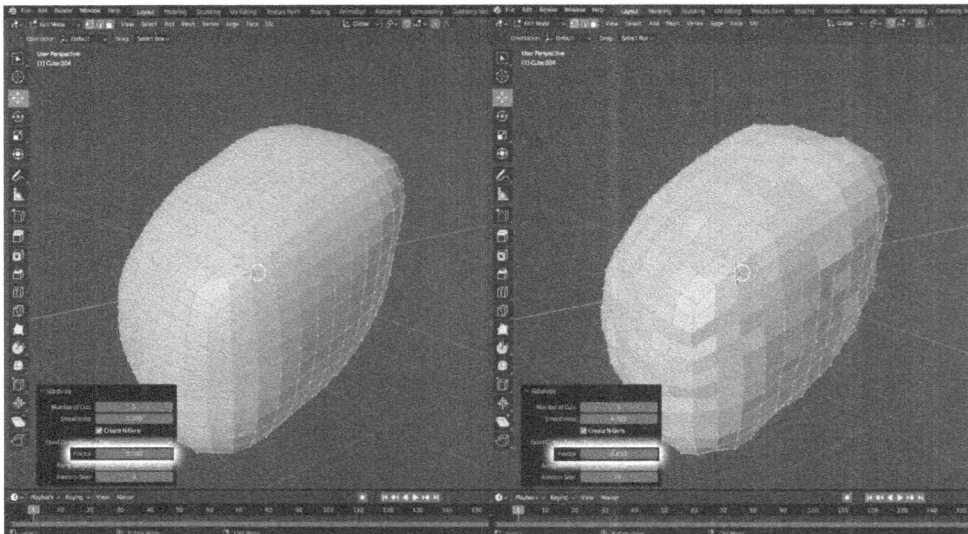

Figure 7.23: Applying Subdivision with Smoothness (left) and adding a Fractal value (right)

Making natural surfaces irregular is key to realism for 3D modeling art, and in game art, it is key to ensuring the immersion of your players.

For example, during terrain creation, I would create a low topology mesh of the general shape of the scene as shown in the first quadrant of *Figure 7.24*.

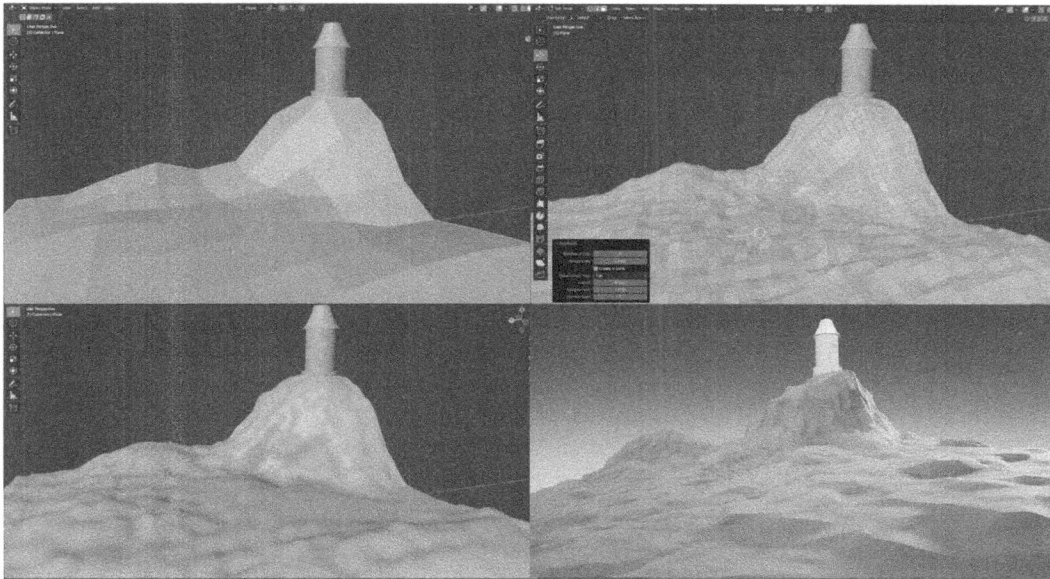

Figure 7.24: Irregular surface design for terrain design

Figure 7.24 is split into four quadrants, showing the following stages:

- *Quadrant 1*: I added a grid plane and used **Proportional Editing** to get a base shape for the scene with as low a topology as possible. This helps you focus on bigger shapes first.

- *Quadrant 2*: I added **Subdivision** with randomness to give this landscape more topology to work with. To boost the detail in the scene using **Subdivide**, I changed its **Fractal** value to **0.94** and **Number of Cuts** to **5**. This got randomly offset to add additional noise to the terrain, which will be picked up by the directional light in the final render, giving us nice shadows within the scene.

- *Quadrant 3*: I added another **Subdivision** with the **Smoothness** value set to **1** and set it to **Shade Auto Smooth** (i.e., shade smooth with angle). This helped soften the terrain surface while preserving some of the harder silhouette shapes, adding variation with larger and smaller forms across the mesh.

- *Quadrant 4*: Here, you can see a quick render and post-processing work. I added the **Auto Smooth** functionality to the terrain. Afterward, I played around with its angle to make certain parts sharper while keeping others smooth. I added directional light to get soft shadows that enhance the terrain's overall shape. Finally, I added a background gradient.

Doing so helps us see how terrain would be broken off in the scene with a more organic shape: the low-poly look we have achieved. With the general noise for terrain done, I could then go on refining the stages of the terrain where needed.

Excessive subdivision

Here, it is worth noting that excessive subdivision without proper planning can result in a messy topology, as shown in *Figure 7.25*, which can pose problems in later modeling stages or animations.

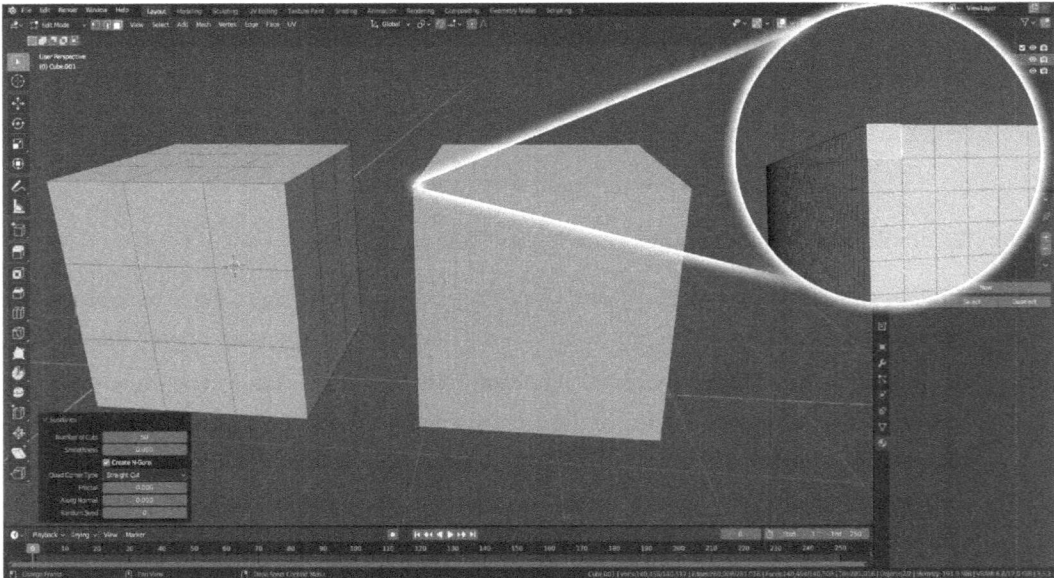

Figure 7.25: Excessive subdivision and resulting topology issues

For something such as animation, excessive use of subdivision levels, other than performance issues, can cause problems for processes such as weight painting (i.e., applying varying levels of influence to specific vertices on a 3D model, affecting how they are deformed by an armature or modifier during rigging or animation). This is because, for weight painting, information is stored on a vertex-to-vertex basis. If you have excessively used subdivision levels, it is more likely that there will be a vertex with incorrect weight painting information. In turn, this will cause a mesh artifact during its animation, like the one in *Figure 7.26*.

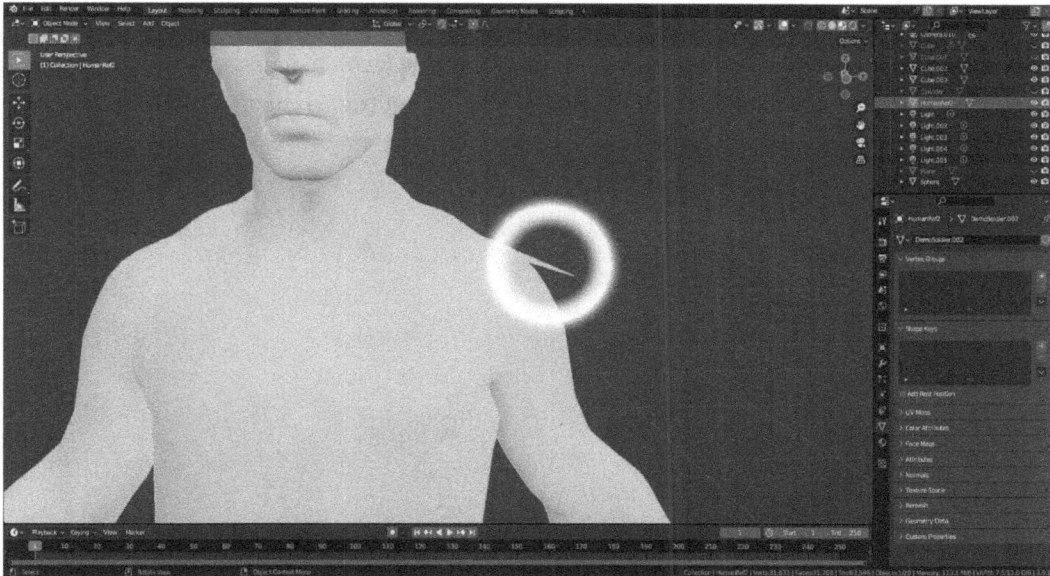

Figure 7.26: What a mesh artifact looks like in animation

We avoid excessive subdivision by using information for our object density as a base for how many times we want to subdivide our mesh. The higher the topology count there is on a mesh before we use subdivision, the less we would want to use **Number of Cuts** on a **Subdivision** operation. For example, with a simple plane made out of 4 vertices, if that was subdivided 5 times, it would give 36 quads in total, but if that same plane had been subdivided once before that same subdivision of 5, it would now give us a total of 144 faces. If the plane had a 4x4 face, and we subdivided it by 5, it would now have 576 faces in total, showing exponential growth when using the tool.

Blender's **Subdivide** tool is a powerful tool in your arsenal, allowing you to carry out local mesh refinement. When you pair it up with the customization options in the **N panel**, you can add a limitless array of nuances to your design. We will move on to discussing the process of triangulation and conversion: two processes that are essential in helping you correct compatibility issues or ensure your models allow for accuracy in 3D printing.

Mastering mesh elements with triangulation and conversion

Triangulation is easily defined as the process of converting faces in a mesh into triangle-based faces. You can see what a mesh looks like before (left) and after (right) triangulation in *Figure 7.27*:

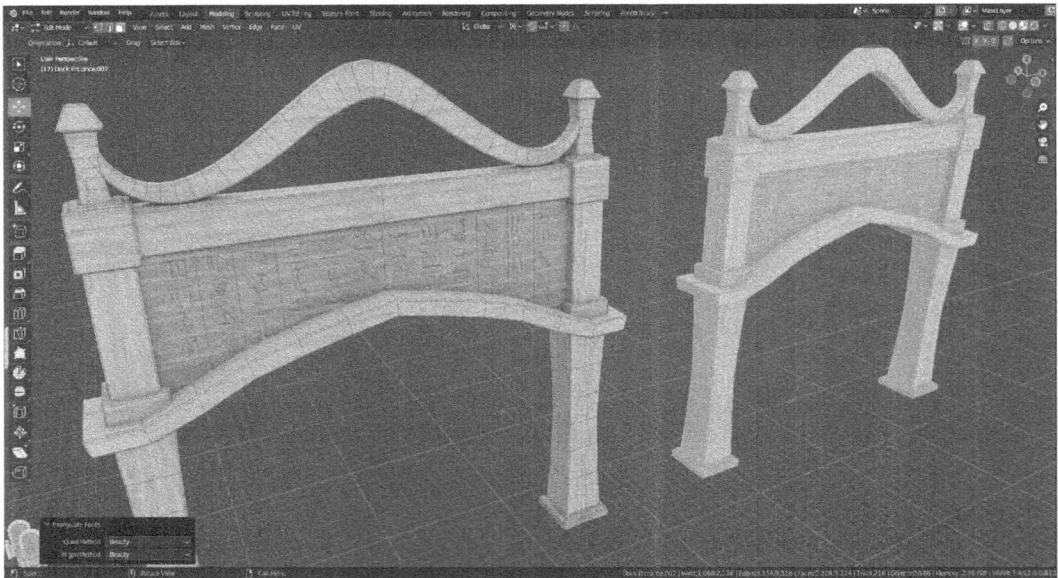

Figure 7.27: Using triangulation on the mesh of an Egyptian sign in Unreal Engine 5 Third Person Game & Stylized Environment by 3D Tudor

The Blender tool that was designed with that in mind is called **Triangulate**, and it ensures that any face in the mesh is represented using just three vertices.

Note

Triangulation is important for 3D models, such as for assets for video games, since topology always gets triangulated when a model is imported into a game engine. So, here's the deal: when you leave an **N**-gon hanging around in your mesh, especially before export, it becomes harder for the game engine to figure out how to break them down into triangles. When the engine has to guess, that guess can go seriously wrong, resulting in nasty little artifacts, shading issues, or faces flipping out in weird ways. That is why it is always a smart move to triangulate your mesh manually in Blender. You get full control over how those N-gons are sliced up, which is super important if you are working on low-poly characters or creatures. One badly triangulated **N-gon** and boom, your mesh deforms like it has just come out of a tumble dryer mid-animation.

To access the **Triangulate** tool, in **Edit Mode**, select the faces you wish to convert to triangles. Then *right-click* to open the context menu shown in *Figure 7.28* and choose **Triangulate Faces**.

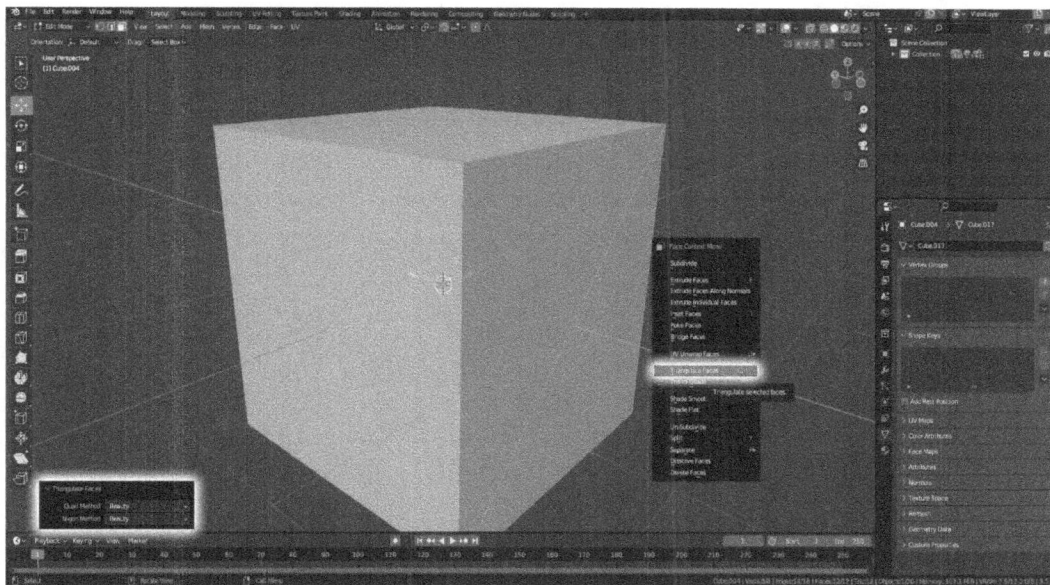

Figure 7.28: Finding and using Triangulate

Triangulate is a specialized tool that you only need to use in certain situations. For example, it is ideal if the game engine you are about to export your model to requires triangle-based geometry to render it out correctly (e.g., Unity or Unreal Engine 5).

Note

Unity and Unreal Engine 5 both triangulate every mesh that is imported into them. Both game engines handle triangulation well, except when it comes to N-gon faces or in certain cases, non-manifold edges. These are issues you should look out for, so by triangulating your entire mesh, or part of it, you can avoid issues such as face stretching and parts of the mesh clipping through.

Triangulate is also good at preventing unexpected shading or deformation and is essential for creating 3D models for 3D printing, so by making sure your model has triangulated geometry, you are saving time and effort. This is because most **Computer-Aided Design** (CAD) programs convert files to the STL format, which converts the content into triangular polygon meshes. Hence, by using **Triangulate**, you are working to prevent unexpected shading or deformation at the same time as streamlining the conversion of models into STL.

When it comes to **Conversion**, simplifying a mesh can be accomplished with the **Tris to Quads** tool, which converts triangles into quadrangles (*Figure 7.29*). To access the tool, in **Edit Mode**, select the triangle pairs you intend to convert to quads, *right-click* to bring up the context menu, and select **Tris to Quads**.

Figure 7.29: Finding menu options for using Tris to Quads

Tris to Quads converts triangle pairs in a mesh into quad-based faces. It is especially useful for cleaning up topology, such as when you need to create a topology with a smoother look using **Surface Subdivision**.

> **Tip**
>
> You need to make sure your topology flow is helping average out the vertices and create an overall smoother shape using its edge topology flow.

You can also use **Tris to Quads** to clean up mesh structures after certain operations. For example, if you decimate your mesh using the **Decimate** modifier, you will end up with a lower topology count, and this will give you a simplified version of the shape you are working on. Using **Tris to Quads** after decimation will instantly combine certain triangles into squares, which will make it much more manageable to continue the modeling process.

Tip

You can gain more control over this conversion process using Blender's options that appear in the operator panel at the bottom left of the **3D Viewport** immediately after using the **Tris to Quads** tool. These settings allow you to control how triangles are merged, adjusting face angle, shape angle, and topology influence, to fine-tune the shape and size limits of the conversion for cleaner results.

Using the **Tris and Quads** tool comes with its benefits, including but not limited to the following:

- Improving your topology flow, which is essential for animations or further mesh editing.
- When you need to animate a character, having a quad-based mesh will allow you to work with and visualize edge loops better.
- It gives you better control over their vertices, and this will result in a more predictable outcome during the deforming process in animation.
- Quad-based meshes look cleaner and are easier to read, which means they might be better if you are planning to submit a 3D project for grading at university or college.

Blender's **Tris and Quads** tool can also make your mesh simpler. This is useful if you are planning to use **Subdivision Surface Modifier** after using **Tris and Quads**, since it works best with quad-based topology.

Note

Quad-based meshes are also better for the 3D modeling process because they speed up the modeling process overall. For example, you want to make sure that edge selection is easier for parts of mesh manipulation. Using **Tris and Quads** does not always give you perfect edge loops in a mesh, but it creates a more manageable flow that you are then able to create faster selection connections out of.

Even if you are not planning to animate what you have created, it is still useful to have quads in a mesh. This is because UVs are used to get textures, and quads can improve UV quality. It is much easier to a) unwrap a surface, and b) follow a certain edge flow to the surface to hide away texture connections (i.e., seams) if it has quads.

> **Note**
>
> You might need to manually adjust your model's geometry after using **Tris to Quads** because it might not always produce the desired results, especially if your geometry is complex. We would advise you to research which game engine or other software you are planning to export your 3D models to before converting your mesh.

Both **Triangulate** and **Tris to Quads** are vital tools for 3D artists in Blender. Knowing which command to use and when will help you optimize your mesh topology, whether for animation, game design, or any other 3D application. Now that you have learned about different ways to optimize your mesh topology, we will look into ways to control surface appearance for aesthetic impact and optimized workflow.

Controlling surface appearance by smoothing or flattening normals

When we talk about smoothing and flattening in this context, we are really talking about normals: those invisible vectors that tell Blender (and game engines) how light should bounce off a surface. Smoothing makes your normals flow smoothly across adjacent faces, giving your object a softer, more rounded appearance. Flattening, on the other hand, keeps the normals sharp between faces, which makes edges and corners pop, great for hard-surface models.

You are not actually changing the geometry here, just the way light interacts with it. That is why a simple cube can look soft and blobby, or hard and mechanical, depending on how its normals are shaded. So, if you want to go stylized or ultra-realistic, getting your normals right is a big part of the look.

As you get initiated into the world of smoothing and flattening, you will come to understand why this is also an introduction to shading. Shading can influence the appearance of an object's surface in terms of smoothness or flatness. Even though you are not changing the geometry of an object when you are shading it, you are influencing how the light interacts with its surface. If you shade an object properly, you can control whether it is a realistic or stylized design and thereby optimize it for the context it's intended for. For example, as you can see in *Figure 7.30*, both models are similar.

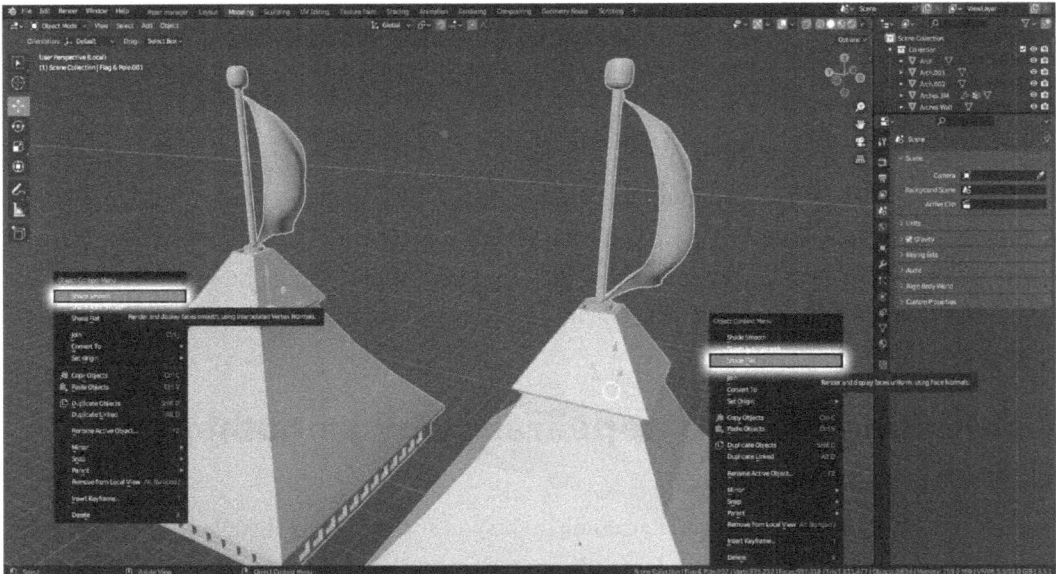

Figure 7.30: Reasons for smoothing and flattening model A versus model B

Model A (left) uses **Shade Flat** to highlight the edges in its topology, whereas Model B (right) uses **Shade Smooth** to create a more realistic surface.

In *Figure 7.31*, you can see **Shade Flat** versus **Shade Smooth** in a simple, up-close way:

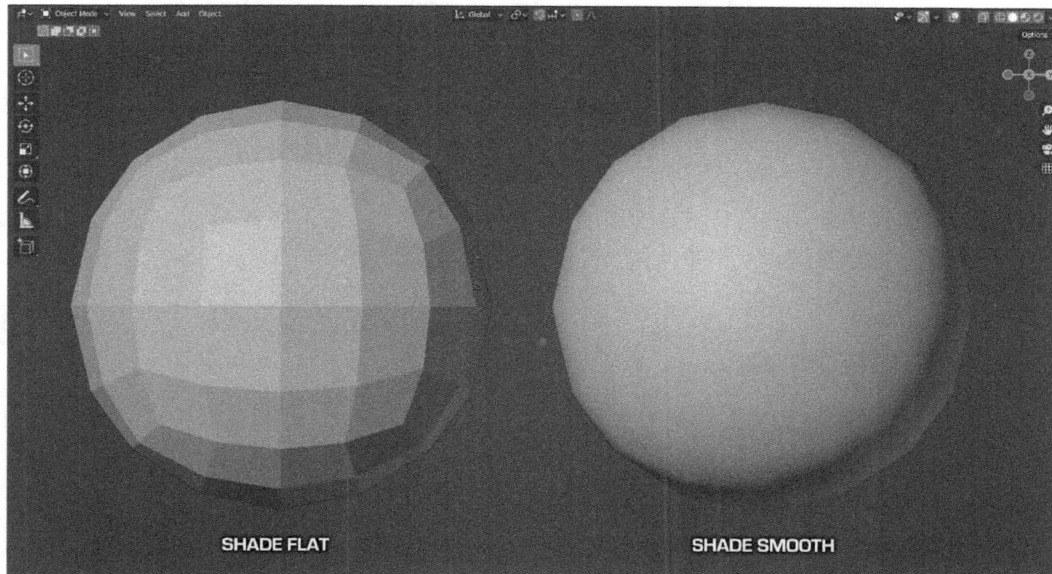

Figure 7.31: Comparing Shade Flat versus Shade Smooth

Let's take a closer look at **Shade Smooth** and **Shade Flat**.

Shade Smooth

Shade Smooth softens the appearance of an object, making edges between faces seem less pronounced. It shades the surface of an object by creating an illusion of smoothness without adding extra geometry.

To use **Shade Smooth**, in **Object Mode**, select the object or specific faces you wish to shade smoothly, *right-click* to open the context menu (*Figure 7.32*), and choose **Shade Smooth**:

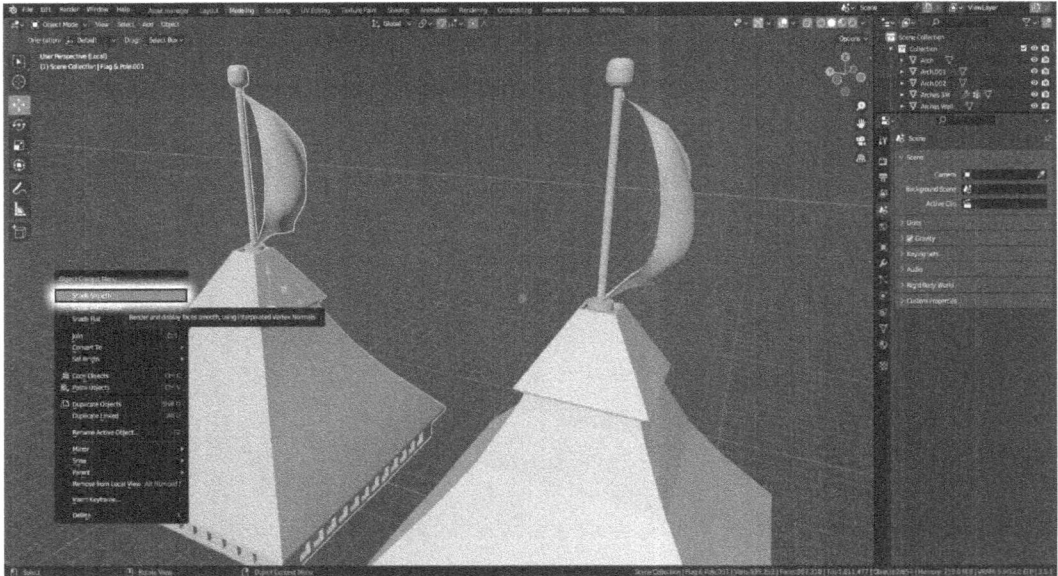

Figure 7.32: Finding and using Shade Smooth

As we delve deeper into the ways of 3D modeling artists, it is important to talk about why we do the things we do. In the case of **Shade Smooth**, this type of shading is good for 3D models of creatures, characters, and other objects with soft or rounded features (i.e., organic models)**, and is** essential if you are creating high-resolution objects and realistic environments, like in *Figure 7.33*.

Figure 7.33: A realistic environment in "Blender 3 The Ultimate Medieval Scene Course" by 3D Tudor

Using the **Shade Smooth** tool on our mesh helps average out its vertex faces, hiding low topology while using the material setup to add realistic detail.

Shade Flat

If you are in a low-poly art world and every polygon counts, you might want to consider using **Shade Flat**. **Shade Flat** returns the shading of an object to a flat appearance, making each face distinctly visible. In making the edges sharp, it emphasizes edges between faces, useful for stylized scenes especially since the aesthetic encourages using distinct faces.

To use **Shade Flat**, follow the same steps as for **Shade Smooth**, but select **Shade Flat** from the list of options instead.

Outside the world of low-poly art, **Shade Flat** (as seen back in *Figure 7.31*) is used for mechanical and hard surface models. This can include machinery or architectural designs whose design benefits from sharp edges. For example, in our course, Blender to Unreal Engine 5, we used **Shade Smooth** and **Shade Auto Smooth** to model all the mechanical parts of a medieval windmill.

You can go a step further and use **Shade Smooth** and **Shade Flat** at the same time. This process is called **Selective Shading**. For the process of selective shading to work, you need to apply **Shade Smooth** and **Shade Flat** on different parts of the same object. This lets you choose which parts of a model appear smooth and which ones stay sharp, great for things such as domes or stylized corners.

Now, if you want even more control, you can use **Mark Sharp**. This tool lets you manually define which edges should stay sharp when using smooth shading. It is not just for previewing: it actually gets exported in most workflows and is super handy when baking normals. **Mark Sharp** helps clearly tell Blender (and other tools) where smooth shading should stop and flat shading should take over.

Note

It is worth noting that normal baking can be directly affected by sharp edges. Using them helps define shading boundaries, making your topology more readable, especially on high-poly meshes prepared for baking. This makes **Mark Sharp** incredibly useful for cleanly splitting surfaces without adding extra geometry.

For example, in *Figure 7.34*, we are in **Edit Mode**, using **Edge Selection**, and marking certain edges sharp. This gives us a clean boundary without needing to mess with extra geometry, especially useful in mid-poly game assets or when preparing clean bakes.

Afterward, we *right-click* in our **3D Viewport** and select **Mark Sharp**, which tells Blender to treat those edges as hard when using **Shade Smooth**, giving them the crisp, defined look of **Shade Flat** while keeping the rest of the surface smooth.

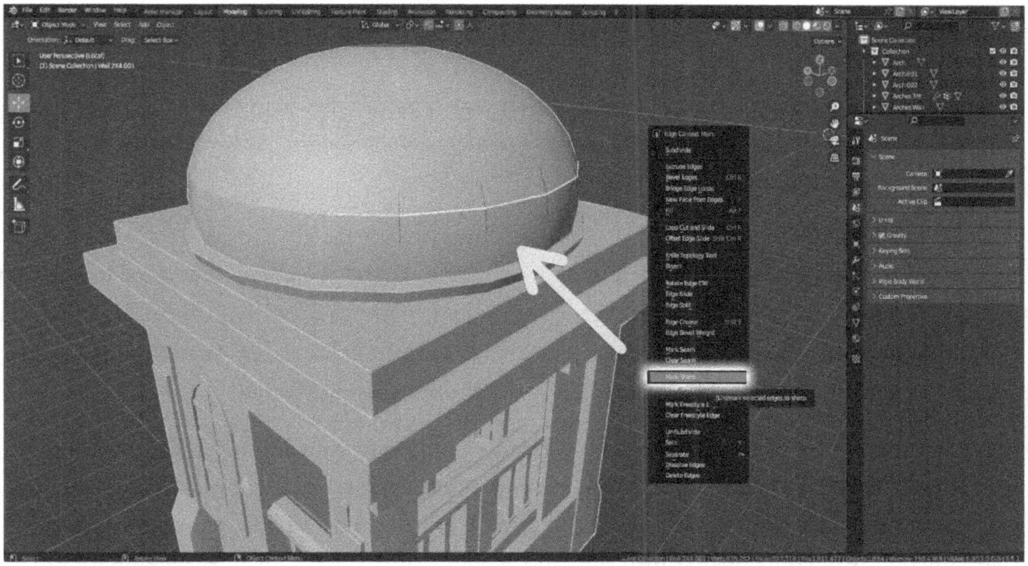

Figure 7.34: Explaining the process of selective shading

As an extra trick up your sleeve, you could use **Auto Smooth**, found in the **Normals** section of an object's **Data Properties** tab (*Figure 7.35*). Alternatively, you could click on **Shade Auto Smooth** on the drop-down options that appear when you *right-click* in **Object Mode**.

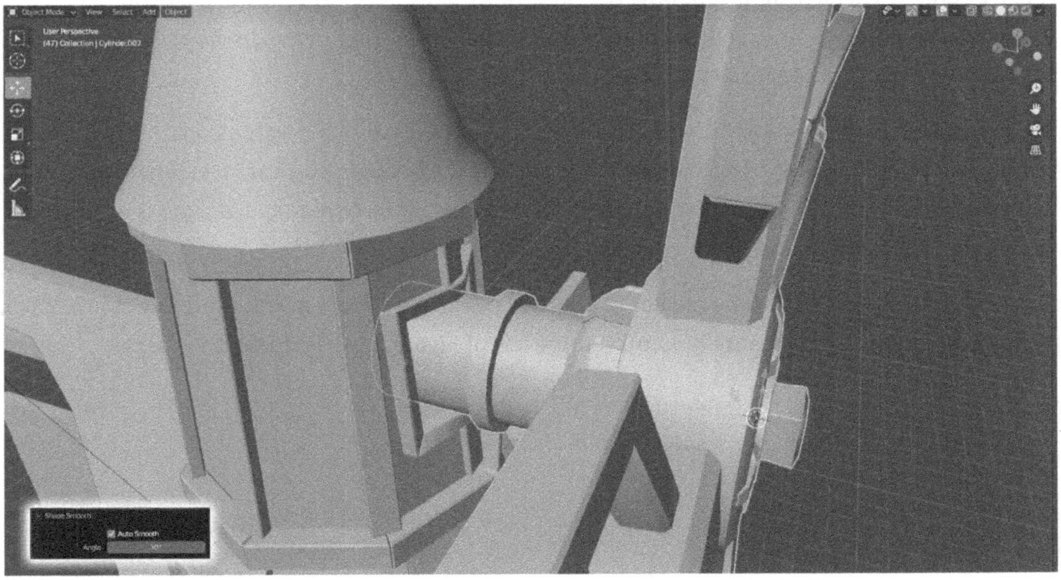

Figure 7.35: Finding and using Auto Smooth in Blender

Tip

Setting the angle threshold in the **Operator** panel (shown in *Figure 7.35*) is important with this option. The default is usually good enough, but I would just mention it in the body text.

This will make sure only some of the angles are smoothed, and the edges that need to be sharp stay that way. For example, this might be something you want to do with a windmill model that has straight and curved sections. In this example, you might want to use **Auto Smooth** to keep the cylindrical form curved while maintaining the timber's straight edge.

By now, you will have noticed that when it comes to making your models look good, shading does a lot of the heavy lifting. It might seem simple, but shading can completely change how a model feels, and more importantly, it can save you loads of time and keep that pesky polycount under control. As we dive deeper into this mid-level territory, you will start picking up how to mix and match tools across different parts of the same model, breaking things down, dissecting geometry, and making smarter modeling decisions overall.

Dissecting geometry using the Separate function

It is a dilemma we have all faced: how do I keep part of this model to reuse elsewhere, but not the whole thing? It is a matter of separation, and I will show you how to divorce sections of your 3D model, hassle- and negotiation-free.

Blender's **Separate** function allows you to detach a selection of a mesh into a distinct object, while both remain in the same scene. This is significant because you can use **Separate** to split complex models and make smaller portions more manageable, or give specific parts of an object individual attention as and when needed.

To use **Separate**, in **Edit Mode**, select the vertices, edges, or faces you intend to detach. *Then, right-click* to bring up the context menu (on the left of *Figure 7.36*) and select **Separate**.

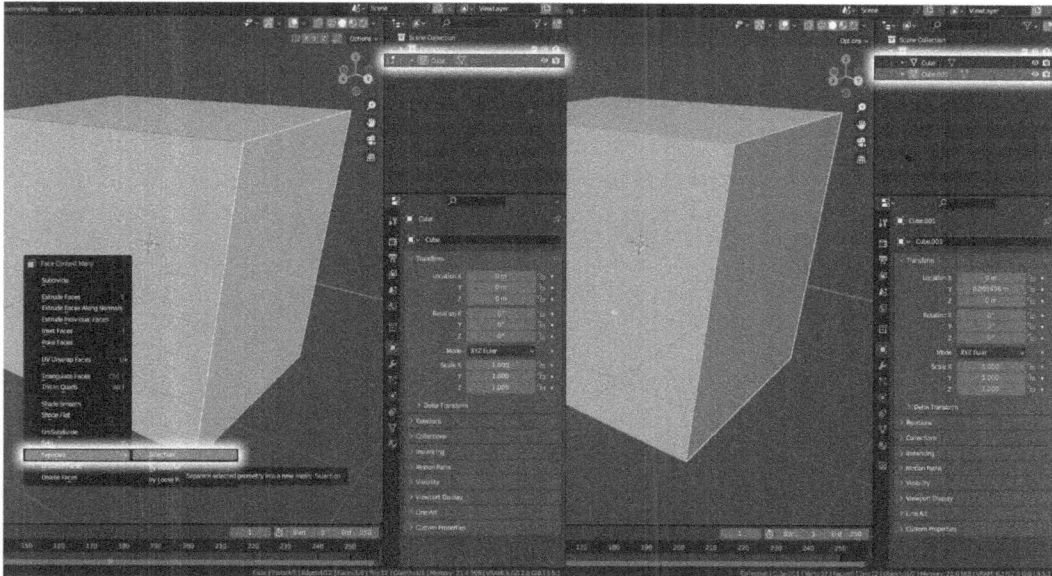

Figure 7.36: Finding and using Separate

Separate works in different modes:

- You can separate objects using **By Selection** (press *P*, then choose **Selection**), which means that you will directly split the selected part of the main object (see the right of *Figure 7.36*). For this type of separation, you need to make sure you have a selection ready beforehand. The best time to use **By Selection** would be if you want to extract a portion of your mesh for focused modification or to create a new element.

- You can also separate objects using **By Material** (*P* > **By Material**). Using **Separate | By Material** is useful if you are segmenting a 3D model with many materials into individual objects for each material, such as a stack of different types of crates (e.g., wooden, metallic, plastic).

  A great example use of separating using **By Material** would be within a building mesh that uses multiple seamless and other textures. By splitting the building into parts based on material, we can make sure that each building part is in its own category. This can help when editing, building, or exporting parts individually to other software.

In *Figure 7.37*, you can see the process of making a boat. In this particular case, we separate the face selection based on the edge loop going around an asset, which we later transform into an individual plank to give it some thickness. So, we start by creating a simple out-of-the-box shape, splitting up its topology, and extruding the faces outward. This is how you would create stylized wood boards.

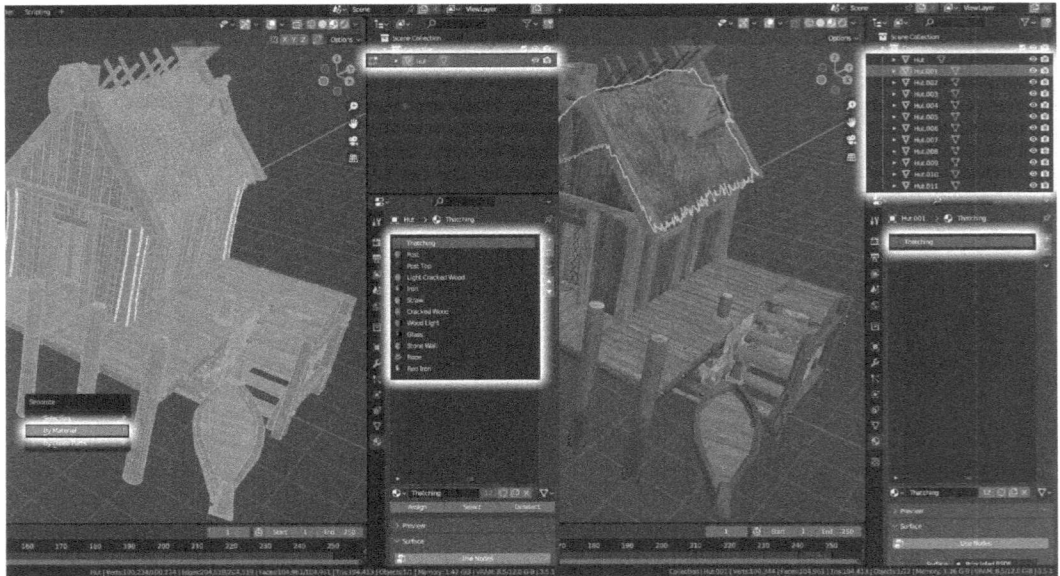

Figure 7.37: Using Separate by Material in Blender to Unreal Engine 5 The Complete Beginner's Guide by 3D Tudor

- A third way to separate objects is using **By Loose Parts** (*P* > **By Loose Parts**), which detaches unconnected parts of a mesh into separate objects. The best time to use **Separate | By Loose Parts** would be if you are splitting an object that consists of unjoined parts, such as a collection of rocks modeled together but not connected, as shown in *Figure 7.38*.

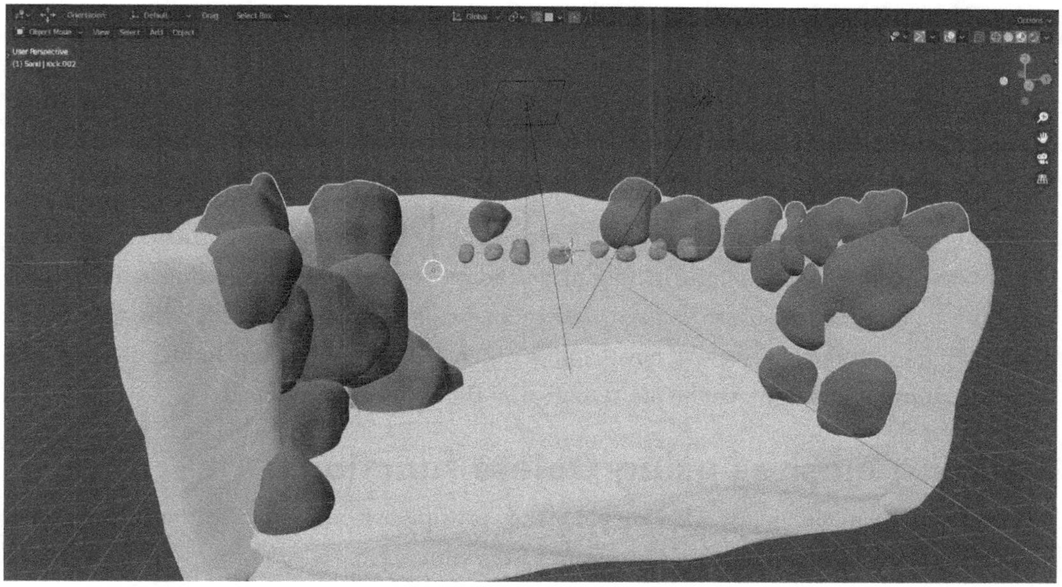

Figure 7.38: Using Separate by Loose Parts in Blender Design & Render a Stylized Water Scene by 3D Tudor

Regardless of which method you use, after separating, the new object will share the same origin point as the original. Adjusting this origin can be necessary for transformations or rotations. This is important because it might lead to an issue with your **Transformation Gizmo** being offset from an object, making object manipulation harder. For example, if you are rotating an object with an offset origin point, the object will not rotate around itself but from the axis of the origin point instead, causing the whole object to offset from its center.

> Tip
>
> To reattach a part that you have used **Separate** on, you need to use the **Join** operation in **Object Mode** (press *Ctrl + J*). Despite this fix, it is important to note that the two parts will still have separated vertices that need to be merged. The easiest way to do that would be using the **Merge By Distance** operation. To use **Merge by Distance**, press *M*, and select **By Distance** from the **Merge** tab, keeping its value close to **0** (i.e., **0.001**) to avoid other vertices joining as well.

Using **Separate** is good if you are working on parts for a modular set or kitbash. This is because you will be able to break down large, intricate designs into modular parts for easier editing and management. You can also use **Separate** to reuse assets by extracting parts of a model to be used in another scene. Plus, **Separate** is useful to split parts of a mesh that have problematic topology for you to resolve the issue and not affect the rest of the model because of reattachment.

Blender is committed to giving 3D modeling artists the tools to be flexible in their art. **Separate** is such a tool, and it is very helpful in helping you adapt your workflow by letting you duplicate parts and separate the details so you can work on them with effortless focus. Taking the process of refining meshes further, we will now explore different **Delete** functions in Blender and why knowing about them might just be the second-best thing since sliced bread.

Refining meshes using Delete functions

Delete functions in Blender do what they say; they provide options to remove various elements (i.e., vertices, edges, faces) or certain structures from your mesh.

To access these functions, in **Edit Mode**, select the desired elements, then press the *X* or *Delete* key to open the **Deletion** menu.

Different **Delete** operations affect the mesh topology differently. For that reason, it is important to understand the results to maintain the structural integrity of your model. Blender's **Delete** functions are highly specialized and have been carefully laid out in *Table 7.1*:

Vertices	Removes the selected vertices and any associated edges or faces.
Edges	Deletes the chosen edges, potentially leaving floating vertices (i.e., floating geometry). This can be problematic because it can create visual artifacts such as unwanted shadows or highlights in your render. To troubleshoot this issue, navigate to the **Mesh** tab, select **Clean Up**, and then **Delete Loose**. Take note that deleting edges deletes vertices too, but if there is another connection to that vertex, it would keep that vertex.
Faces	Erases the specified faces but retains the bordering edges and vertices.
Edge Loops	Eliminates full loops of edges, which can simplify or change the topology dramatically.

Vertices	Removes the selected vertices and any associated edges or faces.
Edge Collapses	Deletes edges, but merges the connected vertices, often used to simplify mesh regions without creating holes.
Limited Dissolve	A versatile cleanup operation that reduces geometry by merging adjacent co-planar faces.
Dissolve Vertices, Edges, Faces	These options dissolve the respective elements, merging them with the adjacent geometry.
Only Faces	Removes only the inner faces, leaving the boundary edges and vertices untouched.

Table 7.1: Choosing the right Delete function

> **Note**
>
> Mistakes can happen, so you will be glad to know that there is an undo command for **Delete** functions. Just press *Ctrl + Z* to undo any accidental deletions.

Blender's **Delete** functions have several practical applications. First of all, they are an essential part of every 3D modeler's workflow after major changes such as fixing meshes, and getting your mesh set up for **Subdivision Surfacing**. **Delete** functions are also essential for performance optimization if you are working on game assets or any other models needing to be rendered in real time. Using a **Delete** function can save you time by rendering a cleaner mesh with fewer issues.

Ensuring a clean base mesh devoid of unwanted elements using one of Blender's **Delete** tools is also essential before entering a sculpting session. This is because it is crucial that the mesh does not have any topology that might cause visual artifacts later down the line.

The **Delete** functions are powerful, but with that power comes the responsibility to use them correctly in a way that ensures the beauty and function of your 3D model. Knowing what to do with each **Delete** function and when is essential for anyone serious about 3D modeling in Blender, as these tools can make or break every modeling project.

Once you have cleared away the elements you no longer need, the next step is simplifying what is left, without wrecking your topology.

Simplifying meshes with Dissolve Faces

Dissolve Faces helps simplify your mesh by removing selected faces, edges, or vertices while trying to maintain the integrity of the surrounding geometry. It is another go-to Blender tool for decluttering unnecessary geometry without changing the form of your model.

To start using **Dissolve Faces**, in **Edit Mode**, make your desired selection (faces, edges, or vertices). Then, *right-click* to access the context menu and choose **Dissolve Faces**. Alternatively, use the *X* or *Delete* key and then choose **Dissolve Faces** from the list, as shown in *Figure 7.39*.

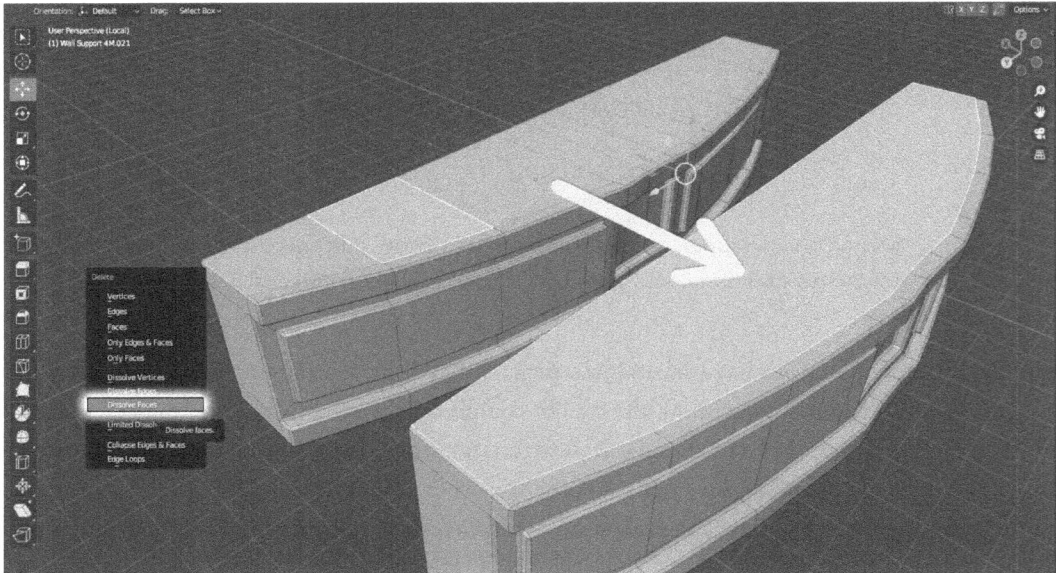

Figure 7.39: Finding and using Dissolve Faces in Blender

One of the things to be mindful of is that **Dissolve Faces** will produce N-gons. While this might be fine for some purposes, it is important to keep in mind the end use of the mesh (e.g., animation, game assets) as N-gons can be problematic in certain scenarios. For models with holes inside, such as apartment windows or door holes (i.e., if a plane is being used for a wall, a hole is referred to as the indent where the window mesh would go in), having an N-gon in the wall will cause issues after the model is imported to a game engine. You will see that the game engine will try to triangulate the mesh, and with this unresolved issue, it will create a face that overlaps the apartment window or door holes, for example.

Tip

To reduce the likelihood of this happening, you can limit N-gons using **Triangulate Faces** (press *Ctrl + T*) and then **Tris to Quads** (press *Alt + J*) on selection.

Dissolve Faces works differently depending on whether you have selected a face, edge, or vertex, as follows:

- **Dissolve Faces:** Removes the selected faces and tries to create an N-gon (i.e., a face with more than four edges) or simpler geometry, depending on the surrounding mesh structure.
- **Dissolve Edges:** Removes selected edges while retaining the surrounding vertices, which may produce N-gons.
- **Dissolve Vertices:** Deletes selected vertices and adjusts surrounding edges and faces accordingly.

Note

Excessively using **Dissolve Faces** can alter the topology of a model, which might affect deformation, shading, and other properties. To make sure you use **Dissolve Faces** within limits, focus on flatter surfaces and areas with higher topology density. By checking your model from various angles, you can ensure your model has not been deformed and that it has a topology setup (i.e., vertex/edge connections) in areas where it would cause N-gons to otherwise act out.

Dissolve Edges is a good Blender tool to use when you are working on removing unnecessary faces in a model as part of your optimization workflow. This can be crucial for real-time rendering since less topology means less computation power. Unlike the **Delete** function, which removes geometry entirely and deletes adjoining faces, **Dissolve** merges the surrounding geometry while preserving the surface. For example, by using **Dissolve Faces**, you can eliminate an entire edge loop or extra face without creating unwanted N-gons, helping keep your mesh cleaner and more efficient.

Another time when **Dissolve Vertices** will be handy is after performing Boolean operations or other modeling tasks that may leave extraneous geometry. This is because Boolean operations connect or remove mesh volumes where vertex connections touch, creating certain vertices in the middle, as shown in *Figure 7.40*.

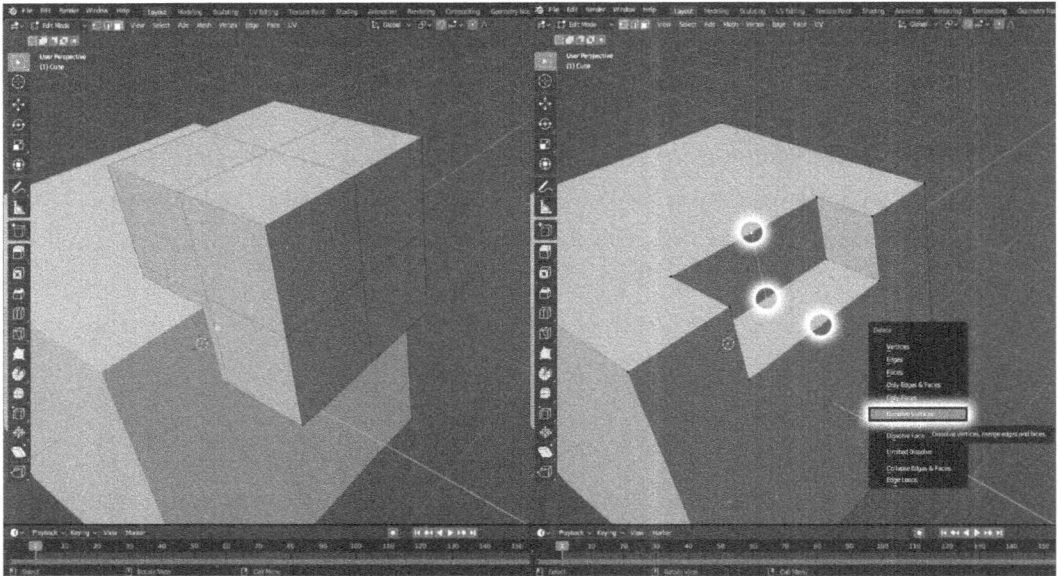

Figure 7.40: The importance of Dissolve Faces to Boolean operations

Finally, **Dissolve Faces** also makes it easier to edit or UV unwrap models (i.e., applying a 2D texture to a 3D model) by reducing the number of faces to deal with. This is important for the UV unwrapping process because each of the faces can act as its own UV island, a part of the mesh that has been unwrapped for texturing. If we are unwrapping UVs automatically, having fewer faces will mean there will be fewer places where UVs can split up, giving us fewer seams in an object. Having fewer seams is important since it will create fewer misaligned texture edges.

Even though **Dissolve Faces** is a potent tool, it is essential to use it with a clear goal in mind to make sure your end model meets all requirements, especially for topology and mesh flow. Understanding and utilizing Blender's **Dissolve Faces** tool properly can lead to quicker, more efficient modeling sessions, especially during the refinement stages of creating a model.

Summary

Many compare learning 3D modeling from scratch to a baptism by fire. This chapter gave us the space to expose you to different mid-level modeling techniques, gradually easing you into the processes and teaching you the real-world relevance of these techniques.

We began with Blender's **Bridge** tool, which allows you to seamlessly connect and mold geometry. From there, we delved into filling faces, using tools such as **Grid Fill**, **Beauty Fill**, and **Poke Faces**. You also learned about **Contextual Subdivision**, **Triangulate**, and **Tris to Quads**. With these tools under your belt, you are now able to optimize and convert your meshes based on whatever your project throws at you. Whether you are going for clean realism or stylized chaos, you have also picked up how to smooth and flatten surfaces in a way that matches your creative direction. It is all about control, and now you have got a lot more of it.

Later on, you got hands-on with breaking things apart the smart way using the **Separate** function, perfect for tackling complex models one chunk at a time. We also looked at how to tidy up your mesh without wrecking it using **Dissolve Faces**, keeping things clean while still holding the form. To wrap things up, we talked about the humble but mighty **Delete** functions, because sometimes the best way to improve a model is knowing what to get rid of.

Equipped with technical know-how and practical applications such as rock and gear generation, it is time to move beyond basic shapes and primitives and try something more advanced, such as generating rocks and utilizing **Pipe Joints** in the next chapter.

Further reading

- If you want to complete a 3D modeling project that will include much of this chapter and let you apply what you have learned, see *Blender Design & Render a Stylized Water Scene* (https://www.udemy.com/course/blender-29-model-render-a-stylized-water-scene/?referralCode=E10AA7712195A6B71D44). Bear in mind that there could be some procedural differences based on the version of Blender used in this course.

- Should you want to learn how to build a modular kitbash in Blender from scratch and use many of the tools we used today, and especially the **Bridge** tool, see *Creating a Modular Kitbash in Blender* (https://www.udemy.com/course/modular-kitbash-in-blender/?referralCode=A256A2F1FDDA5D6B506C).

- If you are looking to find out more about level design and creating an Egyptian harbor town in Unreal Engine 5, see *Unreal Engine 5 Third Person Game & Stylized Environment* (https://www.udemy.com/course/unreal-engine-5-third-person-game-stylized-environment/?referralCode=063EF23C1950D8DB380F).

- Try creating your own 3D environment with a realistic focus and high levels of environmental details in *Blender 3 The Ultimate Medieval Scene Course* (`https://www.udemy.com/course/blender-3-course/?referralCode=BC790C20B043C6B88A7D`).

Subscribe to Game Dev Assembly!

We are excited to introduce **Game Dev Assembly**, our brand-new newsletter dedicated to everything game development. Whether you're coding, designing, animating, or managing a studio, we've got insights, trends, and expert advice to help you create, innovate, and thrive. Sign up now and get exciting benefits.

`https://packt.link/gamedev-newsletter`

Get This Book's PDF Version and Exclusive Extras

UNLOCK NOW

Scan the QR code (or go to `packtpub.com/unlock`). Search for this book by name, confirm the edition, and then follow the steps on the page.

Note: Keep your invoice handy. Purchases made directly from Packt don't require an invoice.

8

Refining Your Mid-Level Blender Modeling Techniques

Now, as we start diving into more advanced modeling and some of the more specialized bits and bobs Blender has tucked away, there are a few tools that are just too good not to mention. What makes these tools stand out is how much easier they make the whole process when you are trying to create something detailed, or downright intricate. These are the tools that let you go from "eh, looks alright" to "yep, that actually looks pretty cool." Not only do they speed things up (which we all love), but they also help you add that extra layer of polish and realism without losing your mind over it.

Take the **Add Extra Objects** add-on, for example, it gives you a bunch of ready-made shapes you can drop straight into your **3D Viewport** and start messing with right away. Then, there is the **Grid Pattern** tool, which is brilliant for anything repetitive and structured. You get full control over tile counts, which makes it perfect for things such as tiled floors, machinery parts, or those fancy architectural facades. And tools such as **Rock Generator** and **Gear Generator**? Total time-savers. They let you create natural-looking rocks or precise mechanical pieces without having to build every detail from scratch.

Think of this chapter as your stepping stone into the deep end of 3D modeling. It is here to help you bridge the gap between where you are now and where you want to be, armed with just enough clever little tricks and specialized know-how to stop you from taking the long way round. The goal? To help you start making smarter decisions in your workflow sooner, without all the trial-and-error detours I took when I was learning.

So, in this chapter, we will cover the following topics:

- Experimenting with the Blender Monkey
- Going through the basics of **Add Extra Objects**
- Introducing extra objects: Grid patterns
- Creating extra objects: **Rock Generator**
- Adding extra objects: Gears
- Exploring Blender's tools: **Pipe Joints**
- Trying out Blender's curves
- Exploring **Non-Uniform Rational B-Splines** (**NURBS**) surfaces in Blender
- Delving into metaballs in Blender
- Harnessing Blender's text capabilities

Technical requirements

As for **Blender 4.5 LTS (Long-Term Support)**, the general requirements include a macOS 11.2 or newer (Apple Silicon supported natively) operating system, or a Linux (64-bit, glibc 2.28 or newer) operating system. Blender now requires a CPU with the SSE4.2 instruction set, at least 8 GB of RAM (32 GB recommended for heavy scenes), and a GPU supporting OpenGL 4.3 with a minimum of 2 GB of VRAM.

For a full list of technical requirements, please refer back to *Chapter 1* of this part.

Experimenting with the Blender Monkey

To start, we are going to mess around with another one of Blender's built-in gems, **Add Monkey**. Good old Suzanne. She is not just a mascot; she is actually super handy for testing out modifiers, materials, and whatever else you feel like throwing at her before you commit to anything serious in your actual project. Think of it as your personal crash-test dummy for Blender, giving you a safe space to break things, experiment, and figure stuff out without wrecking your proper models.

One of the key areas where Suzanne shines is in testing shading techniques. With Suzanne, you can experiment with different shading methods, materials, and lighting setups to see how they interact with the model's geometry.

Here is how you can utilize Suzanne for shading tests:

- **Material assignments**: Apply various materials to Suzanne to observe how different textures and shaders affect the appearance

- **Lighting experiments**: Adjust lighting angles, colors, and intensities to see how light interacts with the model's surface
- **Shader nodes**: Use Blender's powerful shader nodes to create complex materials and observe their impact on Suzanne
- **Rendering techniques**: Test different rendering techniques, such as **Cycles** and **Eevee**, to compare their results on Suzanne

If you want to see how your shaders and lighting setups are going to behave on more detailed models, Suzanne is your best friend. She is perfect for testing out materials before you throw them onto a big scene. Let us say you are working on a metallic shader, you can test the whole thing on Suzanne first and save yourself a headache later. Here is how you might go about it:

1. Go to **Add**, then **Mesh**, then **Monkey**.
2. Select **Suzanne** and go to the **Material** tab.
3. Create a new material and set the base color to a metallic shade. Change the **Metallic** value to 1 and adjust the roughness to see how it affects the shine and reflections. For this exercise, you do not need to worry too much about exact RGB values, but if you are curious, many artists use values close to real-world materials, such as aluminium or copper, for reference.
4. Place different light sources around Suzanne to observe how the metallic shader reacts to various lighting conditions, like in *Figure 8.1*.

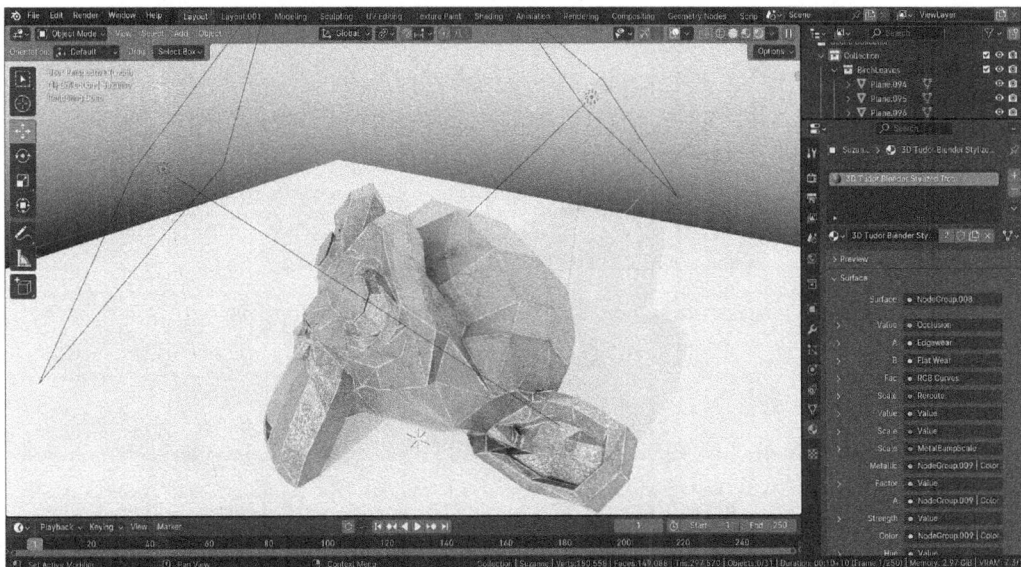

Figure 8.1: Metallic shader preview on Suzanne based on different light sources using 3D Tudor Blender Stylized Ultimate Metal Shader

Blender's **Add Monkey** feature is a great way to test and improve your 3D modeling skills, especially for shading. Suzanne has a perfect mesh and topology, making it easy to try out different materials, lighting setups, and rendering techniques without worrying about fixing initial flaws.

Next, we will look at the basics of the **Add Extra Objects** feature. This tool lets you quickly add a variety of shapes and elements to your 3D scenes, saving you time compared to modeling them from scratch.

Going through the basics of Add Extra Objects

Add Extra Objects is an excellent two-in-one Blender feature:

- First of all, it includes a variety of ready-made geometric shapes that can be added to the **3D Viewport**. This can be useful if you are looking to create a new object or add new elements to an existing object faster than it would take for you to model them from scratch.

- Second, without going into too much detail, each of these extra objects comes with customizable parameters that let you experiment and fine-tune more. All in all, **Add Extra Objects** encourages experimentation by letting you explore new design territories without the need for extensive manual modeling.

To enable **Add Extra Objects**, simply follow these steps:

1. Open Blender and make sure you are in **Object Mode**.
2. Navigate to the **Edit** menu, then from the drop-down menu, select **Preferences**.
3. In the **Preferences** window, click on the **Add-ons** tab and type Add Extra Objects in the search bar. A list of add-ons will appear. Look for **Add Extra Objects** and ensure the checkbox next to it is selected, like in *Figure 8.2*:

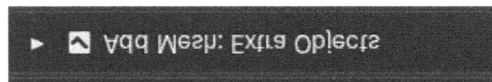

Figure 8.2: Navigating Add Extra Objects in Blender's add-ons

Note

In Blender 4.0 and newer, the **Add Extra Objects** add-on has been renamed to **Add Extra Mesh Objects**. You may also notice additional options, such as **Add Extra Curve Objects**. Just make sure the one you need is enabled in the **Add-ons** tab.

4. Once selected, click the **Save Preferences** button at the bottom of the **Preferences** window to apply the changes.

With **Add Extra Objects** enabled, you will have access to a wide variety of shapes and objects, which can be modified and adapted. Two notable examples are **Torus** and **Honeycomb**:

- **Torus**: This shape has a doughnut-like form with a central hole and rounded, ring-like structure. Blender lets you adjust its major and minor radius, which control the overall size and the thickness of the ring, respectively.

  Its ability to be scaled, twisted, and textured makes it suitable for diverse applications, such as creating bracelets or rings in jewelry design, lifebuoys for nautical scenes, or tyres for cars (*Figure 8.3*).

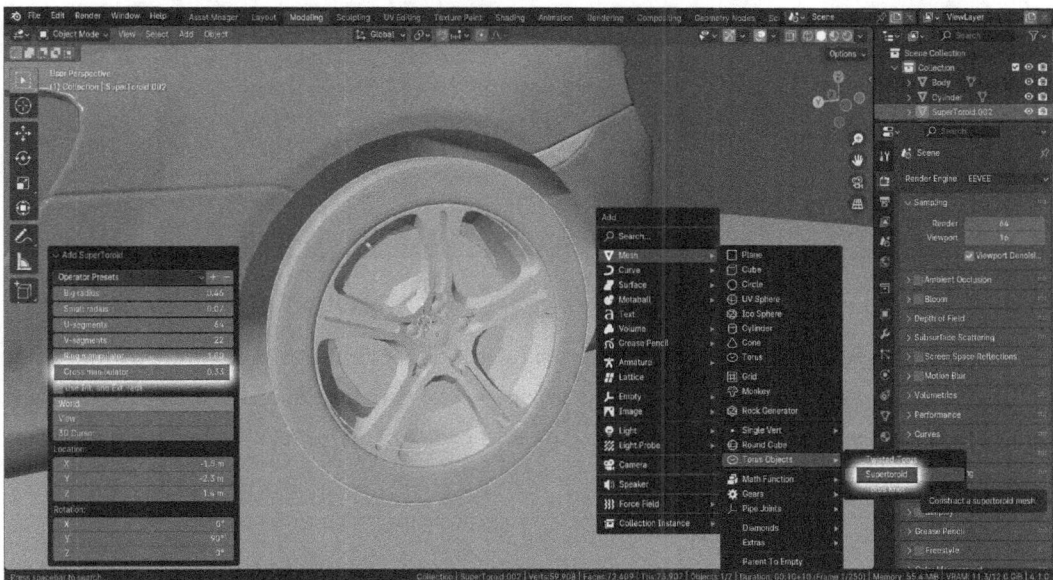

Figure 8.3: Vehicle tires in Blender Lighting & Compositing for Beginners by 3D Tudor

- **Honeycomb**: This shape mimics the hexagonal pattern of a honeycomb, offering a tessellated grid of hexagons. Blender lets you adjust the size of the hexagons and the depth of the grid, like in *Figure 8.4*.

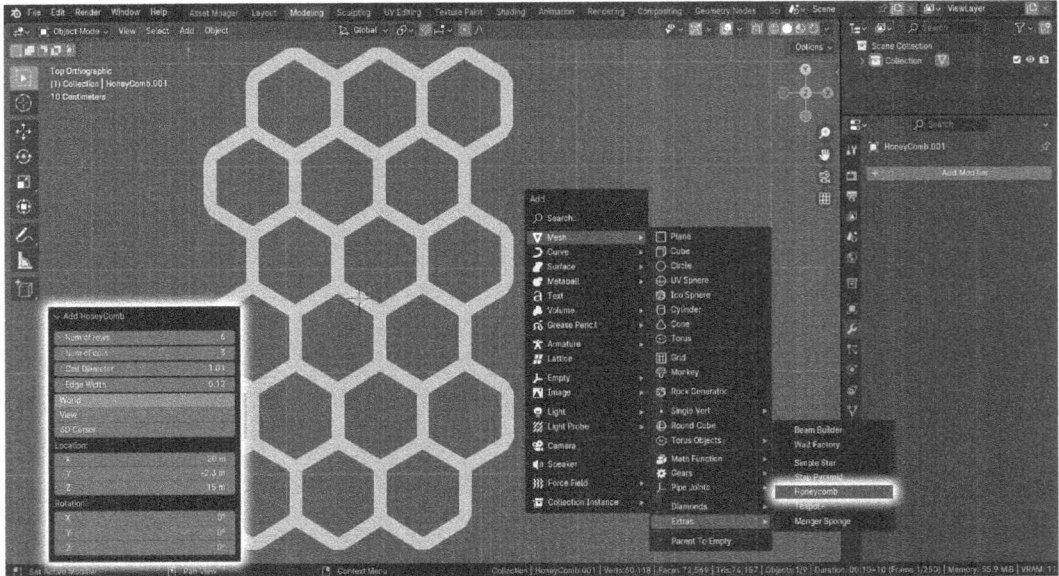

Figure 8.4: Honeycomb shape adjustment options

The **Honeycomb** shape is particularly useful in architectural and environmental modeling. For example, it can be used to create intricate wall panels or flooring. It can also be used to make textures for nature scenes (e.g., the surface of an insect's nest or the pattern on a reptile's skin, like in *Figure 8.5*).

Figure 8.5: Intricate Honeycomb shape uses

So, **Add Extra Objects** empowers you to experiment with unique designs and enrich your scenes with intricate details, taking your creations to the next level. Among these, grid patterns stand out as exceptionally versatile and useful. Now, we will proceed with a detailed discussion of the various grid patterns available in the **Add Extra Objects** feature, exploring how you can use them to create structured, visually appealing designs in your projects.

Introducing extra objects: Grid patterns

Blender's **Add Extra Objects** feature includes **grid patterns**, which can be used to create stand-alone structures or grids that can be integrated into existing 3D models. One of the most important things about grid patterns is that you can adjust the number of tiles in a grid, giving you fine control over how densely populated they will be. This can be useful if you are designing floor vents or fencing, for example.

To fine-tune how many tiles your grid has, follow these steps:

1.   Through the **Preferences** menu, select **Add-ons** and search for `Add Mesh: Extra Objects`. Then, enable **Add Extra Objects**.

2.   With **Add Extra Objects** enabled, press *Shift* + *A* to unveil the **Add** menu.

3.   Navigate to the **Mesh** option and opt for **Grid** to create a grid-based object.

4.   Once the grid-based object is added, customize the tile count via parameter adjustment.

5.   Access the **Operator** panel, typically located in the lower-left corner of the **3D Viewport**, to find various options for configuring the grid's attributes.

6.   Locate the **X** and **Y** parameters, representing the tile count along the horizontal and vertical axes of the grid. From here, refine the values to have as many tiles as you need. Put simply, increasing the **X** value adds more tiles horizontally and increasing the **Y** value boosts the vertical tile count.

Tip

Blender lets you see the grid change in your **3D Viewport** immediately, allowing you to adapt these parameters according to your needs. This feature is indispensable if you are working on a design with specific tile quantities, such as in architectural projects.

Grid-based objects can make 3D objects more detailed and aesthetically pleasing. Here's how you can use grid patterns to create different objects:

•   **Building facade**: Create an array of windows using the grid-based object to go along one side of a building, adjusting parameters such as rows (e.g., 5 rows), columns (e.g., 10 columns), spacing (e.g., 0.01 meter), and window dimensions (e.g., 1.5 meters by 2 meters).

•   **Fences and railings**: Design a fence or railing along a path and define the post count (e.g., 20 posts) and spacing (e.g., 2 meters apart) to make sure it is uniform and structurally sound.

- **Swift pavement tiles:** Quickly generate a grid of pavement tiles for a path or courtyard. Then, change the size (e.g., 0.5 meters by 0.5 meters) and tile arrangement (e.g., herringbone pattern) to give your scene the right feel. For example, larger pavement tiles (e.g., 1 meter by 1 meter) can give an area a more modern and spacious look; they often create a sense of openness and can make a space appear larger than it is. On the other hand, smaller or narrower tiles (e.g., 0.3 meters by 0.3 meters) can give off a more traditional or detailed aesthetic that makes it feel more intimate or cosy, like in *Figure 8.6*.

Figure 8.6: Narrow pavement tiles – a visual representation

Knowing all about the grid patterns feature and its uses helps you simplify the process of making repetitive arrangements in Blender. If you also become good at strategic object placement, you can use grid patterns to gradually improve your scene's composition.

Now that we have covered how grid patterns can bring order and structure to your scenes, let us shift gears and look at something a bit more chaotic but equally useful: rocks, or more specifically, how to generate them procedurally without having to sculpt each boulder by hand like it is the Stone Age.

Creating extra objects: Rock Generator

Rock Generator is an important environment design tool that lets you quickly create naturalistic rock formations and plop them into your scenes, without needing to 3D model each one manually. This is because the generator is **procedural**, meaning that it lets you create different rocks based on an algorithm. The role of the user (i.e., 3D modeling artist) is to input parameters and adjust the **Rock Generator** settings to make rock creation adaptable and to create unique individual rocks, like in *Figure 8.7*.

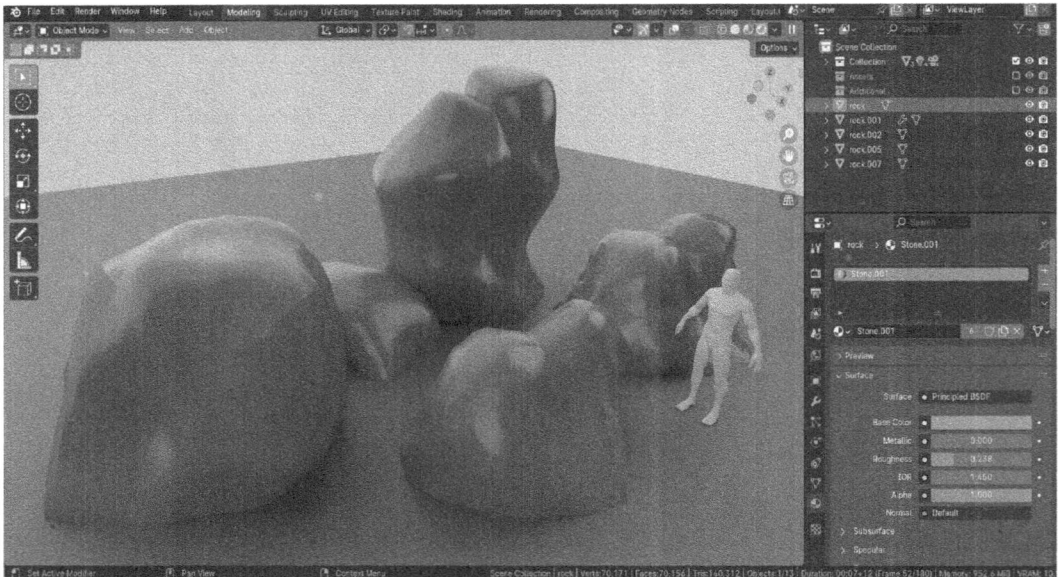

Figure 8.7: Using Blender's Rock Generator to create a versatile rock collection

Since the details are generated algorithmically, procedural tools such as **Rock Generator** can manage large environments or high levels of detail better than manual modeling.

Note

Rock Generator does not just create a static mesh; it generates rocks using modifiers. This approach means that instead of adding a heavy, complex object to your scene, it uses a series of lightweight, adjustable modifications. As a result, the generated rocks have a minimal impact on the overall size and performance of your scene, making it efficient and easy to work with.

Accessing Rock Generator

To make the most of **Rock Generator** in Blender, follow these steps:

1. With **Add Extra Objects** enabled, press *Shift + A* to bring up the **Add** menu.

2. Navigate to **Mesh** and select **Rock Generator** to add a procedural rock to your scene.

3. At this point, you can adjust the **Rock Generator** parameters:

   a. Access the **Operator** panel shown in *Figure 8.8*, typically found in the lower left of the **3D Viewport**, which provides many tools to individualize the rock's characteristics.

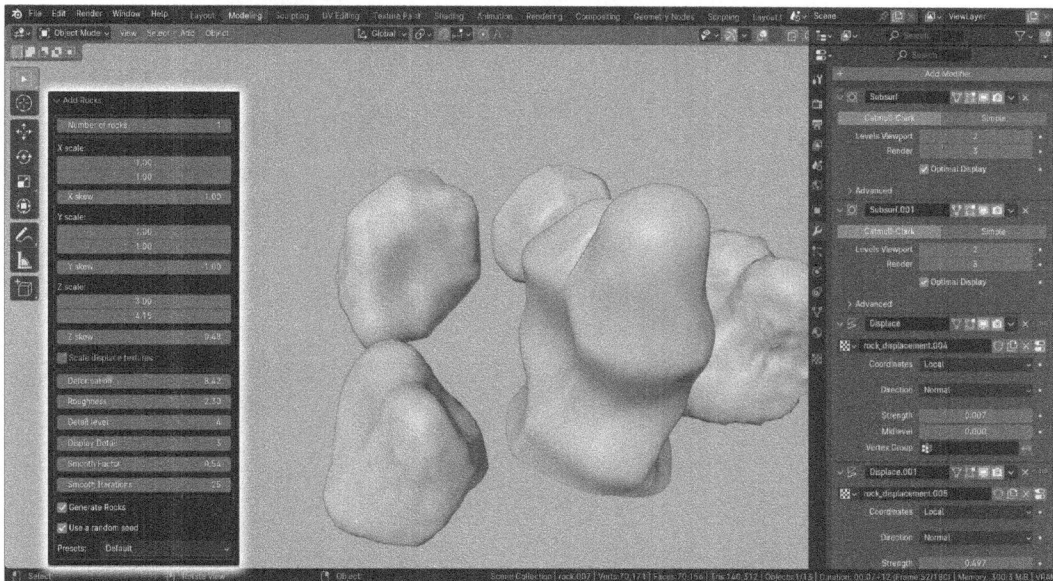

Figure 8.8: Rock Generator Operator panel

   b. Play with the **Rock Generator** settings to get the look you are going for:

   - **Number of Rocks**: Controls how many rocks are generated

   - **Size**: Determines the overall size of the rocks

   - **Scale Variation**: Adjusts the variability in the scale of the rocks, making them appear more diverse

   - **Roughness**: Influences the surface roughness of the rocks, affecting how smooth or jagged they appear

- **Detail**: Adds finer surface features to the rocks, increasing the level of intricacy and making them appear more realistic

Note

Rock Generator can be a bit of a black box. It started out as a third-party plugin, and while it eventually became an official add-on in Blender, most of the original documentation and tutorials were removed along the way. Unfortunately, that means there is no official guide explaining every parameter. The best approach is to experiment with the settings and modifiers it generates; there is no one "correct" way to use it, just what gives you the result you are after.

c. If you want to make your rocks even more detailed, tick **Use Displace Modifier**. The **Displace** modifier adds intricate surface variations by using a texture to displace the vertices of the rock mesh, creating more natural-looking bumps, crevices, and irregularities that are found on real rocks (*Figure 8.9*). The effect seen here likely uses Blender's default displacement texture, which can be scaled and adjusted through the **Texture Properties** tab.

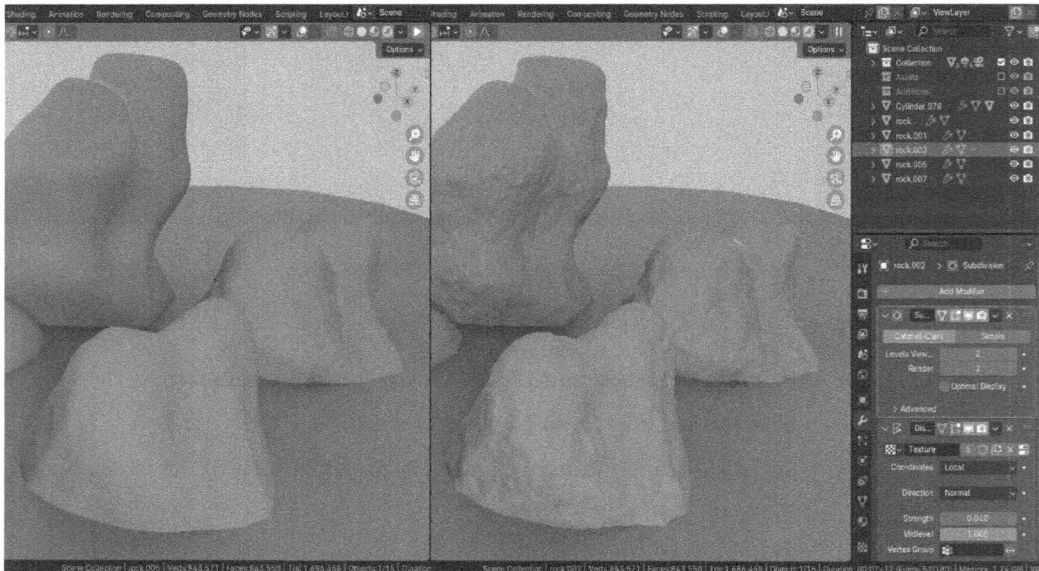

Figure 8.9: Before (left) and after (right) using Displace modifier with Blender's Rock Generator

The **Displace** modifier works by offsetting vertices based on a height texture. When you use a simple noise texture, it simulates the irregular, rocky surface often seen on eroded or weathered stone.

> Tip
>
> When adjusting parameters, the rock will switch seed randomly. In this context, a "seed" is a starting point for the random number generator that creates variations in the rock's shape. Different seeds produce different variations, so the rock's shape will change with each new seed randomly. To disable that and get finer controls over the desired shape, untick **Use a Random Seed**. To have control over the scale of **Displace** textures, enable **Scale Displace Textures**, which will allow you to scale it for the *x, y*, and *z* axes manually.

As you tweak these settings, you will witness the rock transformations in real time in your **3D Viewport**, offering you a dynamic feedback loop.

Examples of Rock Generator usage

Here's how you can make your 3D scenes look more realistic using Blender's **Rock Generator**:

- **Diverse landscapes**: You can use Blender's **Rock Generator** to populate a barren terrain with uniquely shaped rocks. By tweaking the **Number of Rocks** and **Scale Variation** settings, you can quickly achieve a variety of sizes and formations.

- **Riverbeds or oceans**: Take your underwater scenes a step further with rock formations on the seabed. Adjust the **Roughness** and **Detail** settings to simulate water-worn rocks, and enhance the realism of your scene.

- **Architectural elements**: Rocks are not just meant for natural scenes. You could also integrate them into urban environments as part of walls, boundaries, or decorative elements. Change each rock's size and shape to seamlessly blend into man-made structures.

In *Figure 8.10*, you can see an example from our *Build Stunning Medieval Worlds with UE5's Modular Kitbash* course, where rocks placed around the outskirts of the medieval fortress add the necessary environmental detail to make the scene look real.

Figure 8.10: Rock placement for realism in Build Stunning Medieval Worlds with UE5's Modular Kitbash by 3D Tudor

Now that you understand how to effectively use **Rock Generator** to create realistic and varied rock formations, let us move on to another powerful feature in Blender's **Add Extra Objects** toolkit: the **Gear Generator** tool. In the next section, we will explore how to use the **Gear Generator** tool to create intricate gears and worms, enhancing your ability to craft detailed and functional 3D models.

Adding extra objects: Gears

Blender is perfectly suited for making 3D models of mechanical objects, for architectural, engineering, or game purposes. This means that precision, symmetry, and consistency are a must, and this is where Blender's **Gear Generator** tool comes in. Whether you are working on an intricate engine design or experimenting with the steampunk style, the **Gear Generator** tool lets you create gears and worms, like in *Figure 8.11*, quickly and easily.

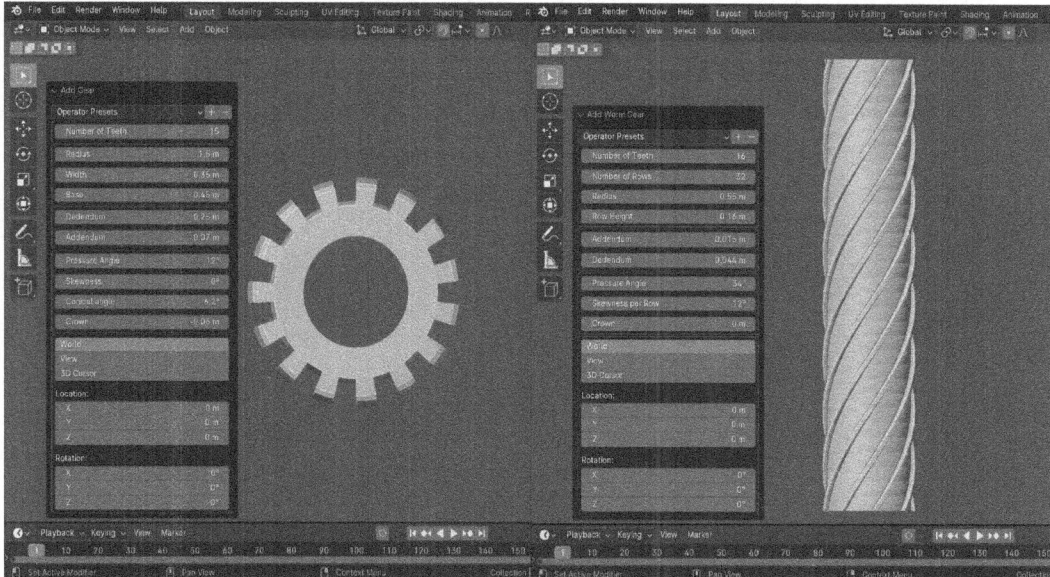

Figure 8.11: Gears, cogs, and sprockets generated with Blender's Gear Generator tool

The best thing about the **Gear Generator** tool is its procedural nature, allowing you to adjust parameters and get the perfect gear without manual modeling.

Accessing Gear Generator

To use the **Gear Generator** tool within Blender's **Add Extra Objects** feature, follow these steps:

1.   With **Add Extra Objects** activated, press *Shift + A* to make the **Add** menu pop up. Then, from **Mesh**, select **Gears** to introduce a procedural gear into your scene.

     Depending on your Blender version, you might have additional options, such as **Gear** or **Worm Gear**. A worm gear is a type of gear that consists of a worm (i.e., a screw-like gear) meshing with a worm wheel, whereas a regular gear has standard toothed wheels that mesh with other gears to transfer motion. The key difference is that worm gears provide smooth, continuous speed reduction and high torque, whereas regular gears are used for direct meshing and transferring motion between parallel axes.

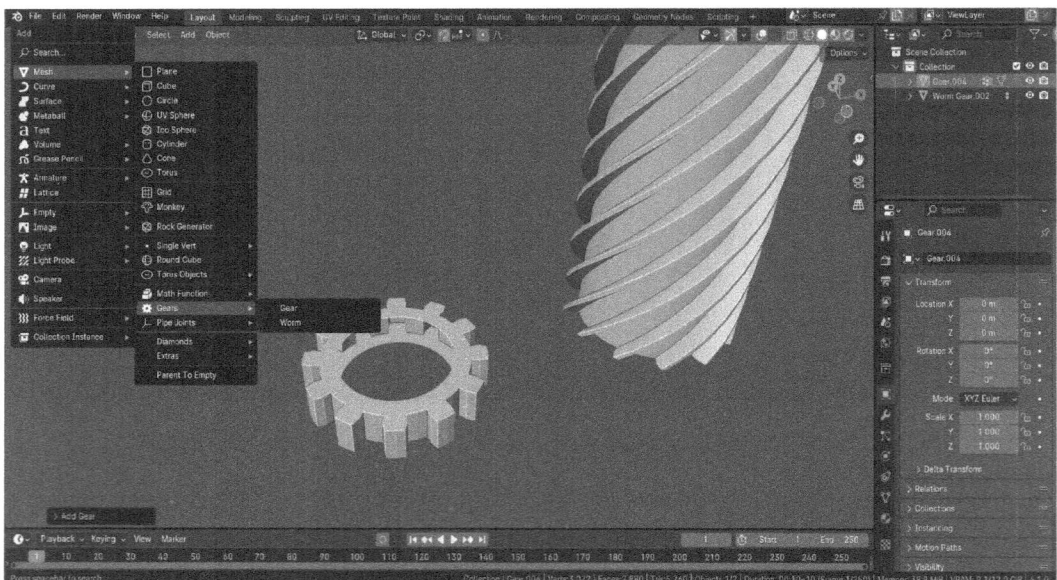

Figure 8.12: How Blender looks when Add Extra Objects is activated

2.   After adding the gear(s) to your scene, you can make parameter adjustments (like you can see back in *Figure 8.11*):

     a.   Access the **Operator** panel: found in the **3D Viewport**.

b. Tinker with the following settings to determine the gear's variables:

- **Number of Teeth**: Controls how many teeth the gear has

- **Radius**: Determines the overall size of the gear

- **Width**: Adjusts the thickness of the gear

- **Crown**: Adjusts the vertical offset of the gear's teeth, affecting their overall curvature

- **Pressure Angle**: Controls how much the teeth taper toward the tips, essentially pinching or spreading the ends

3. As an advanced user, you might want to delve into settings related to the angle of the teeth, convergence, or the type of gear to model more complex mechanisms, as shown in *Figure 8.13*.

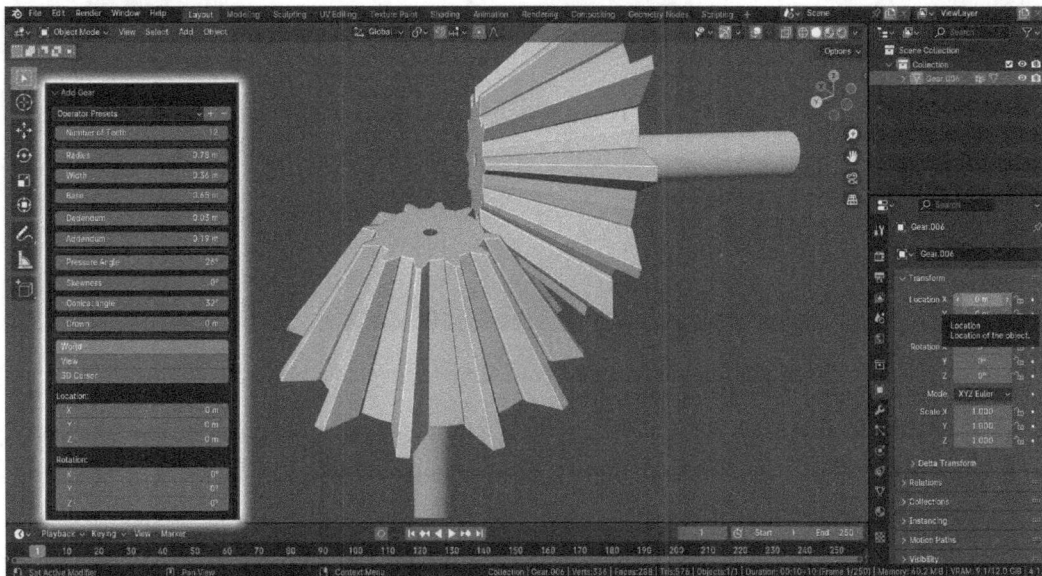

Figure 8.13: Using advanced gear settings in Blender

Examples of Gear Generator usage

Knowing how to generate and customize gears is an essential tool in your 3D modeling toolkit because you would not believe the number of scenarios where that would come in handy:

- **Complex machinery**: Use the generator to quickly generate gears that mesh perfectly by adjusting the **Number of Teeth** and **Radius** parameters, like in *Figure 8.14*:

Figure 8.14: Interlocking gears of different sizes made in Blender

- **Artistic installations**: You could also create wall art, jewelry, or steampunk designs, modifying the **Width** and **Crown** parameters to vary appearance.
- **Animation**: If you are interested in animating the gears you generate, Blender will help you simulate their rotational movements, like in *Figure 8.15*.

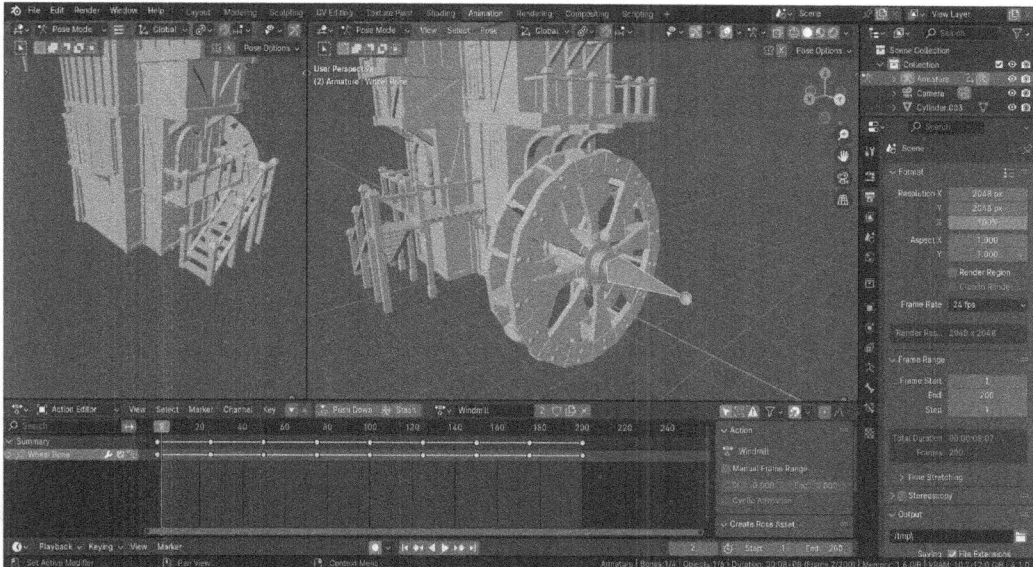

Figure 8.15: Watermill wheel from Blender to Unreal Engine 5 by 3D Tudor

- You can create animations such as turning wheels, conveyor belts, or pendulum clocks. To do so, you will need some foundational knowledge about animation, which we will discuss later in *Chapter 16* of this book.

Blender's **Gear Generator** tool is a perfect example of just how much control the devs have handed over to us lot. Being able to customize gears down to the tiniest detail is a seriously useful skill, and you would be surprised how often it comes in handy. But gears are only half the story. Next up: pipes—yes, like the ones Harry Potter slid through in *The Chamber of Secrets*, minus the giant snake at the end. Yep, those humble cylinders are everywhere, and not just in plumbing. Whether it is cables, tubes, or stylized vents, you will find yourself needing them more than you think. So, let us dive into that next.

Exploring Blender's tools: Pipe Joints

Creating believable pipes from scratch is no walk in the park, even for experienced 3D artists. It is one of those things where the tiniest detail can throw the whole model off. Overlook how the joints connect, and suddenly your industrial scene or fancy bit of machinery starts looking like a plastic toy. Pipe joints might seem minor, but they are absolutely key in making your designs feel grounded, functional, and properly engineered.

Unfortunately, Blender does not have a pipe joint generator in the same way it has a **Gear Generator** or **Rock Generator** tool. This means that you will need a little bit more guidance along the way. That is where this section comes in. Our focus will now shift to discussing how a combination of basic modeling techniques will help you achieve the desired outcome.

Accessing the Pipe Joints tool in Blender

To create a basic pipe joint in Blender, follow the next steps (or a variation thereof depending on your project's needs):

1. Press *Shift + A* to open the **Add** menu, then navigate to **Mesh**, then **Pipe Joints**. This will be the primary basis for your pipe, and you have different options, such as **Pipe Elbow**, **Pipe T-Joint**, **Pipe Y-Joint**, **Pipe Cross-Joint**, and **Pipe N-Joint**, as shown in *Figure 8.16*.

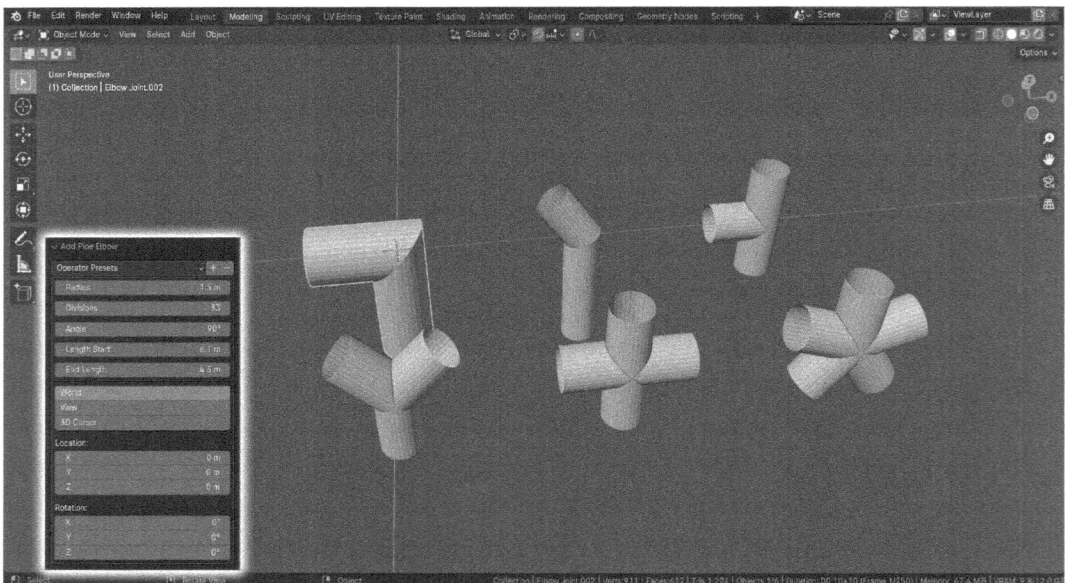

Figure 8.16: Pipe joint options in Blender

Note

It is important to note that the available parameters and their adjustments may vary slightly depending on the type of joint you are using, which can be selected on the bottom left of the **3D Viewport**.

2. After selecting the pipe options that suit your project, use the **Scale** (press *S*) and **Extrude** (press *E*) tools to adjust the cylinder's length and diameter to match the pipe dimensions you are looking for.

3. To create a joint, consider duplicating the pipe segment and positioning it perpendicularly or at the required angle depending on the pipe system you want to make.

4. Then, Blender's **Bevel** tool allows you to smooth out the angles based on an edge loop selection for the corners within each individual pipe joint (i.e., those sharp corners in the first cross to the left of *Figure 8.17*). You can manually select joint edge loops by pressing *Alt + LMB* and then use the **Bevel** tool by pressing *Ctrl + B*. This lets you make custom adjustments to the bevel, as shown in *Figure 8.17*.

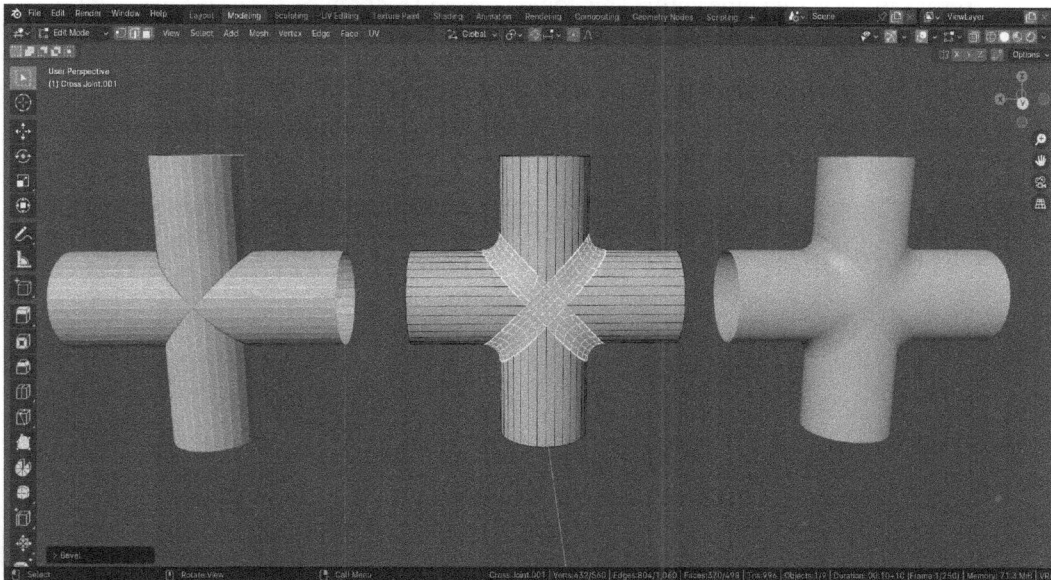

Figure 8.17: Manually selecting edge loops and using Bevel tool

5. Inspect the newly merged object in the **3D Viewport** to ensure the joint is seamless. Rotate and zoom in to verify that there are no gaps or misalignments.

> **Note**
>
> If there are any issues with the seam, you might need to use additional tools such as the vertex or edge merging tools to clean up any small discrepancies manually.

Examples of pipe joint usage

Understanding the different types of projects you can use **Pipe Joints** for takes your 3D modeling projects in Blender to a new level. Here are some examples of pipe joint usage:

- **Industrial scenes**: **Pipe Joints** will help you make your industrial designs more authentic for buildings such as factories, warehouses, or mechanical rooms. You can picture the design of a factory's ceiling where various pipe joints intersect and overlap with the perfect synergy that different types of machinery need to function.

- **Plumbing framework**: Pipe joints are not just for plumbing, but you should certainly also use them for that trade. You could showcase plumbing systems, water pipelines, or HVAC setups using varied pipe joints. This could be useful for architectural visualizations of the interior design of new buildings, for example.

- **Sci-fi and steampunk designs**: As with gears, pipes and their joints can be aesthetic centerpieces in genres such as steampunk or certain sci-fi subgenres, lending a mechanical touch to your creations, like in *Figure 8.18*.

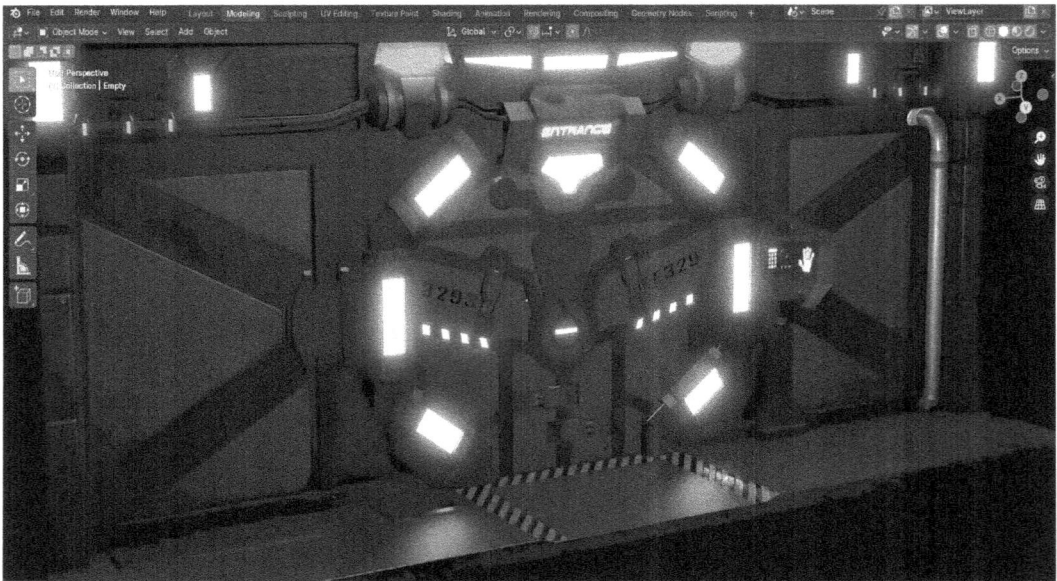

Figure 8.18: Sci-fi pipe point in Blender Sci-fi Scenes with Eevee by 3D Tudor

Building pipe joints in Blender is a perfect example of why you need a solid grip on Blender's modeling toolbox. It is not just about knowing one or two tricks; it is about combining different tools and modifiers to get the result you want without spending your whole weekend wrestling with vertices. The more fluent you are, the faster and cleaner your workflow becomes.

Next up is one of the most underrated bits of 3D modeling magic: curves. Learn to use them right, and your models will stop looking stiff and start feeling alive. Let us get into it.

Trying out Blender's curves

As a 3D modeler, it will be very important for you to be able to create organic, fluid, and custom shapes. Blender's **Curve** functionality offers a flexible way to create and manipulate shapes without the restrictions of mesh vertices, edges, and faces. Mesh vertices, edges, and faces in Blender restrict your modeling by confining shapes to a fixed grid-like structure, limiting the fluidity and organic flow that curves can provide. From basic modeling to sculpting and animation, curves have many uses, some examples of which will be discussed later in this section.

Types of curves in Blender

Before we jump into where curves really shine, it helps to get your head around the different types Blender gives you. Not all curves are created equal, and knowing which one to use can save you a ton of time (and frustration). Once we break down the main types, if you are itching to go deeper, Blender's official docs have you covered with all the nitty-gritty and advanced curve wizardry. This is a list of the most important curve types available in Blender 4: `https://docs.blender.org/manual/en/latest/modeling/curves/editing/curve.html`.

Bezier curves

Bezier curves use two types of points: **anchor points**, which determine the curve's path, and **handle points**, which determine the curve's direction and sharpness.

Bezier curves are often the go-to for design and illustration. The best place to use them would be in creating organic and custom shapes, for example, intricate logo designs such as the elegant curves of a script-based logo, like in *Figure 8.19*.

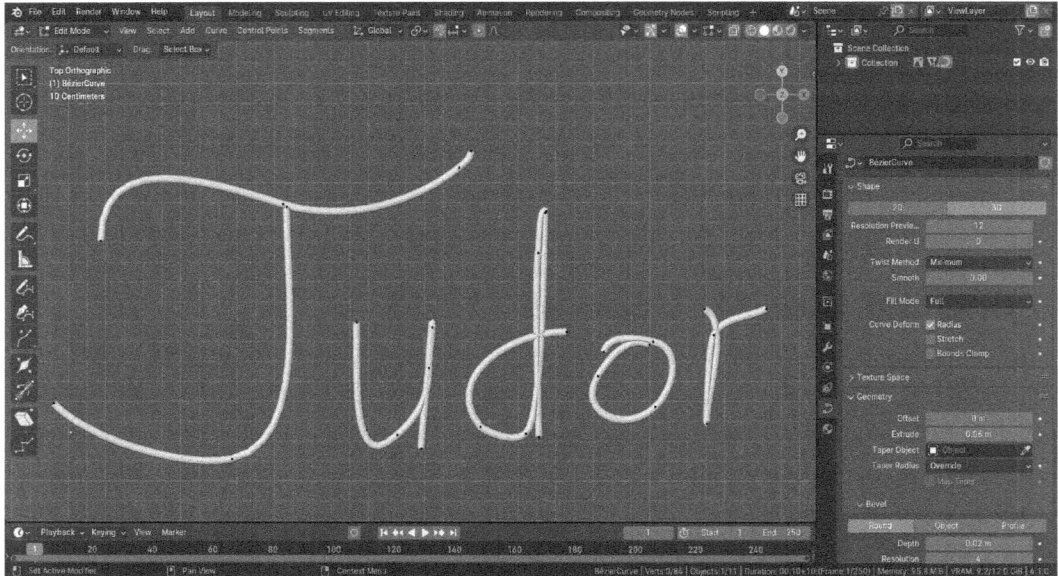

Figure 8.19: Script-based logo design with Bezier curves

A curve can be smoothed or sharpened by manipulating the handles, giving you high levels of control, as shown in *Figure 8.20*.

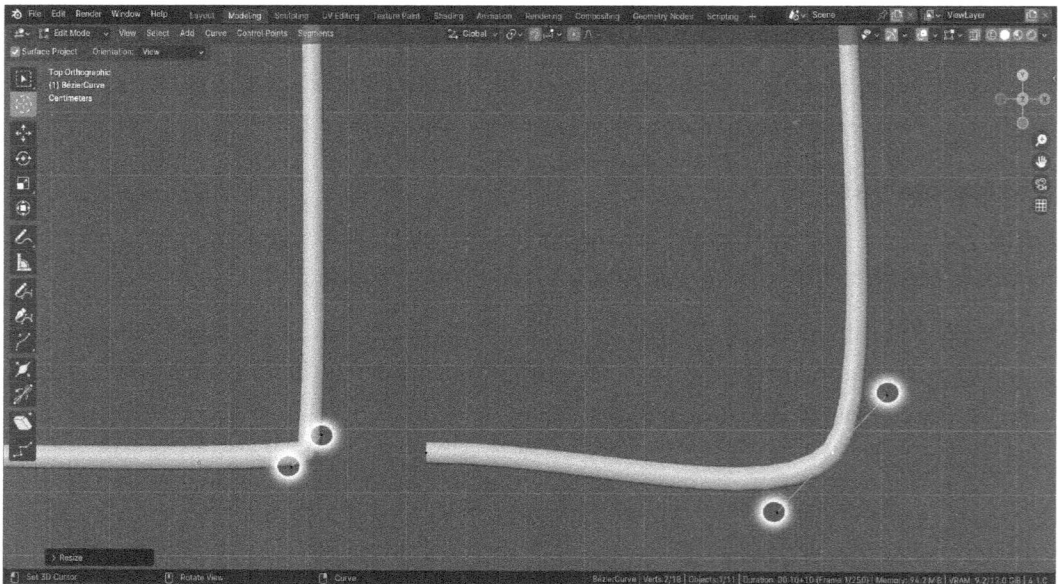

Figure 8.20: Smoothened (left) and sharpened (right) curves

Paths

Paths are a subset of the Bezier curve, consisting of a series of linked anchor points without handles. Paths are normally used as motion paths in animations, including for objects such as cameras, because these structures would follow paths, ensuring a smooth transition. To attach a camera to a curve, use **Follow Path** on the camera, like in *Figure 8.21*.

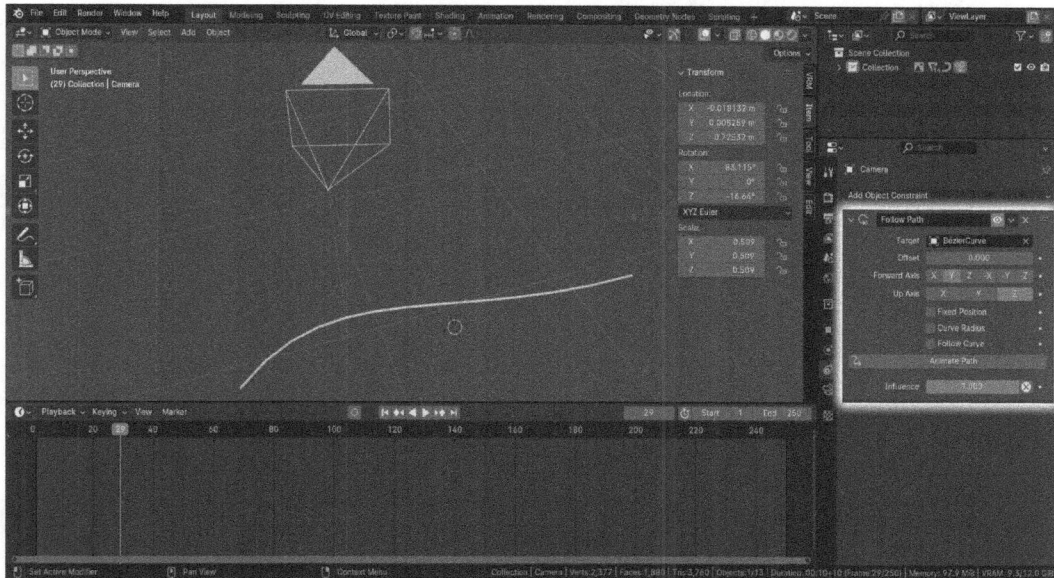

Figure 8.21: Attaching a camera to a curve

You can set the path's duration, allowing for faster or slower animations along the curve.

NURBS curves

Unlike **Bezier** curves, **NURBS** curves use a series of points that influence the curve's shape, but may not necessarily lie on it. NURBS are beneficial when you need a softer, more fluid curve, making them a favorite for industrial design and automotive modeling. In *Figure 8.22*, you can see curves with a geometry preset. We used them to draw out the ivy growth along the bridge wall.

Figure 8.22: Using NURBS curves in Blender to Unreal Engine 5: Fantasy River 3D Diorama Boat Scene by 3D Tudor

Tip

Just a quick tip, if you are using NURBS and plan to apply a **Solidify** modifier, make sure to add a bit of extrusion or bevel first. Without it, nothing will show up in the viewport, and you will be sitting there wondering why your geometry has ghosted you.

You can easily increase the number of control points, refining the curve's path. NURBS can also be closed, creating a cyclic shape.

B-Splines and circles

B-Splines are a simplified version of NURBS, offering a smoother curve by default. They are beneficial for backgrounds or when smoother curves are needed without intensive control, such as in rolling hills for a landscape scene. They can be adjusted using their control points, albeit with less sharpness than NURBS.

A **circle**, on the other hand, is a preset curve type in the form of a closed loop. They can be used for a myriad of purposes, including base shapes, paths, or even architectural elements. Their properties, such as **Radius**, can be easily modified.

Essential attributes of curves

Selecting your desired curve type is only part of the puzzle. To successfully use **curves** in Blender and to get a result you are happy with, you also need to know about **the** attributes of curves. These include the following:

- **Control points**: These define the shape of your curve. Depending on the type of curve, these points might be **Automatic**, **Aligned**, or **Vector**:

    - **Automatic** creates a curve based on an averaged-out angle connection between points. It adjusts the handles automatically, resulting in smooth transitions.

    - **Aligned** keeps the two handles in a straight line, giving you a consistent, averaged-out curve. Moving one handle will move the opposite one to maintain flow.

    - **Vector** lets you move each handle independently, giving you full control to create sharp corners or hard edges where needed.

To change them, you can press *V*, and this will access the **Handle Types** setting. It changes the way curve points interact with one another, as shown in *Figure 8.23*.

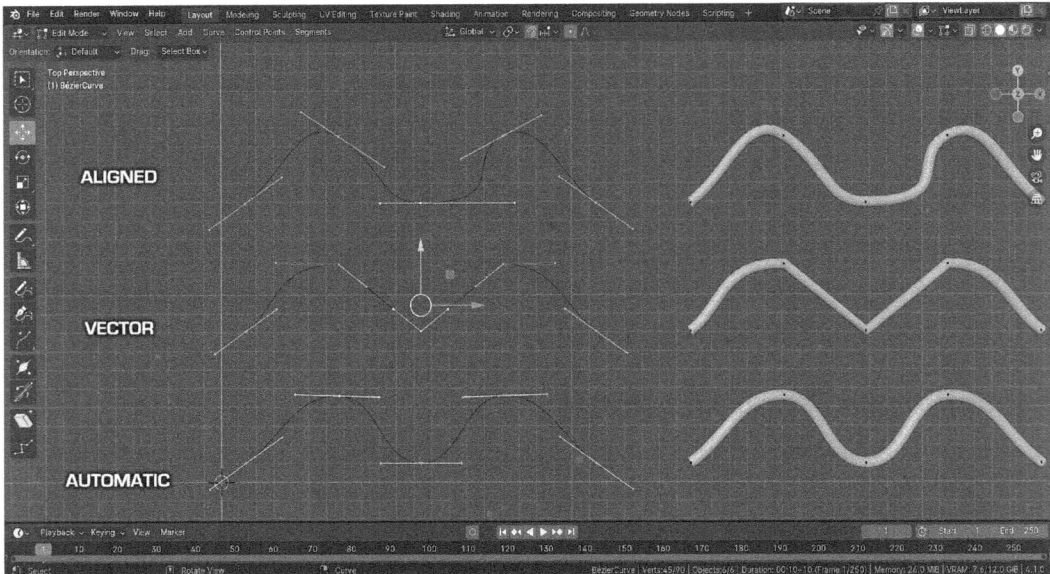

Figure 8.23: Control point handle types illustrated

When you select a control point, you get two points coming out of it, which average how it interacts with the previous and next points to create a line.

- **Handles**: Emergent from control points, they determine the curve's tangency, providing finesse in shaping.

- **Resolution**: Defines how smooth the curve appears, particularly once converted to a mesh or when using bevels.

- **Tilt**: Rotates the curve around its axis, invaluable for twisting effects. This could be useful in situations where you want to create intricate, spiralling designs, such as twisted ropes, spiral staircases, or decorative elements with a helical shape.

Accessing curves in Blender

To start using the **Curve** function, follow these steps:

1. Press *Shift + A* to open the **Add** menu and navigate to **Curve**. Here, you'll find the curve options, such as **Bezier**, **Circle**, **Path**, and **NURBS**, just discussed (see *Figure 8.24*):

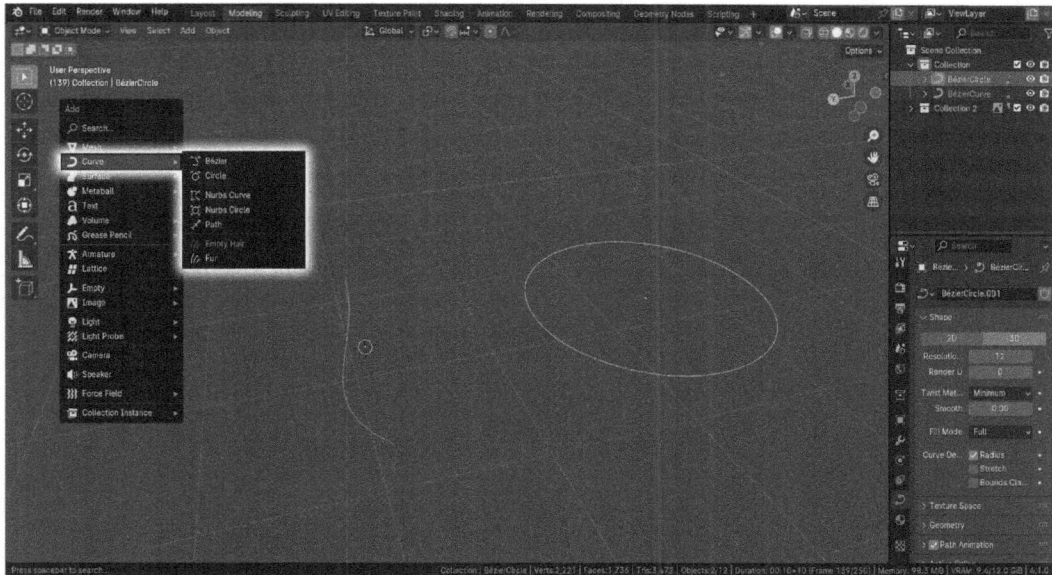

Figure 8.24: Curve options in Blender

2. Once you have created your curve(s), you can utilize **Object Data Properties** located on the right side of UI to refine and customize your project:

- **Bevel: Bevel** adds a 3D profile to a 2D curve, giving it depth and dimension. To adjust the bevel, follow these steps:

  a. In the **Properties** panel, go to the **Curve** tab.

  b. Under the **Geometry** section, set the depth and resolution to define how thick and smooth the beveled edge should be.

  c. You can also select another curve to act as a **Bevel** object, which will define the profile shape that gets extruded along the original curve.

- **Taper: Taper** modifies a curve's width along its length, allowing for variations in thickness. To adjust the taper, follow these steps:

  a. Go to the **Curve** tab in the **Properties** panel.

  b. Under the **Geometry** section, select another curve to act as a taper object, which will influence how the width of the original curve changes along its length.

c. When you hook up a second curve as a taper object, it tells Blender how thick or thin the main curve should be along its length. Blender reads the shape of that taper curve along its *y* axis, higher points make the mesh chunkier; lower points slim it down. Simple as that, but incredibly useful once you get the hang of it, like in *Figure 8.25*.

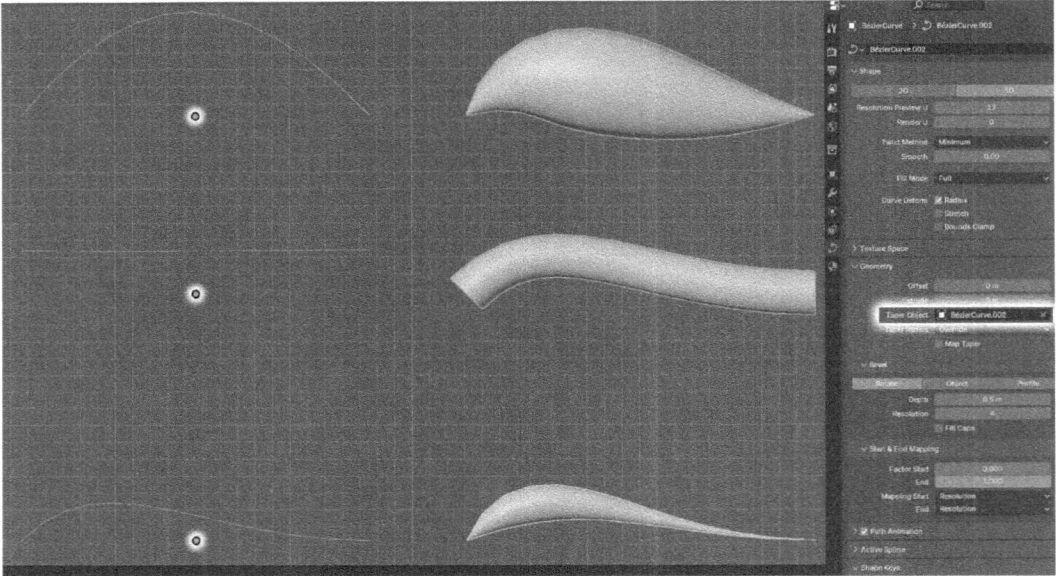

Figure 8.25: Taper object in action – curve thickness controlled by shape

Figure 8.25 shows how different taper curves (left column) affect the thickness of a main curve (right column). Blender reads the *x*-axis shape of the taper curve to decide how wide the mesh should be at each point:

- **Top row**: A high mid-curve makes the center thick and ends thin.
- **Middle row**: A flat taper creates a uniform width.
- **Bottom row**: A downward-sloping taper narrows the end, great for tentacles, tails, or stylized rope. On the right-hand side of the UI, you can see the **Taper Object** field under the **Geometry** settings, where you assign the taper curve. It is all procedural, and once you get the hang of it, it gives you loads of subtle control.

- **Fill Mode: Fill Mode** lets you choose between different fill modes to determine which parts of the curve are visible when it is given a bevel or extrusion. Under the **Shape** section of the **Curve** tab, you can set **Fill Mode** to **Full, Front, Back**, or **Half**, as shown in *Figure 8.26*. Adjusting these settings can control the visibility of the curve's cross-section.

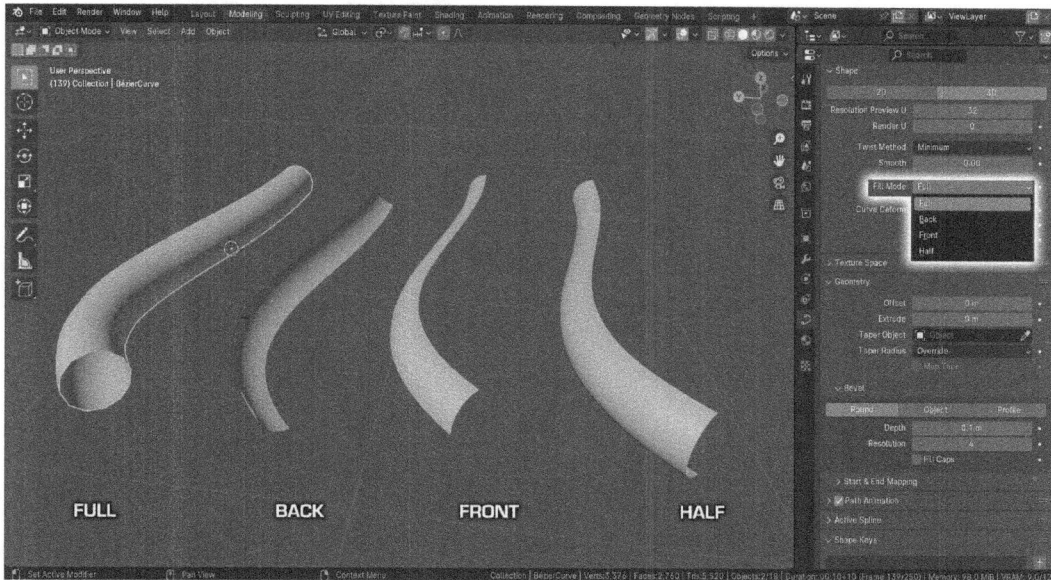

Figure 8.26: Full versus Front versus Back versus Half fill mode in Blender

> **Note**
>
> Make sure to enable the **Bevel** option to give your curve a 3D shape. Without a bevel or extrusion, your curve remains a flat outline, and the **Fill Mode** settings will have no visible effect.

- **Convert to mesh:** Go to **Object** | **Convert** | **Mesh** to transform your curve into a static mesh, useful if you are planning to proceed with advanced modeling or sculpting. For example, you could create a detailed spiral staircase railing with a curve, allowing you to add intricate textures and precise deformations that require mesh editing tools.

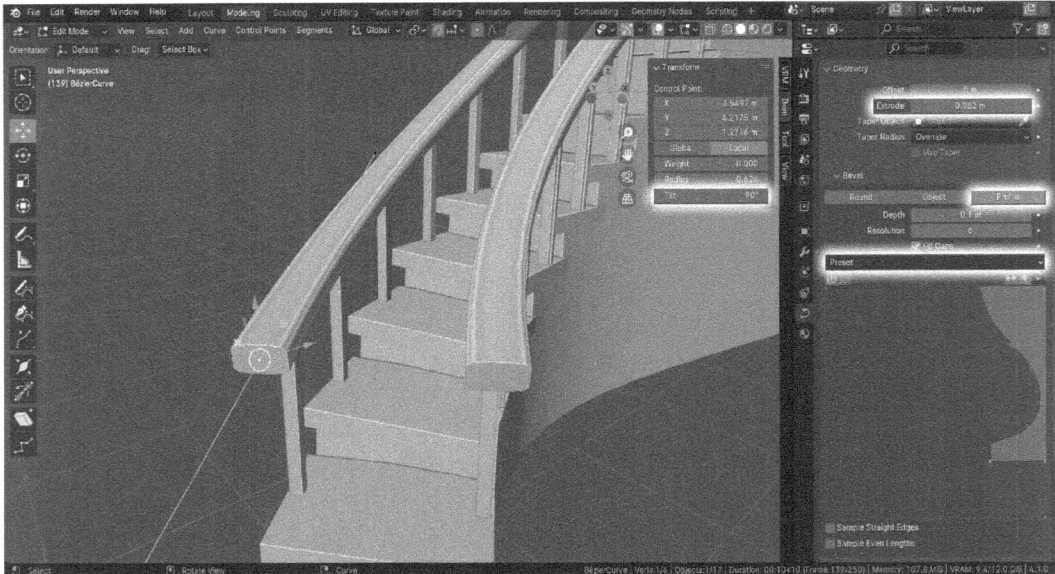

Figure 8.27: Notable curve-specific settings in Blender

Note

Before converting, you might want to finalize any curve-specific settings (see *Figure 8.27*), as these will no longer be available once the curve is transformed into a mesh.

The **Curve Profile** node in Blender is one of those sneaky little gems that quietly does a ton of heavy lifting; you can see all the shape options in *Figure 8.28*.

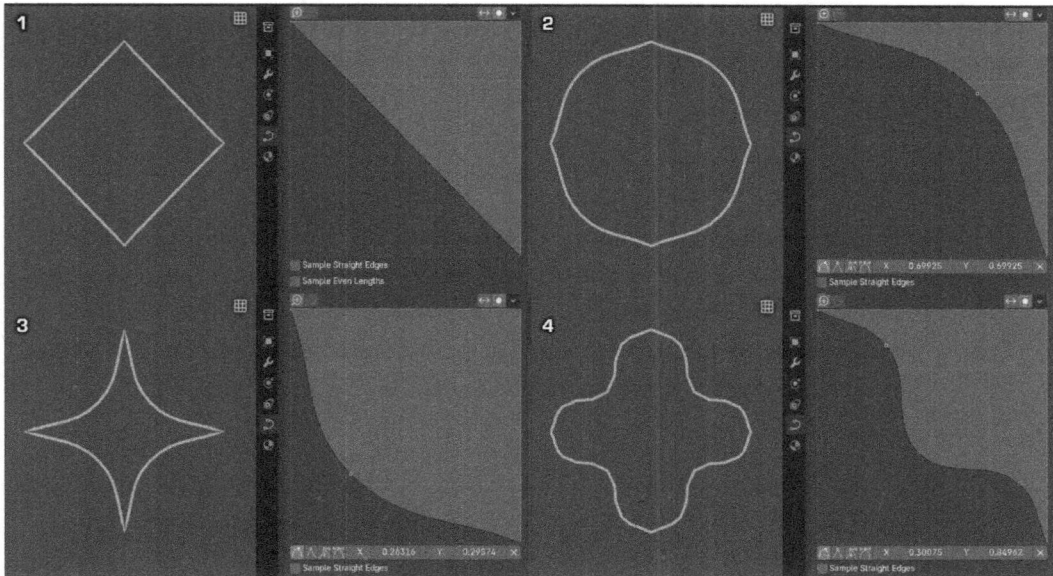

Figure 8.28: Curve Profile node shape options

It lets you sculpt the cross-section of your geometry as it travels along a curve, sort of like giving your mesh a bespoke haircut before it gets extruded. Whether you are going for sharp, smooth, weird, or wonderfully wobbly, this node has you covered. Take a look at the examples in *Figure 8.28*.

All four shapes came from the same base, but with a few nudges to the curve widget, you get wildly different results:

1. **Basic Diamond**: The no-nonsense, sharp-edged profile. Think of it as the "default because I forgot to tweak it" option.

2. **Rounded Form**: Smooth those handles into a soft Bézier curve and voilà: you have got a nice, circular silhouette.

3. **Pinched Star**: Want drama? Push those tangents inward and watch it stretch into something more magical (or slightly menacing).

4. **Stylized Cross**: This one dips, pinches, and pulls its way into a clover-like shape. Great for ornaments, symbols, or if you just feel like adding a bit of flair.

The magic here is all in the graph. Same input, wildly different outputs, all thanks to a bit of curve wrangling. Master this, and you will be well on your way to building procedural assets that look anything but generic.

Tip

To change the *height* of a railing, you can use **Bevel** with the **Extrude** option. **Extrude** does not go lower than a value of 0, meaning you cannot increase the *width* of the curve. In order to bypass that, you can select the points in **Edit Mode**. Go to the **N** menu and select **Item**, and change **Tilt** to 90 degrees. This will rotate the whole profile, allowing you to use **Extrude** as a means to change the width.

- **Curve Data Properties panel**: This section allows you to set the curve type (2D/3D) and switch between cyclic or non-cyclic curves. Here are some of the options:

  - **Twist Method**: Control how the curve twists, with options such as **Minimal**, **Tangent**, and **Z-Up**.

  - **Texture Space**: Adjusts how textures are mapped to the curve, allowing for more intricate visual designs.

  - **Modifiers**: Just like with meshes, curves can also utilize a set of modifiers. Curves are commonly used with the **Mirror, Array**, and **Boolean** modifiers. For example, the **Array** modifier could be used to duplicate a curve along a path, creating a series of repeating elements such as a chain link or a decorative border.

Examples of curve usage

Blender's **Curve** tool will be part of your 3D modeling artist treasure trove. What you need to do now is imagine where best to use them. The following is a list of three typical project areas where curves could be useful:

- **Organic designs**: Curves excel in sculpting fluid and natural forms. They are perfect tools for crafting flowing paths and intricate patterns, such as creating lush, jungle vines that seamlessly integrate with architectural elements or natural environments. We can see this in *Figure 8.28*, which uses **Geometry Nodes** too (we will discuss this later in the book).

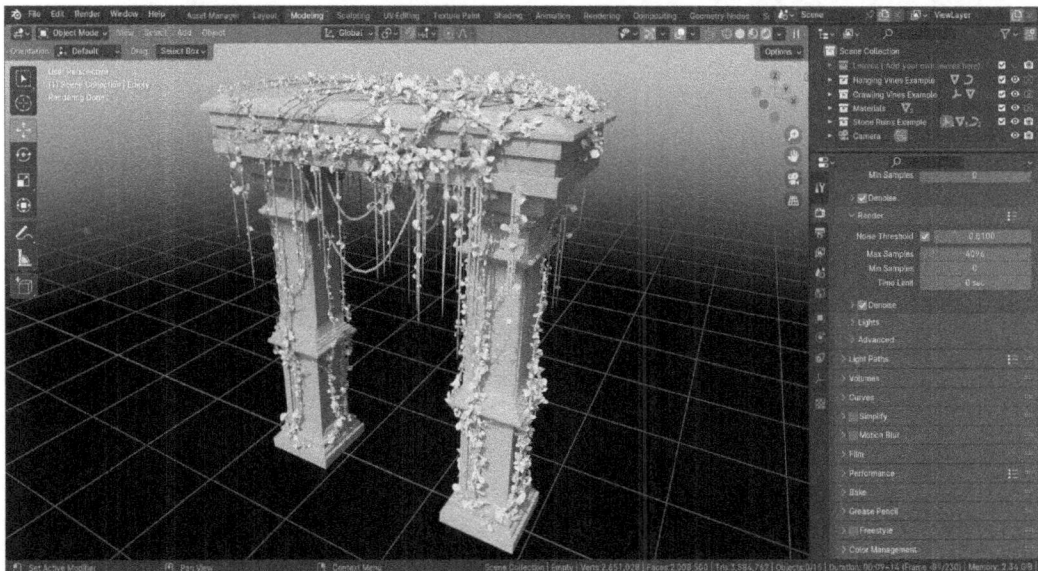

Figure 8.29: Blender 4 Jungle Vines Geometry Node by 3D Tudor

- **Animation trajectories:** Curves can be excellent planning tools and references for 3D animators. In using them as motion paths, artists can ensure smooth transitions and precision-controlled rotations, whether for cameras or animated objects.

- **Architectural accents:** There is nothing better than curves when it comes to moldings, stylized railings, or elaborate frames in architectural design. For example, in *Blender 4 Creator Course Stylized 3D Models*, the **Curve** tool was used to create the intricate wooden railings and the flowing shapes of the lantern supports, enhancing the stylized, whimsical look of the medieval tavern (*Figure 8.30*).

Figure 8.30: Building exterior in Blender 4 Creator Course Stylized 3D Models by 3D Tudor

Curves are brilliant, no doubt about it, but on their own, they are not going to carry you to 3D greatness. As you level up your modeling game, you will start to see that real progress comes from knowing when to mix things up. Great models do not come from one tool, they come from knowing how to blend them instinctively. So, with that in mind, let us move on and talk about surfaces, what they are, how they work, and why they might just be your next secret weapon.

Exploring NURBS surfaces in Blender

Surfaces are basically the next step up from curves. Think of them as 3D shapes that you can bend, twist, and shape using control points, just like curves, but with a lot more depth and flexibility. They are great for creating smooth, flowing forms and are especially handy when you are working on anything organic or complex. If you have never tried them before, they are well worth a go; you might be surprised how much control they give you.

To understand surfaces better, let us dive into NURBS surfaces. These surfaces offer the most versatility and control for complex, organic forms. While Blender includes multiple surface types (such as Bézier and NURBS), this section focuses on NURBS surfaces due to their intuitive control and smooth shaping capabilities. For an overview of all surface types, refer to the Blender documentation on surfaces (`https://docs.blender.org/manual/en/latest/modeling/surfaces/introduction.html`).

Look, NURBS surfaces might not be the go-to for most Blender artists these days, but they are still surprisingly useful, especially for precise, smooth shapes you would struggle to get otherwise. They are a bit niche now, but who knows? Tools change fast, and these might just make a comeback.

Figure 8.31 shows a few basic NURBS surface shapes such as spheres, cylinders, and toruses, but here is the important part: this image lets you visualize the control points. The orange cage-like structures show how Blender defines the surface. Each control point influences a region of the surface, and this interaction is what gives NURBS surfaces their fluid and flexible nature.

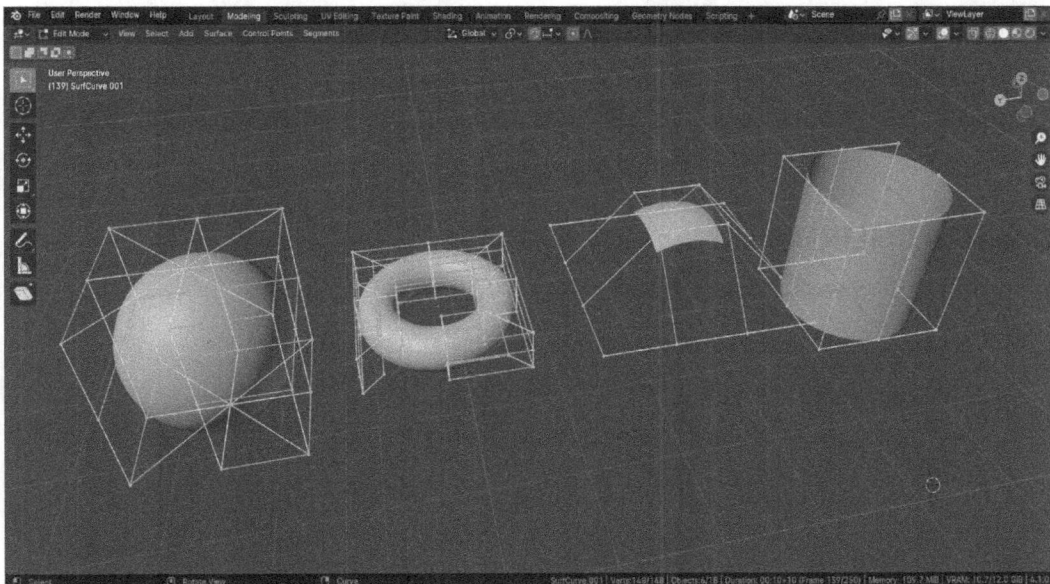

Figure 8.31: NURBS surfaces – visualizing the control points

Figure 8.32 is more of a how-to snapshot. It shows the default Blender menu when you press *Shift + A* and open the **Surface** submenu. This is how you add NURBS surfaces to your scene. The key detail is that most of these surfaces (except for **Curve** and **Circle**) are 2D presets that only display properly once extruded. You can see what they look like when generated, some will appear flat until you give them depth, while others (such as **Sphere** and **Torus**) preview as solid forms.

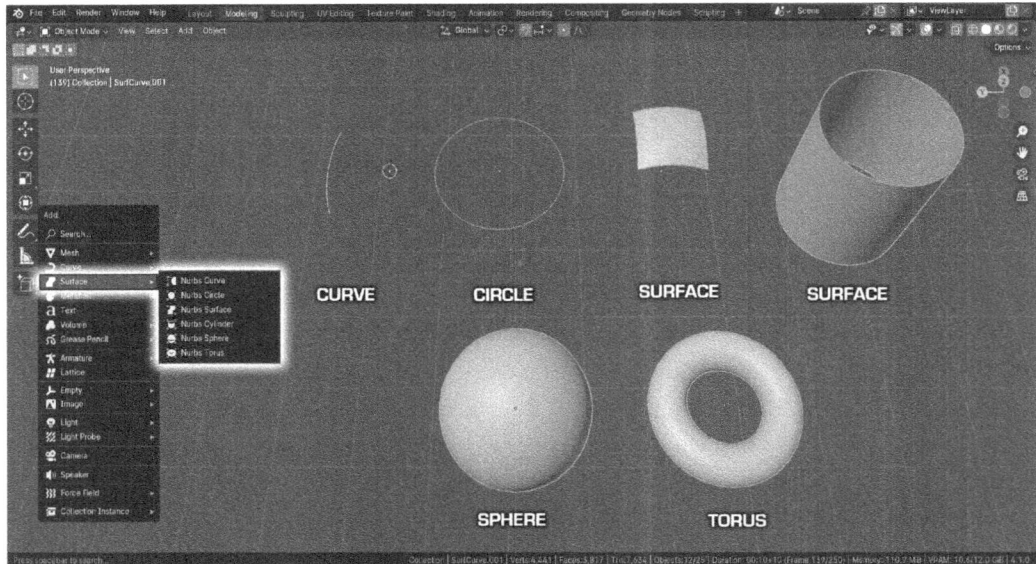

Figure 8.32: Types of NURBS surfaces in Blender

Creating NURBS surfaces

To create a NURBS surface, follow the next steps:

1. Press *Shift + A*, select **Surface**, and then select **NURBS Curve**.

2. Then, go to **Edit Mode** and extrude the vertices.

3. Next, go to the **Modifiers** tab and add a **Solidifier** modifier to add thickness to your 3D shape.

> Note
>
> The **Solidify** modifier will not work on 2D curves such as **Circle** or **Curve** unless they are extruded or converted to geometry first.

4. The main spline controls are located in **Data | Active Spline**. This will give you control over how points connect and interact with one another:

- **Cyclic** enables loop connections
- **Bezier** averages out and smoothens your mesh
- **Endpoint** forces the surface to reach the last points
- **Resolution** changes mesh density
- **Order** changes how many points it uses to average out to **Surface**, a higher count creates a smoother surface but is heavier on performance, so choose carefully

In *Figure 8.33*, you can see which **NURBS Sphere** settings are used and what your mesh looks like without them:

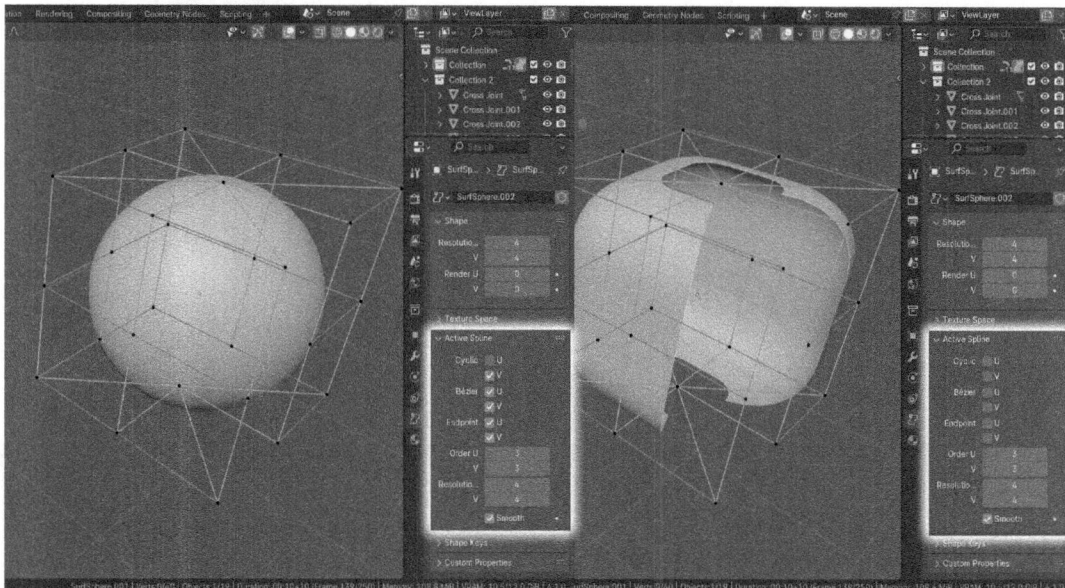

Figure 8.33: NURBS Sphere settings

Manipulating and refining surfaces

This is a crucial section focused on shaping and fine-tuning surfaces to create the 3D model you imagined. For example, if you are working on a project such as designing the sleek sports car in *Figure 8.34*, Blender's **Surface** function would help you sculpt its aerodynamic body with smooth curves and precise contours.

Figure 8.34: Sports car in Blender Lighting & Compositing for Beginners by 3D Tudor

From basic manipulations such as adjusting control points to more advanced settings in the **Properties** panel, each element plays a vital role in crafting the final appearance and quality of your surface. The following is a list of key tools and options available for manipulating and refining surfaces in Blender:

- **Edit Mode**: Allows you to manipulate the control points of the surface, adjusting their positions and the associated handles.

- **U Direction and V Direction**: Surfaces are defined in both the **U Direction** and **V Direction** settings, allowing for two-dimensional manipulation of the form. It basically creates a surface sheet that you can manipulate in 3D space.

- **Degree and Order**: These properties define the mathematical complexity and smoothness of the surface. The **Degree** property is responsible for determining the level of curvature and the influence each control point has over the shape of the surface. A higher **Degree** value usually means a smoother, more complex curve. **Order** changes how the control points' arrangement affects the surface's overall shape, influencing the level of detail and precision in the surface's curvature.

- **The Properties panel options**: As soon as you add a surface, a dedicated set of properties appears in the right-hand panel. This includes options such as setting the **Fill**, **Twist**, and **Texture Space Mapping** properties. Even though we will not discuss these in detail as part of this book, you can find a short overview of each option next:

  - **Fill**: Determines how the surface is filled, letting you choose between various filling methods such as filling only the edges or creating a solid, fully enclosed surface.

  - **Twist**: Adjusts the twist of the surface along its length, which can be used to create interesting spiraling effects or to correct distortions in the surface's geometry.

  - **Texture Space Mapping**: Controls how textures are mapped onto the surface, enabling you to adjust the placement, scale, and orientation of textures.

> Note
>
> If necessary, surfaces can be converted into a static mesh for further sculpting or modeling using the **Object** option, followed by **Convert** and **Mesh**. The old shortcut, *Alt + C*, may no longer work in recent Blender versions unless re-enabled in the **Key Bindings** menu.
>
> Surfaces can also be blended with curves, allowing you to generate complex structures by guiding the surface shape using curve paths. To do this, add a curve (Bezier or NURBS) that will act as the guide for the surface. Then, add a surface object (i.e., **NURBS Surface**, **Bezier Surface**, etc.). Next, apply the **Surface Deform** modifier to the surface object; this allows the surface to be influenced by the shape of the curve. Finally, fine-tune the settings of the **Surface Deform** modifier to ensure the surface follows the curve path the way you want it to.

Examples of surface usage

Surfaces are one of those tools that quietly do a lot of heavy lifting. Whether you are sculpting characters and creatures for a game or shaping out sleek product designs, they are brilliant for getting those smooth, complex forms just right. You will see them used everywhere, from organic creature meshes to curved walls and fancy fixtures. If the shape is tricky and needs to look clean, surfaces are probably what you are after.

Blender's surfaces offer a seamless transition from concept to 3D model, but it is important to understand that there are different types of surfaces that are suited for different kinds of models. As illustrated in *Table 8.1*, surfaces can be categorized based on their application:

Organic forms	Surfaces are perfect for modeling organic forms such as the human body, animal figures, or any 3D sculpture that requires smooth and natural transitions.
Complex topologies	You can also use surfaces to create details such as draped fabrics, intricate roof structures, or any nuanced architectural embellishments.
Architectural details	Think of intricate carvings, detailed clothing, or any other object that needs to be fluid but precise. Surfaces are the best thing for that, too!

Table 8.1: Examples of surface usage in 3D modeling

Surfaces in Blender open the door to a whole new level of organic modeling. In the film world, they have played a big part in bringing lifelike characters and bizarre creatures to life, stuff that feels believable, even when it is totally made up. No matter where you are on your 3D journey, getting comfortable with surfaces is one of those skills you will be glad you picked up. With that sorted, let us move on to another clever mesh tool that flies under the radar, metaballs.

Delving into metaballs in Blender

I will begin this section with a personal anecdote. Dyslexia has not stopped me from being a great teacher, but it has led to some funny bloopers. The first few times I used **metaballs**, I released some posts where I referred to them as *meat*balls! You might even find that post on our Patreon (https://www.patreon.com/3DTudor). Since then, every time I use them, I get an odd craving for meatballs. Now that I have had a chance to make you laugh (hopefully), I will go on to explain what metaballs are.

Unlike traditional meshes, metaballs are forms that blend and fuse based on their proximity to each other. As they move closer together, they merge, and as they move apart, they separate, creating smooth and organic transitions in your mesh. While traditional mesh modeling relies on vertices, edges, and faces, metaballs operate on a field influence, meaning that they create surfaces based on their proximity to one another.

Let's take a closer look at metaballs.

Types of metaballs in Blender

There are different types of metaball elements, including **Ball**, **Capsule**, **Plane**, and **Ellipsoid**, which can all be utilized for various modeling needs. Each type of metaball element has distinct characteristics that make it suitable for various modeling needs. Here's a brief description of the different types:

- **Ball**: This is the most common metaball, just a spherical shape that can be scaled and deformed. The **Ball** metaball is ideal for creating rounded, blob-like structures that you can use to start creating organic forms (e.g., a quick animation of a slime effect, like in *Figure 8.35*).

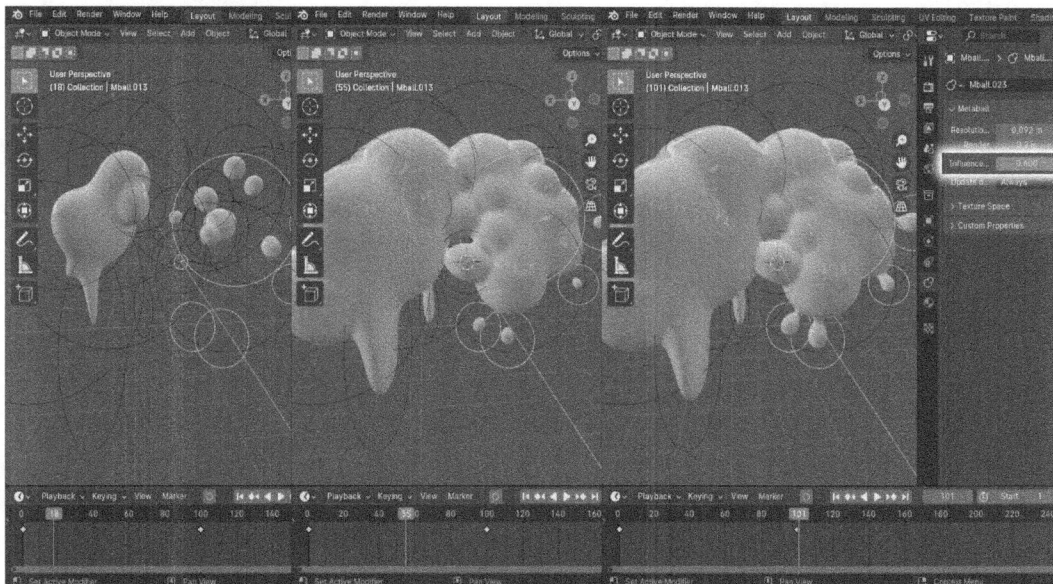

Figure 8.35: Creating a slime effect using the Ball metaball

- **Capsule**: An elongated shape, similar to a cylindrical or pill-like shape. This type is particularly useful for creating structures that require a longer, stretched form, such as limbs or elongated parts of organic creatures.

- **Plane**: A flat, two-dimensional element, useful for creating thin, sheet-like structures. In *Figure 8.36*, you can see how to create a stylized sofa using metaballs. We used **Plane** metaballs with various size scaling and stiffness parameters. We also used the **Negative** option to carve out certain parts, such as splitting the two cushions in the middle.

Figure 8.36: Stylized sofa made using metaballs

The **Plane** metaball is great for laying down the base of something chunky, such as this stylized sofa, giving you a solid foundation to build on. Then, by adding **Ball** or **Ellipsoid** metaballs on top, you can flesh out the cushions, arms, and even those subtle curves that make it look nice and soft. It is a super-intuitive way to sculpt blobby, organic forms without a ton of manual modeling.

- **Ellipsoid:** The **Ellipsoid** metaball is similar to the **Ball** metaball but stretched in one or more directions, creating an ellipsoidal shape. This type of metaball is good for creating oval or egg-shaped structures, or for when you need a more stretched and asymmetrical spherical form.

As you can see from the sofa example, each metaball type can be used on its own or mixed together to build complex, organic shapes. What makes metaballs special is how naturally they blend, giving you smooth transitions and fluid forms that would be a real pain to pull off with standard mesh modeling.

Accessing metaballs in Blender

To start using metaballs in Blender, make sure your **3D Viewport** is clear and follow these steps:

1. To add a metaball, click **Add | Mesh**, then **Metaball**.

2. A submenu will appear, showing the different types of metaballs. When you choose one, by default, it will be placed at the center of the scene.

3. With the metaball selected, you can move it (*G* key), rotate it (*R* key), and scale it (*S* key), just as with any other object in Blender. Use these transformations to position and shape your metaball where you want it to be.

4. In the lower-right corner of the Blender interface, you will find the **Properties** panel. With your metaball selected, you can adjust various properties, such as the resolution, which affects the smoothness and detail level of the metaball.

5. To create more complex shapes, you can add extra metaballs to your scene. Simply repeat *step 1* to add more metaballs.

6. If needed, you can adjust how metaballs appear in your **3D Viewport** and the final render. This is done in the **Properties** panel under the **Data** tab. You can tweak settings such as **Resolution Viewport** and **Render Resolution** to control how dense the mesh appears. **Resolution Viewport** handles what you see while working in the **3D Viewport**, like the lower-res version on the left of *Figure 8.37*, while **Render Resolution** kicks in when you hit **Render**, giving you that smoother final result, like the version on the right.

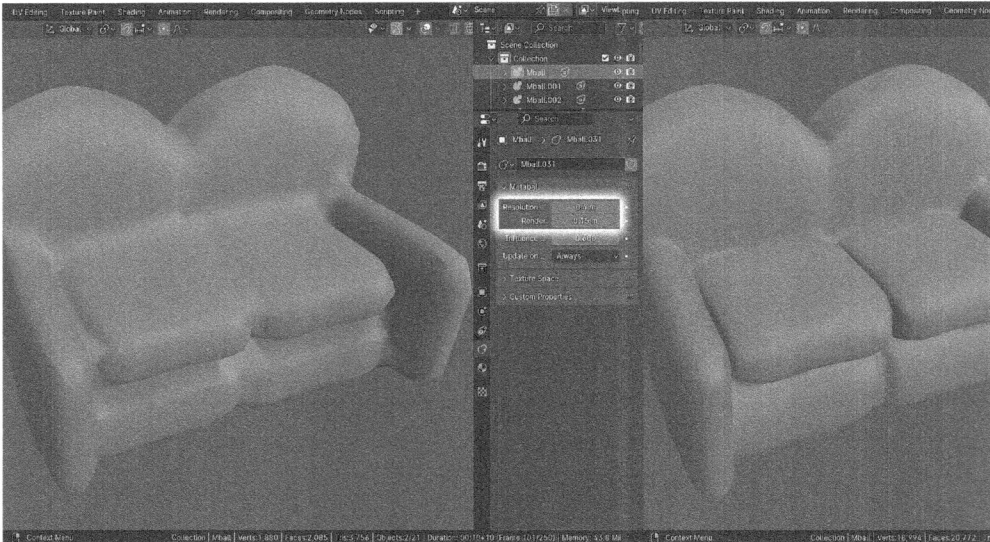

Figure 8.37: Changing how your metaball appears in the final render before (left) and after (right) tweaking settings

7. Once satisfied with the metaball design, use **Convert to Mesh** by navigating to **Object | Convert | Mesh**. This will now be converted into a traditional mesh for detailed sculpting, editing, or further refinements.

Manipulating and refining metaballs

To effectively manipulate and refine metaballs in Blender, it is important to understand the tools and features available. These features allow you to precisely control the shape and behavior of metaballs, ensuring that your modeling process is efficient and accurate.

The following are key aspects of working with metaballs, including editing modes, merging influences, and various properties accessible through Blender's interface:

*   **Editing mode:** Just like other objects, metaballs have an editing mode that lets you add or adjust individual metaball elements within a single object.

- **Threshold and Influence**: The degree to which metaballs merge is determined by a **Threshold** value. Meanwhile, the **Influence** value sets the level at which metaballs will blend together, controlling how seamlessly they merge.

- **The Properties panel options**: The right-hand panel in Blender displays various properties of metaballs when one is selected. The **Data** panel will give you a **Metaball** tab, which controls overall settings of metaballs.

- This includes options such as **Resolution**, **Update Method**, and **Family Grouping**:

  - **Resolution** lets you set the level of detail for metaballs, with separate settings for your **3D Viewport** and **Render** view. Adjusting the **Resolution** setting can impact both the visual quality and the performance of your scene.

  - The **Update Method** option controls how Blender recalculates the shape and surface of metaballs during editing. Different update methods can affect the performance and responsiveness of Blender when working with complex scenes or a large number of metaballs. For example, some methods might offer faster updates at the cost of precision, while others provide more accurate updates but may be slower, especially in high-polygon scenes.

  - **Family Grouping** allows you to control how metaballs merge into a single smooth object by grouping metaballs.

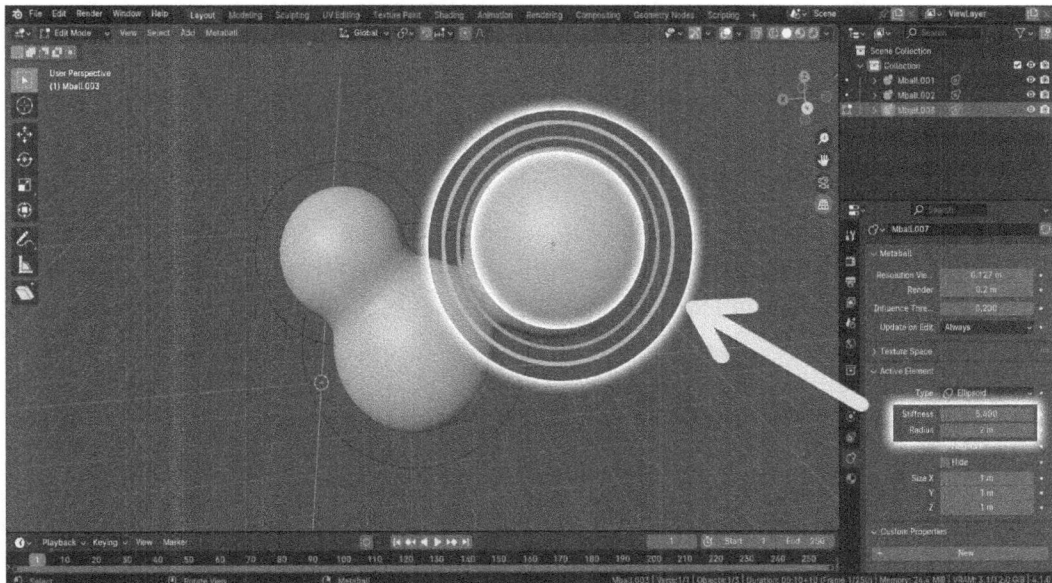

Figure 8.38: Metaball Stiffness and Radius parameter options

Note

If you select a metaball in **Edit Mode**, you can use the **Active Element** option to control parameters for individual metaballs, as shown in *Figure 8.38*, too.

Also, sometimes a metaball will not update when a part was deleted or adjusted in parameters. Hitting *Tab* twice to enter and exit Blender's **Edit Mode** helps to update it and fix this issue.

Examples of metaball usage

Metaballs offer unique advantages because they can form organic and fluid shapes, making them ideal for certain types of projects. Here are some practical uses of **metaballs** in different creative contexts:

- **Organic and fluid shapes**: Metaballs are perfect for creating liquid simulations, soft bodies, or any form that demands fluidity and seamless merging. As a project, you could create a scene of water splashing into a glass, using metaballs to simulate the fluidity and natural merging of water droplets and ripples.

- **Rapid prototyping**: You can quickly mock up shapes and forms using metaballs before refining them further with traditional modeling tools. You might use metaballs to rapidly prototype the concept of a modern building with flowing, organic architectural elements, such as a lobby with a wave-like ceiling structure.

- **Abstract art**: Their unique behavior makes metaballs a favorite tool for abstract and non-traditional designs in digital art. For example, you could create a digital sculpture with different interlocking, fluid forms.

Metaballs will help you think outside the box, helping you create designs that echo the rhythm of nature and look abstract. You might have noticed that the focus of *Chapter 8* is on presenting Blender features that are well suited for organic modeling of living forms, among other uses. As this chapter comes to an end, we will take a short detour to text-based mesh features in Blender.

Harnessing Blender's text capabilities

Blender's **Text** tool lets you add 2D and 3D text in a 3D scene, helping you create descriptive labels and title sequences, or annotate architectural illustrations and product mockups. With this, too, you can choose your font style, size, and thickness, and use **Extrusion** to give it a 3D appearance.

Accessing the Text tool in Blender

To create 3D text using the **Text** tool in Blender, follow these steps:

1. In **Object Mode**, press *Shift + A* and navigate to **Text**.

2. Then, enter **Edit Mode** (*Tab*) and use standard transformation tools (*G* for move, *R* for rotate, *S* for scale) to adjust the position, orientation, and size of the **Text** object.

3. If needed, convert your **Text** object to a mesh. Converting text into a mesh is particularly useful when you need to perform detailed edits or apply modifiers that are not available for **Text** objects. For example, if you want to add intricate 3D effects, Boolean operations, or custom deformations to your **Text** object, converting it to a mesh allows you to leverage Blender's full range of modeling tools. This process is essential for creating complex typography in 3D scenes, customizing fonts, or integrating **Text** objects into more elaborate designs and animations.

4. To convert text into mesh, navigate to the **Object** menu, click on **Convert To**, and then select **Mesh from Curve**, following the smaller steps shown in *Figure 8.39*, from the adjustment options you can see there on the right-hand side.

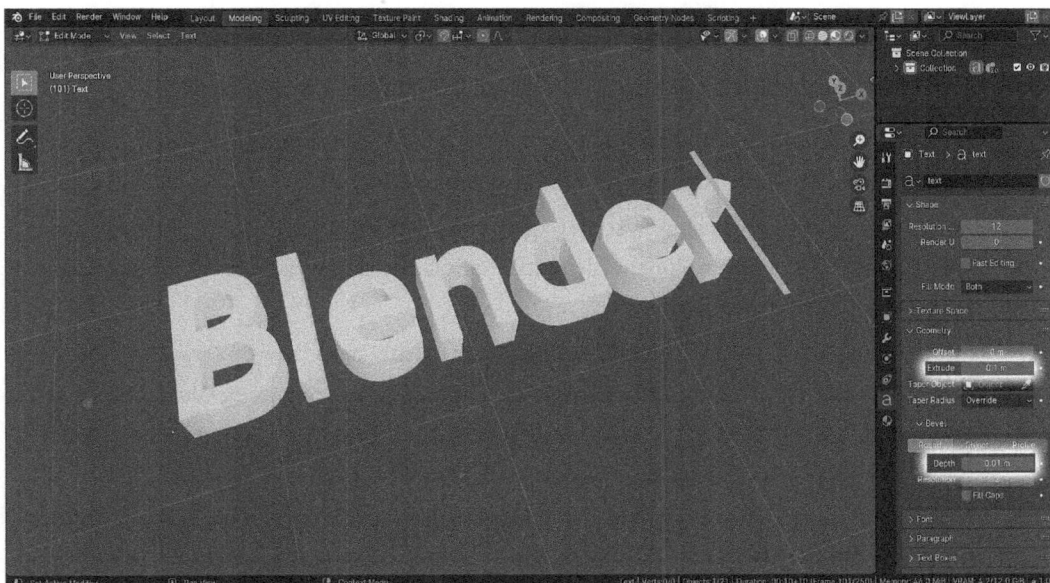

Figure 8.39: Converting mesh to text

Before we get to converting your text into a mesh, let us talk about some powerful tweaks you can make while your text is still editable. Since Blender treats text as a curve object under the hood, you have access to some of the same procedural tools, such as **Extrusion**, **Bevel**, and **Depth**, that you use on curves.

5. You can also use the **Data** tab, then go to **Geometry**, **Extrude**, and, finally, **Bevel** and **Depth**. These settings allow you to do the following:

   - **Extrude**: Add thickness to the mesh by extending the **Text** object along its normal, creating a 3D effect
   - **Bevel**: Smooth out the edges and corners of the **Text** object by applying a bevel, which enhances its appearance and readability
   - **Depth**: Control the overall thickness of the **Text** mesh, giving it more substance and presence in your 3D scene
   - You will want to make all these adjustments before converting your text into a mesh, because once you do that, these options disappear, and you are locked into working with static geometry.

Adjusting text in Blender

To adjust the **Text** mesh you created via the **Text** tool in Blender, follow these steps:

1. First, in the right-hand side of the Blender interface, find the **Properties** panel and click on the α icon for **Data**, representing the text properties.

2. Load custom fonts from your system to give your text a unique style by pressing *Tab* and then navigating to **Open Font**. This feature allows you to choose from a wide range of fonts installed on your computer.

3. Adjust the space between individual characters to fine-tune the appearance of your text. You can do that by pressing *Tab* and accessing **Spacing**, then selecting **Character Spacing** and specifying **Word Spacing**, and then selecting **Line Spacing**. This is particularly useful for achieving precise typography and improving readability.

4. Modify the space between words to ensure that your text layout looks balanced and aesthetically pleasing using the options in the same panel as the previous step. This can help in adjusting the overall density of your text.

5. Determine the gap between lines of text to control the overall vertical spacing of your text blocks using the available **Line Spacing** option. Proper line spacing can make your text more legible.

6. Still inside the **Spacing** tab, go to **Text Boxes**, click on **Add Text Box**, and input values for its size and offset. Blender sets these to 0x0 by default, which means the box might not show up unless you give it actual dimensions. Keep in mind that text content will always appear in **Edit Mode**, but the textbox outline only shows up if you have entered values. So, if your text looks truncated or misaligned, check that your textbox size is big enough and offset properly.

7. Control extrusion (i.e., 3D depth), bevel depth, and resolution. These settings enable you to add depth and detail to your text, transforming it from a flat surface into a three-dimensional object with various levels of detail.

Examples of Text tool usage

Blender's **Text** tool has many creative and practical applications. Whether you are a graphic designer, animator, or 3D artist, understanding how to use this tool can add significant value to your work. Here are some concrete examples of how the **Text** tool can be used in different contexts:

- **3D logos**: You could use Blender's **Text** tool to design a 3D version of a company logo, like in *Figure 8.40*.

Figure 8.40: Easy-to-make 3D logo for a pet shop in Blender Beginner's Bootcamp by 3D Tudor

- You could also go the extra mile and use **Geometry Nodes** to make your text look alive. Imagine effortlessly infusing your scenes with vibrant meadows rich in stylized grass, leaves, stems, and flowers. With **Geometry Nodes**, you can do just that (*Figure 8.41*).

Figure 8.41: Meadow growing on 3D text made with Blender 4 Grass & Flowers Procedural Geometry Node by 3D Tudor

- On top of this, the **Text** tool is also ideal for creating models for 3D printing, such as a physical logo for a store.

- **Scene annotations**: You can use the **Text** tool to label different areas or objects within a 3D scene. This is particularly useful in educational or presentation materials, where you need to identify and explain an architectural model, in larger scenes such as in *Figure 8.42*.

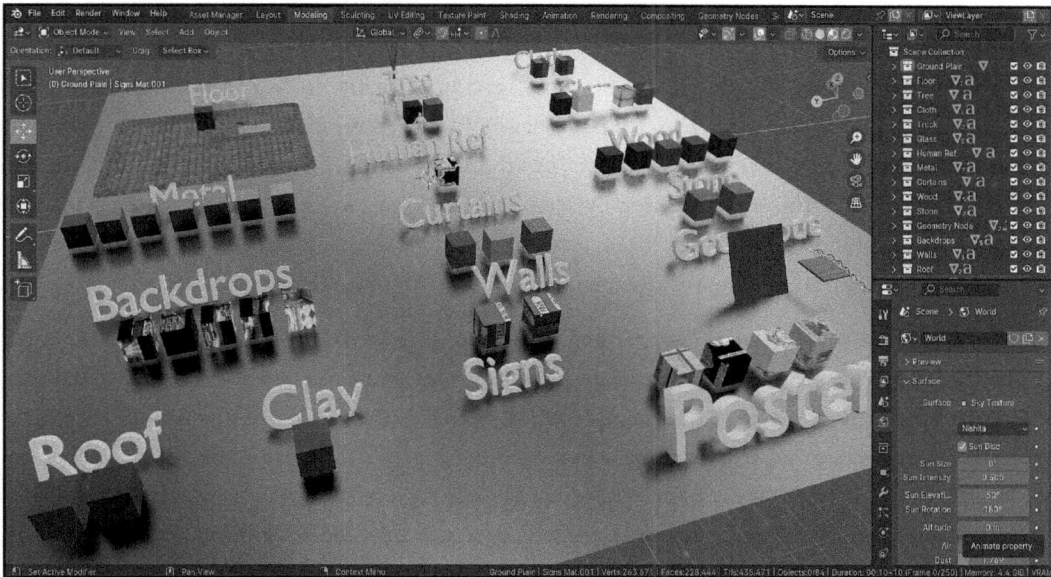

Figure 8.42: Laying out a large architectural scene

- If you are working on a complex environment, you could use the **Text** tool to annotate different quarters or parts of a town during grayboxing.

- **Dynamic graphics**: Combining text with Blender's animation tools can help you create title sequences or text animations. You could animate the text to change size, move through a scene, or morph into different shapes.

Blender's **Text** tool is one of those underrated gems that can seriously level up your creative work. Whether you are crafting slick 3D logos, adding labels to key parts of a scene, or animating text for a title sequence, knowing how to wrangle this tool gives you way more flexibility. It is a small skill that opens up a lot of doors, both for visual polish and practical design.

Summary

This chapter rides on the shoulders of the last one, giving you a bit of a head start with some juicy mid-level modeling tricks. If you had jumped straight in here, it might have felt like being thrown into the deep end with bricks in your pockets, but thanks to *Chapter 7*, you are already swimming. Like before, we broke things down step by step, but this time, we leveled up with mini project mashups, some blending two, even three, techniques into a single design. It is a taste of what is coming next, where things get more advanced, more creative, and — let's be honest, a lot more fun.

We followed a natural progression after initially introducing you to the **Add Extra Objects** function in Blender. From there, we explored some of the most prominent extra objects available in Blender 4 and discussed the purpose of the Blender Monkey: Suzanne. You learned ways of generating rocks and gears and found out how to use curves and surfaces to add mesh details or create new meshes for larger models. This chapter gave you a stack of project ideas to help you put your new skills into practice, with a strong focus on realistic design using Blender's modeling tools, such as, for example, the **Gear Generator** tool, and more organic forms using metaballs and surfaces. It was less about theory and more about getting your hands dirty, applying what you have learned to scenes that actually look like something you would want to show off.

We also touched on how to generate 3D text and the many uses of Blender's **Text** tool, including but not limited to cinematography, logo design, and 3D printing. As this chapter finished, you got a sneak peek into one of the final parts of this book, *Chapter 7* in *Part 2* of this book, where you will see just how powerful Blender is.

Now that you have got the hang of things such as rock and gear generation, and all the practical tricks that came with them, it is time to level up. We are moving past mid-level modeling and into more advanced territory, starting with some seriously useful tools you might have overlooked: **empties** and **lattices**. Trust me, they are way more powerful than they sound.

Further reading

- If you are interested in learning how to create objects such as vehicle tires, lifebuoys, or jewelry pieces using the **Torus** shape, see *Blender Lighting & Compositing for Beginners*. This course will help you master the basics and refine your skills in shaping and fine-tuning surfaces in Blender (`https://www.udemy.com/course/blender-lighting-compositing-for-beginners/?referralCode=7EC5DB0E4AC7A370F003`).

- To enhance the realism of your 3D scenes using Blender's **Rock Generator** feature, explore *Build Stunning Medieval Worlds with UE5's Modular Kitbash*. The course demonstrates how strategically placed rocks can add essential environmental detail (`https://www.udemy.com/course/building-medieval-worlds-unreal-engine-5-modular-kitbash/?referralCode=F936D687808F3AE55AF2`).

- If animating mechanical parts such as gears interests you, Blender will help you simulate their rotational movements effectively. For more details, see *Blender to Unreal Engine 5*, which features a watermill wheel animation (`https://www.udemy.com/course/blender-to-unreal-engine-5/?referralCode=EE62F6FE24732550ACD2`).

- Architectural designers looking to add ornate details such as moldings, stylized railings, or elaborate frames should refer to *Blender 4 Creator Course Stylized 3D Models* (`https://www.udemy.com/course/blender-4-creator-course-stylized-3d-models/?referralCode=1CCFEC9403D6E1B4FB19`).

- For those working on sci-fi or steampunk designs, where pipes and joints play a crucial role, consider *Blender Sci-fi Scenes with Eevee*. This course will help you create intricate mechanical touches (`https://www.udemy.com/course/blender-28-beginners-guide-to-3d-modeling-a-sci-fi-scene/?referralCode=7F31198BF2CCCD95415D`).

- If you aim to create fluid, natural forms such as lush jungle vines that integrate seamlessly into architectural elements or natural environments, see *Blender 4 Jungle Vines Geometry Node* by 3D Tudor (`https://3dtudor.gumroad.com/l/blender4-jungle-vine-geometrynode`).

Subscribe to Game Dev Assembly!

We are excited to introduce **Game Dev Assembly**, our brand-new newsletter dedicated to everything game development. Whether you're coding, designing, animating, or managing a studio, we've got insights, trends, and expert advice to help you create, innovate, and thrive. Sign up now and get exciting benefits.

`https://packt.link/gamedev-newsletter`

Join the 3D Tudor Channel Discord Server!

Join the 3D Tudor Channel Discord Server, a creative hub for learning Blender, Unreal Engine, Substance Painter, and 3D modeling, for discussions with the authors and other readers:

`https://discord.gg/5EkjT36vUj`

9

Discovering Must-Know Advanced Blender Modeling Techniques

This is where things start to level up. In this chapter, you will take your first proper steps into the more advanced side of 3D modeling, and if you have made it this far, you are more than ready.

We kick things off with something a lot of artists overlook: the humble reference image. Now, I know it might not sound exciting, but trust me, learning how to reference properly is a game-changer. We will look at how to turn reference images into solid guides for our modeling, not just decorate the background. Speaking of which, we will also talk about background images. They might not scream "advanced technique," but they are essential when it comes to setting the mood. You will learn how to bring them in, line them up, and make sure they enhance, not distract from, your work.

Next, we will move on to object relationships with **parenting**. It is like setting up a family structure in Blender, parents, kids, and all the fun hierarchy stuff that comes with it. You will learn how to build those connections, why they matter, and how they can make your life a whole lot easier when animating or organizing your scene.

From there, we step into the world of **empties**. These little invisible helpers do not show up in your final render, but behind the scenes, they are doing all sorts of things, controlling deformations, acting as animation handles, and helping you stay organized in complex scenes. They are underrated, but by the end of this section, you will be putting them to work like a pro.

And then there are **lattices**. These things are brilliant when you want to bend, squash, or stretch your mesh without turning it into a mangled mess. Whether you are fine-tuning a character's silhouette or adding a cheeky curve to an otherwise boring shape, lattices let you reshape with style and precision. We will cover how to set them up, bind them to our models, and use them in all sorts of creative ways, from organic characters to weird and wonderful abstract art.

After that, we jump into one of Blender's most unique tools: **Grease Pencil**. It is like Blender handed a sketchbook to your 3D scene and said, "Have at it." **Grease Pencil** bridges the gap between 2D and 3D in the best possible way, letting you sketch, color, and even animate right in your 3D workspace. If you love drawing or just want to plan out your scenes with a bit more visual flair, this tool is going to be right up your alley. Think of it as doodling with superpowers.

Finally, we take a closer look at the *Shift* key. Yes, *that Shift* key. It might not look like much, but once you learn its many tricks, snapping, multiple selections, and modifier tweaks, you will wonder how you ever worked without it.

So yes, this chapter is packed. It is all about broadening your skillset and giving you more tools to handle the creative and technical demands of Blender. By the end of it, you will have a whole new toolkit at your fingertips, and a clearer path toward mastery.

So, in this chapter, we will cover the following topics:

- Dabbling with reference images as blueprints
- Crafting ambience with background images
- Unveiling parenting: A cornerstone of object relationships in Blender
- Embracing empties: The invisible architects of 3D design in Blender
- Harnessing the power of lattices in Blender: A comprehensive guide
- Drawing, sculpting, and more with Blender's **Grease Pencil**
- Refining movement in Blender with the *Shift* key

Technical requirements

As for **Blender 4.5 LTS (Long-Term Support)**, the general requirements include a macOS 11.2 or newer (Apple Silicon supported natively) operating system, or a Linux (64-bit, glibc 2.28 or newer) operating system. Blender now requires a CPU with the SSE4.2 instruction set, at least 8 GB of RAM (32 GB recommended for heavy scenes), and a GPU supporting OpenGL 4.3 with a minimum of 2 GB of VRAM.

For a full list of technical requirements, please refer back to *Chapter 1* of this part.

Dabbling with reference images as blueprints

Referencing was the hardest part of the 3D modeling workflow that I had to get used to, and it is something I avoided like the plague during my early university years. Honestly, though, I should have taken a more mature approach to it. A myth I had to debunk is that referencing is just there for academic subjects and essay writing. However, looking at the process of making 3D art more closely, we all come to realize that many of our best ideas come from one or more ideas of things we have seen through personal experience. Those experiences are then what we add our personal touch to and create 3D models out of. That's how I would put it.

If your goal is modeling precision, then referencing is about closely adhering to concept art or a real-world image of something you are trying to recreate in 3D. Those references would be like visual blueprints for your modeling. But you can reference the same model from different perspectives to create a side, front, and top view of a building, for example, and then add your personal touch to it.

Setting up reference images

I normally use a free referencing tool called **PureRef** (`https://www.pureref.com/`) as part of my referencing routine (*Figure 9.1*).

Figure 9.1: Using PureRef for Blender to Unreal Engine 5 The Complete Beginners Guide by 3D Tudor

Although other tools exist, Blender does come with ready-to-use functionalities for all your referencing needs. To get your referencing resources ready in Blender, follow the next steps:

1. Align your camera. You are creating an image based on the position of your camera. Use the *1* (front camera position), *3* (side camera position), or *7* (top camera position) keyboard shortcut based on your project's needs.

Note

Aligning the camera helps set up the correct perspective or view for the reference images you are using in Blender. When you are working with reference images, it is important to match the camera's angle with the viewpoint that best fits your project: front, side, or top. This alignment ensures that your reference images are positioned correctly relative to your 3D models, letting you model or animate them based on the reference.

2. To add a reference, in the 3D Viewport, press *Shift + A*. Then, from the menu, select **Image**, then **Reference**. This spawns an empty that displays your chosen image.

3. Then, position the reference, aligning the image based on the desired perspective, using *G* to move it.

4. Add more references as needed, ensuring consistent alignment among them.

5. Adjust each image's scale for a uniform modeling base. Use the alignment tools in Blender to position them coherently. You can move (the *G* key), rotate (the *R* key), and scale (the *S* key) just like any other object in Blender. Alternatively, you can use controls on the image itself, you can click on the side of the image to scale it, or you can use *X* in the center of the image to move it.

6. To customize the images, navigate to the right-hand panel in the 3D Viewport. Then, modify the transparency and set the side visibility (i.e., control the sides of the reference image so that it is visible in the 3D Viewport sideways). Here are some options in the **N-panel** to know:

   • **Backface Culling**: This option will make the reference image visible from just the front side, hiding it from the back. You can find this option under the **Object Data Properties** tab (i.e., the green triangle icon), within the **Viewport Display** section.

- **Alpha/Transparency**: Adjusting the transparency of the reference image can also help here. Under the **Image** tab, you can find options to control the opacity of the reference image. This indirectly influences how visible the image is from various angles.

- **Object Visibility**: You can also control the visibility of the entire reference object in specific views (e.g., only in the front view but not the side view) by using the **Local View** mode (activated by pressing /on the numpad) or by manually hiding the object in certain views using layers or collections from the menus.

After adjusting the transparency and side visibility, you should end up with something like what you can see in *Figure 9.2*.

Figure 9.2: An example of preparing your project with Blender's built-in referencing tools

> Tip
>
> Accidentally relocating an image during modeling is common. Ensure they are locked post-setup. You can make an image un-targetable in your 3D Viewport by unticking **Selectable** in the Outliner. If you have already moved it all to a collection, you can simply deselect it from the collection folder.

Expert tips for referencing

To enhance your workflow and do referencing in Blender, consider the following expert tips:

- **Layer management**: For smooth toggling and organization, arrange your reference images in collections or layers, a bit like in **Adobe Photoshop**, if you have used that before (see *Figure 9.3*).

Figure 9.3: Organizing images in collections or layers in Blender

This approach helps you keep your workspace tidy and makes it easier to focus on specific references without visual clutter.

> **Note**
>
> To move references, select all images, press *M*, select **New Collection**, and then tick **Selectable** for the collection. If you do not see the icon, click on the restriction toggles icon (top right) and select **Selectables** to make it visible in your Outliner.

- **Use orthographic view for precision**: Switch to orthographic view (using numpad keys such as *1* or *3*) for an undistorted modeling perspective, as in *Figure 9.4*:

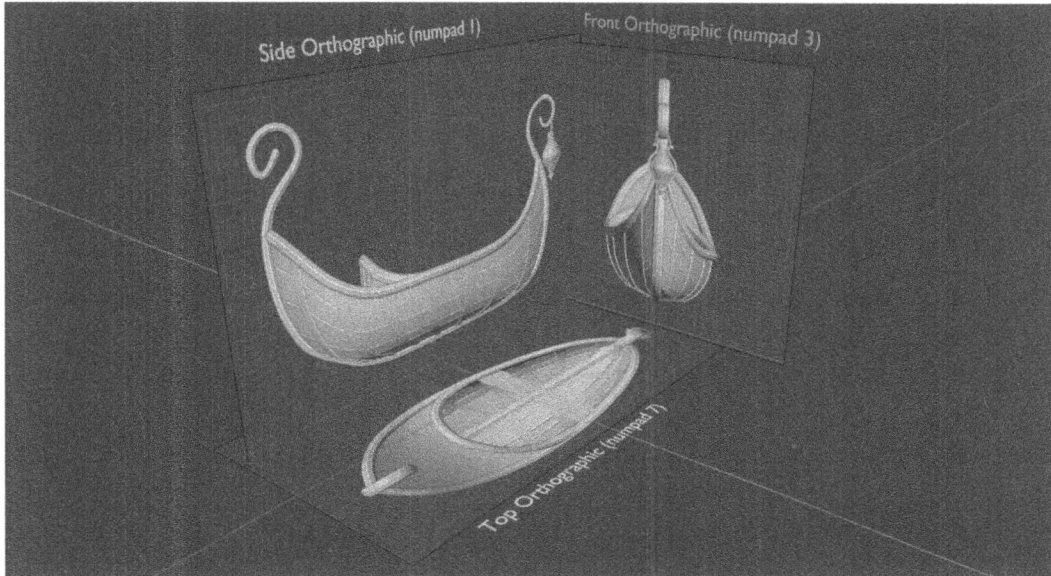

Figure 9.4: Orthographic view for precision in "Blender 3 Stylized Viking Boat 3D Model Complete Guide" by 3D Tudor

This view ensures that your reference images and models align accurately, which is crucial for maintaining correct proportions and details.

> **Tip**
>
> Orthographic view might be useful for a project such as designing a detailed smartphone casing. In this scenario, using orthographic view allows you to align your design precisely with the reference images, ensuring that every port, button, and curve is accurately positioned and scaled according to the real-world dimensions of the device.

Referencing should be part of every 3D modeler's daily diet, right up there with caffeine and *Ctrl + Z*. Whether you are just starting out or have been modeling longer than Suzanne's been staring into the void, good references are essential.

Now, let us talk about background images. These are often treated like the parsley on the side of your modeling steak, nice to have, but not really the star. But trust me, they do some heavy lifting. While reference images help you get your proportions and shapes right, background images quietly work in the wings, setting the tone and mood for your entire scene. Understand what each does and you will not just model better, you will model smarter.

Crafting ambience with background images

Discussing background images in an advanced 3D modeling skills chapter must sound odd. However, that's not the case. Unlike reference images, background images are something that stays as part of your environment or scene, and they are there to create a context or mood. For example, in *Figure 9.5*, you can see how we used post-processing techniques, including the use of background images, to create an appealing course thumbnail:

Figure 9.5: Thumbnail of Blender to Unreal Engine 5 The Complete Beginner's Guide by 3D Tudor

These background images are the canvas upon which you model without influencing the actual composition of the model itself. Let's see how to set one up.

Setting up backgrounds in Blender

To insert a background in Blender, take the following steps:

1. While in the 3D viewport, press *Shift + A*. This will open an **Add** context menu for adding anything to your 3D Viewport, from images to basic objects. Opt for **Image**, and then select **Background**.

2. By default, images stretch to occupy the 3D Viewport. Ensure you adjust them, keeping the aspect ratio intact, and position them according to your needs based on the options in *Figure 9.6*. This creates an image plane with matching image proportions.

Figure 9.6: Options for adjusting images to keep the aspect ratio intact

Note

Background images are great because they allow you to set up the image in front of an object, but it is only visible within an empty space of a scene, as you can also see in *Figure 9.6*.

3. With the background image selected, go to the **Object Data Properties** tab (like in *Figure 9.6*) in the Properties editor. This panel contains all the settings for adjusting how the image appears in the scene, including depth, size, opacity, and offset:

    *   **Depth**: There are three options for image depth:

        *   **Back** places the image behind all objects

        *   **Front** places it in front of all objects

        *   **Default** sets the depth between image empties, but not between mesh objects

    *   **Opacity**: Adjust the slider to make your background image more or less transparent, depending on how prominent you want to make your image in the scene.

    *   **Offset**: Use the **X** and **Y** sliders under the **Offset** section in the **Object Data Properties** panel to reposition the image within the 3D Viewport. This is helpful for aligning the background image without moving the object itself.

    *   **Size**: The **Size** value changes the scale of the image uniformly. If you want more control, you can also move, rotate, or scale the image like any other object using standard transform tools (*G*, *R*, and *S*).

    *   **Rotation** and **Aspect Ratio**: With these, you can rotate the background image and lock its aspect ratio. **Aspect Ratio** refers to the **Scale** parameter, and you can lock any of these values by clicking the lock icons beside the value field. This can be crucial for precise alignment or maintaining the correct proportions of the image.

Leveling up background images with Advanced Uses

There are several advanced uses for background images in Blender. Here are a few examples:

*   **Matchmoving and camera tracking**: In animation and VFX, you can import a real-world image or video into the background to track camera movements and align 3D objects or characters to match the scene.

*   **Blueprints for modeling**: If your 3D modeling project is based on the real world and you need precise images, background images can be used as blueprints. You can import different views (i.e., top, side, and front) of a design and model your 3D objects directly over these images.

*   **Lighting and scene setup**: Background images can be used to mimic real-world lighting conditions. By analyzing the lighting in a background photo, you can set up your scene's lighting to match, creating a more realistic render, as in *Figure 9.7*.

Figure 9.7: Realistic lighting in "Blender 3 Beginners Step-Step Guide to Isometric Rooms" by 3D Tudor

Note

Since this is counted as a UI element and not a plane texture, it does not affect ambient lighting in the way HDRI skyboxes would. Lighting in this scenario would mean establishing the lighting for the background, giving the illusion that the object is brighter/darker (think of the viral golden dress illusion from 2015).

- **Greenscreen and compositing**: For video editing and compositing tasks within Blender, you can use background images as a greenscreen or for chroma keying (i.e., the technique used to remove backgrounds such as greenscreens from video footage). This allows you to integrate 3D elements into film.

- **Texture painting reference**: A background image can serve as a direct reference if you are texture painting. This is useful for 3D artists who are painting textures onto a sculpted 3D model, for example.

- **Animation backgrounds:** For 2D animation or scenes where you do not need a full 3D environment, you can use background images as a static background, as in *Figure 9.8*.

Figure 9.8: Using a background image as a static background in Blender to Unreal Engine 5 Fantasy River 3D Diorama Boat Scene by 3D Tudor

Now, you might be wondering, "Aren't all background images static?" Good question. When we say "static," we are talking about still images that stay put, no movement, no drama. These are perfect for non-animated shots or when you want a consistent visual behind your models.

On the flip side, you can get clever with animated backgrounds too, using image sequences (such as a flipbook) or even video files, to breathe life into your scene with things such as drifting clouds, flickering lights, or looping landscapes. This can be particularly handy if your camera is stationary or doing a simple pan. So, let's summarize:

- **Static background** = a single image that stays still
- **Animated background** = multiple images or a video that plays over time

Both have their place, it just depends on whether you want your background to chill or do the cha-cha.

Now that we have covered background images, and hopefully demystified the whole "static versus not-so-static" debate, it is time to move on to something a bit more behind-the-scenes but just as powerful: parenting and object relationships in Blender. Think of it as giving your objects a family tree. This technique is going to seriously level up your control, making your projects more organized, responsive, and downright clever when things start to get complex.

Unveiling parenting: A cornerstone of object relationships in Blender

The meaning of the term **parenting** in Blender is intuitive: it is all about creating parent and child relationships, like in a family tree, for different 3D objects. We can see this illustrated in *Figure 9.9*.

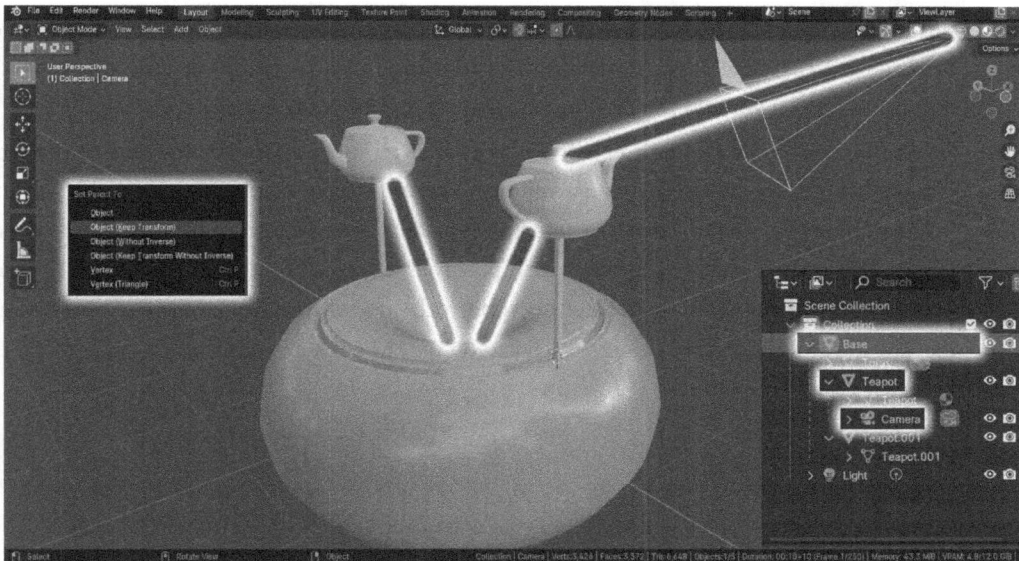

Figure 9.9: Visualizing parent-child relationships

At its core, parenting is about defining hierarchies and relationships. It can influence how objects are structured, how they move, and how they work together in a scene, with applications stretching as far as animation.

Tip

You can always check whether an object is parented to another by looking at the Outliner in Blender. Parented objects will be displayed in a tree-like structure under their parent object, as in *Figure 9.9*.

Setting up parent-child dynamics

To set up a parenting relationship between two or more objects in Blender, follow these steps:

1. First, select the object that you want to be the child. You can do this by *left-clicking* on the object in the 3D Viewport to select it.

2. Next, while holding the *Shift* key, *left-click* on the object you want to be the parent.

> **Note**
>
> This order is crucial: the last object selected becomes the parent.

3. With both objects selected (the child first, then the parent), press *Ctrl + P*. A menu, like back in *Figure 9.9*, will pop up with options that establish the bond between two objects, defining their kinship. In most cases, the **Object** option is the standard choice.

4. Other options in the menu offer different types of relationships. For example, **Bone** lets you parent to a specific bone in an armature, **Vertex** parents the child to a specific vertex in the parent object, and **Keep Transform** maintains the child's current transform when it establishes the parent-child relationship. However, the **Object** option is typically used when you want the child object to fully inherit the transformations of the parent object in a simple and predictable way, which is why we chose this option.

> **Note**
>
> Parenting is powerful, but it does come with a few "gotchas" that can sneak up on you if you are not paying attention. One classic example? You scale the parent, and suddenly the child object stretches like it is being pulled into another dimension. Brilliant. This is especially common when the child has complex geometry or a rig; it just does not take it well. To keep your models from going full Picasso, make sure you use the **Keep Transform** option when parenting. Better yet, apply all your transformations to the parent before you make the connection. Trust me, future you will thank you.

5. If you ever need to detach your objects from each other, press *Alt + P*. A menu will appear with options including **Clear Parent** and **Clear and Keep Transformation**:

    - **Clear Parent**: This option removes the parent-child relationship between the selected child object and its parent. After using this option, the child object will no longer inherit transformations (i.e., position, rotation, or scale) from the parent object. However, the child object will stay in its current position, orientation, and scale relative to the world space.

    Use this when you want to remove the hierarchical link between objects but keep the child object in its current world position. For example, if you have a character holding an object, such as a sword, and you want to separate the sword from the character without moving the sword, you would use **Clear Parent**.

    - **Clear and Keep Transformation**: This option also removes the parent-child relationship but ensures that the child object retains the transformation it had due to the parent. The child object will keep its current world position, rotation, and scale as if it had never been a child of the parent.

    Use this when you want to maintain the appearance of the child object and positioning as it was influenced by the parent but remove the parent-child relationship. For example, if you have a satellite orbiting a planet and you decide to animate the satellite independently from the planet, you would use **Clear and Keep Transformation** to ensure the satellite stays in its orbit while being detached from the planet's influence.

Using parenting as a 3D modeler

Think of parenting in Blender like assigning chores; it keeps everything in line and behaving properly across your scene. You can use parenting in many areas of 3D modeling. For example, with **bone parenting**, you can make sure character leg and arm animations are on-point and natural. By attaching to a bone, you can set up character accessories. These will move alongside the character animation, as in *Figure 9.10 (left)*.

Vertex parenting is a bit like sticking something to a very specific point with superglue; it will follow that exact spot no matter what the parent does. When you attach something to a vertex, you can pinpoint the exact location on an object where you want the child to be attached, as in *Figure 9.10 (right)*.

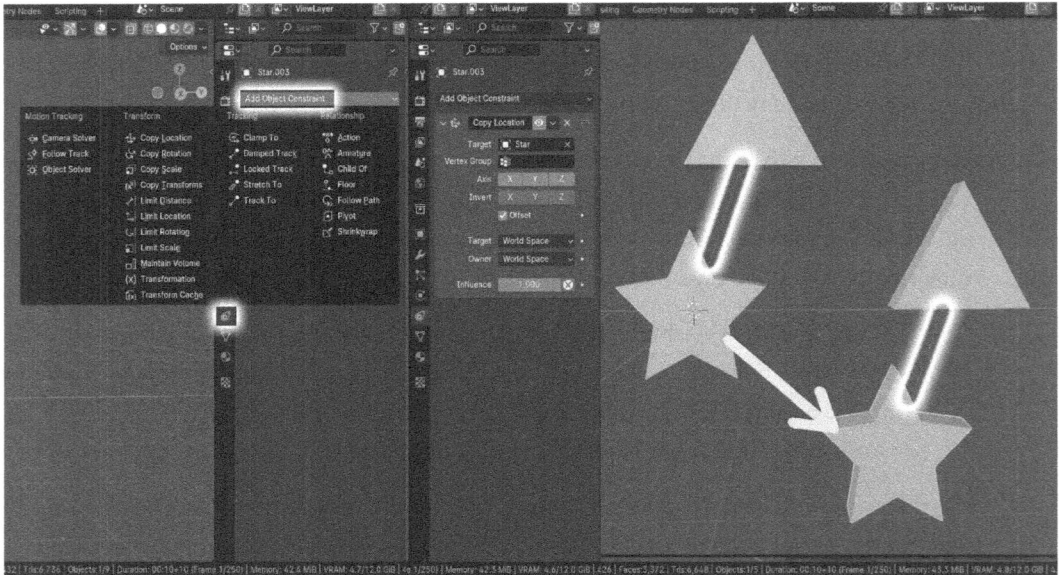

Figure 9.10: Bone parenting (left) versus vertex parenting (right)

Vertex parenting is useful for attaching accessories or details to a character model, such as a scarf or knitting needle, ensuring they move precisely with the character's motion, like in the scene in *Figure 9.11*.

Figure 9.11: Stylized scene Home Is Where the Heart Is Concept by 3D Tudor

I consider **parenting** an advanced Blender feature because of the high levels of control it offers you. Parenting in Blender lets you create detailed and complex relationships between objects. It is like setting up a chain of command, where one object controls others, which can be super powerful but also a bit tricky to get right. Think about a space rover with moving wheels, arms, and antennas, all working perfectly together. That kind of coordination is possible thanks to parenting. But if you do not fully understand how these relationships work, things can go wrong in your scene. So, getting the hang of parenting is key if you want to pull off more intricate and coordinated animations or designs. With great power comes great responsibility, so you need to ensure you know what all the different sub-types of **parenting** do.

> Note
>
> While parenting is powerful, it's essential to be wary of challenges. For example, cyclic dependencies can trap your objects in an endless loop of commands. This happens when you create a parenting chain where an object is parented to another, which is, in turn, directly or indirectly parented back to the first, creating a loop. Blender will warn you if a cyclic dependency is detected. You can fix this issue by reevaluating and restructuring your parenting hierarchy. This is especially true when rigging in Blender, and, to me, a much more prevalent issue than in other software. We will be discussing rigging in *Chapter 16* in *Part 1* of this book so keep your eyes peeled.

Parenting is just the beginning of organizing your 3D models and the way they function. We will continue our discussion with a great tool that you can use as a marker or visual cue in your 3D Viewport, empties.

Embracing empties: The invisible architects of 3D design in Blender

As their name suggests, empties often go unnoticed. **Empties** are non-rendered objects (e.g., arrows, cubes, and spheres) that you can use to annotate parts of your model, a bit like the **Annotate** tool but without writing. They are the silent conductors, unseen yet powerful, influencing how other visible objects behave and interact. The best way to describe empties is as a humble but powerful contender to most of Blender's organizational tools.

Understanding what empties do in Blender

Let us shine a light on this unsung hero in Blender. Sounds like it does nothing, right? But these invisible workhorses are anything but useless.

Through various modifiers, such as the **Lattice** or **Displace** modifier, empties can drive deformations and transformations. This means that in a project where you are designing a character's facial expressions, empties can be used to control the deformation of the face. By attaching a **Lattice** modifier to an empty and then linking it to the character's face mesh, you can manipulate the empty to alter the facial expression without permanently changing the mesh's structure.

This interaction between empties and topology is very powerful. For example, by attaching empties to key points of the character's body and using them to control the displacement and deformation of the clothing mesh, you can create a more realistic and responsive clothing movement that aligns accurately with the character's actions. This saves you time because you do not need complex rigging or vertex-level adjustments.

Empties can also be useful in other areas, taking on different roles every time:

*   Attach a moving object to an **empty**, and you can control its path without altering the object's intrinsic properties. For example, in a project where you are animating a butterfly. You can attach the butterfly model to an **empty** and then animate the path of the **empty**. This way, the butterfly follows the path precisely while maintaining its independent animations, such as wings flapping.

- In a complex scene, empties can become placeholders. For example, in a large-scale architectural graybox, you can use empties to represent furniture pieces. This lets you quickly replace or reposition these elements in the future without disrupting the overall scene layout.

- If you are working on a physics simulation or with modifiers, an **empty** can determine influence zones, guiding how effects unfold across a scene. For example, in a cloth simulation where a flag reacts to wind, an **empty** can be used to control the area where the wind affects the flag, creating a more dynamic and realistic simulation, as in *Figure 9.12*.

Figure 9.12: Creating a dynamic and realistic flag simulation

- Empties become the cornerstone for camera tracking or constraint-based animations, for example. In a project involving a car chase scene, **empties** can be used to track how real cars move, allowing the camera to follow smoothly and realistically, or to manage constraints for objects interacting during the chase.

- In rigging and character animation, empties often become pivotal points guiding movement and ensuring fluidity. In character rigging, empties can be used to control eye movement, making it natural and smooth.

Generating and working with empties

To generate an empty, all you have to do is press *Shift + A* and select **Empty**. But summoning one is the easy part; the real trick lies in knowing what to do with it once it arrives, floating blankly in your scene like a lost balloon. Here is a short list of the main ways to use empties:

- *Positioning the empty*:

  a. Once added, select the empty.

  b. Use the grab (*G*), rotate (*R*), and scale (*S*) commands to position it where you need it in your scene.

  > Note
  >
  > Remember that scaling an empty does not affect its functionality, but it can help you visualize it better in relation to other objects.

- *Linking objects to empties*:

  a. Select the object you want to link to the empty.

  b. While holding *Shift*, select the empty (the order is important as it determines which object is the parent).

  c. Press *Ctrl + P* to parent the object to the empty, and choose the appropriate parenting option described in *Table 9.1*:

Parenting Option	Function
Object	The child object moves and rotates relative to the parent object, inheriting its transform.
Object (Keep Transform)	The child object keeps its current transform (i.e., position, rotation, and scale) but becomes parented to the selected object.
Object (Without Inverse)	The child object moves to match the parent's transform but does not maintain its original transform.

Parenting Option	Function
Object (Keep Transform Without Inverse)	Similar to **Object (Keep Transform)**, but more suitable for armatures. Think of this as the slightly more thoughtful cousin to **Object (Keep Transform)**, the one who shows up to family events but does not make a fuss. It keeps the child object's transform exactly as is, but unlike the usual parenting approach, it skips applying the inverse transformation.
Vertex	The child object is parented to a specific vertex of the parent mesh.
Vertex Triangle	The child object is parented to three vertices of the parent mesh, forming a triangle, which helps in more complex deformations.

Table 9.1: Parenting options and what they do

- *Using empties with constraints*:

    a. Select the object you want to apply a constraint to.

    b. Go to the **Properties** panel and select the **Constraints** tab.

    c. Click **Add Object Constraint** and choose the type of constraint (e.g., **Track To** and then **Copy Location**). There are many constraint options to choose from for specific uses; however, the three most commonly used are listed in *Table 9.2*:

Constraint Type	Function
Copy Location	This makes the constrained object copy the location (i.e., position) of the target object. You can choose to copy all axes or only specific ones (X, Y, or Z).
Track To	It forces the constrained object to always point toward the target object. It is typically used to make objects such as eyes or cameras always face another object.
Follow Path	This makes the constrained object follow a predefined path (e.g., usually a curve). The object moves along the path as the animation progresses, like a camera flying through a scene or a character walking on a path.

Table 9.2: Most common constraint types and their role

d. When you press *I* (yes, that is an uppercase "I", not a slash, backslash, or anything else in disguise. No optical illusions here), it automatically creates a keyframe for location, rotation, and scale.

e. In the **Target** field, select an object or an empty. In *Figure 9.13*, we have done this with a star, which was selected as the triangle's constraint. To apply a constraint, first select the object you want to affect. Then, go to the **Constraints** tab and choose a constraint type, such as **Copy Location**. As shown in *Figure 9.13*, you can then select a **Target** object (such as the targeted triangle or another mesh) that the constrained object will follow. Once the target is set, moving it will offset the position of the constrained object accordingly.

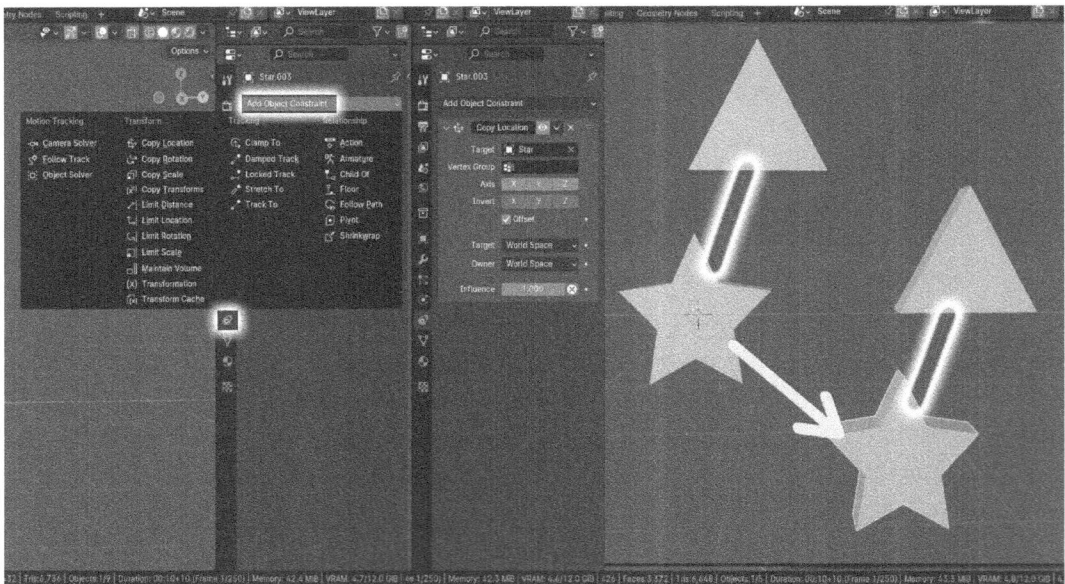

Figure 9.13: Selecting target field options in Blender

Notes

Parenting and constraints can behave similarly. Parenting latches onto the other object. The cool thing is, you can decide whether you just want to link their position, their rotation, or both. Constraints are a bit different: they let you set specific rules for how objects relate to each other, such as keeping one object always a certain distance away or maintaining a particular angle.

While using **Copy Location** with **Offset** activated, your object will not get transported to the center of a target. However, make sure the target object has its transforms applied (using *Ctrl + A*). Otherwise, Blender will act like both objects are still chilling at 0,0,0, even if they look like they are in the right place, and your "offset" will be all smoke and no fire.

    f.   Using the timeline, you can animate your design.

- *Animating empties*:

    a.   Move to the desired frame in the timeline.

    b.   Move, rotate, or scale the empty as needed.

    c.   Press *I* (that is a capital "I" for "Insert," not a rogue backslash or an italicized worm. Blender is quirky, but not that quirky) to insert a keyframe. Choose the type of keyframe (e.g., **Location**, **Rotation**, or **Scale**) and Blender will create the keyframe automatically.

- *Using empties in complex setups*

  Empties can be used to control the behavior of objects in simulations or advanced animations. For example, in a physics simulation, an empty can act as a force field controller, as shown in *Figure 9.14*.

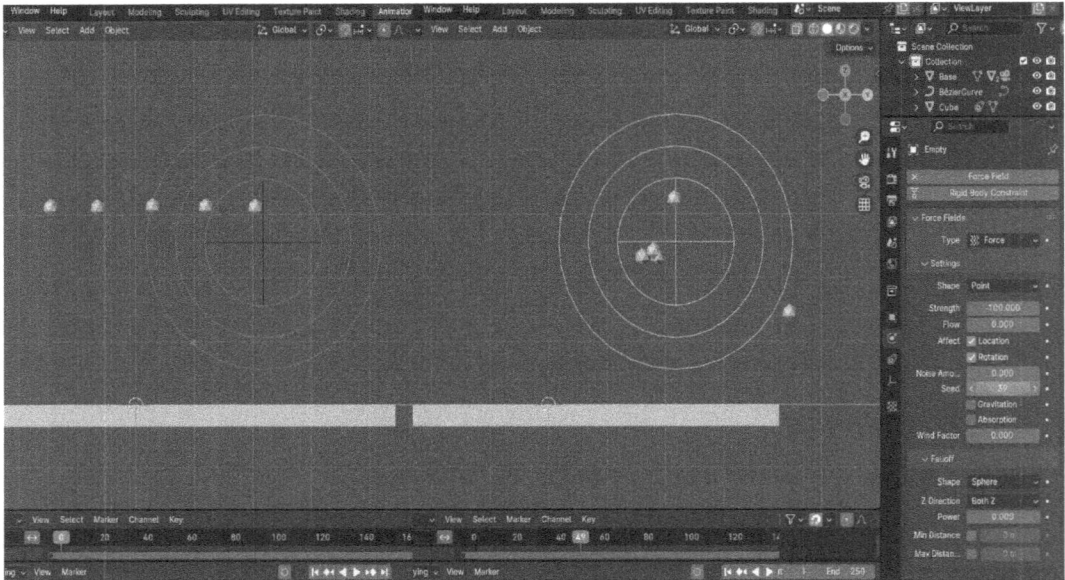

Figure 9.14: Using an empty as a force field controller

Note

To find out more about physics in Blender, refer to the Blender manual, published by the Blender Foundation: https://docs.blender.org/manual/en/latest/physics/.

Also, in rigging, empties can control bone movements or act as **IK** (i.e., **inverse kinematics**) targets. IK is a method used in 3D animation to automate the movement of joint structures, such as limbs. Instead of manually rotating each joint (as in **forward kinematics**), IK lets you define a target point, and the joints adjust themselves automatically to reach this point. An empty can serve as this target point for IK systems.

There is a lot of personal preference (and Blender wrangling) when it comes to rigging with empties as IK targets. Some folks swear by using custom shapes and constraint setups to avoid armature mode altogether. Is it performance-perfect? Maybe not. Is it elegant? Definitely not. But it works, and if you are like me, buried under layers of armature spaghetti, anything that makes your rig behave is worth trying. But that is it for now; more about rigging in *Chapter 16* in *Part 1* of this book.

So, as you can see, empties, despite their invisibility in final renders, carry a weight of significance in the 3D design process. They are the unsung heroes of 3D modeling, so you are encouraged to start using them.

Moving on, we will talk about the **Lattice** tool, which helps you refine 3D models in a non-destructive way.

Harnessing the power of lattices in Blender: A comprehensive guide

Among all other Blender tools, the **Lattice** tool stands out as the go-to tool for deforming and manipulating models. A **lattice** is a 3D grid that envelops an object. Since they do not permanently alter your model, lattices can help you tweak and reshape your meshes for specific effects. By adjusting the lattice point, as in *Figure 9.15*, you can manipulate models in a non-destructive way:

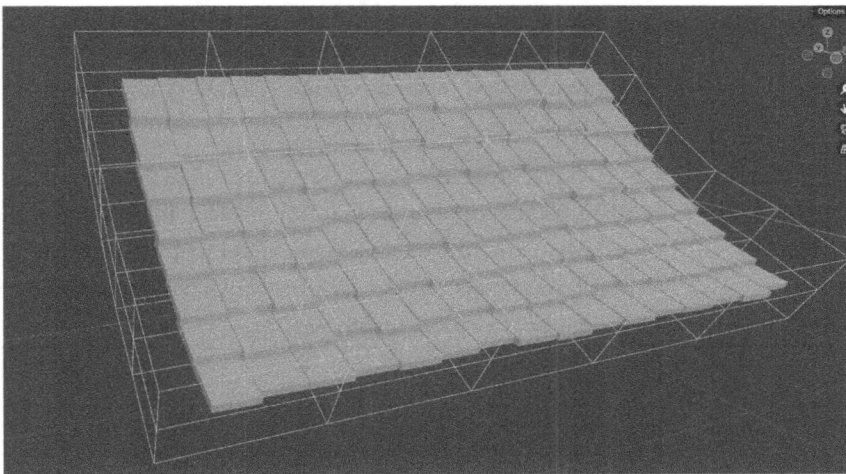

Figure 9.15: Reshaping models non-destructively

Going further, *Table 9.3* will help you understand the uses of lattices and get creative ideas for using them in different projects:

3D Design Processes	Lattice Role	Project Ideas
Non-destructive editing	Lattices let you tweak a model without directly manipulating its topology, preserving the original mesh.	Retouching a character model's posture in an animation without changing the underlying skeletal structure.
Soft and smooth deformations	Perfect for creating natural bends, bulges, or tweaks without hard edges.	Modifying a rubber tire model to show realistic deformations as it rolls over different types of terrain.
Versatility	Lattices can be applied to various objects, including organic shapes (e.g., characters) and abstract shapes.	Applying **lattice** deformations to a spaceship model to easily test different design variations.
Facial rigging in animation	Lattices allow animators to make subtle or extensive facial expressions on characters.	Creating a range of facial expressions for a 3D animated character without changing their basic facial structure.
Real-time shape key adjustments	In projects with morphing or transformation effects, lattices provide a way to adjust **shape keys** on the fly, supporting real-time editing.	Adjusting a fantasy creature's wings in real time during a flight sequence.
Simplified modeling of complex structures	For architectural or mechanical designs with detailed patterns or frameworks, lattices can simplify the modeling process.	Designing a bridge structure for a futuristic building where all parts interconnect.

3D Design Processes	Lattice Role	Project Ideas
Prototype testing in product design	You can quickly modify and test different shapes and sizes of a product prototype without having to make the model from scratch again.	Experimenting with different bottle shapes for a new soft drink brand.
Animation of fluid-like movements	In animations that require fluid-like movements (e.g., a waving flag), lattices make it easier to achieve realistic motion without complex simulations.	Simulating the movement of a silk scarf in the wind.
Custom fit for wearable designs	Lattices can help you adjust the model to different body shapes or sizes, ensuring a custom fit.	Adapting a 3D model of a dress to fit different body types.

Table 9.3: Lattices – 10 common uses and project examples

Setting up and using lattices

The process of setting up a lattice in Blender is straightforward. All you need to do is press *Shift + A* in your 3D Viewport and then choose **Lattice** from the menu. However, depending on what you intend to do with the lattice, the process is different every time:

- **Resizing and positioning**: Scale and place the lattice to envelop the target object. After adding the lattice (press *Shift + A* and select **Lattice**), you will want to scale and move it so that it completely surrounds the object you intend to deform.

  To do this, use the standard scaling (*S*) and positioning (*G*) tools in Blender. Make sure that the lattice closely follows the shape of your object but allows for some space around it, because this gives you more control when deforming. You might need to switch to different view angles (using *1*, *3*, or *7* on the numpad) to accurately align the lattice.

Note

Properly enveloping the object is essential because any part of the object outside the lattice will not be affected by the deformations. If the lattice is too large, the deformations might be too subtle or imprecise.

- **Refining the lattice**: In the **Lattice** option's **Properties** tab, adjust the **U**, **V**, and **W** divisions based on how much deformation control you want to have. These divisions correspond to the lattice's segments along the *X*, *Y*, and *Z* axes, respectively. For example, follow the steps shown here, and illustrated in *Figure 9.16*:

  a. Create a lattice and position the box over an object. Make sure it is done in **Object Mode** because you might get unwanted deformations.

  b. Open up the **Data** tab inside the **Properties** panel for the lattice and increase the **W Resolution** value in the property options. This will give you additional horizontal edge loops to work with.

  c. Attach the **Lattice** modifier to the asset and select the created lattice in the **Object** section.

  d. Select **Lattice**, go to **Edit** mode, and manipulate the points as if they were vertices. Expanding the middle section will give you an inflated object.

Figure 9.16: Refining the lattice walk-through example

- **Binding object(s) to a lattice:** Select your model, then the lattice. Next, press *Ctrl + P* and select **Lattice Deform**. This will establish a parent-child relationship between your 3D model and the lattice, allowing the lattice to control the deformation of the model.

- **Deforming with the lattice:** With the lattice selected, move its points, lines, or planes. The encapsulated object will deform correspondingly. The more divisions (**U**, **V**, and **W**) you have set, the more control you have over the deformation. For more complex shapes, you can combine transformations of multiple lattice points.

Advanced tips for lattices

Should you want to experiment with other advanced 3D modeling techniques that use lattices, you might want to consider the following advanced tips:

- **Modifiers:** You can enhance your lattice using modifiers such as **Simple Deform**, which can bend or twist the lattice itself. This allows you to apply smooth, controlled transformations to any object influenced by the lattice. For more advanced control, combine multiple lattices or parent them to other deformed objects.

- In *Figure 9.17*, a lattice with **Resolution** set to 1 in the **V** axis (think of **U**, **V**, and **W** as **X**, **Y**, and **Z**) is used to gently deform and wrap a piece of mesh around a curved surface, giving it a snug, fitted appearance.

Figure 9.17: Using a low-resolution lattice to warp geometry around an object

Note

By turning the lattice resolution to 1 on one axis, you can deform an entire 3D mesh as if it were a 2D decal, while still preserving its volume and depth. This technique is especially useful when combined with modifiers such as **Shrinkwrap**, allowing the mesh to conform to surfaces without collapsing or flattening in a way you do not want it to.

- **Weight painting**: For precise control over how intense your deformation is, use weight painting on the mesh. By painting areas of the lattice with different weights, you can specify which parts of the model are more influenced by the lattice deformation. For example, in a character model, you might want the facial area to be less affected by the lattice to maintain detailed features, while the body could have more deformation for dramatic effects. We will talk a lot more about weight painting in *Chapter 16* in *Part 1* of this book, so do not worry if this is not instinctual at this stage.

Figure 9.18 shows how I weight painted the limbs. This allowed me to use the lattice to quickly modify the torso without affecting other parts of the body.

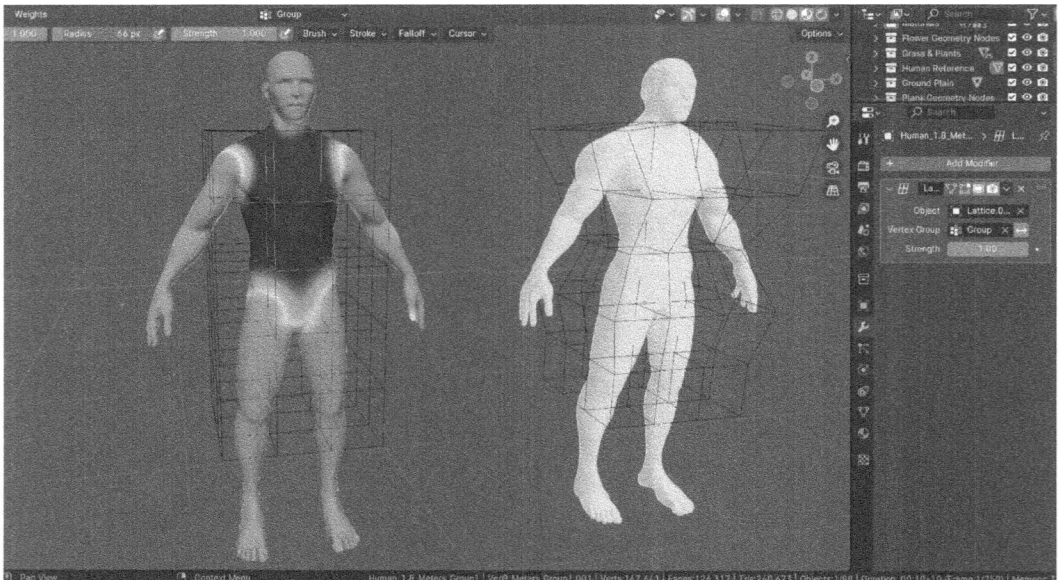

Figure 9.18: Using weight painting to control lattice deformation

- **Animation**: Lattice deformations can be keyframed, allowing for dynamic changes in animations. As a project, you could use a lattice to animate a flag waving in the wind. By keyframing the lattice points, you can create movements that would be difficult to achieve with traditional rigging techniques.

Examples of lattice tool usage

Lattices are particularly useful in three distinct areas of 3D art and design:

- **Character modeling**: Achieve complex facial expressions or postures with ease using lattices. For instance, let us imagine that you are creating an animated character for a short film. Using a lattice, you can easily manipulate the facial features of your character to express a wide range of emotions without the need to individually adjust each vertex.

  As another example, we can use the same technique for animating body postures. Imagine animating a fantasy or sci-fi scene where the character needs to morph into different shapes or perform exaggerated movements. The lattice allows these transformations to be smooth and natural-looking, making your character appear more believable.

- **Abstract art**: Distort shapes smoothly for unique art forms. Imagine working on a digital sculpture about emotions or dreams. You could use a lattice to smoothly distort a basic shape such as a sphere or cube into something that visually represents these concepts (e.g., by elongating, twisting, or warping the form, like the star in *Figure 9.19*).

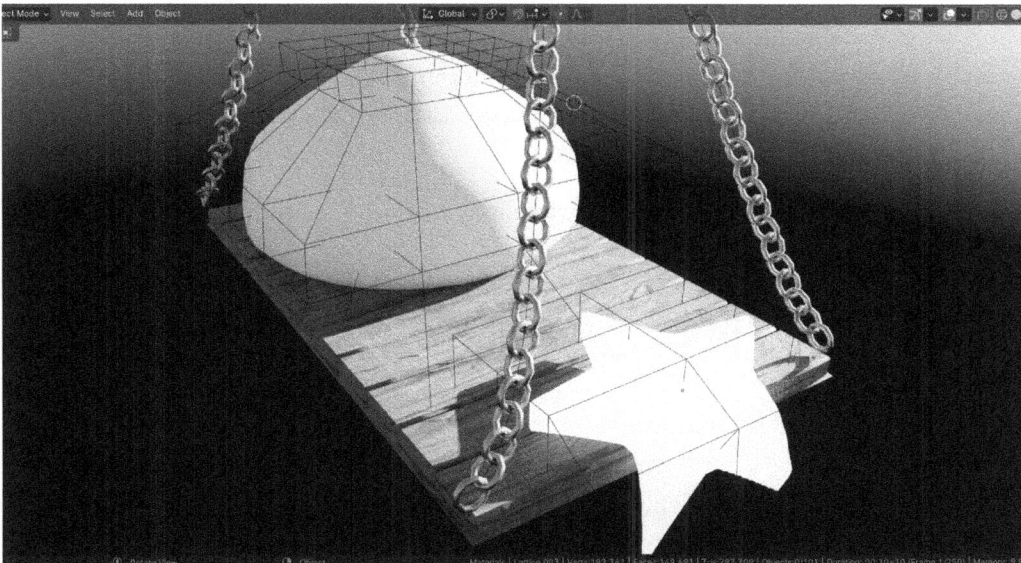

Figure 9.19: Using a lattice on a star

- **Precision modeling**: For projects that need you to pay attention to real-life dimensions, such as car designs, architectural models, or product prototypes, lattices will become one of your go-to tools. In architectural modeling, lattices can be used to model complex curved surfaces such as spiral staircases (e.g., *Figure 9.20*) or undulating facades.

Figure 9.20: Spiral staircase model from Blender Beginner's Bootcamp by 3D Tudor

So, the **Lattice** tool in Blender offers you a unique way to reshape and refine your 3D models. Because it follows a non-destructive approach, you can make sure that your deformations are smooth. Whether you're adjusting a character's expression or tweaking the curve on a vehicle, the **Lattice** tool will be just what you need.

Now, you will find out about a 2D tool you might never have expected to be so versatile in 3D: Grease Pencil.

Drawing, sculpting, and more with Blender's Grease Pencil

Blender's **Grease Pencil** is a fantastic tool that lets you marry 2D sketching with 3D modeling. **Grease Pencil** started as a note-taking tool within Blender and has since transformed into an artist's tool for 2D drawing and animation in 3D space. Although it does not seem that way to the untrained eye, **Grease Pencil** is a Swiss army knife of tools in Blender. Let's dive in!

Accessing Grease Pencil

To access **Grease Pencil** and start working on your first sketch, take the following steps:

1. Press *Shift + A*, then from the **Add** menu, select **Grease Pencil | Blank**.

2. Then, select the upper-left tab (i.e., where **Object Mode** is) and change it to **Draw** mode. Now, you can select the **Draw** icon (it looks like a pencil; see *Figure 9.21*) and start painting.

3. Make sure you have **Strength** set to **100** to see the brush. To change colors, make sure that **Color Attribute** mode is enabled (top of the bar).

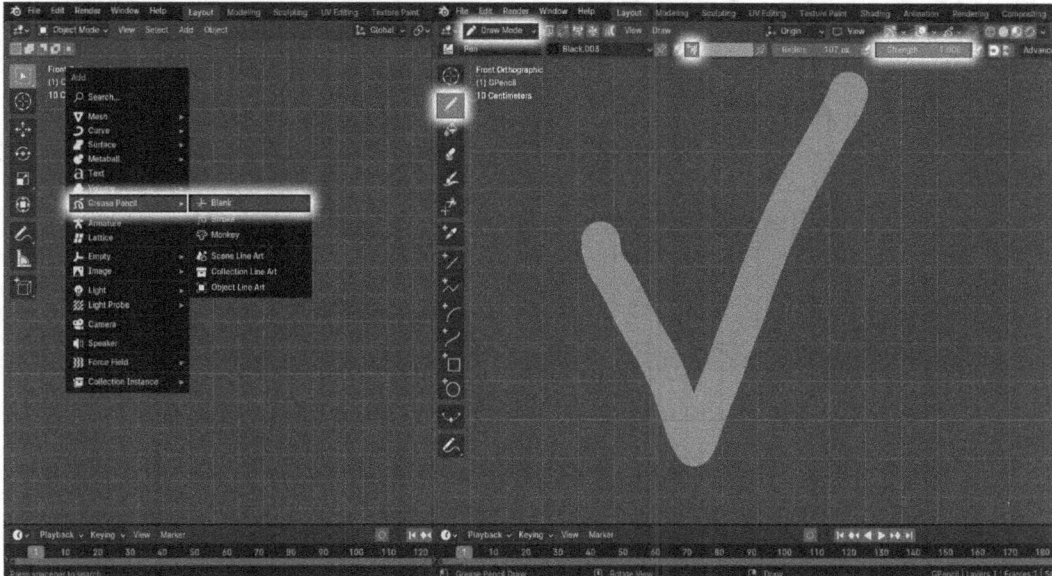

Figure 9.21: Accessing Grease Pencil in Blender

> **Note**
>
> If you are not seeing the color, make sure you are in **Material Preview** mode.

4. If you're using a drawing tablet, **Grease Pencil** will react to pressure, allowing for thicker or thinner lines. You can adjust the stroke thickness of the overall line in the **Properties** panel on the right, as in *Figure 9.22*:

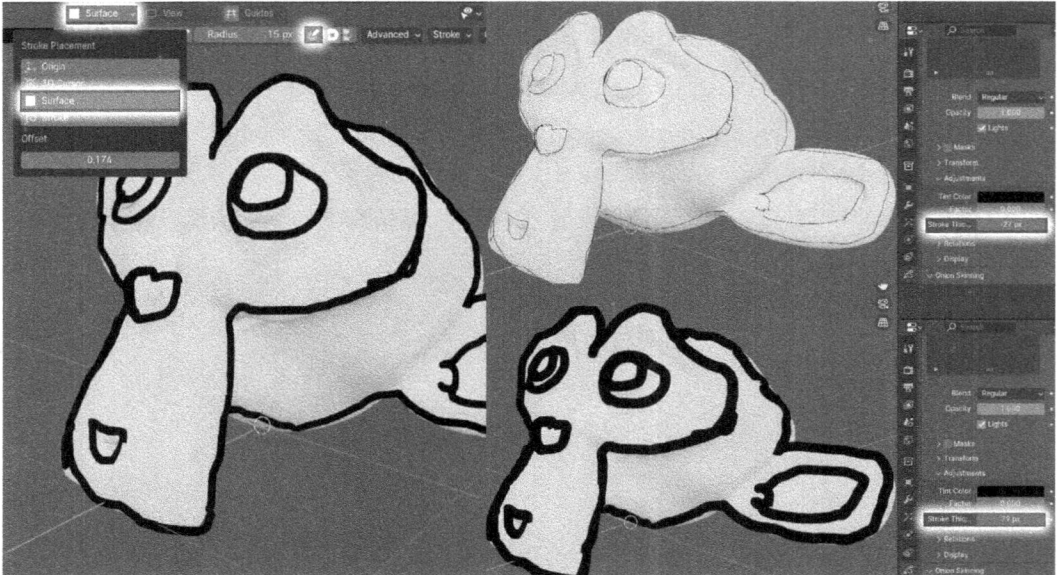

Figure 9.22: Adjusting the sensitivity to create thinner (left) and thicker (right) lines

5. If you are using a drawing tablet, **Grease Pencil** will react to pressure, allowing for thicker or thinner lines, make sure you have **Use Pressure** enabled in the top tab. You can adjust the stroke thickness of the overall line in the **Properties** panel on the right, as in *Figure 9.22*.

6. Now, it is up to you if you choose to go a step further. You can use *Adobe Photoshop* (https://www.adobe.com/cy_en/products/photoshop.html) or *GIMP* (https://www.gimp.org/), where you can use layers to sketch, color, and refine your designs in more detail before bringing them back into Blender.

7. In the **Properties** panel on the right, find the **Grease Pencil** tab.

8. To start organizing your drawing, click the + button to add new layers.

9. Below the layers, you will find a color palette. Click on any color to select or add new colors by clicking the + button.

Note

The **Grease Pencil** tool is used for 2D drawing and animation within a 3D space. When you are drawing or sketching, you can put different strokes or drawings on separate layers. For example, you might do rough sketches on one layer and then make clean, final lines on another. For coloring, you can use layers to keep different colors or shading parts separate. You might have one layer for base colors, another for shadows, and another for highlights. In animation, layers help you separate different parts of your animation. You could animate a character's body on one layer and the facial expressions on another. This makes it easier to tweak each part individually. You can also use layers for special effects, such as glows or blurs. Keeping these effects on separate layers makes it easy to adjust or remove them without affecting the main drawing. Using layers with the **Grease Pencil** tool keeps your work organized, flexible, and efficient, whether you are doing simple drawings or complex animations.

Creating a Grease Pencil outliner

Creating a **Grease Pencil** outliner in Blender 4 is a great way to make your 3D objects pop and give them a cool, hand-drawn look. It helps emphasize the shapes and details, making your work look more artistic and easier to understand, especially if your scene is complicated. Here is how you can do it:

1. Move the mesh you want to outline into a new collection.

2. Then, to create an empty **Grease Pencil**, press *Shift + A*, navigate to **Grease Pencil**, and select **Blank**.

3. In the **Material** properties, create a new material for the **Grease Pencil** and set the base color to black.

4. With the **Grease Pencil** object selected, go to the **Modifiers** tab and add a **Line Art** modifier.

5. In the **Line Art** modifier settings, make sure to specify **Source Type** as **Collection**, and select the collection containing your mesh.

6. Still inside the **Line Art** modifier options, make sure to select the layer you want the outlines to be drawn on. If you have not made one yet, Blender will pick the default (usually the only option). Then, assign the material for the line art effect, yep, the one you just created, as in *Figure 9.23* (skip either of these steps and Blender will act like nothing happened. No lines, no drama, just... silence.)

7. The line art effect is based on the camera view. Create a camera and position it to frame the object you want to outline. Adjust the camera angle to see the outlines clearly.

8. Ensure the camera and mesh are correctly positioned so that the outlines appear as desired in the 3D Viewport and render, as in *Figure 9.23*.

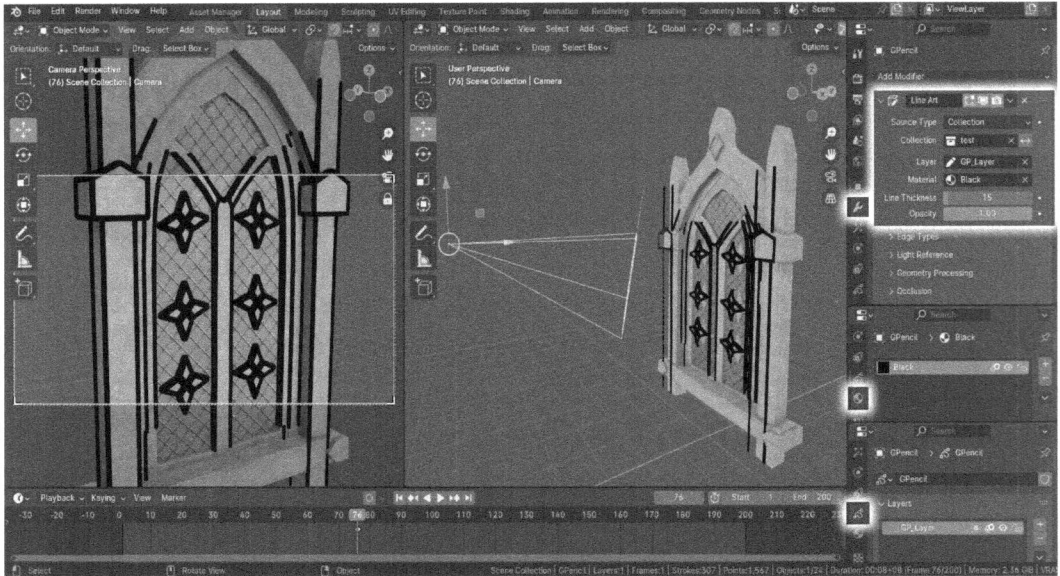

Figure 9.23: Creating a Grease Pencil outliner in Blender 20 Massive Fantasy Windows Asset Pack by 3D Tudor

Advanced tips for using Grease Pencil

Should you want to experiment with other advanced 3D modeling techniques that use Blender's **Grease Pencil**, you might want to consider the following advanced tips:

- **Activating a surface drawing**: In the 3D Viewport, press the *N* key to open the side menu. Under the **Grease Pencil** tab, find the **Draw** dropdown. Here, switch the default **Stroke Placement** option to **Surface**. This lets you draw directly onto 3D objects!

- **Adjusting the offset**: Still in the **Draw** dropdown, you will find an **Offset** slider (see *Figure 9.35*). This determines the gap between your drawing and the object's surface. Slide it to adjust the distance.

- **Animating your Grease Pencil drawings**: Even though this will not be covered in this book, **Grease Pencil** is perfect for more than static images. In the timeline at the bottom (as in *Figure 9.24*), you can enhance 3D environments with 2D VFX.

Figure 9.24: Animation timeline options in the Grease Pencil tab

Blender's **Grease Pencil** is a bit like that quiet kid in class who turns out to be a genius. You do not notice it at first, but once you get familiar with it, you wonder how you ever lived without it. Whether you are doodling storyboards or crafting full-on animations, it is one of the most powerful (and criminally underrated) tools in the Blender arsenal.

Now that we have dipped our toes into the wibbly world of animation, let us roll up our sleeves and dive into a slightly fancier way of making things move, with a bit more finesse and fewer keyframes flailing about like spaghetti in a blender.

Refining movement in Blender with the Shift key

Navigating and transforming objects in Blender's 3D Viewport is generally straightforward, but there are times when you need to be more delicate. This is the best time for you to use the *Shift* key. Even though this chapter section is rather short, it serves as a no-nonsense introduction to how to use this key, using concrete project examples.

Using the Shift key

The *Shift* key is a standard button on all of our keyboards, but it has so many uses in Blender. Although the following list is not exhaustive, it will give you a host of ideas to try out on your different **work-in-progress (WIP)** projects!

- **Precision navigation**: While navigating the 3D Viewport using the middle mouse button, holding down the *Shift* key allows for a panning movement. As an example, imagine you are adding window frames or textures to a building. Using the *Shift* key while navigating with the middle mouse button lets you pan smoothly across the model, ensuring you can focus on specific areas without losing your orientation.

- **Fine-tuned transformations**: When moving (*G*), rotating (*R*), or scaling (*S*) any object or mesh in Blender, holding down the *Shift* key will reduce the transformation speed, giving you more precise control over the adjustments.

  By holding the *Shift* key while moving, rotating, or scaling the butterfly model, you can make subtle, precise transformations.

  > Note
  >
  > Even while using the *Shift* key for precision movement, you can still use the snapping feature (by pressing *Ctrl*) to have a fine-tuned but aligned movement.

- **Delicate slider adjustments**: For many of Blender's settings, you will be adjusting values with sliders. Holding the *Shift* key while dragging these sliders slows down the rate of change, allowing for the more accurate fine-tuning of values.

  In a project where you are creating a nighttime cityscape scene or a building close-up view, the lighting plays a crucial role in setting the mood, as in *Figure 9.25*.

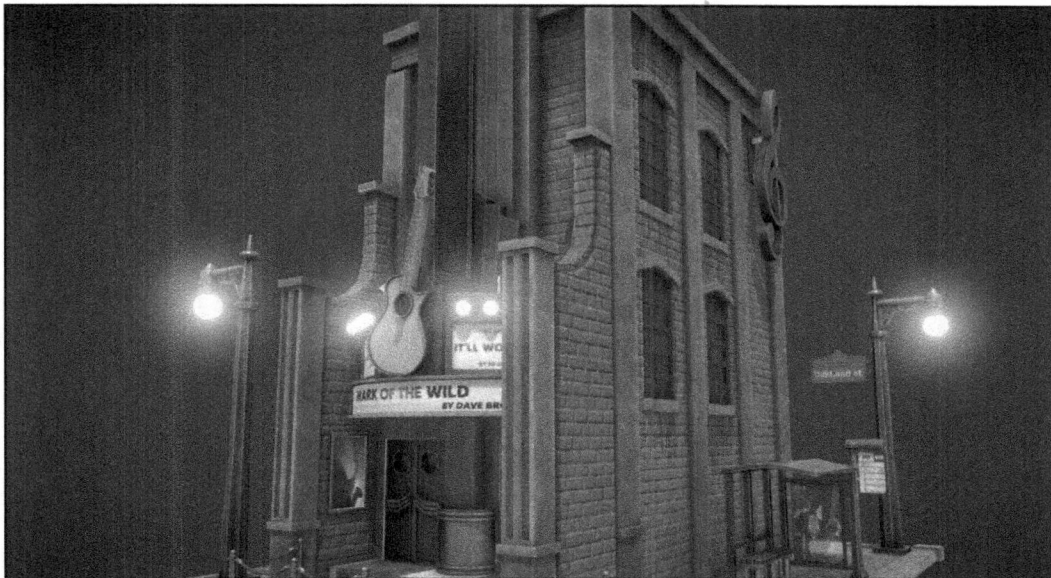

Figure 9.25: Nighttime cityscape scene in "Blender 3 Unreal Engine 5 Vintage Music Hall Building Game Design" by 3D Tudor

Using the *Shift* key while adjusting the light intensity sliders allows for minute changes, letting you get the perfect ambience.

> **Note**
>
> If you find the *Shift* key's precision movement too slow or too fast, you can customize this in Blender's preferences. Go to **Edit** | **Preferences** | **Interface**, and adjust **Zoom Speed** to a value that feels right for you.

Examples of Shift key usage

The *Shift* key might not look like much, but in Blender, it is basically the fine China of keyboard inputs, quiet, unassuming, and only brought out when precision matters. Whether you are nudging vertices into place like a neurotic watchmaker or lining up a camera shot with the obsessive energy of a Kubrick intern, holding *Shift* lets you move things *just enough* without launching them into the stratosphere. Say you are building something fiddly. That *Shift* key? It is your best mate, giving you the micro-control needed to make sure each piece clicks into place like it was born to be there.

And when it comes to framing your scene, *Shift* turns your camera from a clumsy tourist snapping blurry holiday pics into a seasoned cinematographer. You can finesse the zoom, adjust angles, and land that perfect moody close-up or background pan. Even in the Shader Editor, *Shift* pulls its weight. Adjusting lighting intensity or tweaking material values without *Shift* is like trying to ice a cake with a sledgehammer.

Summary

This chapter was your first proper dip into the murky but thrilling waters of advanced 3D modeling. You might have recognized some of the tools from earlier Blender adventures, except now they are wearing capes and demanding more respect.

Take parenting, for example. It is a cornerstone of scene structure, influencing everything from object hierarchy to animation workflows. Once you get the hang of it, you will wonder how you ever got along without it. And then there is **Grease Pencil**, like that cool exchange student who turns up halfway through term and makes you question everything you thought you knew about 2D and 3D. Suddenly, sketching inside your 3D scenes does not feel like witchcraft anymore.

As you were reading this chapter, you must have had many moments where tools or ideas that appeared obvious and seemed like they did not belong in this chapter started to make sense. One of these is the process of referencing: one of the biggest mountains I had to climb as a fledgling 3D modeling artist. Even background images and the process of layering, which are normally associated with Adobe Photoshop or GIMP, will be something you will routinely start to do in Blender. I see this chapter as a way to reprogram the way you think about processes that you might not instinctively link to 3D modeling.

From there, we looked at **empties** and how they can be used as versatile placeholders or reference points in your 3D scenes. You also learned about the **Lattice** tool in Blender, which lets you deform and manipulate your models with greater control and precision. The focus of this chapter was to present you with as many ideas as possible about what you can create with your new knowledge. In the end, you also learned about a worthy contender of many Blender tools that is as humble as it is simple to use: the *Shift* key.

To achieve a professional workflow in Blender, it is essential to delve into advanced modeling techniques. This is what we will continue to do in the next chapter. There are more advanced 3D modeling tools that are readily available in Blender's **Edit Mode**, located in the top toolbar, where you will find options such as **View, Select, Add,** and **Mesh**.

Further reading

- If you are interested in managing and organizing references effectively while working on your projects, you can use **PureRef** (`https://www.pureref.com/`). This free tool simplifies the referencing process and is used in various courses, such as *Blender to Unreal Engine 5 The Complete Beginners Guide* by 3D Tudor (`https://www.udemy.com/course/blender-to-unreal-engine-5-the-complete-beginners-guide/?referralCode=A659E7EEEA61C2DA562A`).

- Orthographic view gives you an undistorted modeling perspective, as demonstrated in *Blender 3 Stylized Viking Boat 3D Model Complete Guide* by 3D Tudor (`https://www.udemy.com/course/blender-to-unreal-engine-5-the-complete-beginners-guide/?referralCode=A659E7EEEA61C2DA562A`).

- If you want to enhance the realism of your renders by mimicking real-world lighting conditions using background images, check out *Blender 3 Beginners Step-Step Guide to Isometric Rooms by 3D Tudor* (`https://www.udemy.com/course/blender-3-beginners-step-by-step-guide-to-isometric-rooms/?referralCode=AB7E2519D26525F1320A`).

- To incorporate static backgrounds in 2D animations or scenes without a full 3D environment, explore the techniques shown in *Blender to Unreal Engine 5 Fantasy River 3D Diorama Boat Scene* by 3D Tudor (`https://www.udemy.com/course/blender-unreal-engine-5/?referralCode=148B2AC2D50591C913A3`).

- For projects requiring attention to real-life dimensions, such as architectural models or product prototypes, using lattices is crucial. See how complex curved surfaces, such as spiral staircases, are modeled in *Blender Beginner's Bootcamp* by 3D Tudor (`https://www.udemy.com/course/blender-beginners-bootcamp/?referralCode=1FEDE1307FCB6BBE265F`).

Subscribe to Game Dev Assembly!

We are excited to introduce **Game Dev Assembly**, our brand-new newsletter dedicated to everything game development. Whether you're coding, designing, animating, or managing a studio, we've got insights, trends, and expert advice to help you create, innovate, and thrive. Sign up now and get exciting benefits.

`https://packt.link/gamedev-newsletter`

Get This Book's PDF Version and Exclusive Extras

UNLOCK NOW

Scan the QR code (or go to `packtpub.com/unlock`). Search for this book by name, confirm the edition, and then follow the steps on the page.

Note: Keep your invoice handy. Purchases made directly from Packt don't require an invoice.

10

Leveling Up with More Advanced Blender Modeling Techniques

This chapter invites you to double up your skills with more advanced Blender modeling techniques. Just as a skilled chef masters a range of culinary tools to create a gourmet dish, you will learn how to use Blender tools and functions in creative ways to meet your goals.

First, we will go over a comprehensive overview of Blender's **Select** menu. Here, you will learn how to target and modify specific areas of your mesh.

Next, we will look at the **Bisect** tool in Blender. This tool acts like a surgeon's scalpel, allowing you to split and modify your models with precision. Then, we will discuss all you need to know about the **Convex Hull** tool. Blender's **Convex Hull** is like a tailor seamlessly draping fabric over a mannequin. By wrapping your selected vertices with a simplified mesh, you will learn how to create a base for you to refine further.

You will also learn about the **Symmetrize** tool, being able to confidently discuss the similarities and differences between the **Symmetrize** tool and the **Mirror** modifier, and when to use each one. Much like polishing a gemstone, you will learn about how Blender's **Clean Up** tools can transform your model. We will also talk about the **Bevel** tool. This technique adds realism and detail to your models by softening edges and corners, much like how a carpenter smooths out the edges of a piece of furniture to give it a finished look.

Next, you will find out how to rip meshes, introducing you to a method to create openings or separations in your models. Afterward, you will learn about the **Hook** tool. By attaching vertices to objects or bones, you can manipulate parts of your mesh as if they were on strings, providing a powerful way to animate or modify specific areas of your model.

Finally, we will cover how to convert different object types in Blender. This process is comparable to an alchemist transforming one substance into another, giving you the flexibility to switch between mesh, curve, text, and surface types, adapting your models to fit the needs of your project.

Chapter 10 will be the point where you will tell yourself that you can finally connect all of what you have learned about 3D modeling techniques together and that it makes sense.

So, in this chapter, we will cover the following topics:

- Delving deep into Blender's Select menu
- Dissecting meshes with the Bisect tool in Blender
- Exploring Blender's Convex Hull tool in depth
- Guaranteeing symmetry in Blender with Symmetrize
- Cleaning up your meshes in Blender
- Beveling vertices in Blender
- Ripping meshes in Blender
- Mastering control over vertices with the Hook tool
- Converting different object types in Blender

Technical requirements

As for **Blender 4.5 LTS (Long-Term Support)**, the general requirements include a macOS 11.2 or newer (Apple Silicon supported natively) operating system, or a Linux (64-bit, glibc 2.28 or newer) operating system. Blender now requires a CPU with the SSE4.2 instruction set, at least 8 GB of RAM (32 GB recommended for heavy scenes), and a GPU supporting OpenGL 4.3 with a minimum of 2 GB of VRAM.

For a full list of technical requirements, please refer back to *Chapter 1* of this part.

Delving deep into Blender's Select menu

Contrary to (un)popular opinion, by now, you will be well aware that 3D modeling artists do more than build structures made out of cubes. Sometimes, your models are so intricate that you need to select just the right spot to modify with pinpoint accuracy. Blender offers a wide range of selection tools. The **Select** menu, located in the top toolbar in **Edit Mode**, hosts several of these tools (*Figure 10.1*).

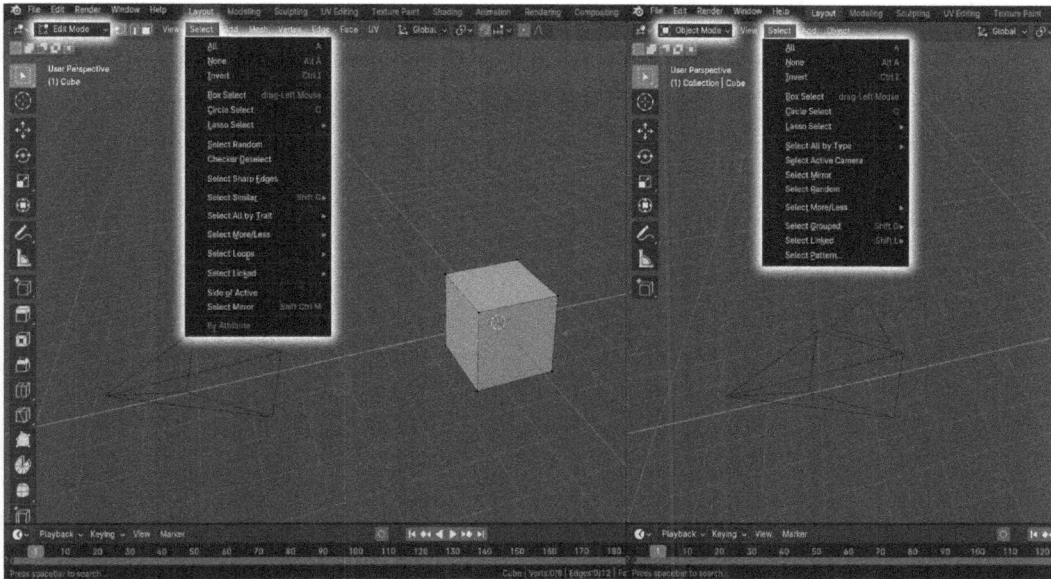

Figure 10.1: Select menu tools in Edit Mode (left) and Object Mode (right)

> **Note**
>
> Blender's **Object Mode** also contains the **Select** menu, although the options are limited to object selection.

In the list that follows, we will discuss the most popular selection tools and mention in which scenarios they would be most useful:

- **Box Select** (shortcut: *B*): You can use this to draw a rectangular selection area to select vertices, edges, or faces within that region.

  It is ideal for selecting specific portions of a mesh quickly and is particularly useful for selecting and modifying large contiguous regions. For example, in a model where you need to modify the side of a building, **Box Select** would be useful because it allows for fast and efficient selection of the entire area without missing any parts, like in *Figure 10.2*.

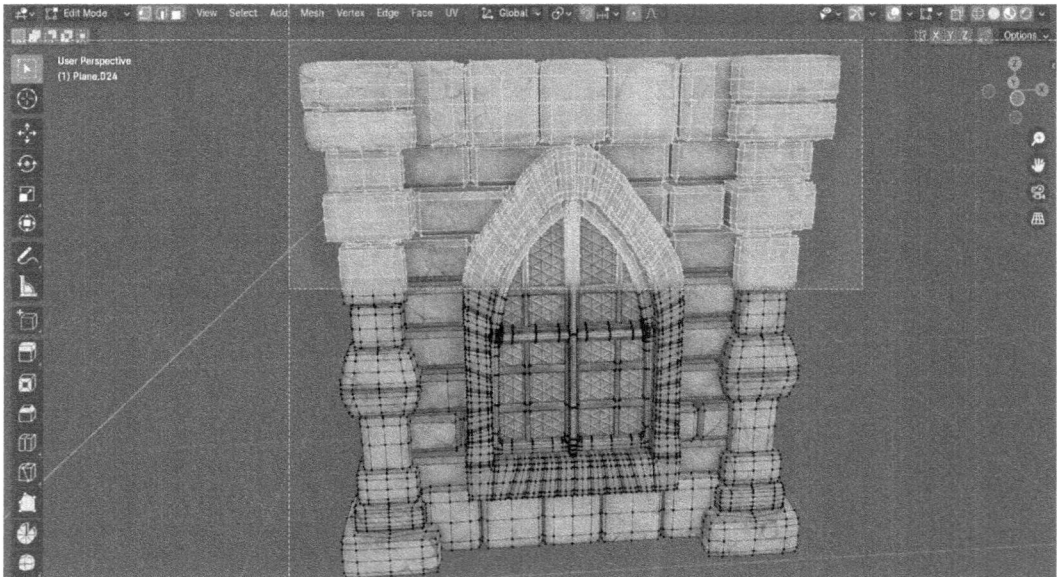

Figure 10.2: Using Box Select to modify the side of a building

- **Circle Select** (shortcut: *C*): You can use this to paint a selection using a circular cursor, like in *Figure 10.3*.

Figure 10.3: Using Circle Select in Blender 20 Massive Fantasy Windows Asset Pack by 3D Tudor

Circle Select is best for more refined and organic selections, such as a character's face or the foliage of a tree 3D model. This selection tool is also ideal if you are selecting the vertices on a curved surface or if you need a softer, more controlled selection, such as the body of a car.

- **Lasso Select** (shortcut: *Ctrl + Left Mouse Button*): You can draw a freeform shape. For example, outlining the silhouette of a complex object is like an intricate piece of jewellery. This is perfect for selecting irregularly shaped regions of a mesh that do not conform to box or circle shapes, such as organic shapes such as animals or twisted tree branches.

- **Checker Deselect** (located within the **Select** menu): As soon as you use **Checker Deselect**, a box will pop up at the bottom left, showing you all the options. You can select and deselect components in a pattern (*Figure 10.4*), creating a checkerboard effect.

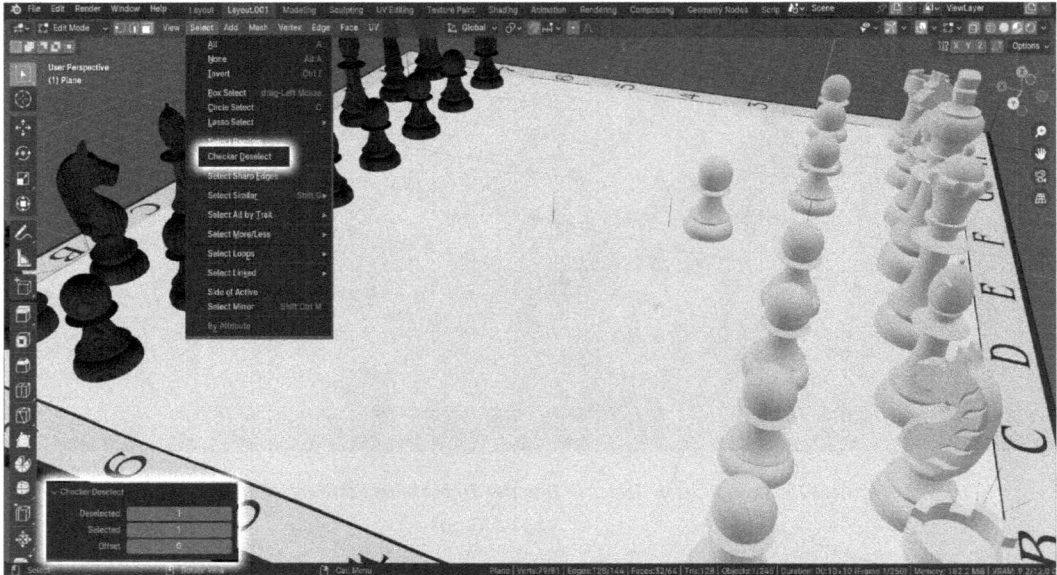

Figure 10.4: Using Checker Deselect in Blender

Although the grid shown in the screenshot does not have a visible checker pattern, it represents a selection made using **Checker Deselect**, which alternates the selected vertices to create a grid-like topology.

This is useful when you want to apply a periodic effect to a mesh, such as making alternate faces on a grid transparent. For instance, if you have a plane divided into numerous subdivisions, using **Checker Deselect** and then scaling the selected faces can create an interesting tiled pattern, like a geometric facade (*Figure 10.5*).

Figure 10.5: A geometric facade

- **Select Sharp Edges** (go to **Select | Select Sharp Edges**): There, you can select the edges where two adjacent faces form an angle sharper than the threshold you set (usually meaning more acute), as *Figure 10.6* shows.

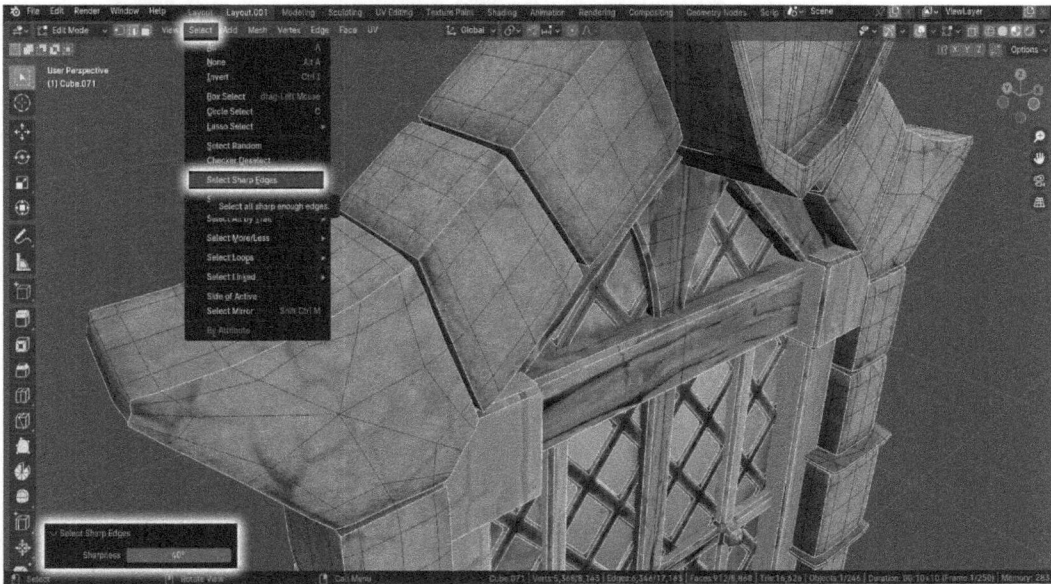

Figure 10.6: How Select Sharp Edges works

This is valuable for selecting edges that form sharper angles between faces, what we often call "hard" edges of a model, especially if you want to apply a bevel or mark those edges on a low-poly object using **Smooth Shading**. For example, this project could be a mechanical part where emphasizing the sharp edges can highlight its angular design.

- **Select Linked** (shortcut: *L*): You can use this to select all elements connected to the current selection. This is essential when working with multi-part objects and you want to select all the parts of a specific mesh. For example, if you have a character model and need to select all parts of an arm without affecting the rest of the body, **Select Linked** is ideal for ensuring continuity in your selection.

- **Select All by Trait** (go to **Select** | **Select All by Trait**): This tool is a bit of a time-saver, really. Instead of tediously clicking your way around a model to find all the sharp bits or seams, you can just tell Blender, "Oi, grab everything with this trait," and it does the heavy lifting for you. Handy, right? The panel in *Figure 10.7* shows where to pick your trait, seam, sharpness, crease, and then off it goes, doing exactly what you asked, for once.

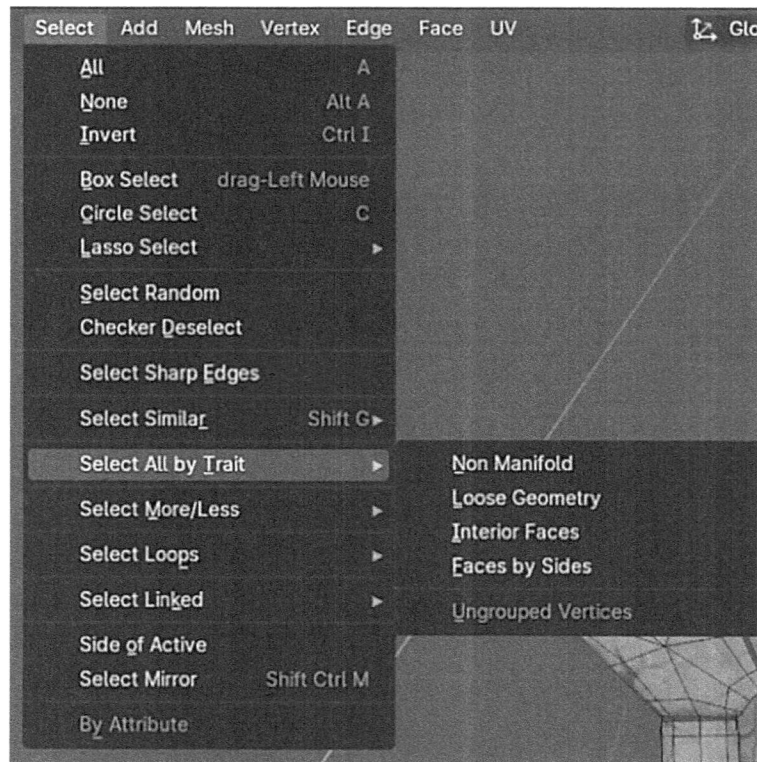

Figure 10.7: Navigating to Select All by Trait

This tool is brilliant for sniffing out sneaky problems in your mesh. You can highlight non-manifold edges in seconds; those little gremlins that love to ruin your 3D print or crash your simulation. It also helps catch things such as leftover interior faces from a dodgy extrusion, or those pesky verts that refuse to merge because they are just barely apart. Basically, it saves you the pain of chasing mystery glitches later on. A quick scan here keeps your mesh clean and drama-free before you move on to UVs, rigging, or exporting.

The tools available in Blender's **Select** menu are considered advanced 3D modeling tools because they let you select parts of your scene or individual models with pinpoint accuracy. They also cater to the specific needs and geometries of different models. By understanding when and how to use these selection tools, you can significantly speed up your modeling process. Familiarize yourself with these tools, especially the shortcuts, to see a substantial boost in the quality of your work.

Now, we will move on from selecting meshes to dissecting them. Sounds cool, right?

Dissecting meshes with the Bisect tool in Blender

The **Bisect** tool in Blender is an advanced 3D modeling feature that allows you to split and dissect meshes. This tool works by drawing a line or plane through the mesh to create a cut, like slicing bread with a knife. The cut is made along the plane you define, dividing the mesh into two parts. This functionality is ideal for creating detailed models, refining geometry, and preparing models for further detailing or animation

Accessing and using the Bisect tool

To start using the **Bisect** tool, follow the next steps:

1. With your object selected, enter **Edit Mode**.

2. Before using the tool, you need to make a selection. Blender's **Bisect** tool will only affect selected parts of a mesh.

3. Navigate to the tool shelf on the left side and select the **Bisect** tool. Alternatively, you can access it from the **Mesh** menu (**Mesh | Bisect**) or by pressing the shortcut *W* and choosing **Bisect**.

4. With the **Bisect** tool active, click and drag across your mesh to create a bisecting line. Release to make the cut.

Now, if you want to be a super fruit-slashing ninja instead, then let's explore how to adjust the **Bisect** cut.

Adjusting the cut

After making the initial cut, the tool settings will appear in the lower-left corner, allowing you to adjust parameters, as shown in *Figure 10.8*.

Figure 10.8: Adjusting the cut with Blender's Bisect tool

When you start using the **Bisect** tool, a gizmo for its controls will also appear. This will allow you to visually control the **Bisect** location position. For better accuracy, I recommend you control the **Bisect** location using the options at the bottom left instead. Let's break down these options:

- **Plane Point & Normal**: This adjusts the starting point and orientation of the cut. Making these adjustments can help you align the cut with complex geometries or specific design elements of your model. Let's say you are cutting through a cylindrical object and want the cut to align perfectly with the axis. In this case, adjusting **Plane Point & Normal** is essential; if you did not adjust it, you would risk having a misaligned or skewed cut that does not follow the desired path, potentially compromising the symmetry or aesthetic of your model; this could result in an uneven or unrealistic appearance.

> Note
>
> Use **Bisect** for more freehand and arbitrary cuts. For straight cuts along a mesh's topology, consider using the **Loop Cut** tool.

- **Clear Outer** and **Clear Inner**: This will remove the vertices either on the outer or inner side of the bisect, giving you a clean cut. You might want to do that if you are creating a sectional view of a model or removing unwanted parts of a mesh, like trimming the excess from a 3D scanned object to isolate part of the model you want to keep.

- **Fill**: When enabled, Blender will fill the area of the cut with new faces. This could be useful if, for example, you are creating a cross-sectional view of an object and need a solid face to visualize its internal structure, such as a eukaryotic cell.

- **Threshold**: This determines how close vertices need to be to the cut line before they are considered part of the bisect. This is important because it allows you to control the precision of the cut, ensuring that small details near the cut line are either included or excluded based on your specific requirements. For example, in a densely detailed model, a lower threshold can help avoid accidentally including nearby vertices that should not be part of the cut.

> Tip
>
> Use **Snapping** (by pressing *Ctrl*) along with the **Bisect** tool to ensure your cuts align with specific vertices or edges.

Examples of Bisect tool usage

Although we have already covered some possible project examples, in the following table, we will look at the reasons why you might want to use the **Bisect** tool, alongside some different examples:

Bisect Tool	Reason for Using the Tool	Project Example
Model Symmetry	If you want to ensure symmetry (e.g., for a face or a car), you can use the **Bisect** tool to split the mesh in half, modify one side, and then mirror it by navigating to Object and then selecting Mirror.	Creating a character's head for an animated movie. You can model one half of the head, use the **Bisect** tool to create a symmetrical half, and then make adjustments to ensure the facial features are perfectly aligned.

Bisect Tool	Reason for Using the Tool	Project Example
Breaking Objects Apart	For visual effects, such as breaking glass or a splitting rock, the **Bisect** tool can help achieve that appearance by dividing the mesh into random patterns.	Designing a scene in a short film where a window shatters upon impact. Using the **Bisect** tool, you can create realistic, random fracture patterns on the glass mesh before applying physics simulations for the shattering effect.
Creating Openings	If you are modeling architectural designs or vehicles and need to create a door or window opening, the **Bisect** tool can be used to cut out precise portions of your mesh.	Let's say you are working on an architectural visualization of a modern house. You can use the **Bisect** tool to precisely cut out window and door openings in walls, ensuring they fit the architectural plan's dimensions accurately.
Geometry Optimization	For dense meshes, the **Bisect** tool can be handy in slicing off unwanted or unnecessary portions of the model to optimize the geometry.	In this example, you are preparing a highly detailed 3D model of a car for a mobile game. To reduce the model's complexity without compromising its appearance, use the **Bisect** tool to remove unseen or less important parts of the mesh, such as the bottom side of the chassis.
Artistic Stylization	For a more artistic approach, the tool can be used to create stylized breaks or splits in models, especially for abstract art or sculptures.	You are designing a fantasy character for a video game. You can use the **Bisect** tool to add distinctive features to the character's armour or clothing, such as asymmetrical cuts or angular shapes, creating a stylized look.

Table 10.1: Examples of Bisect tool usage and reasons for using it

Tip

After bisection, tools such as **Bevel** can be applied at the cut edges to create interesting effects.

Blender's **Bisect** tool is your chance to perfectly slash fruits without playing the popular mobile game *Fruit Ninja* by Halfbrick Studios. Whether you are aiming for precision edits or more freeform artistic expressions, understanding the depths of this tool can make or break your next 3D project.

We will now look at another powerful feature in Blender's arsenal: the **Convex Hull** tool. This tool complements the **Bisect** tool by quickly generating a simplified outer boundary around complex shapes.

Exploring Blender's Convex Hull tool in depth

Blender's **Convex Hull** tool streamlines and simplifies many 3D modeling processes. Its absence would make a variety of processes more labor-intensive and complex when they do not need to be.

The **Convex Hull** tool creates simple structures that envelop a set of points. It can be visualized as a tightly stretched elastic band, like in *Figure 10.9*.

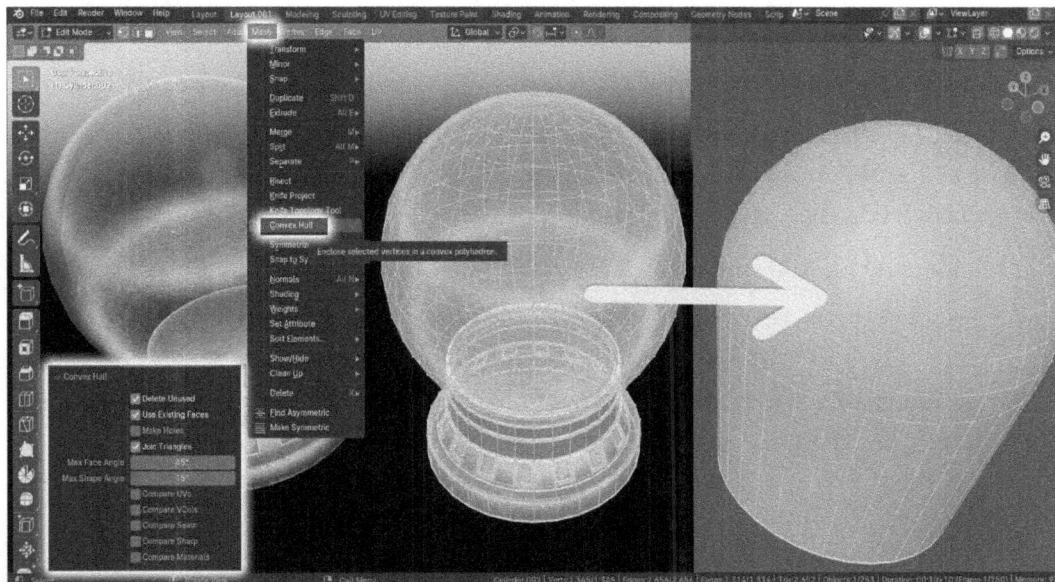

Figure 10.9: Visualizing the Convex Hull tool in Blender

When released, this band wraps around the points, forming the most external boundary without any indentations. The **Convex Hull** tool generates a new mesh that surrounds the selected vertices, edges, or faces. The following list includes the three most common uses of this tool:

- *Creating collision boundaries*: In game development, **Convex Hull** is used to create simplified collision boundaries around complex models, making physics calculations more efficient. This is useful because it reduces the computational load on the game engine.

- *Preparing for 3D printing*: **Convex Hull** can be used to determine the minimum volume of material needed to encase a model. This has significant implications in texturing, meaning that the surface area requiring texture or finishing is minimized, thereby reducing printing time and costs.

- *Geometric analysis*: In architectural modeling or design, **Convex Hull** can help in space analysis. This will make sure you are using the space you have with optimization in mind, a bit like custom-built IKEA kitchens.

Note

By encapsulating the outer limits of data points, 3D modelers can identify key areas that require more attention or detail in their models. This is particularly useful in complex projects such as urban planning models or detailed product designs, where understanding the overall scope and outliers is crucial.

Accessing and using the Convex Hull tool

The process of using Blender's **Convex Hull** tool is straightforward if you have already grasped the basics of using Blender for 3D modeling and are used to the terminology. To minimize errors, make sure to follow these steps exactly:

1. Enter **Edit Mode** (by pressing the *Tab* key).

2. Using any of the selection methods, select the set of vertices, edges, or faces you want to encase within **Convex Hull**.

3. With your selection made, press *F3* and, with the search box function, search for **Convex Hull**. Alternatively, in the **Mesh** menu, select **Convex Hull**.

> Tip
>
> For a complex object, consider breaking it into parts and generating multiple **Convex Hulls**. For example, if you are working on a robot with different moving parts in an action game, it is often more efficient to break the model down into segments and create individual convex hulls for each part.

4. After activating the **Convex Hull** operation, a set of options will appear at the bottom left, which you can explore (you can see these back in *Figure 10.9*):

    -   **Delete Input:** Determines what happens to the original selection (e.g., you can keep or delete it)
    -   **Make Holes:** If set, it will create holes in places where the convex shape is not obstructed by the original geometry

> Tip
>
> Honestly, this feature is a bit pants. If enabled, it tries to punch holes wherever the convex shape overlaps with the mesh, but results are hit-and-miss. Sometimes it fills in random gaps or just leaves you wondering what on Earth happened. You are much better off using **Geometry Nodes** or a proper volume-to-mesh workflow if you actually want control over the outcome. Read more about it in *Chapter 1* in *Part 2* of this book!

    -   **Join Triangles:** Merges triangles into quads where possible, simplifying the mesh's geometry

> Note
>
> Using the **Convex Hull** tool in combination with modifiers such as **Subdivision Surface** can lead to interesting, smoothed forms. This technique is particularly effective for organic shapes, such as creatures or natural elements. The initial **Convex Hull** gives you the basic form, and the **Subdivision Surface Modifier** smooths and refines this form, making it appear more lifelike and detailed.

Examples of Convex Hull usage

Using the **Convex Hull** tool helps avoid the time-consuming effort of manually creating simplistic envelopes or boundaries around complex shapes. Here are some key examples of how **Convex Hull** usage significantly impacts the workflow and creative process of 3D artists in various fields:

- *Quick base mesh*: If you have an idea or a set of points for a structure but not a defined shape, **Convex Hull** can quickly generate a base mesh to start with. Imagine a project where you are designing an alien landscape for a sci-fi game. You have a collection of points representing the rough location of rocks and terrain features, but no defined shape. Using the **Convex Hull** tool, you can quickly generate a base mesh for these landscapes, forming the fundamental shapes of cliffs and ground formations.

Tip

After applying the **Convex Hull** tool to get the basic shape, using the **Displace Modifier** can add intricate textures and details to the surface. This is particularly useful for creating realistic terrains, scales on creatures, or intricate bark textures on trees.

- *Physics simulations*: In physics, particularly collision detection, objects are often approximated using **Convex Hull** to simplify calculations. Consider a racing game with intricate car models. By approximating the cars' shapes using **Convex Hull**, you make the gameplay smoother and all car-to-car interactions more realistic without overloading the game engine with complex geometry.

- *Optimization in games*: Game engines sometimes use the **Convex Hull** of complex objects for collision detection to enhance performance. In an action-packed adventure game, where the environment is filled with detailed structures such as ancient ruins or dense forests, using **Convex Hull** for collision detection becomes crucial (i.e., for ensuring that the game runs smoothly even in graphically intensive scenes, like in *Figure 10.10*).

Figure 10.10: Escape room animation project in "The Ultimate Guide to Blender 3D Rigging & Animation" by 3D Tudor

Tip

If you are working on a model of a river stone, **Convex Hull** provides the initial shape, and the **Smooth** modifier can be applied to mimic the natural smoothness and roundness of the stone.

- *Abstract art and sculpting*: **Convex Hull** can also be used for more abstract purposes, creating unexpected and organic forms by generating hulls from various selections. This could work in a puzzle or exploration game where forms are subsequently sculpted and modified to create unique and intriguing art assets.

Note

The resulting mesh from a **Convex Hull** operation can sometimes have unnecessary vertices or faces. **Limited Dissolve** (i.e., simplifying a mesh by reducing its number of vertices and faces) and **Decimate Geometry** (i.e., simplifying a mesh by reducing the vertex and face count of a mesh) can help you to optimize the mesh. This is especially important for mobile games or VR applications, where resource efficiency is key. Should you want to find out more, check out our 3D Tudor *Performance and Optimization Guide* video here: `https://youtu.be/JSU42gTJp_c`.

Blender's **Convex Hull** tool is simple but powerful, with many applications, ranging from practical physics simulations to abstract art. Whether you are a beginner or a seasoned pro, knowing how and when to use this tool can change how you do things from the ground up.

We will now tackle a similar tool, called **Symmetrize**, to find out how to generate geometry that mirrors your original selection.

Guaranteeing symmetry in Blender with Symmetrize

I am sure that we could all agree that, except for some abstract art, pretty much every structure has an element of symmetry to it. Blender's **Symmetrize** tool helps you create mirrored copies of your mesh based on its topology. When you work on one side, it automatically replicates your work on the other. This is especially useful when modeling symmetrical objects, characters, or components.

For example, in a course where you are learning to model a medieval castle, the **Symmetrize** tool would be invaluable for creating the two symmetrical towers on either side of the main gate. Each tower would need to be identical in size, shape, and detail, and the **Symmetrize** tool allows you to model one tower and then instantly create a mirror image for the other, ensuring perfect symmetry and saving significant time and effort.

Accessing the Symmetrize tool

To start using the **Symmetrize** tool, follow the next steps:

1. Change your origin points to wherever you want to make your model mirror over, because the **Symmetrize** operation is done based on the mesh origin point.

2. Select the object you want to symmetrize, then press *Tab* to enter **Edit Mode**.

3. Choose the specific vertices, edges, or faces that you want to symmetrize or select the entire mesh using *A*.

4. With your desired geometry selected, go to the **Mesh** menu in the header, then **Symmetrize**. Alternatively, you can press *F3* to search for **Symmetrize**.

5. Once activated, a tool settings panel will appear at the bottom left, like in *Figure 10.11*.

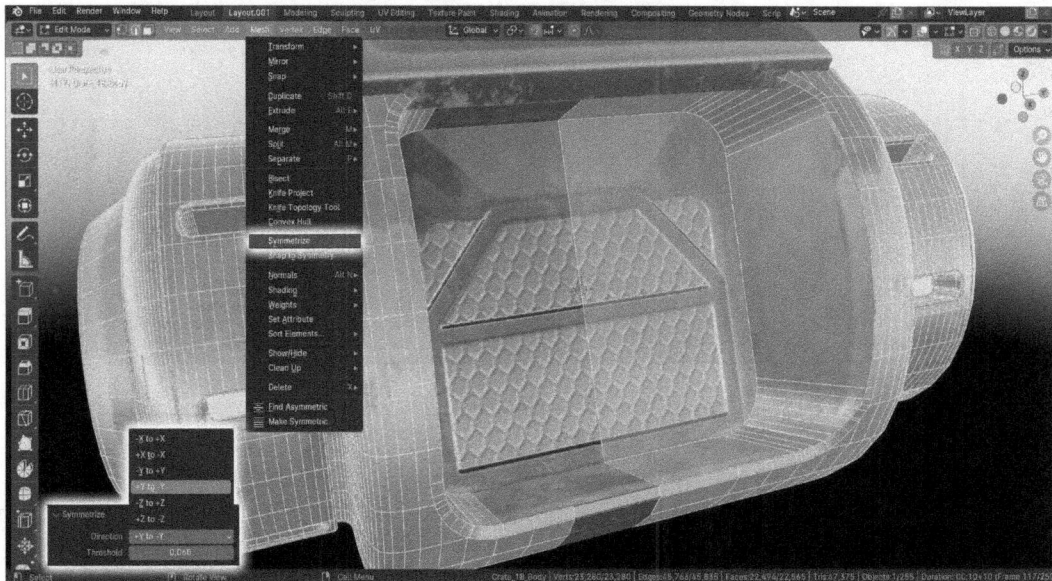

Figure 10.11: Symmetrize tool settings panel

Here, you can define the direction of the symmetry. For instance, **-X to +X** would mirror the negative X side of your mesh to the positive X side, like in *Figure 10.12*. You will see that the origin point was highlighted using a circle. By placing the origin point on the upper edge of the mesh, I could use **Symmetrize** to mirror both the corner and the top section of the model: handy when you want to duplicate details cleanly without fiddling around with manual snapping. See how it lines up in the image?

Figure 10.12: Defining the direction of symmetry in action, showing -Y to +Y and -Z to +Z

Note

Symmetrize uses your mesh's topology to make things symmetrical. If your mesh topology is uneven or has **Ngons**, the results might be unpredictable. To make sure this does not happen, it is important to maintain a clean, even topology with **Quads** (i.e., four-sided polygons). Before using **Symmetrize**, check for and correct any irregularities, such as **N-gons** (i.e., polygons with more than four sides) or uneven edge loops. You can do that using tools such as **Knife** or **Loop Cut** to add necessary edges, and by dissolving or merging vertices to eliminate **N-gons**. You can read more about these tools in *Chapter 6* in *Part 1* of this book.

Examples of Symmetrize usage

Blender's **Symmetrize** tool is crucial in numerous scenarios where symmetry is a key component of the design, such as in the following example projects:

- *Character modeling*: Using the **Symmetrize** tool, you can model one-half of a character's face. This will ensure that detailed features such as ears, eyes, and facial expressions are perfectly mirrored on the other side.

- *Creating symmetrical objects*: The **Symmetrize** tool can help by making sure that elements such as doors, headlights, and aerodynamic curves are identical on both sides of a car.

- *Fixing asymmetrical errors*: If one side of your model gets distorted or has mistakes, you can correct one side and then use **Symmetrize** to correct the other. If you accidentally distort a window frame on one side of a building, you could use the **Symmetrize** tool to correct it.

Deciding when to use Symmetrize

The **Symmetrize** tool effectively mirrors a section of your mesh across a chosen axis, replacing the geometry on the target side. This ensures that the model is perfectly symmetrical based on the defined axis.

> Tip
>
> Ensure your mesh's center aligns with the intended axis of symmetry. If it's off-center, the **Symmetrize** tool may not work as expected.

You might say, this sounds a lot like Blender's **Mirror** modifier to me; why should I not use that instead?

Here, we will explore the individual roles of Blender's **Symmetrize** tool and the **Mirror** modifier. This will help you distinguish which situations are suited for using either methodology and why. Blender's **Symmetrize** tool and the **Mirror** modifier serve similar but distinct purposes in 3D modeling, and each has its advantages depending on the situation:

- **Symmetrize**: This tool is primarily used to make one side of a mesh a mirrored copy of the other. It is a one-time operation that immediately applies the changes to the mesh.

Unlike the **Mirror** modifier, which assumes a clean centerline and tends to just reflect geometry across an axis, the **Symmetrize** tool can create or fill in geometry if one side is missing. It is not shy about adding faces when needed, and can be a bit aggressive if your model is messy. Also, if your object does not have a perfect center, **Symmetrize** still tries to enforce symmetry based on direction and threshold. In short, think of it as a brute-force symmetry fix, it gets the job done.

Here are some examples of when to use it:

- *Correcting asymmetrical edits*: If you have edited one side of a model and want to quickly apply the same changes to the other side, **Symmetrize** can instantly make your model symmetrical.

- *Fixing asymmetry in a non-mirrored object*: For models that were not initially created with symmetry or a **Mirror** modifier, **Symmetrize** can be used to enforce symmetry after the fact.

- *Sculpting workflows*: In sculpting, especially if you are working on organic models, you might sculpt details on one side and then use **Symmetrize** to copy those details to the other side.

Note

If your object has modifiers such as a **Mirror** modifier, you might want to apply or remove them before using **Symmetrize** for more predictable results. If you forget to remove the modifiers, it will mirror the already mirrored geometry, potentially leading to overlapping vertices, extraneous geometry, or other modeling anomalies.

- **Mirror**: This modifier is used for creating a dynamic, mirrored duplicate of the mesh. It is a non-destructive tool, meaning the original mesh can still be edited independently.

Here are some examples of when to use it:

- *Creating symmetrical models from scratch*: The **Mirror** modifier allows you to work on one half while automatically replicating changes to the other half.

- *Maintaining flexibility*: Since it is non-destructive, you can toggle the **Mirror** modifier on and off, adjust its settings (see *Figure 10.12*), or remove it without changing the original mesh so much that you cannot go back. The **Mirror** modifier also lets you control the **Mirror** operation origin point. By default, Blender's **Mirror** modifier would use the origin point of its object, but you can use the **Mirror Object** option, highlighted in *Figure 10.13*, to create a mirror operation on its side even though the object has its origin at its center.

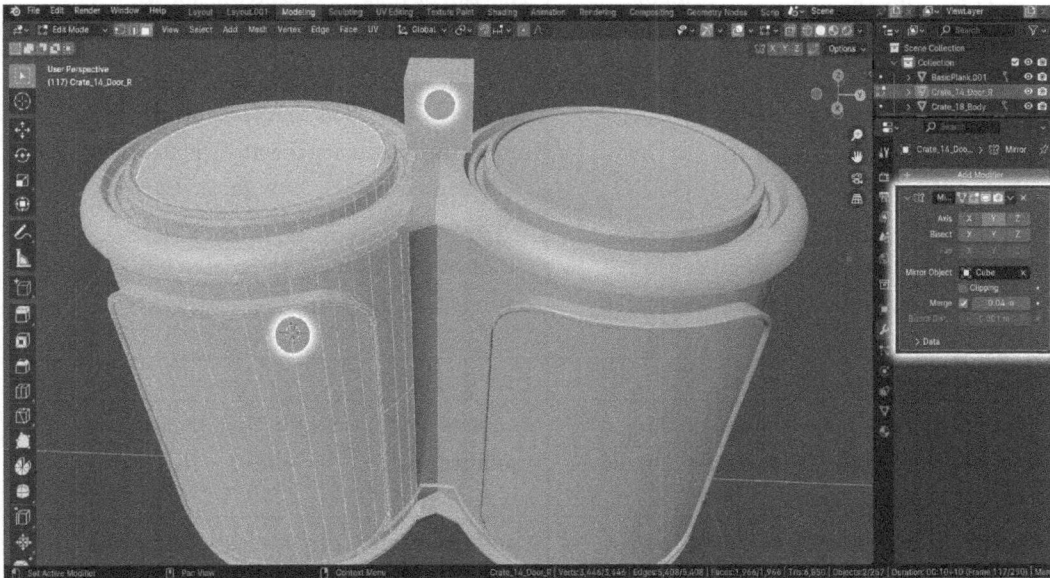

Figure 10.13: Available Mirror modifier settings in Blender

- *Complex modeling workflows*: In more complex models, where you may want to keep the symmetry dynamic for a longer period during the modelling process, the **Mirror** modifier is more suitable. For example, when designing a character model that requires frequent adjustments to its pose or anatomy, the **Mirror** modifier allows you to make continuous symmetrical updates across the model without permanently applying these changes.

You can use *Table 10.2* to decide whether to use **Symmetrize** or the **Mirror** modifier based on the situation:

Symmetrize Tool	Mirror Modifier
Advantages	**Advantages**
Quickly makes one side of a mesh a mirrored copy of the other, applying changes instantly.	Mirrors changes made from one side of the model to the other with real-time updates.
Ideal for correcting asymmetries in models that you did not originally create with symmetry in mind.	This can be toggled on and off, allowing for flexible editing without permanently altering the original mesh.
Beneficial in sculpting workflows, especially for organic models.	Excellent for models that you will adjust multiple times, since the modifier lets you maintain symmetry throughout the design process.
Does not require ongoing management, making it user-friendly for quick symmetry fixes.	Offers control over the symmetry axis, clipping options, and merging thresholds.
Disadvantages	Disadvantages
Permanently changes the mesh, making it unsuitable for models that require ongoing symmetry adjustments.	Requires management within Blender's modifier stack.
It mirrors the geometry of your model based on its current state at the moment of application. This means that any changes or modifications you make to the mesh after using the tool will not be automatically mirrored to the other side.	Less effective for correcting asymmetry in models that were not initially created with the modifier.
Once the tool is applied, it creates a fixed, mirrored version of your model as it exists at that moment. Any asymmetrical changes made afterward, such as adding a new feature on one side or altering the shape of a specific part, will not be automatically replicated on the mirrored side.	Sometimes, the modifier can create vertices, edges, or faces that need manual cleanup, especially near the mirror plane. Clean-up options will be discussed in the next section of the current chapter.

Table 10.2: Deciding between the Symmetrize tool and the Mirror modifier

In summary, use the **Symmetrize** tool for quick, one-time symmetry corrections or in situations where you do not need the ongoing flexibility of the **Mirror** modifier. The **Mirror** modifier is more suitable for ongoing, dynamic symmetrical modeling where you want to maintain the ability to adjust or remove the symmetry at any point in the workflow.

Blender's **Symmetrize** tool is great when your mesh is behaving. But if your topology is a mess, think double verts, hidden faces, or dodgy edges, you are going to get some very weird results. That is why it pays to run a quick cleanup before you start mirroring parts of your model. Luckily, Blender comes with a whole set of **Clean Up** tools built for exactly this. Let us take a look at how to use them to keep things tidy and predictable.

Cleaning up your meshes in Blender

A clean topology should be at the top of your to-do list as a 3D modeling artist. You will not only improve your 3D model's quality but also its performance if you are planning to animate it, create simulations, or export your model to a popular game engine. Blender has a built-in suite of **Clean Up** tools (*Figure 10.14*) to help identify and correct issues in a mesh.

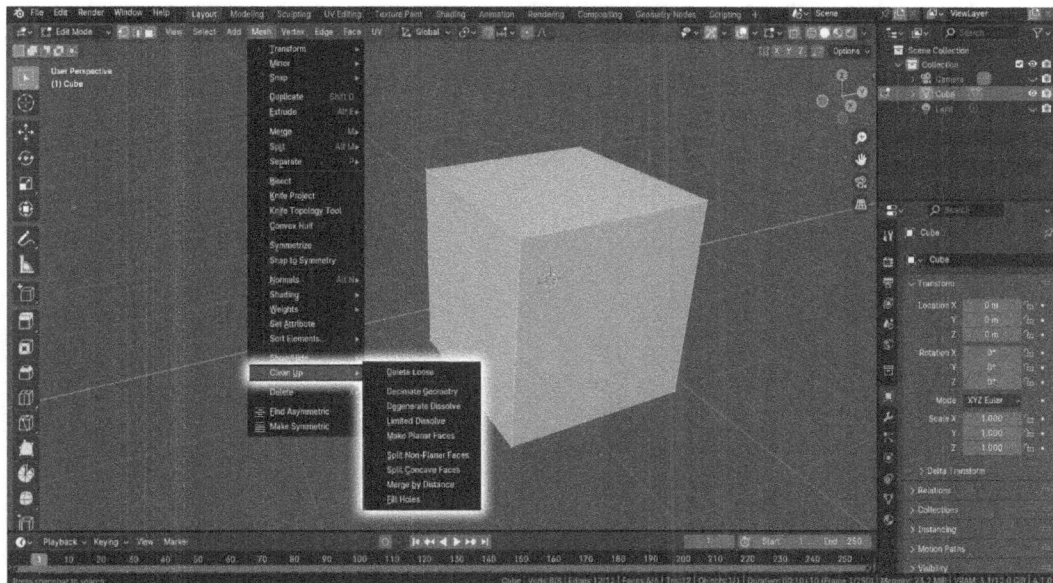

Figure 10.14: Blender's Clean Up tools

A cleaner mesh uses fewer vertices, edges, and faces, which translates to improved performance in real-time applications such as games. Other benefits of clean topology include that models deform correctly when animated, and that a clean mesh is easier to edit and modify. Eliminating unnecessary vertices and faces can also lead to faster rendering times.

Both **Cycles** and **EEVEE** appreciate clean topology, but **EEVEE** is the one that really throws a tantrum if your mesh is a mess. Since it is a real-time engine, performance is everything; clean geometry means faster previews, better frame rates, and fewer headaches when building interactive scenes or game assets. **Cycles** is a bit more forgiving. It is built for realism and can chew through more complex geometry without blinking. That said, keeping things tidy still helps speed up renders and saves your system from doing unnecessary heavy lifting.

Here's how to access the **Clean Up** tool:

1. Select the object you want to clean and press *Tab* to enter **Edit** mode.

2. Go to the **Mesh** menu in the header and hover over **Clean Up** to view the drop-down menu with various cleanup options.

3. Ensure that all the faces in your mesh are correctly oriented. Misoriented faces (i.e, normals pointing in the wrong direction) can cause shading and rendering anomalies. Use the **Recalculate Normals** function to correct them.

    In *Figure 10.15*, you can see how to identify which normals are facing the wrong way, using **Face Orientation** under the **Viewport Overlays** menu.

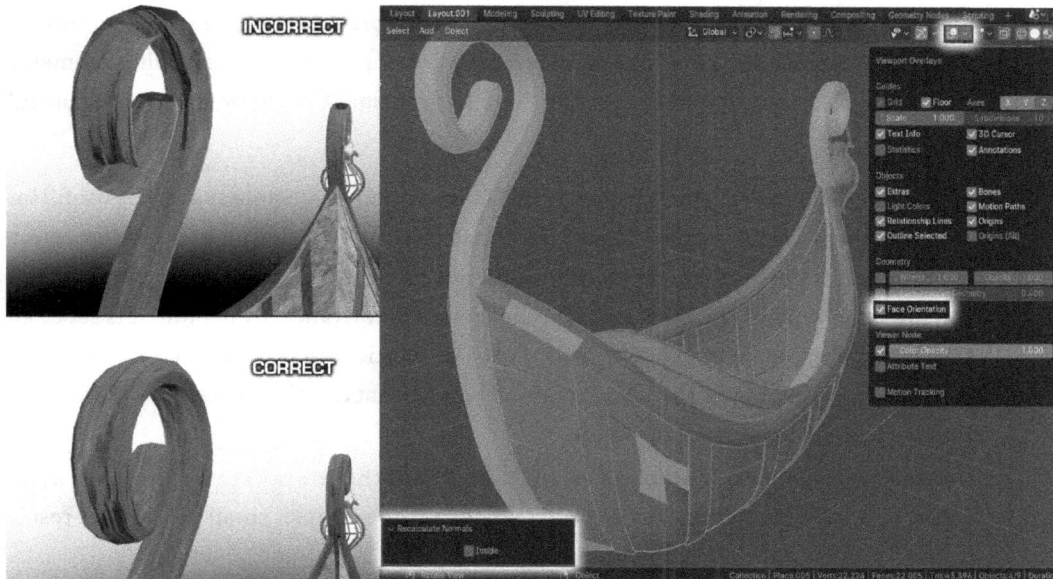

Figure 10.15: Identifying misorientated faces in 3D Tudor Blender Boat Geometry Node Build Any Boat in Seconds by 3D Tudor

The ones that show as red will be facing the wrong way. This will cause issues with preview, especially with real-time rendering engines, if we export it from Blender. By default, Blender uses a two-sided shader, which will not visually show up as an issue when previewing. Regardless, it will still cause issues in modeling if you use modifiers or any other operations that require normal data (e.g., the **Inflate** operation). To avoid errors, good practice dictates that you keep all parts shaded in blue when you are previewing your work on **Face Orientation**.

> **Note**
>
> There are a few exceptions, however. If you are creating window planes or foliage leaves, they would have to be visible from both sides. This means that you cannot avoid having visible red sides. If you are using **Recalculate Normals** (*Shift + N*), and you are still getting red parts, select the red sections and use the operation with **Inside** checked on.

Before diving into more advanced modifiers, it is good practice to make sure your mesh is clean. Blender includes several mesh cleanup tools designed to fix overlapping geometry, stray vertices, and other modeling gremlins that can sneak in. Some of the most useful are as follows:

- **Merge by Distance**: This tool removes vertices that occupy the same space. It is useful for ensuring there are no overlapping vertices that can cause rendering issues. After selecting it, adjust the distance in the bottom-left corner if needed. **Merge by Distance** allows you to merge vertices that are close together, based on distance. By default, it is set to an extremely low value (i.e., 0.0001). This makes the vertices that are in the same location merge because it is based on a small radius. If you see that certain vertices are not merging, you might need to increase the value.

- **Delete Loose**: Removes loose vertices, edges, and faces that are not connected to the main mesh. It is ideal for getting rid of stray geometry, for example, small pieces that result from sculpting or **Boolean** operations.

- **Degenerate Dissolve**: Dissolves vertices and edges that do not contribute to the mesh's form. This helps in removing unnecessary geometry. This could be tiny slivers or redundant edges that complicate the mesh without adding detail, like the ones in *Figure 10.16*.

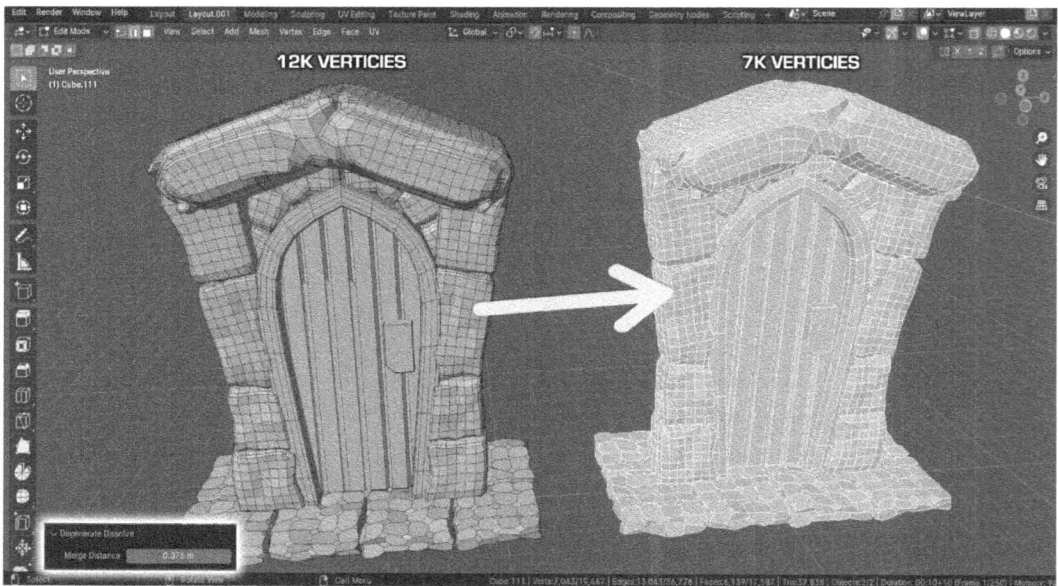

Figure 10.16: Mesh issues like tiny slivers and redundant edges

Tip

Tip

While not a tool, limiting your polygon count is best practice. Keeping the polygon count optimal without compromising on detail will help you balance your 3D model.

- **Fill Holes:** Identifies and fills any gaps or holes in the mesh, which might happen if certain faces were deleted or if there was incomplete modeling. This is a vital tool for ensuring manifold geometry, especially important for 3D printing. The practical reason for this is that non-manifold geometries can lead to print errors or structural weaknesses in the printed object.

Tip

Non-manifold geometry can cause issues in various 3D modeling tasks. To check for non-manifold geometry, from the **Select** menu, use **Select Non-Manifold** to find and address these issues.

- **Make Planar Faces:** Adjusts selected faces to lie in the same plane, like in *Figure 10.17*, realigning faces that may have become slightly skewed during modeling.

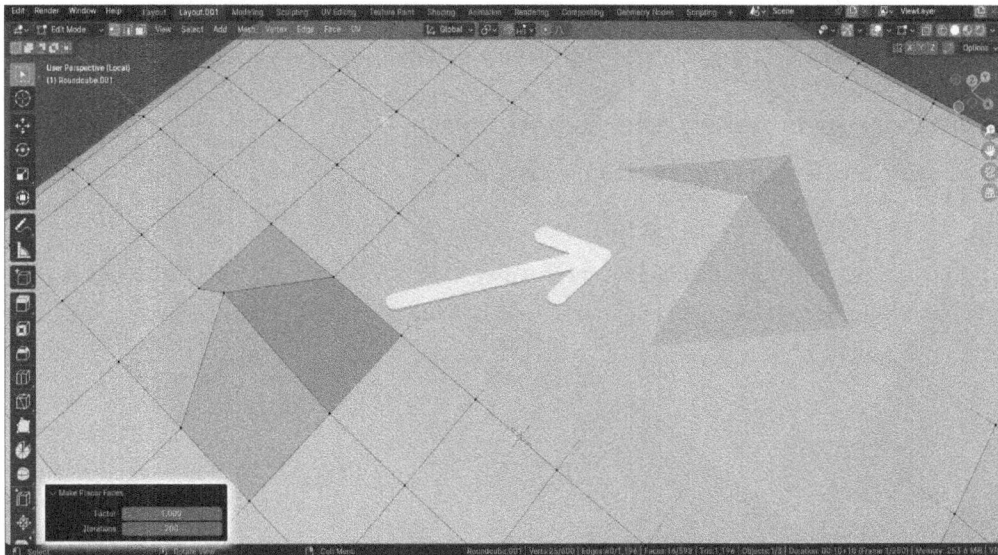

Figure 10.17: Adjusting faces that lie on the same plane

- This is useful for models that need flat surfaces. architectural elements, mechanical parts, or any design requiring precision and uniformity in surface planes.

The process of cleaning up a mesh in Blender is crucial for optimal results in any 3D project. This might seem like a rudimentary piece of advice at first, but I am sure that we can all agree that you would not eat food off a grime-infested floor. Following that logic, why should we not clean up our models to make sure we can enjoy them?

Our next stop on this journey will be Blender's **Bevel** tool, where, once again, we will focus on optimizing our models by focusing on shape rather than the elimination of errors.

Beveling vertices in Blender

Take a moment to look around your house. From kitchen counters to steps and coffee tables, you will see that many of these corners have been bevelled. The reasons for bevelling edges are often aesthetic. Bevelling, by softening sharp edges and corners, not only contributes to a more realistic appearance but also plays a crucial role in mechanical and functional designs, where smooth transitions are often essential. This is where Blender's **Bevel** tool comes in.

In high-poly modeling, especially in close-up renders or detailed sections of a model, the **Bevel** tool can add subtle edge details and boost its photorealism. This is because perfectly sharp edges rarely exist in the real world, so this is what we should emulate through our work as 3D modeling artists too. The **Bevel** tool can also be used to create more realistic interactions with light. Bevelled edges catch and scatter light in a way that sharp edges cannot, which is crucial for creating realistic materials and surfaces, especially those with reflective properties.

Accessing and using the Bevel tool

To start using the **Bevel** tool, follow the next steps:

1. Go to **Edit Mode** (by pressing the *Tab* key).
2. Ensure you are in **Vertex Select** mode (press *1* on the keyboard or click the vertex icon in your Blender **3D Viewport** header). Your **3D Viewport** should look like what you can see in *Figure 10.18*.

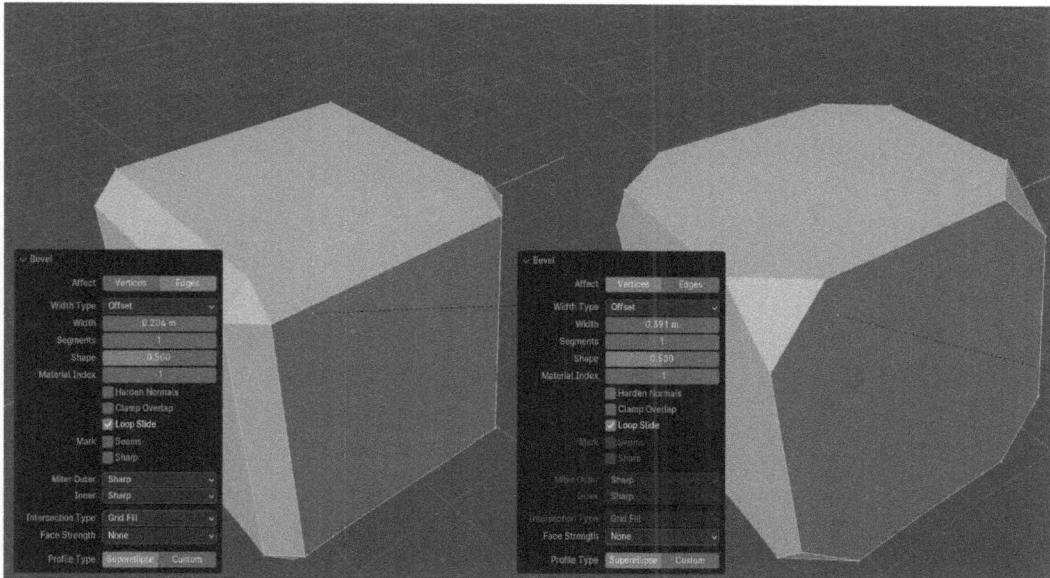

Figure 10.18: Visually identifying Vertex Select mode

3. Select the vertices you want to bevel. Then go to **Mesh** | **Vertices** | **Bevel Vertices**. Alternatively, with the desired vertices selected, simply press *Ctrl + Shift + B*. This will bevel the vertices of the selection itself.

> **Note**
>
> Pressing *Ctrl + B* will bevel the edges of a selection.

4. Now move the mouse to adjust the bevel's size:

   - When moving the mouse, the further you move from the center point of your selection, the greater the effect.
   - While moving the mouse, hold *Shift* for greater accuracy.

- Use the scroll wheel to adjust the number of segments or divisions in the bevel, which will make the bevelled edge smoother, like in *Figure 10.19*.

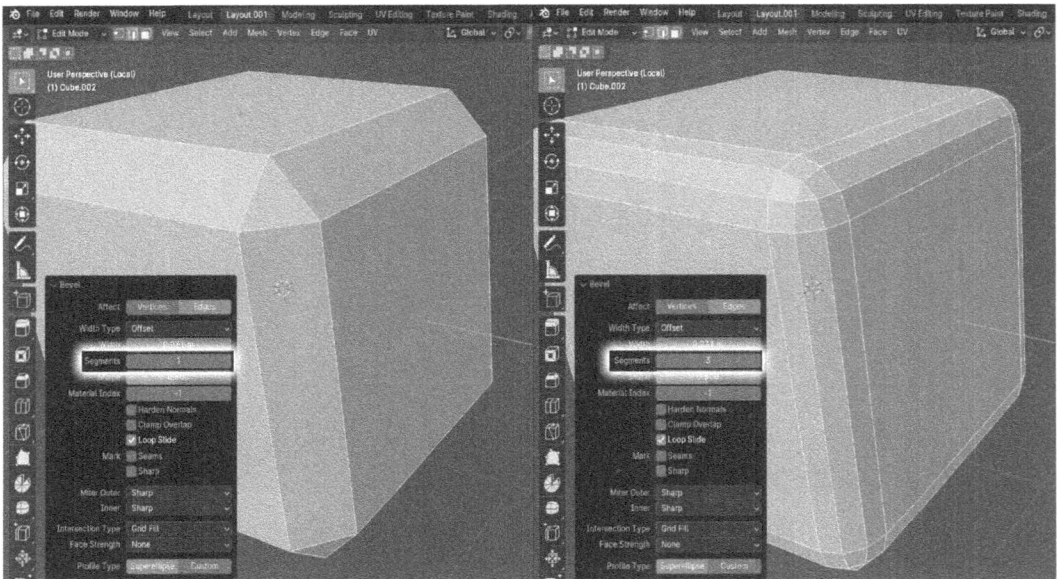

Figure 10.19: Beveling edges – a visual example

5. Once you start the **Bevel** operation, clicking and dragging with your mouse, a panel will appear in the bottom-left corner, allowing you to adjust various parameters (*Figure 10.21*), such as the following:

   - **Offset**: Controls the distance the bevel extends. This means that you can determine how far from the original edge or vertex the new bevelled surface will be created, effectively setting the width of the bevel itself.

     > **Note**
     >
     > Be mindful of the bevel's size. Large bevels on closely spaced vertices might result in overlapping geometry.

   - **Segments**: Controls the number of cuts in the bevel. More segments will result in a smoother bevel.

- **Profile:** Adjusts the curve of the bevel. A value of 0.5 will give a straight bevel, values less than 0.5 will curve inward, and values greater than 0.5 will bulge out, as shown in *Figure 10.20*.

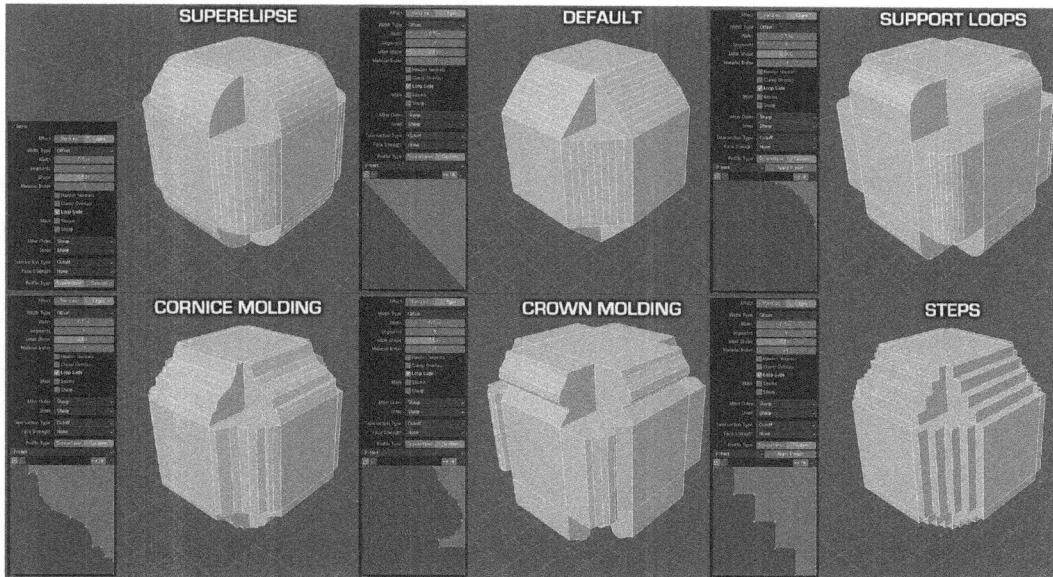

Figure 10.20: Adjusting the bevel curve in six ways

There are six presets in total: **Default**, **Superellipse**, **Support Loops**, **Cornice Molding**, **Crown Molding**, and **Steps**. By default, **Superellipse** is active. **Profile Type** is a curve profile, so you can also set it to **Custom** and define your own curve that will become the profile of the bevel. That is how you access the other presets, by switching to **Custom**, you will see the editable curve graph. From there, click on the **Preset** tab to access the five additional shapes. You can also draw your own shape directly in the graph for full control over the bevel's profile. Each preset offers a distinct silhouette, allowing for both technical and decorative results.

Each of the six presets changes the profile curve, which in turn gives different shapes for your bevel, but you can adjust the curve yourself to customize it. Specifically, **Superellipse** disables the profile graph and allows you to use the **Shape** option.

Note

If you need to adjust the bevel after applying it, you can use the **Operator** panel (i.e., the small panel that appears at the bottom left of the **3D Viewport** after a tool operation). It is, however, important to note that this only works immediately after the action and before any other operations are performed.

Examples of Bevel tool usage

Like all 3D modeling tools, there is more than one way that the **Bevel** tool can be useful. So far, we have discussed how Blender's **Bevel** tool can help you achieve photorealism, and what its role is in achieving photorealism. Now, we will go over a list of other benefits of using the **Bevel** tool for your 3D modeling workflow:

- *Enhancing texturing and UV unwrapping*: Beveling can help you when you are texturing, particularly if you are using baking techniques, as will be discussed in *Part 3, UV Unwrapping and Texturing in Blender* of this book. Bevelled edges can help in creating more accurate normal maps, as they provide additional geometry for capturing finer details. This is especially important in game asset creation, where textures often need to convey detail that is not there if you have a low-poly model.

- *Improving structural integrity for 3D printing*: In 3D printing, adding bevels to edges can increase the structural integrity of the printed object. Sharp corners can be points of weakness. Bevelled edges are better because they help distribute stress more evenly.

- *Subdivision surface modeling*: If you intend to subdivide a model, bevels can help you maintain edge hardness. This is crucial in organic modeling, such as character design, where certain areas need sharper definition without adding too much to the model's geometry.

- *Stylizing 3D models*: Bevels can be used as part of creating a stylized aesthetic, like in *Figure 10.21*.

Figure 10.21: Bevels in Blender 4 Creator Course Stylized 3D Models by 3D Tudor

- *Creating text and logos*: Blender's **Bevel** tool can enhance text and logos, giving them a three-dimensional, embossed, or engraved look.

- *Collision physics and game development*: In game development, bevelling edges can help in creating more accurate collision physics. This is because overly sharp edges can cause unrealistic or glitchy interactions in a simulated environment.

Bevelling vertices in Blender is one of those deceptively simple tricks that packs a punch. With just a few tweaks, you can soften those harsh corners and instantly give your models a more grounded, believable look, less "default cube," more "this belongs in a proper scene."

Now that we have rounded things off a bit, let us talk about the opposite, introducing gaps in your mesh, and why you might actually want a hole or two.

Ripping meshes in Blender

The **Rip** and **Slide** functions in Blender are a trick up your 3D-modeling-workflow sleeve because they allow you to create gaps, adjust edge flow, and reposition vertices without changing the model's overall form.

The **Rip** tool is used to create gaps or splits in your mesh by pulling apart vertices, edges, or faces. This is especially useful when you need to add more detail to a specific area without altering the surrounding geometry. The **Slide** tool, on the other hand, allows you to reposition vertices, edges, or faces along their current geometry, making subtle adjustments without changing the overall shape of the model.

For example, in a project where you are creating a character model with complex clothing, you would use **Rip** on the areas where the clothing folds or overlaps. You could also use **Slide** to subtly adjust the position of vertices along the clothing edges, gently nudging the edges of the clothes to make them sit more naturally and look more realistic, as if the clothing is being worn by the character.

In a few words, **Rip** and **Slide** can impact your 3D modeling workflow by giving you more control and flexibility in shaping and refining your models. Let's start!

The Rip function

Ripping is the process of disconnecting or tearing vertices, edges, or faces to create a gap in your mesh. This is helpful when you need to isolate a part of your model for detailed editing or when creating openings such as windows or doors in architectural models. You can use **Rip** in various 3D modeling projects unless the integrity of the mesh needs to remain intact for animation or simulation purposes, where such gaps could cause issues.

Accessing the Rip tool

To start ripping, you need to follow the next steps:

1. Enter **Edit Mode** (by pressing the *Tab* key).

2. Make sure that your mouse is on the section where you want the ripping to occur, like in *Figure 10.22*. As the screenshot shows, I have my mouse on the right side of the selected vertex, which causes it to rip off a vertex of the right-side face. The top and left faces of that vertex will stay connected.

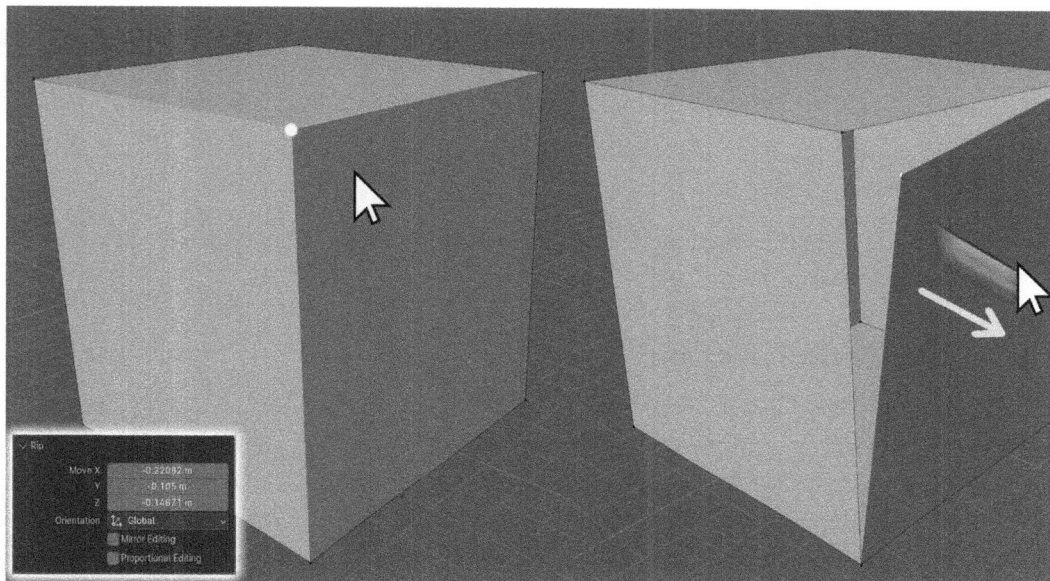

Figure 10.22: Using the Rip tool before (left) and after (right)

3. Press the *V* key (there's no need to hold it) and drag the ripped section to the desired location.

> Heads up
>
> When you use the **Rip** tool, it does not just visually separate the mesh, it actually splits the vertices apart. So, if you are wondering why you suddenly have extra geometry floating around, that is why. Think of it like tearing paper: you are not just making a flap, you are actually creating two edges where there used to be one. Also, be aware that ripping can create non-manifold edges, which might be an issue for certain applications such as 3D printing or animation.

Examples of Rip tool usage

The **Rip** tool lets you quickly modify your models by creating gaps or adjusting edge flows. If you were editing your vertices manually, that would be more complex. Despite its advantages, the **Rip** tool is not always as precise as manual editing, particularly for intricate details. The following are two typical examples of using the **Rip** tool that you can try for yourself:

*   *Creating gaps*: If you are modeling a torn cloth or any object with intentional gaps, the **Rip** tool comes in handy. For a project such as designing a dilapidated building, use the **Rip** tool to create realistic cracks and holes in the structure, simulating years of wear and tear.

- *Adjusting edge flow*: Sometimes, you may want to reroute the edge flow without adding new geometry or deleting existing elements. For example, the tool can be used to reposition the flow of fabric on clothing, making it drape more naturally on the character's form.

Tip

Use Blender's **Snapping** feature to precisely align the ripped elements with other parts of the mesh.

The Edge Slide function

Blender's **Edge Slide** tool (i.e., sliding) involves moving vertices, edges, or faces along the surface of the mesh without altering the surrounding geometry's form. It is a great tool for tweaking the position of elements while maintaining the mesh's overall shape. If you are smoothing the edges of a roof or aligning window frames, **Edge Slide** can help you make detailed adjustments to specific parts of the structure. For example, if a window frame is slightly misaligned or not level with the building's facade, **Edge Slide** can be used to move the edges of the frame along the surface of the wall, like in *Figure 10.23*.

Figure 10.23: Misaligned window frames before (left) and after using Edge Slide (right)

Accessing the Edge Slide tool

To use **Edge Slide**, follow the next steps:

1. In **Edit Mode**, select the vertices, edges, or faces you wish to slide.

2. Press the *G* key to initiate the move, and then double-press the *G* key again, to initiate **Edge Slide**. So, basically, press *G* three times, which would cycle back to move.

3. Move the mouse to slide the selection along the mesh.

> **Note**
>
> Alternatively, you can use the *Shift + V* keys for vertices specifically.

4. Experiment with the **Influence** setting, which can control how much the surrounding geometry is affected by the slide. *Figure 10.24* shows both **Edge Slide** and **Vertex Slide**.

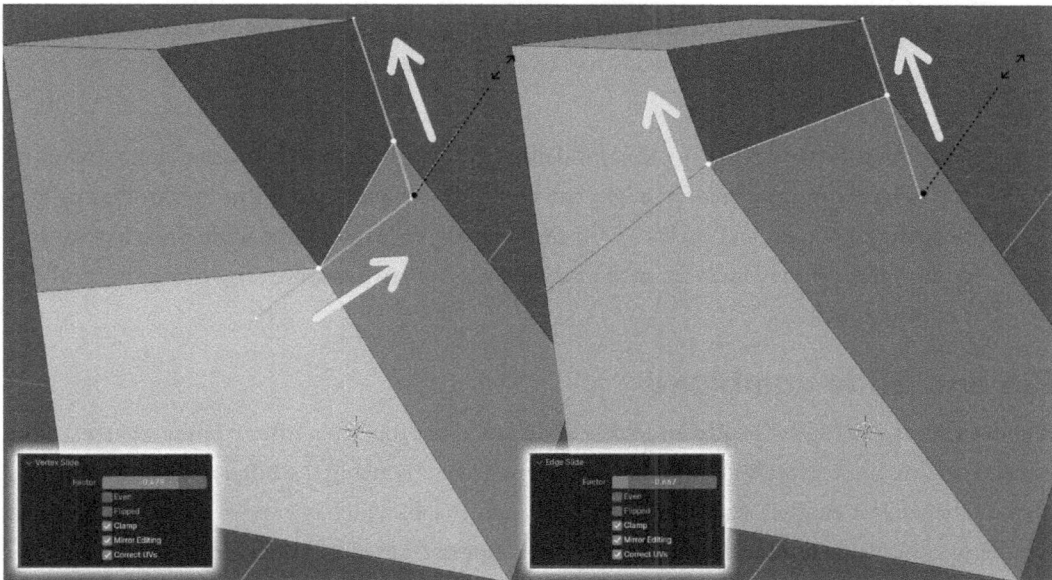

Figure 10.24: Differentiating between Edge Slide (right) and Vertex Slide (left)

5. **Edge Slide** will treat the surrounding geometry all as one and move it all in the same direction. **Vertex Slide** will also move it in the direction closest to the slide of a mouse, but it will treat each vertex as an individual operation, causing the vertices to move in separate directions.

Examples of sliding usage

Blender's **Edge Slide** tool offers smooth and quick adjustments to mesh topology. However, I would not recommend using **Edge Slide** for highly detailed or complex edits because it lacks the granular control of manual vertex manipulation. Here are two typical examples of using the **Edge Slide** tool that you can try for yourself:

- *Refining topology*: If you have added new **Loop Cuts** or geometry and need to adjust their position without distorting the model, sliding is your best bet. For instance, imagine working in an environment featuring a realistic kitchen. You have just added new loop cuts to represent tiles or cabinet details. Using **Edge Slide**, you can adjust the positions of these cuts to align the tiles perfectly or to make the cabinet doors symmetrical, all without changing the overall layout and dimensions of the kitchen.

> Tip
>
> For a smoother transition in adjustments, use **Proportional Editing** together with the **Edge Slide** tool to affect a broader area around the slide.

- *Smoothing out areas*: For organic modeling, you might find some areas look pinched or too sharp. Sliding vertices or edges can help soften these areas without introducing new geometry. For a project such as sculpting a character's face, **Edge Slide** is perfect for softening sharp or uneven areas, such as cheekbones or jawlines, creating a more natural and lifelike appearance.

Rip and Slide combined

Blender allows you to use the **Rip** and **Edge Slide** functions together. After ripping a vertex, edge, or face, you can immediately slide it along adjacent geometry using the **Edge Slide** function. This is useful because it enables seamless reshaping of the mesh, which is important. After all, seams can disrupt the visual flow and realism of a model, especially in highly detailed or organic designs.

Figure 10.25 shows how to use **Rip** with **Edge Slide** to open up a mesh to see the interior of computer parts. To use the **Rip** and **Edge Slide** functions, press *V*, followed by *G*.

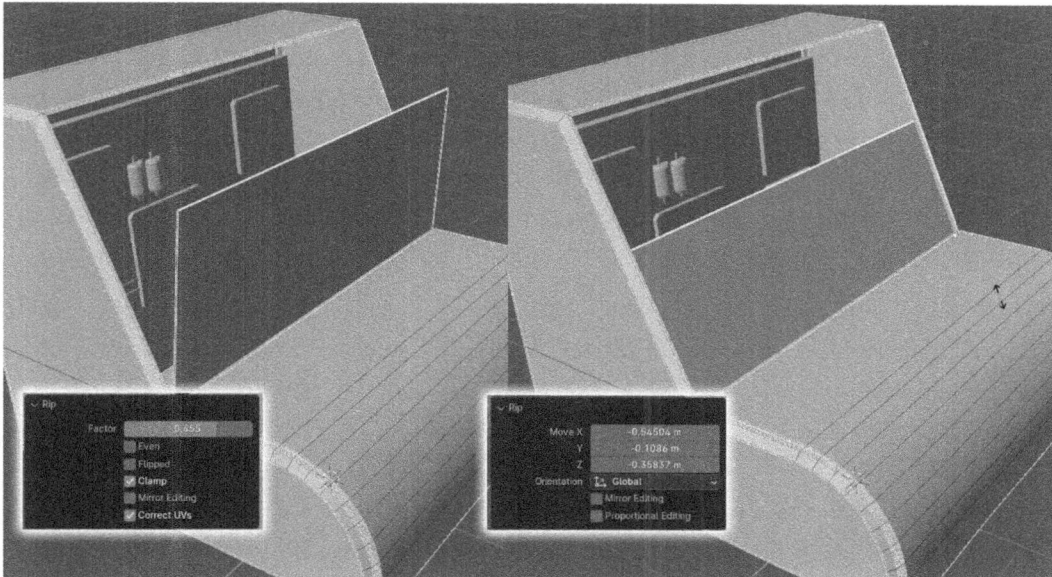

Figure 10.25: Using Rip and Edge Slide together for a computer part illustration

Using **Rip** and **Edge Slide** separately would mean that you cannot smoothly integrate the changes or ensure a natural transition in the mesh's modification. Combining **Rip** and **Edge Slide** is ideal for projects such as sculpting detailed landscapes, where precise control over both the separation and positioning of mesh elements is crucial.

To combine the **Rip** and **Edge Slide** functions and use them together, follow the next steps:

1. Enter **Edit** mode (by pressing the *Tab* key).

2. Select the vertices or edges you wish to rip.

3. Rip your desired vertices or edges using the *V* key.

4. Without clicking anywhere else, press the *G* key twice (or *Shift + V* for vertices). This activates the **Edge Slide** function.

5. Move your mouse to slide the ripped section along the adjacent geometry. The position and alignment can be adjusted as you drag the mouse.

6. *Left-click* to confirm the new position of the ripped and slid section.

Blender's **Rip** and **Edge Slide** functions provide quick ways to adjust topology, create gaps, and refine the position of elements. They are included in this advanced 3D modeling techniques chapter because they are clever methods for altering mesh topology. **Rip** and **Edge Slide** are two underrated heroes when it comes to shaping up your mesh with precision. Whether you are carving out details, nudging geometry into place, or fine-tuning flow, these tools save you the headache of constantly redoing topology. If you are working on a detailed model with lots of custom cuts and angles, they will quickly become part of your core toolkit.

Up next, we will take a look at the **Hook** tool, which gives you direct, dynamic control over specific parts of your mesh: great for animation, deformations, or just getting a handle on complex forms without wrecking your topology.

Mastering control over vertices with the Hook tool

A **Hook** in Blender creates a relationship between selected vertices and another object, often an empty. When you move the controlling object, the hooked vertices move with it. This provides dynamic control over specific parts of your mesh without affecting the entire object.

Accessing the Hook tool

To start using the **Hook** tool, do the following:

1. Enter **Edit Mode** (by pressing the *Tab* key) on your object.
2. Select the vertices you wish to hook.
3. Press *Ctrl + H* to bring up the **Hook** menu (*Figure 10.26*).

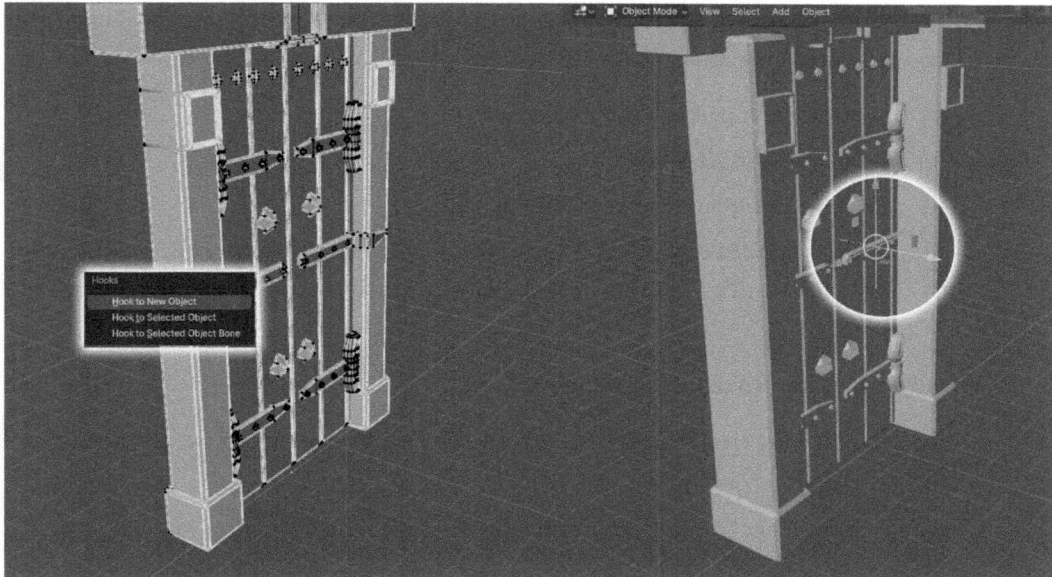

Figure 10.26: Hook menu in Blender in Blender 20 Massive Fantasy Doors Asset Pack by 3D Tudor

4. Choose **Hook to New Object** to create a new empty and automatically hook your vertices to it. Alternatively, you can choose **Hook to Selected Object** if you already have another object selected to act as the hook controller.

5. Once the hook is set up, make sure you switch to **Object** mode and select the empty (or whichever object you are using as a hook). Then move, rotate, or scale the object; the hooked vertices will follow its transformations.

> **Note**
>
> Too many hooks can make the scene complicated to manage. Use them carefully, for specific, dynamic parts of the mesh.

6.   There are also advanced **Hook** controls you can use. If you want only partial control over the vertices using the hook, do the following:

    a.   Select the main object (not the empty).

    b.   Go to the **Modifiers** tab.

    c.   Find the **Hook** modifier that has been added.

    d.   Adjust the **Influence** slider. A lower value will mean the empty has less influence over the vertices, leading to more subtle transformations when you move the empty.

7.   Finally, here's how to remove clear hooks:

    a.   In **Edit Mode**, select the vertices from which you want to remove the hook.

    b.   Press *Ctrl + H*.

    c.   Choose **Clear Hook** to remove the hook relationship.

Examples of Hook tool usage

The **Hook** tool in Blender gives you control over specific mesh areas, making it ideal for animations and interactive scenes. However, its less precise nature compared to manual vertex editing might not suit highly detailed sculpting tasks. These are the three most common uses of Blender's **Hook** tool:

- *Rigging and animation*: Hooks can be instrumental in rigging models for animation, offering a simplified way to control certain mesh parts without a full rig. For a project such as creating a cartoon character, hooks can be used to control facial expressions; by attaching hooks to key facial features, you can quickly animate facial expressions.

- *Dynamic modeling adjustments*: If you're sculpting or modeling and want to reposition part of a mesh without affecting everything else, hooks provide a great way to do that. In a landscape modeling project, hooks can be used to dynamically adjust elements such as rolling hills or shifting sand dunes, helping you perform quick and non-destructive changes to the terrain.

- *Interactive scenes*: For interactive scenes or simulations, hooks can be keyframe animated, giving dynamic changes. As an example, if you are creating an interactive architecture project. Hooks can be keyframe animated to demonstrate moving parts such as elevator doors or window shutters.

Whether you are animating, modeling, or just playing around, understanding how to use hooks effectively gives you a lot of control over what you create.

Next, we'll delve into Blender's **Convert** function. **Convert** will let you seamlessly convert between different object types such as meshes, curves, and text.

Converting different object types in Blender

Blender is known for offering a fully customizable user experience with few exceptions. Whether you are working with meshes, curves, text, or even **Grease Pencil** strokes, Blender provides the tools to seamlessly convert between them.

Accessing the Convert function

To convert one object type to another, follow these steps:

1. Make sure you are in **Object** mode (if you are in **Edit** mode, press *Tab* to toggle back to **Object** mode).

2. Click on the object you wish to convert.

> Tip
>
> All modifiers get applied instantaneously when you use **Convert to Mesh**. We often use that option to quickly apply all modifiers. Particles and geometry nodes might not convert properly, however. If your geometry node does not have **Realize to Instances** at the end of its node tree, the conversion will fail, leaving you with an empty object. This step ensures Blender bakes the instanced geometry into something real, so always place it at the bottom of your node tree before converting. We will talk more about node trees in *Chapter 1* in *Part 2* of this book, so buckle up!

3. Next, go to the **Object** menu located at the top, navigate to **Convert To**, and choose the desired conversion option from the dropdown, like in *Figure 10.27*:

    -   **Curve**: Converts the selected object into a curve. This can be useful for using the object as a path or for specific curve-based modifiers.

    -   **Mesh**: Converts the selected object into a mesh. This is particularly useful when you want to perform detailed edits on these object types using mesh tools.

- **Grease Pencil**: Converts the selected object into a **Grease Pencil** object. It is useful for stylized representations or planning out changes to your mesh.

- **Curves**: Allows for conversion to the new curve system introduced in recent Blender versions, which might offer enhanced control and features.

- **Trace Image to Grease Pencil**: This converts an image to a **Grease Pencil** object, useful for creating hand-drawn effects or planning out animations.

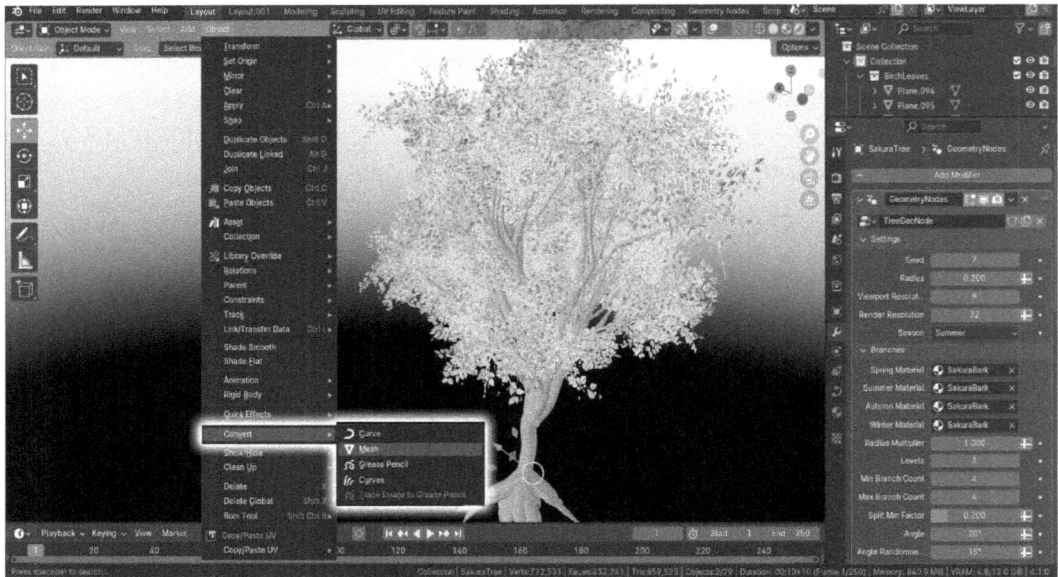

Figure 10.27: Convert options in Blender

Note

Converting objects might require adjustments to materials and textures to ensure they display correctly on the new object type. Also, converting between types can lead to a loss of specific object information. For example, converting a curve to a mesh means you can no longer edit it using curve controls.

Blender's **Convert** function in **Object** mode is a bit like a cup of tea in a crisis, surprisingly effective, often overlooked, and capable of fixing more problems than you might expect. It lets you hop between object types without throwing your project into chaos. Whether you are locking in a sculpt, baking down modifiers, or trying to stop your geometry from misbehaving before render time, knowing how and when to convert objects gives you far more control over your workflow.

Under the hood, it does all the quiet, unsung work, like the intern nobody appreciates until they go on holiday.

Summary

This chapter has been an adventure, much like *Chapter 9* in this part of the book, where familiar tools were used in new and innovative ways. We ventured beyond the basics, and you learned how to approach 3D modeling differently.

Here, you were introduced to advanced functions in Blender's **Edit** mode, delving into tools such as **Bisect**, **Convex Hull**, and **Bevel**. We also demystified the concepts of ripping meshes and using the **Hook** tool, expanding your ability to animate and modify specific areas of your model with puppeteer-like control.

As you move forward, remember that each tool, each technique, is a part of a larger toolkit at your disposal. The world of 3D modeling is vast and full of possibilities, and now you are better equipped than ever to explore it with confidence and creativity.

In the next chapter, we will explore Blender's **Particle System**. **Particle System** can be used to simulate various natural phenomena such as hair, fur, grass, fire, smoke, rain, snow, and even more abstract effects such as magic spells or flowing water.

Further reading

- If you are curious about dynamic architectural elements and how to rig modular assets in Blender, check out *Blender 20 Massive Fantasy Doors Asset Pack* (https://3dtudor.gumroad.com/l/blender_fantasy_doors_asset_pack).

- To dive deeper into stylized modeling and see bevels used to bring life to whimsical buildings, *Blender 4 Creator Course* (https://www.udemy.com/course/blender-4-creator-course-stylized-3d-models/?referralCode=1CCFEC9403D6E1B4FB19) is packed with examples and hands-on lessons. It is a fantastic course for learning stylized asset workflows.

- For those working with game-ready assets and geometry nodes, *Blender Boat Geometry Node – Build Any Boat in Seconds* (https://3dtudor.gumroad.com/l/blender-boat-geometry-node) can help you experiment with common issues such as face orientation and how to handle them.

- Want to animate entire scenes in Blender? The *Ultimate Guide to Blender 3D Rigging & Animation* (https://www.udemy.com/course/blender-3d-rigging-animation/?referralCode=39A1E0B8F07B474DFE0F) walks you through an escape room project where modular animation meets puzzle-game logic, brilliant if you like your projects with a bit of mystery.

- If you love the fantasy aesthetic and want to build out modular worlds with detail and charm, *Blender 20 Massive Fantasy Windows Asset Pack* (`https://3dtudor.gumroad.com/l/blender_fantasy_windows_asset_pack`) will be right up your alley: great for using tools such as **Circle Select** and **Box Select** to shape detailed environments.

Subscribe to Game Dev Assembly!

We are excited to introduce **Game Dev Assembly**, our brand-new newsletter dedicated to everything game development. Whether you're coding, designing, animating, or managing a studio, we've got insights, trends, and expert advice to help you create, innovate, and thrive. Sign up now and get exciting benefits.

`https://packt.link/gamedev-newsletter`

Join the 3D Tudor Channel Discord Server!

Join the 3D Tudor Channel Discord Server, a creative hub for learning Blender, Unreal Engine, Substance Painter, and 3D modeling, for discussions with the authors and other readers:

`https://discord.gg/5EkjT36vUj`

11

Exploring Blender's Particle System

Right, let us get back to basics. A particle system in Blender is essentially a controlled way of spewing out lots of tiny objects, or instances over time. Think of it like a smart emitter that can simulate anything from sparks flying off a welding torch to a fluffy field of dandelions.

A particle system is pretty much an animated simulation. You tell Blender: "Here's a mesh, now throw particles out of it over 100 frames and try to make it look like a swarm of bees." The particles themselves can be just simple points, full mesh objects, or hair strands, and how they behave depends entirely on how you play with the settings.

We are going to cover all the ways you can use this system to create believable motion, sticking to the basics. Particle systems in Blender could be a book of its own, so this will just be an introduction.

But before we dive into fancy tricks, we will talk about the logic behind how particle systems work, how to control them using weight maps and vertex groups, and what all those dropdowns actually do. Later in the chapter, we will explore advanced topics such as **Force Fields**, scripting behaviors with keyframes and modifiers, and how to stop your simulation from setting your GPU on fire. While this chapter sticks closely to Blender's particle systems, we also take a quick peek at some advanced physics simulations toward the end. Yes, it is technically outside the core particle toolkit, but it felt like a natural leap rather than a random detour.

Let us crack on. Whether you are an aspiring technical artist, a seasoned developer, or simply a curious enthusiast eager to learn a little bit about particle systems, this chapter will act as your compass.

So, in this chapter, we will cover the following topics:

- Introducing the basics of particle systems

- Introducing emitters and hair in Blender's particle system
- Exploring the emitter particle system
- Exploring the hair particle system

Technical requirements

As for **Blender 4.5 LTS (Long-Term Support)**, the general requirements include a macOS 11.2 or newer (Apple Silicon supported natively) operating system, or a Linux (64-bit, glibc 2.28 or newer) operating system. Blender now requires a CPU with the SSE4.2 instruction set, at least 8 GB of RAM (32 GB recommended for heavy scenes), and a GPU supporting OpenGL 4.3 with a minimum of 2 GB of VRAM.

For a full list of technical requirements, please refer back to *Chapter 1* of this part.

Introducing the basics of particle systems

A **particle system** in Blender is a collection of small objects or points that can simulate various kinds of *fuzzy* phenomena, such as fire, smoke, rain, dust, or abstract visual effects (*Figure 11.1*).

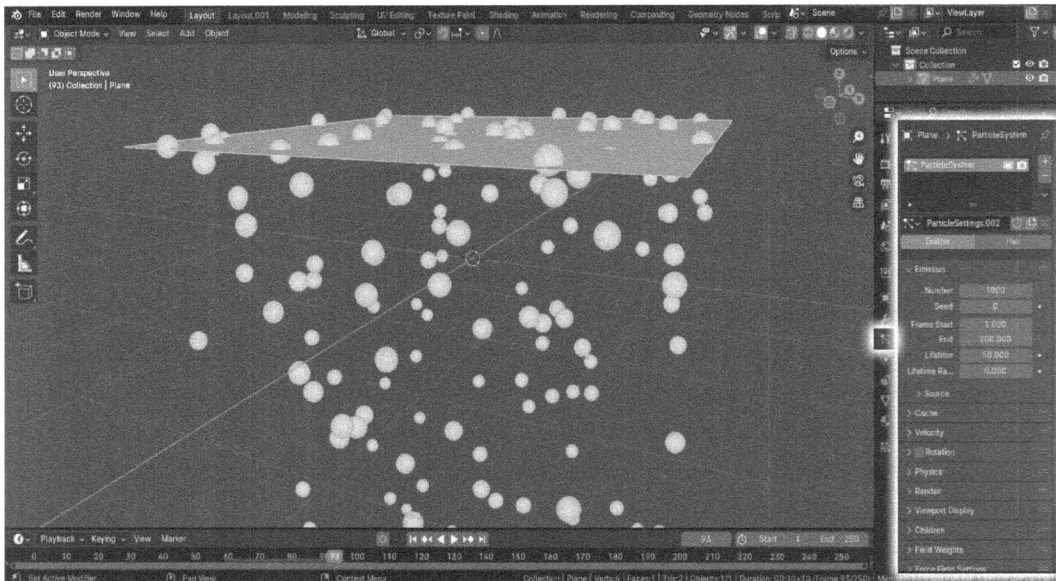

Figure 11.1: Particle system options in Blender

Each particle represents a unit of the effect and is governed by physics and user-defined settings.

The key components of a particle system are as follows:

- **Emitter**: The object from which particles are emitted. The emitter can be any mesh object, and its shape, size, and surface properties can influence the initial properties of the particles. For example, a plane can emit particles evenly across its surface, while a sphere might emit them along its radius.

- **Particles**: Individual elements that make up the system. You have got control over pretty much everything: how long they stick around, how big they are, what colour they show up as, and how they move through the scene.

- **Physics**: Rules that govern the behaviour of particles. Physics settings determine how particles move and interact with what is around them. This includes collisions with other objects in the scene to create realistic interactions.

- **Render settings**: This is how particles are visualized in the final render. Render settings control the material, lighting, and shading of particles, determining their final appearance in the scene. You can choose between different render types, such as halo, path, or object, and apply materials and textures.

As a beginner in Blender, setting up a particle system might seem like a tall mountain to climb, but it is straightforward when you get the basics. The following instructions will guide you through setting up a particle system from a basic plane (i.e., a flat, two-dimensional surface):

1. Open Blender and create a new project. In the default scene, you will typically find a cube: select and delete it by pressing *X* or *Delete* on your keyboard.

2. Next, add a plane by going to **Add** (which you can find at the bottom of the **3D Viewport**, or by using the shortcut *Shift + A*), then selecting **Mesh | Plane**.

3. Now select **Plane** and then go to the **Properties** panel on the right side of the screen, on the **Particle Properties** tab, represented by a small star icon.

4. From here, add a new particle system by clicking the + button.

5. To see your emission particle, click the **Play** button on your screen or your spacebar on your keyboard.

You are now ready to explore the two primary modes within this system: **Emitters** and **Hair**. We should go over the fundamental differences between these modes and why you might choose one over the other. We will concentrate on the emitter first.

Introducing Emitter and Hair in Blender's particle system

While both **Emitter** and **Hair** can share some settings (e.g., rendering and physics; see *Figure 11.2*), what they do and the scenarios in which you might use them are different.

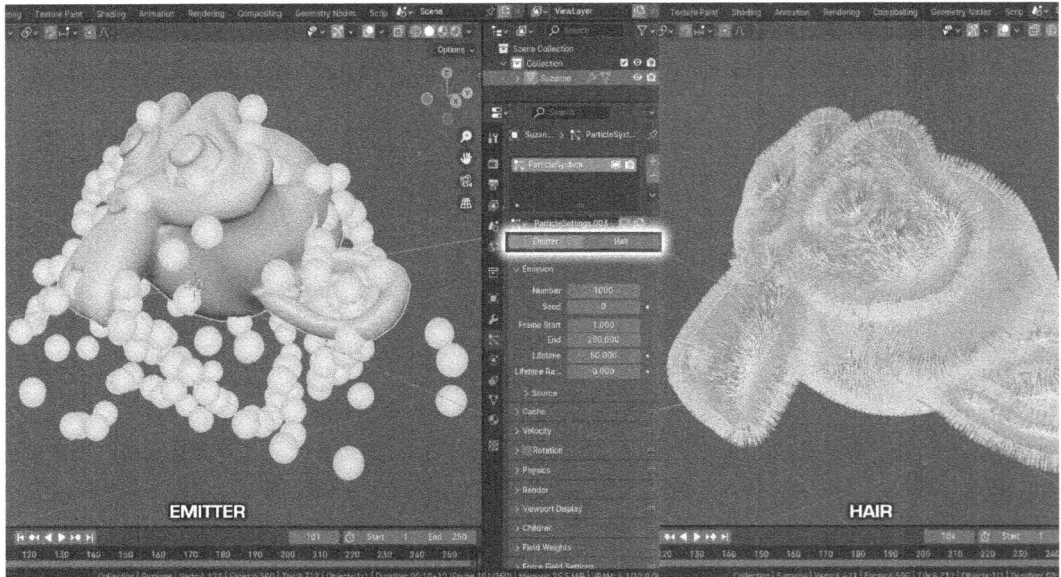

Figure 11.2: Emitter (left) versus Hair (right) settings overview

First of all, we will focus on Blender's **Emitter** mode. I will show you how to set up an emitter, manipulate its behavior, and apply various settings for effects such as explosions, water flows, or floating particles.

After a thorough exploration of **Emitter**, we will move on to the **Hair** mode. **Hair** in Blender is primarily used for static particle effects, such as fur, hair, or grass, which require particles to remain attached to the source object. Once we start discussing **Hair**, we will concentrate only on aspects that differ from or extend beyond what we have covered with emitters, making sure that the knowledge capstones of this chapter are clear.

Now, we will move on and turn our focus to **Emitter** and the emission settings in Blender's particle system. As we talk about each setting, you will understand how to precisely tailor your emitter's behavior to what you need, whether it is a gentle snowfall or an explosion.

Blender's emitter system

An **emitter** in Blender is a type of particle system used to create particles that move and behave independently. This mode is your go-to for anything that needs to move, drift, scatter, or explode. Emitter particles shoot out from the surface or volume of an object, and unlike hair, they are not tied down. That means you can fling them around using forces, gravity, or other physics settings to create dynamic, animated chaos.

For example, in a project with a blacksmith's shop, you would expect to see sparks flying from the anvil as the blacksmith hammers a piece of metal, as in *Figure 11.3*.

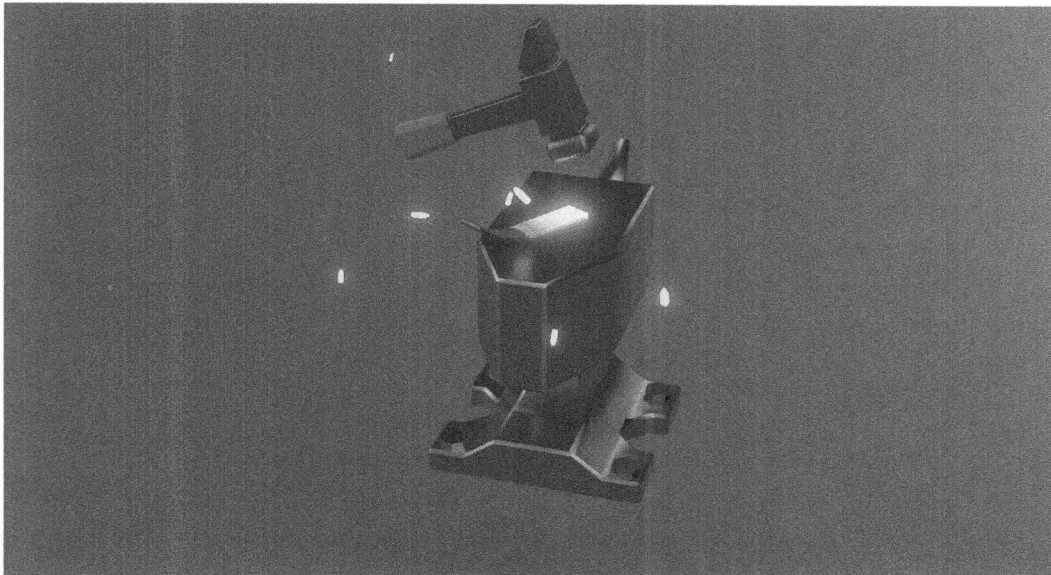

Figure 11.3: Sparks flying off an anvil in "Blender 3 Animated Stylized Blacksmith House 3D Modelling Guide" by 3D Tudor

By using **Emitter,** these sparks can be realistically simulated to move dynamically, mirroring the way actual sparks scatter and fall. The particles can be adjusted to glow and fade out over a short duration. That is the wild and unpredictable world of emitters. Now, let us turn our attention to hair particles. These stick around for the long haul, quite literally.

Blender's hair system

The **Hair** mode is designed for static particles that stay attached to the emitting object, such as fur or grass. Hair particles do not typically move independently after they are generated, although they can be affected by physics to simulate motion such as swaying grass, as in *Figure 11.4*.

Figure 11.4: Swaying grass in "Blender 3D Model a Ghibli Art Stylized Scene" by 3D Tudor

For example, if you were working on a large outdoor environment such as a flying island, you would see lush grasses and perhaps wildflowers or moss covering the ground. **Hair** mode allows for the static particles to remain attached to the ground or rocks, giving the flying island a natural, overgrown appearance. By adjusting the **Hair** settings, the length, density, and direction of the grass can be altered to match the environment's desired look.

Tip

You can also apply physics to the hair particles to simulate the effect of wind, making the grass or other foliage sway gently. You can do this by adding a force field to your scene in Blender. Select the object with the hair particles and then go to the **Physics** tab in the **Properties** panel. Here, you can add a force field, such as **Wind** or **Turbulence**, which will affect the way the hair particles move. You can then adjust the strength and direction of the force field to get to what you want. Just do not blame us if you end up knee-deep in comb settings and wonder why your hedgehog looks like it lost a fight with a leaf blower.

Note

Hair particles work in a very similar way to an emitter, with one key difference: they are anchored directly to the object and do not respond to forces in the same way. Just keep in mind that they are designed to stay put, which makes them ideal for things such as fur, grass, or glorious digital beards.

Now that you have got the basics of hair particles down, let's jump into Blender's emitter particle system and see how we can really push it to create some cool, dynamic effects.

Exploring the emitter particle system

In this section, we are going to dive into Blender's emitter particle system, where the real magic happens. Whether your goal is to simulate sparks, rain, or a full-blown explosion, emitters give you the tools. We will walk through the key settings and techniques that let you control how particles behave, interact with their environment, and achieve the exact look you are going for.

Reviewing the Emitter and Source settings

In this section, we will look at the particle system's **Emitter** and **Source** options. We will start with the **Emitter** options, as you can see in *Figure 11.5*.

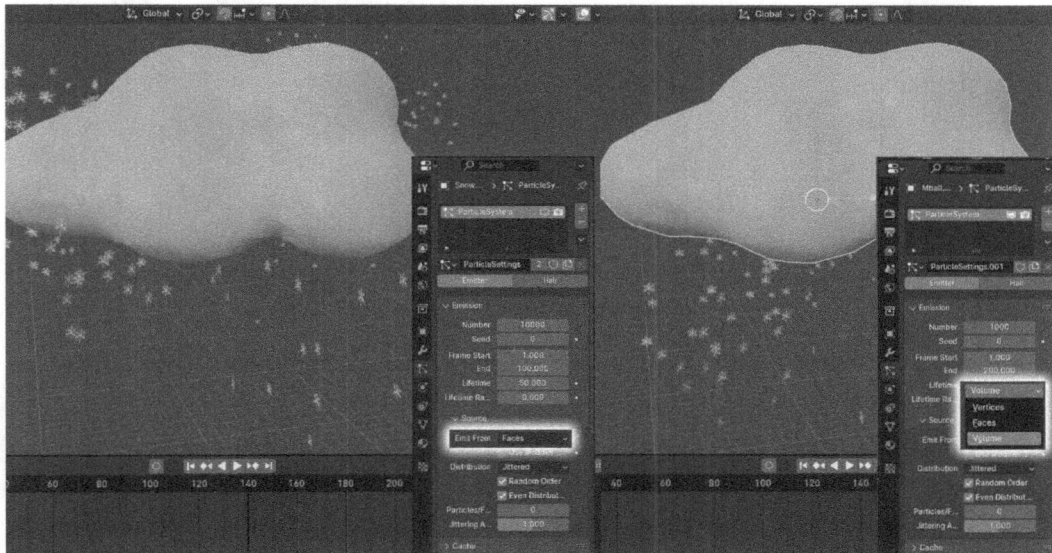

Figure 11.5: Emission settings overview

Let's break down the **Emitter** options:

- **Number**: This sets the total number of particles that the emitter will produce. Setting it to 1000, for example, means the emitter will release 1,000 particles over its active period, as in *Figure 11.6*.

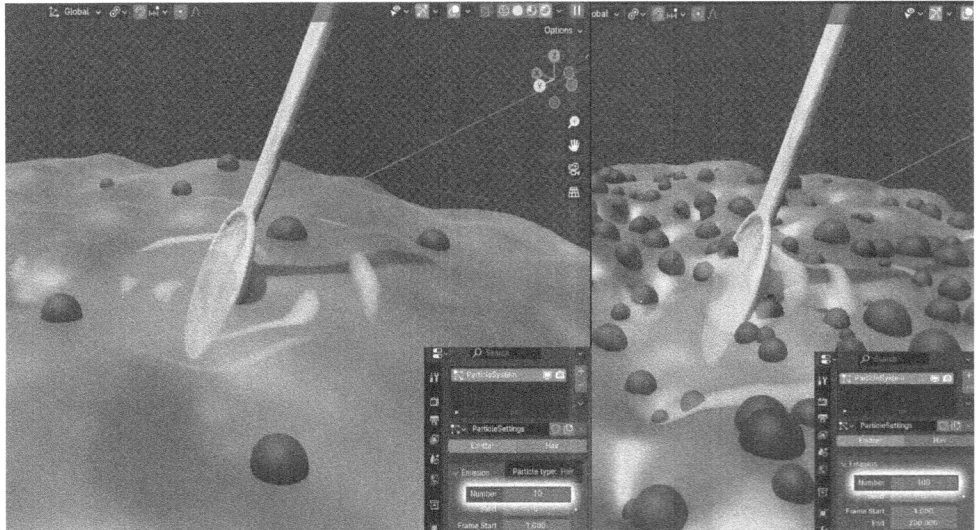

Figure 11.6: Changing the Number setting on Emitter in Blender 4 Magic Potion & Cauldron Liquid Geometry Node by 3D Tudor

- You could use this setting for a fireworks display, where each firework needs to release a specific number of spark particles.
- **Frame Start/End**: This determines the frame range during which the particles start and stop being emitted. If set from frame 1 to frame 100 (*Figure 11.7*), the emitter will only release particles between these frames. Once the frame goes over 100, the emitter for the snow will stop spawning particles.
- **Seed**: This changes the random pattern of particle emission without altering other settings.

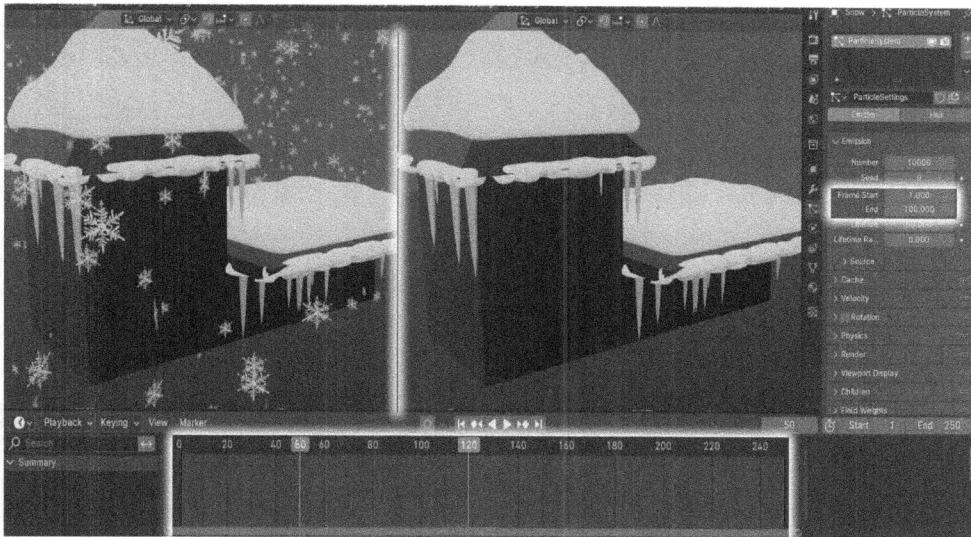

Figure 11.7: Visualizing Frame Start/End settings for emitters

Such a setting is useful if, for example, you are creating a scene where a car speeds off, kicking up a cloud of dust in a brief, concentrated period.

- **Lifetime:** This specifies how long, in frames, each particle will exist after being emitted, as shown in the settings in *Figure 11.8*.

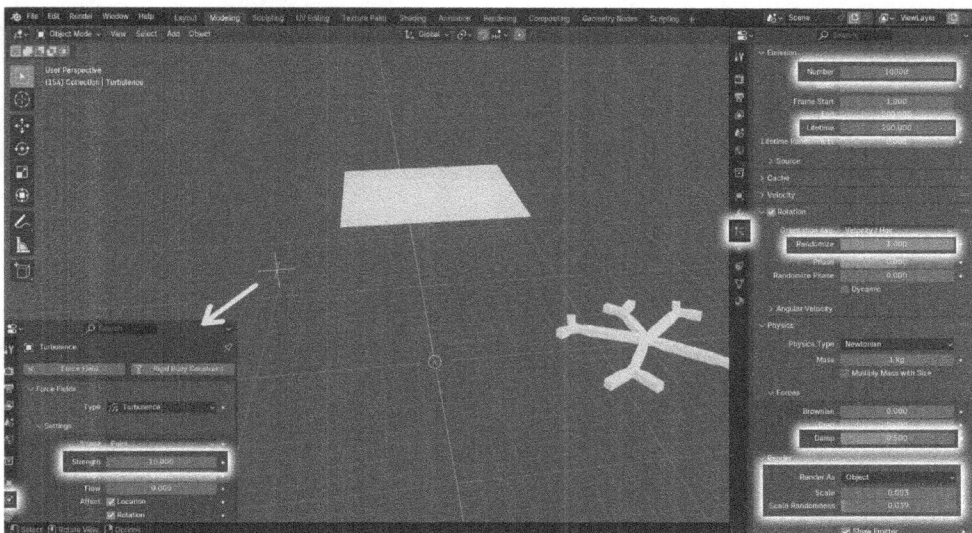

Figure 11.8: Lifetime and other settings for emitters

A lifetime of 50 frames, for example, means each particle will last for 50 frames before disappearing. You might see this in a project with a fountain, where the water droplets need to vanish after reaching a certain height.

- **Lifetime Randomness**: This introduces variability to the lifetime of individual particles. A value of 0 means no randomness: all particles will live for the exact duration specified, whereas higher values increase the randomness.

With **Lifetime** of **50** frames and **Lifetime Randomness** of **0.5**, some particles might last only 25 frames, while others could last up to 75 frames, creating a more varied and natural-looking effect. This is helpful in scenarios such as simulating a campfire (*Figure 11.9*).

Figure 11.9: Fire sparks in "Blender 3 Unreal Engine 5 Complete Guide Stylized Camping Trip Gone Wrong Environment" by 3D Tudor

The **Source** setting under the **Emission** options is crucial as it determines from where the **Emitter** object particles are generated. Each option within **Source** offers a unique method of particle distribution, suitable for different effects (*Figure 11.10*).

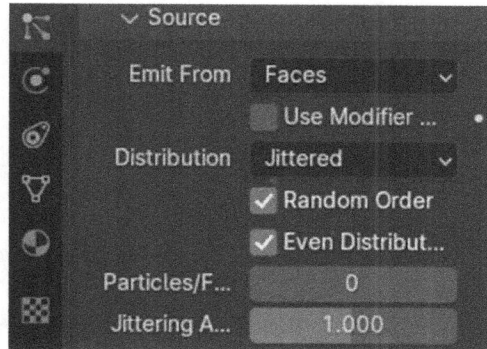

Figure 11.10: Source setting options

Here's an in-depth look at each option with examples:

- **Emit From**: This setting lets you choose where the particles are emitted from. You can choose from the following options:

  - **Verts (Vertices)**: Particles are emitted from the vertices of the mesh. If you have a cube, particles will only emit from the cube's eight corners. This is useful for effects such as sparks flying off specific points, such as glowing energy particles emitting specifically from the object's corners to signify power or magic.

  - **Faces**: Particles are emitted from the faces of the mesh, providing a more even distribution over the surface. This is ideal for effects such as a surface shedding water droplets. This could be something you might see in a scene involving a rain-soaked car.

  - **Volume**: Particles are emitted from within the volume of the mesh. Particles will emerge from inside the cube, filling it up and spilling out, like foam in a container. This could work with a magical cauldron or a science-fiction container where a substance such as a magical mist or potion is brewing and bubbling from within.

- **Distribution**: This setting determines how particles are spread across the surface of your object. It is like deciding how you want to sprinkle particles, whether you want them placed in an orderly grid, scattered randomly, or something in between:

  - **Jittered**: This option places particles in a semi-regular pattern with a slight randomness. It is a balance between uniformity and variability. For example, instead of particles being perfectly aligned in rows and columns, a **Jittered** distribution will create a more organic look, such as pebbles spread along a path, where they are evenly distributed but not perfectly placed, as in *Figure 11.11*.

Figure 11.11: Path of pebbles in Blender 4 Modeling and Geometry Node Workshop by 3D Tudor

If used on a plane, particles will be distributed in a pattern that is orderly but with slight variations in position. This can simulate effects such as seeds scattered in a row in a garden, where there is an underlying order, but it is not perfect (*Figure 11.12*).

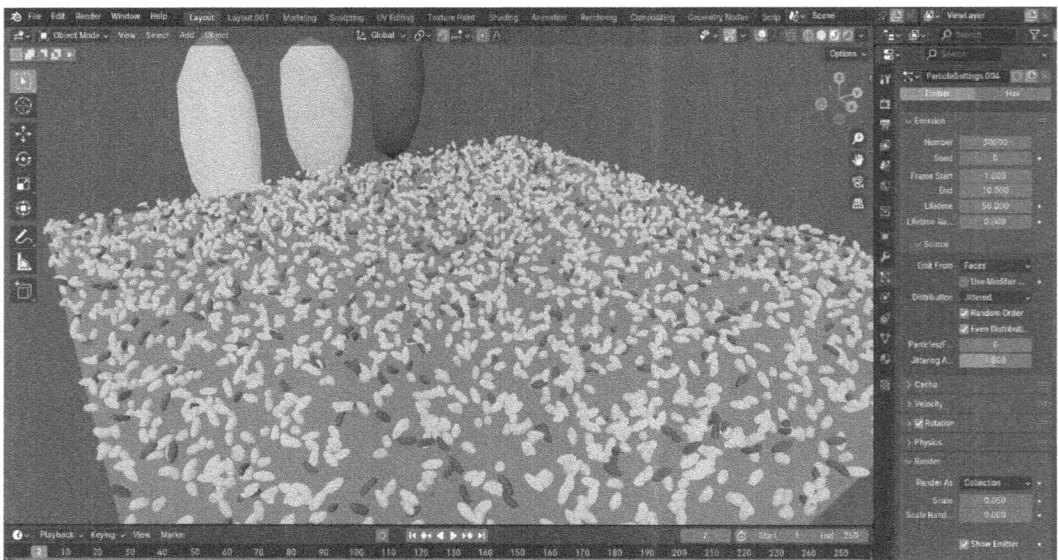

Figure 11.12: Visual scattered seeds demonstration

- **Random**: With this option, particles are placed in a completely random way across the emitting surface. This is ideal for creating random raindrops hitting the surface (*Figure 11.13*) or stars scattered in the night sky.

Figure 11.13: Raindrops landing on the floor in Blender 4 Procedural Rain Geometry Node Pack by 3D Tudor

- **Grid**: This option makes it so that particles are arranged in an orderly, grid-like pattern. This is the most uniform distribution method.

On a flat plane, particles will be aligned in neat rows and columns, resembling a grid. This distribution is perfect for architectural models, such as evenly spaced windows on a building facade or tiles on a floor.

> **Note**
>
> Your **Emission** settings control where particles spawn from, be that **Faces**, **Vertices**, or **Volume**. **Distribution** methods are different in that they control how particles get distributed within those spawn locations.

- **Random Order**: When enabled, particles are emitted in a random sequence instead of one after another. It does not directly affect the location where particles are emitted; the location is still determined by distribution settings such as **Jittered**, **Random**, and **Grid**.

On a plane emitter, we are talking about where particles are emitted instead of the order in which they are. Instead of particles being emitted from one end to the other, they will appear at random points on the plane, creating a more natural and less predictable emission pattern. When you enable **Random Order** on a plane emitter, it affects the sequence in which the particles are emitted, not their locations. This would be ideal if you had a video game environment with a magical forest, where random bursts of mystical particles appear around various trees and plants (*Figure 11.14*).

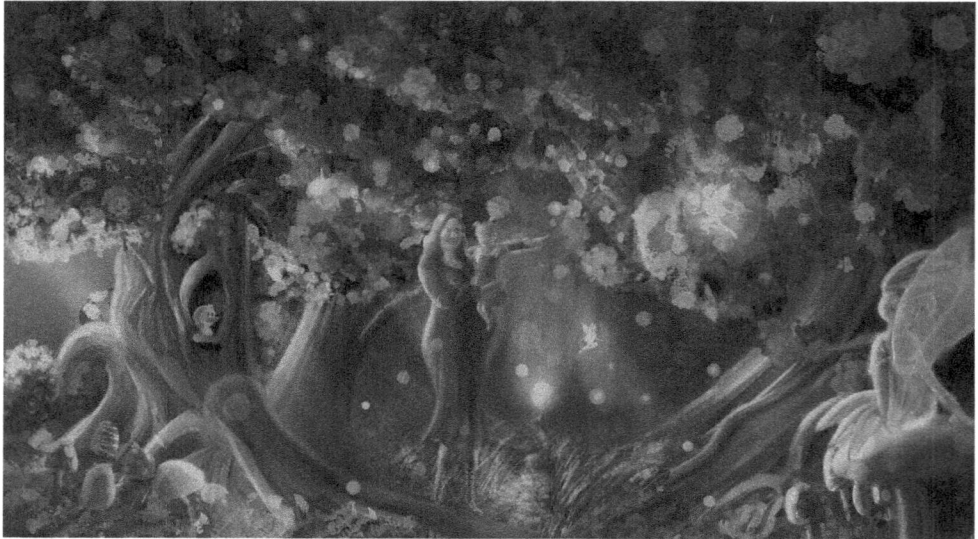

Figure 11.14: Custom Fantasy Steampunk Character Illustration by Brenda Strummer

- **Even Distribution**: This option will make sure that you have an even spread of particles across the emitting surface. If you are emitting particles from a sphere, enabling this option will distribute particles over the sphere's surface, avoiding clustering or uneven gaps. This would work for a project with a globe with twinkling city lights placed evenly on a path.
- **Particles/Face**: This setting determines the number of particles emitted per face of the mesh. On a subdivided plane, setting a higher **Particles/Face** value means more particles will be emitted from each face, leading to a denser particle distribution. In a project, this might look like a field where each patch of ground emits a high number of grass blades.

Note

This setting still works even when **Even Distribution** is enabled.

- **Jittering Amount:** This introduces randomness to the particle distribution. This is even more useful when **Even Distribution** is used, because it allows you to introduce irregularity, to make things look more real.

- With **Even Distribution**, particles are placed at regular intervals on a grid. But by adding jittering, you disturb this regularity, making the distribution appear more random while still being evenly spaced overall.

Figure 11.15 shows you what different spawn point setups look like:

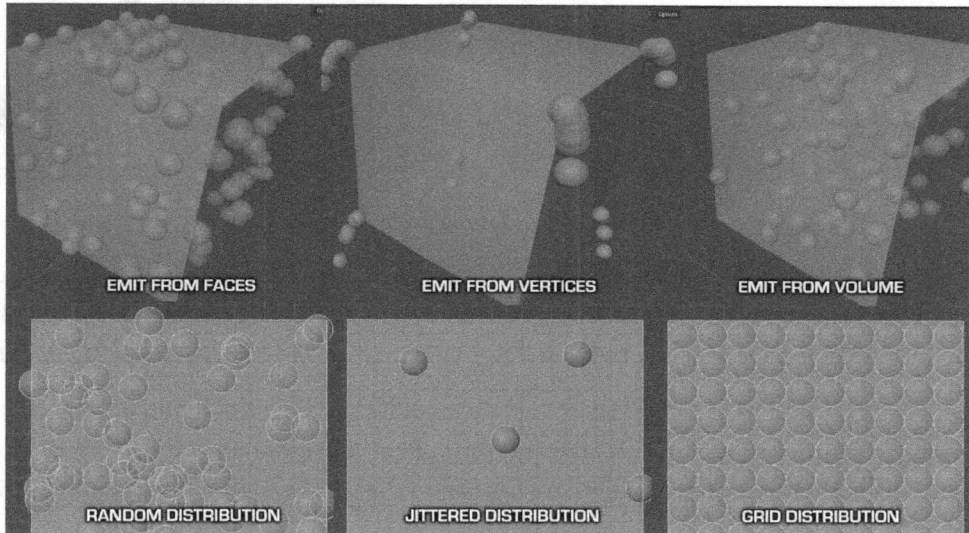

Figure 11.15: Spawn point differences – a visual representation

I think this would work for an orchard where fruit trees are arranged in uniform rows. With jittering, the trees' positions are subtly varied, creating slight differences in spacing and alignment.

Once you have set up your initial spawn points and adjusted the distribution settings, it is important to understand how modifiers affect particle emission. This is where **Modifier Stack** comes into play.

Within the **Source** settings is the **Modifier Stack** option, which plays a crucial role in how particles are emitted from the object. For example, if **Subdivision Surface** is set within the mesh, it will apply modifiers to a smoothened, denser mesh first, before spawning particles.

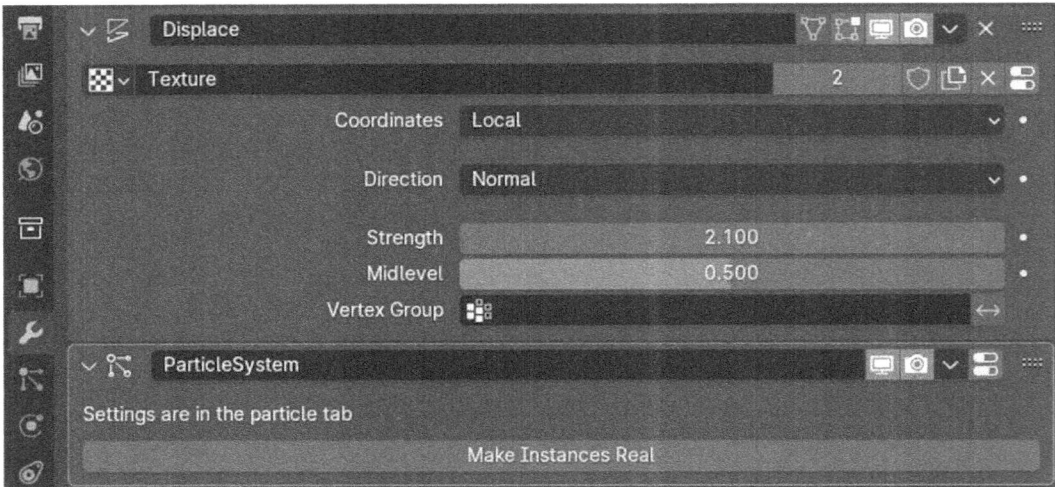

Figure 11.16: Particle location in the modifier hierarchy

Turning on the **Modifier Stack** option allows the particle system to acknowledge and use the modified geometry of the object. This means that you will see the geometry of your model after all the modifiers have been applied. It follows a hierarchical order, as shown in *Figure 11.16*.

You might want to use a **Subdivision Surface** modifier to create resolution on a mesh or a **Displace** modifier for simulating ocean waves on a plane. If you are simulating surface motion or fluid-like behaviors, other modifiers are further up the pecking order. For example, a **Displace** modifier could be used to create uneven terrain, which would affect how particles are distributed across the surface.

Without **Modifier Stack**, particles will be emitted based on the object's original, unmodified mesh. This means that any changes made by modifiers such as bevels, twists, or bends are not considered. Blender's **Modifier Stack** works in layers, where you can move items forward or backward depending on how prominent you want them to be.

Tip

Emitting particles without **Modifier Stack** might be better suited to a project such as a simple architectural model, where the basic geometry is more important than detailed surface variations.

But with the **Particle System** being applied at the bottom of all layers, particles will take into account the final shape and structure of the object after all modifiers have been applied. Your particle emission will now follow the modified contours and details of the object.

A project example could be a landscape with rolling hills and valleys. With **Modifier Stack** enabled, the particles (e.g., fog) would follow the landscape structure.

Let's look at a couple of practical uses of **Modifier Stack**:

- *Complex shapes*: For objects that you have modified significantly (e.g., a simple cube turned into a twisted, organic shape using modifiers), enabling **Modifier Stack** ensures that particles will follow this new complex shape. For example, if a cube is modified to have a swirling, vortex-like shape using a **Twist** modifier, enabling **Modifier Stack** would ensure that particle emission, such as energy streams or wind effects, accurately follows the twisted shape.
- *Animation and dynamics*: If the modifiers on the object are animated (e.g., a wave modifier causing a mesh to undulate), enabling **Modifier Stack** will make the particle emission adapt to these changes frame by frame. This might look like a fantasy cloak with a **Cloth** modifier where the fabric is animated to puff in the wind. With **Modifier Stack** enabled, a mystical aura emitted from the cloak would move and flow in a way that matches how the fabric moves.

In a few words, the **Modifier Stack** option within the emitter's **Source** settings is essential for making sure that the particle emission matches the current, modified state of the emitting object (e.g., a transforming car).

Understanding the Cache settings and their role in baking

In Blender's particle system, the **Cache** settings are the bread and butter for managing the playback and stability of particle simulations. **Cache** settings store and retrieve pre-calculated particle physics data. This pre-calculation allows for smoother playback and editing of complex particle systems without recalculating the physics each time. If this sounds too technical, do not worry, you are not alone.

Put simply, the **Cache** settings act like memory for your particle simulations, storing the movements and interactions so you do not have to wait for the computer to calculate them each time you play back your scene.

For a complex smoke simulation, recalculating the particle movement each time you make a change can be time-consuming. Using **Cache**, Blender can remember and replay the simulation quickly. This means that you can focus on creative adjustments and view the results instantly.

Note

The process of caching makes sure playback is consistent, and that is crucial for reviewing and rendering final animations.

Under the **Particle** setting, let us take a look at the **Cache** options, as shown in *Figure 11.17*:

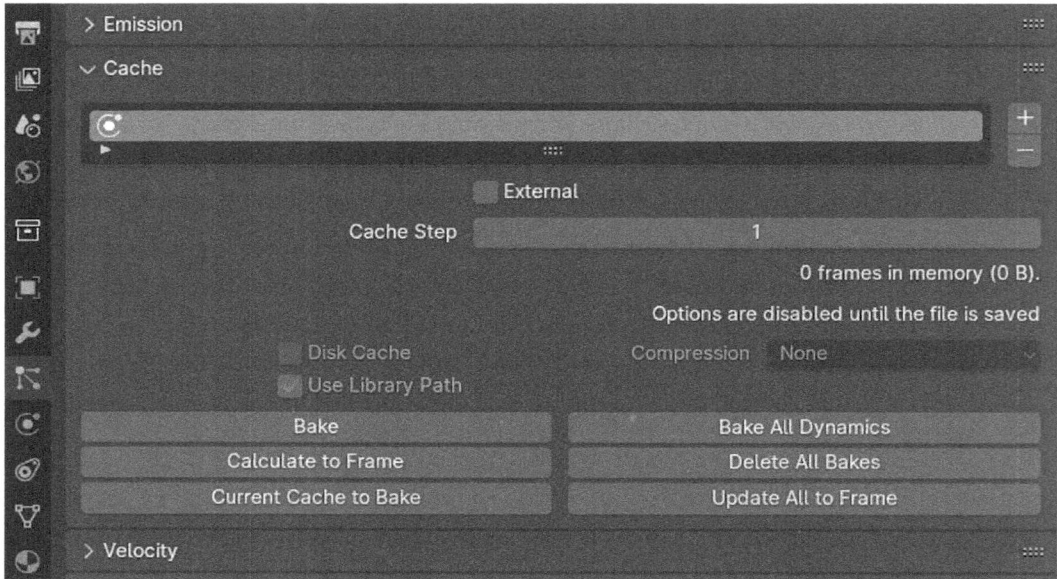

Figure 11.17: Cache options in Blender

- **Frame Start/End**: Determines the frame range for which the cache is valid. This is where your particle simulation will begin and end.

- **Cache Step**: Controls the resolution of the cache. If you set a lower **Cache Step** value (e.g., 1), Blender saves particle data for every frame, giving you a more accurate simulation but using more memory. A higher value (i.e., 2 or more) caches less often, saving memory but possibly losing a bit of simulation detail.

Note

Lower **Cache Step** values calculate the simulation more precisely but take longer to compute.

- **File Path:** When using **Disk Cache**, assuming you have **External** checked on, you can specify the location to use external baked particle data.

- **Disk Cache:** This enables saving the cache to disk, which is useful for very large simulations. If you are editing and tweaking your particle settings, caching saves time by avoiding constant recalculations. You could use it in a project where you are simulating complex weather patterns over a large landscape, making sure that each playback of the simulation matches. **Disk cache** also allows you to share simulation data with other team members or transfer it between different computers.

Disk Cache and baking have different functions in Blender's particle system, but they complement each other. Both caching and baking aim to save time and resources by storing simulation data, but **Disk Cache** is more flexible if you are planning to work on the project more or collaborate with someone, while baking locks in the simulation, ready for final production or rendering.

Baking will process and store the particle movement data for the specified frames, ready for smooth playback. This process calculates the entire particle simulation within the specified frame range and stores it in the cache. Once baked, the simulation plays back consistently.

Here's how to bake the simulation:

1. In the **Particle** settings, go to the **Cache** section.
2. Choose your frame range.
3. Click **Bake**.
4. If you make changes to the simulation settings, you will need to clear the previous bake, by clicking **Delete All Bakes**, update the settings, and rebake.

Getting a handle on Blender's **Cache** settings is absolutely vital when working with complex particle systems. If your scene is juggling thousands of particles or packed with intricate physics interactions, **Cache** is your best friend. It stores baked simulation data so Blender is not recalculating things every time you press play, saving you both time and your sanity.

Delving into the Velocity settings in Blender's particle system

In Blender's particle system, the **Velocity** settings play a critical role in defining the initial motion of particles upon emission. In a few words, **Velocity** settings determine the initial speed and direction of particles as they are emitted from the source object:

- **Normal:** Sets the speed of particles along the normal vector of the emitting face.

Note

The **normal vector** is a line that points straight out from the surface at a right angle. Imagine the top of a table. The normal vector is an imaginary line going straight up from the table. If particles are emitted from this surface, a higher normal value will make the particles shoot up faster along this straight line.

Increasing the **Normal** value on a **Plane** emitter will make particles shoot upwards more quickly, like sparks flying off a surface. You might see this in a wizard's duel, where magical energy bursts from the ground around the wizards.

- **Tangent**: Controls the velocity of particles along the tangent vector of the emitting surface, as in *Figure 11.18*.

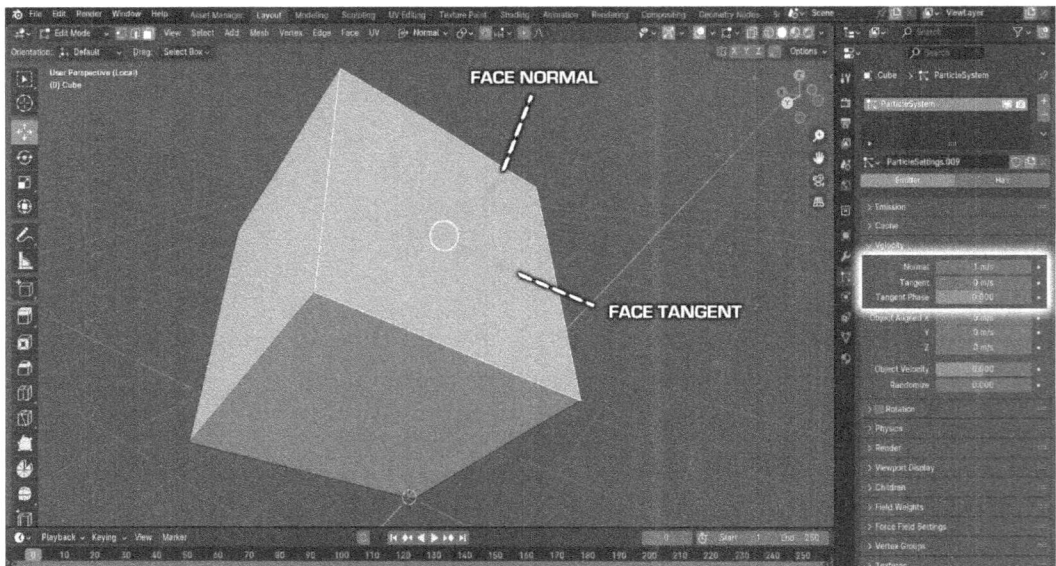

Figure 11.18: Tangent and Normal direction within a face plane of a cube

This setting is particularly useful when you want particles to follow the surface they are emitted from, such as hair strands growing along a scalp or moss clinging to a rock. A **Tangent** vector, in simple terms, is a direction that runs along the surface rather than cutting through it.

- While in the **Tangent** section, add **Tangent Phase**, to rotate the surface tangent direction.

  By adjusting **Tangent Phase**, you can control the orientation of the tangents on the surface, influencing how the material appears, especially with anisotropic shading.

  Blender gives you full control over the direction of the particles, making them follow the surface in a way that enhances the scene. On a curved surface, increasing the **Tangent** velocity allows particles to glide smoothly along the curve, which is ideal for simulating effects such as water flowing over a rounded rock.

- **Object Aligned X/Y/Z**: These settings allow you to control the direction in which particles are emitted based on the local rotation of the emitter object, as in *Figure 11.19*.

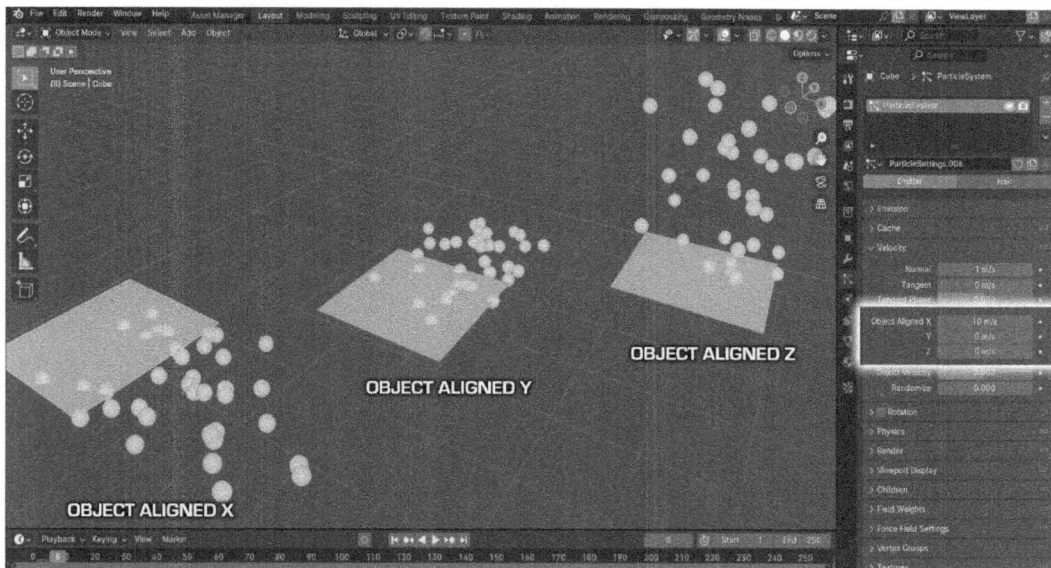

Figure 11.19: Using alignment to rotate the surface tangent direction

By aligning the particle velocity with the local X, Y, or Z axis of the emitter, you can make the particles move in a direction that corresponds with the object's own orientation. This is particularly useful for creating a stream of particles that move along the length of an object.

- **Object Velocity**: Allows particles to inherit some velocity from the movement of the **Emitter** object itself. If the **Emitter** object is moving, activating **Object Velocity** causes particles to emit in the direction of the object's motion, such as smoke trailing from a moving train.

Note

By tweaking the **Normal**, **Tangent**, and **Object** velocities, you can tailor the behavior of particles to match what you need for your scene. For example, adjusting these settings for a space simulation scene can create the effect of debris and particles moving realistically in zero gravity.

- **Random**: Adds a random component to the velocity, making the particle emission less uniform and more natural-looking. For example, adding randomness to the velocity of a fire emitter can simulate the unpredictable nature of flames and sparks (*Figure 11.20*).

Figure 11.20: Realistic flames and sparks in Blender Geometry Node Fire Animation by 3D Tudor

Tip

The **Random** velocity setting is particularly useful for achieving a natural, organic feel in particle systems, essential for realistic simulations. This is essential in projects such as open-world fantasy environments and inter-active sci-fi cities that require a big focus on making the environment look as if it could exist in front of you.

As you can see, the **Velocity** settings give you a lot of control over the movement of particles, ranging from subtle drifts to explosive movements.

Exploring Rotation settings in Blender's particle system

The **Rotation** settings in Blender's particle system are crucial if you want to make your particle animations look real. Put simply, **Rotation** settings control how particles spin and rotate as they move through the scene. Adjusting rotation settings can simulate effects such as swirling leaves, tumbling debris, or chaotic fire sparks.

Let's take a look at some specific rotation settings in *Table 11.1*:

Setting	Function	Tip
Randomize	Adds randomness to the rotation of each particle, making their motion look more natural and less uniform.	Applying **Randomize** to a particle system of falling leaves will give each leaf a unique orientation.
Dynamic	Enables **Dynamic** rotation, meaning particles rotate based on their movement. You will see this in a scene with effects such as fluttering butterflies or spinning debris.	**Dynamic** rotation applied to a whirlwind of debris will make each piece spin in response to its velocity, making it look more chaotic. In Blender, you can further control particle spin by adjusting the angular velocity of the **Emitter** object or through advanced scripting.
Phase	Controls the initial rotation angle of particles as they are emitted.	Adjusting **Phase** is useful when you want particles to start with a specific orientation, such as aligning confetti pieces before they start spinning in the air.
Angular Velocity	Sets the speed at which particles spin around their own axes.	Increasing **Angular Velocity** can create effects such as fast-spinning sparks or slow-rotating snowflakes, depending on what you are looking for.

Table 11.1: Selecting the right rotation settings in Blender

Now let's take a look at some practical examples:

- *Natural motion*: Randomization makes sure your particles do not look too uniform or mechanical. This is useful in projects such as a virtual forest scene, where falling leaves need to have varied and random orientations to mimic the chaotic nature of nature.

- *Enhancing dynamics*: Dynamic rotation is your go-to option for effects where particles respond to their environment or initial conditions. You might see this in an interactive environment such as a forest, where leaves and twigs interact as characters move through.

- *Visual effects in film and video*: In VFX, especially for film and video, **Rotation** settings can be critical for adding realism to scenes involving explosions or collisions, where debris needs to have a chaotic look, such as in a car accident simulation.

- *Weather simulations*: In weather simulations, such as tornadoes or cyclones, the **Dynamic** rotation of particles can be used to create more realistic representations.

Rotation settings in Blender's particle system are a powerful tool for bringing lifelike motion and complexity to particle animations. Through settings such as **Randomize** and **Dynamic**, you can infuse your scenes with realism and natural movement, both of which are crucial for immersive visual storytelling.

Bringing particle effects to life in Blender

Once your particles are behaving themselves in the **3D Viewport**, the next step is to make sure they look the part when rendered. You can tweak their appearance in a number of ways, from how they are shaded to how they interact with lighting in your scene.

- **R.**

    Particles can have materials and shaders applied to control their appearance. To picture this better, imagine a project with a fireworks display, where each firework particle changes color and brightness over its lifespan until it disappears completely. You get that satisfying glow-trail effect without needing to animate each spark by hand.

    Lighting plays a big role here, too. The same particle system can look completely different depending on your lighting setup. Want drama? Try a three-point lighting system. Want something softer and more ambient? A gentle HDRi or ambient light might be all you need. Experiment with different lighting setups, such as a three-point lighting system for a dramatic scene or soft ambient lighting for a calming landscape (*Figure 11.21*).

Figure 11.21: Soft ambient lighting in Unreal Engine 5 Beginners Guide to Building an Environment by 3D Tudor

- **Motion Blur**

  Enabling **Motion Blur** can add realism to fast-moving particles by creating streaks in their path. For a high-speed car chase, the motion blur effect adds a sense of speed and intensity to the particles representing dust and debris kicked up by the racing cars.

Instancing and shader tricks

It is also worth noting two rendering techniques. If you are spawning a ridiculous number of particles (think flower fields, flocks of birds, or anything that might cause Blender to raise an eyebrow), instancing is your friend.

Rather than rendering a fully detailed mesh for every single particle, instancing swaps them for a simpler stand-in, much easier on your hardware, and no one's the wiser. Instead of rendering each particle as a complex object, you can use **instancing** to replace particles with simple objects or even entire scenes. This reduces rendering complexity. For example, in a project with a large field of flowers, you would use instancing to replace each flower particle with a simplified model.

- Another trick up Blender's sleeve is the **Particle Info** Node in **Cycles** (refresh what you know about rendering in *Chapter 5* in *Part 1* of this book). This lets you control shader behavior based on particle properties. For example, you could have a shader respond to a particle's age by changing its color, opacity, or glow over time, as in *Figure 11.22*.

Figure 11.22: Using the Particle Info node on a magic cauldron

- *Figure 11.22* shows how we use information about your particle's lifetime to change the glow of bubbles in a magic cauldron. In this example, we make them glow more at the start, and we lower their brightness as they fade away. All in all, Blender's **Particle Info** node is perfect for those little touches that add storytelling and realism, such as a glowing spark that flickers out or a slime trail that fades behind a creature.

Before we dive into Blender's physics settings, let us connect the dots. We have talked about how particles look, how to shade them, light them, and even fake complexity with instancing. But great visuals are only half the story. What really sells a particle effect is how it moves. Whether it is a spark drifting with the wind or a clump of grass swaying, the magic happens when motion meets meaning. That is where Blender's physics settings come in, and where things start to get properly clever.

Unpacking physics settings in Blender's particle system

In Blender's particle system, the **physics** settings control the behavior of particles in response to forces, collisions, and other physical interactions within the simulation.

Table 11.2 shows which physics settings to pay attention to and why:

Setting	Function	Example
Newtonian Physics	This simulates particle motion based on classical physics principles, considering forces, acceleration, and collisions.	For example, in a scene with a waterfall, **Newtonian** physics can be used to simulate the natural downward movement and impact of water droplets, while considering gravity and interactions with the environment.
Keyed Physics	This gives you precise keyframe control over your particle animation.	For example, you can create a magical spell where particles move in a specific, predetermined path with scheduled timings.
Boids Physics	This emulates flocking behavior like you might see in birds or fish. If you choose **Boids** physics, your particles will follow simple rules such as cohesion, separation, and alignment.	In a scene simulating a flock of birds, each bird (i.e., particle) will move with the others, naturally forming and changing formations.
Fluid Physics	This makes particles look as if they were part of a fluid, accounting for viscosity, turbulence, and surface tension.	For example, you could generate realistic flowing water, splashing liquids, or swirling smoke in fluid simulations.
Mass	This defines the weight of each particle: heavier particles respond differently to forces than lighter ones.	In a rain simulation, particles with higher mass will fall faster and create larger splashes upon impact.
Size	This determines the dimensions of each particle: larger particles occupy more space and interact differently with what is around them.	In a crowd simulation, particles with larger sizes may represent people, while smaller ones could depict debris.
Brownian	This motion introduces random movement to particles, simulating the effect of molecules colliding with each other.	For example, when applied to dust particles in the air, **Brownian** motion makes them appear to move erratically, like in real air molecule collisions.
Damping	This controls how quickly particles lose energy: here, high values cause particles to slow down rapidly.	In a bouncing ball simulation, increasing **Damping** will make the ball stop bouncing more quickly.

Table 11.2: Physics settings in Blender's particle system

Tip

Keyed physics settings are ideal for scripted or stylized effects. Basically, scripted means the animation follows a set plan or script, while stylized means the animation is designed to look a certain way, focusing more on looks than realism.

Let's take a look at some practical applications:

- *Realistic behavior*: Adjusting **Mass**, **Size**, and **Damping** can create particle behavior that replicates real-world physics, making simulations more lifelike, like the water in *Figure 11.23*

Figure 11.23: Realistic water made with geometry nodes in Blender for Unreal Engine 5 The Complete Beginner's Guide by 3D Tudor

- *Biological simulations*: Blender's physics settings can simulate blood flow in vessels, the movement of microscopic organisms, or pollen dispersing in the air
- *Architectural visualization*: Physics settings can simulate how leaves or debris accumulate in certain areas of a structure, or how water flows through and around a building
- *Complex interactions*: Physics can simulate fluid dynamics, soft body deformations, or the behavior of fine particles in the wind

Advanced physics simulations

Advanced physics simulations in Blender offer a sophisticated level of realism and detail in animations. Let us look at some of these simulations more closely:

- *Fluid simulation*: Blender's **Fluid** physics settings include not just water-like liquids, but also viscous materials, gaseous substances, and smoke, like in *Figure 11.24*.

Figure 11.24: Gaseous smoke in Blender for Unreal Engine 5 Stylized Monster Hot Spring Environment Game Dev by 3D Tudor

Key features of **Fluid** physics include the following:

- *Liquids*: Simulate realistic water flow, including splashes, waves, and interactions with objects. Adjustable viscosity settings help you simulate thicker fluids such as honey or lava.
- *Gases and smoke*: Create dynamic smoke and gas simulations for effects such as fire, fog, or explosive blasts. You can control the diffusion, buoyancy, and turbulence of smoke or gas.
- *Fluid-object interaction*: Blender allows fluids and other objects within the scene to interact. This means that your fluids can flow around or collide with these objects realistically.

- *Cloth simulation*: Blender's **Cloth** simulation brings fabric to life with realistic physics-based animations. You can also simulate any fabric-like objects in a scene, such as flags, curtains, or tablecloths, a bit like in *Figure 11.25*.

Figure 11.25: Cloth simulation in Blender for Unreal Engine 3D Props Medieval Market Stall by 3D Tudor

Key features of a **Cloth** simulation include the following:

- *Motion and dynamics*: The cloth model can react to forces such as wind or gravity, flowing and fluttering in a lifelike manner.

- *Material properties*: You can simulate different types of fabric, from heavy velvet to light silk, letting it bend, stretch, and get dampened.

- *Collision and interaction*: The cloth can interact with other objects, ensuring it drapes, folds, or wrinkles upon contact, including self-collision (e.g., cloth interacting with other cloth).

- *Stress and strain*: Advanced settings can help you simulate stress and strain on the fabric, like cloth that is meant to tear or stretch under pressure.

Fluid and **Cloth** simulations help you create animations that are realistic, no matter how complicated they are. Both systems pull their weight when it comes to realism, whether it is the gentle flutter of fabric or the way particles catch the light.

Different tools, the same goal: fool the eye, and do it convincingly.

Particle interaction with materials

In Blender's particle system, you can control how particles interact with different materials to create a variety of effects. Here are some key settings you can adjust:

- *Transparency*: Particles can be made partially or completely transparent to create effects such as smoke, mist, or glass shards

- *Reflection and refraction*: Control how particles interact with reflective and refractive surfaces in your scene to achieve realistic glass, water, or gem effects

    For example, if you were working on gem effects, you would adjust the reflection and refraction settings to mimic how light interacts with each gemstone, making sure that they sparkle and reflect the environment (*Figure 11.26*).

Figure 11.26: Gem effects in Blender for Unreal Engine Become a Dungeon Prop Artist by 3D Tudor

Note

So, here is the deal, while the idea of using reflection and refraction settings to make gem particles dazzle like they are auditioning for a fantasy film sounds fun: it might be a bit much in practice. In high-end film work, sure, you would be looking at volumetrics and 3D textures for this. But in our world of practical Blender magic, there are often easier, more efficient ways to get a similar result. Using these nodes for sparkle might be clever, but let us not overdo it. Sometimes, subtle lighting tricks can give you the same bling with half the render tears.

– Skylar, a thoughtful technical reviewer of this book.

Compositing and post-processing

Once you have the physics and particles nailed down, the next step is all about making those particles look awesome in the final render. That is where compositing and post-processing come in:

- **Compositing**: Blender's **Compositor** allows you to enhance your rendered images by adding effects such as color grading, depth of field, and lens distortion. In the context of particle systems, this is useful because, for example, you can adjust the color of smoke or fog to match the lighting and mood of the environment.

- **Post-processing**: External software such as *Photoshop* (https://www.adobe.com/products/photoshop.html) or *GIMP* (https://www.gimp.org/) can be used for further image enhancement, such as retouching, color correction, and adding special effects. You might want to consider post-processing if your project requires a specific artistic style or additional visual effects that cannot be achieved within Blender (e.g., advanced image retouching or detailed texturing that requires you to work on the pixel level). We will talk about post-processing more in *Chapter 7* in *Part 2* of this book.

Tip

If you need to add specific wear-and-tear or ageing effects to a rendered object or particle system, tools such as *Photoshop* offer more precise control for adding scratches, smudges, or other fine details that require editing on a per-pixel basis.

In essence, after you have nailed the physics, compositing and post-processing help you polish and perfect your final render.

Discovering Blender's Viewport Display for particle systems

Now that we have tackled the underlying physics of how particles move and react, let us zoom out, just a little, and talk about how to actually see what they are doing while you work. Before you ever hit render, Blender gives you a sneak peek right in the **3D Viewport**. It is time to zero in on a very practical tool: Blender's **Viewport Display**.

This might seem like a step backward in the pipeline, but trust me, it is not. Once particles are flying around and doing their physics thing, the **Viewport Display** helps you debug, tweak, and visualize those chaotic swarms in real time, without waiting for a render every time you adjust a setting. So, if the physics settings were about how your particles behave, **Viewport Display** is about how you see and interact with them as you build your scene. Think of it as your particle system's HUD.

Viewport Display helps you see and control the fairy dust (i.e., particles) while you are creating your scene.

Here are some ways you can use **Viewport Display** to work with your particles:

- **Particle Size**: You can decide how big or small you want your fairy dust to look in the 3D world. It is like choosing the size of your magical stars. For example, if you want your fairy dust to be tiny like fireflies, you make it small, and so on and so forth.

- **Color**: You can control how each particle's color is determined in the **3D Viewport**. You can set it to the following:

  - **None**: All particles will appear the same default color.
  - **Material**: Particles will display the color of their assigned material.
  - **Velocity**: Particles will be colored based on their speed and direction.

- **Shape**: While the actual shape of your particles is set elsewhere, **Viewport Display** helps you visualize them in the scene using basic forms. This makes it easier to see how your fairy dust will move and behave, even if it is not showing the final render shape just yet.

> Note
>
> We would change the particle shape in the **Render** tab using the **Render As** menu and specify an **Object** or **Collection** of objects.

Viewport Display is like having a playground where you can test and see your magical particles in action before using them in a project or making a movie. It is one of those unknown giants in Blender, and even though the role of **Viewport Display** might appear very small, think again. Blender's **Viewport Display** offers immediate visual feedback.

Having children in Blender's particle system

The **Children** options rule how your particles come together to create effects in your animations. Instead of simulating and rendering many individual particles, Blender generates a smaller number of parent particles and then automatically spawns the **Children** particles around them. There are three set options to choose from:

- **None**: When you choose **None**, it means every particle is on its own, just like each block in your tower standing alone. If you want each raindrop to be separated and fall individually, you could pick **None**.

  Also, in a scene depicting a light snowfall, choosing **None** would allow each snowflake to drift independently.

- **Simple**: **Simple** is like making some particles work together as a group. They stay close to each other. If you wanted your stars to form clusters or groups (like constellations), you would choose **Simple**.

In *Figure 11.27*, you can see how **Simple** works. It is used to populate the scene with palm trees in an Aztec temple environment.

Figure 11.27: Simple particle children in Blender 4: The Modular and Kitbash Environment Guide by 3D Tudor

- **Interpolated: Interpolated** makes your particles look like they are smoothly connected, like drawing a line between dots.

  If you wanted a smooth trail when your superhero flies across the screen, you would choose **Interpolated**. It is like connecting the dots to show the path. Another example is a simulation of the trajectory of a comet soaring through space, where the particles create a seamless, glowing tail.

Field Weights in Blender's particle system

Field Weights decides how much each force, such as gravity and turbulence, can push or pull your particles.

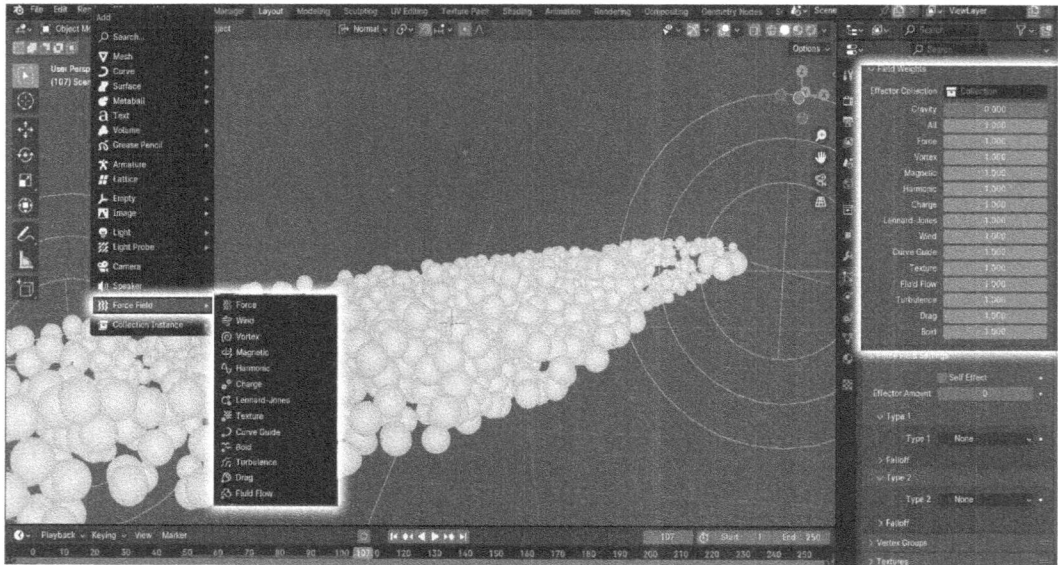

Figure 11.28: Field Weights options – a complete perspective

If we explored every **Field Weights** option (see *Figure 11.28*) in detail, it would be like opening a whole new chapter. You can read more about them in the Blender manual (https://docs.blender.org/manual/en/latest/physics/fluid/type/domain/field_weights.html).

Since this is a larger chapter about Blender's particle system, we will touch briefly on a couple of examples to understand **Field Weights** better. How your particles interact relies on the setup of physics forces. We will quickly go over key settings such as **Gravity** and **Turbulence** to see how they influence particle behavior, and then move on to explore how **Force Fields** can further refine and direct these interactions in the subsection that follows:

- **Gravity**: The force, just like when you drop a ball, gravity makes it fall to the ground. In Blender, you can adjust the **Gravity** field weight to make your particles (e.g., raindrops) fall faster or slower.

- **Turbulence**: This is the force of the wind blowing in different directions. It can make your particles move in a wavy, swirling way. The **Turbulence** field weight controls how strong this wind is.

If you wanted your magic sparkles to flutter around gently, you would increase the **Turbulence** field weight. If you wanted them to stay still, you would decrease it.

My advice is to think of **Field Weights** as volume knobs for different forces in your particle world: you can turn them up or down to make your particles dance, float, or zoom around when there is a force field present. Without a force field acting as the source of a force, the knobs do nothing, like turning up the volume on a speaker that is not plugged in.

On the other hand, force fields can be thought of as the sources of these forces, acting as invisible magnets that directly interact with your particles. They offer a more direct and hands-on approach to manipulating how your particles move.

Explaining force fields in Blender's particle system

If you ask me, I would compare **force fields** to invisible magnets that can push or pull your particles in different ways. The main types of force fields are as follows:

- **Force**: This pushes particles away or pulls them closer, like a magnet or a repelling force.

  If you wanted your particles to scatter when they get close to an object, you would use a **Force** force field. This might be useful in a project with a magical barrier in a fantasy scene. The **Force** force field can be used to create an effect of particles, such as mystical energy or debris, that are deflected by the barrier.

- **Wind**: This can make particles move as if they are being carried by the wind.

  If you wanted leaves to be blown by the wind in your animation, you would use a **Wind** field.

> Tip
>
> Force fields work together with other particle settings. For example, adjusting the mass of particles and using a **Wind** force field can change how particles respond to the wind.

- **Magnetic**: This behaves like a magnet, attracting or repelling particles based on their charges (i.e., positive or negative).

  If you were making a sci-fi scene with particles being pulled toward a spaceship, you would use a **Magnetic** force field.

Note

When using multiple force fields, it is crucial to balance their strengths and directions for a realistic effect. Overpowering one field can overshadow the effects of others.

Here's how to simulate external forces for particles:

1. Go to the **Particles** tab in Blender.

2. Press *Shift* + *A* to access the **Add** menu. Under the **Field Weights** section, select the desired item. In this case, we want to select **Vortex**, to create an empty object with a **Vortex** force field applied.

3. To adjust the controls of it, you can use the **Physics** tab on a **Vortex** force field, which will allow you to change things such as **Strength** and **Noise Amount**.

4. By default, all forces will affect the particles. To limit this, you can use **Effector Collection**:

    a. Simply move all forces to a new collection (select forces, press *M*, then **Move to Collection** and choose **New Collection**).

    b. Afterwards, select the created collection and click on **Effector Collection**. This is where you can add your force fields.

Note

While most of the force field primary controls are handled in the **Physics** tab, this note is particularly important after setting up your force fields in the **Field Weights** section. The **Particle Field Weight** tab allows you to fine-tune or dampen the influence of these forces on your particles. This allows you to fine-tune how much each type of force field affects your particles, for example, turning **Gravity** down while keeping **Wind** strong. Unlike vertex groups or weight painting, these weights are not visualized with color but are just numerical sliders that influence the simulation behind the scenes.

5. Click the **New** button to create a new collection for your force fields.

Want your force fields to play nicely together? To group force fields into a collection for controlled influence, follow the next steps:

1. Go to the **Layout** workspace to see your 3D scene.

2. Create or import objects to represent your force fields. For example, a sphere could be a **Wind** force field.

3. Select the force field object, *right-click*, and choose **Move to Collection**, or you can press *M*.

4. Select the collection you created earlier in **Effector Collection**.

Then, here's how to set up force fields:

1. With the force field selected, go to the **Physics Properties** tab in the **Properties** panel.

2. Here, you can choose the type of force field you want, such as **Force**, **Wind**, or **Magnetic**.

3. Adjust the strength and other settings to control how the force field affects your particles.

By setting up and adjusting force fields, you can make your particles interact with your 3D world based on physics. Each type of force field, from **Wind** to **Magnetic**, is specialized in how it makes particles interact with the world around them. While force fields act like invisible forces that impact particle behavior, vertex groups serve as specific zones on objects that precisely control where particles appear. This level of control is more localized and specific.

Explaining vertex groups in Blender's particle system

Vertex groups are like special zones on objects where you can control where your particles appear or do not appear. They help you decide where your particles should go in your 3D scene.

Here's how to create a **vertex group**:

1. Select the object to which you want to attach particles.

2. Go to the **Properties** panel and find the **Object Data Properties** tab (it looks like a triangle).

3. In the **Vertex Groups** section, click the **+ New** button to create a new group.

4. Name your group something such as Particle Zone.

Then, here's how to assign **vertices** to the group:

1. In **Edit** mode, select the vertices (i.e., points) on your object that you want to be part of the particle zone.

2. In the **Vertex Groups** section, select the group you created earlier.

3. Click the **Assign** button to attach the selected vertices to the group.

Here's how to adjust the particle settings:

1. Go to the **Particles** tab and find the **Vertex Groups** section.

2. Under **Density**, choose the vertex group you created earlier (e.g., **Particle Zone**).

3. Adjust the **Density** value to control how many particles appear in that zone.

Vertex groups are like invisible paintbrushes that tell Blender where to place particles. You can use them creatively in various types of projects, such as the following:

*   *Hair on a character*: If you have a character model and want to add hair, you can create a vertex group on the character's head to control where the hair particles should grow.

*   *Vegetation on a landscape*: You can make a vertex group on the ground where you want the trees to appear in a forest, and then use it to control tree placement.

*   *Particle textures*: Vertex groups can also be used with textures. You can paint a texture on an object, and the areas with certain colors will determine where particles appear, like in *Figure 11.29*.

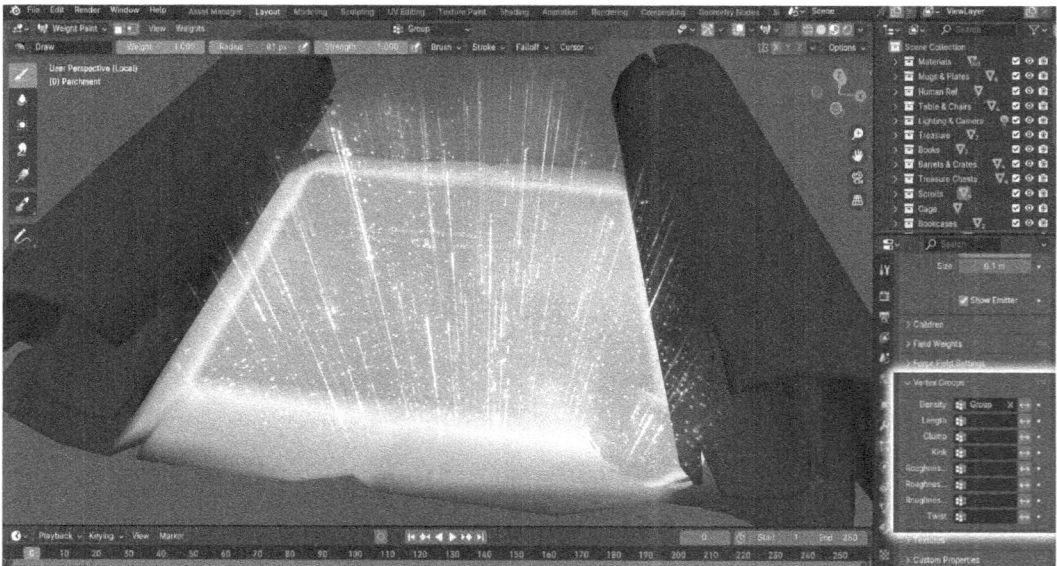

Figure 11.29: Using textures to determine where particles appear

By setting up and using **vertex groups**, you have control over where your particles show up in your 3D world. Textures can be used to add color variations, create patterned distributions, or even influence the growth and decay of particles.

Setting up textures in Blender's particle system

Textures are like digital paintings or patterns that you can use to control how your particles look and behave. They add detail, color, and interesting effects to your particles.

Here's how to create a texture:

1. Go to the **Texture Properties** tab in Blender (it looks like a checkerboard).

2. Click the **+ New** button to create a new texture.

3. Name your texture something such as Particle Texture.

Then, here's how to adjust the texture:

1. In the **Type** dropdown, choose the type of texture you want. *Figure 11.30* shows you all options, but among them are options such as **Image** or **Movie** for using pictures as textures, and **Clouds** for generating patterns.

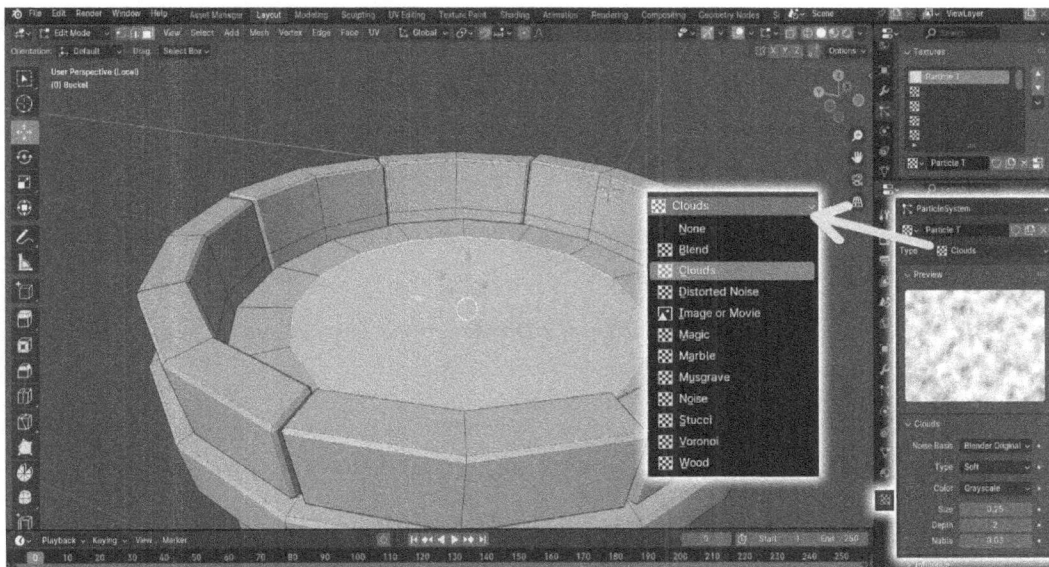

Figure 11.30: Type drop-down menu options

2. Depending on the texture type you choose, you will have other settings to customize. For example, if you use an **Image or Movie** texture, you will need to load an image file.

3. You can also make changes to properties such as **Color**, **Contrast**, and **Size**.

Here's how to use textures with particles:

1. In the **Particles** tab, find the **Texture** section.

2. Under **Density, Size,** or other parameters, click the dropdown and select the texture you created (e.g., **Particle Texture**).

3. Adjust the texture's influence to control how much it affects your particles.

You can use textures in different ways to achieve various effects:

- *Color variation*: You can use textures to give your particles different colors, creating a more natural or artistic look. For example, you can use a texture to make leaves on trees vary in shades of green.

  In an animated garden scene, you can apply a gradient texture to a group of flower particles. This texture can gradually change the color of the flowers from vibrant pinks at the base to softer whites at the tips.

- *Patterned distribution*: Textures can help you distribute particles following the pattern or shape you choose. Imagine creating a texture with circles and then using it to distribute particles in circular patterns.

  For a sci-fi space animation, you could use a texture that has a star-shaped pattern.

- *Displacement*: Some textures can push particles around, making them look bumpy or wavy. It is like adding texture to a surface.

  In a project simulating ocean waves, a **Displacement** texture can be used to make the water particles move up and down.

- *Growth and decay*: Textures can control how particles grow or disappear over time. You can create effects such as particles growing from the center and spreading out.

  Imagine a magical orb that emits particles. A texture can be applied to control the growth of these particles, making them emanate slowly from the orb's center and then dissipate as they move outwards.

As you can see after that deep dive, Blender's emitter **system** lets you create cool particle effects such as smoke, fire, and fairy dust. You can change how particles look by adjusting their size, color, shape, and more. Plus, **Viewport Display** helps you see and tweak these particles easily while you work.

But there's more! Blender also has a hair system for creating things such as realistic hair, fur, and other detailed strands. Let us check out how the hair system can add even more effects to your scenes.

Exploring the hair particle system

The hair system shares many of the options available in the emitter system. However, in Blender's particle system, there are options specifically tailored to control the behavior, appearance, and styling of hair particles.

Blender's hair system is there for creating strands that remain static or gently animated, making it ideal for simulating hair, fur, grass, or similar structures. The hair system focuses on the detailed styling and grooming of strands, offering tools to control their length, shape, and flow.

Here are some key options available for hair particles that are unavailable for effects you create via the emitter system:

- **Regrow**: This is an option that determines whether particles can reappear or regrow after they have died or been removed in a particle simulation.

  This option is cool if you want particles to appear over time, even after some of them have vanished. For example, in a grass simulation, **Regrow** can ensure that grass particles reappear after they have been cut or removed by a character walking through them.

- **Advance**: This option allows particles to advance to the next frame in the simulation even if they have not fully lived out their lifespan.

  The **Advance** option helps particles move faster than their lifespan. For example, in a fast-moving smoke simulation, you might enable **Advance** to make sure that smoke particles can move quickly, even if they have not been around for very long.

Table 11.3 shows another dedicated set of controls and features to create and style realistic hair-like structures in Blender:

Need	Emitter Particles	Hair Particles
Hair Length	They emit other types of particles, such as smoke, fire, or sparks, which do not have a hair-like appearance. Emitter particles do not have a **Length** setting.	They will help you create realistic hair in character models or furry creatures. Hair particles have a **Length** setting that lets you control the length of individual hair strands.

Need	Emitter Particles	Hair Particles
Hair Styling	Their appearance is usually determined by size, color, and velocity. Emitter particles are not designed for hair styling.	**Children** options allow you to control how **Child** hairs are styled and distributed, while **Kin** settings let you add curls and waves to hair strands.
Clumping and Clumping Force	**Clumping** and **Clumping Force** settings do not typically apply to emitter particles.	The **Clumping** settings simulate the natural tendency of hair to form into clumps. The **Clumping** and **Clumping Force** parameters will help you control how hair groups together.
Bristle and Bristle Length	There are no specific options for bristle-like structures.	You can add additional short hairs (i.e., bristles) on the surface of each hair strand. You can also adjust **Bristle Length** to control the length of these bristles.
Strand Shape	There are no settings to define the shape of strands.	Hair particles include options to control the shape of individual hair strands. You can use settings such as **Strand Shape** to make hair strands thicker at the base and taper towards the tips, achieving a more natural look.
Hair Dynamics	There are no settings for hair dynamics.	They can react to wind or gravity, for example. Hair dynamics make hair particles respond realistically to movement and collisions.
Hair Rendering	They have simpler rendering options, often resembling points or objects.	Hair particles have specialized rendering options for hair. There, you will find settings for rendering as strands, with options for thickness, shading, and root-to-tip color variation.

Table 11.3: Features and controls of the Blender hair system

Blender's hair system is a great tool for creating and styling realistic hair and other similar effects. With features such as **Regrow** and **Advance**, you can make particles reappear or move faster for more lifelike animations, such as grass growing back or fast-moving smoke. The system also has easy-to-use tools for combing, cutting, and shaping hair.

Summary

This chapter introduced you to Blender's particle system. We discussed basic setup tips, followed by talking about emitters, hair, and force fields. You learned how to control particle distribution, movement, and various interactions. We also discussed Blender's **Hair** mode and its role in rendering static particles such as fur or grass through physics simulations.

Our focus was on how Blender functions influence particle interactions with their environment. We explored how textures can be used in Blender's particle system to simulate various effects, from hair and fur to chaotic fire and smoke, magic spells, and flowing water. We delved into **Emitter** and **Hair** base settings, source settings, velocity, and rotation settings. The importance of managing cache settings for baking simulations was also discussed. The chapter also covered compositing and post-processing techniques to enhance particle effects. You learned about Blender's **Viewport Display** for visualizing particle systems, adding secondary particles (i.e., children) for more detailed effects, and using **Field Weights** and **Force Field** to influence particle behavior.

You learned how to set up simulations from scratch, style convincing hair and fur, and bring your effects to life with smart rendering and materials. You also explored the more advanced side of things, tapping into Blender's physics engine and mastering force fields. Whether you are scattering magical dust or simulating stampedes, you now have the tools to do it with confidence (and maybe a touch of flair).

As we move forward, the next chapter introduce you to sculpting and retopologizing in Blender. There, we will talk about shaping your models like a digital sculptor, and how retopology will refine your sculpted models to make them animation-ready.

Further reading

- If you are interested in creating dynamic particle effects such as sparks flying from a blacksmith's anvil, explore the **Emitter** settings in Blender. You can see an example of this in *Blender 3 Animated Stylized Blacksmith House 3D Modelling Guide* (https://youtu.be/N8HLjYGK0jQ).

- To simulate static particles, such as fur or grass that remains attached to an object but sways with physics, you can use **Hair** mode. This technique is demonstrated with swaying grass in *Blender 3D Model a Ghibli Art Stylized Scene* (https://www.udemy.com/course/blender-ghibli-beginners-3d-model-guide-oriental-stylized-scene/?referralCode=6EECBC38724A19C061C5).

- Adjusting the particle number in an **Emitter** system is crucial for controlling the density of particles in your scene. You can find out more in *Blender 4 Magic Potion & Cauldron Liquid Geometry Node* (`https://3dtudor.gumroad.com/l/blender4_magicpotion_cauldron_geonode`).

- If you are looking to create simulations such as campfires where the sparks' lifespan differs, a good place to start is *Blender 3 Unreal Engine 5 Complete Guide Stylized Camping Trip Gone Wrong Environment* (`https://youtu.be/QnDpIXQxmiY`).

- Jittered distribution is perfect for creating natural effects, such as a path of pebbles, seen in *Blender 4 Modeling and Geometry Node Workshop* (`https://www.udemy.com/course/blender-4-modeling/?referralCode=2ECBF4BA115166314468`).

- For realistic fire effects, adding randomness to the velocity of particles can simulate the chaotic nature of flames and sparks. A full and comprehensive walkthrough guide can be found in *Blender Geometry Node Fire Animation* (`https://www.udemy.com/course/blender-geometry-node-fire-animation/?referralCode=CCE4248DBF37B3DBF567`).

- Proper lighting is key to making particle systems stand out. This approach is demonstrated in *Unreal Engine 5 Beginners Guide to Building an Environment* (`https://www.udemy.com/course/unreal-engine-5-beginners-guide-building-environment/?referralCode=9B5652DD3928EDEDD5A8`).

- For fluid simulations, Blender's settings allow you to create realistic water, splashing liquids, or swirling smoke. Find out more in *Blender to Unreal Engine 5 The Complete Beginner's Guide* (`https://www.udemy.com/course/blender-to-unreal-engine-5-the-complete-beginners-guide/?referralCode=A659E7EEEA61C2DA562A`).

- Blender's **Fluid** physics settings extend beyond water to include viscous materials and gaseous substances, perfect for creating smoke effects. This is shown in *Blender to Unreal Engine 5 Stylized Monster Hot Spring Environment Game Dev* (`https://youtu.be/10W_pU8yTlc`).

- Cloth simulation in Blender adds realism to fabric animations, such as flags or curtains. Try it with our quick walkthrough course: *Blender to Unreal Engine 3D Props Medieval Market Stall* (`https://www.udemy.com/course/blender-to-unreal-engine-5-3d-props/?referralCode=92DD6C744ECF6621836C`).

- To achieve sparkling gem effects, adjusting the reflection and refraction settings in Blender is essential. See more in *Blender to Unreal Engine Become a Dungeon Prop Artist* (`https://www.udemy.com/course/blender-to-unreal-engine-become-a-dungeon-prop-artist/?referralCode=979CA6D3C71A4B2BB8CD`).

Subscribe to Game Dev Assembly!

We are excited to introduce **Game Dev Assembly**, our brand-new newsletter dedicated to everything game development. Whether you're coding, designing, animating, or managing a studio, we've got insights, trends, and expert advice to help you create, innovate, and thrive. Sign up now and get exciting benefits.

https://packt.link/gamedev-newsletter

Get This Book's PDF Version and Exclusive Extras

UNLOCK NOW

Scan the QR code (or go to packtpub.com/unlock). Search for this book by name, confirm the edition, and then follow the steps on the page.

Note: Keep your invoice handy. Purchases made directly from Packt don't require an invoice.

12

Introducing Digital Sculpting and Brushing Up on Your Retopology Skills

Imagine your favorite story is written in a language that not everyone understands. You decide to translate this story into a more common language, such as *Common* in *World of Warcraft*, making sure to keep the story's heart and soul, every plot twist and cheeky joke, so the whole pub can enjoy it.

Retopology in 3D modeling is a lot like the translation process. You start with a complex, detailed model (i.e., the original story) and simplify it (i.e., translate it) into a form that computers and games can easily handle without losing what makes the model special. Just like translating a story makes it accessible to more readers, retopology makes your models ready for action in games and animations, ensuring they look great and run smoothly on all kinds of devices.

In this chapter, we will cover both manual and automated retopology techniques, starting with the hands-on approach of the **Poly Build** tool for direct mesh manipulation. This chapter also brings you up to speed with the latest advancements in Blender, including new tools and features, such as **Retopology Overlay**. Mastering these tricks sets you up to build lean, mean meshes that won't bring your frame rate to its knees.

Once your low-poly cage is sorted, it is time to swap the ruler for a rolling pin, Blender's **Sculpt** mode lets you push and pull digital clay just like the real stuff, minus the mess on your desk. Sculpting in Blender is quite similar to this hands-on experience. You start with a basic digital shape, like a virtual ball of clay, and use Blender's sculpting tools to mold it into a character, an animal, or anything else your imagination conjures up. Just as with real clay, you can add or subtract material, smooth surfaces, and refine shapes.

Here, we will cover everything from the interface and key sculpting brushes to remeshing techniques. Each brush is a stand-alone tool, designed for specific tasks to build up forms, add details, smooth transitions, and reshape your sculpted 3D models. You will also use project examples to imagine these brushes in action.

So, in this chapter, we will cover the following topics:

- Introducing retopology in Blender
- Introducing Blender sculpting for beginners

Technical requirements

As for **Blender 4.5 LTS (Long-Term Support)**, the general requirements include a macOS 11.2 or newer (Apple Silicon supported natively) operating system, or a Linux (64-bit, glibc 2.28 or newer) operating system. Blender now requires a CPU with the SSE4.2 instruction set, at least 8 GB of RAM (32 GB recommended for heavy scenes), and a GPU supporting OpenGL 4.3 with a minimum of 2 GB of VRAM.

For a full list of technical requirements, please refer back to *Chapter 1* of this part.

Introducing retopology in Blender

Retopology is not just another box to tick, it is the bit that turns a show-pony sculpt into a workhorse mesh that your software can actually run. Your character might look gorgeous, but try dropping it straight into a game engine and prepare for an instant slideshow. Retopology steps in, pares away the excess, and rebuilds the surface with tidy, efficient loops.

Even when you start a model in high-density mode, a quick pass with retopo tools trims the fat and leaves you with a model that animates, UV-unwraps, and bakes textures without kicking up a fuss. It turns your detail-rich showpieces into streamlined work, assets that drop straight into any scene and plug neatly into **Level-of-Detail (LOD)** chains, progressively lighter versions of the same model that a game or render engine swaps in as the camera moves farther away.

Preparing your model

First, you need to prepare your model. We are doing that because modifiers get affected based on your object's transformation. This means that even if we are using **Voxel Remesh**, the density parameters would be vastly different. Follow these instructions:

1. Open your high-poly model in Blender. Make sure that its location, rotation, and scale are set to the default values of 0, 0, and 1 by selecting the model, pressing *Ctrl + A*, and applying all the transformations, as in *Figure 12.1*.

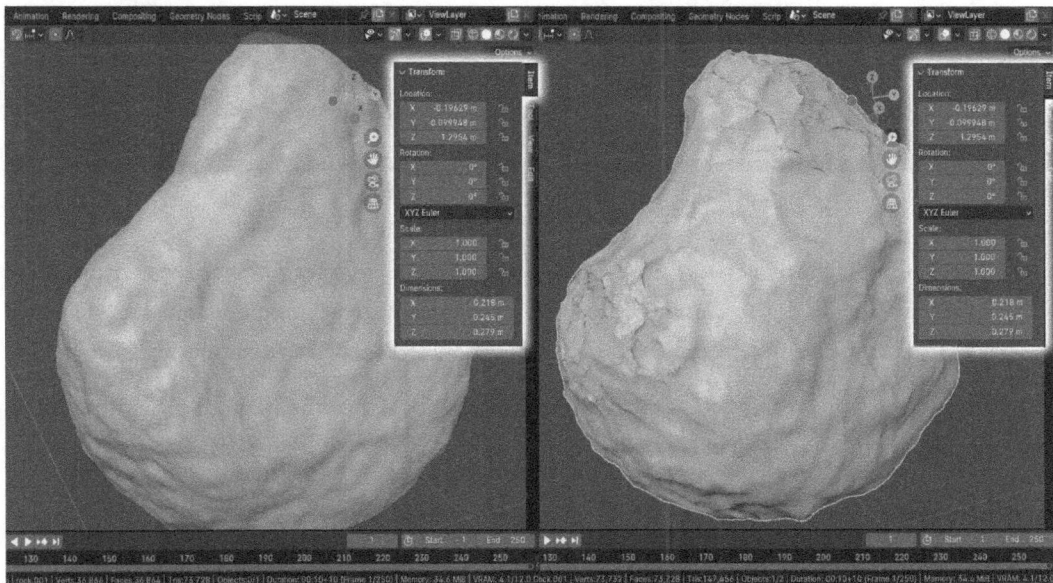

Figure 12.1: A visual checklist of preparing your model for retopology

In this example, you can see how transformations have affected a rock generator.

2. Enter **Edit Mode** (by pressing *Tab*) and inspect the mesh for any anomalies or errors that might complicate the retopology process. Use the **Mesh** menu to clean up any issues, using some of the options in *Figure 12.2*.

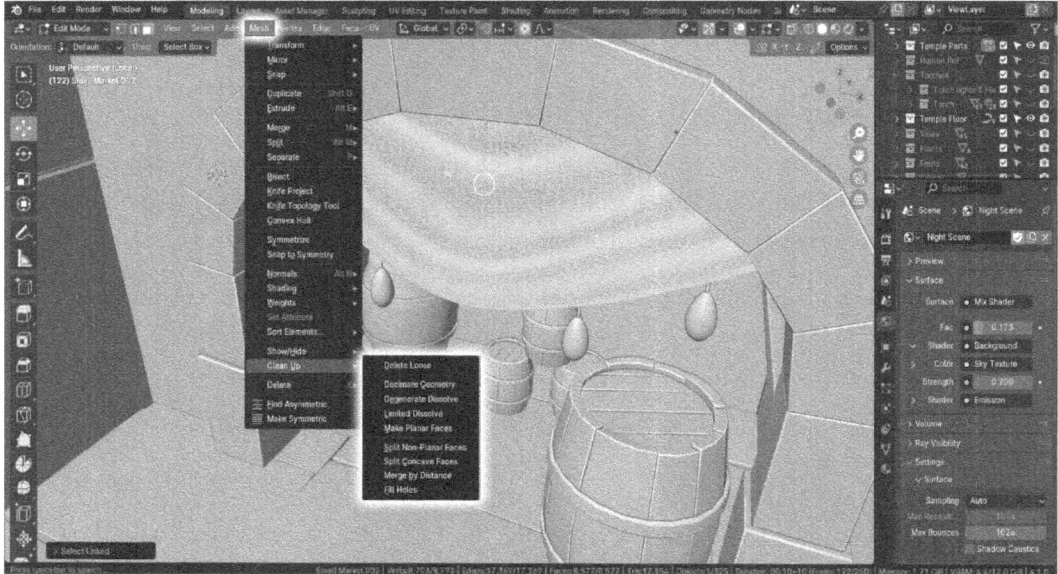

Figure 12.2: Mesh menu options for Clean Up

Merge by Distance cleans up overlapping geometry by merging vertices within a set distance. On the other hand, **Fill Holes** closes gaps by generating new faces, and **Delete Loose** simplifies the mesh by removing unconnected vertices, edges, or faces.

After tidying up your mesh, you are ready to continue with either the manual or automated retopology approach. Let's look at both.

Automated retopology in Blender

Now, let's explore various retopology approaches, ranging from hands-on techniques to advanced automated tools. These methods are essential if you are looking to refine and animate your models further to boost their quality.

Voxel remeshing modifier

Voxel remeshing is Blender's automated approach to making your topology uniform. By converting the mesh using the **Voxel Remesh** modifier (which can be found in **Modifier | Remesh | Voxel**), your polygons are processed in a very concise way, as in *Figure 12.3*. The **Voxel Remesh** modifier does not change the actual topology of the mesh until it is applied, making it especially useful for testing different settings non-destructively or preserving your original geometry while experimenting.

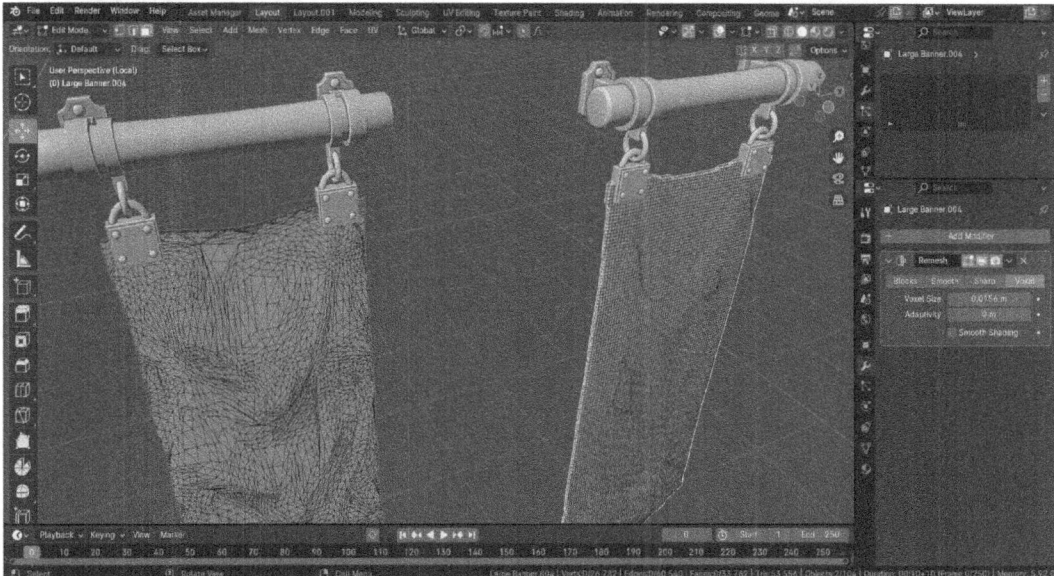

Figure 12.3: Original topology (left) versus remeshed mesh (right)

A smaller **Voxel** size will give you a more detailed mesh but will also have more polygons. A larger **Voxel** size will have less detail and fewer polygons. To make a visual comparison of different **Voxel** sizes, see *Figure 12.4*, where an increasing **Voxel** size shows an increase in detail preservation together with an increase in topology count.

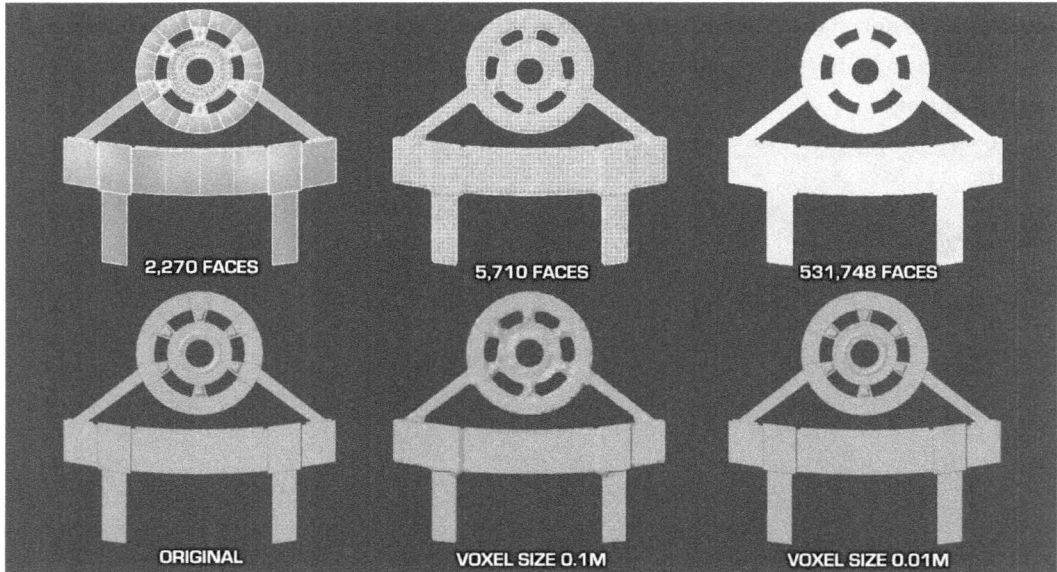

Figure 12.4: Original mesh (left) versus two different Voxel sizes (middle and right)

Tip

Voxel remeshing is very helpful if you are planning to sculpt or do more detailed modeling work on your 3D model. You can access remeshing from the dropdown or the sidebar tool menu.

Voxel takes in the volume of a selection as a whole and recreates a mesh based on volume detail or **Voxel** size. **Remesh Quad** is different because it will retopologize mesh faces based on its surface, giving a new flow to the topology.

Voxel is great for items with thickness, or when you have multiple objects and want to combine them into one solid mesh. Its biggest drawbacks are that it does not handle thin meshes or mesh planes and it creates holes in assets.

Let us go over some options for **Voxel**:

- **Voxel Size**: This value determines the resolution of the **Voxel** grid that will be used in **Voxel** mode.

- **Adaptivity**: This slider gives you control over how adaptive the remeshing process is. A higher value will give you a mesh with more variance in polygon sizes, with smaller polygons in areas of higher detail and larger polygons in flatter areas.

Sculpt mode options

- **Fix Poles**: This checkbox, when enabled, will attempt to fix **poles** (i.e., vertices where a non-standard number of edges meet). This might happen if the mesh has been edited manually, leading to irregularities in its topology.

> Note
>
> These, and the next few settings, only show up in **Sculpt** mode's **Voxel Remesh**. Don't go hunting for them in the **Remesh** modifier; they simply are not there. You might also see poles in your mesh if you have used complex operations such as Boolean operations, extrusions, or merging of vertices. Complex operations such as that might mean that your vertices connect to more or fewer edges than is typical for a smooth mesh.

- **Preserve**: under this section, you have two options:
- **Volume**: If you enable this, the remeshing process will attempt to preserve the volume of the original mesh as closely as possible. This could be helpful if you have detailed sculpting work where maintaining the overall shape and form is critical to the character or object's appearance. For example, imagine that you are working on a character's face; any significant volume loss during remeshing could affect its expression or features.
- **Attributes**: This will preserve all mesh data and recreate it onto a new mesh, including seam and sharp data, as well as vertex color information.

If you need a more precise, animation-friendly approach, **Quadriflow Remesh** is your next stop. Let's check out how it improves on automated remeshing.

Quadriflow Remesh

Quadriflow Remesh takes automation a step further. It uses advanced algorithms to generate a uniform topology that maintains the original model's curvature and flow.

Quadriflow Remesh is the third remeshing option we are tackling. Unlike the **Remesh** modifier, it runs directly on the object's data, much like **Voxel Remesh** in **Sculpt** mode, and that means it is destructive. Once you apply it, there is no modifier stack to dial back, so work on a duplicate if you need a safety net. Be aware, too, that **Quadriflow Remesh** lives in a different corner of the interface (i.e., **Object Data Properties** and then **Remesh**), so it is easy to miss if you are expecting another modifier-style panel.

> Tip
>
> **Quadriflow Remesh** is particularly good at preparing models for deformation. This is because it makes sure that the topology supports the model's intended motion range without distorting it or losing details.

Quadriflow Remesh uses the **Quad** mode in Blender, referring to the **Quadriflow** remeshing algorithm. The **Quad** mode is designed to convert the mesh into a quad-dominant mesh, meaning the mesh will primarily consist of quadrilateral faces. This type of remeshing is ideal for models that you are planning to animate or add detailed sculpting details to. This is because quads tend to deform more predictably and smoothly than triangles.

Now, let me go over some basic **Quadriflow Remesh** options with you:

- **Use Mesh Symmetry**: This option, when checked, instructs **Quadriflow** to create a symmetrical mesh along the object's symmetry axis. This is useful for objects that have a symmetrical shape, such as characters or vehicles, to ensure uniform topology on both sides.

- **Preserve Sharp**: If enabled, this will preserve sharp edges and corners in the model. It is useful when you want to maintain the definition of certain features after remeshing. For example, **Preserve Sharp** would be ideal in a project with mechanical parts or architectural elements that need sharp edges.

- **Preserve Mesh Boundary**: When selected, the boundaries of the mesh are preserved during remeshing. I imagine this being useful if you are working on a piece that needs to fit precisely with other parts or models, such as character models where costume elements need to align perfectly.

- **Preserve Attributes**: If you have areas of the mesh painted with a mask (e.g., in **Weight Paint** or **Vertex Paint** mode), checking this will ensure that these areas are considered during the remeshing process to preserve detail where it is needed. **Preserve Attributes** is good if you are sculpting detailed characters or objects where specific regions require higher detail preservation, such as facial features or texture details.

- **Smooth Normals**: When this is checked, the normals of the resulting mesh are smoothed out. **Normals** are vectors that define the orientation of the surface at each point and are important for how light interacts with the material. Smoothing normals can lead to a softer appearance where the faces meet. This is essential if your model is going to be part of animations where lighting plays a key role in the presentation, such as characters, vehicles, or other assets in a 3D environment.

- **Mode**: This drop-down menu allows you to select the criteria **Quadriflow** uses to determine the density of the new topology, as in *Figure 12.5*.

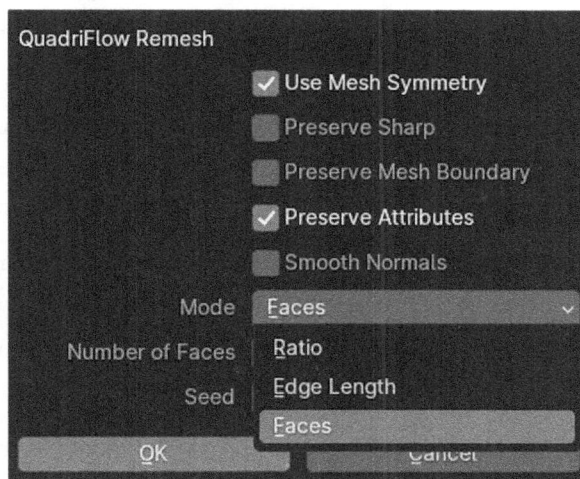

Figure 12.5: Quadriflow drop-down menu

- **Number of Faces**: This numeric input allows you to set the target number of faces for the remeshed model. **Quadriflow** will try to generate a topology that meets this face count, which gives you control over the LOD and the complexity of the mesh.

- **Seed**: The **Seed** value is used to start the random number generator that is part of the remeshing algorithm. Changing the **Seed** value can lead to slightly different quad distributions for the same mesh. This can be useful for troubleshooting issues with the remeshing process or for trying to achieve a slightly different result without changing the other parameters.

> Note
>
> Using **Quadriflow Remesh** in Blender is particularly beneficial for creating a clean, animation-friendly topology that simplifies further sculpting or rigging processes. It can also help optimize meshes for real-time rendering by reducing the polygon count while preserving essential details.

Quad is great when you want multiple parts of a mesh within an asset to be kept separated even after the operation. It is great for use on 2D planes or thin meshes. You either use one or the other, but sometimes, it is great to use both.

For example, if you have an asset with multiple parts, use **Voxel** with high density to combine them into a solid piece without losing much detail. Afterward, you could use **Quad** to fix its topology flow. This hybrid technique will allow you to convert a multi-asset piece.

Now that we have seen how **Voxel** and **Quadriflow** each do their own thing, let us check out how Blender actually puts them together in one toolset. We will dive into the settings that let you merge thick objects, maintain volume, and even preserve fine details, all with a couple of clicks. Buckle up; automated retopology just got simpler!

Automated retopology with Voxel and Quadriflow Remesh

Remeshing can be done by accessing **Data** and then **Remesh**. In the **Remesh** panel, you find **Mode**. The **Mode** option allows you to choose between the different types of remeshing algorithms:

- **Voxel** mode uses a **Voxel** data structure to create a new mesh that encapsulates the volume of the original mesh
- **Quad** mode tries to create a mesh composed of mostly quadrilateral faces, as shown in *Figure 12.6*

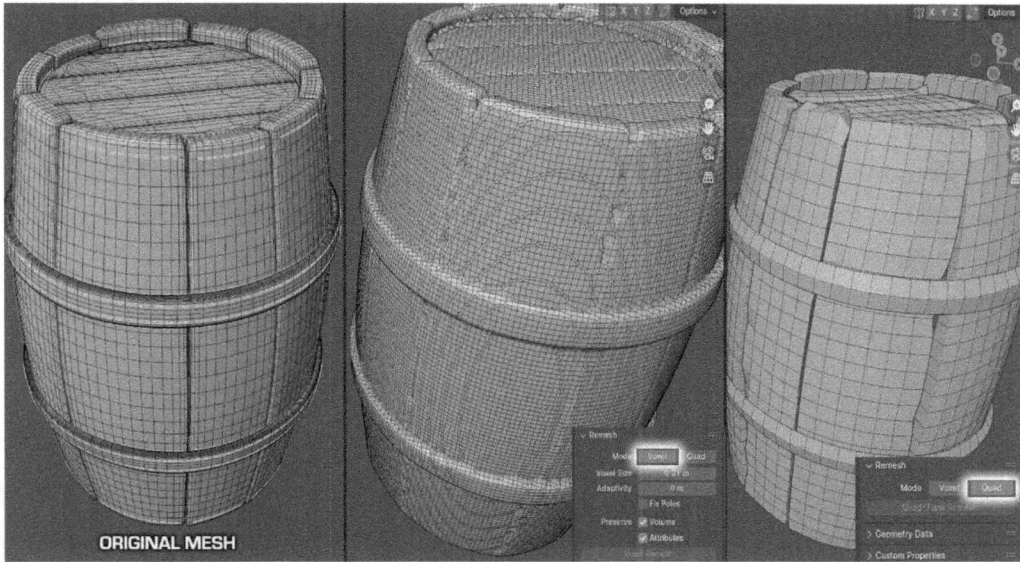

Figure 12.6: Original mesh versus Voxel versus Quad remeshing

- **Voxel Remesh** is used to execute the **Remesh** operation with the currently selected options.

  - You can access these tools by going to **Remesh | Quad | Quadriflow Remesh**. It might help you to look through the **QuadriFlow Remesh** options in *Figure 12.7*.

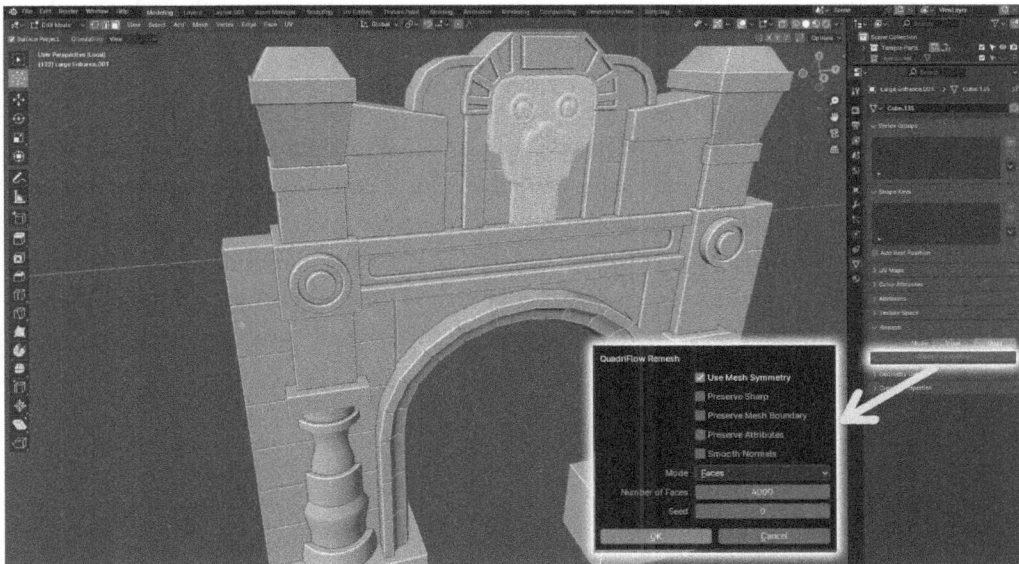

Figure 12.7: Quadriflow Remesh options in Blender in Blender 4: The Modular and Kitbash Environment Guide by 3D Tudor

Voxel Remesh: automated retopology step by step

To follow the automated retopology approach, use the following steps as your guide:

1. For a quick, uniform topology over the entire model, go to the **Properties** panel, find the **Object Data** tab, and find the **Remesh** section.

2. Click on **Voxel Remesh**. Adjust the **Voxel Size** value to control the mesh's detail level, as in *Figure 12.8*.

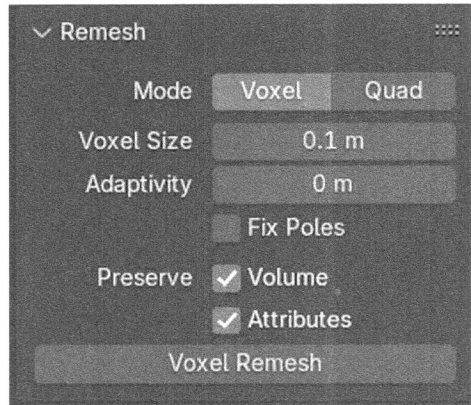

Figure 12.8: Controlling Voxel Size during Voxel Remesh

3. Smaller **Voxel** sizes will give you more detail but will make your mesh more complex.

Note

Higher values, such as 0.1 or higher, will simplify the mesh, reducing the number of polygons and potentially making the model less detailed but easier to manage and sculpt on a broader scale. On the other hand, lower values, such as 0.01 or less, will increase the mesh's detail level, creating a denser polygon distribution that is ideal for capturing fine details, but may result in a higher computational load and slower performance on less powerful systems.

4. Click on **Voxel Remesh** to combine your mesh into a single, unified object, effectively closing up holes and merging disconnected parts. Adjust the **Voxel Size** value to control the LOD.

> **Note**
>
> Using a higher **Voxel Size** value will close up holes more effectively and simplify the mesh, but it will reduce fine details. Lower values will preserve details but may not be as efficient at closing gaps.

These are some other **Voxel Remesh** options you might want to consider:

- **Adaptivity**: Cuts down on polygons in flatter areas while keeping detail where surfaces are curved. It speeds up your workflow, but you might lose a little precision
- **Fix Poles**: Helps avoid odd pole artifacts in your mesh
- **Preserve: Volume**: Makes sure your remeshed object keeps its general shape and size, even if the topology changes
- **Preserve: Attributes**: Tries to keep things such as UV maps and vertex colors after remeshing

Quadriflow Remesh: automated retopology step by step

For a cleaner and more structured topology, use **Quadriflow Remesh**, which can be found in the same **Remesh** section. This will generate a more optimized quad-based mesh, improving edge flow for sculpting and animation:

1. Set your desired detail level through the **Face** count or **Edge Length**.
2. Click **Quadriflow Remesh** to apply and look through the options you saw in *Figure 12.8*. You can choose to define the mesh by the number of faces, edges, or vertices.

Depending on your choice, the next option (i.e., **Number of Faces**) will change accordingly, as in *Figure 12.9*, where we show an original mesh with 80,000 faces and the process of remeshing it into 10,000 faces and 5,000 faces.

Figure 12.9: Changing the Number of Faces option in Quadriflow before (left) and after (middle and right)

Next, we will look at the newest Blender tools that make retopology easier and more precise. These features help you work faster and more accurately, improving your overall workflow.

Manual retopology in Blender

So far, so good! Now, you will go through a detailed walk-through of the retopology process in Blender. Before we wade into the nuts and bolts, take a look at the following cheat-sheet and keep it handy. It is an at-a-glance guide to when you should reach for automated remeshes versus rolling up your sleeves for manual patching:

Quick note: auto versus manual retopo cheat-sheet

- Organic stuff (creatures, cloth) → start with **Voxel Remesh/Quadriflow**, then tidy by hand.
- Hard-surface (bevels, panels) → jump straight to **Poly Build** for laser-placed loops.
- One-off concept render → auto-remesh + light polish is usually plenty.
- Animation/game asset → manual patches round joints and deforming areas, clean flow everywhere else.
- Mobile/VR→ low-poly manual cage plus auto-decimated LODs.
- Film/marketing stills → auto pass, quick manual sprucing.
- Auto gives pinching or spirals? → fix that zone manually.
- LOD tip: Stash those mid- and low-poly auto outputs, they double as ready-made LOD levels.

Armed with that perspective, let's roll up our sleeves and walk through the hands-on retopology process step by step.

We will start from the initial setup of the high-poly model and go as far as the final adjustments of the retopology mesh. Each step would be explained in depth, with clear instructions, tips, and best-practice notes to make sure you have the necessary support through the complex process of retopology.

Creating a retopology base

Creating a retopology base means you are building a simple mesh that will become the scaffold for the new topology. In this way, you are making sure that the foundational geometry is in place before the more intricate work begins.

Creating a retopology base is not a new feature, but Blender 4 includes enhancements that make this process more efficient. For example, the improved **Poly Build** tool helps you add and adjust geometry more easily, while better grid snapping and dynamic topology options ensure your base aligns well with the original model. New shortcuts and context menus shave minutes off the setup, while built-in edge-flow guides highlight exactly where your loops should land. With live mesh previews and adjustable templates for common asset types, you can jump straight into detailing on a rock-solid base instead of fiddling with the basics.

Basic retopology techniques

Now, let's dive into essential retopology techniques that streamline the process of transforming complex models into optimized, manageable assets:

- **Poly Build** lets you directly manipulate your mesh geometry. It provides a hands-on approach to retopology, allowing you to add, remove, and adjust vertices and edges with precision (e.g., *Figure 12.10*).

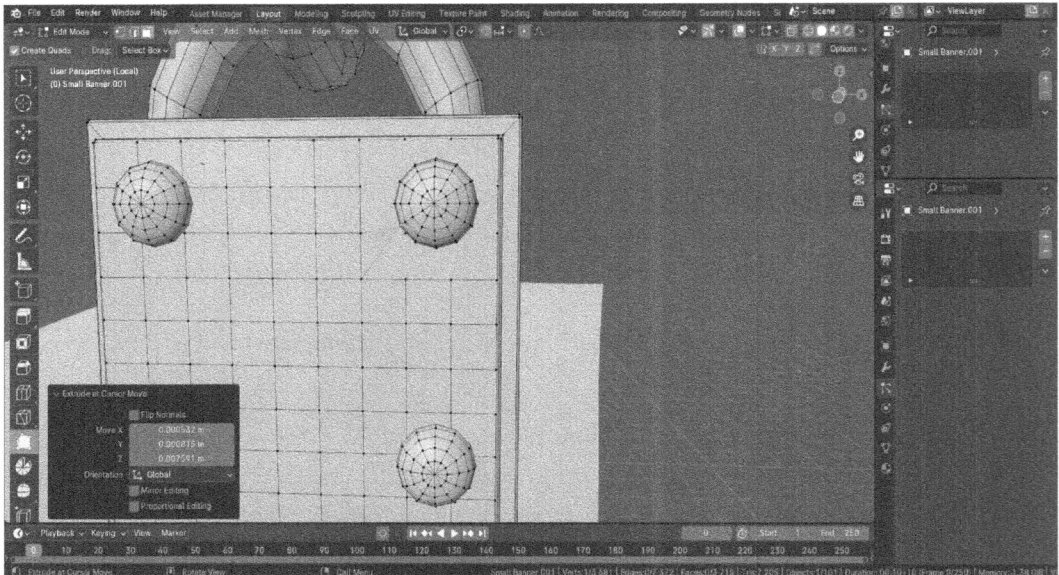

Figure 12.10: Poly Build in action

> Note
>
> **Poly Build** is best for retopologizing organic shapes, where the subtleties of their form are at the top of your agenda.

- **Edge loops** are like the skeleton of each mesh, as shown in *Figure 12.11*.

Figure 12.11: Edge loops on a medieval chest

- They define your mesh's structure and influence its behavior. In animation, where you place your edge loops is what determines how a model deforms in response to movement. Creating loops is, therefore, a key skill in the retopologist's toolkit. You can revisit *Chapter 6* in this part of the book, where we talked about them in more detail. This will help you anticipate how the model will need to move so that you can structure the topology accordingly.

> **Tip**
>
> Creating and adjusting loops is important if you want to make sure that the mesh deforms correctly during animation. Later in this chapter, we will discuss strategies for optimizing loop placement.

- Snapping and mirroring are Blender tools that make sure that your retopology is symmetrical and accurate. **Snapping** makes sure that the new vertices match the contours of the original model. The **Mirror** modifier then helps you by taking that new form and reflecting it across the model's axis of symmetry, halving your workload at the same time as making sure both sides of your model are the same.

Note

This combination of tools is especially valuable in character modeling, where symmetry is often a foundational aspect of the design. Snapping is a tool/feature you activate in the **3D View** (i.e., it is not a modifier), while **Mirror** is an actual modifier in Blender.

Manual retopology with the Poly Build tool

Manual retopology is about placing polygons where they matter the most so that your model can move and bend naturally later on. Here is a quick but comprehensive walk-through that blends the "how" with the "why" of the manual retopology approach:

1. With your high-poly model selected, switch to **Edit Mode** (by pressing *Tab*), and select the **Poly Build** tool from the toolbar on the left side of the **3D Viewport**. This tool lets you *click and drag* right on the model's surface to drop in new vertices and edges.

2. Start where you need the most detail, such as a character's face or places that bend a lot (knees, elbows, etc.). *Click and drag* on the surface of your high-poly model to start creating new vertices and edges. Focus on areas that require the most detail first, such as the facial features of characters.

3. Use the **Poly Build** tool (by pressing *Ctrl + R*) to create edge loops around essential features. Aim for smooth, even loops so the model moves naturally instead of getting weird kinks in important areas. For more information on how to do that, refer back to *Chapter 6* in this part of the book.

By blending these steps together, placing loops where detail really counts, using the tools effectively, and building outward, you will keep your topology nice and clean. Plus, it sets you up for smoother rigging, animation, or whatever else you want to do next.

Advanced snapping and projection

As *Figure 12.12* shows, **advanced snapping** and **projection** (i.e., when Blender takes the newly created geometry and projects it onto the original model surface) ensure that the new topology conforms to the original model like a hand in a glove. You can use features such as **Snap Individual Elements To | Face Project** or **Snap Individual Elements To | Face Nearest**.

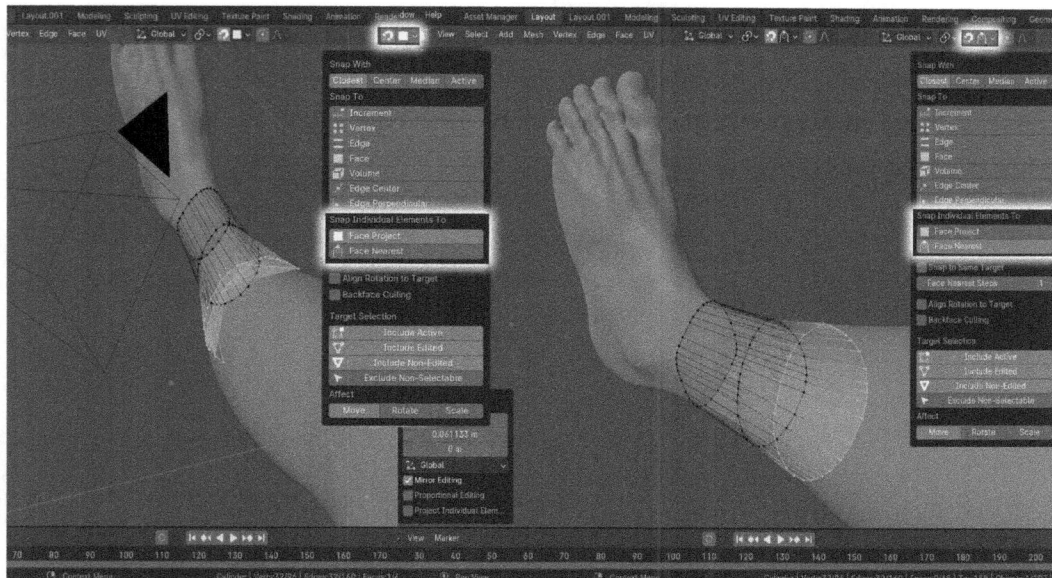

Figure 12.12: Advanced snapping (left) and projection (right) and their role in topology

These tools let you accurately place vertices and edges to make sure that the retopologized mesh keeps the form and detail of the original even though you are optimizing it for performance.

> **Tip**
>
> Manipulating vertices and edges is part and parcel of the retopology process. Extrusion, merging, and snapping are techniques for efficiently expanding the retopology mesh. They are critical for building the new topology quickly and without error.

Vertex smoothing

Vertex smoothing is a technique used to refine the mesh. It makes your topology evenly distributed and takes away irregularities. Vertex smoothing is particularly useful for evening out sharp edges and irregularities, creating smoother transitions between vertices. This is not always required, but you should consider it if you are preparing the mesh for UV mapping, texturing, and rigging.

Blender 4 and beyond

Blender advancements bring with them new tools for you to enjoy. This includes new tools focusing on the retopology workflow, such as **Retopology Overlay** (*Figure 12.13*).

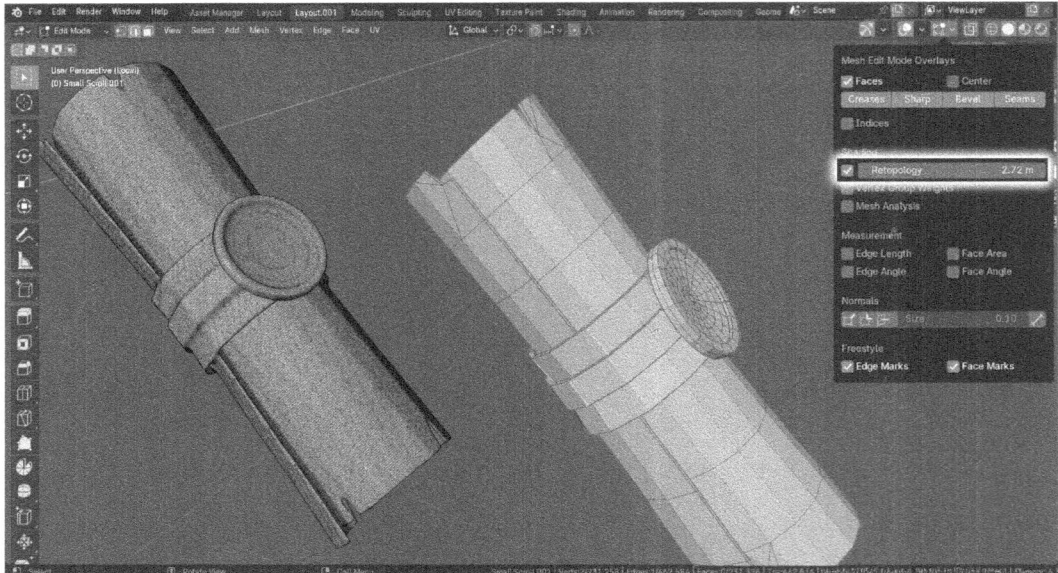

Figure 12.13: Using Retopology Overlay and available options

This new feature improves how visible your retopology mesh is, giving you more confidence as you are working on your model, even if your model includes densely detailed areas. You can adjust the opacity of the overlay to make the new mesh more or less visible against the original model you started with.

Another useful feature is the ability to highlight specific parts of the mesh. This lets you focus on small areas without losing track of the overall structure. Overall, **Retopology Overlay** helps make the retopology process more transparent and manageable.

Alright, we have just tackled the wild world of manual retopology! But neat wires are not the only reason we do this. Next comes the part that every engine and GPU truly cares about: how light the final mesh is on system resources. So, before we dive into sculpting brushes and clay-like fun, let us talk numbers and frame rates.

Retopology and performance: Why it matters

Retopology is not just about clean geometry, it is a fundamental requirement for keeping your scenes responsive and game-ready. In *Figure 12.14*, we duplicated an anvil model 400 times to simulate a typical production environment where objects are reused heavily.

Figure 12.14: High-poly anvils (left) versus their retopologized twins (right)

On the left, the high-poly version of the anvil was used without any optimization. This unreto-pologized model results in over 23 million triangles, consuming 6.25 GB of system memory and 5.3 GB of VRAM, a massive performance hit that would quickly bog down most real-time engines or even Blender's **3D Viewport**.

The right side of the image uses a retopologized low-poly version of the same anvil. With the same number of duplicates (400), the triangle count drops to just 17,616, while memory usage shrinks to 1.57 GB, and VRAM usage drops to 4.7 GB. Visually, the difference is minimal thanks to proper normal baking, but the performance savings are dramatic.

Table 12.1 compares and contrasts performance metrics for the original high-poly anvil against its retopologized counterpart:

Attribute	High Poly (Left)	Retopologized (Right)
Object Count	400	400
Triangle Count	23,249,600	17,616
System Memory	6.25 GB	1.57 GB
VRAM Usage	5.3 GB	4.7 GB

Table 12.1: Comparison table of high poly versus retopologized asset attributes

This example makes it clear: retopology is essential for scalable, performant scenes. Whether you are working in games, animation, or even Blender's **3D Viewport**, optimizing your assets allows you to build richer environments without compromising how fast you model or how stable their structure is.

We have built a solid foundation with our retopology base, got cozy with tools such as **Poly Build** and edge loops, and even flexed some snapping and mirroring magic to keep everything looking symmetrical and slick. These bad boys make sure you are working efficiently while keeping your models neat and optimized like a pro!

Refining your mesh and finalizing your retopology

Before we wrap up this topic, let's quickly look at how to refine your mesh, making sure it is squeaky clean and well structured. Here are some tips on how to do that:

- **Snapping**: Activate the **Snap** tool (by pressing *Shift + Tab*) and set it to **Face** with **Project Individual Elements** on the surface of other objects for precise vertex placement.
- **Mirroring**: Enable the **Mirror** modifier from the **Modifiers** panel for symmetrical models.
- **Adjusting and smoothing vertices**: As you work, regularly adjust vertices for even distribution. Use the **Smooth Vertices** option (by *right-clicking* in **Edit Mode**) to soften any harsh edges or irregularities in your topology.

To complete your retopology, ensuring your mesh is optimized and ready for use, here are some final steps:

1. Ensure your mesh's topology has your edge loops correctly placed around areas of deformation. Do not skip this step if you are animating your models.

2. Then, to ensure the new topology closely conforms to the high-poly model, apply the **Shrinkwrap** modifier from the **Modifiers** panel. Set your high-poly model as the target and adjust the modifier settings for the best fit. The **Shrinkwrap** modifier will dynamically wrap the low-poly mesh around the high-poly target, thereby transferring the detailed surface contours at the same time as maintaining the simplicity of the base mesh.

3. Now, make any final adjustments to your topology by moving vertices and adding or removing edge loops. This is to make sure that your mesh is as clean and efficient as possible.

Even though we are only halfway through this chapter, you have been equipped with an arsenal of techniques, tools, and insights that are fundamental for transforming complex meshes into optimized, animation-ready assets. With a step-by-step walk-through of the retopology process, you used practical tips and notes about adjusting your workflow to learn how to tackle any retopology challenge.

Now, we will go through a brief overview of sculpting in Blender. Although Blender is not specifically designed for 3D sculpting, it offers powerful and free tools to help you along the way.

Introducing Blender sculpting for beginners

Welcome to a brief introduction to sculpting in Blender! Sculpting lets you mold and shape your digital creations in a way that mimics clay sculpting, making the process intuitive and transferable if you have traditional sculpting skills. This chapter will cover the basics to get you started, including navigating Blender's interface, understanding the key sculpting brushes, and the process of remeshing to refine your models.

Getting started with sculpting in Blender

Before you start the creative process of sculpting in Blender, you need to properly prepare your 3D model, and this is a step you should not skip. This preparation phase makes sure that your mesh has the right structure and resolution to support detailed sculpting work:

1. Begin with a simple mesh that closely represents the basic form of your final model. Blender's default cube is a good starting point. However, choosing a shape that is closer to your intended sculpture (e.g., a UV sphere for heads or cylindrical shapes for limbs) can save time in the early sculpting stages.

    Tip

    You can create a combination of primitive shapes first, and then use the Boolean modifier to join the topology. Afterward, you can use **Remesh**, which is explored in detail later toward the end of this chapter, to get consistently dense topology. This would be a great starting point for adding additional detail using Blender's sculpting functions.

2. To make your mesh density higher before sculpting (i.e., to make it look more organic), apply a **Subdivision Surface** modifier. This modifier smooths the model by subdividing its polygons, providing more geometry for detailed sculpting. To apply it, go to the **Modifiers** tab (indicated by the wrench icon) in the **Properties** panel, select **Add Modifier**, and choose **Subdivision Surface**.

    Note

    This method will only give a preview of the **Subdivision Surface** modifier, as in, it will not let you sculpt on it. Instead, it will blur out any smaller detail. To enable **Subdivision** while you are sculpting, simply *right-click* on your mesh while in **Edit Mode** and select **Subdivide**. The modifier will be applied on top of your sculpt in a non-destructive way.

3. For more control over the sculpting process, consider adding a **Multi-Resolution** modifier. This modifier allows you to sculpt at various LODs, letting you make broad changes without affecting finer details or vice versa.

4. After adding the **Multi-Resolution** modifier, click **Subdivide** to increase the resolution. You can switch between different LODs using the **Sculpt** and **Preview** settings within the modifier.

5. When applying the **Subdivision Surface** modifier, you have the option to use the **Catmull-Clark** or **Simple** subdivision type:

    -   The **Simple** option subdivides the mesh without smoothing, retaining the original form while increasing the polygon count. This option is useful when you need more geometry for sculpting but want to maintain the mesh's basic shape. I imagine using this option for adding fine details to a mechanical object, where preserving the precise, hard edges and flat surfaces is needed.

    -   The **Catmull-Clark** option smooths the mesh by averaging the vertices. It is particularly beneficial when you aim to create high-quality, smooth models with rounded features and a more organic appearance. You want to use this option if you are modeling complex organic shapes, such as characters, animals, or smooth, flowing design details, where you want to keep smooth transitions and surfaces.

    To select either option, go to the **Subdivision Surface** modifier settings and choose **Simple** or **Catmull-Clark** from the **Subdivision Type** drop-down menu.

6. Finally, before starting your sculpt, consider using the **Remesh** tool if your base mesh has uneven or stretched topology. Remeshing creates a new, uniform topology that makes sculpting easier. Access the **Remesh** tool in **Sculpt Mode** under the **Remesh** options.

Trying out different sculpting brushes

Whether you are a complete beginner or have some experience in 3D modeling, knowing what sculpting brushes are available in Blender and how to use them is something you must know. Think of sculpting brushes as your digital sculpting tools, each made for different tasks. Here, we will explore the most useful sculpting brushes Blender has to offer. We will look into their options, including **Fall Off** in 3D sculpting.

The sculpting workspace in Blender is optimized for sculpting tasks, with tools and settings arranged for easy access, as shown in *Figure 12.15*.

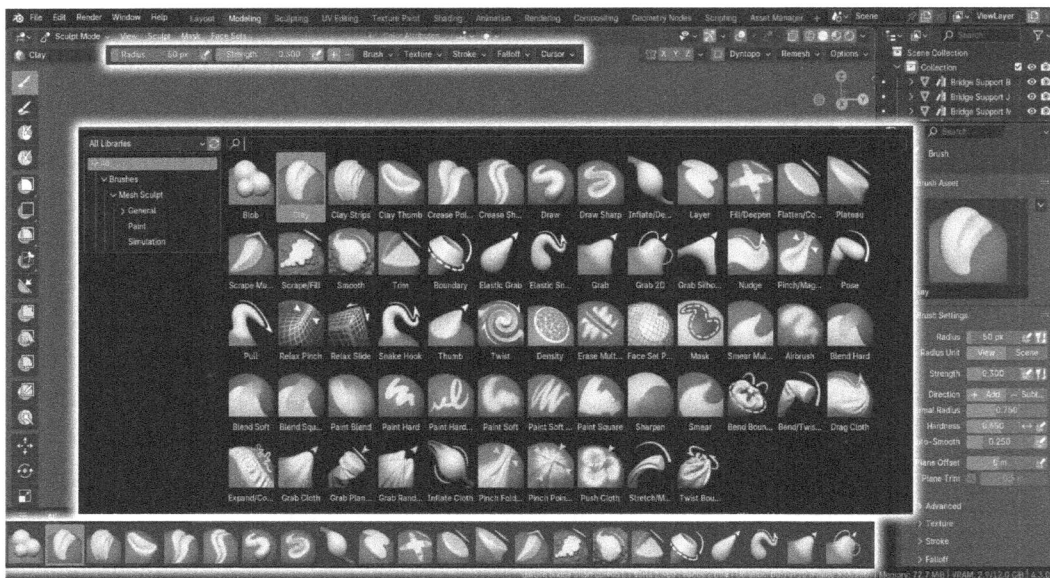

Figure 12.15: Understanding the sculpting workspace

On the bottom, you will find the **Toolbar**, which houses various sculpting brushes and tools. The top and right panels provide quick access to brush settings, symmetry options, and **3D Viewport** navigation controls (you can also use the *Shift* + spacebar shortcut to bring this menu up).

Note

In Blender 4.x, the spacebar triggers timeline playback only if the spacebar default **Play** action is still assigned. If you have remapped spacebar to **Search** (a legacy key-map common before version 3.0), the playback shortcut changes as well, so either keep the default layout or remap both keys together to avoid confusion.

With your model prepared and your workspace set up, you are ready to dive into the fun part: trying out different sculpting brushes and exploring the techniques they offer.

Exploring essential sculpting brushes

Now, let me introduce you to the most essential sculpting brushes that you will use frequently. In Blender's **Sculpt Mode**, there are several basic brushes:

- **Draw** (shortcut: *V*): This is your fundamental sculpting tool, letting you add material to your model. Think of it as your chisel, perfect for building up forms, adding details, or refining your model's surface.

  For example, you can use this brush while creating muscle definition on a character model, emphasizing the bicep and tricep areas.

- **Smooth** (shortcut: *Shift* while using any brush): You can use this to smooth out rough areas, eliminate bumps, and blend brush strokes seamlessly. It is an essential brush for refining shapes and softening transitions between details.

  For example, you can use this brush for smoothing the transitions between facial features in a portrait sculpt.

- **Clay Strips** (shortcut: *C*): This brush lets you add strips of virtual clay to your model's surface. It is excellent for building volume, defining shapes, and creating intricate details.

  For example, you can use this brush to sculpt the folds of a draped cloth on a statue, layering clay strips to mimic how fabric moves depending on its volume.

- **Grab** (shortcut: *G*): This brush is like physically grabbing and moving clay, allowing you to click and drag parts of your mesh. It is ideal for making large-scale changes to your model's form and repositioning elements.

  For example, you can use this brush to adjust the overall silhouette of a fantasy creature, repositioning limbs and the head to create a dynamic pose.

- **Crease** (shortcut: *Shift* + *C*): The **Crease** brush is used to create sharp folds or creases. This brush is especially useful for adding definition and sharp details to your model.

  For example, you could use this brush to add wrinkles to an elderly character's face.

- **Snake Hook** (shortcut: *K*): This is similar to the **Grab** brush, but it lets you make more extreme deformations. It is perfect for pulling out elongated shapes, such as horns or limbs.

  You could use the **Snake Hook** brush to create exaggerated features such as long, twisted horns on a mythological creature, utilizing **Dyntopo** to ensure detailed topology during the process.

Note

The **Snake Hook** brush is particularly useful if you use it with **Dyntopo** (i.e., **Dynamic Topology**). This is because this will generate topology while dragging it out. To enable it, simply tick the relevant box next to the **Dyntopo** bar at the top right of your **3D Viewport**.

- **Inflate** (shortcut: *I*): The **Inflate** brush is used to expand the volume of your mesh, making it appear as if it's being inflated. This brush is great for adding bulk to certain areas of your model.

You could use the **Inflate** brush to correct collapsed areas on a character's arm by inflating the mesh, restoring the intended muscular volume.

Tip

Blender's **Inflate** brush is also great for fixing issues. If you use a brush that is too large, you sometimes end up affecting the topology under the mesh, causing it to collapse toward the area where the brush was used. This creates a hole on the opposite side. You can use the **Inflate** brush to fix it by pushing that topology back out.

- **Flatten** (shortcut: *T*): The **Flatten** brush is used to compress high areas and fill in low areas, effectively flattening the surface of the mesh. It is useful for creating flat surfaces and sharp edges.

For example, while sculpting armor plates on a warrior model, you could use the **Flatten** brush to achieve clean, hard surfaces and sharp edges.

Note

Remember, you can quickly switch between brushes by pressing the assigned shortcut key while in **Sculpt Mode**. Also, Blender is highly customizable, meaning that these shortcuts can be changed in your Blender preferences if needed.

Using sculpting brushes

To effectively use sculpting brushes in Blender, you also need to know about all the available settings:

- To use a brush, select it from the brush menu, typically located in the **Toolbar** or the **Brushes** panel. Then, *left-click* and drag on your 3D model to apply the brush strokes. Adjust the brush size using the radius slider for fine details or broader strokes.

- The **Strength** slider determines the intensity of the brush's effect on the mesh. A higher **Strength** value results in more pronounced changes, while a lower value provides subtler alterations.

- Understanding the concept of **Fall Off** is crucial. Alright, so imagine you are sculpting in Blender and you want your brush strokes to either be super smooth and soft or really sharp and defined. That is where **Fall Off** comes in. It is basically how your brush strength fades out from the center to the edges. For example, a sharp **Fall Off** (*Figure 12.16*, right) will create a distinct edge, while a smooth **Fall Off** will produce a gradual transition (*Figure 12.16*, left).

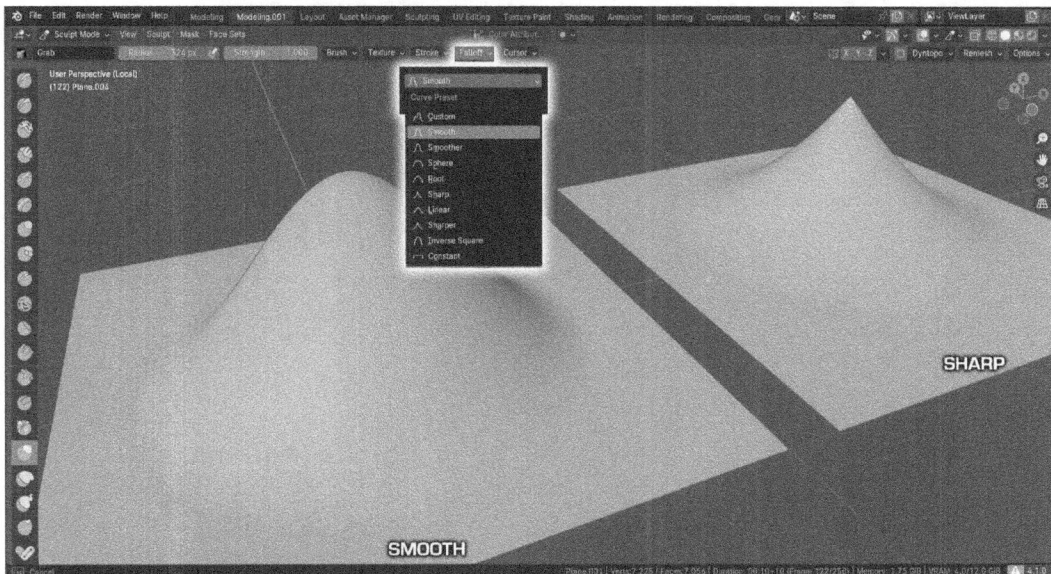

Figure 12.16: Smooth (left) versus sharp (right) Fall Off

- For models that require symmetry, Blender offers a **Symmetry** option. Activating **Symmetry** makes sure that your brush strokes are mirrored across a chosen axis, making all changes to your model uniform on both sides.

The importance of symmetry

When you are working on 3D models that require perfect symmetry, such as characters or creatures, making sure everything is uniform can be a challenge. I have good news, though! Blender's sculpting tools offer a convenient solution through the **Symmetry** option.

Imagine you are sculpting a character's face and you want both sides to be perfectly symmetrical. Activating **Symmetry** in Blender makes sure that any brush stroke you make on one side of the model is mirrored precisely on the other side.

To make the most of **Symmetry** in Blender's sculpting mode, first, you need to activate **Symmetry**. Head to the **Sculpting** settings panel, which is typically located on the right side of the Blender interface. There, you will find the **Symmetry** options. Once you are in the right place, enabling **Symmetry** is just a click away (*Figure 12.17*).

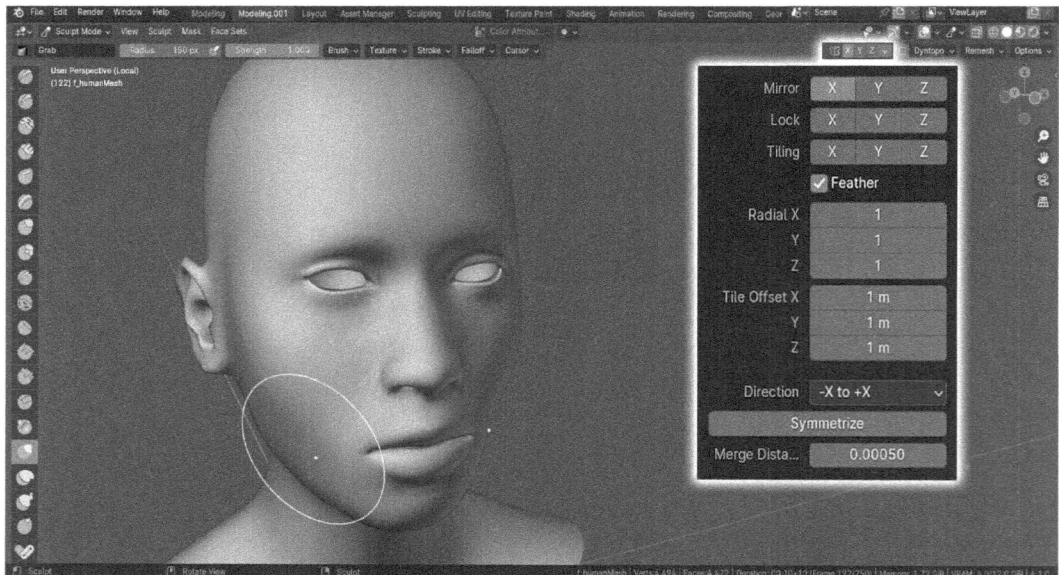

Figure 12.17: Sculpting settings and Symmetry options

What is interesting about this **Symmetry** bar in Blender's **Sculpting** mode, unlike **Edit Mode**, is that you can open additional settings to help with your sculpting workflow:

- **Mirror** will give you the usual **Mirror Along Axis** option.

- **Lock** will stop you from affecting the mesh along a specific axis of the mesh.

- **Tiling**, combined with the **Tile Offset** option, will let you make seamless patterns as your brush gets used multiple times along the specified axis.

- **Feather** will use less strength on a brush as it gets closer to the center point of symmetry.

- The **Symmetrize** operation will allow you to do a quick mirror operation on a model, to control this function. To do that, use the **Direction** bar (allows you to control the way the mirror gets applied +X to -X of an axis) and **Merge Distance**, letting you control how close to the center of symmetry the vertices start to merge.

Next, choose the appropriate axis for your symmetry. Blender allows you to select the axis across which you want the symmetry to occur. For example, if you are sculpting a character's face, you might want to choose the x axis to ensure symmetry from left to right. This helps maintain a balanced and even look on both sides of your model.

With **Symmetry** activated, any changes you make with your sculpting brushes will be mirrored along the chosen axis. This allows you to focus on one side of the model, knowing that the other side will automatically stay symmetrical.

Remeshing your model

As you dive into sculpting, you will notice that your model's geometry can become stretched, uneven, or messy in some areas. This is a common challenge in sculpting, and you can easily resolve these issues using Blender's **Remesh** tool.

> Note
>
> You might think, "*Wait, didn't we already talk about 'fixing' the mesh?*" Retopology and remeshing might sound the same, but they are actually a bit different. Retopology is usually about manually (or semi-manually) rebuilding your mesh so that it has clean edge flows for animation or deformation. You are focusing on placing loops exactly where you need them. On the other hand, remeshing is more of an automated process that works quickly and easily but might not always be perfect. Blender takes your sculpt and redistributes polygons for you, keeping everything uniform. Both methods can fix messy geometry, but retopology gives you ultimate control over your mesh flow. Remeshing and retopology complement each other, but they are not the same tool for the same job.

Remeshing recalculates the mesh topology of your model, making your polygons more uniformly distributed.

Here's how to use the **Remesh** tool in Blender:

1. Make sure you're in **Sculpt Mode** in Blender, where you perform your sculpting.

2. In the **Sculpt Mode** settings, you will find the **Remesh** tool. It typically appears as an option in the top panel, and you can adjust its settings from there.

3. The key decision when remeshing is selecting the detail size. This parameter determines the size of the newly created polygons. A smaller detail size preserves finer-sculpted details but results in more polygons, potentially making your model heavier. A larger detail size simplifies the mesh but may sacrifice some finer details.

4. Once you have selected your desired detail size, click the **Remesh** button to recalculate the mesh topology. You will notice that the mesh becomes more even and better suited for further sculpting.

Tip

By periodically remeshing your model, you can maintain a balanced polygon distribution. This will make sure that your sculpted details are preserved while keeping your mesh manageable and easy to work with.

Dynamic Topology (Dyntopo)

Dyntopo, or **Dynamic Topology**, offers dynamic geometry adjustments as you sculpt. This makes it especially useful for detailed sculpting work where new geometry is needed on the fly. **Dyntopo** can be found in Blender's **Sculpt Mode** settings. Activate it to enable **Dynamic Topology** sculpting.

An important thing to remember is that **Dyntopo** allows you to control the LOD by adjusting the **Detail Size** parameter, like in remeshing. A smaller detail size adds more geometry where you are sculpting, but a larger size simplifies it.

As you sculpt, **Dyntopo** dynamically adds or removes geometry based on your brush strokes and the chosen detail size. This guarantees that you always have the right LOD where you need it most.

Dyntopo is invaluable when you want to focus on intricate sculpting without worrying about manually adjusting the mesh topology. With all power comes a responsibility, so I am here to give some of that as well. When you are sculpting, you do not normally need to worry about topology. Therefore, use **Dyntopo** with caution. My first reason for this is that it is costly to use; with every brush stroke, it updates the area with a new topology. If you have a dense topology, this might not be a viable option.

> Tip
>
> **Dyntopo** works based on s0creen space. In a few words, the closer you zoom into the mesh, the higher the topology you will get out of **Dyntopo**. Mix this up with **Detail Size** and you will have good control over the mesh density.

So, at this point, you have a good handle on **Symmetry**, remeshing, and **Dyntopo**, each one tackling different sculpting challenges in its own way. Need both sides of your model to stay perfectly even? Flip on **Symmetry**. Noticing your mesh getting stretched or messy? A quick remesh will smooth things out. Want more flexibility to add detail as you go? **Dyntopo** has your back. The cool thing is, you do not have to stick to just one, mix and match them depending on what you are working on. Play around, find what works best for you, and keep sculpting!

Summary

This chapter was a quick but comprehensive guide to retopology and sculpting in Blender. In the first half of the chapter, you took a crash course on the principles of retopology. Our focus was on preserving the detail and character of the original model and optimizing it. We explored techniques such as manual retopology with the **Poly Build** tool, creating edge loops, and snapping and mirroring. This also included a brief discussion of automated retopology tools such as **Voxel** and **Quadriflow Remesh**. Although Blender is free and open source, it is updated regularly. Updates include new tools such as **Retopology Overlay**, which we discussed.

In its second half, we introduced you to sculpting in Blender. We began with preparing 3D models for sculpting. We talked about using the **Subdivision Surface** and **Multi-Resolution** modifiers for mesh density management. You explored Blender's essential sculpting brushes, such as the **Draw**, **Smooth**, **Clay Strips**, and **Grab** brushes. As the chapter came to a close, you saw an overview of the **Symmetry** tool, and we introduced **Dyntopo** for dynamic topology adjustments.

Overall, this chapter offered a deep dive into the retopology and sculpting processes in Blender. Across a single, jam-packed chapter, with hands-on demos, clear steps, and plenty of pro tips, you have wrangled the trickier bits of retopology and digital sculpting.

As we move on, in the next chapter, we will look at the process of shading and materials. You will become familiar with key areas such as the **Material Properties** panel, the **Shader Editor**, and **3D Viewport**, and you will find out about their role in creating materials.

Further reading

- If you are looking to optimize your sculpting workflow in Blender, understanding how the sculpting workspace is designed for ease of use is essential. *Blender 4: The Modular and Kitbash Environment Guide* (`https://www.udemy.com/course/blender-4-the-modular-and-kitbash-environment-guide/?referralCode=D17399836E8352DFBBD2`) shows why the sculpting workspace offers organized access to key tools, such as remeshing algorithms.

- For a more detailed look into remeshing techniques and how they can enhance your sculpting projects, *Blender 4: The Modular and Kitbash Environment Guide* (`https://www.udemy.com/course/blender-4-the-modular-and-kitbash-environment-guide/?referralCode=D17399836E8352DFBBD2`) is an invaluable resource here also.

Subscribe to Game Dev Assembly!

We are excited to introduce **Game Dev Assembly**, our brand-new newsletter dedicated to everything game development. Whether you're coding, designing, animating, or managing a studio, we've got insights, trends, and expert advice to help you create, innovate, and thrive. Sign up now and get exciting benefits.

`https://packt.link/gamedev-newsletter`

Join the 3D Tudor Channel Discord Server!

Join the 3D Tudor Channel Discord Server, a creative hub for learning Blender, Unreal Engine, Substance Painter, and 3D modeling, for discussions with the authors and other readers:

`https://discord.gg/5EkjT36vUj`

13

Introducing Shaders in Blender

Throughout this book, you have navigated many parts of the Blender multiverse. Now, it is time to look at shaders. **Shaders** are like your set of paints and tools that help you add colors, textures, and effects to your 3D models. They tell the computer how to draw the surface of your 3D model by defining its color, how shiny or dull it should be, and how it interacts with light. The paint and technique you use can make your model look wet, metallic, or even translucent. In the same way, shaders help you achieve these effects on your 3D models, making them look as realistic or stylized as you want.

Blender has a specialized interface optimized for shading tasks, and we will go through it in this comprehensive guide. Some key areas include the **Material Properties** panel, the Shader Editor, and the 3D Viewport. You will find out how to access and use different shading tools through project examples and visualizations. You will learn about the process of adding materials to objects, and about how different render views, such as **Material Preview**, **Eevee**, and **Cycles**, can dramatically change what your 3D models look like.

You will also explore the roles of materials and material slots and discover the versatility of the **Principled BSDF** shader. This is the main tool used to define and adjust the appearance of these materials. We will focus on the importance of shader properties because of their role in defining how your models look.

The chapter begins by setting the stage for more advanced topics, such as nodes and node-based workflows. As you go along, you will learn how to create and tweak complex materials, which will help you get a solid grasp of these advanced techniques.

So, in this chapter, we will cover the following topics:

- Understanding Blender's interface for shading
- Adding materials to objects and understanding different render views
- Mastering nodes and node-based workflows in Blender
- Creating your first material and shader in Blender
- Exploring advanced material properties in Blender
- Creating PBR materials
- Using Blender's Node Wrangler for efficient workflow
- Understanding Ambient Occlusion
- Introducing Blender's shader nodes
- Understanding and using displacement in Blender shaders
- Familiarizing yourself with shader baking in Blender

Technical requirements

As for **Blender 4.5 LTS (Long-Term Support)**, the general requirements include a macOS 11.2 or newer (Apple Silicon supported natively) operating system, or a Linux (64-bit, glibc 2.28 or newer) operating system. Blender now requires a CPU with the SSE4.2 instruction set, at least 8 GB of RAM (32 GB recommended for heavy scenes), and a GPU supporting OpenGL 4.3 with a minimum of 2 GB of VRAM.

For a full list of technical requirements, please refer back to *Chapter 1* of this part.

Understanding Blender's interface for shading

Before you start exploring the world of shading in Blender, you need to pinpoint the specific areas of Blender's interface that you will be using. Blender's interface is thoughtfully organized into various panels and workspaces, each specialized for different aspects of 3D modeling and rendering. For shading, you will be focusing on the **Material Properties** panel, the Shader Editor, and the 3D Viewport.

First up, the **Material Properties** panel, which is represented by an icon resembling a red ball on the right-hand side of the Blender interface (*Figure 13.1*). This panel is crucial for shading as it displays all the materials assigned to your selected object. In this panel, you can add new materials or edit existing ones. It serves as the starting point for defining the appearance and feel of your entire scene, based on each individual object it is made up of.

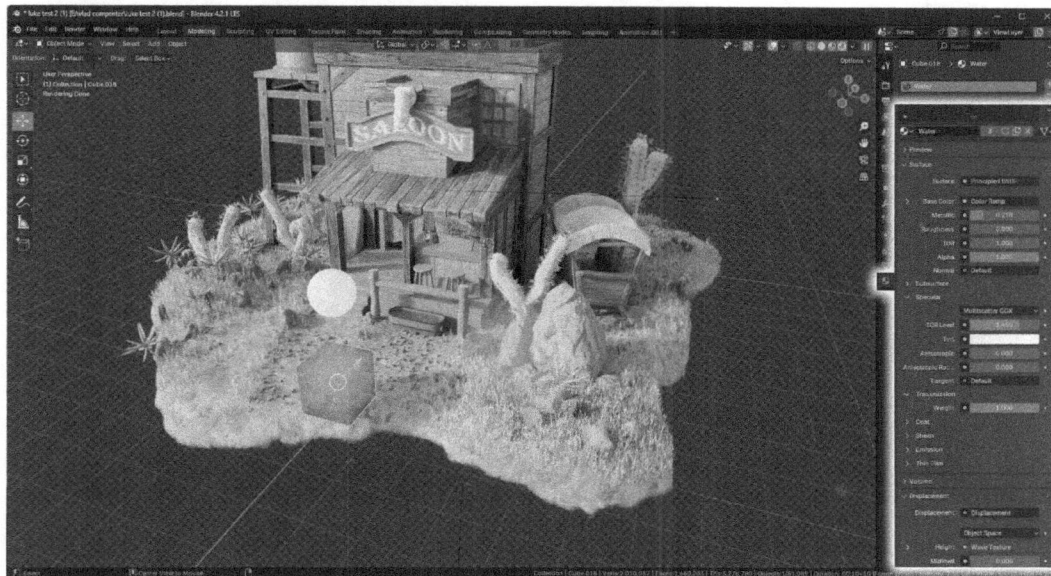

Figure 13.1: Blender's Material Properties panel in Substance Painter Beginner's Guide to Game Texturing by 3D Tudor

Imagine you are a chef in a kitchen, and you keep all your spices and ingredients in a single cupboard. Each dish you prepare needs a specific set of these ingredients. In Blender, the **Material Properties** panel is like that cupboard. It is where you select and adjust all the ingredients for your 3D model's appearance, such as color, shininess, and texture.

Blender's **Shader Editor** comes next. It is the heart of material creation in Blender. The Shader Editor is a node-based system, which might look complex at first, but it offers you detailed control over the materials. It is a more advanced and detailed space where you can visually connect and adjust different nodes (such as sliders and knobs) to create complex materials and textures for your 3D models.

Within the Shader Editor, you will connect different nodes (i.e., small boxes representing various material properties, as shown in *Figure 13.2*) to create complex materials. Each node affects the material's properties, and how they are connected can drastically change how your model looks.

Figure 13.2: Example node structure in the Shader Editor in "Master Blender 3D with Wild West Environments" by 3D Tudor

Note

You can find the Shader Editor by changing your workspace to **Shading** at the top of the Blender window.

Last but not least comes the **3D Viewport**. It is the large central area of the Blender interface, where you can see your 3D scene from various angles. You can watch your models, see how the lighting affects them, and preview how changes in materials and textures made in the Shader Editor or the **Material Properties** panel will look in real time, as shown in *Figure 13.3*.

Figure 13.3: Blender's 3D Viewport in action in Substance Painter Beginner's Guide to Game Texturing by 3D Tudor

Tip

For shading purposes, you will want to set this to the **Material Preview** mode. This mode, which can be activated by clicking on the sphere icon located toward the top right of the 3D Viewport (shown in *Figure 13.4*), allows you to see the effects of your shading changes in real time. The **Material Preview** mode will help you understand how your materials interact with the lighting and objects in your scene.

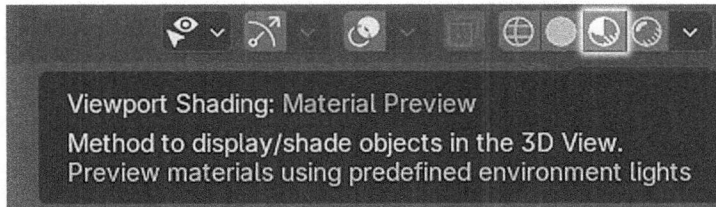

Figure 13.4: Material Preview mode options

In this section, we covered Blender's interface for shading, including the **Material Properties** panel, the Shader Editor, and the 3D Viewport. These tools help you manage materials, create complex textures, and preview your scene in real time.

Your first material: making raw bronze in seconds

When you create a new material in Blender, you will notice something waiting for you in the Shader Editor: a **Principled BSDF** shader. This is Blender's all-in-one material node, and it is powerful enough to handle everything from skin to plastic to metal, with just a few tweaks.

Let us start by turning this default material into something that already looks great: raw bronze.

Step 1: Base Color

Base Color is the starting tint of your material. Click on the **Color** box and shift it toward a yellowish-bronze tone. You can go with something like a muted golden brown, or simply drag the hue slider toward yellow and slightly desaturate it. Do not worry about getting it perfect, it is meant to look raw and a bit imperfect.

Step 2: Metallic

Next, find the **Metallic** slider and crank it all the way to **1**. This tells Blender that your material is fully metallic, not a painted surface or plastic.

You will immediately see the shader come alive, reflecting light more like real metal.

Step 3: Roughness

Now drag the **Roughness** slider down, but not too far. Something around **0.25** is a great start. This controls how smooth or scratched up the metal looks. A lower value means shinier reflections. Higher values make it more matte.

For raw bronze, we want a slightly polished look, so you still get nice highlights without it looking like chrome.

And just like that, in *Figure 13.5*, you have a believable, stylized bronze surface, all with three tiny tweaks.

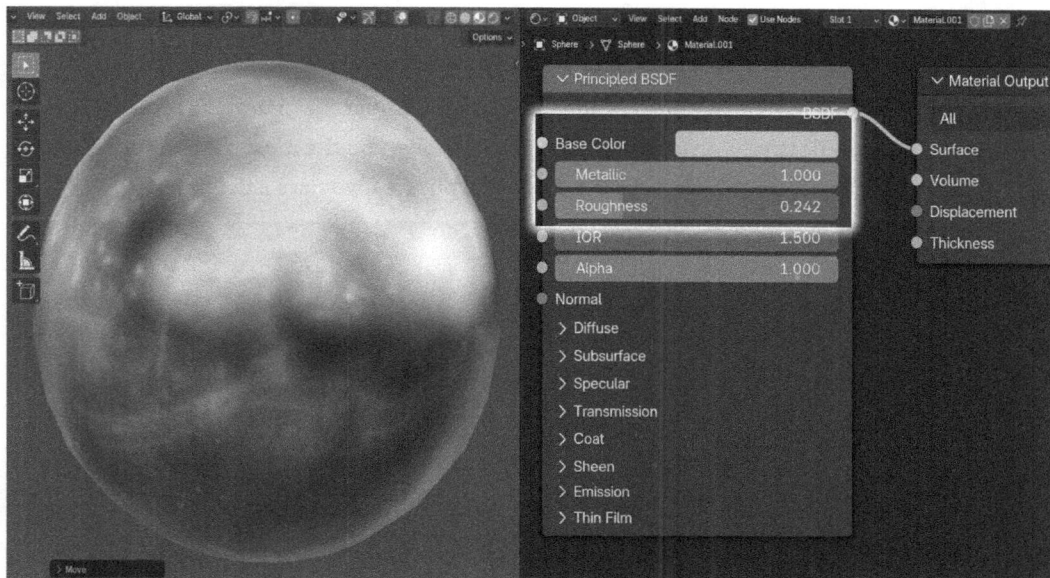

Figure 13.5: Guided walkthrough of making a stylized bronze material work

This is the power of **Principled BSDF**: it is like a Swiss army knife for materials. Once you understand how to guide it, you can build almost anything, from dirty wood to sci-fi glass. But starting with a simple bronze is a great way to build confidence. Next, we will explore adding materials to objects and understanding different render views, such as **Material Preview**, **Eevee**, and **Cycles**.

Adding materials to objects and understanding different render views

In Blender, adding materials is what takes your 3D models from bland to something special. Understanding the different render views, such as **Material Preview**, **Eevee**, and **Cycles**, is also important since they each offer different ways to visualize what you have made. We will now explore how to add materials to objects and the differences between these views.

Adding decal materials to objects

To add a material to an object in Blender, follow these steps:

1. Click on the object to which you want to add a material.

2. Open the **Material Properties** panel (identified by a red ball icon on the right-hand side of the Blender interface).

3. Click on the **New** button in the **Material Properties** panel. This will create a new material slot and assign a default material to your selected object.

4. Use the settings in the **Material Properties** panel to adjust the material's properties, such as its color, reflectivity, and texture. *Figure 13.6* shows you the most basic setup of a decal plane with just a few nodes, which is easy to replicate if you are a beginner.

Figure 13.6: Blender's Shader Editor options

5. To access more advanced features, open the Shader Editor, where you can use nodes to create complex materials, as shown in *Figure 13.6*.

Understanding different render views

Blender offers several ways to preview and render your scene, each with its advantages. In *Part 7, Rendering and Lighting Optimization in Blender*, we will discuss all of Blender's rendering engines, their options, and how to optimize them in full detail. For now, we are focusing on the role of rendering engines in shading.

First of all, let us talk about the **Material Preview** mode. This mode, accessible in the 3D Viewport, gives you a quick way to see what materials you applied to objects without fully rendering the scene. Blender's **Material Preview** mode is useful for fast, approximate previews of how your materials look under generic lighting conditions. For example, back in *Figure 13.6*, you can see a black and white image set up as an alpha texture (i.e., one of the **Shader** inputs that we will look into later) that was used to create a decal.

For simplicity, it can still work with a call-out that explains the black and white image works like a mask or stencil, and the alpha channel uses white to gray values to tell the shader what to show/render, and black to tell the shader what to mask/hide/make transparent.

> Tip
>
> Use the **Material Preview** mode when you need a fast check on how your materials look. It is also less demanding on your computer's resources.

Now, we should talk about the quickest rendering engine. Eevee is Blender's real-time render engine. It is designed to provide a high-quality preview of your scene in real time, making it great for fast rendering and animation previews. Eevee is less computationally intensive than Cycles, but does not calculate light and shadow as accurately as Cycles.

> Tip
>
> Choose **Eevee** when you need a balance between speed and quality. It is ideal for animation previews or when working on less complex scenes.

Last but not least, Cycles is Blender's physically-based, ray-tracing render engine. It calculates light and shadows more accurately, producing more realistic results, especially for scenes with complex lighting. However, Cycles is tougher on your computer and can take longer to render a scene.

> Tip
>
> Use **Cycles** for your final renders or when working on scenes where realism and lighting accuracy are crucial. Keep in mind that rendering with Cycles can be time-consuming, especially for high-resolution images or complex scenes.

Adding materials in Blender is a straightforward process that can dramatically change the appearance of your 3D models. By understanding the different render views Blender offers, you can choose the most appropriate one for your project's needs, whether it is a quick material preview, a real-time render, or a high-quality final image. Next, we will look at the basics of creating and changing materials to change how objects appear in your 3D scene.

Basic concepts of material shading

Shading in Blender is a fascinating process that involves creating and adjusting materials to define how objects appear in your 3D scene. To get a deeper understanding, we need to expand on some of the fundamental concepts, starting with materials and material slots.

In Blender, **materials** are what give your 3D objects color, texture, and reflectivity. Materials are assigned to objects through **material slots** (*Figure 13.7*).

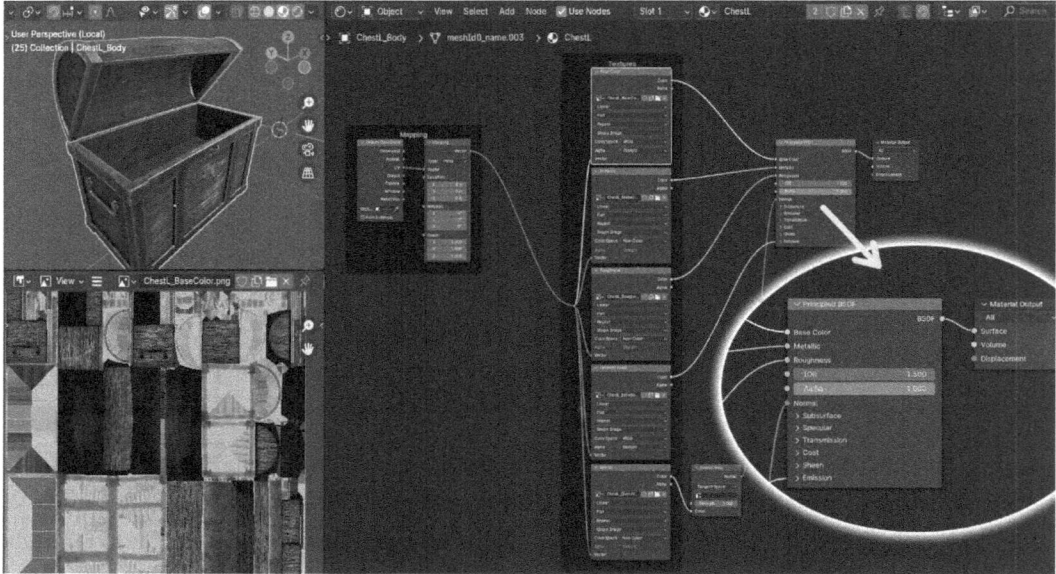

Figure 13.7: Material assignment in Blender 4 using a wooden chest example

Think of each slot as a container that holds a specific material. A single object can have multiple material slots. This means that different parts of the object can have different materials. For example, a car model could have separate materials for the body, windows, and tires, each in its own slot.

The next fundamental concept you need to know about is the **Principled BSDF** shader. This is the go-to shader in Blender, and you will be using it for most material creation tasks. The **Principled BSDF** shader combines multiple shader properties into one node, making it easier to create realistic materials. It is a great starting point for beginners and a powerful tool for advanced users. It will save you time because you can make quick changes to how things look, such as making them shiny, see-through, or metallic, all in one place. Instead of having to mess around with lots of different settings and mix them to get what you want, you can do most of it with just one tool. This is handy when you are in a hurry or trying to figure out the best look for something.

You should also know about **Shader Properties**. These properties are what you adjust to change how your materials look. Some of the key properties under **Shader Properties** are the following:

- **Base Color**: This defines the primary color of your material. It is the most straightforward way to change how a material looks. This is as simple as changing a red cube into a blue one.

- **Metallic**: This gives your material a metallic sheen. Increasing this value makes the material look more like metal, affecting how it reflects light. An example project where you would use **Metallic** could be a realistic car model, as in *Figure 13.8*. The body of the car can be given a metallic paint effect, simulating how real car paint looks with a mix of a base color and a metallic sheen.

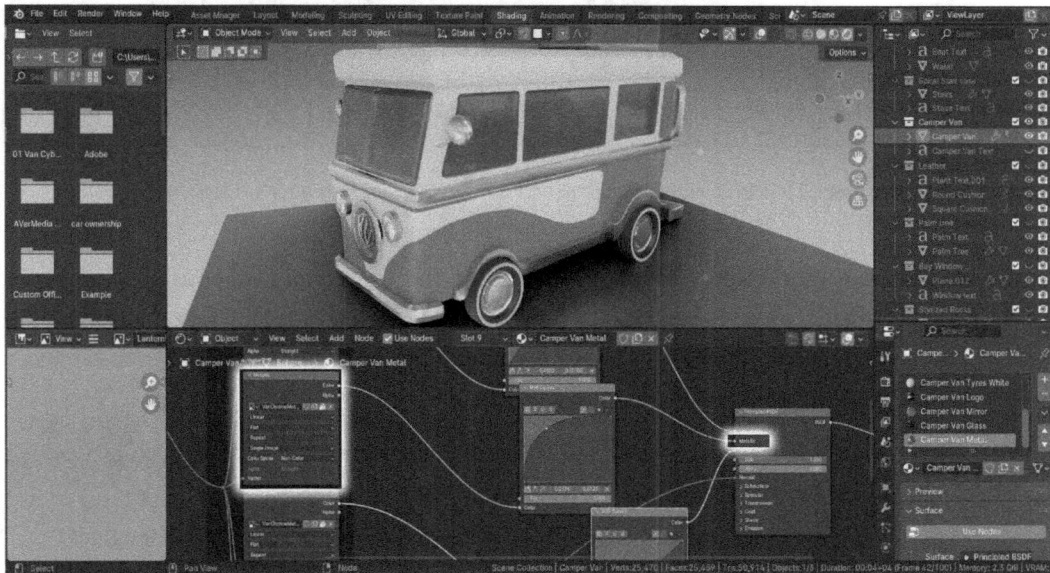

Figure 13.8: Car model using a Metallic material in Blender Beginner's Bootcamp by 3D Tudor

- **Specular**: This controls the reflectivity of the material. Higher values result in a more reflective surface, which is essential for creating materials such as glass or polished surfaces. For example, you might use this if you are modeling a mirror. The high **Specular** value would help to simulate the light-reflective properties of the mirror's surface, and by using the **Anisotropic** parameter, you will give extra depth to your mirror (*Figure 13.9*).

Figure 13.9: Mirror with a Specular material in Blender Beginner's Bootcamp by 3D Tudor

- **Roughness:** This affects how rough or smooth the material's surface appears. A lower value results in a smoother surface, which reflects light sharply, while a higher value scatters light, giving a more diffused reflection. With wooden floors, **Roughness** plays a crucial role in their appearance:

    - A lower **Roughness** value might be used to simulate a well-polished, shiny wooden floor, such as what you might find on basketball courts
    - A higher **Roughness** value could represent an old, weathered wooden deck

Blender includes many other shaders, each with its unique purpose and set of properties. *Table 13.1* includes some example shaders, their purpose, and example projects for each one:

Shader name	Purpose	Example projects
Emission	Makes your material emit light	Light bulbs, glowing signs
Transparent BSDF	Used to create transparent materials	Glass, water
Diffuse BSDF	Ideal for non-reflective, matte surfaces; scatters light evenly	Materials with a soft appearance
Glossy BSDF	Used for creating shiny, reflective surfaces	Surfaces that require a shiny look
Mix	Blends two different shaders; does not create a material on its own	Complex materials with multiple characteristics

Table 13.1: Shaders, their purpose, and example projects

Remember, these are just a few examples of what Blender has to offer in terms of shaders. Each shader can be used on its own or combined with others to achieve a wide range of effects. For example, you could combine the **Glossy BSDF** and **Diffuse BSDF** shaders using a **Mix** shader to create a material that has both a shiny reflective surface and a soft, matte finish, mimicking the appearance of satin or semi-gloss paint. This **Mix** shader could be used on smartphones or laptops to create realistic materials that mimic the look of metallic bodies with a satin finish. Digging into Blender's shader palette and tweaking each setting is the quickest way to get comfortable with material shading.

In the next section, we will explore Blender's node-based workflow for shading.

Mastering nodes and node-based workflows in Blender

Blender's node-based workflow for shading lets you create and change materials in a creative way. **Nodes** are the building blocks of this system, and each node represents a specific function. When connected, nodes form a network like a tree that defines how your materials look and behave. This part of *Chapter 13* will help you understand what nodes are, their common types, and the basics of working within the Node Editor.

Understanding nodes: a comprehensive snapshot

Blender's node-based workflow for shading lets you create and change materials in a creative way. Nodes are the building blocks of this system (a sort of visual coding, basically), and each node represents a specific function. When connected, nodes form a network, called a **node tree**, that defines how your materials look and behave. This part of *Chapter 13* will help you understand what nodes are, their common types, and the basics of working within the Node Editor.

Each node has a set of inputs on the left and outputs on the right, as shown in *Figure 13.10*. **Inputs** are parameters that the node can receive from other nodes, while **outputs** are the results of the node's function, ready to be passed on to other nodes. For example, an **Image Texture** node has an output that sends the texture information to the next node in the chain.

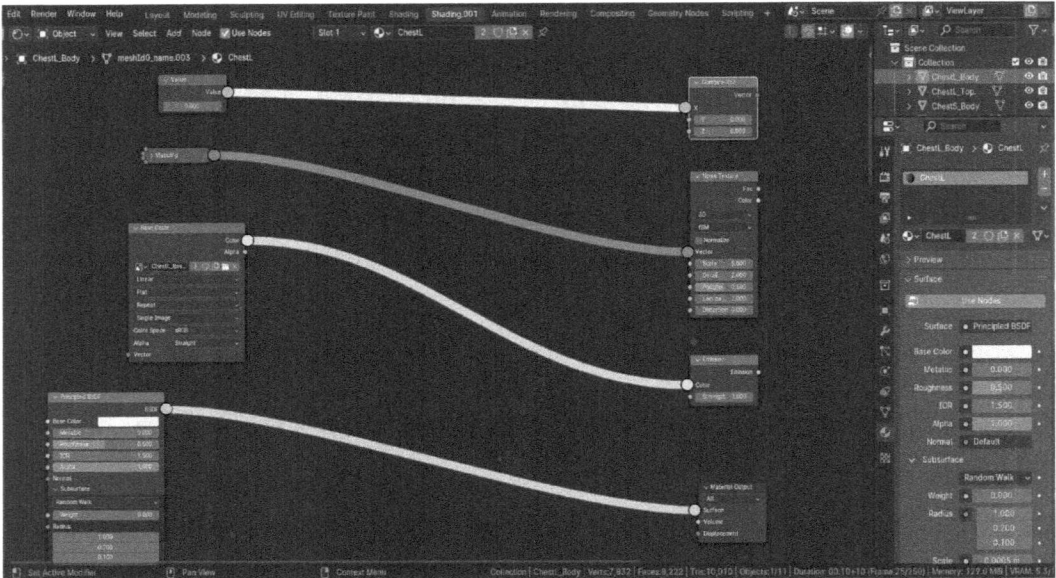

Figure 13.10: Example node settings preview

Note

Depending on the node, you might only have **Input** or just **Output** options to play with.

You can find out more about the color coding of nodes in *Table 13.2*:

Color	Type	Usage
Yellow	Color (RGB)	Typically used for anything related to color, such as textures or base colors.
Gray	Scalar (Value)	Used for controlling scalar properties such as roughness, specular values, and so on.
Green	Shader	Used for connecting shaders within a material. Represents the surface properties of a material.
Purple	Vector	Used for any data consisting of three values, including vector-based tasks such as normals, displacement, transformations, or RGB values. These are often used in normal mapping, UV mapping, or to pass XYZ coordinate data.

Table 13.2: Color coding of nodes in Material Design

To create a material, you connect the output of one node to the input of another. Connect the output of an **Image Texture** node to the **Base Color** input of a **Principled BSDF** node that applies the texture as the material's color. This will map the texture onto your 3D model, giving the surface a detailed and realistic appearance based on what image you used.

Tip

Controls within the middle of a node allow you to adjust specific properties or parameters of that node. These adjustable fields or sliders let you modify the behavior of the node itself. They are internal controls that define how the node processes the data and can often be linked to external inputs.

Common nodes and their uses

Understanding the essential nodes for creating materials is key to your shading workflow. Here are some key nodes you will frequently use:

- **Principled BSDF**: This node is used for creating a wide range of materials. It combines multiple shader properties (i.e., **Base Color**, **Roughness**, and **Alpha**) into one node, simplifying the material creation process. The shader properties included in **Principled BSDF** are shown in *Figure 13.11*.

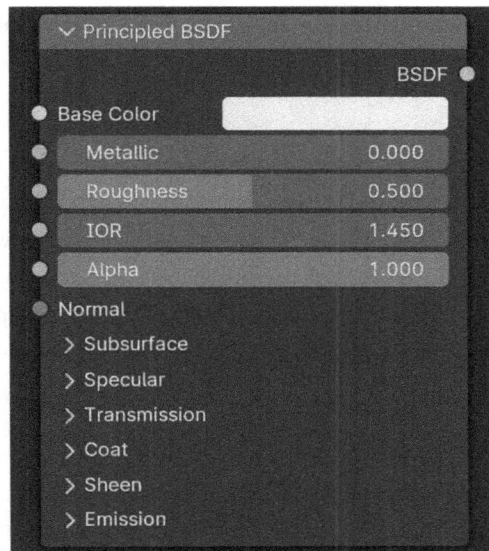

Figure 13.11: Principled BSDF properties in Blender 4

Note

Principled BSDF is a versatile shader suitable for most materials. It is designed to work well in different and varied lighting conditions, making it ideal for any scene.

For example, you can use **Principled BSDF** to create a photorealistic wooden table through **Roughness**, **Specular**, and **Sheen**.

Tip

Combine **Principled BSDF** with an **Image Texture** node that contains a high-quality wood texture. Experiment with the **Roughness** and **Specular** values to achieve a realistic look. Adding a slight bump or normal map can enhance the realism of the wood grain.

- **Image Texture**: This node is used to import texture images into your material. It is crucial for adding realism through images such as diffuse maps, bump maps, or normal maps.

  For example, you could use it to design a vintage leather book cover. You could apply a high-resolution leather texture image to give a book a realistic and aged appearance.

  Tip

  The **Image Texture** node can be connected to the **Base Color** property of **Principled BSDF**. Use a bump map or normal map together with the original texture to simulate the uneven surface of aged leather. Make sure the image texture has enough resolution to avoid pixelation at close views. For example, you might want to choose a 4K (4,096 x 4,096 pixels) image texture over a standard HD (1,280 x 720 pixels) image texture for this reason.

- **Mapping**: This node controls how textures are placed and oriented on your object. It is important for adjusting the scale, rotation, and position of your textures. Experiment with non-uniform scaling to create variations in textures. This is especially useful if you are trying to avoid a tiled look.

Note

Node Wrangler will be covered later, since the **Mapping** and **Texture Co-ordinate** nodes can be generated together with that. Without the **Mapping** node, you might come across problems such as textures appearing stretched or squashed and misaligned textures that do not fit properly on the model's surface.

For example, you could use the node to design custom wallpaper for interior design. You can adjust the scale, rotation, and position of a floral wallpaper texture to fit perfectly on a room's walls.

Tip

Connect the **Mapping** node between the **Image Texture** node and the **Texture Coordinate** node. Use it to tile the texture seamlessly across large areas. Pay attention to the texture's scale to avoid unrealistic repetition patterns.

- **Texture Coordinate**: This node provides different methods of mapping textures onto objects. The **Texture Coordinate** node determines how the texture is wrapped around the 3D model.

For example, you could use this node to animate water for a pool, using generated coordinates to apply a moving water texture that wraps around the pool.

Tip

For dynamic textures such as water, the **Texture Coordinate** node's **Generated** or **Object** output can be keyframed or driven by an animation node to simulate motion. Combine with a **Mapping** node for more control over the texture's movement and orientation.

Node Editor basics and techniques

Learning the basics of the **Node Editor** is super important for creating and managing materials in Blender. Here are the key steps to get you started:

1. To add a node, press *Shift + A* in the Node Editor. This brings up the **Add** menu, where you can search for and select the node you need. For example, searching for `Principled` will bring up the **Principled BSDF** node.

2. To connect nodes, click and drag from an output socket of one node to an input socket of another. A line will appear, showing the connection. This line represents the flow of data between nodes, as shown in *Figure 13.10*.

3. To duplicate a node, select it and press *Shift + D*.

4. To delete a node, select it and press *X* or *Delete* on your keyboard.

Organizing node graphs

As your node tree grows, keeping it organized will be the bread and butter of your workflow:

- Click and drag nodes around, and use *Ctrl + J* to create a frame around your selected nodes. Select the frame by pressing *G*, this will let you move all the nodes within it together.

- You can rename the frame by selecting it and pressing *F2*. To add an item to the frame, simply move it inside the frame's boundaries. To remove an item from the frame, select the item and press *Alt + P*.

- Label nodes and frames to keep your workflow clear.

Organizing shaders

You can also manage nodes with Blender's **Node Wrangler** add-on. We will discuss this in more detail later in this chapter, but it is good to introduce you to it now. It adds shortcuts and features that make working with nodes faster and more intuitive.

For example, with **Node Wrangler** enabled, you can quickly join nodes using different drag shortcuts depending on what you want to achieve:

- *Alt + right mouse button* drag creates a direct connection between two compatible sockets (e.g., **Color → Color**, **Shader → Shader**). Simply drag a line from one node's output to another node's input. If they are compatible, you will see a green line before releasing, and the connection will be made cleanly, ideal for fast, automatic wiring between common node types.

- *Ctrl + Shift + right mouse button* drag goes a step further: it inserts a **Mix** node (such as a **Mix Color** or **Mix** shader) between the two nodes based on context. For example, connecting two textures will create a **MixRGB** node, and connecting a texture to a shader input might create a **Mix** shader. This shortcut is perfect when you want to blend or combine two sources without manually setting up the node structure.

These two drag shortcuts make node creation and editing much faster, streamlining your shader workflow significantly.

As a second example, connecting two textures will create a **Mix Color** node. Using that **Mix Color** node on a **Principled BSDF** shader will create a **Mix** shader. This feature streamlines the process of applying textures, saving significant time and effort.

Before we move on, since we are talking about frames and groups, we should also talk about Blender's **Reroute** node. The **Reroute** node in Blender is simple but powerful because it helps organize complex node setups by allowing you to manage and streamline connections between nodes.

To create a **Reroute** node in Blender, hold *Shift* and drag a dotted line across an existing route link (i.e., the line connecting two nodes). This will create a **Reroute** node at your desired point.

Note

If you hit the slash (/) key (next to the right *Shift* key) with a node selected, you can add a **Reroute** node directly to the output socket(s). It is maybe not as useful as the typical **Reroute** because you have to select the behavior you want from a pop-up menu, but it is an alternative.

You can move the **Reroute** node by selecting it and pressing *G* to adjust its position within your node setup. To keep your node tree organized, you can also straighten multiple **Reroute** nodes at once. Select the nodes you want to align, and then press *S* + *Y* + *0* for vertical straightening or *S* + *X* + *0* for horizontal straightening. This will give you a clean and orderly layout, making your node tree easier to navigate and understand. If you are working on large projects where many nodes are interconnected, a **Reroute** node will help reduce visual clutter and make the node setup easier to navigate and debug.

Tip

You can create multiple outputs from a single **Reroute** node, letting you split and direct the same data to different parts of your node tree efficiently.

Mastering the node-based workflow in Blender will help you form complex materials. With practice, you will find that nodes are incredibly versatile and powerful. Now that you have acquired the basic knowledge behind the process of shading in Blender, I will guide you through creating your first material and shader.

Creating your first material and shader in Blender

This section will guide you through the process of creating your first material and shader in Blender. We will start with a basic object and step-by-step instructions to help you understand each part of the process. You will learn how to use different nodes, connect them to form a shader, and even add some animation to your material. So, let's get started:

1. Start with a basic object in your scene; here, we will use a cube. This will be the object to which you will apply your material.

2. In Blender's interface, switch to the **Shading** tab.

3. With the cube selected, add a new material. You can do that in the **Material Properties** panel.

4. The new material comes with a **Principled BSDF** shader by default. Delete this shader since you will be creating a custom one.

5. Add an **Emission Shader** node. This shader makes your object emit light. To do that, hover over the shader window, press *Shift + A*, and search for Emission. Select **Emission Shader**.

6. Add a **Color Ramp** node to blend colors in a gradient by pressing *Shift + A* and searching for Color Ramp.

7. Add a **Noise Texture** node to create a procedural texture. This means that you will be able to add random, organic variations that can mimic surfaces such as rock, water, or clouds to your material.

8. Link the **Factor** output of the **Noise Texture** node to the **Factor** input of the **Color Ramp** node. This might sound confusing at first, but essentially, this will control how the noise pattern affects the color transition in **Color Ramp**.

9. Connect the **Color** output of **Color Ramp** to the **Color** input of the **Emission** shader.

10. Finally, link the **Emission** output to the **Surface** input of the **Material Output** node, as shown in *Figure 13.12*.

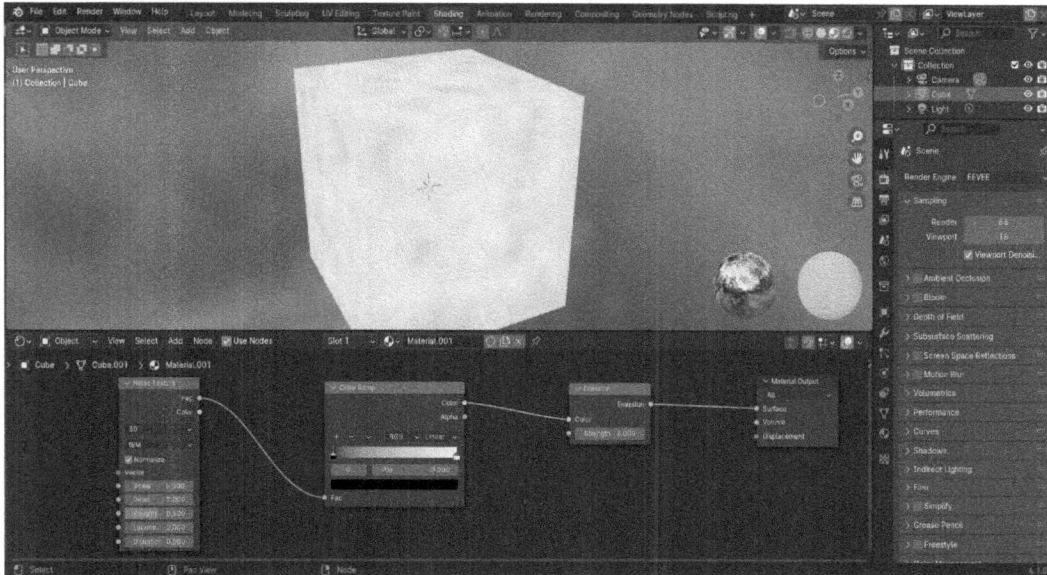

Figure 13.12: Visual representation of connecting the nodes

11. Increase the strength of the **Emission** shader to 3. This will make your material significantly brighter.

12. Select the **Color Ramp** node, click the + icon to add a new stop in the middle of the gradient, select that new stop, and change its color to blue using the parameter below.

13. In the **Noise Texture** node, set **Scale** to 12, **Detail** to 1.5, **Roughness** to 0.7, and **Distortion** to -2. These settings will affect the appearance of the noise pattern on your material.

14. Switch back to the **Layout** tab and go to frame 1 in your timeline.

15. Return to the **Shading** tab, hover your mouse over the **Lacunarity** parameter in the **Noise Texture** node, and press *i* to insert a keyframe. The default is **2**, and once you have inserted this frame, it should now be highlighted in yellow.

16. Switch back to **Layout** and change the frame to 100. Afterward, go back to **Shading**, and change **Lacunarity** to 1.99 and press *I* while hovering over it.

17. Move to a different frame, adjust the **Lacunarity** value slightly, let us say to 1.99, and press *I* again to insert another keyframe. This creates a basic animation for your material.

18. Upscale the cube by 100. To do that, select your cube, press *S*, and set the value to 100.

19. Now, add a camera to the scene and use **Render**, followed by **Render Animation** to see the final result. The material you have created should result in a stylized, animated sky with good ambient lighting, giving it a dynamic and visually appealing look (*Figure 13.13*).

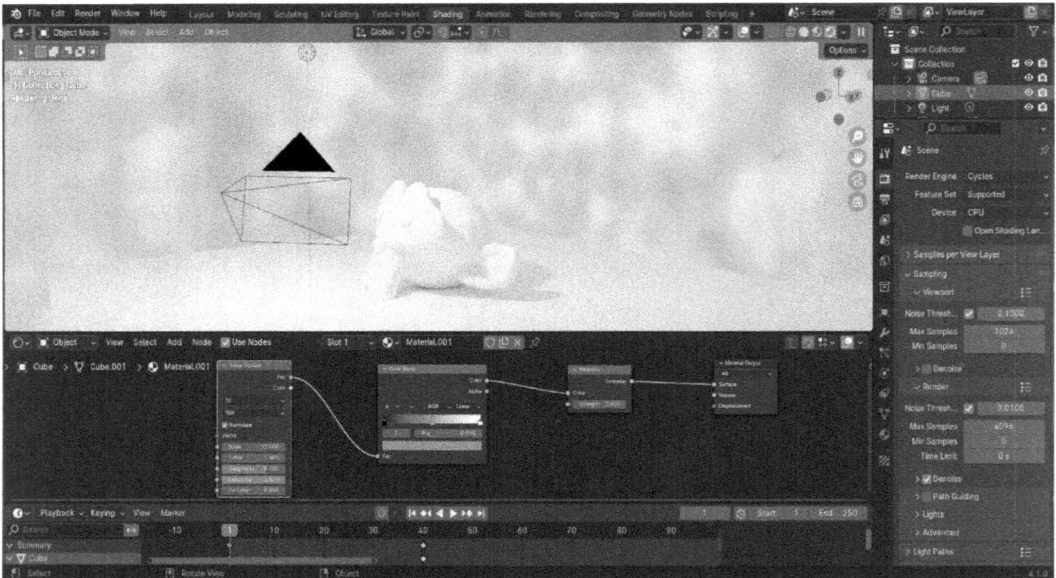

Figure 13.13: Rendering the scene with your first material made from scratch

By following these steps, you have created and animated your first material in Blender. As we move on, we will look at advanced material properties.

Exploring advanced material properties in Blender

Advanced material properties help you to simulate a wide range of physical characteristics. This could be anything from the way light interacts with skin to the reflective qualities of metal. When you are trying to replicate a specific material, use real-world references. Take notes of how light interacts with different materials in the real world and try to replicate those observations in Blender. The most important advanced material properties to know about are **Subsurface Scattering (SSS)**, **Metallic** and **Specular**, and **Specular Reflection**.

Tip

The key to getting better at using these advanced properties is experimentation. Try combining different values and observe how they interact with each other and the 3D environment around them.

Using **Subsurface Scattering (SSS)** can make the skin of your 3D characters look lifelike by simulating how light penetrates the surface and scatters beneath it, just like it does in real human skin. In **Subsurface Scattering (SSS)**, light penetrates the surface of a translucent object, scatters by interacting with the material, and exits the surface at a different point. This effect is crucial for materials such as skin, wax, marble, and leaves, where light does not just bounce off the surface.

> Note
>
> You can implement **SSS** in your materials using the **Principled BSDF** shader. You can adjust the subsurface scattering radius and color to simulate different kinds of materials. For example, skin would have a scattering radius that gives a reddish hue at shallow depths, while marble would have a larger, more uniform scattering effect.

The **Metallic** and **Specular** material properties let you replicate the shiny, reflective surface of the car's paint. First of all, **Metallic** in the **Principled BSDF** shader determines how *metal-like* your material appears. A value of 0 represents non-metallic materials, while a value of 1 represents metals. Metals reflect light in a specific way, often tinting the reflected light with their color. Next, **Specular Reflection** is the mirror-like reflection of light from a surface. In Blender, **Specular** controls the intensity and sharpness of these reflections. You will find it very useful for creating materials such as polished surfaces, glass, or water.

Metallic/Specular (Blender ≤ 3.6)

Older Blender versions offered a **Specular Reflectivity** slider to control how strongly non-metallic surfaces reflected light.

Metallic/Roughness (Blender 4.0 +)

From 4.0 onward, that slider was replaced by the modern **Specular Roughness** workflow:

- **Metallic** (0–1) still decides whether the surface behaves like a metal or a dielectric.
- **Roughness** now governs the size and clarity of the specular lobe. Lower values give crisp, mirror-like highlights; higher values blur them.
- If you are following along in 3.x, you will still see the old **Specular** field; in 4.x, you will work entirely with **Metallic** and **Roughness**.

Tip

Adjusting the **Specular** value and **Roughness** at the same time can help you achieve the desired level of reflectivity and clarity for materials such as polished surfaces, glass, or water.

There are two more advanced properties for materials that could change the fate of your 3D project. First, **Transmission** is used to create transparent materials such as glass or clear plastic. By increasing the **Transmission** value, you allow light to pass through the material, simulating transparency.

Tip

Transmission combined with **Roughness** can create effects ranging from clear, sharp glass to frosted glass.

The last advanced property for materials that we will talk about in this section is **Emission**. Put simply, **Emission** turns the material into a light source. This is useful for light bulbs, screens, or glowing signs, for example. You can control the color and intensity of the light.

Note

Emission is also used together with other properties for creating materials such as neon. To do that, you can add a **Glow** effect in the compositor, adjust the **Emission** strength for the desired intensity, and use a **Color Ramp** node to refine the neon color gradient.

By working through the scenarios where these advanced material properties can be used, you can create more realistic materials. Taking it a step further, we will now look at **Physically Based Rendering (PBR).** This is a cornerstone in 3D modeling and rendering because **PBR** textures let you create materials that react realistically to lighting conditions based on real-world data.

Creating PBR materials

PBR textures are a collection of image maps that work together to accurately simulate how a material interacts with light. Unlike simpler texturing methods that might just apply a flat color or basic shininess to an object, PBR materials use a combination of detailed image maps and mathematical models to reflect, absorb, or scatter light like real-life materials. PBR is the gold standard for digital rendering because it gives a predictable and realistic way for materials to behave.

> **Tip**
>
> For the best results, use high-resolution textures, especially for close-up shots where details are crucial. However, be mindful of your system's capabilities, as higher-resolution textures can increase render times and require more memory.

While many places are offering PBR textures, **3D Tudor** (`https://3dtudor.gumroad.com/`) stands out. It provides a variety of high-quality PBR textures suitable for different projects. Other popular sites include **Poliigon** (`https://www.poliigon.com/`) and **Ambient CG** (`https://ambientcg.com/`), which offer both free and premium textures.

Poliigon has a vast library and high-resolution textures, while Ambient CG offers a wide range of free options. 3D Tudor, on the other hand, is an excellent resource for those starting on their 3D modeling journey or working on projects with a tight budget.

Exploring PBR texture types

I will now talk you through what PBR textures are, how they are created, and where they can be sourced. PBR textures include, but are not limited to, **Base Color** (or **Albedo**), **Roughness**, **Normal**, **Metallic**, and **Ambient Occlusion** maps, as shown in *Figure 13.3*:

PBR texture types	Function
Base Color/Albedo	Represents the color of the material without any lighting or shadow information
Roughness	Determines how rough or smooth the material's surface is, affecting how it reflects light
Normal Map	Adds surface detail and texture without adding additional geometry, simulating bumps and dents
Metallic	Defines the metallic nature of a surface, differentiating between metal and non-metal areas
Alpha	Controls the transparency of a material

Table 13.3: Commonly used PBR textures

To read more about different PBR texture types, including **Specular**, **Transmission**, and **Diffuse**, you can find out more from the Blender Foundation (`https://docs.blender.org/manual/en/latest/render/shader_nodes/shader/principled.html`). If you would like a deeper dive into photorealism, Packt's *Photorealistic Materials and Textures in Blender Cycles* (4th ed.) by Arijan Belec (`https://www.amazon.com/Photorealistic-Materials-Textures-Blender-Cycles/dp/1805129635`) walks through full-production case studies and shader ideas that pair perfectly with what we cover here.

Sharing brief advice about PBR textures

Even though you can get ready-made PBR textures from many different places, creating custom textures offers more control, and you can make sure no one has a texture like yours. Software such as **Adobe Photoshop** (`https://www.adobe.com/products/photoshop.html`) and **Substance Designer** (`https://www.adobe.com/products/substance3d-designer.html`) are widely used for creating PBR textures. Adobe Photoshop is powerful if you are editing and creating textures, and Substance Designer offers a node-based environment for more complex materials.

On a side note, AI tools such as **Midjourney** (`https://www.midjourney.com/home`) can be used to create unique textures. AI-generated textures can be used to create stylized or realistic properties for a **Color Map**. These AI-generated images can then be transformed into PBR textures using software such as **Substance 3D Sampler** (`https://helpx.adobe.com/substance-3d-sampler.html`), which allows you to generate PBR data (e.g., **Roughness**, **Normal**) from AI-generated images.

Once you set up your PBR textures, you can apply them in Blender by mapping these textures to the corresponding slots in the shader, such as connecting the roughness map to the **Roughness** slot in the **Principled BSDF** shader. One thing to keep in mind is that, often, textures need adjustments to fit the specific needs of a project. Blender tools, such as the Shader Editor, will help you fine-tune PBR textures, adjust their scale and orientation, and combine them with other shader nodes for more complex materials.

Note

When you are rendering scenes with PBR materials, you need to consider the lighting setup and render engine being used. PBR materials often look their best under realistic lighting conditions. You can set up realistic lighting conditions using HDRI environments or carefully placed light sources.

In a few words, PBR materials offer a level of realism based on the physical properties of materials. However, knowing how to apply PBR principles is key because it makes all the difference in creating uninspiring versus lifelike 3D scenes.

> **Note**
>
> Pay attention to the color space settings in your **Image Texture** nodes. Color maps (such as **Base Color**) should typically be set to **sRGB**, while non-color data maps (such as **Roughness**, **Metallic**, and **Normal** maps) should be set to **Non-Color Data** to make sure that everything renders accurately.

Setting up PBR materials in Blender can be a detailed process, especially if your goal is to achieve high realism in your 3D projects. I will help you out with that by showing you how to use the **Node Wrangler** add-on to efficiently import and map textures that can significantly streamline the process of setting up PBR materials.

Using Blender's Node Wrangler for efficient workflow

Node Wrangler is a powerful add-on built directly into Blender, offering many functionalities designed to simplify and speed up working with node-based materials. Blender's **Node Wrangler** will help you quickly set up PBR materials and set up or adjust precise texture maps and adjustments. Put simply, **Node Wrangler** gives you the tools to create highly realistic materials in the most efficient way possible.

In this section, we will explore the steps you need to take to activate **Node Wrangler**. To not leave any stone unturned, we will also cover the manual setup of textures for those who prefer a hands-on approach.

Activating Node Wrangler and automating the PBR texture setup within a shader

To get started on streamlining your PBR texture setup in Blender, you need to activate the **Node Wrangler** add-on. Here's how to do it in just three steps:

1. Navigate to **Edit | Preferences | Add-ons**.
2. Search for **Node Wrangler** in the **Add-ons** section.
3. Check the box next to **Node Wrangler** to activate it.

Once **Node Wrangler** is activated, you can use it to quickly set up PBR materials. Follow these steps:

1. Select the **Principled BSDF** node in your material setup.

2. Press *Ctrl + Shift + T* to activate the **Node Wrangler** quick PBR setup feature.

3. Choose multiple texture maps (e.g., **Base Color**, **Roughness**, and **Normal**) from the file browser that opens.

4. **Node Wrangler** will automatically create and connect the nodes for these textures, streamlining the PBR material setup (*Figure 13.14*).

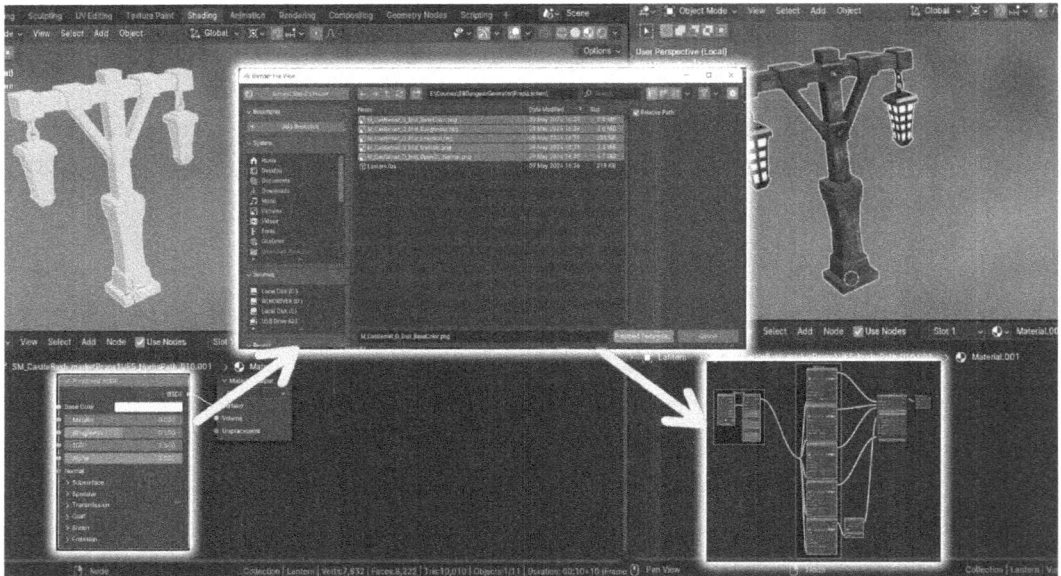

Figure 13.14: Node Wrangler automation in action

It detects the type of textures by looking at their filenames. You can edit the tags used for this matching process in the add-on preferences.

Importing and mapping textures manually

To import and map textures manually in Blender, ensuring each texture map is accurately applied to your material, follow these detailed steps:

1. With your object selected, open the Shader Editor.

2. Make sure you are in the **Material** tab to see the material nodes.

3. Press *Shift + A* to open the **Add** menu in the Shader Editor.

4. Navigate through **Texture | Image Texture** to add an **Image Texture** node.

> **Note**
>
> You will need to repeat this step for each texture map you plan to use (e.g., **Base Color**, **Roughness**, and **Normal**).

5. For each **Image Texture** node, click **Open** to browse and select the corresponding texture map from your files.

> **Tip**
>
> In newer Blender versions, you can also drag and drop image files directly into the Shader Editor, and Blender will automatically create and connect the **Image Texture** node for you. This is often faster and more intuitive.

Note that **Normal** maps are used to add detail to surfaces without increasing the polygon count. However, OpenGL and DirectX handle the orientation of these **Normal** maps differently. Because of this difference, **Normal** maps created for one system might look wrong when used in another.

Blender uses OpenGL by default. However, it can be difficult to identify which **Normal** map format an asset is using. If the lighting and details on an object look incorrect, try converting the **Normal** map from one format to the other. To do this, invert the green channel (*Y* axis) of the **Normal** map. This will adjust the orientation to match the target system, correcting the appearance of the lighting and detail, as in *Figure 13.15*.

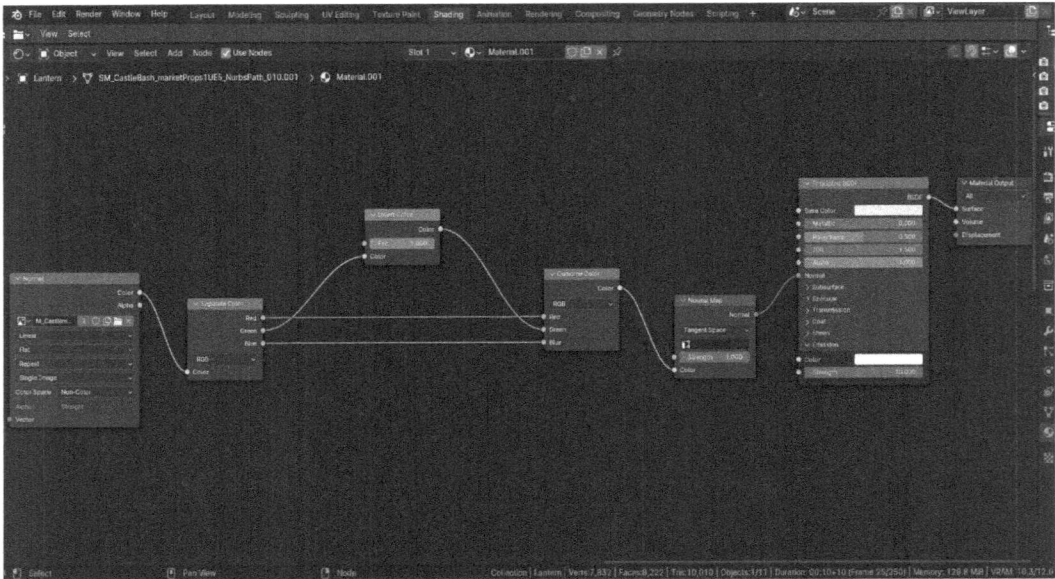

Figure 13.15: Troubleshooting a common Normal map orientation issue

Connecting textures to Principled BSDF

After importing your texture maps, the next step is to connect them to the **Principled BSDF** shader. This shader acts as a comprehensive material model that can simulate a wide variety of materials. Here's how to connect each texture map:

1. First, let us define the main color of your material:

    a. Drag the **Color** output of the **Image Texture** node intended for the **Base Color** map.

    b. Connect it to the **Base Color** input slot of the **Principled BSDF** node. This defines the main color of your material.

2. Next, we will control the material's shininess and reflectivity:

    a. For the texture map that represents the roughness of the material, connect the **Color** output of its **Image Texture** node.

    b. Plug it into the **Roughness** input slot of **Principled BSDF**. This controls the material's shininess and reflectivity, affecting how matte or glossy it appears.

3. Finally, let us add fine surface details and textures:

    a. Normal maps require an additional node to interpret the map correctly. Add a **Normal Map** node by pressing *Shift + A*, and navigating to **Vector | Normal Map**. This converts the color information of a texture into **Vector** information.

> **Note**
>
> Make sure the color space is set to **Non-Color**.

    b. Connect the **Color** output of the **Image Texture** node, which holds your **Normal Map** node, to the **Color** input of the **Normal Map** node.

    c. Then, connect the **Normal** output of the **Normal Map** node to the **Normal** input slot of **Principled BSDF**. This simulates fine surface details and textures without adding geometric complexity to the model.

Adjusting texture settings for realism

Blender lets you control how textures adhere to the complex surfaces of its models. To make sure that your textures are correctly mapped onto your 3D model, use **Texture Coordinate** and **Mapping** nodes. The **Texture Coordinate** node provides various options for how the texture is projected onto the object, with **UV** being the most common. The **Mapping** node lets you adjust the position, rotation, and scale of the texture. I recommend that you adjust the settings in the **Mapping** node to make sure that the texture fits your model correctly, as shown in *Figure 13.16*.

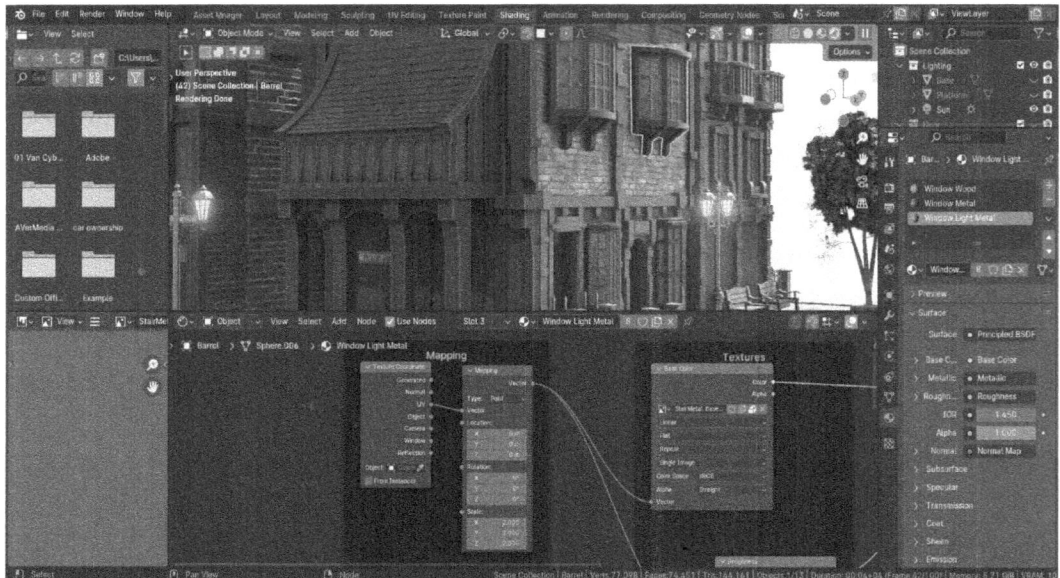

Figure 13.16: Wood grain textures in Blender 4 The Ultimate Environment Artist's Guide by 3D Tudor

For example, if a wood grain texture is stretching unnaturally, you can scale it on the appropriate axis to correct its appearance. Let's say your wood grain texture looked like it was being pulled too thin across a wide surface. In this case, you would adjust the **Mapping** node by increasing the scale along the axis that is stretched, making the texture appear more compact and natural.

Normal maps are another thing you should consider when you are adjusting texture settings for realism. When you are using **Normal** maps, make sure that you add a **Normal Map** node between the **Image Texture** node and the **Principled BSDF** shader. This node will convert the color information from **Normal Map** into proper normal data that Blender can use to simulate surface details. This avoids problems such as the flat appearance of textures that lack depth or incorrect lighting reflections that can make materials look unrealistic or out of place. Properly using a **Normal Map** node makes sure that the tiny bumps, grooves, and other surface details are accurately represented.

By leveling up and getting better at using these techniques for setting up PBR materials in Blender, you will be able to create highly realistic and visually appealing materials for your 3D models. Whether you are working on a simple project or a complex scene, these skills are essential for stepping up your 3D modeling game.

The next section shifts our attention to **Ambient Occlusion**, focusing on the soft shadowing effects that occur in natural and tight spaces where direct light struggles to reach. Understanding its common misconceptions and its correct usage in different rendering engines, such as Eevee and Cycles, will give you insight into another dimension of realism.

Understanding Ambient Occlusion

Ambient Occlusion (AO) represents the occlusion (i.e., blocking) of ambient light in tight spaces and crevices where light has difficulty reaching. It adds depth and realism to your scene because it brings attention to soft shadows in those darker areas.

AO accentuates the depth and contours of models, much like how proper texture mapping and **Normal** maps move your viewer's attention to the surface detail you created.

Tip

Often, AO maps are incorrectly used by simply multiplying them over the **Albedo** (i.e., **Base Color**) texture, affecting the material under all lighting conditions. This is not how AO works in real life. To avoid this mistake, you can use shader nodes to control when and where the AO effect goes.

Using AO in Eevee

To set up **AO** in Eevee, follow the next steps:

1. Start by adding in texture maps using **Node Wrangler**. Select **Shader** and then press *Ctrl + Shift + T* to import a texture map.

2. Start by adding a **Mix Color** node to the **Albedo** texture and plug the **AO** map into the second slot.

3. Set the blend mode to **Multiply**. Make sure your process is the same as in *Figure 13.17*.

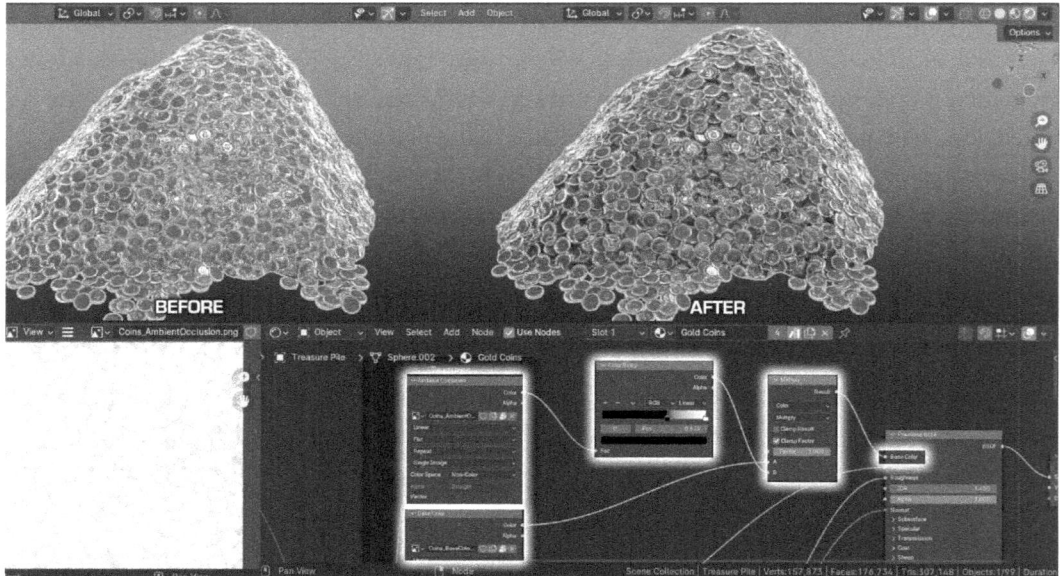

Figure 13.17: Setting up AO in Eevee – initial settings

4. Press *Shift + A* to add a **Color Ramp** node and drop it in between the **AO** and **Mix Color** nodes.

5. Plug the **Color Ramp** output into the factor input of the **Mix Color** node (i.e., where the **AO** map is connected). Adjust the **Color Ramp** to control the **AO** effect by moving the black arrow closer to the center to intensify the effect, or vice versa. If you do this right, this will make sure that your AO is only visible under ambient lighting conditions.

6. You can further adjust the **AO** map's appearance by adding a **Brightness/Contrast** node or changing **Color Ramp** to a constant type for different effects.

7. Connect the **Color** output of the shader to the first slot of the **Color Mix** node. If you do this right, this will make sure your **AO** is "faking" additional shadow depth in your real-time renderer.

Note

Ambient Occlusion maps do not always get their own fancy input slot in Blender. But that does not mean they are useless! You can still make your textures look way better by combining the **AO** map with your **Base Color** map.

The trick is to either multiply or mix **AO** with **Base Color**. This adds some nice visual complexity without needing to mess around with complex lighting. It is a simple way to make your textures pop, giving them that extra realism or stylized details, depending on what you are going for.

Using AO in Cycles

In **Cycles**, **AO** is often naturally integrated due to path-traced rendering. However, you can use an AO pass for additional control.

Note for Eevee users

The **Ambient Occlusion** shader node is in **Cycles** only:

- For real-time previews, enable **Screen-Space AO** in the **Eevee Render** settings.
- For final shaders, bake an **AO** map and mix it in a texture node; this is engine-agnostic and faster than the **Cycles** node.

To set up **AO** in **Cycles**, follow the next steps:

1. First, create and set up the material:

    a. Switch to **Cycles Render** by selecting it from the **Render Engine** dropdown in the top-right corner of the screen.

    b. Then, open the Shader Editor by navigating to the **Shading** workspace or switching any window to the Shader Editor.

    c. Select your object and check whether it has a material. If it does not, create one by clicking **New** in the **Materials** tab.

2. Next, add the **Ambient Occlusion** node:

    a. In the Shader Editor, press *Shift + A* to open the **Add** menu, and select **Input** and then **Ambient Occlusion** to add an **Ambient Occlusion** node.

    b. Place the **AO** node in your shader graph, but do not connect it just yet, as we will modify it further.

3. Now, we want to add and control the mix for color blending:

    a. Add a **Mix Color** node by pressing *Shift + A*, going to **Color** and then **Mix Color**, and placing it in your shader setup.

    b. Connecting the **AO** map to the **Factor** input of a **Mix Color** node allows you to control the color of the **AO** information, enabling customization of shading and depth by blending it with different colors.

    c.   Insert a **ColorRamp** node by pressing *Shift + A*, selecting **Converter**, and then **ColorRamp**.

    d.   Place it between the **AO** and **MixRGB** nodes. This gives you control over the intensity and distribution of the **AO** effect.

    e.   Connect the output of **ColorRamp** to the **Factor** input of the **MixRGB** node for more refined color blending.

4.   Finally, connect and adjust the colors:

    a.   In the **MixRGB** node, set two colors to control the **AO** effect. Typically, you would choose a light color for the base and a darker color for the occluded areas.

    b.   Connect the output of the **MixRGB** node to the **Base Color** input of the **Principled BSDF** shader, completing the setup and allowing you to see the **AO** effect in your material.

Note

This might be useful in a project such as designing the interior of a rustic cabin, where you want to give attention to the texture of wooden beams and stone flooring. By applying the **AO** pass, you can highlight the natural shadows in the crevices between the wood planks and stones. Using the **Gamma** node can accentuate the warm, soft lighting more than **AO** on its own.

Whether you are working in Eevee or Cycles, without **AO**, your 3D scenes would look flat and less engaging. Now that ambient occlusion is ticked off the list, let's zoom out and explore the rest of Blender's shader node toolbox, the tricks that turn a plain material into something worth a double-take.

Introducing Blender's shader nodes

Blender's node system for shader nodes is as close to programming as you are going to get as a 3D modeler. You will need to pay attention to detail since tweaking the most inconspicuous value can make a huge difference in how your material will look.

Table 13.4 tells you a bit more about each shader node, and why and when to use it:

Shader node	Properties and uses	Example Blender project
Add Shader	Combines two shaders, useful for adding emission to existing materials	A neon sign glowing in a cityscape
Add Shader	Simulates materials with anisotropic reflections, such as brushed metal	A futuristic car with brushed metal surfaces
Diffuse BSDF	Basic diffuse shader, representing matte surfaces	A cozy living room with matte-painted walls
Emission	Makes objects emit light, used for creating light sources	A scene with glowing lanterns in a garden
Glass BSDF	Creates transparent materials with reflective properties, such as glass	A glass vase with flowers on a table
Hair BSDF	A specialized shader for rendering hair and fur	A character with detailed, realistic hair
Holdout	Creates a transparent hole in the final render, used for masking	A scene with a character in front of a green screen
Mix Shader	Blends two shaders based on a factor, useful for mixing different material properties	A marble statue with a mix of glossy and rough areas
Principled BSDF	A versatile shader combining multiple properties, suitable for most materials	A photorealistic wooden table with various textures
Principled Hair BSDF	An advanced shader for rendering hair with realistic properties	A lion with a detailed mane
Principled Volume	Creates volumetric materials for effects such as smoke, fog, and fire	A smoky forest with volumetric lighting effects
Refraction BSDF	Simulates the bending of light through transparent materials, such as water or glass	An underwater scene with realistic light refraction
Subsurface Scattering	Simulates light scattering within materials, used for skin, wax, and other translucent objects	A close-up of a human face with realistic skin rendering
Toon BSDF	Creates a cartoon-like shading effect, used for stylized renders	A colorful animated scene with cartoon characters
Translucent BSDF	Allows light to pass through the material, creating a soft, glowing effect	A scene with frosted glass windows
Transparent BSDF	Makes objects completely transparent, often used for alpha masks	A butterfly with transparent wings

Shader node	Properties and uses	Example Blender project
Volume Absorption	Creates a volumetric effect that absorbs light, used for effects such as murky water or fog	A dark, foggy forest scene
Volume Scatter	Simulates light scattering within a volume, used for effects such as mist and atmospheric lighting	A forest with volumetric mist and god rays

Table 13.4: An overview of shader nodes in Blender

Note

Some legacy shaders (e.g., **Glossy** and **Diffuse**) were rolled into **Principled** in Blender 4.0+. For historical nodes, see the official docs (`https://docs.blender.org/manual/en/latest/render/shader_nodes/index.html`).

You can use a **Principled BSDF** shader node to create the surface material for a dragon. By simply adjusting the **Roughness** value within the same node setup, you can dramatically alter the appearance of the dragon's scales. With a low **Roughness** value, the scales appear shiny and reflective, like a freshly molted dragon basking in sunlight (*Figure 13.18*).

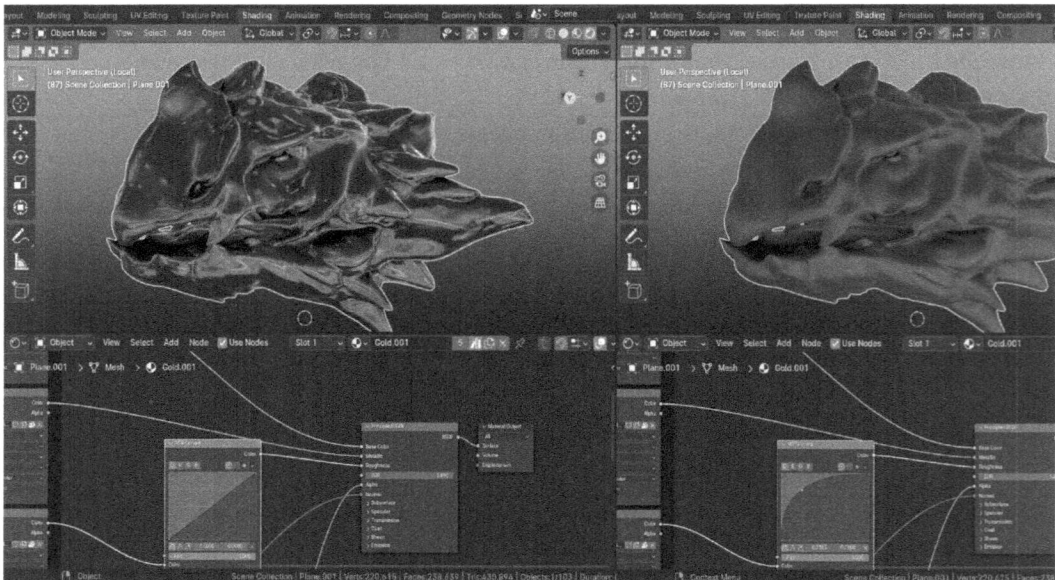

Figure 13.18: Dragon with shiny and reflective scales based on a low Roughness value (left) and a high Roughness value (right)

On the other hand, increasing the **Roughness** value gives the scales a matte, rugged look.

As you have seen, this subtle change in the **Roughness** value on an otherwise identical node setup completely transforms the narrative and visual impact of the dragon in your scene.

In *Table 13.5*, you can compare the important parts of Blender's node system. This will help you understand how to use it, step by step, through practicing the different projects discussed in this chapter.

Node	Function	Project example
Ambient Occlusion node	Generates **Ambient Occlusion** as color or black-and-white data. Controls include samples, inside, only local, color, distance, and normal input. Note that in Cycles, it works automatically, but in Eevee, you need to enable ambient occlusion in render settings.	Can bring attention to the crevices between stones and rubble in ancient ruins
Attribute node	A testing node for developers to use attributes such as **Normal**, vertex colors, and **UV** maps. Outputs color, vector, or black-and-white data based on the attribute name.	A custom character model where vertex colors define different zones for makeup or tattoos
Camera Data node	Provides data based on the camera's position and view. Includes view vector, view Z depth, view distance, and **Fresnel** outputs (the **Fresnel** node in Blender is a function used within the shading system to simulate the way light reflects off surfaces at different angles).	Creating a depth-of-field effect in a camera fly-through animation of a forest, where the focus point changes depending on the camera's distance from objects
Geometry node	Offers various outputs such as position, normal, true normal, back facing, and hair info. Geometry nodes are useful for accessing different aspects of an object's geometry (we will discuss geometry nodes fully in *Part 5*, *Geometry Nodes in Blender*).	Simulating realistic snowfall and icicle formation on different objects

Node	Function	Project example
Layer Weight node	Similar to **Fresnel** but with more options, such as facing output and linear falloff. Useful for mixing materials based on the angle of view.	Designing a car paint material that shifts color based on the viewing angle, like a pearlescent finish.
Light Path node	Provides information about the light's interaction with surfaces. Outputs include camera ray, shadow ray, diffuse ray, glossy ray, reflection ray, transmission ray, ray length, and ray depth.	A magical orb that glows differently when viewed directly versus when seen in reflections or shadows
Object Info node	Gives information about the object, such as location, color, object index, material index, and random value. Useful for randomizing aspects of materials for multiple similar objects in the same scene.	Randomizing the color of leaves in a forest scene
Particle Info node	Provides data about particles such as index, random, age, lifetime, location, size, and velocity. Your go-to node for creating particle-based materials.	Creating a firework simulator where each particle displays different colors and sizes based on how long ago each particle started firing
RGB node	Outputs a color value chosen from a color wheel.	Designing a simple material for a cartoon sun, where the RGB node provides the base color for the **Emission** shader, making it brightly glow
Tangent node	Creates a custom tangent for **Anisotropic BSDF**. Allows control over how light is bent around a point.	A metallic vase with an anisotropic finish, where the custom tangent controls the direction of light streaks, as with brushed metal
Texture Coordinate node	Defines where a texture should be placed on an object. Outputs include generated normal, **UV**, object, window, reflection, and **UV Map**.	Mapping a decal onto a racing car model, using UV coordinates to place the decal without affecting the paint material underneath

Node	Function	Project example
Value node	Outputs a single value.	Controlling the intensity of a lamp in an interior design project based on the time of day
Wireframe node	Provides the wireframe of an object. Allows control over the size of the wireframe on the object.	Creating a holographic display effect with a **Wireframe** node outlines objects in a sci-fi room
Material Output node	This is the end product of all other nodes in a material setup. Includes surface, volume, and displacement inputs.	Compiling a complex shader for a dragon's skin that combines **Subsurface Scattering, Glossy Reflection**, and detailed textures for a single material
Texture nodes	Include **Brick Texture, Checker Texture, Environment Texture, Gradient Texture, IES Texture, Image Texture, Magic Texture, Musgrave Texture, Noise Texture, Sky Texture, Voronoi Texture**, and **Wave Texture**. These nodes are used to create various textures and patterns on materials.	Making a procedurally generated alien landscape, using various texture nodes to create the terrain, sky, and vegetation patterns
Color nodes	Include **Brightness/Contrast, Gamma, HSV, Invert, Mix RGB, Light Falloff**, and **RGB Curves**. Used for color correction and manipulation of materials.	Post-processing a rendered scene to adjust the mood, using color nodes for correction and effects, such as making a sunset scene feel warmer
Vector nodes	Include **Bump, Vector Curves, Displacement**, and **Mapping**. Used for manipulating vectors and normals in materials.	Simulating wind affecting a field of grass, using **Vector** nodes to manipulate the direction and strength of the grass movement

Node	Function	Project example
Converter nodes	Include **Blackbody, Clamp, Color Ramp, Separate/Combine RGB, Separate/Combine XYZ, Separate/Combine HSV, Map Range, Math, RGB to Black and White**, and **Wavelength.** Convert one type of data to another, such as color to black and white or temperature to color.	Using a **Blackbody** node to convert temperature values into color to show heat distribution in a 3D model
Script nodes	Used for custom **Open Shading Language** (**OSL**) node-based shader setup	Creating a custom glass shader that simulates realistic relationships with light

Table 13.5: Important nodes and their functions

Understanding the function of these nodes and how they interact with each other is what will make or break your material creation in Blender. This overview did not cover everything, but it prepared you for what we will do next: displacement mapping.

Understanding and using displacement in Blender Shaders

Displacement mapping can help you add intricate detail and texture to 3D models. It physically alters the geometry of 3D models based on a texture. Displacement is good for creating realistic surfaces, but the process of displacement is different depending on which Blender rendering engine you use.

> Tip
>
> For both Cycles and Eevee, using high-resolution textures for displacement maps ensures more detail and a more realistic effect. If your project requires rendering in both Cycles and Eevee, test your displacement setups in both engines to ensure consistency in the look and feel of your materials.

Displacement in Cycles

Cycles is a ray-tracing render engine, so it offers more advanced and realistic **Displacement** options. Think of it like adding real-life bumps and grooves to objects so they look more natural.

You would want to use Cycles for projects where you need things to look super detailed and realistic, such as a picture of a house that shows all the textures of the walls and floors, or a close-up of a rock where you can see every little crack and crevice. This is because Cycles can make these tiny details on the surface of objects, which helps make your 3D models look like they could exist in the real world.

> **Note**
>
> Displacement, especially true displacement in Cycles, can be resource-intensive. Only use **Displacement** if it is necessary, and balance your texture resolutions with performance needs.

In Cycles, displacement is typically set up using the **Displacement** node in the Shader Editor. This node is connected to the **Displacement** input of the **Material Output** node. The **Displacement** effect is driven by a texture, often a black-and-white image, where the white areas represent higher points, and the black areas represent lower points, as shown in *Figure 13.19*.

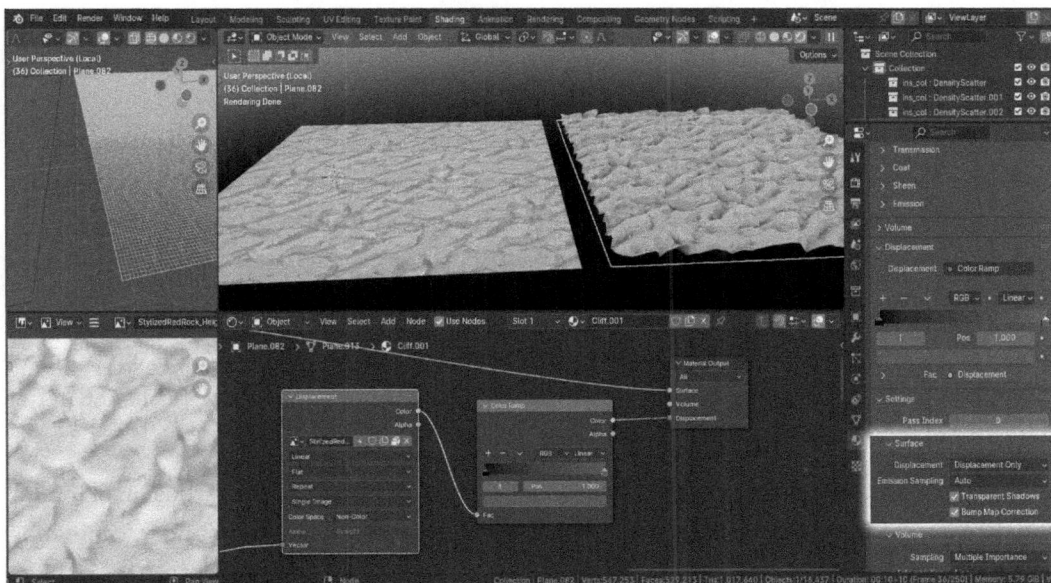

Figure 13.19: Displacement effect in action, white vs. black areas

Cycles supports two types of displacement. First, you have **Bump,** which is a simulation of **Displacement** and does not alter the actual geometry. The other type of displacement available in Blender is true or actual displacement, which physically modifies the mesh by offsetting vertices.

Note

True displacement requires a highly subdivided mesh to work effectively. This can be done using the **Subdivision Surface** modifier. If you are on a shiny-new build, you do not have to dive into the experimental rabbit anymore. Just drop a **Subdivision Surface** modifier on your mesh, tick **Adaptive Subdivision**, and Cycles will now slice the geometry on the fly based on camera distance and **Dicing** scale. From there, you can change the **Dicing** scale, but it bricks and crashes pretty easily if you go below 1. The end result is a crisper displacement in the close-ups, saner poly counts in the distance, and a GPU that doesn't wheeze like an asthmatic badger.

In Blender's **Material** settings, under the **Settings** tab, you can find the **Displacement** method, where you can choose between **Bump Only**, **Displacement Only**, or **Displacement and Bump**.

Tip

For true displacement, choose **Displacement Only** or **Displacement and Bump**.

Displacement in Eevee

Eevee is a real-time render engine. It does not support true displacement in the same way as Cycles. While earlier versions did not support true displacement, Eevee 4.2 LTS now includes limited real-time displacement capabilities. However, this feature still requires an extremely high poly count to produce meaningful results and may not be practical for most workflows because of how performance-heavy it is.

As a result, Eevee relies on **Bump** mapping and **Parallax** mapping to simulate the effect of **Displacement** without changing the actual geometry. These techniques are much faster and better suited for development or animation previews.

Bump mapping changes the way light interacts with the surface to create the illusion of bumps and dents. **Parallax** mapping shifts the texture's appearance as you move around it, simulating depth without actually modifying the model's surface. These methods allow Eevee to simulate the look of detailed textures quickly. For example, if you are creating a forest scene for a game, the way that Eevee uses **Bump** and **Parallax** mapping can quickly give the ground and tree bark textures a realistic look of depth and complexity. This will help your game run smoothly on various devices without needing heavy computational power to render true geometric changes.

To set up **Bump** mapping in Eevee, you can use a texture connected to a **Bump** node, which then connects to the **Normal** input of the shader, such as **Principled BSDF**. Using this method will give you the appearance of depth by changing the light's behavior. This technique can make the stones and bricks of the castle walls appear rough and weathered, and this would be great for scenes where the camera pans or zooms over the castle walls.

> Tip
>
> For a more enhanced **Displacement** effect in Eevee, **Parallax** mapping can be used. This technique uses a grayscale height map to create an illusion of depth by shifting textures based on the viewer's angle. One of the drawbacks of **Parallax** mapping is that it needs more complex node setups and is more resource-intensive.

By understanding and using **Displacement** mapping in Blender, you can boost the realism and detail of your 3D models. As you found out, you can choose **Cycles** for true geometric displacement or **Eevee** for simulated effects. Either way, displacement is essential if you want to create lifelike materials. Despite its benefits, **Displacement** mapping can sometimes be too resource-intensive for real-time rendering, such as in games. This is where the next step in our exploration comes into play: shader baking in Blender.

Familiarizing yourself with shader baking in Blender

Shader baking converts the visual information of a shader, such as colors, textures, and lighting effects, into a flat image texture. You want to do that if you are optimizing 3D models for video games or interactive simulations, where you need to keep your computer from overstraining itself. The process of baking is like taking a photo of all the fancy effects (such as colors, textures, and how light bounces off things) on a 3D model and sticking that photo onto the model. This is super helpful when you are making things for video games or virtual reality, where you cannot use a lot of computer power. By baking, you make everything look good without making the computer work too hard every time the game is played, keeping things running smoothly while still looking great.

I will guide you through the entire process of preparing your 3D model, setting up and creating your shaders, and then baking them into a single, easy-to-use texture. Here is how to get started:

1. First, prepare your 3D model:

    a. Make sure your model is properly UV unwrapped. UV unwrapping is the process of projecting your 3D model onto a 2D plane to apply textures accurately.

    b. If necessary, subdivide the model to add more geometry for finer details.

2. Next, in the **Shading** workspace, create your desired material using Blender's shader nodes. This could be a combination of various textures, colors, and procedural effects.

3. Now, set up your shader for baking:

    a. Switch to the **Cycles** render engine.

    Note

    Cycles offers more comprehensive baking options compared to **Eevee**.

    b. In the Shader Editor, add an **Image Texture** node to your material. Do not connect this node to the shader; it will serve as the target for the baked texture.

    c. Create a new image in the **Image Texture** node. This image will store your baked texture. Set the resolution (e.g., 2048x2048 pixels) according to your needs.

4. Then, bake the shader:

    a. Go to the **Render Properties** panel and find the **Bake** section.

    b. Choose the bake type that corresponds to the information you want to capture (e.g., **Diffuse**, **Glossy**, or **Normal**).

    c. For the **Selected to Active** option, ensure only the object with the shader you want to bake is selected.

    d. Click **Bake**. Blender will render the shader information onto the image texture you created.

5. Once baking is complete, save the image texture. Go to the Image Editor, select the baked image, and use **Image** and **Save As**.

6. You can now use this baked texture in a new material setup. Simply add the saved image texture to a **Principled BSDF** shader, connecting it to the appropriate inputs (e.g., **Base Color** or **Normal**). If you want to avoid baking lighting information into your textures, make sure to disable **Direct** and **Indirect** lighting contributions in the **Bake** settings, especially when baking **Diffuse**. This gives you clean, lighting-agnostic maps that are easier to reuse across different lighting setups.

You can now bake shaders in Blender, transforming complex materials into lightweight, versatile textures. In short, it is a two-for-one win: your mesh stays lean enough to keep frame rates happy, but it still has the look!

Summary

This chapter brought the art of shading into the spotlight. We started off getting comfy with Blender's controls, kind of like finding the right seat in an art class. Then, we covered the basics, understanding how shaders are your digital paints and brushes. Through hands-on project examples, you have seen how to apply materials, use the **Principled BSDF** shader, and harness the power of nodes to create complex, lifelike textures. Put simply, shading lets you dictate how models reflect light, appear wet or metallic, and even how translucent they seem.

Imagine we went on a treasure hunt together, looking for the secrets to make our 3D models come to life. We learned how to mimic the way light plays on different materials, making them look real enough to touch. It was like discovering the right shade of blue for a sunny sky or the perfect texture for an old brick wall. And with PBR materials, it was as if we found a whole new set of high-quality paints that make everything look even more real.

Now that *Chapter 13* is finished, it is time to roll up our sleeves for *Chapter 14*. Imagine you are making a custom-fit suit. In 3D modeling, we use seams to tell Blender how to unfold our model into a flat image for texturing. *Chapter 14* is your friendly guide on this journey, showing you the ropes, from marking those seams correctly so your model lays out flat like a well-pressed shirt, to using sharps to keep those edges as crisp as a fresh dollar bill. Whether you're a Blender newbie or just looking to brush up on your skills, these techniques will help take your models from "good" to "wow."

Further reading

- If you are aiming to break into photorealism in Cycles, reach for *Photorealistic Materials and Textures in Blender Cycles* (https://www.amazon.com/Photorealistic-Materials-Textures-Blender-Cycles/dp/1805129635).

- If you want a full bake-to-paint workflow that bounces between Blender and Substance, dive into *Substance Painter Beginner's Guide to Game Texturing* (https://www.udemy.com/course/substance-painter-beginners-guide-to-game-texturing/?referralCode=861FE7C558A5F530D284). You will see every step: baking, layering smart materials, and piping the finished maps back into Blender for final-look dev.

- If you need to manage dozens of shared materials in a production-scale scene, tackle *Master Blender 3D with Wild West Environments* (https://www.udemy.com/course/master-blender-3d-with-wild-west-environments/?referralCode=3C8C3D3700AC8174742B). It shows how trim-sheet-driven node groups keep GPU memory low while texturing entire towns.

- If you are ready to master metallic, glossy, and specular cheats on smaller props, try *Blender Beginner's Bootcamp* (https://www.udemy.com/course/blender-beginners-bootcamp/?referralCode=1FEDE1307FCB6BBE265F).

- If your goal is rock-solid texture scale, normal map fixes, and mapping node tricks for large environments, try *Blender 4: The Ultimate Environment Artist's Guide* (https://www.udemy.com/course/blender-4-the-ultimate-environment-artists-guide/?referralCode=FF4B83F7AB5B90390273).

Subscribe to Game Dev Assembly!

We are excited to introduce **Game Dev Assembly**, our brand-new newsletter dedicated to everything game development. Whether you're coding, designing, animating, or managing a studio, we've got insights, trends, and expert advice to help you create, innovate, and thrive. Sign up now and get exciting benefits.

https://packt.link/gamedev-newsletter

Get This Book's PDF Version and Exclusive Extras

UNLOCK NOW

Scan the QR code (or go to packtpub.com/unlock). Search for this book by name, confirm the edition, and then follow the steps on the page.

Note: Keep your invoice handy. Purchases made directly from Packt don't require an invoice.

14

Mastering Seams and Sharps in Blender

In this chapter, you will learn how to use **seams** and **sharps** in Blender to effectively unwrap models and define edges. **Seams** are edges marked to define where a 3D model will be cut to create a flat, 2D representation, much like unfolding a map. This process is known as **unwrapping**, and it is something you need to do to prepare your models for adding colors and textures. **Sharps**, on the other hand, are edges marked to define where the geometry of the model should appear sharp or creased. This helps in controlling the smoothing of the model during rendering and boosts realism and detail.

Understanding how to use seams and sharps properly will help you create detailed, textured, and visually appealing 3D models, which is a big step in making them look awesome. If you do not plan where the edges of the sticker for a soccer ball should go, it might end up wrinkled or not fit right. That is what I could compare seams in 3D modeling to. You must plan where to cut your model so you can spread it out flat for texturing.

For sharps, think about when you are drawing and want to make one part of your drawing stand out by making the line thicker or darker. Put simply, that is what sharps do in 3D modeling. They make some edges more defined, so your model has more depth and looks more interesting.

This chapter is going to show you step by step how to use these tools, including bevel weights, creases, and fine-tuning edges. You will learn the basics of seams, understand sharps and why you use them, master creases and bevel weights, fine-tune your model's edges with bevel weights, and try and test common pitfalls in Blender modeling. This will teach you the best ways to fold and cut so your projects turn out just the way you want them to.

So, in this chapter, we will cover the following topics:

- Getting down to the basics of seams
- Understanding sharps and why you use them
- Mastering creases and bevel weights: advanced techniques in Blender
- Fine-tuning your model's edges with bevel weights
- Navigating common pitfalls in Blender modeling

Technical requirements

As for **Blender 4.5 LTS (Long-Term Support)**, the general requirements include a macOS 11.2 or newer (Apple Silicon supported natively) operating system, or a Linux (64-bit, glibc 2.28 or newer) operating system. Blender now requires a CPU with the SSE4.2 instruction set, at least 8 GB of RAM (32 GB recommended for heavy scenes), and a GPU supporting OpenGL 4.3 with a minimum of 2 GB of VRAM.

For a full list of technical requirements, please refer back to *Chapter 1* of this part.

Getting down to the basics of seams

Seams are like the lines you draw on paper to help fold it into a shape; they help us turn a 3D shape into a flat 2D image. This process, known as UV unwrapping, is super important and will be explained in detail in *Chapter 15* in *Part 1* of this book. For now, you only need to know that seams are the big first step in getting good at adding textures to your models. They are there to help you plan where to put these lines so that when you spread your model out flat, everything lines up correctly and looks good, without any stretchy or squishy parts.

Doing this right means your model will not have any weird-looking areas where the texture does not fit properly. Whether you are making a car, a character, or a building, knowing how to use seams means you can wrap your texture around it just right. It is a basic skill in 3D modeling that opens the door to helping your models go from looking okay to looking amazing.

Marking seams: a beginner's tutorial

Marking seams is a straightforward process in Blender:

1. Begin by entering **Edit Mode** (by pressing *Tab*), then, from the **3D Viewport** heading, select **Edge Select** mode (or press *2*). This mode will let you choose the edges where seams will be most effective.

2. Select the edges you want to mark as seams (use *Shift + click* for multiple selections).

3. *Right-click* anywhere in your **3D Viewport** window to open the **Edge Context** menu (or use *Ctrl + E*) and select **Mark Seam**.

   You should place your seams at the edges of clothing pieces, where different materials or components meet. These are perfect spots for seams because they are natural separations within the model. Marked seams will appear in red, meaning that they are ready to guide UV unwrapping, as shown in *Figure 14.1*.

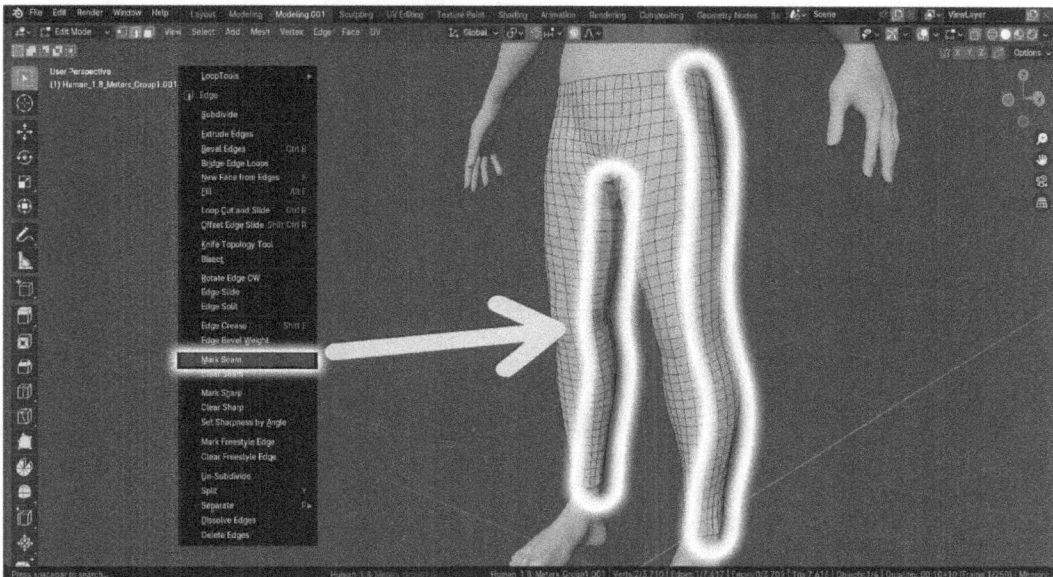

Figure 14.1: Marking seams in red – color coding as your guide in Blender

> **Tip**
>
> Because of the high likelihood of texture stretching in these spots, marking seams along the inner edges of the arms where they connect to the torso can greatly improve how textures distribute across the model.

4. Should you need to unmark a seam, *right-click* anywhere in your **3D Viewport** window and select **Clear Seam**.

For more complex models, such as those with detailed facial features, you might need to use seams around the head or neck, as in *Figure 14.2*. This makes sure that your facial textures lay out smoothly without distortion. By carefully considering where you place your seams, your character model can have a more polished and realistic look when you texture it.

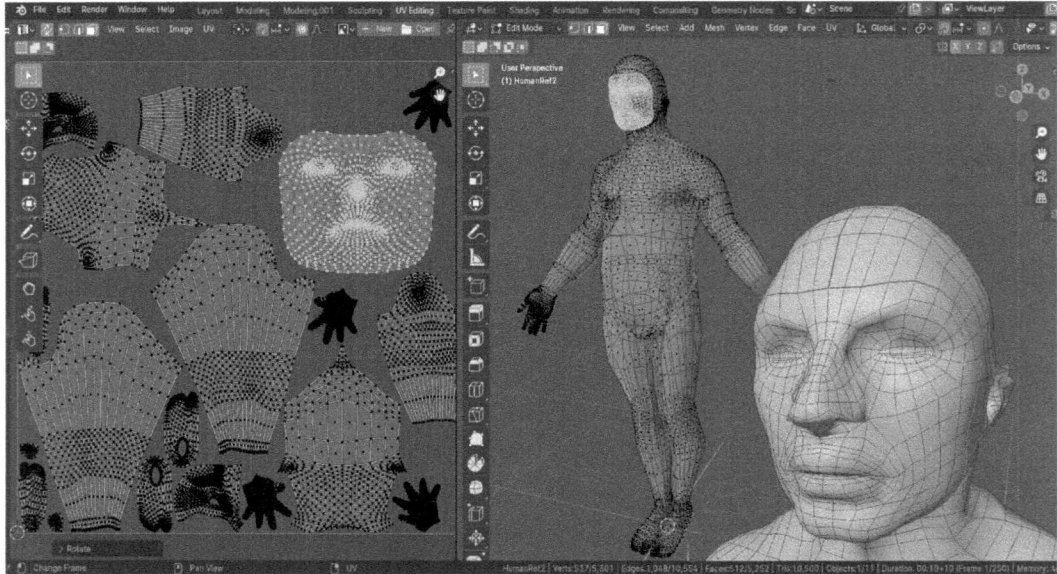

Figure 14.2: Marking seams on complex models, such as on a face

Tip

If your mesh is properly set up, it is best to create seams from **Edge Loops**, selecting continuous, circular paths around your model where it makes sense to cut the mesh for unwrapping. If you do not select an entire loop and only choose partial sections, **Mark Seam** will break off UVs into chunks. This can lead to uneven textures and visible seams on your model, making it harder to have a smooth and realistic appearance when the texture is applied.

Preparing for UV unwrapping

After you have put in your seams, you are ready to start UV unwrapping. This part of the chapter just gives a quick look at the process, but you can find out all about UV unwrapping in *Chapter 15* in *Part 1* of this book:

1. First, make sure you select everything on your model by pressing *A*. This makes sure you include every part of your model in the unwrapping.

2. Then, press *U* and click **Unwrap** to start the process. This step uses the seams you have marked to spread your model's surface flat, getting it ready for texturing. How you have placed your seams is important for a good unwrap. Doing this step right means your textures will look better and fit the model without being stretched or squished.

3. After unwrapping, you might need to tweak the UV map a bit to make sure the textures sit just right. You can do this in the UV Editor, where you can move, scale, or spin the pieces of your model's surface to make them fit better, as in *Figure 14.3*.

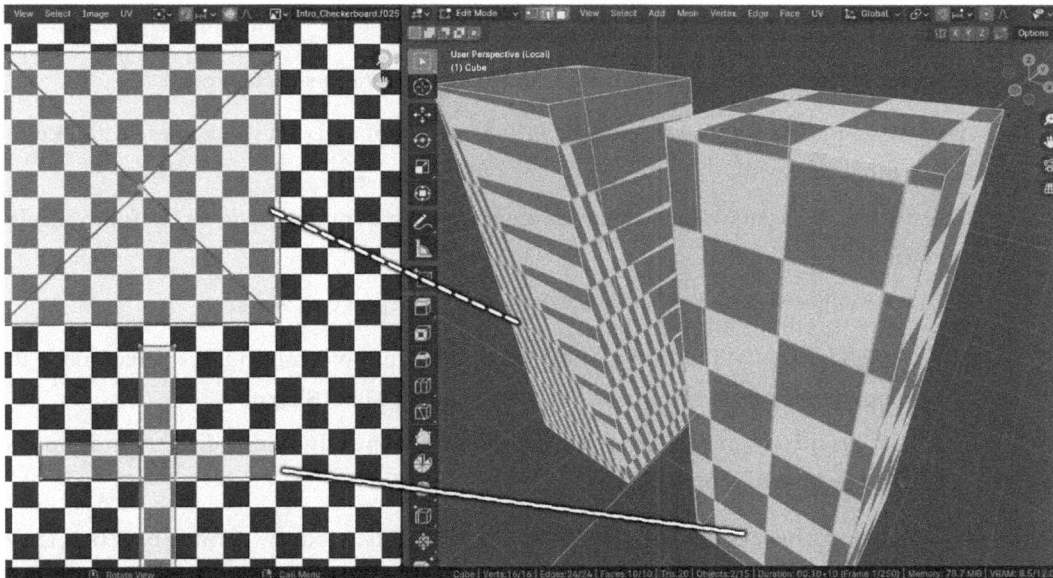

Figure 14.3: UV map before (left) and after (right) adding seams onto a shape

This introduction to seams sets the stage for UV unwrapping in the next chapter. Experiment with various models to see how different seam placements affect the UV layout and, with that, the texturing process.

If you know how to effectively use seams, you have laid the groundwork for the next crucial step: managing the edges of your model. Now, we will look at how to use sharps to get that perfect mix of smooth areas and sharp, clear lines.

Understanding sharps and why you use them

In 3D modeling, sharps are edges that you mark to stay crisp or sharp, especially during smoothing. Sharps make your model's edges look just right through a perfect mix of smooth areas and sharp, clear lines. They are useful for things such as machine parts or objects with hard surfaces, where you need edges to be nice and precise, but still want the rest of the model to look smooth.

Sharps let you pick which edges should stand out as sharp and clear, and I will show you exactly how. This trick is great for making your models look more like real-life objects, which often have sharp edges here and there.

Marking edges as sharp: step by step

The process of marking edges as sharp in Blender follows several distinct steps:

1. As with seams, ensure your model is in **Edit Mode** (*Tab*) and that you have selected **Edge Select** mode (press *2*).

2. Choose the edges you wish to define as sharp (remember to use *Shift* + *click* for multiple selections).

3. With your edges selected, you can mark them as sharp in two ways:

    *   *Right-click* anywhere in your **3D Viewport** window while in **Edge Select** mode to open the context menu and select **Edge**, then **Mark Sharp**
    *   Alternatively, use the shortcut *Ctrl* + *E* to open the **Edge** menu directly and choose **Mark Sharp** from the list

    After marking, these edges will visually stand out in **Edit Mode** by turning blue (i.e., they have been successfully defined as sharp), as shown in *Figure 14.4*.

Figure 14.4: Sharp edges in Blender. Left: mesh with no marked sharp edges. Middle: same mesh in Wireframe view showing marked sharp edges (lighter edges). Right: same mesh in Solid view with sharp edges enabled for comparison.

4. For the sharp edges to impact your model's rendered appearance, you need to enable the **Shade Smooth** feature. This can be found by *right-clicking* on your **3D Viewport** area while in **Object Mode**. Check the **Shade Smooth by Angle** option, and you can adjust the angle threshold to control which edges Blender considers sharp based on their angle. This setting allows Blender to apply smooth shading to the model while preserving the sharpness of the marked edges.

Practical application: mechanical and hard surface models

Sharps are super helpful when you want part of your model to be smooth and other parts to have crisp, clear edges. In mechanical and hard surface modeling, sharps are exactly what you need to use if you want your 3D model to look real. With a computer mouse, you would use sharps on the edges where the buttons meet the body of the mouse. This makes the buttons stand out against the smooth, curved surface of the mouse, as in *Figure 14.5*.

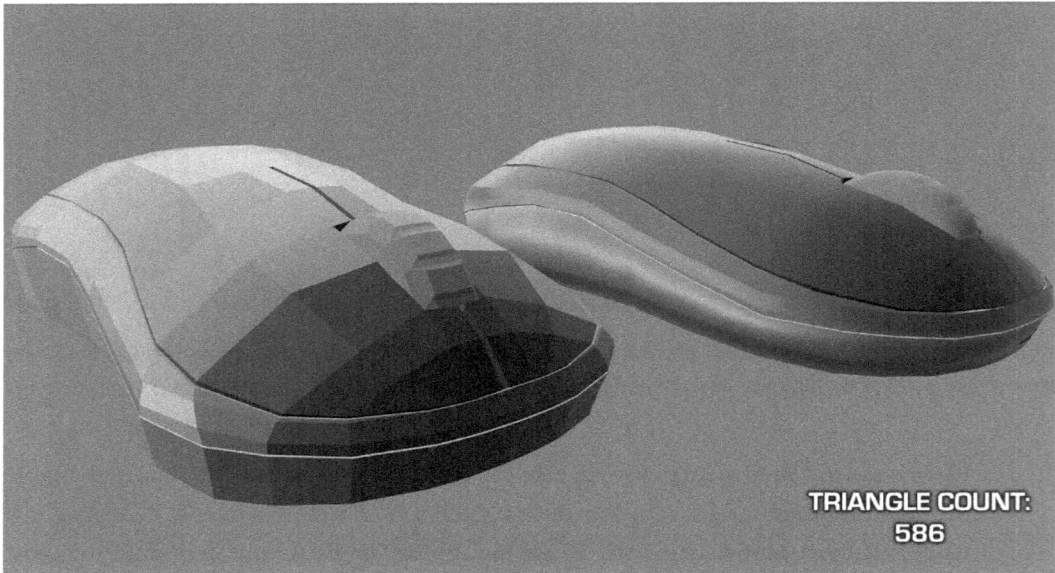

Figure 14.5: Sharps on a computer mouse

Sharps will make your mouse look more realistic because it reflects light like a real computer mouse would.

Note

Normally, **Shade Smooth** averages out the surface normals across the model, which is great for creating soft, organic shapes, but can make hard edges appear too soft or undefined. By marking edges as sharp, you override the smoothing in those areas. Using **Shade Smooth** with this example helps you create the illusion of higher topology density without actually increasing the polygon count.

Another example is modeling a car. Sharps can be used on the edges of doors, windows, and other body parts to create a distinct separation between different components. Modeling cars is one of the best examples of mechanical and hard surface modeling. In these cases, using sharps helps create the appearance of multiple distinct components within a single mesh. This level of control can make a 3D car model look more like it is in real life, reflecting light realistically and showcasing how it has been engineered.

You can also apply sharps to architectural models, such as the edges of a building's windows, doors, and rooflines. These sharp edges make the architectural details pop, clearly showing where different materials meet, such as stone against glass or metal, making the whole design look more realistic and interesting.

As you get more comfortable with sharps, try them out on various models to see the difference sharp edges can make. Practice on objects such as furniture, electronics, or even characters with distinct armor or clothing pieces. The key to getting better with Blender is to keep practicing and exploring different ways to use sharps in your work. Go ahead and experiment to discover how they can enhance the realism of your models.

With a solid understanding of sharps, you are ready to try more advanced techniques such as creases and bevel weights. These tools will further enhance your ability to shape and refine your models with precision.

Mastering creases and bevel weights: advanced techniques in Blender

Blender is not just about simple modeling; it is packed with cool tricks such as creases and bevel weights to make your 3D stuff look even better. They help you shape your model with more precision, making it look nicer and work better.

Sometimes, though, if you add too much crease to an edge, your model can end up with super sharp, unnatural-looking corners where you want a smooth transition. Or, if you get carried away with bevel weights, parts of your model might look too bulky or oddly pinched, ruining the realistic look you were going for.

Table 14.1 is a quick reference guide for you to keep in mind before we go into each of these in detail:

Technique	Best used for	Pros	Cons/watch outs	Example use case
Creases	Subdivision surfaces where edges need to stay sharper	Non-destructive Works well with the **Subdivision Surface** modifier	Can produce artifacts if overused Not supported in all exports	Making a sci-fi panel with hard edges but smooth corners
Sharpened edges	Hard surface models, bevel modifiers, and baking workflows	Great for defining UV seams and smoothing groups Works well with auto-smooth	Can be destructive if applied early Needs careful control	Baking a normal map from a high-poly hard surface model
Support loops	Clean subdivision topology and animation-ready models	Physically accurate results Fully compatible with all render engines	Adds geometry Slower to model and edit	Modeling a stylized character for animation or rigging

Table 14.1: A cheat sheet of advanced techniques for mastering creases and bevel weights

As with everything in 3D modeling, it is all about finding the right balance to make your model come to life just the way you imagined.

Controlling subdivision surfaces with creases

Creases let you define which edges remain sharp in a smoothed model. This is important for designs that have a mix of hard and soft edges. For example, if you are creating doors, you want each plank of the mesh to have distinct contrast against one another while maintaining softened edges.

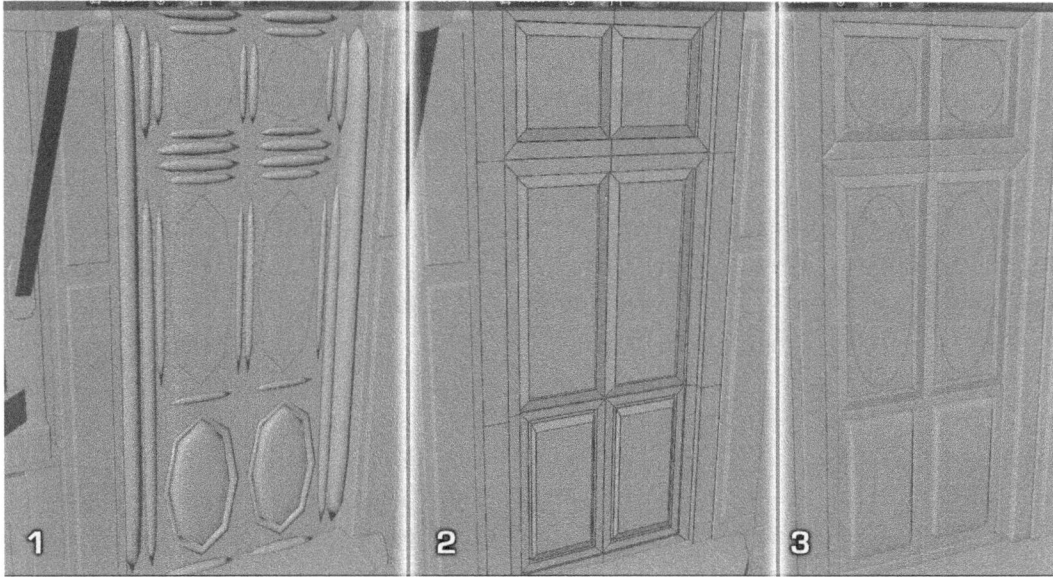

Figure 14.6: Controlling subdivision surfaces with creases for a door model

As shown in *Figure 14.6*, the first part shows a simple mesh of a door with a **Subdivision** modifier applied, which naturally smoothens the geometry and creates rounded, spherical forms. In the second part, we see creases applied to specific edges, allowing control over how much smoothing will be applied to each edge. The final part demonstrates the results of the same **Subdivision** modifier, but with **creases** in place. Using this visual example, you can see how this non-destructive workflow effectively balances smooth and sharp features in the model.

To apply creases to a model in Blender, follow the next steps:

1. In **Edit Mode** (press *Tab*), switch to **Edge Select** mode (press *2*) to choose the edges you want to crease. These edges are typically where you want to maintain sharpness amid a generally smooth surface.

2. With your edges selected, access the **Crease** tool by pressing *Ctrl* + *E* to open the **Edge** menu, then select **Edge Crease** (or just use the *Shift* + *E* shortcut).

3. As you drag your mouse or use your keyboard to input a value, you will see the **Crease** value adjust in real time.

4. Once you create a crease, you can adjust its value with a temporary crease menu found at the bottom right of the **3D Viewport** window, as seen in *Figure 14.7*.

Figure 14.7: Applying creases in Blender

Edges with creases will not smooth, even with subdivision, so you can use them to create a blend of sharp and smooth surfaces on your model (e.g., a leather couch with detailed stitching). The overall couch should appear smooth and soft, but the stitches need to have defined, sharp lines to stand out as realistic details (*Figure 14.8*).

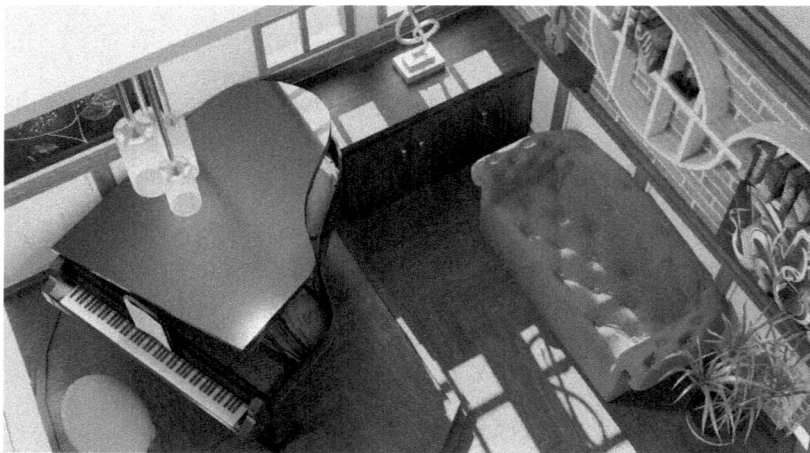

Figure 14.8: Leather couch in "Blender 3, Beginners Step by Step Guide to Isometric Rooms" by 3D Tudor

Fine-tuning your model's edges with bevel weights

Bevel weights provide an additional layer of control, letting you specify the intensity of the bevel effect on individual edges. This is handy for making small, cool details on your model, such as making parts of machines or buildings look like they catch the light just right.

For a wooden table, adjusting the bevel weight on the edges can give it a worn look (see *Figure 14.9*), as if it has been used and slightly softened over time, rather than having sharp, brand-new edges.

Figure 14.9: Medieval Tudor era-style table by 3D Tudor

Bevel weights can enhance the realism and visual appeal of what you create, whether you are working on mechanical parts, architectural elements, or any design that benefits from varied edge treatments. The following step-by-step guide will walk you through the process of selecting edges, adjusting their bevel weight, and configuring the **Bevel** modifier to achieve the desired effect on your model:

1. Start by selecting the object, then apply the **Bevel** modifier and set the **Limit Method** to **Weight**. You will not see any changes to the mesh at this point, as bevel weights have not been applied yet.

2. Make sure to have **Clamp Overlap** ticked off. If needed, select **Switch to Edge Selection Mode**.

3. Select all edges and *right-click* and choose **Edge Bevel Weight**, then set the factor to 1. This will apply a bevel to all the selected edges.

    This weight dictates how strongly the **Bevel** modifier will affect each edge, allowing for a controlled application of bevels across your model. For example, in a model of a kitchen knife, a high value would sharpen the edges of the blade, making it look more realistically thin and sharp. In the same model, a low bevel weight would softly round the handle edges, making the handle look more comfortable to grip and less sharp.

4. To refine the selection, go to **Select** and then **Sharp Edges**. By default, **30** degrees of sharpness will be sufficient while in **Edge Selection Mode**.

5. Next, invert the selection using *Ctrl + I* to select all the non-sharp edges.

6. With the non-sharp edges selected, *right-click* and choose **Edge Bevel Weight**. Drag the slider inward to apply a negative factor, ensuring that no bevel is applied to the smooth edges, as in *Figure 14.10*.

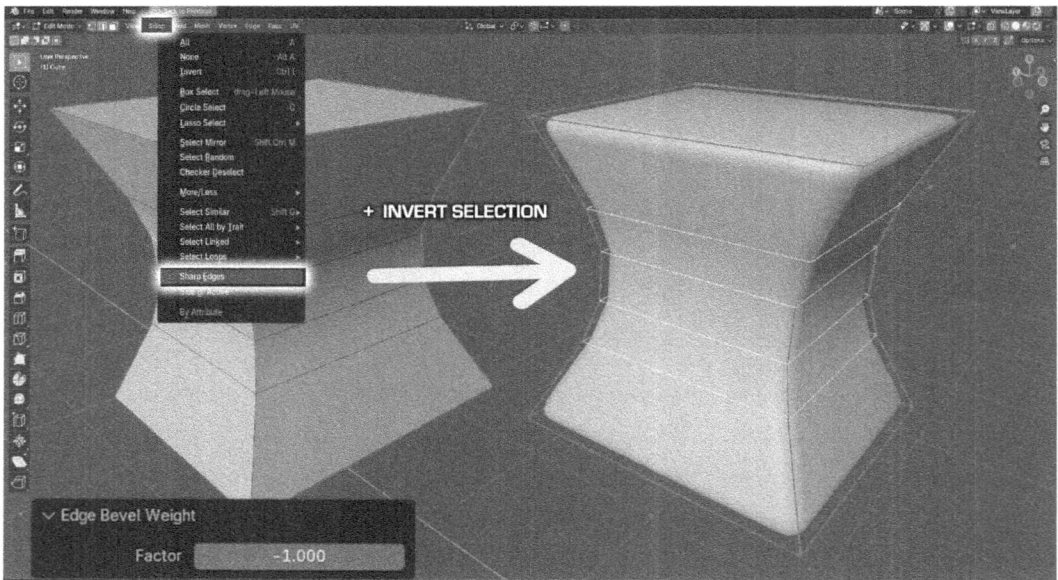

Figure 14.10: Following along steps 4 to 6

7. Finally, manually select any specific edges where you would like to apply a custom bevel or further sharpen an existing bevel and adjust their bevel weight as needed. This workflow lets you control which edges receive a bevel while preserving the smoothness of others.

In the example shown in *Figure 14.11*, we use a -1 factor weight to ignore the edge of the beveling so that it sharpens out the inner edge. We also use a factor of 0.5 for the inner ring of the cup to give it a partial bevel and sharpen the edge.

Figure 14.11: Using bevel weights on a coffee cup

Using creases and bevel weights can up your game in 3D modeling. The more you use these tools, the better your models will look. As we move on, in the next section, we will talk about the common mistakes beginners often make and will give you tips on how to avoid them.

Navigating common pitfalls in Blender modeling

Getting the hang of Blender can be tricky, and it is easy to slip up, especially when you are just starting. Mistakes with basics such as seams, sharps, creases, and bevel weights happen to everyone. When you are learning to ride a bike, sometimes you will wobble, maybe even fall, but that is just part of the learning process. This chapter is like your training wheels.

We have all been there with seams, marking too many or too few, and ending up with a model that looks like a patchwork quilt. That is what can happen if you apply sharp edges without thinking about the overall shape of your model.

We will look at four main areas: overusing seams in UV unwrapping, misapplying sharp edges, overreliance on creases for detail, and incorrectly applying bevel weights. Each section will start with a pitfall, basically, a trap that is easy to fall into if you are not careful, and then possible solutions.

Overusing seams in UV unwrapping

One mistake you are highly likely to make is using too many seams. If you do that, you will have UV maps that are more complicated than they need to be. This will also inadvertently overcomplicate the texturing process (as in *Figure 14.12*).

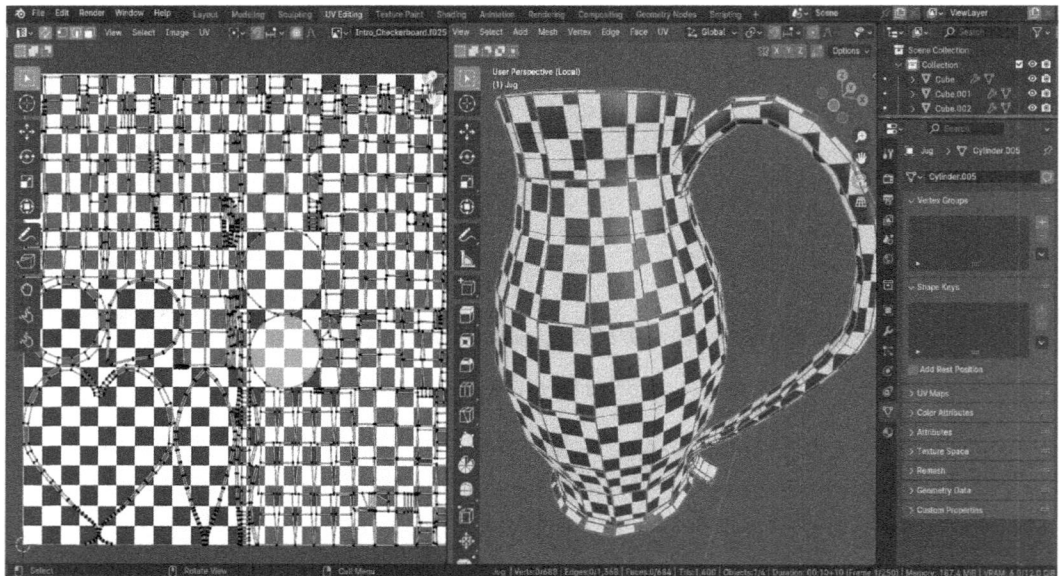

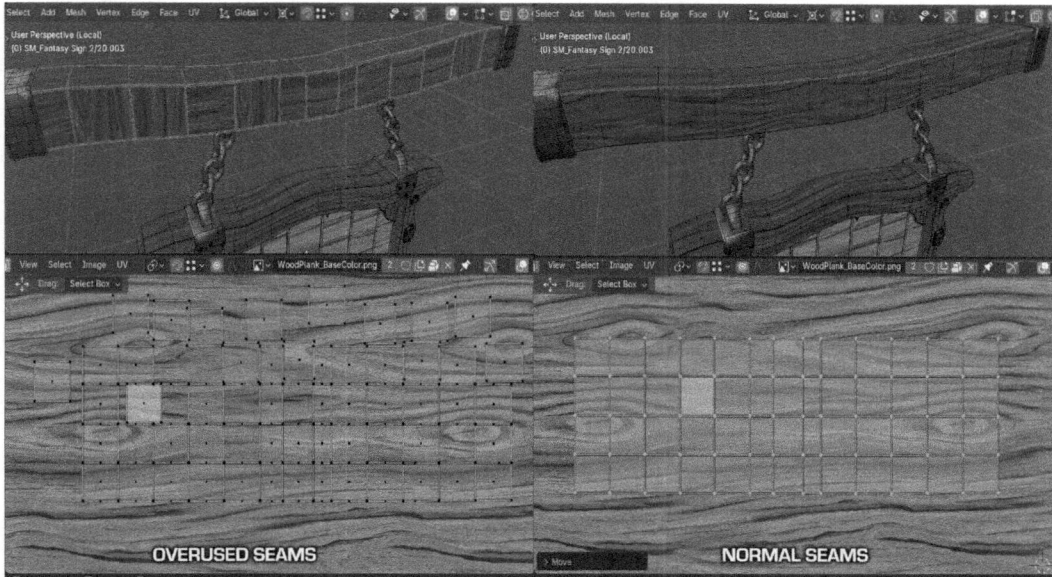

Figure 14.12: Overusing seams in UV unwrapping (left) and solving the problem (right) on a carafe (top) vs. a wooden sign (bottom) in UV Mapping Bootcamp: Unwrapping & Texturing in Blender by 3D Tudor

Note

Seams are visible in the textures of a mesh. More chunks mean less pixel density and lower resolution on textures. This is because each UV island has to be separated with a small gap to avoid texture bleeding; more gaps mean less of a texture map is being used.

To avoid this problem, you can do the following:

- Before marking seams, imagine the most efficient way to unfold your model. Try to use the least number of seams needed to lay out the UV map flat without distortion.
- Place seams at natural or less visible parts of the model, such as where clothing meets skin or under hidden areas.

Misapplying sharp edges

Incorrectly applying sharp edges can disrupt your model's flow, as in *Figure 14.13*. This will make your model look unnatural. You will be able to see it after you apply **Smooth Shading** because your face normals will have been averaged out.

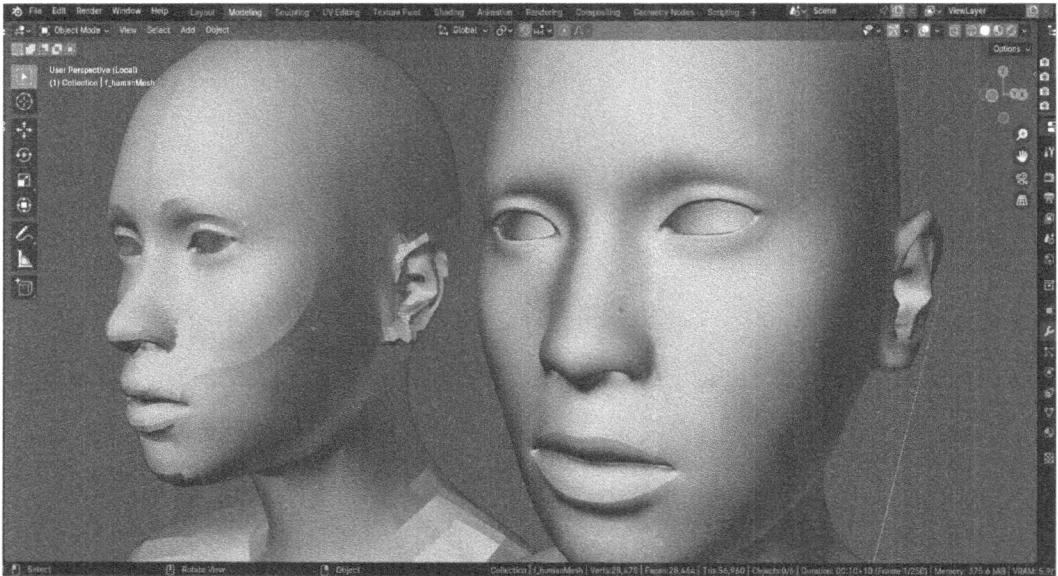

Figure 14.13: Misapplying sharp edges (left) and solving the problem (right)

To avoid this problem, only apply sharp edges where absolutely necessary. For example, if you are working on a robot arm, you would only want to apply sharp edges around the joints and panels. To find out more about that, make sure you read through the next chapter.

> Tip
>
> Every once in a while, switch to the **Smooth Shading** view to assess how sharp edges affect the model's appearance, adjusting as needed to maintain a natural flow.

Overreliance on creases for detail

Using too many creases to make a model detailed can make your model look artificial. This is because you might make your edge flow go a way you did not want it to, as in *Figure 14.14*.

Figure 14.14: Overrelying on creases for detail (left) and solving the problem (right)

This can slow things down and make rendering take longer. To avoid this problem, you can do the following:

- Use creases to maintain edge definition in key areas, but consider adding geometry for finer details. For example, for a keyboard key, instead of just using creases, you could build those details into the model using a bevel edge and additional edge loops. This makes your shape easier to control without needing to add a bunch of extra steps that make everything slower. When you mix in real details with the basic shape and subdivision, your control over the edge flow will determine how smooth the corners are.

- For surface details that do not alter the silhouette, consider using edge loops instead of increasing geometry with creases and subdivisions.

> **Tip**
>
> Slide your edge across the surface for additional control. You can do that by double-tapping *G* with an edge selected.

Baking normal maps: capturing high-detail model intricacies

To do that in Blender, you will need to go through a process that captures the intricate details of a high-detail model onto a **Normal Map**, which you can then apply to a lower-detail version of the same model. Since we will talk about UV unwrapping in detail in *Chapter 15* in *Part 1* of this book, here is a simplified breakdown of how to do it:

1. You will need two versions of your model: one with high detail and another with lower detail. Make sure both models have the same overall shape and size, but the high-detail model should have all the extra bumps, dents, and textures you want to capture.

2. Before you can apply a **Normal Map**, the low-detail model needs UV mapping. This process tells Blender how to wrap the **Normal Map** around the model. In **Edit Mode**, select all faces of the low-detail model, then unwrap it by going to **UV | Unwrap**.

3. Place both models in the same location in your **3D Viewport** window. The high-detail model should overlap the low-detail model perfectly. This way, when you bake the normal map, the details correspond correctly to the surface of the lower-detail model.

4. Select the high-detail model first, then hold *Shift* and select the low-detail model so both are selected, with the low-detail model being the active selection.

5. Now, it is time to bake the normal map:

   a. Go to the **Properties** panel, find the **Render Properties** tab, make sure you are in **Cycles**, and scroll down to the **Bake** section.

   b. Choose **Normal** as **Bake Type**.

   c. Make sure to select **Selected to Active** since you want to bake details from the high-detail (selected) model to the low-detail (active) model.

   d. Set **Ray Distance** to 0 to give yourself maximum distance.

   e. Create a new material for the low-detail model if it does not already have one. To do that, go to the Shader Editor. Add an **Image Texture** node, click **New**, and set **Resolution** to **2048 by 2048**.

   f. Select your **Image Texture** node and then click the **Bake** button to start the baking process. Blender will render a **Normal Map** that captures the surface details of your high-detail model.

6. Next, apply the **Normal Map** to the low-detail model:

    a. Create a new material for the low-detail model if it does not already have one.

    b. In the Shader Editor, add an **Image Texture** node and open the baked normal map.

    c. Add a **Normal Map** node (found under **Vector**) and connect the **Image Texture** node to the **Normal Map** node, then connect that to the **Normal** input of the model's shader, such as the **Principled BSDF** node shown in *Figure 14.15*.

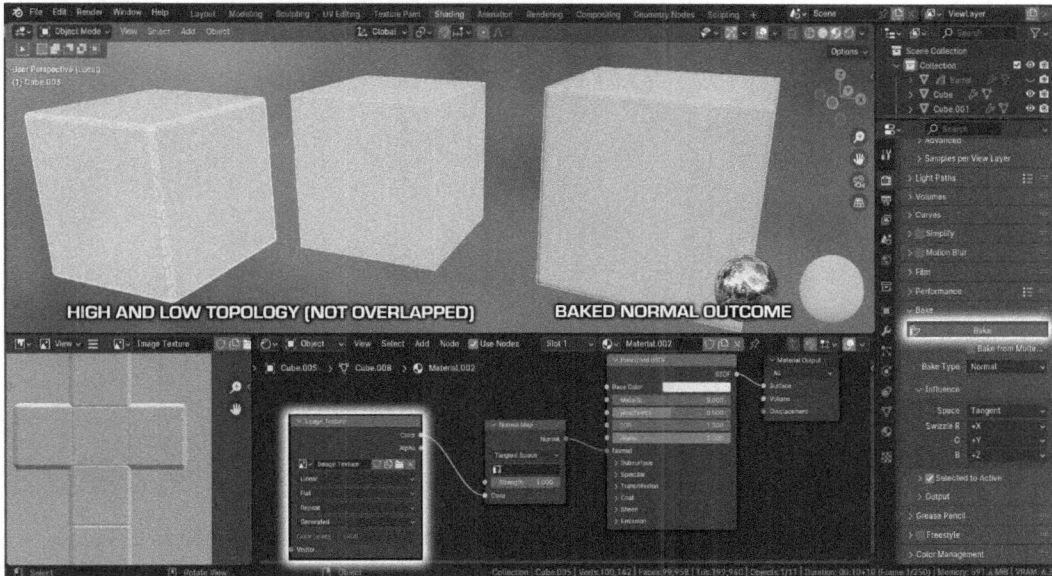

Figure 14.15: Applying a baked normal map to a low-detail model

> **Note**
>
> Ensure that the **Normal Map** node is set to **Tangent Space** for the correct interpretation of the map.

Following these steps will enhance your low-detail model with the visual complexity of the high-detail version, without adding extra polygons, keeping your scene efficient and easier to render.

Incorrectly applying bevel weights

Smoothing every edge without thinking about where your model actually needs it might mean that you are inaccurately applying bevel weights. For example, imagine you are making a bookshelf such as the one in *Figure 14.16*.

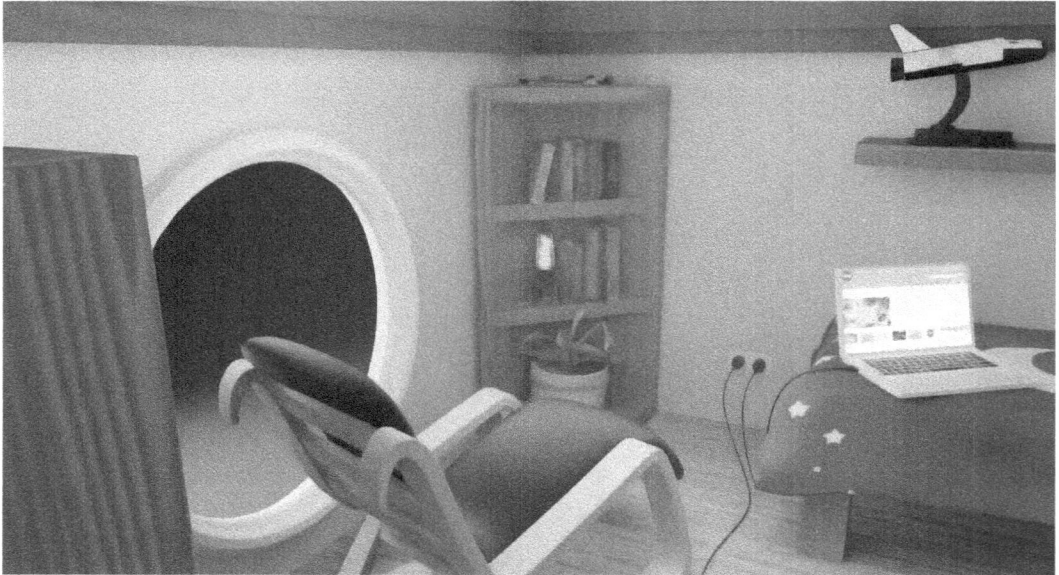

Figure 14.16: Bookshelf from "Mastering the Art of Isometric Room Design in Blender 3" by 3D Tudor

If you apply the same amount of **Bevel** (or **Smoothing**) to the edges where the shelves meet the side panels as you do to the decorative trim on the top, the bookshelf might not look right. The edges where the shelves meet should be sharper to show a clear definition. Doing it all the same way can make the bookshelf lose its detailed appearance.

To avoid this problem, you can do the following:

- Adjust bevel weights based on the edge's role in the model. For example, edges forming a mechanical part's interface might require a heavier bevel.

- Use the **Bevel** modifier together with **Bevel Weight** for a way of modeling that lets you make changes easily without permanently altering the model.

Blender can be a bit of a rollercoaster when you are learning the ropes, and mistakes are pretty much part of the process! In this section, we explored how to avoid common pitfalls with each of these tools to keep your models looking natural and realistic.

Overusing UV seams can complicate your texturing and leave models looking fragmented, while applying sharp edges without consideration can disrupt a model's flow. Creases are helpful for detail but can make things look rigid if overdone, and normal maps let you capture fine details without overloading your model with geometry. Finally, we wrapped up the section with bevel weights, which are best used strategically to balance your edges and keep your details as they should be.

So, as you continue working in Blender, remember these tips to avoid common modeling snags and improve your workflow!

Summary

This chapter introduced you to the world of seams and sharps, guiding you through the sometimes tricky terrain of preparing your models for texturing. You learned how to strategically use seams to lay out your models flat and sharps to give them that extra bit of character. We also talked about creases and using Blender's **Bevel Weight** function to balance the softness and sharpness of your model's geometry.

Along the way, we also uncovered some common pitfalls in using seams and sharps. For every challenge presented, we also discovered tips and strategies to keep our work on track. Armed with that knowledge, you are now ready to texture your models with confidence, bringing them to life with colors and details that tell a story all their own.

As we close *Chapter 14*, we are now ready to tackle UV unwrapping. The next chapter promises to be a comprehensive guide to UV unwrapping, where you will learn how to apply detailed maps to your models, bringing them to life with color and texture.

Further reading

- If you want to see how bevel weights sharpen or soften furniture details, jump into *Mastering the Art of Isometric Room Design in Blender 3* (https://www.udemy.com/course/blender-3-mastering-the-art-of-isometric-room-design-in/?referralCode=663C5F3BD974 A0124FB7). The lesson shows exactly where to dial weight values so bookshelves are crisp without over-smoothing the whole piece.

- If you are battling seam placement on round assets such as a Viking shield, watch the shield demo in *UV Mapping Bootcamp: Unwrapping & Texturing in Blender* (https://www.udemy.com/course/uv-mapping-bootcamp-unwrapping-texturing-in-blender/?refer ralCode=BD129B8744D8DA188A38). You will learn how to hide cuts, keep the checkerboard tidy, and avoid the quilting effect that kills texel density.

Subscribe to Game Dev Assembly!

We are excited to introduce **Game Dev Assembly**, our brand-new newsletter dedicated to everything game development. Whether you're coding, designing, animating, or managing a studio, we've got insights, trends, and expert advice to help you create, innovate, and thrive. Sign up now and get exciting benefits.

https://packt.link/gamedev-newsletter

Join the 3D Tudor Channel Discord Server!

Join the 3D Tudor Channel Discord Server, a creative hub for learning Blender, Unreal Engine, Substance Painter, and 3D modeling, for discussions with the authors and other readers:

https://discord.gg/5EkjT36vUj

15

Mastering the Art of UV Unwrapping in Blender

UV unwrapping in Blender is a really important step when you are working with 3D models and want to put images or textures on them. It involves transforming a 3D object into a flat 2D surface, enabling it to map pictures or textures accurately onto the model.

Think of UV unwrapping like wrapping a present, but in reverse. Instead of wrapping paper around a gift, you are taking the outer surface of your 3D model and laying it out flat. This flat version is called the **UV map**. Once you have this map, you can easily paint or apply textures to it, knowing that everything will line up perfectly when it is wrapped back around the 3D model.

We will start simple, opening Blender and setting up a basic model, so you can follow along step by step. Then, you will see how textures work with UVs, and you will create texture atlases, a way to pack multiple textures into one space. This chapter will also cover **U Dimension (UDIM)**, a method that takes your texture detail to the next level, and finish with tips on optimizing your UV space to make everything look its best without wasting any texture space.

With UV unwrapping, you can make sure every detail of your texture appears exactly where you want it on your model. It is what allows you to place textures, whether it is wood grain, fabric, or detailed patterns, onto your models in the right way.

So, in this chapter, we will cover the following topics:

- Demystifying UV unwrapping
- UV unwrapping a simple model

- Applying textures based on UV placement
- Initiating you into the world of Magic UV in Blender
- Creating and applying texture atlases in Blender: a comprehensive guide
- Mastering UDIM in Blender: enhancing texture detail and efficiency
- Optimizing UV space for texture quality and efficiency

You may think you need a *Book of Shadows* to unlock the secrets of UV unwrapping, but don't worry, this chapter will *be* your *Book of Shadows*! Let's jump in!

Technical requirements

As for **Blender 4.5 LTS (Long-Term Support)**, the general requirements include a macOS 11.2 or newer (Apple Silicon supported natively) operating system, or a Linux (64-bit, glibc 2.28 or newer) operating system. Blender now requires a CPU with the SSE4.2 instruction set, at least 8 GB of RAM (32 GB recommended for heavy scenes), and a GPU supporting OpenGL 4.3 with a minimum of 2 GB of VRAM.

For a full list of technical requirements, please refer back to *Chapter 1* of this part.

Demystifying UV unwrapping

Before we look at the practical aspects of UV unwrapping in Blender, you need to understand some key terms and concepts that will form the foundation of your knowledge. These definitions will help you grasp the basic ideas behind how UV unwrapping works and why it is such a vital part of 3D modeling.

The term *UV* refers to the coordinates used to describe points on a flat 2D surface, analogous to the X, Y, and Z coordinates used for 3D space. In UV mapping, *U* and *V* are the axes for the flat surface's width and height. This system makes sure that every point on the 3D model corresponds to an exact point on the flat texture.

UV mapping is the process of projecting a 2D image texture onto a 3D model. By unwrapping the 3D model into a flat 2D representation, artists can easily apply textures so that the details and patterns match up correctly with the 3D form.

The **UV layout** refers to the arrangement of all the UV islands on the UV map. It is essentially how the UV islands are positioned and organized within the UV space. An efficient UV layout minimizes wasted space and ensures that textures are applied smoothly and without distortion.

On the other hand, **UV islands** are the individual pieces of the unwrapped mesh. These pieces are created based on the seams marked on the 3D model and can be moved, scaled, and rotated within the UV layout to optimize texture placement and alignment.

Last but not least, UV unwrapping is the technique of flattening out a 3D model to create its UV map. UV unwrapping is simple: you unfold the 3D model's surfaces. This minimizes distortions and overlaps, making it easier to paint or apply textures so that what you see in the flat, 2D version is reflected in the 3D version when UV unwrapping is finished.

Without a good UV map, textures can appear stretched, distorted, or misaligned, detracting from the realism and visual appeal of your model. Proper UV unwrapping ensures that every detail of your texture looks just right. Now, let us dive into the steps that will take you from marking seams to applying textures.

The steps that follow will guide you from the initial cut to a finished UV map to which you can apply textures:

1. **Marking seams:** The first step in UV unwrapping is to mark seams on your 3D model. **Seams** are edges where the mesh will be cut to lay flat. If you place them correctly, seams can minimize visible texture seams in the final model. For example, placing seams in less noticeable areas, such as where clothes meet the skin or under the arms, can help make the texture appear more natural on the 3D model. To read more about seams, go back to *Chapter 14* in this part of the book.

   > Note
   >
   > Marking seams only affects the **UV Unwrap** operation. All other UV techniques create UVs from different projection functionalities. It is also worth saying that marking seams does not affect **Smart UV Project** or cube projection.

2. **Unwrapping:** Once the seams are marked, the model can be unwrapped. In Blender, this is typically done using the **Unwrap** operation, which calculates how to lay out the 3D surface in 2D space based on the marked seams. The result is a UV map, which is a flat representation of the model's surface.

3. **Editing the UV layout:** After unwrapping, the UV layout can be adjusted in the **UV Editing** tab. This involves moving, scaling, and rotating the UV islands (i.e., the individual pieces of the unwrapped mesh). Make sure you have the desired object/objects selected, then go to **Edit Mode** and select all faces (press *A* while in the 3D Viewport) to see the objects' UVs, as shown in *Figure 15.1* with a default cube, which already comes with preset UV data. This way, you will use the texture space without gaps and align the texture patterns where you want them.

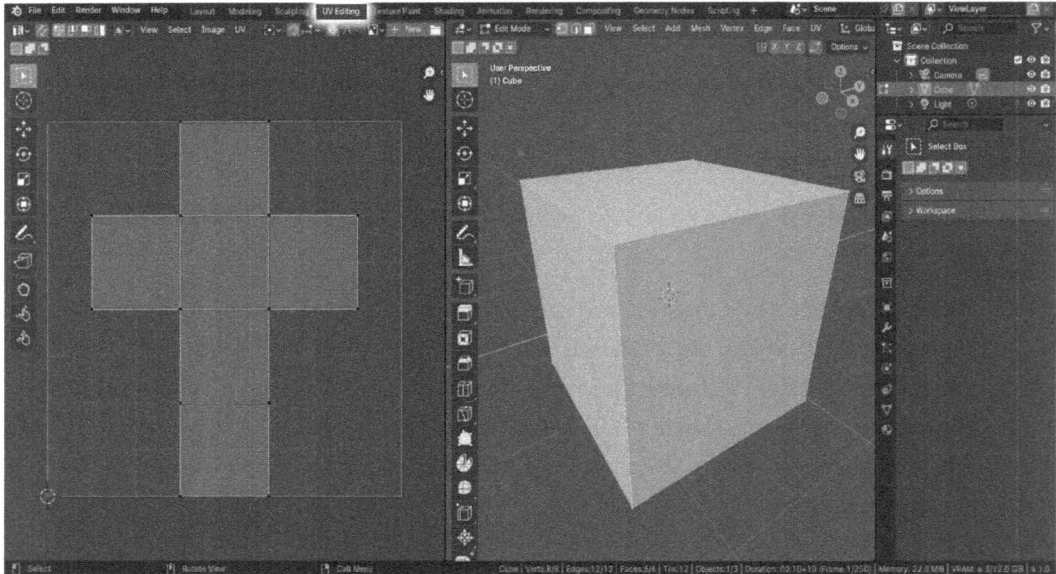

Figure 15.1: Visualizing a UV map

4. **Applying textures:** With the UV map prepared, textures can be applied. **Textures** are 2D images that cover the surface of the 3D model, and they will be discussed in more detail throughout the chapter. Because the UV map tells Blender how these textures map onto the model, careful use of **UV Layout** can change a simple clay figurine to a lifelike character. This way, you can add detailed skin textures that show wrinkles and pores or realistic fabric textures for clothes with visible threads.

Now that we have covered how to unwrap UVs (marking seams, unfolding models, adjusting layouts, and adding textures), let us take a step back and dive into texture baking. Before we get to why UV unwrapping is so important (we will cover that soon, I promise), understanding how texture baking fits into the process will give you a clearer picture of how these techniques work together to make your models look amazing. Whether you are creating assets for games, animations, or any other 3D project, learning this step will level up your workflow in no time!

UV unwrapping versus texture baking

While UV unwrapping is essential for getting textures in the right place, it is only part of the bigger picture when it comes to making your models look polished and detailed. That is where **texture baking** comes into play. This is essential knowledge before we continue, kind of like knowing a good diversion when a slipway on the motorway is closed. Miss it, and you might end up stuck in a traffic jam of stretched textures and misaligned UVs!

Let us imagine you are working on a cube. When you apply a texture to a 3D model in Blender, the program looks at the UV map to determine how to project the 2D texture onto the 3D surface. Each point on the UV map corresponds to a point on the model's surface, and the texture image is mapped to it. Put simply, the position and layout of your UV islands within the UV Editor need to be on point.

If you have unwrapped a cube and laid out its UV map in a cross formation, which is a common approach for cubes, the texture will be applied to each face of the cube based on the corresponding section of the texture image. If you move or rotate the UV islands in the UV Editor, the texture's appearance on those cube faces will change based on the changes you have made. This manual process provides control over how textures wrap around the model, making it a vital step in 3D modeling.

UV unwrapping prepares the model for texturing, while texture baking captures and transfers details, often relying on the UV map created during unwrapping. At this point, I recommend watching *The ONLY Normal Map Baking Tutorial You Need to Watch* (https://www.youtube.com/watch?v=e2aCEbcA7q8), which we created for free on YouTube.

On the other hand, texture baking, such as in **Substance Painter** (https://www.adobe.com/products/substance3d-painter.html) or Blender, involves transferring details (e.g., colour, lighting, and shadows) from a high-poly model to a texture map that can be used on a low-poly version of the model. Texture baking lets you keep complex visual details without the computational cost of rendering a high-poly model in real time. We will talk about it again in *Chapter 3* in *Part 2* of this book.

Despite their different priorities and roles in the process, UV unwrapping and texture baking work hand in hand to make your models look detailed and polished. Still, UV unwrapping is where it all starts. Think of it as that life-saving diversion keeping you on the right path. Now, let us cruise into why UV unwrapping is so important!

Understanding the importance of UV unwrapping

UV unwrapping gives you the most control over how a texture is applied to a model. Without UV unwrapping, textures might stretch or compress in ways you do not want them to. For example, if you directly apply a texture to a 3D model such as a window without unwrapping it first, you might notice that the texture stretches unevenly across the frame or warps around the edges, making the window look unrealistic and distorted, as in *Figure 15.2* on the left.

Figure 15.2: Medieval window with applied texture with UV unwrapping used (right) vs. without (left) in the Blender 20 Massive Fantasy Windows Asset Pack by 3D Tudor

Also, by unwrapping a model, you can paint or apply detailed textures directly to the 2D UV layout. This means that you can add specific details exactly where you want them on the model. For example, in a video game such as *Sims 4*, because of UV unwrapping, you might see characters with unique tattoos that wrap perfectly around their arms or scars that follow the lines of their faces perfectly.

The impact of UV unwrapping on the quality of your model can only be as good as you make it. With a well-organized UV layout, you can have higher-resolution textures without wasting space. Imagine you are using a single sheet of paper to wrap a gift, and you cut and fold the paper to cover it completely without any leftover paper. This is similar to organizing your UV layout, where you make sure every bit of your texture space is used effectively to make your texture placement better.

By being careful about that, you make sure every leaf, rock, and bit of ground looks as good and realistic as possible, making the game world feel alive and inviting, by hiding hiding how repetitive textures are.

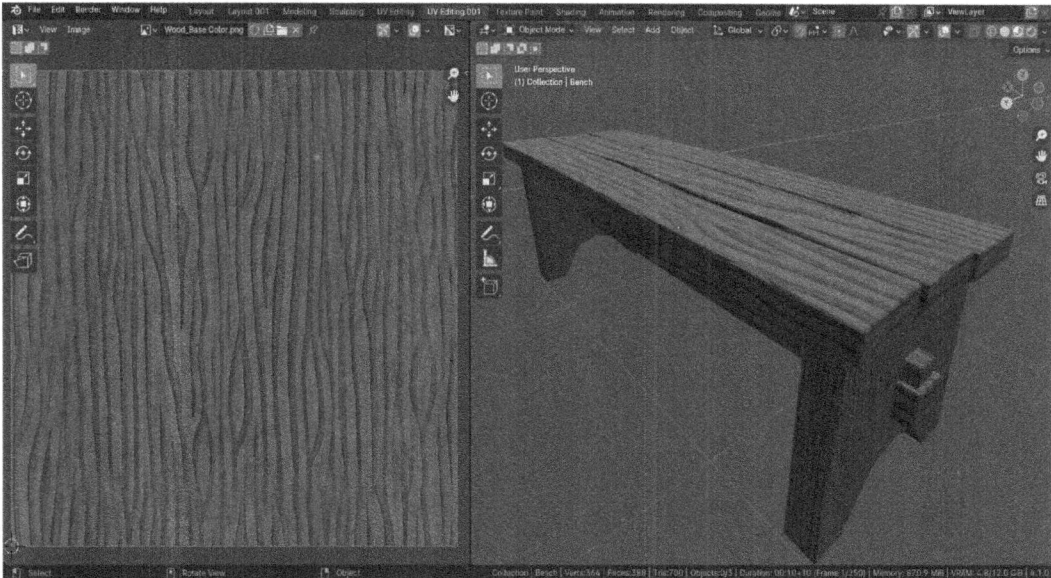

Figure 15.3: Effective UV unwrapping results

Figure 15.3 shows a single wood texture map being used on a bench. By changing your scaling and wrapping your UVs, you can make the same pattern look different on parts of the model. For example, the bench has a larger pattern on the top, making the wood seem coarser and weathered. The side of the bench has a much finer pattern, making it seem smoother. As you wrestle with UVs and textures, you will discover that even the most perfect models can throw a tantrum, but do not worry; with the right tricks up your sleeve, there is always a solution.

Complex models can be difficult to unwrap without stretching or distortion. This is one of those challenges that you can mitigate by carefully placing seams and by using Blender's various unwrapping algorithms to find the best fit. For example, if you are building a detailed medieval castle model with stone walls and wooden beams, I would place seams around areas that are less likely to draw attention, such as the junctions where the stone walls meet the ground or behind the wooden beams (*Figure 15.4*).

Figure 15.4: Wooden meeting stone walls in building medieval worlds – Unreal Engine 5 Modular Kitbash by 3D Tudor

Another common challenge you will come across is visible seams where the edges of the UV islands meet. Fortunately for you, this issue can be managed effectively with the right techniques and practices. Visible seams in UV mapping can be effectively managed by using these techniques:

- Strategically placing seams in less noticeable areas (i.e., less visible areas of the model). Follow natural lines and breaks in the geometry, such as edges of clothing or accessories, where seams would naturally occur.

Figure 15.5 shows how bad visible seams can be. Placing them in less noticeable areas, such as on the inside of the legs and on the top where the parts touch, will make it seem like they are two unique pieces and make the error less noticeable.

Figure 15.5: A visualization of strategically placing seams in less noticeable areas with a hidden seam in the crevice of the stool on the right

- Using texture painting to hide seams and make sure your models look smooth and polished. Here are some techniques to make the most of it:

  - Use texture painting tools in software such as Blender, Substance Painter, or Photoshop to paint or blend textures directly on the model.

  - Manually paint over the seams to match the surrounding texture, ensuring a seamless look between UV islands.

  - Try gradient techniques to gradually blend the texture colours at the seam lines.

  - Try using different layers for base color, details, and blending.

  - Adding **triplanar projection** can help since you are using 3D spaces to apply texture data onto UV coordinates. This means that if you are creating a detailed dragon model with scales and horns, triplanar projection allows you to wrap the scale textures smoothly around its body and horns. In doing so, you will not have awkward lines or gaps where the texture pieces meet.

Choosing the right UV unwrapping method

The UV unwrapping method you choose, whether it is auto/smart, seam-based, or projection-based, should meet the specific needs of your project:

*   **Smart UV unwrapping**: This is great for when you need something quick and do not need everything to be perfect. It creates UV maps for you automatically, so it is perfect for rough drafts or simple models where you do not need to tweak things manually.
*   **Seam-based UV unwrapping**: This gives you full control by letting you choose where to place seams on your model. It is perfect for tricky shapes, such as characters or detailed objects, because you can customize the UV layout and avoid weird stretching.
*   **Projection-based UV unwrapping**: This is a fast option for simple shapes such as cubes or cylinders. It projects the texture straight onto the model from a set angle, making it super handy for straightforward models such as walls or pipes.

Knowing which method to use and when will take your texturing skills to the next level, whether you are working in Blender or any other 3D tool!

UV unwrapping is key to making your 3D models look realistic. It lets you control exactly how textures wrap around your model, so nothing looks stretched or out of place. By organizing UV layouts and blending seams, you can create smooth, natural-looking surfaces.

In the next section, we will be taking a practical approach to UV unwrapping by preparing a simple model.

UV unwrapping a simple model

Blender typically opens in the **Layout** workspace, which is designed for general 3D modeling tasks, as we discussed in *Chapter 1* in this part of the book. You will see a default scene that often includes a camera, a light, and a cube. This cube is a good starting point because of its straightforward geometry, making it easier to see the effects of UV unwrapping, as shown in *Figure 15.6*.

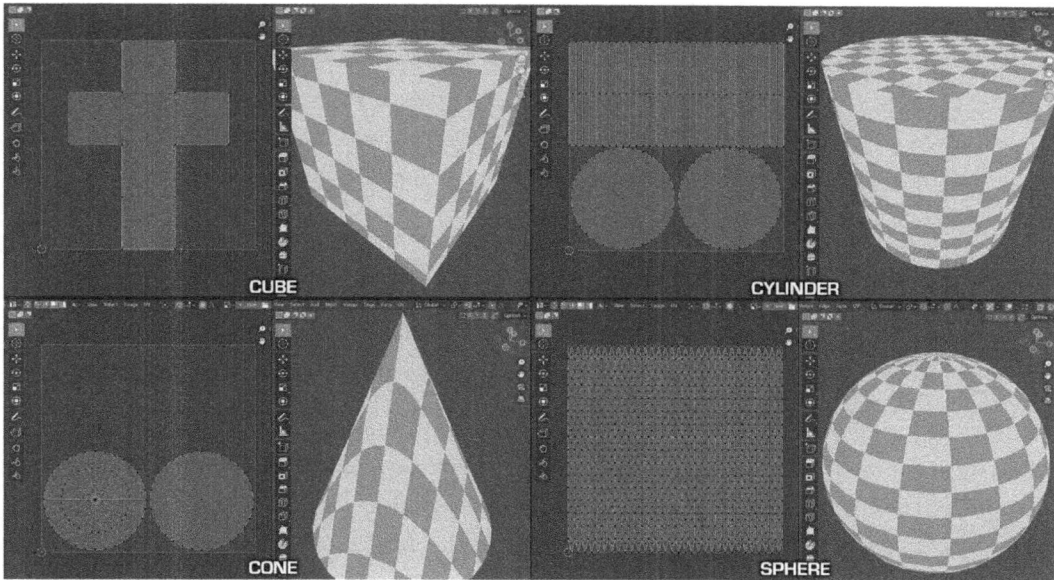

Figure 15.6: UV unwrapping a cube (top left) versus a cone (bottom left)

If you were UV unwrapping a 3D model that has the shape of a cone instead, you would need to take into account the tapering sides and the pointy top, as you can also see in *Figure 15.6*.

Note

In Blender, primitive shapes such as cubes, cylinders, cones, and spheres come with their own unique UV maps, allowing you to apply textures directly without issues, as long as the shape has not been distorted afterward. These basic shapes also serve as useful previews of how different geometries are unwrapped (as seen in *Figure 15.6*). For example, a cube typically unwraps into a six-sided, unfolded cardboard packaging-like shape, while a cylinder creates a circular top and bottom with a rectangular side that wraps around its circumference. The cone unwraps by squishing from the top down into a circular shape, and the sphere's UVs resemble an atlas map with a single vertical UV split going from top to bottom. By understanding these UV layouts, you can break down more complex assets into simpler parts, using the unwrapping techniques of these primitives.

Alright—primitives unpacked, seams sliced, and checkerboards looking tidy. Now, let's zoom out for a minute. Instead of clicking straight into the next tool, we will step back and ask *why* we unwrap the way we do. A bit of theory goes a long way: when you understand the logic behind UV layouts, every cylinder, sphere, and lumpy fantasy prop suddenly makes a lot more sense. With that mindset, let us dive into the guiding principles that turn guess-and-check unwrapping into a strategy.

The theory behind UV unwrapping strategies

Before we start to do all that UV unwrapping involves, it is important to understand that every 3D model needs to be unwrapped to accurately map 2D textures onto its surface. Without proper unwrapping, textures can appear distorted, stretched, or misaligned.

When unwrapping a complex object such as a human body, it is helpful to think of the body parts as simplified primitives. For example, you can treat the neck as a cylinder, use cylinders for the limbs, and think of the head as a sphere. This approach makes it easier to unwrap and manage the UVs. However, this method does not work as well for smaller, detailed objects such as the hand (see *Figure 15.7*).

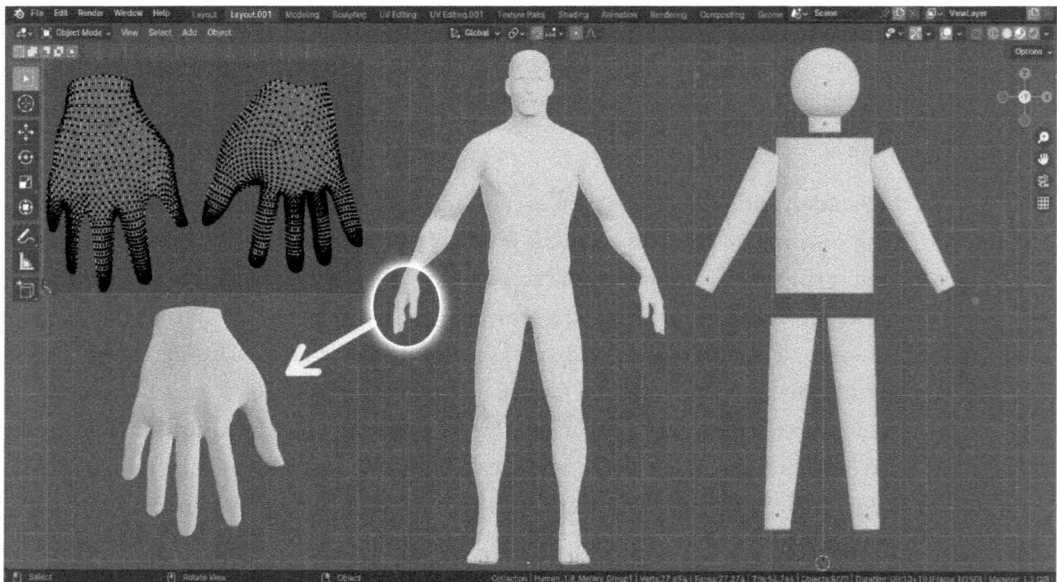

Figure 15.7: UV unwrapping a hand and visualizing a body as a collection of primitives

While each finger can technically be unwrapped as a cylinder, this would create numerous UV islands, which can reduce the overall texture resolution. Instead, it is often better to unwrap the hand by splitting it into two main pieces with a seam, dividing it between the top and bottom of the hand. The unwrapping strategy also depends on the intended use of the mesh. For example, if the model is meant for extreme close-up shots in film CGI, it may be better to use multiple texture maps for each limb and combine them using UDIM. **UDIM** is a system that allows you to organize and use multiple texture maps seamlessly across a single model. We will look at UDIM more closely later in this chapter.

Now that we have explored how to unwrap a simple model, let us take a closer look at the **UV** menu in Blender. Think of it like a toolbox, where each tool exists for a specific reason, whether it is stitching islands together, scaling UVs evenly, or packing them neatly to save space. Let's break down some of these tools and how they can help you get the most out of your textures.

UV menu overview

The **UV** menu in Blender's UV Editor includes many tools and commands for editing UV maps. They will help you fine-tune your UV layout so that textures are applied correctly. *Table 15.1* shows some of the notable options and their functionalities:

UV Editor tools	Function
Weld/Align	These options allow you to modify the positions of selected UV vertices. Welding can help you merge close vertices. Aligning is different because it helps in organizing UVs in a straight line, either horizontally or vertically.
Stitch (*V*)	Stitching is used to connect separate UV islands along shared edges. This is handy for reducing seams in your texture by maximizing how continuous your model looks along the edges. You can control **Stitch** using options such as limiting by selection or using the active UV as a pivot.
Seams	From this submenu, you can mark or clear seams directly within the UV Editor. Marking seams tells Blender where to cut the model to lay it flat.
Pin (*P*)/**Unpin** (*Alt + P*)	Pinning lets you fix certain UV vertices in place. This can be helpful if you are making adjustments to other parts of the UV map. Unpinning releases these vertices, letting you move them again.

UV Editor tools	Function
Pack Islands (*Ctrl* + *P*)	This command rearranges the UV islands within the UV space to minimize wasted space. This is the crème de la crème tool for optimizing texture resolution.
Average Islands Scale	This adjusts the scale of the UV islands to make their density consistent across the UV map. Consistent density helps textures appear with an identical resolution across different parts of the model.
Minimize Stretch	Allows you to mirror selected UV islands along the *U* or *V* axis. This is useful for creating symmetrical UV layouts, such as on models with mirrored geometry.
Merge/Split	Merging combines selected UV vertices into a single vertex at a specified location (e.g., average, center, cursor, etc.). Splitting separates connected vertices into individual elements.

Table 15.1: UV Editor tools in Blender 4

Blender's UV Editor also includes tools that give you the power to transform, mirror, and export UV layouts. These features enable artists to adjust, optimize, and utilize UV maps outside of Blender. The rest of this section will focus on exploring these tools in detail.

Transform

The **Transform** tools let you manipulate UV maps. This means that you move, scale, and rotate UV islands to better fit the texture space or to align textures with specific parts of the model. You might need to transform a model such as a medieval building. In this case, you would use **Transform** to adjust the UV islands so that the stone textures for walls and wooden textures for beams and doors are perfectly scaled and positioned.

Blender's **Transform** tool has four key operations, listed here:

- **Move** (*G*): You can move selected UV vertices, edges, or islands by pressing *G* and then dragging your mouse. This is useful for positioning UV islands within the texture space.
- **Scale** (*S*): Scaling is performed by pressing *S* and then moving your mouse to adjust the size of the selected UV elements. Scaling UV elements can be done uniformly or non-uniformly, each affecting the texture application on the model in different ways. By default, this scales them uniformly, meaning all directions are scaled at the same rate.

- Uniform scaling (press *S*) affects texture tiling. This means that the texture will repeat more or less frequently over the surface of the model, changing how many times the texture appears or how big the texture patterns look on the model.

  You can also scale non-uniformly by constraining the direction. To scale in the *U* direction (i.e., horizontally), use *S X*, just like you would in your 3D Viewport. Use *S Y* for scaling in the *V* direction (i.e., vertically). This is helpful when adjusting textures on stretched shapes such as benches, planks, or long tables, where you want to avoid texture distortion.

  By scaling the UVs more in one direction than the other, you can make sure that the wood grain texture looks correct and is not stretched or squashed, making the table look more natural and realistic.

- **Rotate** (*R*): Rotating UV elements is done by pressing *R* and then moving your mouse. This will help you align textures with the model's geometry.

These **Transform** operations can be constrained to the *X* (*U*) or *Y* (*V*) axis for more precise adjustments by pressing *X* or *Y* after initiating the transform. In other words, the coordinate system becomes relevant when you are matching wood grain direction on furniture or adjusting fabric patterns on clothing, for example.

Mirror

Mirroring UV islands is a technique used to apply symmetrical textures on both sides of a model. This is your go-to tool if you are modeling characters and objects with mirrored features. Blender's UV Editor lets you mirror selected UV islands across the *U* or *V* axis.

To mirror something in Blender, follow the next steps:

1. Select the UV islands you want to mirror.
2. Access the **Mirror** function either through the **UV** menu or by using the shortcut keys (*Ctrl + M*).
3. Press *X* to mirror along the *U* axis or *Y* to mirror along the *V* axis. This flips the selected UV islands, creating a mirrored effect in the texture application.

Blender's **Mirror** function significantly speeds up the alignment process, transforming hours of careful texture adjustment into a task that takes only seconds.

UV Editing workspace: a quick overview

Now, look for the workspace tabs at the top of the Blender interface and click on the **UV Editing** tab to change your workspace. The **UV Editing** workspace is organized into two main sections: the 3D Viewport and the UV Editor, as shown in *Figure 15.8*.

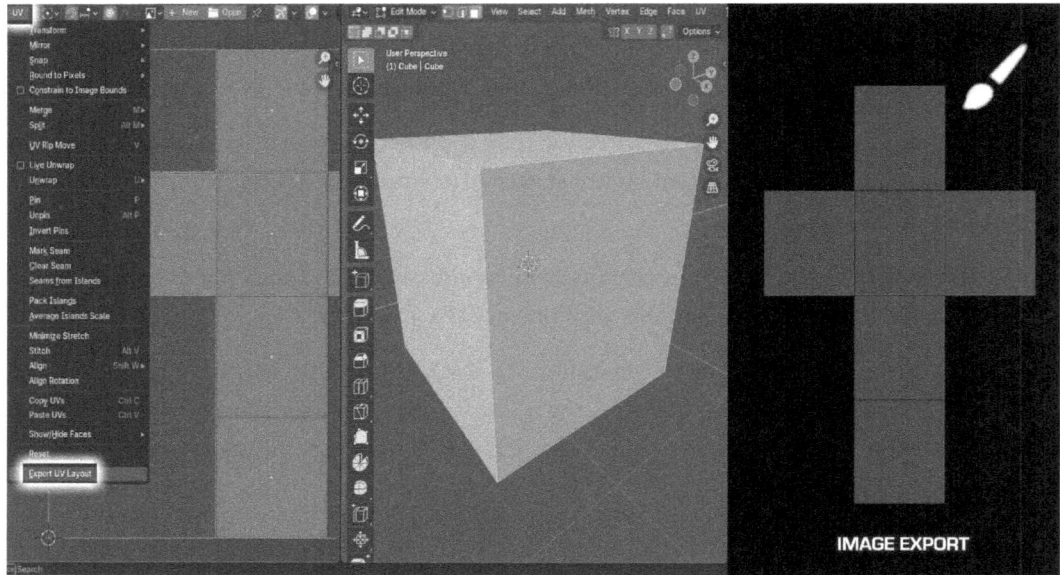

Figure 15.8: UV Editing workspace

The UV Editor shows the UV map of the selected object. After unwrapping your model, this is where you will see its 2D representation. You can edit this 2D representation to control how textures are applied to the model.

Refining UV maps before exporting

Before exporting, the UV Editor helps you refine your UV map to ensure that the layout is clean and accurate. Using tools such as **Move**, **Scale**, and **Stitch**, you can make sure everything lines up perfectly. We also covered how to mark seams, pin vertices, and pack islands to save space. Plus, we saw how mirroring can help with symmetrical textures and how exporting UV layouts lets you work on textures in other software.

Exporting UV layouts

Exporting a UV layout is crucial when you need to create a texture in an external image editing software, as the exported UV layout becomes a guide for where to paint or place texture details.

Exporting a UV layout is something you might want to do in a project such as a custom skin for a video game character in a video game such as *Smite* (https://www.smitegame.com/). Exporting your UV layout will let you apply detailed textures, logos, or patterns in specific areas, ensuring that they align perfectly with the model's geometry once imported back into Blender.

To get started and export your first UV layout, make sure you are in the UV Editor, then go to **UV | Export UV Layout**. A file dialog will appear, allowing you to choose the export location, file format (commonly .png), and other options such as the fill opacity or the inclusion of UV and texture borders.

> **Note**
>
> You might want to include UV and texture borders if you are working on detailed architectural models for a virtual reality tour. This extra step makes sure that when textures, such as brick patterns or window frames, are applied, they do not bleed over or leave unexpected gaps at the edges.

The exported image will show the edges of your UV islands, which you can then use as a template in the image editing software you prefer.

Practical applications of UV unwrapping

Now that you understand the theory behind unwrapping strategies, let us practice. By practicing with a simple cube, you will see how marking seams and unwrapping shapes the UV layout.

In the next steps, you will learn how to mark seams on your cube, unwrap it, and then manipulate its UV map in the UV Editor:

1. Make sure your model (e.g., the default cube) is selected in the 3D Viewport of the **UV Editing** workspace. It should be highlighted, indicating that it is the active object. If it is not, you can select it by clicking on it with the **right mouse button** (**RMB**) or, depending on your Blender keymap settings, this might be the **left mouse button** (**LMB**).

2. Then make sure you are in **Edit Mode**. Here, you can select individual vertices, edges, or faces of your model to manipulate them directly.

3. In **Edit Mode**, you can select the faces of your model that you want to unwrap. The faces you select will determine how the UV map is created.

    You can select multiple faces by holding *Shift* and clicking on them. Unwrapping multiple faces at once will create a more complex UV map that represents the part of the model you have selected.

4. When unwrapping, you can also set a specific face as active, which lets you unwrap based on the active face's orientation and alignment, as shown in *Figure 15.9*.

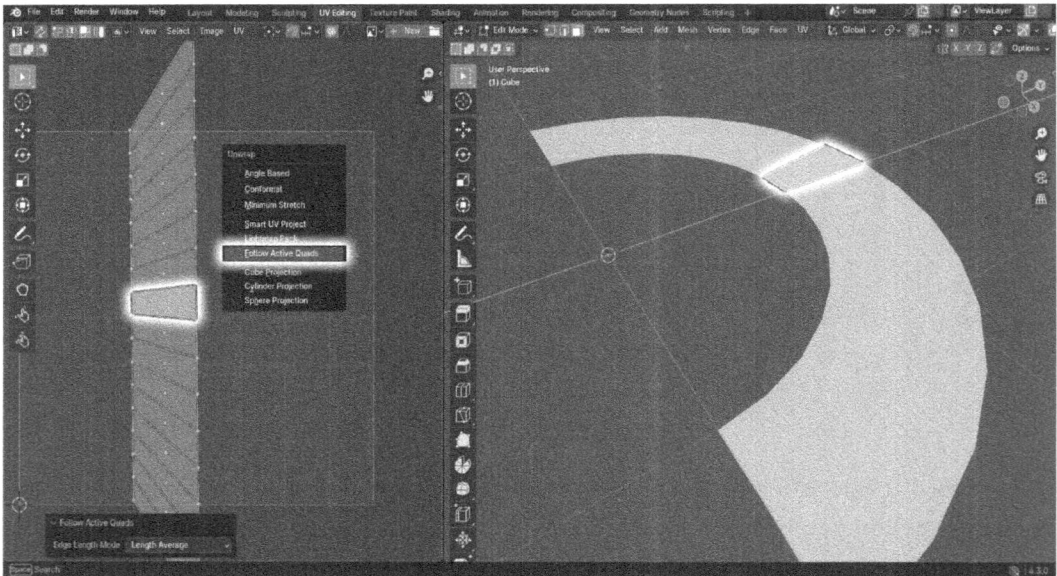

Figure 15.9: Setting specific faces as active during UV unwrapping

5. This can be useful for aligning UVs across different parts of your model. And that's not all; the UV Editor includes options to control face selection and visibility, letting you isolate certain faces for detailed adjustments. Use the **UV Sync Selection** button to toggle between selecting faces directly on your model or within the UV Editor.

6. Now, you can access various UV unwrapping methods by pressing *U*, as shown in *Figure 15.10.*

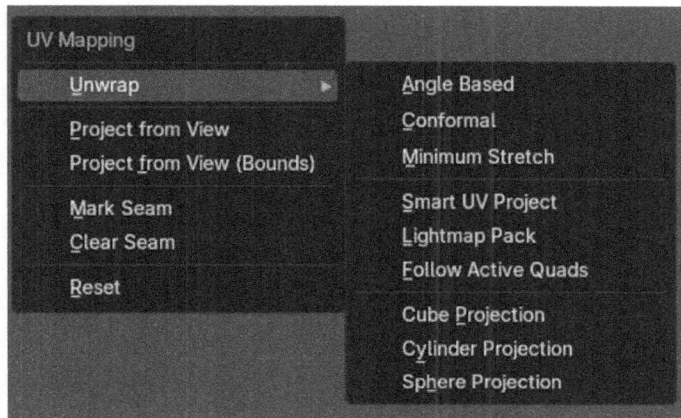

Figure 15.10: UV Mapping menu overview

Each method is designed for specific shapes and use cases, so knowing when to use them can make all the difference in your workflow:

- **Unwrap**: This basic unwrapping option uses the seams that you have marked on your model to unfold it into a 2D UV map. In Blender 4.3, **Unwrap** has been broken into three separate algorithms:

  - The **Conformal** algorithm is the same as **Unwrap** in previous Blender versions. It prioritises flat surfaces and minimal distortion. It will be your go-to choice for hard-surface models or assets where you need to have precise scaling.

  - The **Minimum Stretch** algorithm, however, is ace for organic meshes (e.g., characters). It lets you iteratively relax UV islands, which is great for reducing stretching and conforming UVs to complex shapes.

  - **Angle Based** strikes a balance between these approaches. It preserves angular relationships, which means that it works well for models that need moderate distortion control (e.g., assets with a mix of curved and flat surfaces). **Angle Based** is a practical middle option for UV unwrapping various projects.

Tip

If no seams are marked, Blender will attempt to unwrap the model based on its geometry. This means that you might see unexpected or inefficient UV layouts, where the texture appears stretched, distorted, or broken up in ways that do not correspond to the model's actual shape.

- **Smart UV Project**: This automatically unwraps the selected mesh without the need for predefined seams. It allows you to adjust parameters such as the angle limit, which determines how Blender decides to split the mesh into UV islands. **Smart UV Project** is useful for quick unwraps or for objects with less complex geometry. For example, if you were creating a basic environment asset, such as a rock or a simple building for a video game, you would use **Smart UV Project** and see that it provides a fast and decently accurate UV map. This will let you quickly texture in a way that looks good enough in a game engine (as shown in *Figure 15.11*) without needing to spend a lot of time on seam placement.

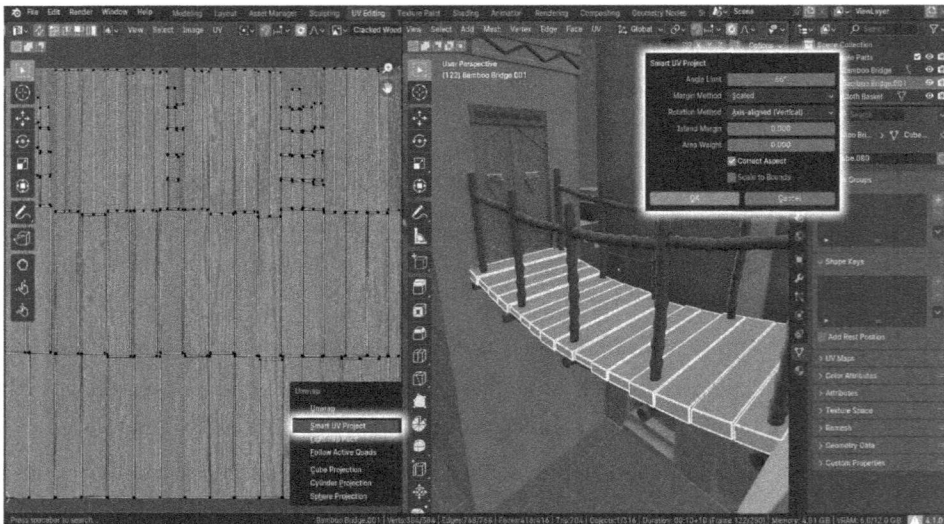

Figure 15.11: Using Smart UV Project on a suspension bridge in Blender 4: The Modular and Kitbash Environment Guide by 3D Tudor

- One of the primary controls of **Smart UV Project** is the ability to rotate UV islands based on, for example, their length. This will ensure that your textures align properly with the model's shape. You can also scale and pack the UV islands within the UV space to maximize texture resolution, minimizing empty areas and texture wastage.

- Another important option is the ability to define how Blender handles overlaps and seams. **Smart UV Project** also allows for margin adjustment between UV islands to prevent bleeding between textures. Margin adjustment is also commonly referred to as **UV island padding**, and it helps ensure that textures do not bleed onto the wrong coordinates. This is especially important when working with game engines, which use mipmaps (lower-resolution versions of textures) to improve performance. As resolution decreases, the likelihood of texture bleeding increases, making proper padding a vital part of clean UV workflows.

> Note
>
> These controls appear in a pop-up menu after you click the **Auto UV** button, but you can also access them in the bottom-right corner of your 3D Viewport.

- In the example shown in *Figure 15.12*, you can see how using an angle limit of 30 for a sphere may be more beneficial to avoid certain distortions on the mesh.

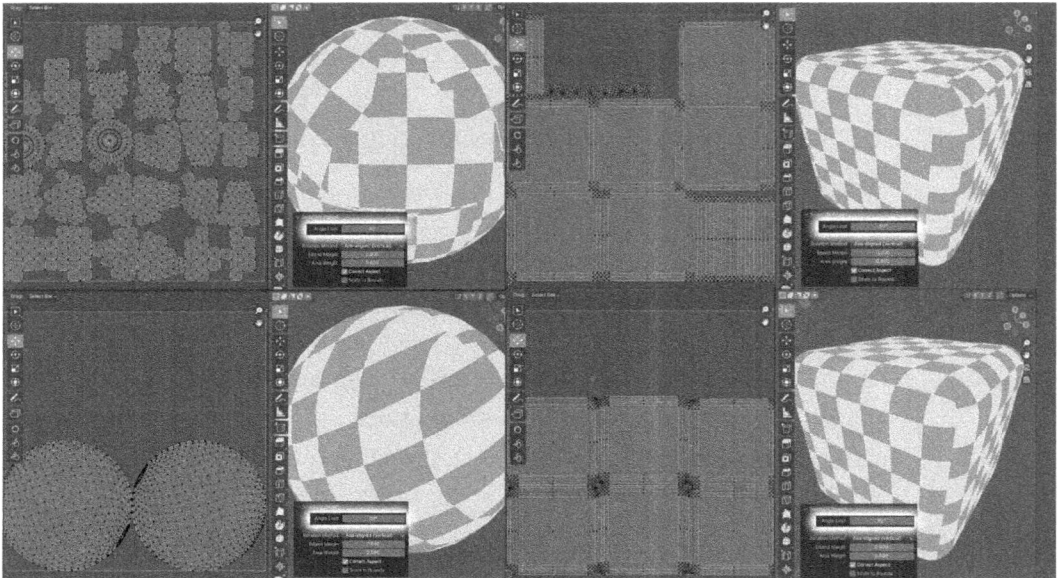

Figure 15.12: Smart UV Project with a cube vs. a sphere

- However, for the beveled cube shown next to it, it might be better to use an angle limit of 80 to create fewer pieces, as distortion is less noticeable within its angles. Adjusting the angle limit based on the shape can help optimize the UV layout and texture quality of your work.

- **Project From View**: This projects the UV map based on your current view in the 3D Viewport. **Project From View** is what you would use on flat surfaces or when you need precise control over a texture. If you were working on a detailed cityscape for a background scene in an animation, **Project From View** would be your go-to, too. It allows you to align the texture of buildings, roads, and landscapes exactly as seen from the camera's perspective, so that the textures fit perfectly with the view that will be shown in the final animation.

- There are variations such as **Project from View (Bounds)**, which fits the UV map to the UV bounds, ensuring that the entire texture covers the object equally and maximizes texture space. You might use this one if you are working on a project that involves applying a detailed map or pattern to a complex object, such as texturing a cloth draped over a frame, as you would find on a market stall (*Figure 15.13*).

Figure 15.13: Cloth draped over a frame in Blender to Unreal Engine 5 | 3D Props | Medieval Market by 3D Tudor

Figure 15.13 shows that you need to be careful when you are using **Project from View (Bounds)**. For example, if it is using the perspective of your 3D Viewport (top right) to project UVs onto the texture (left), it might look good, but if you look at it from another angle (e.g., bottom right), it will show UV distortion.

> Tip
>
> Use the numpad shortcuts *1*, *3*, *7*, and *9* to switch to the front, right, top, and bottom views, respectively. This will help you to get a straight angle on an object's side. From there, you can select the topology facing you and apply functions to avoid distorted textures on angles that cannot be seen from your current perspective at the one time.

- **Cube Projection**, **Cylinder Projection**, and **Sphere Projection**:
    - **Cube Projection** maps a texture onto a 3D object by projecting it from six sides, like wrapping a cube around the object. **Cube Projection** is ideal for objects with boxy shapes, such as crates, buildings, or boxes in a video game. Here, each face of the cube receives a proportional and accurate section of the texture, minimizing distortion.

- **Cylinder Projection** maps a texture onto a 3D object by wrapping it around the object as if it were a cylinder. **Cylinder Projection** is best suited for cylindrical objects such as barrels, pipes, or columns. It wraps the texture around the sides of the cylinder while projecting flat textures onto the top and bottom faces. This makes sure that the cylindrical surface is textured evenly without distortion.

- **Sphere Projection** is like tossing a stretchy, perfectly printed balloon over your model and letting it shrink-wrap itself evenly from every angle. It shines on anything vaguely globe-like (planets, marbles, dragon eyeballs, etc.) because the texture radiates outward in all directions, smoothing itself around the curvature instead of bunching up at the poles. The result? No nasty pinching, no polar smears, just a clean, consistent coverage that looks right no matter how you spin the model.

- **Lightmap Pack**: This option is designed for creating lightmaps, packing the UVs in a way that maximizes space usage and ensuring that no two faces overlap. **Lightmap Pack** is useful for baking lighting information onto textures. It might not seem straightforward at first, but you could use this in a project such as an intricate interior scene where accurate lighting is crucial. By using **Lightmap Pack** to bake the lighting into your textures, you can simulate complex lighting effects, such as soft shadows and ambient occlusion, without real-time lighting calculations.

- **Follow Active Quads**: This method unwraps the mesh based on an active quad (i.e., four-sided face) you have selected. It is useful for grids or continuous surfaces. For example, as seen in *Figure 15.14*, if we want to create a wooden arch above a window, we will place seams like you would on a cylinder, creating a large, elongated UV island. After unwrapping, we focus on this island by selecting only it.

To make one part of the UV space the active selection (preferably the straightest section, often the middle), hold *Shift* and double-click the face in **Face Selection** mode while the rest of the island is selected. Then, you can choose one of three unwrapping options:

- **Length Average**, which averages the length of quads for consistent scaling.
- **Even**, which evenly distributes UVs for a uniform layout.
- **Length**, which preserves the original aspect ratio of the geometry.

Once you click **OK**, the tool will unwrap the entire island to follow the shape of the active face, warping the texture detail smoothly along the arch's form.

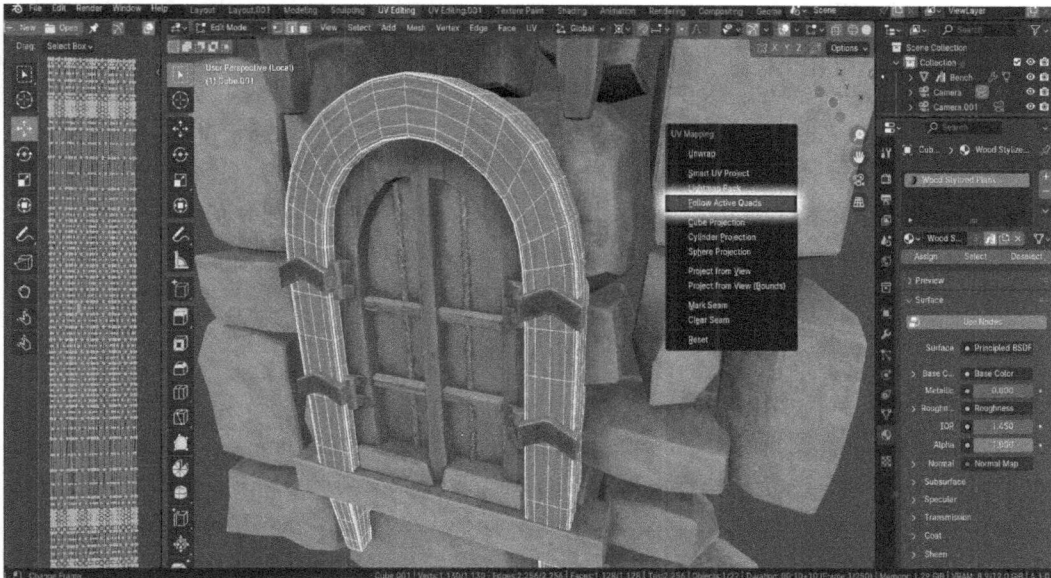

Figure 15.14: Wooden arch above a window in Blender 20 Massive Fantasy Windows Asset Pack by 3D Tudor

Using the UV Pack tool for optimization

UV Pack optimizes the layout of UV islands after the model has been unwrapped, even after using **Smart UV Project**. Even though this ensures that the UV islands fit within the UV space, **UV Pack** refines it even more by minimizing wasted space. This reduces texture distortion and improves overall texture resolution.

Like **Smart UV Project**, **UV Pack** also includes a **Rotation Method** option, which controls how UV islands are rotated when they are arranged in the UV space. Using the right rotation settings means that you can align your UV islands to fit the texture's directional patterns better. This is particularly important for textures with directional features such as wood grain or fabric patterns, because it helps the patterns follow the natural flow of the model's surface. You can find **UV Pack** by going to the UV Editor and accessing it from the **UV** menu at the top, and choosing **Pack Islands**.

Applying textures to a cube or any 3D model in Blender depends significantly on how the UV map is laid out. Mastering the different projection methods, such as **Cube Projection**, **Cylinder Projection**, and **Sphere Projection**, and understanding when to use each is crucial for creating accurate textures without any weird distortions.

Now, let us talk about add-ons. Blender's ecosystem includes many add-ons, both community-developed and built-in. Each add-on is specialized and can extend 3D modeling and texturing. Add-ons are useful for UV mapping, offering advanced unwrapping techniques, layout optimization tools, and more. Because talking about the different add-ons available would be a chapter of its own, we will use this space to focus on one of the best: Magic UV.

Initiating you into the world of Magic UV in Blender

I would confidently call Blender a powerhouse in the 3D software world. It offers robust tools for UV mapping, but it can sometimes be time-consuming. This is where **Magic UV**, an inbuilt Blender add-on, comes in. Magic UV introduces a suite of advanced tools and features that address a wide range of UV mapping needs.

Why Magic UV is useful

Magic UV is designed to make the UV mapping process faster. Automating certain tasks and providing shortcuts for complex operations significantly reduces the time spent on UV mapping. One of the tasks it automates includes copying/pasting UV maps between objects. This is because Magic UV lets you duplicate texture coordinates from one model to another quickly. For example, if I were working on a project with a fleet of identical spacecraft, Magic UV would let me unwrap one spacecraft and then apply the same UV map to the rest.

Another good point is that Magic UV is an add-on that extends Blender's UV capabilities with a range of advanced features that you cannot access in the default setup. This includes UV sculpting, which gives you more control over the UV layout by treating it similarly to mesh sculpting. Without this advanced feature, adjusting the UV map would be more time-consuming. Another notable example is the advanced **UV Packing** tool, which optimizes the arrangement of UV islands to make the most efficient use of texture space.

How to access Magic UV

Follow these steps to access and enable Magic UV within Blender:

1. Navigate to **Edit | Preferences**. In the **Preferences** window, click on the **Add-ons** tab.

2. In the **Add-ons** tab, type `Magic UV` into the search bar to find the add-on quickly.

Note

In the newer 4-series builds, Magic UV (and many other community add-ons) is not bundled by default. Instead, hit **Edit**, go to **Preferences** and **Add-ons**, then jump over to the shiny new **Get Extensions** tab. Give Blender permission to phone home (we are with team E.T.), type Magic UV into the search bar, and let it install itself. Same toolset, just living in a different cupboard these days.

3. You will see an entry named **UV: Magic UV** or similar. Check the box next to this entry to enable the add-on.

Once enabled, you will have access to a variety of powerful UV mapping tools within Blender's UV Editor. These tools include advanced options for unwrapping, aligning, copying and pasting UV coordinates, transferring UV maps between different objects, and more, all designed to make your UV mapping workflow faster and better.

Key features and capabilities of Magic UV

Magic UV significantly enhances the UV mapping workflow in Blender. By integrating this add-on into your texturing process, you can face different texturing challenges. Its main features are summarised in *Table 15.2*:

Feature	Function	Project idea
Unwrap Constraint	Facilitates unwrapping with constraints. It is useful for maintaining specific proportions or alignments in texture layouts.	Designing a modular building system with interchangeable parts that need to align perfectly, such as in the online course *Creating a Modular Kitbash in Blender* by 3D Tudor
Copy UV/Paste UV	Enables easy copying of UV maps between objects, streamlining your workflow if you are dealing with multiple objects that share textures.	Creating a crowd scene with characters wearing the same outfit but with variations in colour or pattern

Feature	Function	Project idea
UVW Mapping	Provides UVW mapping tools for more control over texture projections. In other words, it lets you adjust the way the texture covers each part of your model, making sure it looks just right from every angle.	Applying complex textures to a vehicle model where different parts require different projection types
Preserve UV Aspect	Ensures the aspect ratio of textures is maintained when you are scaling UVs.	Texturing a character where the uniformity of fabric patterns or logos across different body parts is crucial
Texture Lock	Allows for editing UVs while keeping the texture locked in place, offering real-time feedback on texture placement adjustments	Adjusting the texture on a character's clothing during an animation to prevent sliding or stretching
World Scale UV	Calculates **UV Mapping** scale based on world coordinates, making sure you end up with uniform texture scaling across different objects in a scene.	Creating a large-scale environment where textures on various elements, such as buildings, roads, and landscapes, need to remain consistent in scale

Table 15.2: Magic UV key features and project ideas

Magic UV will help you become more efficient at UV mapping, whether you are conjuring up your first model or are a wizard of the craft. Magic UV acts as a powerful spellbook by automating routine tasks and offering advanced features. As we move from mastering the arcane arts of UV mapping to the practical magic of creating and applying texture atlases, you will learn how to consolidate textures into a single image. This will be a time-saver, improving rendering performance and streamlining your workflow for game engines such as Unity or Unreal Engine.

Creating and applying texture atlases in Blender

Creating a texture atlas is the bread and butter of optimizing 3D models, especially if you are planning to use them in game engines such as Unity or Unreal Engine. A **UV texture atlas** consolidates multiple textures into a single image, as in *Figure 15.15*.

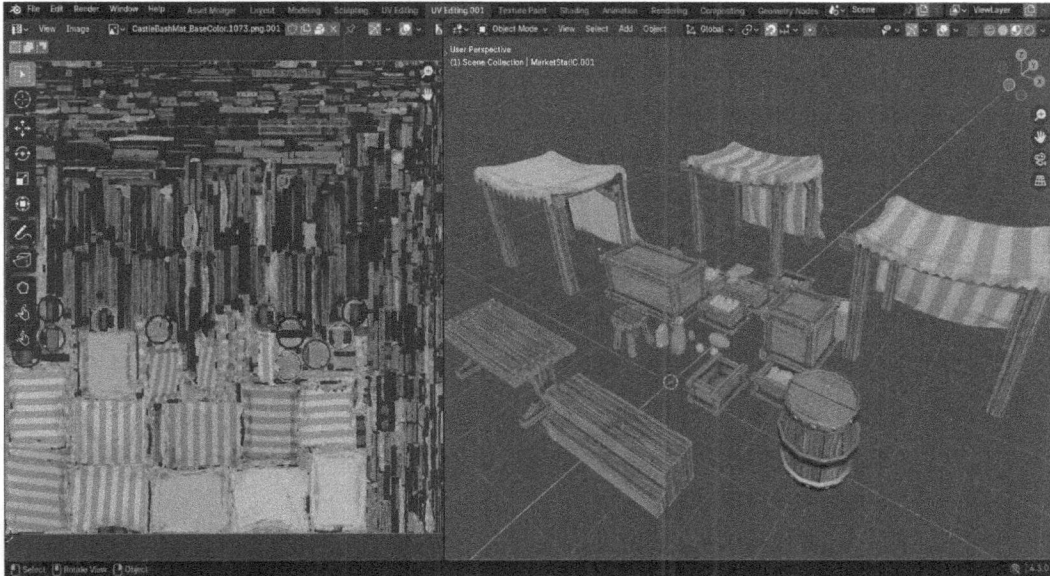

Figure 15.15: A UV texture atlas with assets that use 1 material and 0-1 UV space in Blender to Unreal Engine 5 | 3D Props | Medieval Market by 3D Tudor

They reduce the number of materials and draw calls, and by doing that, texture atlases significantly enhance rendering performance. A UV texture atlas needs to use a single material and be within 0 to 1 of the UV space.

Initial steps for creating a texture atlas

Creating a UV texture atlas is a detailed but simple process. You might look at these steps like an impossible mountain to climb, but you will see that you will warm up to the idea as we go through each one. Let's get started:

1. First, pick the objects you want to include in the UV texture atlas. Make sure they are scaled, rotated, and positioned correctly in your scene.

2. To keep things clean, apply all transformations by pressing *Ctrl + A* and choosing **All Transforms**. This step makes sure your UV unwrapping will go smoothly.

Note

Ultimately, you want your UV texture atlas to be unified because it stream-lines the rendering process by reducing the number of texture swaps the engine has to make.

3. Assign a single material to all the objects you have chosen for the UV texture atlas. Go to the **Material Properties** tab and make sure each object is using this material. You can either create a new one or reuse an existing material. This way, when you bake textures later, everything will fit together in the same UV space.

4. Next, assign the same material to all the objects you are adding to the UV texture atlas. To do that, open the Shader Editor, create a new material, and link it to all the selected objects. This keeps things simple and makes texturing and baking easier later.

5. Now, go to the **UV Editing** tab to see your 3D model on one side and its UV map on the other.

6. Pick an unwrapping method:

    •   **Smart UV Project** is great for quick and simple unwrapping. It is automated but may scatter UV islands.

    •   **Manual Unwrapping**: If you want more control, mark seams (*Ctrl + E* and select **Mark Seam**) and unwrap manually. This is best for detailed models where the UV layout matters.

Alright, you have got the mesh peeled open like a digital orange, nice work. Now, let's shuffle those peels into something the texture gods will actually thank you for and dive into wrangling your UV islands.

Organizing your UV islands

To understand UV islands better and to know how to organize them, take a moment to study *Figure 15.16*.

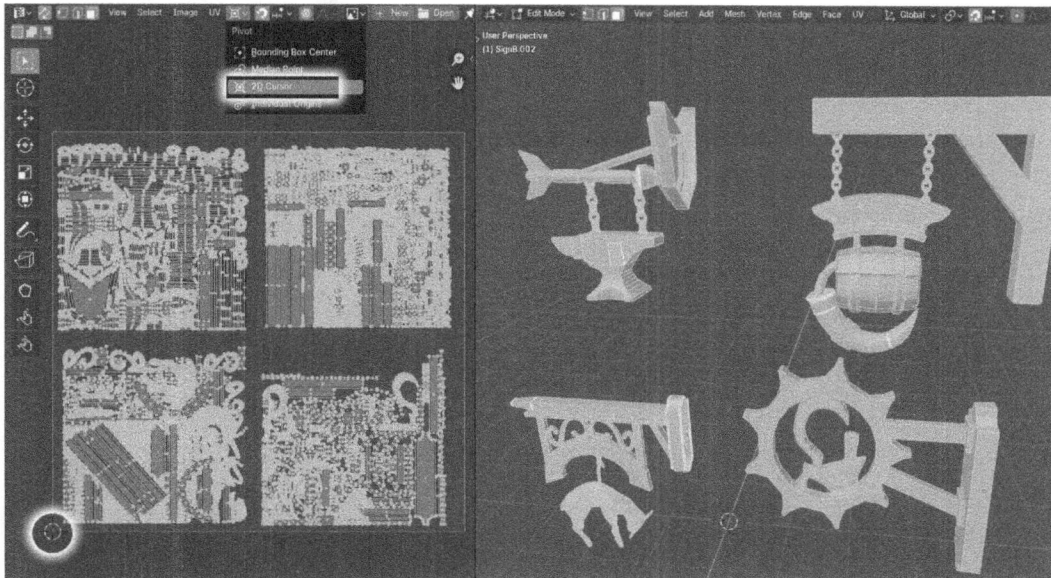

Figure 15.16: Individually packed islands for each object in building medieval worlds – Unreal Engine 5 Modular Kitbash by 3D Tudor

Here, you can see individually packed UV islands for each object. After moving each UV island to its respective section, we used **2D Cursor** as a pivot to scale it down to a 0–1 UV space. For the sake of the preview, each object-packed island was scaled down to better represent each of the four separate fields.

Think of this as a lightning-round tidy-up after your main unwrap, the same goal, with three focused moves:

1. **Straighten edges:** Use the **Align X/Y** tool to tidy up UV islands for cleaner texturing.

2. **Keep UVs consistent:** Use **Average Island Scale** to make sure all parts of your model have the same texture density.

3. **Pack UV islands:** Use *Ctrl + P* to neatly pack UV islands into the UV space. For extra control, you can move sections out of the main UV space (using *G, X* or *G, Y*) and scale them down to fit everything back into the 0–1 UV area later.

4. Follow this trio in order (straighten > scale > pack), and your UV layout will look as sharp as your final bake.

Tip

For programs such as Substance Painter, you can pack all UVs together, but if you are working on something complex, separating objects into sections makes it easier to paint and tweak textures.

Alright, islands squared away and snug in the 0–1 grid? Sweet, let's lock that layout in and ship it off so we can start painting:

1. Once your UVs are set, in the UV Editor, go to **UV**, then **Export UV Layout**.

2. Choose your resolution (e.g., **2048x2048**) and save it as a PNG file. This file acts as a guide for painting textures in Photoshop or other software.

3. Open your exported UV layout in a program such as Photoshop. You can paint directly on the UV guide, making sure each part lines up with the UV islands to preserve clean texture alignment. Alternatively, the hand-painted color texture can be brought into Substance Painter, where you can also define roughness, normal, and other material properties. When you export it, you will have a stylized, hand-painted look, as in *Figure 15.17*, which shows an atlas containing a door, its frame, and a window.

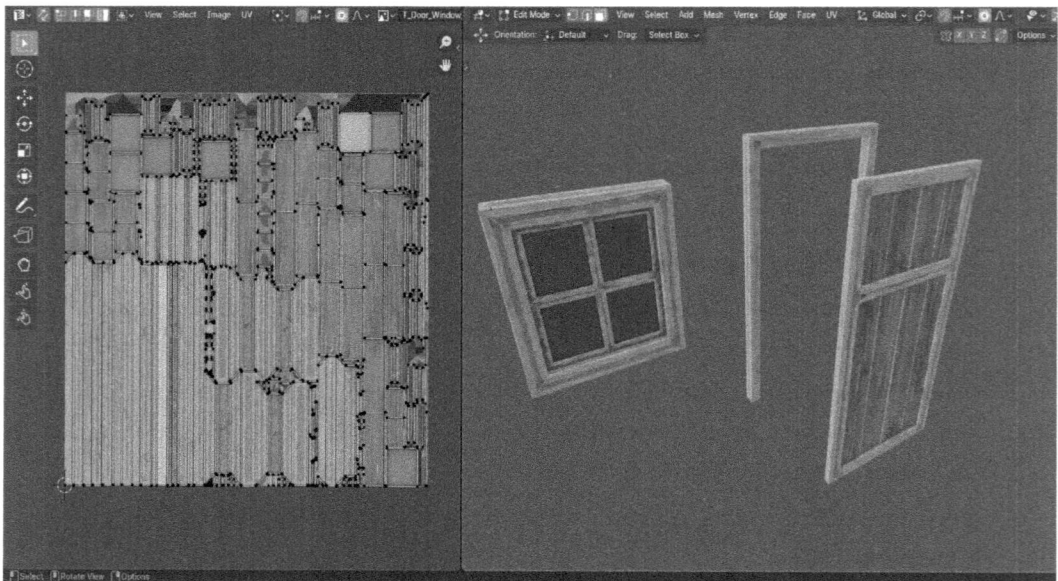

Figure 15.17: Painted textures on a wooden door

4. Save the result as a PNG or JPEG file, then link it back to your material in Blender to pre-view the textures on your model.

> **Note**
>
> Instead of the workflow described in the previous steps (i.e., manually arranging and editing UV islands in Blender or painting textures on a 2D guide via Photoshop), you can use a 3D texturing tool. Programs such as Substance Painter let you texture multiple objects at once.
>
> As some general steps, select your objects in Blender, assign them a single material, and optionally join them (*Ctrl + J*). Then, export them as an FBX or OBJ file and load it into Substance Painter. Now, you can bake and paint your textures, then export the final atlas to apply back in Blender.

Once you have your UV texture atlas ready, it is time to think about what it means for your work-flow. Sure, they are great for making things faster and smoother, but they are not all sunshine and rainbows; there are a few downsides you need to know about.

Advantages and disadvantages of texture atlases

Texture atlases offer several advantages, one of which is optimizing performance. By consolidating multiple textures into a single atlas, your engine will need to process fewer materials and textures. This will give you fewer draw calls during rendering, meaning that you will be able to maintain high frame rates. However, this optimization comes with a trade-off: all objects in the atlas must share the same texture, which can limit customization for individual objects.

Using a UV texture atlas improves performance, enhances memory efficiency, and streamlines workflows. By consolidating multiple textures into a single image, they reduce the number of texture swaps needed during rendering, which, in turn, speeds up the rendering process and decreases the load on the GPU. Texture atlases also help by reducing texture memory. They also make it so that you can work on a single image file instead of juggling multiple texture files. This makes it easier for you to see how different textures interact with each other.

Using a texture atlas can contribute to a more consistent and cohesive look for models that share similar materials or textures. For example, in a project such as a detailed village for a video game, by using a texture atlas, all the buildings, roads, and environmental elements can share textures such as wood, stone, and foliage from the same source. This simplifies material management by reducing the number of individual textures you need to track and manage, making it easier to ensure consistency across assets.

By packing multiple textures into one image, you can also have higher-resolution textures without increasing the memory required too much. This can help in mobile gaming, where you might be adding assets to environments with strict memory limitations. However, editing textures for one object can become more challenging, as changes often require you to adjust the entire atlas.

Another downside to consider is that packing all textures into one atlas can lead to resolution issues, especially if the UV space is tight. Textures might appear blurry or pixelated if there is not enough room to maintain detail for all objects. And that is not all: a UV texture atlas supports visual consistency across models because all textures are managed within a single image file. This technique, often called batching, reduces overhead by loading fewer texture files and streamlining rendering.

All in all, when deciding whether to use a UV texture atlas for your project, it is helpful to weigh up the pros and cons. *Table 15.3* highlights the key advantages and disadvantages:

Advantages	Disadvantages
Boosts performance by reducing draw calls and memory usage	Limits customization since all objects share the same texture
Makes material management easier with fewer textures	Can cause resolution issues if the UV space is tight
Speeds up texturing since multiple objects can share the same atlas	Editing textures for one object might require changes to the whole atlas
Reduces material count, which simplifies real-time engine exports (e.g., for Unity/UE)	Inefficient UV packing can waste texture space and increase memory usage
Enables batching and instancing more effectively in game engines	Large atlas sizes (e.g., 8K) lead to higher file sizes and longer loading times

Table 15.3: Advantages and disadvantages of texture atlases

While texture atlases are incredibly useful, sometimes you need a different approach, especially for repetitive patterns or modular designs. That is where trim sheets come in handy.

What are trim sheets?

Trim sheets are like specialized texture atlases designed for repeating patterns and modular designs. They are perfect for things such as buildings or decorative objects. If you want to push a single trim sheet even further, remember you are not married to the original layout, by nudging and warping those UV shells, you can bend the sheet's details to match bespoke meshes (e.g., see the crate makeover in *Figure 15.18*).

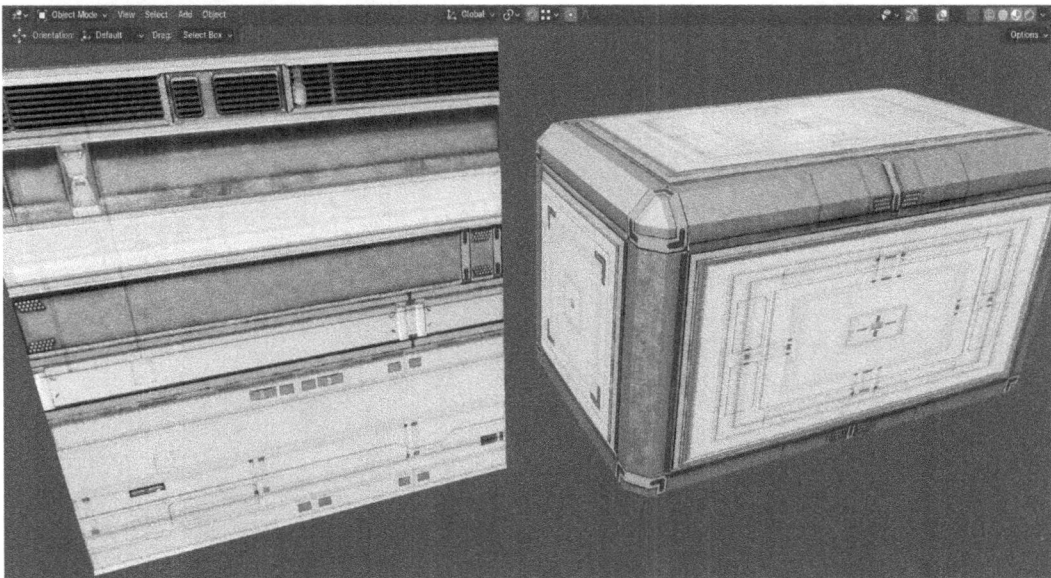

Figure 15.18: Trim sheet manipulation for a crate texture

Here is how to use trim sheets:

1. Plan the layout so sections are divided for patterns, edges, and unique details.
2. Straighten the UVs and snap them to gridlines in the UV Editor for perfect alignment.
3. Paint the trim sheet in Photoshop or Substance Painter, then apply it in Blender by aligning your UVs to the trim sheet texture.

Trim sheets are great when you need precise and flexible designs, especially for things such as buildings or decorative details. They are all about reusing patterns smartly, which makes your work easier and faster on big projects. While trim sheets are perfect for structured, repetitive layouts, seamless textures are your go-to for natural, organic surfaces such as stone or wood.

Before we finish this section, let us talk about seamless textures and how they play a crucial role in creating detailed, efficient texture atlases.

Seamless textures

Seamless textures are images that can be tiled without visible seams, making them ideal for large or repeating surfaces. Seamless textures can be applied to models with relatively simple UV maps since they can forgive minor mismatches in the UV layout. You will come across seamless textures in projects involving natural elements such as stone, wood, or fabric, such as in *Figure 15.19*.

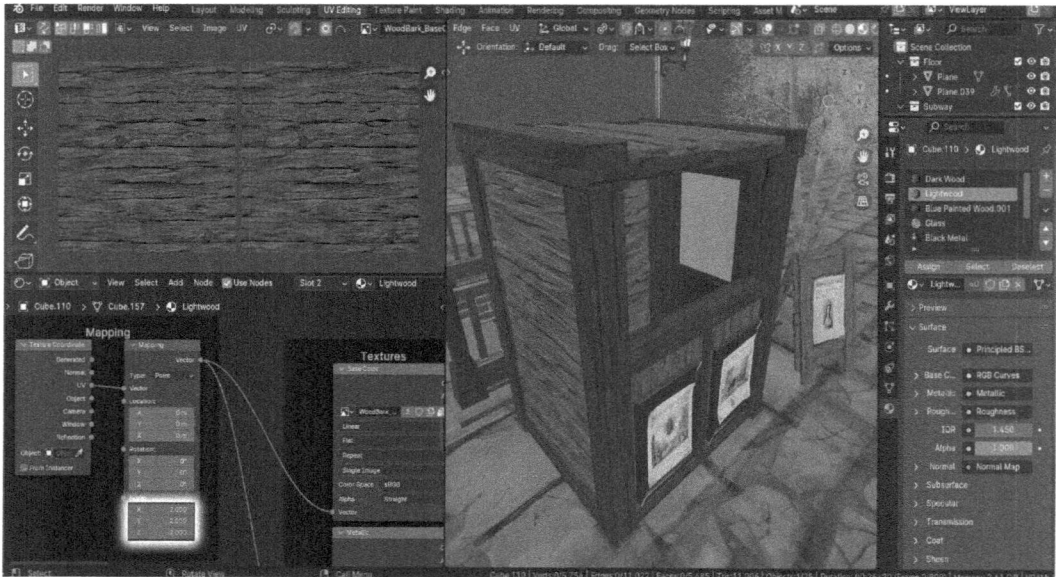

Figure 15.19: Seamless texture in wooden beams featured in Blender 4: The Ultimate Environment Artist's Guide by 3D Tudor

These are projects where you want a continuous texture without the labor-intensive process of aligning every detail in the UV map.

For seamless textures, you have two main options:

- You can upscale the UVs or scale up the texture pattern through the **Shader** settings using the **Mapping** node. If you added the texture with **Node Wrangler**, this **Mapping** node would have been created automatically. Upscaling UVs will give you more control over individual elements of your model, allowing you to fine-tune the texture.

- You could also scale the texture pattern within the shader. This lets you adjust the level of detail across the entire asset in a non-destructive way.

> **Tip**
>
> Keeping your asset within the 0–1 UV space allows you to reuse the UV layout for other processes, such as **Ambient Occlusion (AO)** baking.

At the top left of *Figure 15.16*, you can see a wood texture alongside its duplicate for preview purposes. This shows how the seamless pattern can connect and maintain consistent detail across the model.

Hence, when you are working with seamless textures in Blender, you do not need to pay as much attention to how good your UV unwrapping is. Still, even without the issue of Seams, it is important not to be too lax if you are UV unwrapping a model with large or repeating surfaces because UV unwrapping is important for the overall distribution and scale of the texture on the model.

Even with seamless textures, attention to UV unwrapping is important for the overall distribution and scale of the texture on the model. While seamless textures forgive minor mismatches, proper unwrapping ensures the texture looks natural and well distributed. When you are working on projects that need super-detailed, high-resolution textures, regular UV mapping can only take you so far. That is where UDIMs step in; they are a game-changer for handling texture detail more effectively.

Mastering UDIMs in Blender: enhancing texture detail and efficiency

The concept of UDIMs will help you improve texture detail without compromising performance. UDIMs were first used at *Weta Digital* during the production of *The Lord of the Rings*, and they have been widely adopted by the **computer-generated imagery (CGI)** industry. They are your antidote for a real time-sink in 3D modeling by allowing for multiple texture tiles instead of cramming details into a single, limited-resolution texture.

UDIMs are, as such, an extension of traditional UV mapping. Each tile in the UDIM workflow is identified by a unique number. This number is like a marker for its position in a grid layout that extends beyond the standard 0–1 UV space.

Figure 15.20: Unique numbers in the UDIM workflow on a door in Blender 20 Massive Fantasy Doors Asset Pack by 3D Tudor

They look like coordinates, as in *Figure 15.20*, where the first number represents the *U* direction, and the second number increments for each tile in the *V* direction, starting from 1001 for the first tile, 1002 for the second, and so on. This numbering system makes sure that textures are accurately applied and easily managed across the tiles.

Setting up UDIMs in Blender: a beginner's guide

UDIMs are a powerful way to manage textures, and this step-by-step guide is designed to help you understand and set up UDIMs in Blender. Let's get started:

Note

Before diving into UDIMs, make sure you are familiar with all there is to do in the UV Editor in Blender. This is where you will manage your model's UV maps and textures.

1. In the 3D Viewport, select the model you want to work with by clicking on it.

2. Press *Tab* to switch to **Edit Mode**, where you can edit the model's geometry and UVs.

3. If you are not already in the **UV Editing** workspace, change one of your panels to the UV Editor or select **UV Editing** from the workspace tabs at the top of the Blender interface.

4. In the UV Editor, open the **Show Overlays** menu (found in the top-right corner of the UV Editor), then adjust the **Tiles X** and **Tiles Y** values to increase the number of visible UV tiles.

> Note
>
> This step does not create UDIM tiles yet, but gives you a visual guide for laying out UVs across what will become multiple UDIM tiles.

5. If your model is not already unwrapped, you can unwrap it by selecting all faces in **Edit Mode** (*A*) and then pressing *U* to unwrap. Choose a method that suits your model, such as **Smart UV Project**, for a quick unwrap.

6. Then, click and drag UV islands in the UV Editor to position them across the expanded grid:

   - Ensure that each UV island is fully within a grid square, which will become a UDIM tile.

   - Use the grid lines as guides to avoid overlapping UV islands across tiles. If they overlap, you might face issues such as textures bleeding over from one island to another. This can lead to parts of your model showing the wrong texture or having distorted textures. You want to avoid that at all costs.

7. Now, in the UV Editor, go to the **Image** menu and select **New**. In the dialog that appears, you can name your image, set the resolution, and importantly, check the **Tiled** option to enable UDIMs.

8. After creating your first image, you will see a + button next to the image name in the **UV Editor Image** drop-down menu. Click this to add new tiles. Each new tile will automatically be assigned the next number in the UDIM sequence.

9. Alternatively, you can also assign an existing image as a UDIM base by opening the **N** panel (press *N* in the UV Editor), going to the **Image** tab, and setting **Source** to **Tiled**.

10. Once you have a UDIM image set up, you can add new tiles in a couple of ways:

    - If using the header drop-down in the UV Editor, a + button may appear next to the image name. Click it to add tiles one by one.

    - A faster way is to use the **Count** field (available when you are first creating the image or via the **N** panel) to add multiple tiles at once. You can then remove any extras using the – button. Each tile is automatically assigned the next number in the UDIM sequence.

11. With your UDIM tiles set up and your model's UVs laid out across them, you are now ready to begin texturing:

    - You can start painting directly onto your model in **Texture Paint** mode. Blender will automatically use the correct UDIM tile based on where you paint on the model.

    - If you have external textures you want to apply, you can assign them in the Shader Editor by creating an **Image Texture** node for each UDIM tile and loading the corresponding image.

Setting up UDIMs in Blender might seem complex at first, but it is a straightforward process once you understand the steps. It is a bit like learning how to solve a jigsaw puzzle after someone mixed two different boxes; once you start recognizing the edge pieces and separating the cats from the dinosaurs, the whole scene starts to make sense.

Practical applications of UDIMs

UDIMs are useful in a variety of scenarios:

- They are very good for organic models (i.e., models based on life forms, be it humans, fauna, or flora). Splitting UVs across multiple tiles means that you can have increased texture resolution where it is most needed (e.g., for faces or other details on a model).

Note

Quick heads-up: if you are laying out a sprawling environment rather than a single hero asset, hop back to the *Seamless textures* and *What are trim sheets?* sections we covered earlier. Layered tileables and mask-based blends usually beat UDIMs for memory footprint and authoring speed in those big, repeating spaces.

- They can efficiently handle displacement maps, transferring sculpted details from high-poly models to their lower-poly versions without missing out on the detail.

- They are also helpful from a technical perspective. By spreading UVs over several tiles, you can work on large sections of a model at the same time. Now, on to the juiciest benefit of using UDIMs: they are highly adjustable. For example, imagine you are working on the main character for a video game. You later decide that the character's face needs to be more expressive for close-up cut scenes. UDIMs allow you to go back and increase the texture resolution of the face without having to redo the entire texture work. Now, who doesn't like that?

However, even though UDIMs have several attractive advantages, you need to balance detail with performance:

- First and foremost, you should avoid overusing UDIMs. Use UDIMs on hero assets or areas requiring high detail. If you use them excessively, you might end up with overly complicated setups and high resource demands on your device or game engine.

- You also need to make sure that you are optimizing your tile count. A practical approach is to create a test model, apply a range of UDIM tile configurations, and look at how your texture quality and performance change.

- Finally, use UDIMs together with procedural textures. For example, you might use UDIMs to allocate higher-resolution textures to a dragon's head, claws, and scales where players will focus their attention. Then, blend these detailed textures with procedural techniques to add variety and depth to the scales and skin.

All in all, UDIMs can help you achieve stunning results that were previously out of reach due to technical limitations. UDIMs are like a hot sauce on your breakfast, a little goes a long way, so use it wisely where it counts! We will now focus on maximizing texture quality and efficiency through UV space management.

Optimizing UV space for texture quality and efficiency

Optimizing UV space is fundamental to 3D modeling and texturing. Before you start doing pretty much anything, you need to understand why you are using it.

Benefits of UV space optimization

By packing UV islands efficiently, you can allocate higher resolution textures to critical areas, enhancing the overall detail of the model. For example, in an urban landscape, efficiently arranging the UV islands of buildings and street elements will give you the space to allocate higher resolution textures to areas that you want to draw the viewer's attention to, such as storefronts and signage (*Figure 15.21*).

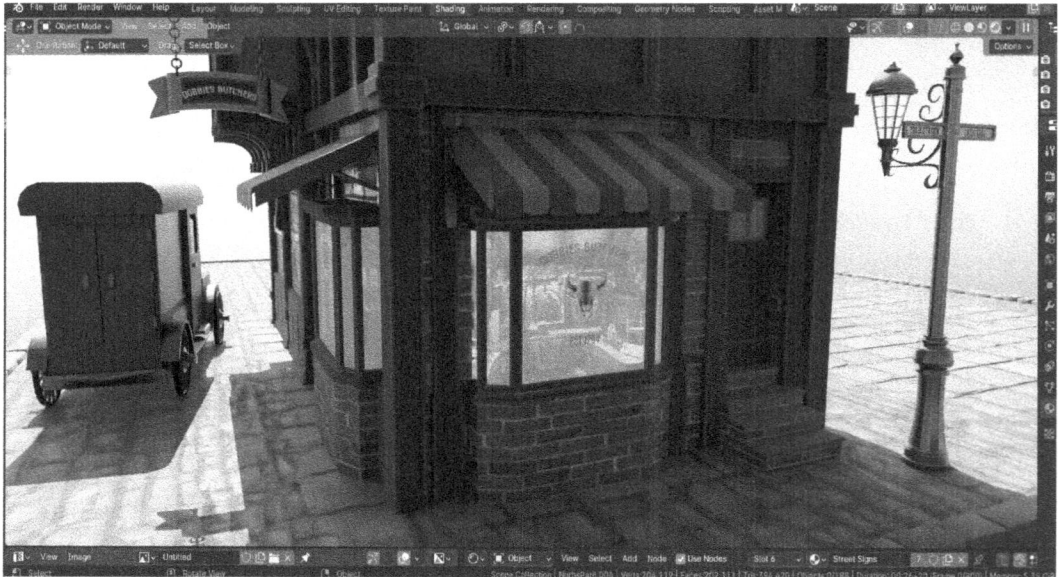

Figure 15.21: Storefronts and signage in Blender 4: The Ultimate Environment Artist's Guide by 3D Tudor

You also need to try and get consistent texture detail. Uniform scaling makes sure that the texture resolution is the same across the entire model. This avoids issues where textures appear blurry on large parts and too sharp on smaller parts. For example, let's say you are working on a car model that includes the main body and smaller parts such as wheels and headlights. If you make sure these parts are all scaled the same way in the UV map, it helps keep the textures from looking too blurry on big parts or too sharp on small parts, as in *Figure 15.22*.

Figure 15.22: Stylized Victorian truck in Blender 4: The Ultimate Environment Artist's Guide
by 3D Tudor

A third benefit of UV space optimization is enhanced visual appeal. Strategic seams placement can help hide them in less noticeable areas, making the model appear more seamless and professional.

Last but not least, proper UV unwrapping and minimizing distortion ensure that textures follow the model's contours smoothly. For example, in a detailed tree model, proper UV unwrapping means that the bark texture follows the way the tree bends smoothly, as in *Figure 15.23*.

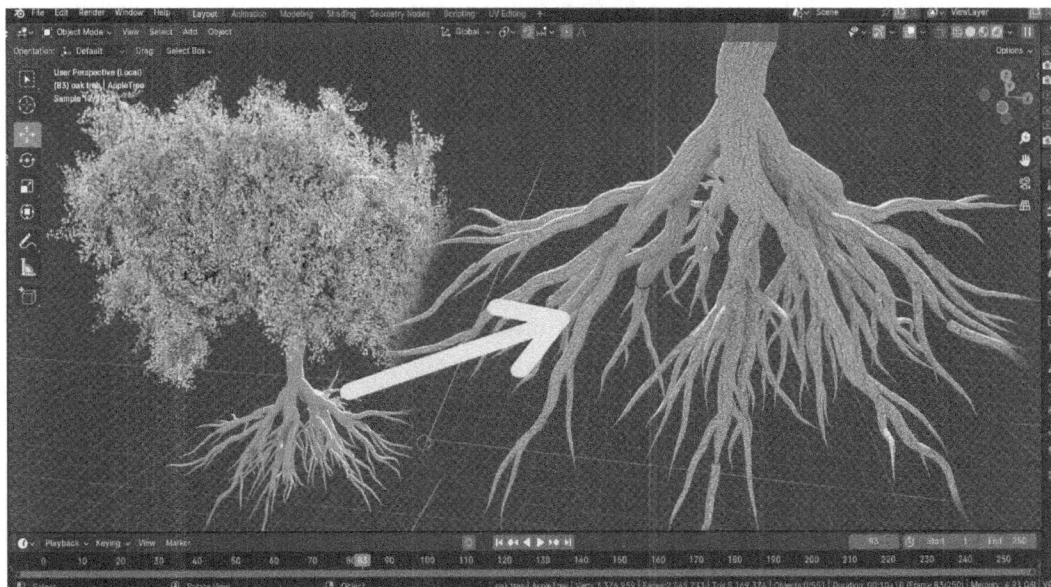

Figure 15.23: Tree generated using Geometry nodes in 3D Trees with Blender Geometry Nodes
by 3D Tudor

Techniques for optimizing UV space

To achieve the benefits mentioned previously, you can use different techniques depending on the situation:

- **Efficient packing of UV islands**: Limiting wasted UV space through efficient packing will let you add more texture detail where needed. This technique is crucial for environments such as city landscapes, which are made up of many parts.

- **Uniform scaling**: Ensuring that all parts of a model are scaled uniformly in the UV map helps maintain consistent texture detail across the entire model. Uniform scaling is ideal if you have models with components of different sizes, such as different cars, vans, or bulldozers.

- **Strategic seam placement**: Placing seams in less noticeable areas can help make seams less visible and integrate better with the model's natural lines and textures.

- **Minimizing distortion**: Proper UV unwrapping techniques minimize texture distortion, making sure that your textures follow the model's natural contours. This is super important for organic models such as trees or characters.

All in all, optimizing UV space is key to making 3D models look great. By packing the UV islands efficiently and keeping the scale uniform, you ensure textures are sharp and consistent across the model. Hiding seams in smart places and reducing distortion helps the textures look natural and smooth. These tricks make your models look more realistic and professional.

Summary

As we wrap up this chapter (pun intended!), we have looked through the essential and more advanced tools of UV unwrapping in Blender. The size of this chapter allowed us to explore UV unwrapping as a craft of its own. We started with the basics. This set the stage for topics such as the importance of UV unwrapping, how to start with a simple model in Blender, and how to apply textures based on UV placement. We also introduced you to the world of Magic UV, a toolset within Blender that simplifies and enhances the UV mapping process.

You also learned about texture atlases in Blender so that you can optimise your 3D models for game engines such as Unity or Unreal Engine. UDIMs were another highlight of this chapter, showing you how to boost your model's texture detail and be efficient, especially for models that need close-up detail or high-resolution textures.

Finally, we summarized all those different ways of optimizing UV space in a well-rounded section. On reflection, just like we unfold a 3D object into a 2D plane in UV mapping, we have unfolded the complexities of UV unwrapping in Blender, laying them out in a way that hopefully makes them more accessible and understandable.

In the next chapter, now that we have completed our texturing workflow marathon, we will take a short weekend trip to animation in Blender.

Further reading

- To explore UV unwrapping techniques on real game-ready 3D models, *Blender 20 Massive Fantasy Windows Asset Pack* (https://3dtudor.gumroad.com/l/blender_fantasy_windows_asset_pack) and *Blender 20 Massive Fantasy Doors Asset Pack* (https://3dtudor.gumroad.com/l/blender_fantasy_doors_asset_pack) provide excellent insights into seam placement and unwrapping methods.

- For an introduction to **Smart UV Project** and how it simplifies the UV mapping process for basic assets, *Blender 4: The Modular and Kitbash Environment Guide* (https://www.udemy.com/course/blender-4-the-modular-and-kitbash-environment-guide/?referralCode=D17399836E8352DFBBD2) is a must-have 3D modeling course. It explains how to efficiently unwrap objects such as bridges or basic architectural elements with minimal effort.

- Dive deeper into projection-based techniques with *Blender to Unreal Engine 5 | 3D Props | Medieval Market* (https://www.udemy.com/course/blender-to-unreal-engine-5-3d-props/?referralCode=92DD6C744ECF6621836C). This guide demonstrates how to apply detailed textures to challenging objects such as fabric draped over frames or market stalls, ensuring optimal use of UV space.

- For maintaining consistent texture detail across models, *Blender 4: The Ultimate Environment Artist's Guide* (https://www.udemy.com/course/blender-4-the-ultimate-environment-artists-guide/?referralCode=FF4B-83F7AB5B90390273) provides practical advice on uniform scaling and texture allocation, ensuring your projects look sharp and professional.

- Learn how to tackle the challenges of unwrapping complex models such as medieval castles in *Building Medieval Worlds - Unreal Engine 5 Modular Kitbash* (https://www.udemy.com/course/building-medieval-worlds-unreal-engine-5-modular-kitbash/?referralCode=F936D687808F3AE55AF2). This course covers seam placement strategies for minimizing texture distortion, including hiding seams at natural junctions such as where stone walls meet wooden beams. This is perfect for creating detailed and polished architectural assets.

- If you need to unwrap and texture procedurally generated organic forms, such as the tree, check out *3D Trees with Blender Geometry Nodes* (`https://www.udemy.com/course/3d-trees-with-blender-geometry-nodes/?referral-Code=AA0F261DB44076B21A2D`). This course guides you through building tree meshes with **Geometry** nodes, then unwrapping bark and leaf UVs so your textures follow every twist and curve seamlessly.

Subscribe to Game Dev Assembly!

We are excited to introduce **Game Dev Assembly**, our brand-new newsletter dedicated to everything game development. Whether you're coding, designing, animating, or managing a studio, we've got insights, trends, and expert advice to help you create, innovate, and thrive. Sign up now and get exciting benefits.

`https://packt.link/gamedev-newsletter`

Get This Book's PDF Version and Exclusive Extras

UNLOCK NOW

Scan the QR code (or go to `packtpub.com/unlock`). Search for this book by name, confirm the edition, and then follow the steps on the page.

Note: Keep your invoice handy. Purchases made directly from Packt don't require an invoice.

16

Animating Your First Scene in Blender

Learning 3D animation is a bit like stepping into a world you have never visited before. It is not just about picking up a few new tricks, you are entering a field with its own terminology, tools, and way of thinking.

With animation, you are entering a world where you can create anything you can think of. You could animate anything from the simple bouncing of a ball to a character's emotions on their face. You could even go on to animate short films such as *Big Buck Bunny* (https://studio.blender.org/films/big-buck-bunny/) and *Sintel*, both created by the Blender Foundation (https://durian.blender.org/about/).

This chapter is a short but comprehensive overview of the animation process without going into the nitty-gritty. You will start by familiarizing yourself with Blender's **Animation** workspace, learning how to navigate the Timeline, Graph Editor, and other key features. The chapter covers the basics of keyframing, where you define start and end points for an object's movement, allowing Blender to generate smooth transitions automatically. You will then create your first animation, such as a cube sliding across the screen, rotating, and growing in size.

Even though this is a short overview, we will also dive into more advanced techniques. This includes refining motion with the Graph Editor and adjusting keyframe timing. Finally, the chapter walks you through rendering and exporting your work, making sure your finished animation is ready to share, whether as a high-quality video or an editable image sequence.

This chapter is your chance to branch out into a fresh part of 3D art. We will get you moving in the right direction, and who knows, you might end up enjoying it enough to carry on well past this quick reference guide.

So, in this chapter, we will cover the following topics:

- Acquainting yourself with Blender's **Animation** interface
- Understanding the basics of keyframing
- Animating a simple object
- Raising the bar with advanced animation techniques
- Rendering and exporting your animation in Blender

Technical requirements

As for **Blender 4.5 LTS (Long-Term Support)**, the general requirements include a macOS 11.2 or newer (Apple Silicon supported natively) operating system, or a Linux (64-bit, glibc 2.28 or newer) operating system. Blender now requires a CPU with the SSE4.2 instruction set, at least 8 GB of RAM (32 GB recommended for heavy scenes), and a GPU supporting OpenGL 4.3 with a minimum of 2 GB of VRAM.

For a full list of technical requirements, please refer back to *Chapter 1* of this part.

Acquainting yourself with Blender's Animation interface

Before you start creating animations through Blender, you need to familiarise yourself with Blender's animation setup. Blender even comes with its own **Animation** workspace, which means that you can quickly switch gears between creating a scene and bringing it to life in a workspace with all the tools you might need. You can find the **Animation** workspace at the top of Blender's window, as shown in *Figure 16.1*.

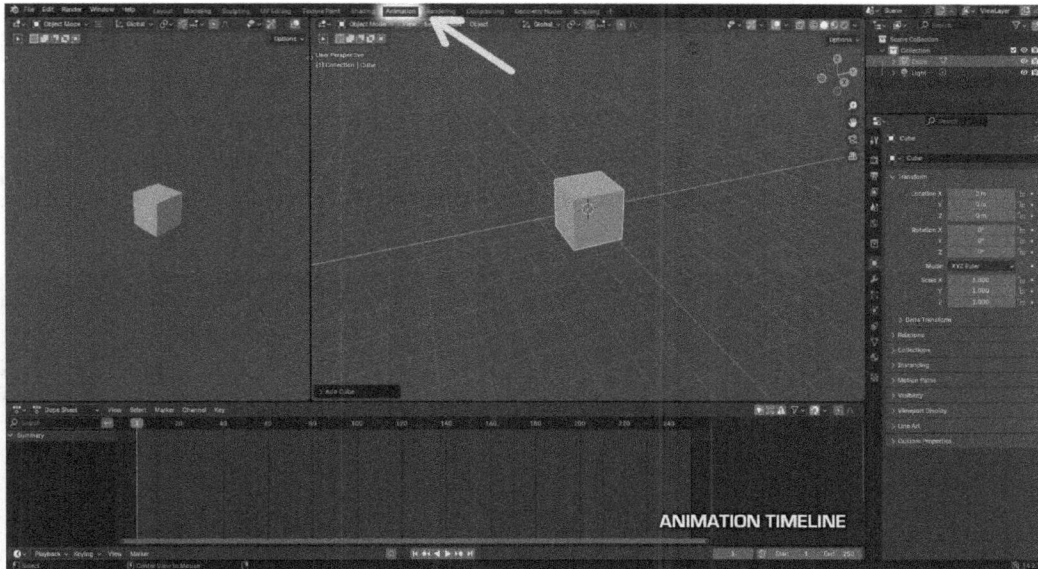

Figure 16.1: Locating the Animation workspace in Blender

It will show you the tools and areas that are key to animation. This includes the 3D Viewport, Timeline, Dope Sheet, and Graph Editor, each having a special job in making animations. We will go into each one of these in detail now.

3D Viewport

The **3D Viewport** is where you model and set up scenes, but it is also where you animate your objects. It shows your animation as you work on it, updating live when you change keyframes or move through your animation.

The 3D Viewport allows you to select and manipulate objects directly. This is incredibly useful for animators who need to position characters, props, and cameras precisely. You can grab, rotate, and scale any part of your scene to fit your vision.

You can also play your animation within the 3D Viewport to see how your scene unfolds in real time. This instant feedback is invaluable for tweaking motions and ensuring smooth transitions. Using Blender's 3D Viewport, you can view your scene from the perspective of the camera set up for rendering. This is great because it helps ensure that all animations are framed exactly as they will appear in the final output.

Timeline

The **Timeline** is your main animation tool in Blender, and you can find it at the bottom of the **Animation** workspace. Here, you can go through your animation, add keyframes (i.e., the main points of your animation), and control how the animation plays. The Timeline has buttons for play, pause, and repeat, and markers to set the beginning and end of your animation, as you can see in *Figure 16.2*.

Figure 16.2: Functionalities offered by Blender's Timeline in 3D Tudor Blender Conveyor Belt Geometry Node by 3D Tudor

To better understand what the Timeline does, let us go through an example. Your character winds up and throws a ball across the screen:

1. **Starting position**: At the beginning of the Timeline, you place keyframes for the character in a standing position, with their hand back, ready to throw the ball.

2. **Winding up**: As you move a few frames forward in the Timeline, you add keyframes where the character's arm is further back, emphasizing the wind-up motion before the throw.

3. **The throw**: At the key moment when the character releases the ball, you place another set of keyframes. For the character, these keyframes capture the arm's forward motion. For the ball, you set its starting position in the character's hand.

4. **Follow-through**: Moving further along the Timeline, after the ball has been released, you add keyframes showing the character's arm continuing its motion, following through after the throw.

5. **Ball in motion**: For the ball, as you progress frame by frame along the Timeline from the point of release, you add keyframes to capture its arc through the air, its peak, and its descent toward the ground, as in *Figure 16.3*.

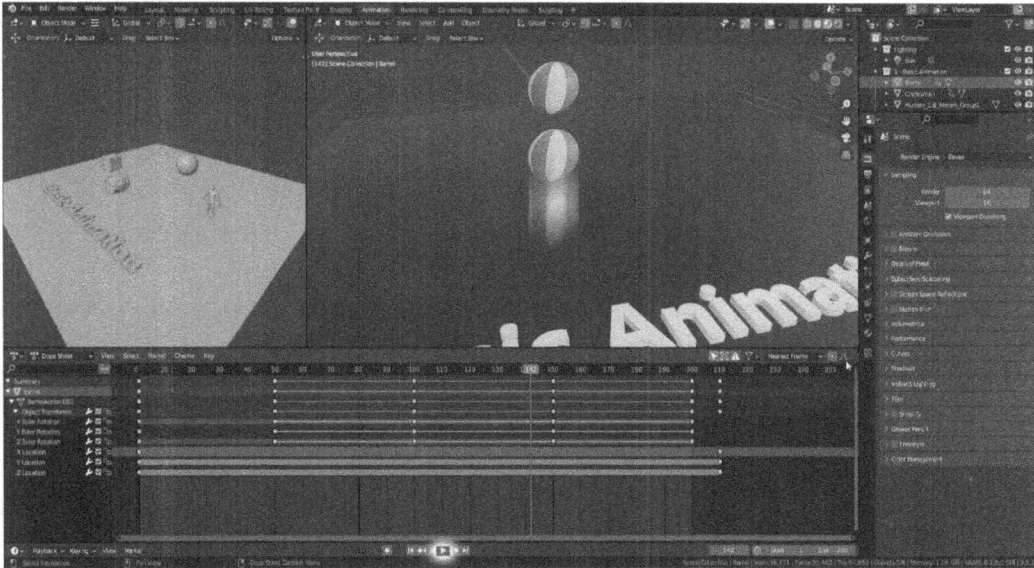

Figure 16.3: Ball in motion in Blender, step by step

The Timeline will let you scrub back and forth through these keyframes. This means that you can review the animation in real time. Scrubbing means dragging the playhead across the Timeline to see how the animation looks at different points in time. This feature is crucial for understanding the pacing of the throw and the motion of the ball. If the ball moves too slowly or too quickly, you can adjust the spacing of the keyframes along the Timeline to speed up or slow down specific parts of the animation.

Dope Sheet and Graph Editor

The **Dope Sheet** is an essential tool for you to use alongside the Timeline. The Dope Sheet is a big, detailed list that shows every single movement or change (i.e., keyframes) that you have planned for your animation. Whether it is a character jumping, a ball bouncing, or a light flickering, every action that happens over time is listed here.

The beauty of the Dope Sheet is how it lets you see all these keyframes at once, laid out across different channels for each thing you are animating, like separate tracks in a music editing program. This makes it super easy to see the big picture of your animation. You can spot whether a movement starts too early or too late, or use it if you want to make several things happen at the same time.

For example, if you are animating a character waving while walking, the Dope Sheet shows you the keyframes for the waving hand and the walking legs. If the wave needs to start a second later, you can simply select those keyframes and move them over. This is much simpler than tweaking each frame one by one, especially for complex animations with lots of elements.

The Dope Sheet also works closely with the Graph Editor. While the Dope Sheet is great for organizing *when* things happen, the **Graph Editor** dives into *how* they happen. We will talk about the Graph Editor more later. For now, all you need to know is that it shows the speed and flow between keyframes, represented by curves, as in *Figure 16.4*.

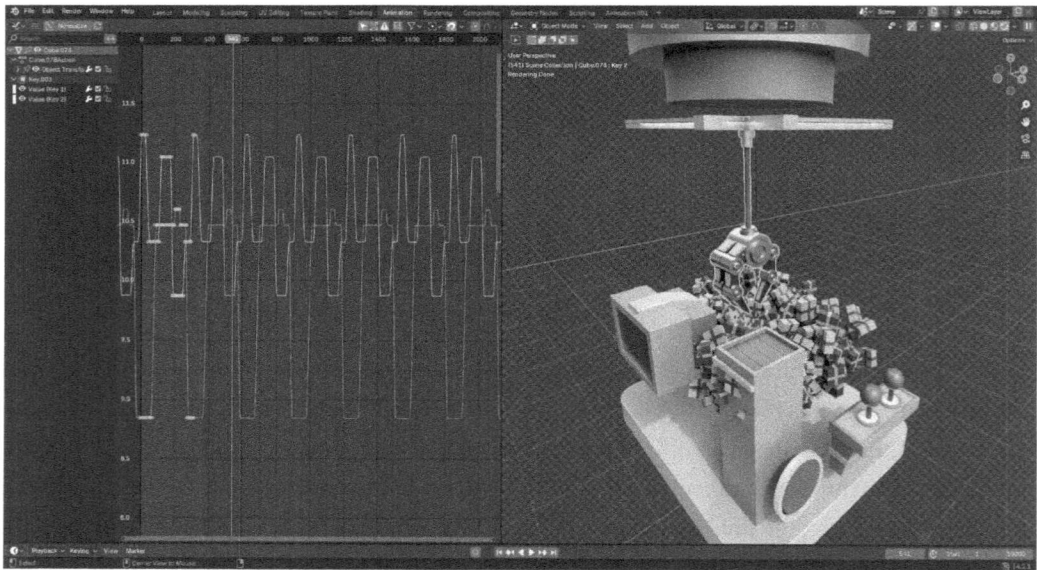

Figure 16.4: Graph Editor curves in 3D Tudor Blender Conveyor Belt Geometry Node by 3D Tudor

If you want a ball to bounce more softly or a character to move more smoothly, you would tweak these curves in the Graph Editor. Together, the Dope Sheet and Graph Editor give you full control over the timing and quality of your animation, making it possible to fine-tune all the details.

Properties panel

In Blender, you can animate almost any setting in the **Properties** panel, which gives you tons of flexibility for creating cool animations. For example, you can animate things such as an object's position, material colors, modifiers, or even how bright a light is. All you have to do is *right-click* on the property you want to animate and select **Insert Keyframe** (or hover over it and press *i*). This lets you set values at different points in the Timeline, and Blender will automatically create smooth transitions between them. This is great for bringing complex movements and effects, whether you are chasing gritty realism or going all-in on a stylized look.

The **Properties** panel is the control center for the technical aspects of your objects and animations, containing lots of settings such as the following:

- **Object Properties**: From this panel, you can adjust the precise location, rotation, and scale of objects, with the ability to set keyframes for each property. This is where the smallest of movements are defined.

- **Bone Properties**: For character animators, this panel is essential for rigging and animating with bones. The panel offers advanced settings for armatures, bone constraints, and inverse kinematics.

- **Material Properties**: You can animate material settings, such as roughness, to show changes in the environment, such as a surface getting wet from rain. For example, you could set keyframes on the roughness of a material to make it look glossier and more reflective as rain builds up. This way, it gradually looks wetter and shinier over time. By adjusting roughness like this, you can go from a dry, matte look to a slick, shiny surface, which really boosts the realism of your scene.

Using **Material Properties** in this way is a great trick for adding weather effects or making the environment feel more alive in your animations, as in *Figure 16.5*.

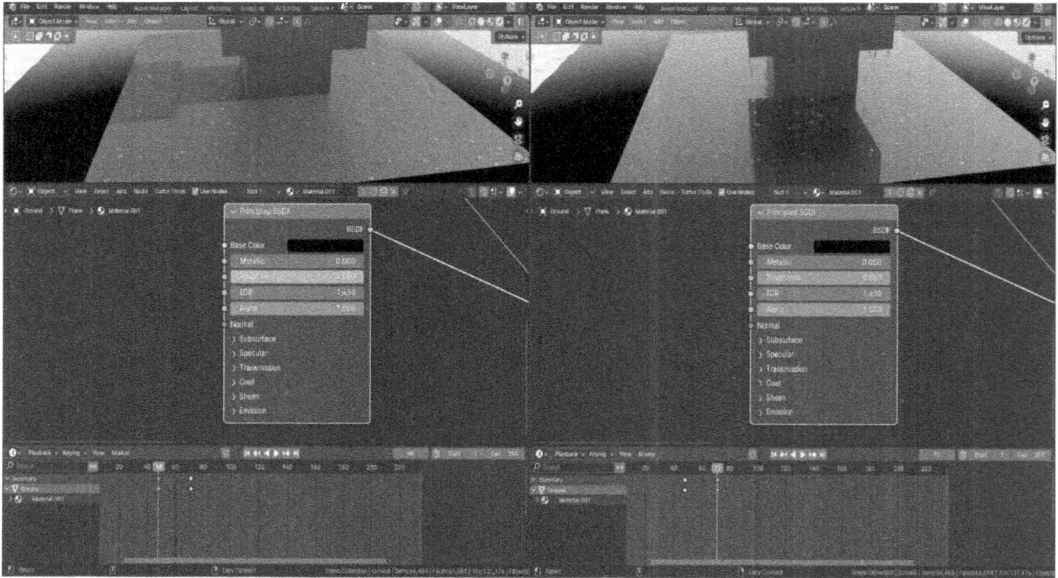

Figure 16.5: Using Roughness to create a dry (before) and wet (after) material animation

- **Physics Properties**: This panel is where you set up physics simulations such as cloth movement, hair dynamics, or particle effects.

- **Rendering Settings**: In the end, your animation needs to be rendered into a final video or sequence of images. The panel includes rendering settings, including **Motion Blur** settings, which affect the viewer's perception of motion within our animation (*Figure 16.6*).

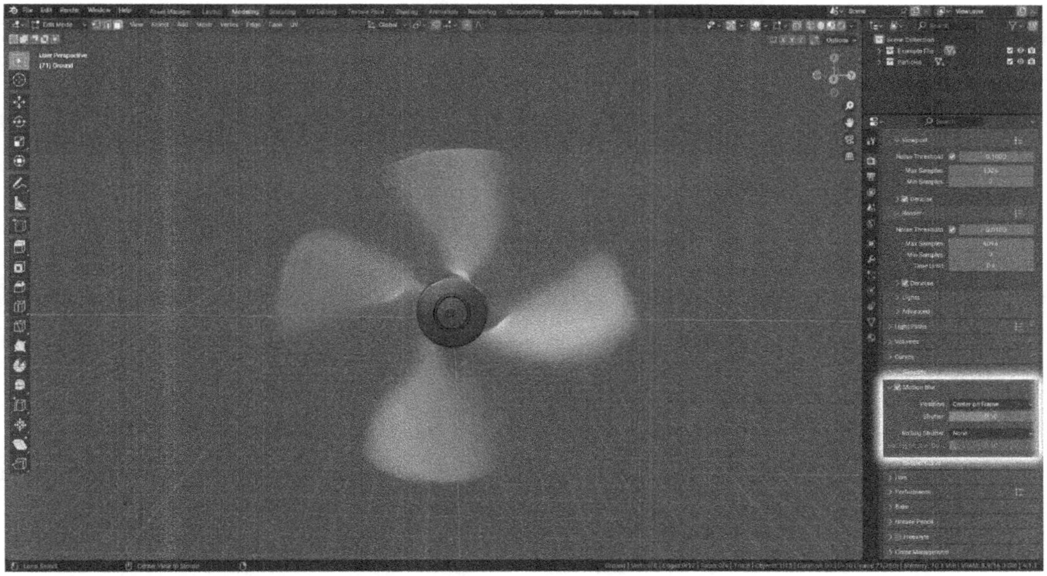

Figure 16.6: Motion Blur rendering settings for animation in the Properties panel

Quick access to animation tools

Blender makes animating faster with keyboard shortcuts. For example, pressing *i* lets you add a keyframe, *Shift + Left Arrow* moves you to the start of your animation, and the spacebar plays or pauses the animation. Getting used to these shortcuts can speed up making animations.

You can also use the *up* and *down* arrow keys to quickly jump between keyframes in your animation. This is super handy for spotting keyframes that are close together, so you can easily adjust timing or make sure nothing is overlapping too tightly.

The *left* and *right* arrow keys nudge you through your animation one frame at a time. It is a simple trick, but perfect for ironing out the little details and making sure everything plays back smoothly. Once you get used to it, hopping around and fine-tuning your keyframes becomes a whole lot easier.

Understanding these parts of Blender will help you a lot as you start to animate and bring your creations to life. Now, let us talk about one of the most important parts of animation in Blender: keyframing. It is how you create and control movement. In the next section, we will go into more detail about keyframing by animating a simple cube moving across the scene.

Understanding the basics of keyframing

Keyframing is like your magician's wand since you will need it to do pretty much anything to do with animation in Blender. It is the fundamental technique through which movement is created and controlled, think of it as the stop-motion magic of *Wallace and Gromit*, only without the thumbprints and lumps of clay.

Keyframes are markers that show Blender where the start and end points of any change in animation are. They specify the location, rotation, and scale at a particular frame in your animation timeline. Blender then interpolates the values between these keyframes to create smooth transitions and motion.

Let us understand keyframing in action by animating a simple cube moving across the scene. This step-by-step tutorial will introduce you to adding keyframes for an object's location, rotation, and scale:

1. Open Blender and select the **Animation** workspace.

2. Make sure the default cube is at the centre of your 3D Viewport.

3. In the Timeline, move the playhead to frame **1**. This will be the starting point of our animation.

4. Find the **Auto Keyframe** button in the Timeline header (it looks like a hollow gray/white circle that changes to blue-white when it is on), as in *Figure 16.7*, and click it. This will let you automatically add keyframes when you change an object's properties.

Figure 16.7: Locating the Auto Keyframe button

5. With the cube selected, press *G* to grab it and move it to the left side of the 3D Viewport. Release the mouse to set its starting position. Since **Auto Keyframe** is enabled, Blender automatically inserts a keyframe for the cube's location at frame **1**.

6. Now, move the playhead to frame **60** to define the end of our animation.

7. Press *G* again and move the cube to the right side of the 3D Viewport. Releasing the mouse confirms the cube's end position, and Blender automatically adds another keyframe.

8. Let's make the cube rotate and grow as it moves. Go back to frame **1**. Press *R*, then *X*, and rotate the cube slightly. Press *S* to scale the cube down a bit. These transformations are instantly keyframed.

9. Then, move to frame **60**, rotate the cube more significantly on the *X* axis, and scale it up. Blender adds keyframes for these changes, too.

10. Press the spacebar or the **Play** button on the Timeline to watch your cube move, rotate, and grow across the scene.

Keyframing in Blender is powerful, but it also makes intuitive sense, so you can pick up the basics of the skill quickly. By practicing with simple animations such as moving a cube, you are laying the groundwork for more complex animations.

Animation is one of those key areas involved in 3D modeling that I will invite you to experiment with the most. Experimenting with different properties and observing how they create changes in your project over time will help you imagine time and movement in a creative way that makes your work stand out more. At this point, you have pretty much grasped the basics of keyframing.

> **Tip**
>
> To adjust the speed of an animation, remember that closer keyframes result in faster motion, while farther-apart keyframes create slower motion.

Now, to take your animations further, you will learn how to move and edit keyframes in the **Timeline** and use the **Graph Editor**. This will give you detailed control over interpolation (i.e., filling in frames between keyframes) and velocity (i.e., speed of movement).

Leveling up with intermediate animation techniques

At this point, you have pretty much grasped the basics of keyframing. Now, to take your animations further, you need to have a look at adjusting the timing and flow of your animations with precision. Here, I will talk you through intermediate techniques that are essential for refining your animations. You will learn how to move and edit keyframes in the Timeline and use the Graph Editor. This will give you detailed control over interpolation (i.e., filling in frames between keyframes) and velocity (i.e., speed of movement).

Adjusting timing in the Timeline

Once you have set your keyframes, you might find that the timing of your animation is not quite perfect. Maybe the action in your scene moves too slowly or too fast. Blender makes it easy to adjust the timing directly in the Timeline:

1. Click on the Timeline where your keyframes are displayed. You will see diamond-shaped markers representing each keyframe.

2. Click on a keyframe to select it; it will turn orange to indicate it is selected (*Figure 16.8*).

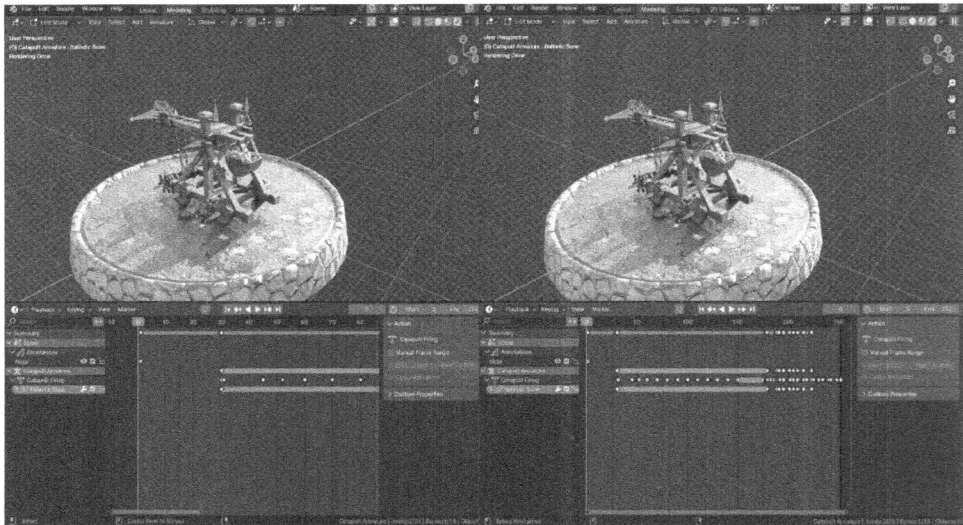

Figure 16.8: Selecting keyframes and adjusting the speed of an animation in "Blender 3D Model a Medieval Catapult Full Simulation Guide" by 3D Tudor

3. With a keyframe selected, you can simply click and drag it left or right to adjust its timing. Moving it closer to the previous keyframe speeds up the action, and vice versa.

4. To select multiple keyframes, you can simply *left-click* and drag your mouse over the keyframes in the Timeline or the Dope Sheet. This will create a box that highlights and selects all keyframes within that range.

5. Once selected, you can move them by pressing *G* (grab) and dragging the keyframes left or right along the Timeline. This shifts their timing, allowing you to adjust when the animated actions take place.

6. To adjust the speed of the animation, you can scale the selected keyframes. Press *S* (scale) and move the mouse to adjust their spacing. By default, Blender uses the current frame indicator (i.e., the vertical blue line in the Timeline) as the pivot point for the scale operation.

This means keyframes will scale outward or inward relative to that point:

- Scaling up (dragging outward) will spread the keyframes apart, slowing down the animation by increasing the time between actions.
- Scaling down (dragging inward) will compress the keyframes, speeding up the animation by reducing the time between them.

You could use this technique when creating an animation such as a sunrise and sunset. By selecting and adjusting the keyframes in the Timeline, you can speed up the sunrise, making it feel more dynamic.

Using the Dope Sheet for complex edits

The Dope Sheet will become your new favourite toy for more complex animations involving multiple objects or properties. It gives you a bird's-eye view of all your keyframes across all animated properties and objects.

Open the editor-type menu at the bottom of the window (where the Timeline is), and switch to the Dope Sheet, as highlighted in *Figure 16.9*. In the example, we animated a catapult made up of different components that move together. We used Blender's Dope Sheet to boost the animation's impact and create the illusion of the parts interacting with one another.

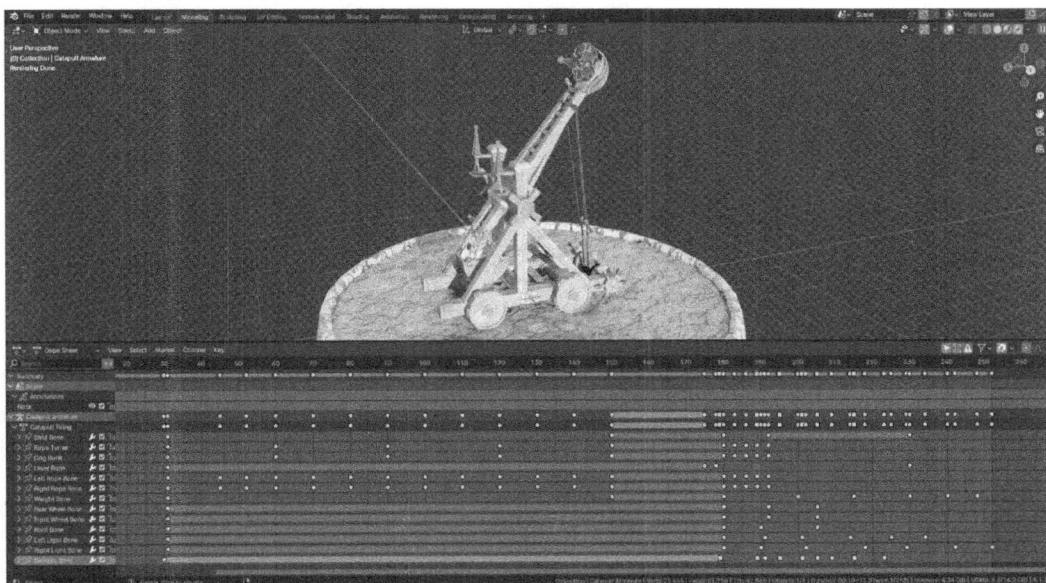

Figure 16.9: Accessing the Dope Sheet in "Blender 3D Model a Medieval Catapult Full Simulation Guide" by 3D Tudor

In the Dope Sheet, you can do the following:

- Box-select multiple keyframes across different objects and properties by clicking and dragging over them. Then, move them as a group by clicking and dragging.

- Copy keyframes with *Ctrl + C* and paste them with *Ctrl + V*, making it easy to replicate parts of your animation.

Tip

A good time to use a Dope Sheet to your advantage would be if you are creating a scene where multiple characters are performing similar actions at different times, such as in a dance sequence. You can animate one character's dance moves and then use the Dope Sheet to copy and paste those keyframes to the other characters.

- Use the Action Editor, which is useful for managing and reusing animations across different objects or scenes. For example, if you have animated a walk cycle for one character, you can save this as an action and apply it to other characters. This greatly speeds up the animation process for scenes with multiple characters.

As you can see, to make the animation more impactful and create the illusion of the parts interacting with one another, we utilized the Dope Sheet. The Dope Sheet gives us the power to adjust the timing of multiple items, making it easy to tweak and fine-tune the overall animation for a cohesive and polished result.

Using the Graph Editor

The **Graph Editor** lets you adjust the interpolation and velocity of keyframes. This is where you can polish the feel of your animations, making them smoother or more interactive.

One of the advanced features of the **Graph Editor** is the ability to apply modifiers to animation curves. For example, the **Noise Editor** introduces randomness into the movement of objects. This would be perfect for simulating the flickering of flames or leaves swaying. Before we move on, also, think of the **Noise** modifier when you want to add a more realistic or unpredictable element to movements, such as the trembling hands of a character who is nervous.

The **Graph Editor** also lets you create custom interpolation curves. This lets you carefully manage how fast or slow animations start and stop. Custom interpolation curves are useful in a project such as animating a flying bird. They give you control over the bird's acceleration as it leaps into the air and the gradual deceleration as it lands. Let's say custom interpolation curves are unavailable; you would have to manually adjust each keyframe, which would be much more time-consuming and likely less smooth.

Types of interpolation in the Graph Editor

Like the Dope Sheet, you can switch to the Graph Editor from the editor-type menu, which is located in the top-left corner of each editor window. This menu lets you choose from various editor types, allowing you to customize your workspace for different tasks.

In the Graph Editor, each animated property is represented as a curve, showing how its value changes over time. These curves give you a visual representation of your animation's motion and let you make precise adjustments. The slope of the curve indicates the velocity of change (*Figure 16.10*), while the handles on each keyframe allow you to adjust the interpolation method. The interpolation methods available in Blender include the following:

- **Linear**: Imagine animating a conveyor belt in a factory setting, where boxes move. **Linear** interpolation would ensure that the movement of the boxes along the conveyor belt is steady.

- **Bezier**: If you want to create a more natural-looking animation, such as a bird flying, **Bezier** interpolation is a great choice. It lets you control how smoothly the bird goes up and down, so the motion feels more lifelike. Even though it takes a bit longer to set up than the usual methods, it is totally worth it because you can really fine-tune the movement.

- **Constant**: For a stop-motion animation effect in a digital project, **Constant** interpolation could be used to mimic the abrupt, frame-by-frame transitions. This could apply to a character performing a robotic dance.

- **Ease-In** and **Ease-Out (or Ease-in-Out)**: These interpolation curves could be used to animate the car accelerating out of a standstill and coming to a smooth stop.

- **Bounce** and **Elastic**: You could use these for a playful animation of a cartoon character bouncing on a trampoline. **Elastic** interpolation could be used for a scene in which the character stretches an elastic band, where it stretches and snaps back.

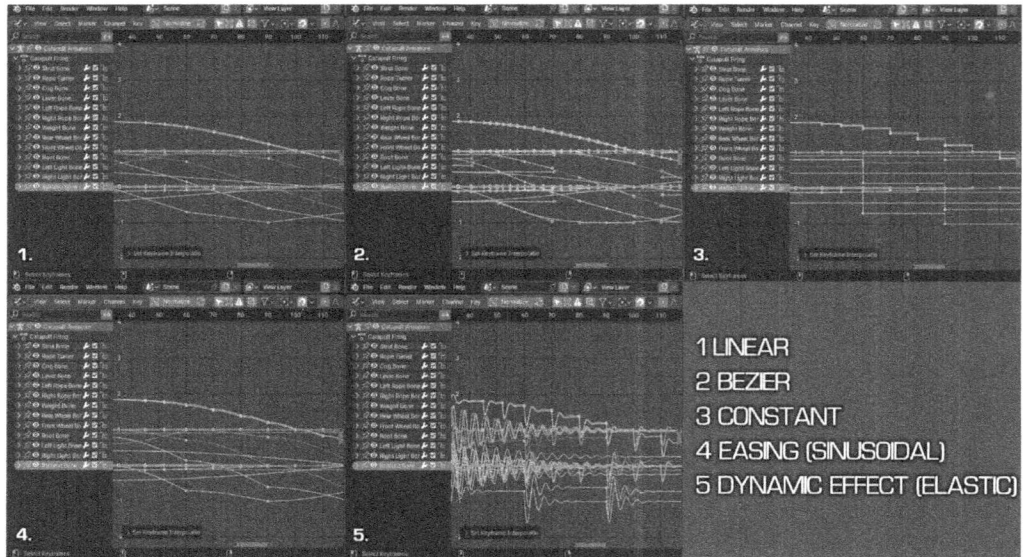

Figure 16.10: Interpolation curves in Blender's Graph Editor

To see how interpolation curves actually change the feel of movement, check out the following comparison. In this example, a ball moves upward along the Z axis, with two different interpolation types running the show: **Bezier** and **Linear**. Let us look at *Figure 16.11*. On the left, you have the rendered animation; on the right, the matching curves in Blender's Graph Editor.

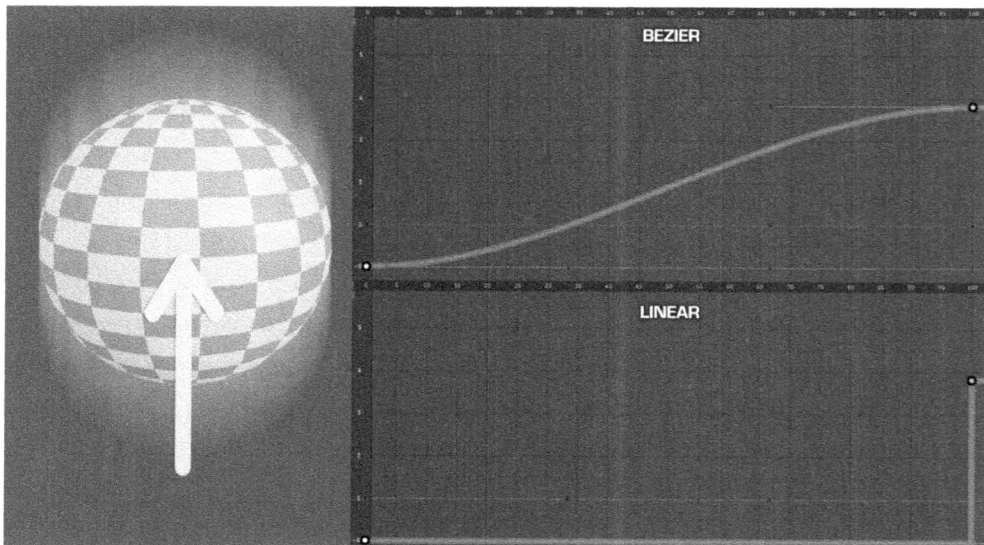

Figure 16.11: Visual representation of a Linear vs. a Bezier curve

Table 16.1 compares **Bezier** and **Linear** interpolation side-by-side, so you can see exactly how each one affects motion, both in the animation and in the Graph Editor.

Bezier interpolation	Linear interpolation
The top graph has that classic smooth curve, slow at the start, picking up speed in the middle, then easing to a stop. The result is a ball that glides naturally into and out of motion, which is exactly what you want if you are aiming for realistic or physically believable animation.	The bottom graph is a straight line, which means there is no easing at all, just a constant rate of change. In practice, the ball stays frozen, then suddenly snaps to its new position on the very next keyframe. No gentle build-up, no slowdown, just a hard cut in motion. Great if you want a mechanical or snappy effect, but not if you are going for natural movement.

Table 16.1: Bezier versus Linear interpolation – a quick reference

Adjusting interpolation and velocity

To control the velocity of an animation, one simple method is to adjust the spacing of keyframes (i.e., the individual dots on the graphs). Selecting a keyframe will expose its interpolation handles, as seen in *Figure 16.12*. By bringing keyframes closer together, you increase the speed of the transition between them, making the movement faster. Looking at it the other way, by moving keyframes further apartment, you slow down the transition.

Put simply, for fine-tuned adjustments, you can select multiple frames and use the **Scale** (*S*) tool to scale them down, compressing the timeline and increasing the overall velocity.

Interpolation is one of those sneaky little tools that can completely change the feel of your animation. By tweaking it, you control how your motion flows from one value to the next, dialing in the smoothness, speed, and style so your scenes have more personality and punch.

The **Graph Editor** provides powerful tools for refining your animations. Here is how to start making adjustments:

1. Click on a keyframe in the Graph Editor. Handles will appear, which you can drag to adjust the curve.
2. With one or more keyframes selected, press *T* to choose an interpolation type.
3. By adjusting the handles, you can control how quickly an object accelerates or decelerates.

For more advanced control over your animations, you can use the Graph Editor, as shown in *Figure 16.12*. In this example, a gun barrel has a vertical motion, which we can enhance by manipulating the interpolation curves in the graph. By tweaking the curve, you can adjust the velocity to create smoother or more exaggerated effects.

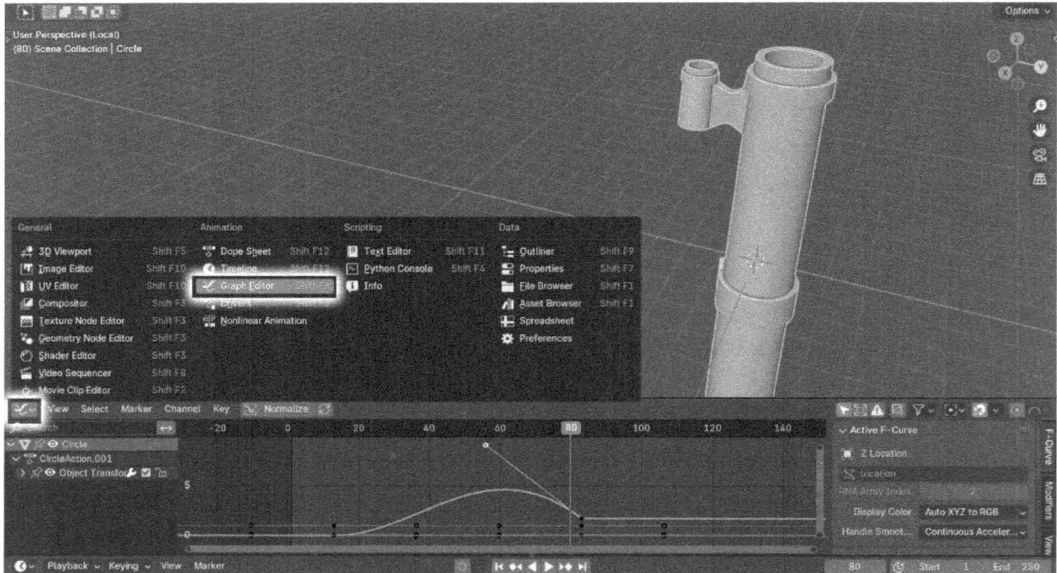

Figure 16.12: Animating a gun barrel using Blender's Graph Editor

Here, we exaggerated the interpolation to simulate a barrel kickback effect. By allowing the value to overshoot its original position before returning to its frame's final value, we added a dynamic recoil effect. This overshooting creates a realistic sense of force and rebound, enhancing the visual impact of the animation.

Motion paths in Blender

Motion paths are a great way to actually see where your animation is going, literally. They draw a trail of points showing where an object or bone sits at each frame, so you can follow its path through time. It is like having a breadcrumb trail for your animation, making it much easier to tweak complex moves, smooth out transitions, and nail the timing.

Motion paths give you a clear picture of how things flow, so you can catch any unnatural movements and have better control over where your keyframes go and how consistent the motion looks overall.

To use the **Motion Paths** tool, follow these steps:

1. Select the object or bone whose motion path you want to display.

2. The next settings differ if you are setting up a motion path for an object or a bone, as follows:

   - *For objects*: Go to the **Object Properties** tab on the right-hand side.

   - *For bones*: Select the bone and go to the **Bone Properties** tab.

3. Scroll down to the **Motion Paths** section.

4. Click the **Calculate** button to generate the motion path. You will be prompted to set the start and end frames for the path.

5. After calculating, you will see the motion path displayed as a series of points in the 3D Viewport, which correspond to the object's or bone's positions over the selected frame range. *Figure 16.13* is a good visualization of that.

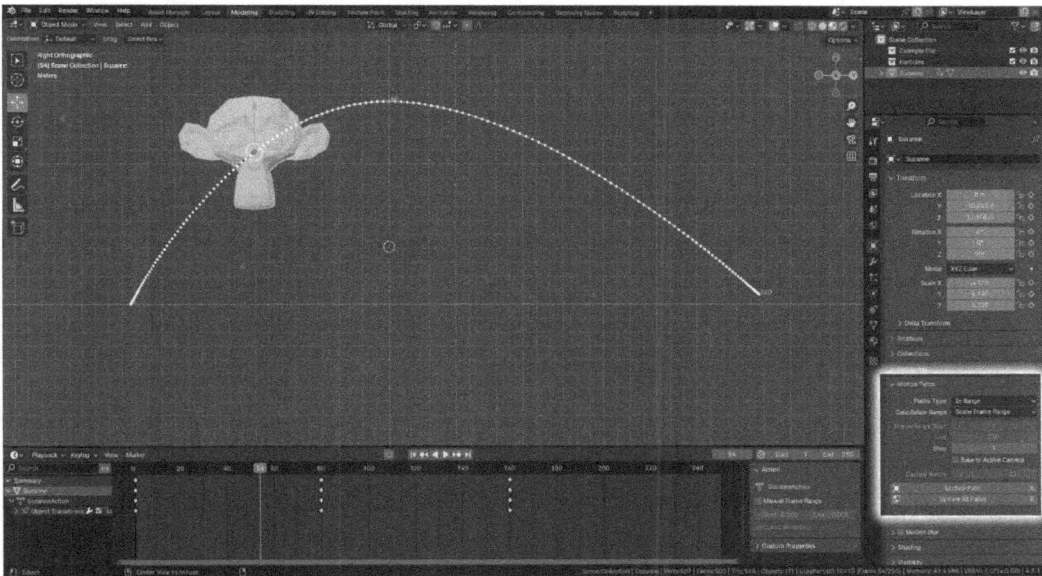

Figure 16.13: Visualizing motion paths in Blender

6. To update or recalculate the motion path after changes, simply click **Update Paths** under the same **Motion Paths** section.

By learning how to move and edit keyframes effectively, you gain control over the pace of your animations. The Dope Sheet gives you the tools to manage complex animations, and the Graph Editor acts as your Swiss army knife for adjustments to interpolation and velocity. Now that you have a good grasp of creating animations, we will create our first full animation project in Blender from start to finish.

Animating a simple object

Animating objects in Blender is not just about moving them across the screen. It is also about telling a story through the movement itself. In this section, we will talk about animating a simple object, from the planning stages to the final animation, using a bouncing cube as our example.

Planning your animation

Before we dive into animating, it is crucial to have a clear plan. This means understanding exactly what you want to create and why it matters. Think about the story or action you want to show your viewers through your animation. For our bouncing cube, take the time to ask yourself the following questions:

- **Personality**: Is the cube energetic, cautious, or perhaps a bit clumsy? Its personality can influence how high it bounces, how it lands, and how it prepares for the next jump.
- **Environment**: Where is the cube bouncing? Is it on a hard surface, which might make for high, less frequent bounces, or is it on something softer, such as a mattress, resulting in quicker, smaller bounces?
- **Reaction**: How does the cube react to its surroundings? Does it look around curiously, or does it have a goal it is bouncing toward?

Sketching a simple storyboard or jotting down notes about these aspects can help get a better picture of your vision and guide your animation process. You might recall that we spoke about *PureRef* (https://www.pureref.com/) earlier in this book, and this free tool might help here, too. Try it out!

Step-by-step animation of a ball

Now, let us bring our ball to life in Blender. Our goal is to make it bounce across the scene and react to its environment as it moves. Follow these steps:

1. Open Blender and select the **Animation** workspace.
2. Make sure you have a default ball (i.e., **UV Sphere**) placed at the starting point of your scene, as in *Figure 16.14*.

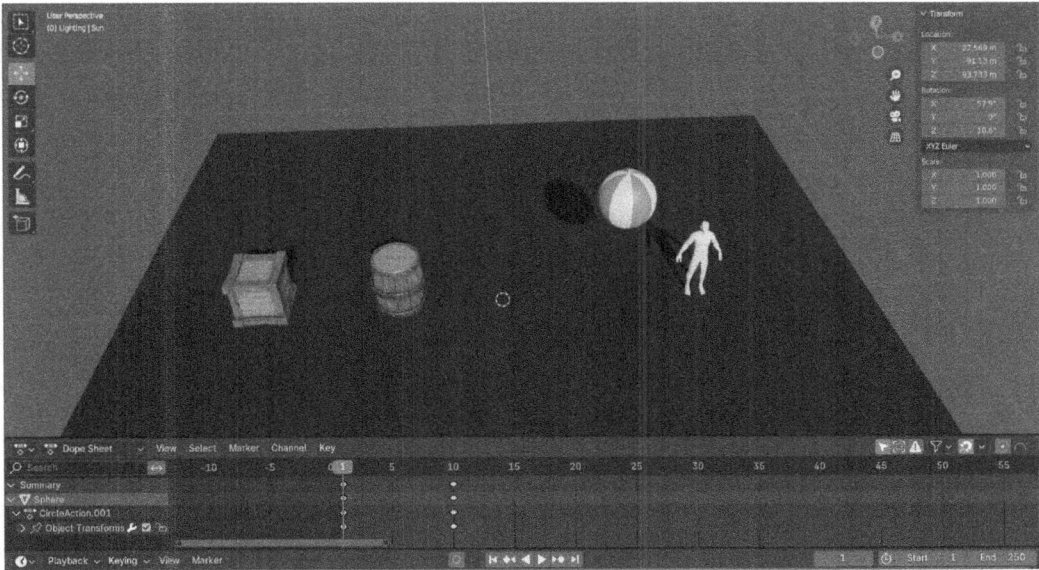

Figure 16.14: Example animation scene preparation for a bouncing ball in "The Ultimate Guide to Blender 3D Rigging & Animation" by 3D Tudor

3. To create a **UV Sphere** ball in Blender, press *Shift + A*, navigate to **Mesh**, and then select **UV Sphere** from the drop-down menu.
4. Move to frame **1** in the Timeline. Then, with **UV Sphere** selected, press *I* and choose **Location** to insert the first keyframe. This is how you are marking the cube's starting position.
5. Decide on the frame where the **UV Sphere** ball will reach the peak of its first bounce. Let's say frame **10**.

6. Move the **UV Sphere** ball up along the *Z* axis to simulate the bounce's peak. Press *I* again and insert a keyframe for the location of frame **10**.

7. Continue this process, moving the **UV Sphere** ball down to the ground at frame **20**, up again at frame **30**, and so on, creating a series of bounces across the Timeline. With each bounce increasing or decreasing in height, you are controlling the intensity of the overall bouncing movement.

8. To add personality, let us adjust the interpolation. Set it to **Bezier Interpolation**. When the **UV Sphere** ball reaches its highest point, increase the size of the Bezier handles. This will make the **UV Sphere** ball appear to hang in the air longer, giving it a lighter, floatier feel.

9. At the landing frames (e.g., frame **20**), scale the **UV Sphere** ball down slightly on the *Z* axis to simulate squashing (press *S*, then *Z*), and insert a scale keyframe.

10. To quickly add a visible texture for rotation, go to the **Shading** tab, create a new material, and add an **Image Texture** node. Load or create a texture, then connect the **Color** output of the **Image Texture** node to the **Base Color** input of the **Principled BSDF** shader. You are doing the last step to ensure the texture appears when the sphere rotates.

11. To make the **UV Sphere** ball look around, select a frame where the cube is on the ground, resting between bounces. Then, rotate the cube as if it were looking around and insert a rotation keyframe.

Note

You can animate the rotation on the *Z* axis for simplicity. Go to the **Object Properties** panel, and under **Transform**, locate the **Rotation Z** parameter. Adjust the value to your desired rotation, and when you like what you see, hover your mouse over the parameter and press *i* to insert a keyframe.

12. Repeat this at various points in the animation to make the **UV Sphere** ball appear more lifelike and aware of its surroundings.

13. Use the Dope Sheet and Graph Editor to adjust the timing and smoothness of your bounces, rotations, and scale changes.

14. Experiment with different interpolation types in the Graph Editor to make the motion more dynamic or fluid.

You know, starting with something simple, such as animating a **UV Sphere** ball, is a great way for beginners to get the hang of animation. The secret sauce to nailing animation? Just keep watching the world around you, try out new things, and tweak your animations. This way, you will get good at spotting what makes movements look natural and how to tell a story through motion.

To take you a step further, we will now look at some advanced skills for Blender animators.

Raising the bar with advanced animation techniques

As I have said before, Blender is like a magic wand for animators. Think about the nitty-gritty details, such as a character's eyebrow twitching or a flag waving with all its textures flowing just right. With Blender's advanced tools, you can get as detailed and expressive as you want.

Shape keys for detailed deformations

Shape keys let you make detailed deformations in an object. They do that by mimicking the smallest movements and transformations (simple keyframes cannot do that). In facial animations or any scenario requiring smooth transitions between shapes, you want to be using shape keys.

For example, when a character blinks or speaks, the movements involved are small but complex. Just think of all the subtle shifts in the skin, muscles, and features around the eyes and mouth. Regarding blinking, shape keys can capture the exact curvature and motion of the eyelid as it closes and reopens. This would be challenging to do with basic bone rigging alone because eyelids are soft and flexible. Regarding talking, shape keys let you create precise mouth shapes (i.e., phonemes) for characters to look like they are talking.

Within the **Object Data** properties of your selected object, you can add and manage shape keys to create and control deformations for your mesh. Here is how it works:

1. Start with a **Basis** key that represents the original, undeformed shape. You can then add additional keys to represent various deformations.

2. Create a new shape key, which will store the deformed version of the mesh. Once added, set **Value** to 1 to fully enable this shape key for editing.

3. With the new shape key selected, enter **Edit Mode** and adjust the vertices to create the desired deformation. Any changes you make to the vertices will be stored within this shape key.

4. You can now adjust the **Value** slider of the new shape key to smoothly transition between the original mesh (i.e., **Basis**) and the deformed version. This process is called **blending**, and it allows you to dynamically mix the two states.

By following these steps, you can sculpt the specific deformation that the key represents, as shown in *Figure 16.15*.

Figure 16.15: Editing the mesh with shape keys selected

Note

For shape keys to work, the vertex count and order must remain identical across all keys. This means you cannot delete or add vertices to the mesh after creating shape keys. Any changes to the topology will invalidate the shape key functionality.

Animating textures

Almost any texture property can be animated in Blender. This means that you can add anything from flickering flames to shifting landscapes, as in *Figure 16.16*, into your project.

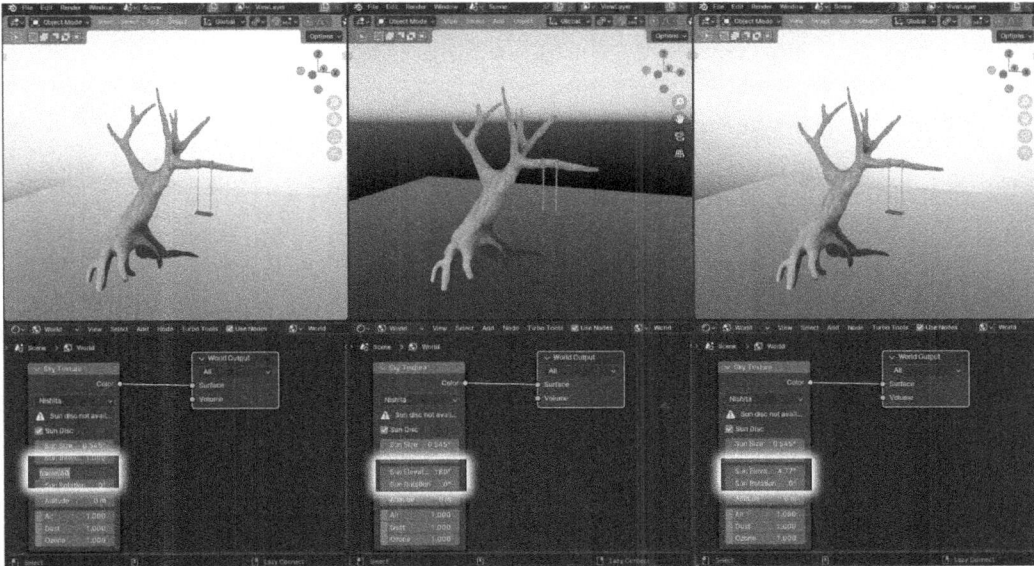

Figure 16.16: Controlling a shifting landscape in Blender by animating textures

By hovering over a property in the **Texture** tab and inserting a keyframe, you can decide how that property changes over time (e.g., **Scale**, **Offset**, and **Texture**).

You might also want to experiment with changing the color of the sky from dawn to dusk in a time-lapse-style animation.

> Tip
>
> You can also animate properties using expressions within the parameter field. One commonly used function is **#frame**, which inputs the current frame number as the parameter's value. To control the speed of the change, you can divide or multiply the frame number. For example, using *#frame/60* for the air value in a sky texture creates a gradual dawn effect, while *#frame*10* would make the transition happen in seconds.

Animating modifiers

You can animate any modifier in Blender, including custom **Geometry** nodes. For example, you can animate the growth of vines up a light post by gradually increasing the number of leaves from the base to the top, as seen in *Figure 16.17*. This technique brings life and progression to your scenes by showing changes over time.

Figure 16.17: Vines growing on the side of a building using Blender 4 Jungle Vines Geometry Node, by 3D Tudor

For more complex texture animations, such as synchronizing texture movement with object animation, you can use drivers. This means you can make a texture change directly tied to how another part of your scene moves or changes. For example, you might see this in a project where the intensity of a character's glowing eyes increases as they power up for a special move. Even though the full process of using drivers for more complex texture animations is beyond the scope of this chapter, a good place to start your research would be Blender's official documentation (`https://docs.blender.org/manual/en/latest/animation/drivers/drivers_panel.html`) or online tutorials focused on drivers and animation.

Now, before we close this brief introduction to animation, we will look at rendering and exporting animations.

Rendering and exporting your animation in Blender

After you have poured all that creativity and skill into your Blender animation, guess what? We are hitting the final stretch, rendering and exporting your masterpiece. I will walk you through getting your scene ready for the big render, picking the best settings so it looks awesome, and then, the fun part, showing you how to send your animation out into the world for everyone to see.

Preparing for rendering

Rendering transforms your animated scene from a collection of objects, lights, and shaders within Blender into a standard video or image sequence.

First of all, you need to look at setting up your camera angles. Your scene's camera determines what will be visible in the final render. Position and angle your camera to frame your animation effectively. Use the *Numpad 0* shortcut to view through the camera and adjust its location and rotation to capture your scene from the best perspective. You might find another read of *Chapter 1* of this part useful here.

Once you have your camera angles set up, the next step is to fine-tune your render settings for the best possible output. Blender's **Render Properties** panel offers a multitude of settings that affect the quality and speed of your render. Key settings include the following:

- **Render Engine:** Choose between **Eevee** (faster, real-time engine) and **Cycles** (more realistic, ray-traced engine).
- **Sampling:** Higher samples in **Cycles** will give you higher quality but longer render times. Eevee's samples affect effects such as shadows and reflections.
- **Resolution:** Set the dimensions of your final output. Using higher resolutions will give you more detail but increase render times.
- **Output Properties:** Here, you can select the file format for your render, such as **PNG** for an image sequence or **FFmpeg** video for a video file.

Your final decision will be deciding what output format you want to use. Decide whether you want your final animation as a video file or an image sequence. For example, in a project focused on creating a cinematic for a short film, your output format could be **PNG** if you need high-quality frames for further compositing. Alternatively, if you are creating content for social media sharing, you would use an **FFmpeg** video output format because it provides a ready-to-upload video file that balances quality with file size for quick sharing.

Tip

Video files are convenient, but image sequences offer more flexibility for post-processing and are safer. Using image sequences means you will not lose the entire render if the process is interrupted.

Exporting your finished animation

Once your scene is prepared and render settings are configured, it is time to render and export your animation. Blender's got your back, whether you are going straight to video or want to play around with an image sequence for more flexibility. Think of rendering as this mix of art and tech, play around with it, practice a bit, and you'll find the sweet spot for your project.

When it comes to rendering your animation:

- **For a video file**: In **Output Properties**, set the file format to **FFmpeg**, choose your encoding settings, and specify the output path. Then, render your animation by going to **Render** and then **Render Animation** or pressing *Ctrl + F12*.

- **For an image sequence**: Set the file format to **PNG**, specify the output path, and render the animation. Each frame will be saved as a separate image file.

If you rendered your animation as an image sequence and wish to compile it into a video file, you can use Blender's **Video Editing** layout. Switch to the **Video Editing** workspace, add your image sequence as a strip in **Sequencer**, and set the end frame of your sequence, as shown in *Figure 16.18*.

Figure 16.18: Rendering your animation as an image sequence in Building Medieval Worlds - Unreal Engine 5 Modular Kitbash, by 3D Tudor

Make sure the output settings match your desired video format and resolution, and then render the animation. Still confused? You can read all about rendering in *Chapter 5* in *Part 2* of this book.

Summary

If *Part 1* of *Blender for Beginners* felt like the starting point of learning to ride a bike, *Chapter 16* was the moment you took your hands off the handlebars and noticed the wheels were taking you somewhere. In *Chapters 1–15* you built your 3D artist foundations: a clean, speedy Blender setup, dependable modelling habits, shading that behaves, UVs that make sense, and scene hygiene that does not fall apart the minute you add detail. *Chapter 16* then stitched it all together with motion, keyframes, timing, interpolation, and some good, old-fashioned polishing.

You learned how to set keys with intent, manage timing in the **Timeline** and **Dope Sheet**, and shape motion with interpolation instead of beginner's luck. Motion blur and preview settings gave you quick actionable results. You touched shape keys for controlled deformation and even tried out animated lighting and simple **Geometry Node** movements. In a few words, you closed *Part 1* with a complete "from still to moving" loop that you can repeat any time you need a shot that works the way it should, just like that!

Part 1 of *Blender for Beginners* is a stack of habits. You can navigate around Blender with confidence, model cleanly, unwrap without fear, shade with principled materials, and organise scenes like someone who plans to finish. When you press play, you now understand why things move and how to fix problems you may come up against. These are the habits of professional 3D artists, keep growing them.

Why Part 2 is a necessary companion

Part 2 picks up exactly where you are standing and carries those skills into building better systems and portfolio presentation. You will rig with simple, reliable IK so posing does not fight you. You will build beginner-friendly **Geometry Nodes (GN)** that scatter, instance, and generate without tanking performance. You will light and render in **Eevee** or **Cycles**, then push final polish in the **Compositor** with reusable node stacks. In the end, you will learn the optimisation knobs that keep scenes responsive and hand-off friendly.

Before you turn the page

Save your *Part 1* practice files. Take one scene you like and write a plan for how you will make it better or bigger in *Part 2*. Add a few poses with IK, a **GN** scatter pass for depth, a lighting target, and a compositing pass as a cherry on top. That is the muscle memory you are here to build, small, deliberate steps that add up to work you are proud to show.

In the next chapter, *Chapter 1* in *Part 2* of *Blender for Beginners*, we will look into rigging. Rigging is the process of creating a skeleton for your 3D models so they can move in a realistic way. Let's step into new territory and push the limits of your 3D art, preferably without pulling a *Jurassic Park* and realizing too late that we were so preoccupied with whether we *could* that we never stopped to think whether we *should*.

Right then, let's hoist the sails and make for *Part 2*. Ahoy! We'll chart the cleanest course, catch a fair wind, and dock those shots in your portfolio looking proper shipshape.

Until next time, happy modeling, everyone!

Neil and Vanessa

Further reading

- If you are ready to dive deeper into animation in Blender, the possibilities are endless. You could even go on to animate short films such as *Big Buck Bunny* (https://studio.blender.org/films/big-buck-bunny/) and *Sintel*, both created by the Blender Foundation (https://durian.blender.org/about/).

- To explore the essentials of animation workflows, including using the Timeline and Dope Sheet effectively, check out *Blender 3D Model a Medieval Catapult Full Simulation Guide* (https://www.udemy.com/course/blender-28-model-texture-animate-simulate-complete-guide/?referralCode=A4E33A5BAA75AB5E31A5).

- If you are interested in animating with **Geometry** nodes, you can animate custom **Geometry** nodes to create dynamic effects, such as the growth of vines up a light post, as shown in *Blender 4 Jungle Vines Geometry Node* (https://3dtudor.gumroad.com/l/blender4-jungle-vine-geometrynode).

- For a comprehensive look at rigging and animation techniques in Blender, *The Ultimate Guide to Blender 3D Rigging & Animation* (https://www.udemy.com/course/blender-3d-rigging-animation/?referralCode=39A1E0B8F07B474DFE0F) provides step-by-step projects to try out. It covers everything from basic animation principles to advanced rigging workflows.

- Finally, if you want to render your animations as a video, learn how to compile image sequences using Blender's **Video Editing** layout in *Building Medieval Worlds - Unreal Engine 5 Modular Kitbash* (https://www.udemy.com/course/building-medieval-worlds-unreal-engine-5-modular-kitbash/?referralCode=F936D687808F3AE55AF2).

Subscribe to Game Dev Assembly!

We are excited to introduce **Game Dev Assembly**, our brand-new newsletter dedicated to everything game development. Whether you're coding, designing, animating, or managing a studio, we've got insights, trends, and expert advice to help you create, innovate, and thrive. Sign up now and get exciting benefits.

https://packt.link/gamedev-newsletter

Join the 3D Tudor Channel Discord Server!

Join the 3D Tudor Channel Discord Server, a creative hub for learning Blender, Unreal Engine, Substance Painter, and 3D modeling, for discussions with the authors and other readers:

https://discord.gg/5EkjT36vUj

17

Unlock Your Exclusive Benefits

Your copy of this book includes the following exclusive benefits:

- ☁ Next-gen Packt Reader
- 📄 DRM-free PDF/ePub downloads

Follow the guide below to unlock them. The process takes only a few minutes and needs to be completed once.

Unlock this Book's Free Benefits in 3 Easy Steps

Step 1

Keep your purchase invoice ready for *Step 3*. If you have a physical copy, scan it using your phone and save it as a PDF, JPG, or PNG.

For more help on finding your invoice, visit https://www.packtpub.com/unlock-benefits/help.

> **Note:** If you bought this book directly from Packt, no invoice is required. After *Step 2*, you can access your exclusive content right away.

Step 2

Scan the QR code or go to `packtpub.com/unlock`.

On the page that opens (similar to *Figure 17.1* on desktop), search for this book by name and select the correct edition.

<packt>   🔍 Search...   Subscription 🛒 👤

Explore Products   Best Sellers   New Releases   Books   Videos   Audiobooks   Learning Hub   Newsletter Hub   Free Learning

Discover and unlock your book's exclusive benefits

Bought a Packt book? Your purchase may come with free bonus benefits designed to maximise your learning. Discover and unlock them here

Discover Benefits   Sign Up/In   Upload Invoice

Need Help?

✦ 1. Discover your book's exclusive benefits   ∧

🔍 Search by title or ISBN

CONTINUE TO STEP 2

👥 2. Login or sign up for free   ∨

☁ 3. Upload your invoice and unlock   ∨

Figure 17.1: Packt unlock landing page on desktop

Step 3

After selecting your book, sign in to your Packt account or create one for free. Then upload your invoice (PDF, PNG, or JPG, up to 10 MB). Follow the on-screen instructions to finish the process.

Need help?

If you get stuck and need help, visit https://www.packtpub.com/unlock-benefits/help for a detailed FAQ on how to find your invoices and more. This QR code will take you to the help page.

> **Note:** If you are still facing issues, reach out to customercare@packt.com.

‹packt›

Other Books You May Enjoy

If you enjoyed this book, you may be interested in these other books by Packt:

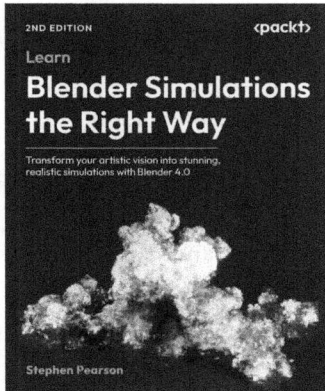

Learn Blender Simulations the Right Way

Stephen Pearson

ISBN: 978-1-83620-005-5

- Create a realistic campfire simulation with sparks and motion blur
- Simulate a chaotic explosion using smoke, fire, and particle effects
- Implement Fluid simulation for a waterfall with waves and foam
- Use the Soft Body system to simulate a sphere moving through obstacles
- Apply Cloth physics to animate a waving flag attached to a pole with ropes
- Master the Rigid Body system to create a Rube Goldberg machine-like animation
- Animate painting effects and raindrops using Dynamic Paint
- Combine multiple simulation effects to create a burning effect animation

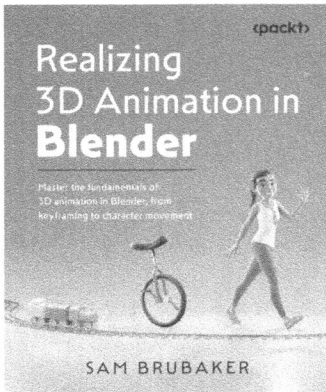

Realizing 3D Animation in Blender

Sam Brubaker

ISBN: 978-1-80107-721-7

- Become well-versed with the simple rules of keyframing and interpolation
- Understand the function and behavior of Blender's animation curves
- Bring a character to life with Blender 3D character animation
- Utilize multiple cameras and the video sequence editor for advanced shot composition
- Get to grips with Blender's mysterious non-linear animation tool
- Explore advanced features such as physics simulation and camera techniques

Packt is searching for authors like you

If you're interested in becoming an author for Packt, please visit authors.packt.com and apply today. We have worked with thousands of developers and tech professionals, just like you, to help them share their insight with the global tech community. You can make a general application, apply for a specific hot topic that we are recruiting an author for, or submit your own idea.

Share your thoughts

Now you've finished *Blender for Beginners, Part 1*, we'd love to hear your thoughts! Scan the QR code below to go straight to the Amazon review page for this book and share your feedback or leave a review on the site that you purchased it from.

https://packt.link/r/1837631093

Your review is important to us and the tech community and will help us make sure we're delivering excellent quality content.

Index

S